FIFTH EDITION

Psychology A Level
Year 1 and AS

The Complete Companion Student Book

Mike Cardwell • Cara Flanagan

OXFORD
UNIVERSITY PRESS

OXFORD
UNIVERSITY PRESS

Great Clarendon Street, Oxford, OX2 6DP, United Kingdom

Oxford University Press is a department of the University of Oxford. It furthers the University's objective of excellence in research, scholarship, and education by publishing worldwide. Oxford is a registered trade mark of Oxford University Press in the UK and in certain other countries

British Library Cataloguing in Publication Data
Data available

ISBN 978-0-19-843632-4

10 9 8 7 6 5 4 3 2 1

Paper used in the production of this book is a natural, recyclable product made from wood grown in sustainable forests.
The manufacturing process conforms to the environmental regulations of the country of origin.

Printed in Italy by L.E.G.O SpA

The questions in this book allow students a genuine attempt at practising exam skills, but they are not intended to replicate exam papers. Where questions have been taken from AQA exam papers, any commentaries or possible answers have neither been provided nor approved by AQA, nor do they constitute the only possible solutions.

Dedication
To Thomas Cardwell, my grandson (MC)
To my cats (CF)

Author acknowledgements
Bringing projects such as this to fruition is never easy and we owe a huge debt of gratitude to Sarah Flynn, Alison Schrecker, Rebecca DeLozier, Kate Buckley and the rest of the OUP family for continuing to believe in what we are trying to achieve with *The Complete Companions* series.

About the authors

Cara Flanagan has decades of experience as a teacher and senior examiner and is a widely published educational author, conference organiser and speaker, and CPD trainer.

Mike Cardwell is Senior Lecturer in Social Psychology at Bath Spa University. Mike is a former Chief Examiner, a widely published textbook author and an experienced conference speaker.

Oxford University Press would also like to thank Dave Latham for his contribution and advice.

Dave Latham has been an A level specialist in Psychology for 15 years and currently works at a large sixth form college in Birmingham. He has been an examiner for 12 years on a number of specifications and is part of the senior examining team. He lives with his wife and two boys, Charlie and Alfie, where his main specialism is building Lego Star Wars.

The Oxford Impact Framework is a systematic approach to evaluating the impact of Oxford University Press products and services. It was developed through a unique collaboration with the National Foundation for Educational Research (NFER) and is supported by the Oxford University Department of Education.

OXFORD IMPACT FRAMEWORK
EVALUATING EDUCATIONAL PRODUCTS AND SERVICES FROM OXFORD UNIVERSITY PRESS

CREATED WITH  Evidence for Excellence in Education

SUPPORTED BY  Department of Education University of Oxford

About our cover cat

Weighing in at little more than a couple of bags of sugar, Coco is a pedigree Birman. She and her her sister, Misty were rescued by their owner, Sharon, when they were just two years old. They divided their time between proofreading their owner's business reports, sleeping for England and drinking tea. Like her sister, Coco was a constant reminder that you never own a cat, a cat always owns you.

CONTENTS

HOW TO USE THIS BOOK

The book is called 'The Complete Companion' because we have written a book which we hope will be like having a friendly teacher and examiner by your side, providing you with everything you need to do well at AQA AS and A Level psychology. The contents of this book are mapped exactly onto the AQA AS and A Level (Year 1) specifications. The book is divided into seven chapters that map onto the AQA psychology specification. Rather than writing separate AS and A Level (Year 1) books, we have integrated the two approaches into the same text. The content covered by AS and A Level students is exactly the same, but A Level students have some additional material that AS students will not need to cover. You will be guided through the book so you know which material is appropriate for AS and which is only for A Level.

Each chapter begins with an **introductory spread** where you will find:

Introduction
On each spread is an **introduction to the topic**, at the top left. This explains what the topic is about and what some of its main issues are.

Description (AO1)
The **main descriptive text** (i.e. **AO1**) for the spread is on the left-hand page. We have provided more detail than you would require for an exam question for the topic. The questions on the page (Can you...?) aim to help you select appropriate material to prepare for exam questions, and the diagrammatic summaries at the end of each chapter précis this down to the bare bones of each topic.

An image to give you a flavour of what the chapter is about.

A starter activity to get you thinking about what is to come.

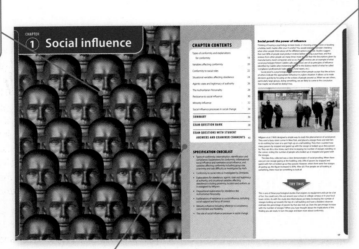

Chapter contents and a specification breakdown for these contents so you can see how each double page spread maps on to the specification.

The **content** of each chapter consists of a number of double-page spreads. All the features in these chapters are illustrated on the two sample spreads on the right. The main text and all the other features together will help turn your psychological knowledge into effective exam performance. Each chapter ends with some more useful features – an **end of chapter review** consisting of:

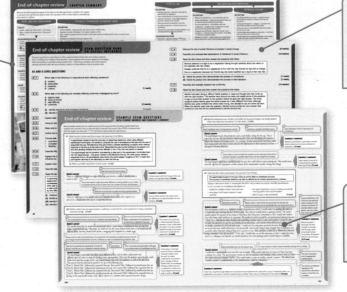

A diagrammatic summary of the chapter.

Example examination questions to give you an idea of how the chapter's contents might be assessed in an exam.

Sample student answers to some of these questions with examiner's comments.

Suggested answers for questions throughout the book can be found on our website:
www.oxfordsecondary.co.uk/aqa-companions

4

Meet the researcher

It is easy to forget that the psychologists whose research and theories you will read about in this book are real people. We have included brief biographies of some of the **researchers** covered in this book – and even sometimes included a message from them with an interesting or amusing anecdote.

Insider tips

We have provided occasional **insider tips** to give you some extra insight into the requirements of the exam and how you might cope effectively with these.

Key terms

We have given on the page definitions of the **key terms** used in the specification plus some others that we think are very important.

Can you...? questions

On each spread we ask you some **Can you...?** questions to help focus you on the level of knowledge and understanding that you will need for the exam. We have tried to ask questions that will be useful for your exam. You will not be required to reproduce the amount of detail that is on the spreads, but to select just enough to be effective in answering each question. These boxes ensure that you have at least that minimal level of understanding that will enable you to perform well in the exam.

Evaluation/Discussion (AO3)

The text on the right-hand page of each spread has the title **Evaluation/Discussion**. Each evaluation/discussion point is split into different parts (the three point rule), which **identify**, **elaborate** and then draw a **conclusion** about that point. This material is the AO3 content for that particular spread.

On most spreads we have provided some extra points of evaluation/discussion for answering the 16-mark essay questions on the A Level specification. These can be identified by the **'AO3 plus' icon**. Although this extra material is mainly intended for A Level students only, AS students also have the option of using it in their 12-mark essays (i.e. 'stretch and challenge').

Research methods, Upgrade and Apply your knowledge (AO2)

We have included regular extra features on each spread. These can either be on **Research methods**, within the context of a particular spread; an **Upgrade** feature, giving advice to make your exam performance more effective; or an **Apply your knowledge** feature, presenting novel scenarios and asking you to consider some of the issues that arise from these scenarios. This feature gives you valuable practice for any **AO2** questions on the exam.

If content is A Level only this will be clearly indicated with the **A Level only** feature.

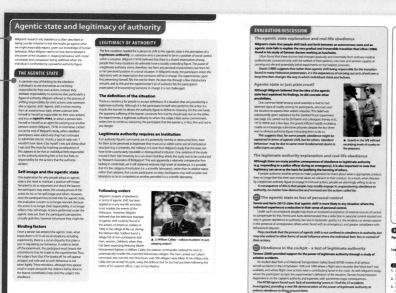

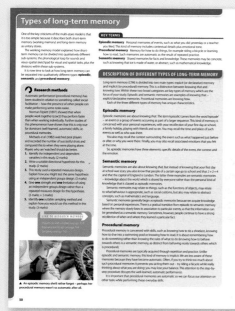

Assessment objectives

- **AO1** is your ability to demonstrate your **knowledge and understanding** of the specification content. AO1 questions typically ask you to describe or outline something.
- **AO2** is your ability to **apply** this knowledge and understanding in a variety of different scenarios. AO2 questions typically ask you to engage with some stimulus material in a psychological way.
- **AO3** is your ability to **analyse, interpret and evaluate** the specification content. AO3 questions typically ask you to criticise something (e.g. by looking at the strengths and limitations of a theory or approach) although there are many other ways of demonstrating AO3.

THE AS EXAMINATION

There are two AS exams (7181/1 and 7181/2).
- In both exams, all the questions will be compulsory.
- You will have one-and-a-half hours to answer all the questions in 7181/1 and one-and-a-half hours to answer all the questions in 7181/2 (many of the questions in both papers will be split into parts).
- The total mark for each paper will be 72 marks.

Paper 1 (7181/1) Introductory topics in psychology

This exam paper is divided into three sections, each worth 24 marks.

Section A Social influence

In this section you will be asked questions on the topic of social influence, i.e. any change in an individual's beliefs, attitudes or behaviours that results from interaction with another individual or a group. Questions can be on any of the different aspects of social influence that make up the specification (e.g. conformity, obedience, social change). Not all topics will appear in the exam (as the Principal Examiner for this paper can only sample them), but you need to learn about them all as they are all equally likely to be selected for the exam. Questions on research methods (which can include maths) can also be incorporated into this section, where they will be set in the context of social influence research.

CHAPTER 1:

Social influence (pages 16–41)

Section B Memory

This section focuses on one aspect of cognitive psychology – memory. Questions can be set on any of the different aspects of memory that are detailed in the specification (e.g. working memory, forgetting, the cognitive interview). Questions set in the exam will sample this material in different ways, ranging from single mark identification questions through to a 12-mark extended writing question. As with social influence, questions testing your research methods (and potentially your mathematical ability) may also turn up in this section.

CHAPTER 2:

Memory (pages 42–67)

Section C Attachment

In this section you will be asked questions on the topic of attachment and the closely associated concept of maternal deprivation. As with the other sections in this paper, questions range from single mark identification or selection questions through to 12-mark extended writing questions and may include research methods questions set in the context of either real or hypothetical attachment research.

CHAPTER 3:

Attachment (pages 68–95)

Paper 2 (7181/2) Psychology in context

This exam paper is divided into three sections, each worth 24 marks.

Section A Approaches in psychology

Questions in this section will be on the different psychological approaches detailed on the specification (e.g. learning approaches, the cognitive approach and the biological approach) as well as the origins of psychology. It is worth noting that the specification also includes a specific subsection on biopsychology, so you can expect some questions on that material. Questions range from low-tariff identification questions (e.g. identifying different parts of a neuron), through mid-tariff questions (e.g. outlining the strengths or limitations of a specified approach), to high-tariff, 12-mark extended writing questions (e.g. 'outline and evaluate the cognitive approach to psychology').

CHAPTER 5:

Approaches in psychology (pages 122–145)

Section B Psychopathology

This follows a similar pattern to Section A, with a mix of low, medium and high-tariff questions (e.g. 2 marks, 4 marks and 12 marks) and a mix of AO1 (description), AO2 (application) and AO3 (evaluation) questions. The content includes definitions of abnormality, characteristics of different disorders, and explanations and treatments of these disorders.

CHAPTER 4:

Psychopathology (pages 96–121)

Section C Research methods

Questions in Section C can be asked on any of the content of the Research methods part of the specification. Most of the marks in this section are AO2 (application) marks, where you are presented with specific scenarios and asked research methods questions on these. Some of the questions will be assessing your mathematical skills (e.g. through simple calculations, selecting a sample, interpreting a graph).

CHAPTER 7:

Research methods (pages 176–231)

THE A LEVEL EXAMINATION

There are three A level exams (7182/1, 7182/2 and 7182/3). The material for papers 1 and 2 are covered in this book, and paper 3 is covered in our Year 2 book.
- On papers 1 and 2, all the questions will be compulsory.
- You will have two hours to answer all the questions in 7182/1 and two hours to answer all the questions in 7182/2 (many of the questions in both papers will be parted).
- The total mark for each paper will be 96 marks.

A LEVEL ONLY ZONE

If you see this on a page, it means you only need to cover this material if you are doing the full A Level course.

Paper 1 (7182/1) Introductory topics in psychology

This exam paper is divided into four sections, each worth 24 marks.

Section A   Social influence

In this section you will be asked questions on the topic of social influence, i.e. any change in an individual's beliefs, attitudes or behaviours that results from interaction with another individual or a group. Questions can be on any of the different aspects of social influence that make up the specification (e.g. conformity, obedience, social change). Not all topics will appear in the exam (as the Principal Examiner for this paper can only sample them), but you need to learn about them all as they are all equally likely to be selected for the exam. Questions on research methods, or on maths, can also be incorporated into this section, where they will be set in the context of social influence research.

CHAPTER 1:
Social influence (pages 16–41)

Section B   Memory

This section focuses on one aspect of cognitive psychology – memory. Questions can be set on any of the different aspects of memory that are detailed in the specification (e.g. working memory, forgetting, the cognitive interview). Questions set in the exam will sample this material in different ways, ranging from single mark identification questions through to a 16-mark extended writing question. As with social influence, questions testing your research methods skills and your mathematical ability may also turn up in this section.

CHAPTER 2:
Memory (pages 42–67)

Section C   Attachment

In this section you will be asked questions on the topic of attachment and the closely associated concept of maternal deprivation. As with the other sections in this paper, questions range from single mark identification or selection questions through to 16-mark extended writing questions and may include research methods questions set in the context of either real or hypothetical attachment research.

CHAPTER 3:
Attachment (pages 68–95)

Section D   Psychopathology

This follows a similar pattern to the other sections on this paper, with a mix of low, medium and high-tariff questions (e.g. 2 marks, 6 marks and 16 marks) and a mix of AO1 (description), AO2 (application) and AO3 (evaluation) questions. The content includes definitions of abnormality, characteristics of different disorders, and explanations and treatments of these disorders.

CHAPTER 4:
Psychopathology (pages 96–121)

Paper 2 (7182/2) Psychology in context

This exam paper is divided into three sections: Approaches in psychology and Biopsychology are worth 24 marks each and Research methods is worth 48 marks.

Section A   Approaches in psychology

Questions in this section will be on the different psychological approaches detailed on the specification (i.e. learning approaches, the psychodynamic approach and humanistic psychology) as well as the origins of psychology. Questions range from low tariff identification questions (e.g. identifying different aspects of classical conditioning), through mid-tariff questions (e.g. outlining the strengths or limitations of a specified approach), to high tariff, 16-mark extended writing questions (e.g. 'outline and evaluate the psychodynamic approach to psychology').

CHAPTER 5:
Approaches in psychology (pages 122–145)

Section B   Biopsychology

This section focuses on different aspects of the biological bases of behaviour. Questions can be set on any of the different aspects of biopsychology that are detailed in the specification (e.g. the divisions of the nervous system, localisation of function in the brain, biological rhythms). Questions set in the exam will sample this material in different ways, ranging from single mark identification questions through to a 16-mark extended writing question.

CHAPTER 6:
Biopsychology (pages 146–175)

Section C   Research methods

Questions in Section C can be asked on any of the content of the Research methods part of the specification. Most of the marks in this section are AO2 (application) marks, where you are presented with specific scenarios and asked research methods questions on these. Some of the questions will also be assessing your mathematical skills (e.g. through simple calculations or interpretation of data).

CHAPTER 7:
Research methods (pages 176–231)

TYPES OF AS AND A LEVEL EXAM QUESTION

Question type	Example	Advice

Simple selection/ recognition

Which **one** of the following is a dispositional factor affecting obedience?

A   Location
B   Personality
C   Proximity
D   Uniform

[1 mark]

Which of the following types of memory is being used in each of the examples below? Choose **one** type of memory that matches each example and write A, B or C in the box next to it. Use each letter once only.

- Justin remembers how to brush his teeth without consciously thinking about it.   ☐
- Justine remembers how awful she felt when she went to the dentist surgery yesterday.   ☐

A   Episodic memory
B   Procedural memory
C   Semantic memory

[2 marks]

Questions such as these should be straightforward enough, so the trick is making sure you have selected the right answer to gain maximum marks. If you aren't sure which answer is the right one, try crossing through those that are obviously wrong, thus narrowing down your options.

It is well worth reading each question very carefully (and then reading it again) to make sure you follow the exact instructions in the question. For example, you might, contrary to instructions, be tempted to use the same answer in both boxes.

Description questions
(E.g. Describe, Outline, Identify, Name)

Give **two** features of the concept of the critical period.
[2 marks]

Identify and outline **two** techniques that might be used in a cognitive interview.   [4 marks]

Outline the fight or flight response.   [4 marks]

These AO1 description questions can come in lots of different forms, but will never be worth more than 6 marks for any one part of a question.

To judge how much to write in response to a question, simply look at the number of marks available and allow about 25 words per mark.

However, where the sole command word is 'Name' or 'Identify', there is no need to develop a 25 word per mark response, simply identifying or naming (as required by the question) is enough.

Sometimes the phrasing of a question (such as the second question) is a prod to get students to go beyond just naming or identifying something and to offer additional detail to flesh it out.

Differences/ Distinguish between

Distinguish between proactive and retroactive interference as explanations of forgetting.   [2 marks]

Identify **two** differences between insecure-resistant and insecure-avoidant attachment.
[2 marks]

Students often ignore the instruction to 'distinguish between' or 'identify differences' and simply outline the two terms or concepts named in the question. This is not what is required, and would not gain credit.

The word 'whereas' is a good linking word to illustrate a difference between two things. However, the difference must be related to the same thing, e.g. it would not be appropriate to point out that an insecure-resistant infant displays high levels of stranger anxiety whereas an insecure-avoidant infant avoids contact with the caregiver at reunion. This is because the two types are not being compared on the same thing (e.g. stranger anxiety). (For further advice on this type of question have a look at page 236.)

Applying knowledge

Nadia is passionate about a charity that supports children living in developing countries. However, most of her classmates want to raise money for an animal charity. The class are due to vote for the class charity at the end of the week.

Using your knowledge of minority social influence, explain **two** ways in which Nadia could try to persuade her classmates to vote for her charity.   [6 marks]

Kelly was chatting to her friend about her new son, Henry, who was now 3 months old. She told her friend how amazing it was that when she smiled at Henry, he smiled back, and when she poked her tongue out, so did he. 'It's as if he's trying to copy everything I do', Kelly said to her friend.

With reference to Kelly's conversation with her friend, outline two features of caregiver-infant interaction.
[4 marks]

In these AO2 questions, you will be provided with a scenario (the question 'stem') and asked to use your psychological knowledge to provide an informed answer.

*You must make sure that your answer contains not only appropriate psychological **content**, but that this is set explicitly within the **context** outlined in the question stem.*

In the first example on the left, some students would ignore the question stem and simply provide a description of minority influence research for changing attitudes. Other students might ignore the underlying psychology completely and simply engage with the material in the stem in some other way. Neither approach is appropriate, and would result in a disappointingly low mark. (For further advice on this type of question have a look at page 233.)

The same warning applies to the second example. There is a temptation to either ignore Kelly's conversation with her friend completely or just mention it in passing. Examiners will be looking for total engagement with the question stem, so ignore it at your peril!

We have included a number of 'Apply your knowledge' features throughout the book so you can practise your skills in this area as well as going a little deeper with some of the issues of the page. The scenarios in these features tend to be lengthier than in actual exam questions, but the skill in answering them is the same.

Question type	Example	Advice
Research methods questions	For at least part of the Research methods section, it is likely that you will be given a description of a study and then a number of short questions such as: (i) Write a suitable hypothesis for this study. [3 marks] (ii) Identify the experimental design used in this study and outline **one** strength of this experimental design. [3 marks] (iii) Name a measure of dispersion the researcher could use. [1 mark] (iii) At the end of the study the researcher debriefed each participant. Write a debriefing that the researcher could read out to the participants. [6 marks]	*Most research methods questions are set within the context of a hypothetical research study. This means that your answers must also be set within the context of that study. If you don't set your answers within the specific context of the study, you cannot receive full marks.* *Most research methods questions have a fairly low tariff (i.e. 1, 2 or 3 marks), although they can be worth as much as 6 or even 12 marks.* *We have included a large number of sample research methods questions throughout the book. The more you practice these, the better you will become at them, and with mastery comes increased confidence.* *You could also be given a scenario and asked to design a study based on that scenario. It might, for example, ask you to outline what method you might use, what design or behavioural categories you might decide on, the sampling method and so on. There is some advice in the problem pages (page 235) on how to answer this type of question.*
Maths questions	Time taken (secs) for six different participants to complete a task over consecutive attempts: 24, 22, 19, 16, 15, 12. Calculate the mean time for participants to complete the task. Show your calculations. [2 marks] **Table 1** Median accuracy scores for anxious and non-anxious participants. |	Anxious	Non-anxious
Median	18	28 | Sketch an appropriate graphical display to show the median accuracy scores in Table 1. [6 marks]	*'Maths' questions can appear anywhere on the paper, and can assess your ability to carry out simple calculations, construct graphs and interpret data. For example, in the first question, a correct answer and appropriate working are necessary for maximum marks.* *Six marks may seem a lot for the second question, but 1 mark is given for each of six aspects of the requested graph, e.g. displaying the data as a bar chart, correct plotting of the bars, labeling axes correctly, having an informative title etc.*
Evaluation questions	Briefly evaluate Bowlby's theory of maternal deprivation. [4 marks] Explain **one** strength and **one** limitation of the biological approach in psychology. [6 marks] Briefly discuss **two** limitations of the cognitive approach in psychology. [6 marks]	*Evaluation can be 'general' as in the first question on the left, or specific as in the second. For the latter question, marks will only be given for that specific content. Miss part of it out and you miss out on marks, put more than one strength or limitation and it won't be creditworthy.* *It is important that you elaborate your evaluative points for maximum marks. We have shown you how to achieve this in some of the 'Upgrade' features throughout this book.*
Mixed description and evaluation questions	Briefly outline and evaluate the cognitive interview as a technique for improving the accuracy of eyewitness testimony. [4 marks] Briefly outline and evaluate **one** explanation for the working memory model. [6 marks]	*Not all questions are straightforward 'description only' or 'evaluation only', but may be mixed.* *The command words (e.g. outline, evaluate) will tell you that description and evaluation are required.* *As a rule of thumb, in short questions like these you should divide your AO1 and AO3 content equally.*
Extended writing questions	Outline and evaluate research into the effects of anxiety on the accuracy of eyewitness testimony. [8 marks] Describe and evaluate **two** studies of social influence. [12 marks] Describe and evaluate the multistore model of memory. [16 marks] Discuss the cognitive approach in psychology. [16 marks]	*Although the distinction between this and the previous category is somewhat arbitrary, questions worth more than 6 marks are usually referred to as extended writing questions.* *As a rough guide, you should write 25–30 words per mark, so for an 8-mark answer 200–240 words would be appropriate and 300–360 words for a 12-mark answer. Three well-developed AO3 points are usually sufficient for a 12-mark question, and that is the approach we have taken throughout this book.* *In the A Level exam you may face a 16-mark question. The difference between this and a 12-mark question is the requirement for further evaluation, taking your word count to around 400–480 words. It is important to remember that for 16-mark questions, AO1 and AO3 are not evenly split, so you should be looking at about 150–180 words of AO1, but 250–300 words of AO3.* *If the instruction is to 'discuss', you are required to go beyond just stating strengths and/or limitations in your AO3 content. You could, for example, look at the implications of these points or counter evidence for their claims.*
Extended writing questions with specific instructions	Describe and evaluate the two-process model as an explanation of phobias. Refer to evidence in your answer. [12 marks] Read the item and then answer the question that follows. Thomas has a phobia of clowns. He relates this to a scary experience he had as a child. He was at the circus when a clown jumped up from the row behind Thomas and startled him so much that his parents had to leave before the show ended. Thomas was so disturbed that he has not even been able to look at a picture of a clown since, let alone go anywhere near one. Describe and evaluate the two-process model as an explanation of phobias. Refer to the example of Thomas in your answer. [12 marks]	*Some extended writing questions have an extra specific instruction, as in the two examples on the left. Both require a discussion of the two-process model (i.e. AO1 and AO3), but each has a slightly different additional requirement.* *The first simply asks you to include evidence (e.g. research evidence as AO3) in your answer. You might well have been going to do this anyway, but now it is required. It doesn't mean that all your AO3 has to be 'evidence', but a couple of research studies that either support or challenge the two-process model would suffice.* *The second question requires you to discuss not only the model but to do this in the context of the stimulus material provided. Although the model is the key requirement of the question, don't make the mistake of assuming the applied aspect of the question is less important. You can include the application as part of the description and/or as part of the evaluation.*

THE WAY YOUR ANSWERS ARE MARKED

Questions and mark schemes

Examiners mark your answers using mark schemes. The mark schemes vary from question to question, depending on the specific demands, but below are some examples.

1-mark questions: 1 mark is given for an accurate selection of the right answer or an appropriate identification. Giving the wrong answer or selecting more than one alternative from those available (if it is a multiple choice question) would result in 0 marks.

2-mark questions: For questions such as 'Explain which type of conditioning is being investigated in this experiment', 1 mark would be given for identifying the correct type of conditioning, and the second mark for further elaboration (in this case explaining *why* this is the case). Other 2-mark questions such as 'Calculate the mean score from this data, and show your calculations' have two requirements (i.e. correct answer and appropriate workings), which would receive 1 mark each.

3-mark questions: Again, these can appear in many guises. For example, 'Briefly discuss **one** strength of...', where the mark awarded is determined by the criteria outlined in the evaluation questions in the mark allocation table below. At other times the question might focus on a descriptive point, e.g. 'Outline **one** explanation of...', where the mark awarded would reflect the detail, accuracy and overall organisation of your answer. Three-mark questions can also simply be a collection of three 1-mark points, so marks would simply be awarded for accuracy.

4-mark questions: Sometimes 4-mark questions are simply 2 x 2 mark questions in disguise, i.e. they contain two specific components, each worth 2 marks. Consider the question 'Identify and outline **two** techniques that may be used in a cognitive interview. (4 marks)'. There are clearly **two** techniques required, so that is immediately 2 marks for each technique, but how would an examiner determine what mark to give for each? Look again at this question, and you will see two distinct instructions, i.e. 'Identify' and 'outline'. So, an examiner would give 1 mark per technique for identification (e.g. 'report everything') and the second mark for adding some elaboration about what is involved in that technique. They then repeat this assessment pattern for the second technique. Some 4 mark questions will ask you to apply your knowledge to a particular scenario or conversation between two people. Focus on the key points of the theory or study you are being asked to apply and make sure you clearly link these points to the scenario or conversation you have been given.

6-mark questions: These can have very different requirements (e.g. description only, description plus application, evaluation only), in which case their actual wording varies. An indication of how marks are awarded for description only questions can be seen in the 'Description' column at the bottom of this page. For 6-mark evaluation questions (such as 'Evaluate research into...'), marks would be awarded as shown in the following table.

▲ Want a high grade? Make life easier for the examiner (and more beneficial for you) by making sure your answer demonstrates the criteria detailed in these mark schemes.

Evaluation questions (AO3: 3 or 6-mark questions)

Level	3-mark question	6-mark question	Evaluation	Organisation	Specialist terminology
3	3	5–6	Clear and effective	Coherent and well-organised	Used effectively
2	2	3–4	Mostly effective	Mostly clear and organised	Used appropriately
1	1	1–2	Lacks detail and/or explanation	Poorly organised	Either absent or used inappropriately
	0	0	No relevant content		

Other 6-mark questions might be 'applying knowledge' questions which require some description of your knowledge (AO1) and application to the stem (AO2). There are examples of such questions on page 8. Examiners do not award the AO1 and AO2 marks separately, they just look for how well your answer fits the criteria below. A word of warning: don't treat the application component of questions as less important; they need at least the same attention as any AO1 component, and frequently more.

Description and application questions (AO1 + AO2: 6-mark questions)

Level	6-mark question	Description	Explanation	Specialist terminology
3	5–6	Generally detailed, clear and coherent	Thorough and appropriate	Used effectively
2	3–4	Mostly clear although some details missing	Mostly sound and appropriate	Some effective use
1	1–2	Lacks detail and clarity	Limited	Minimal, absent or used inappropriately
	0	No relevant content		

8, 12 and 16-mark questions: Questions worth more than 6 marks are generally referred to as 'extended writing' questions. They always have more than one requirement, so examiners will be assessing (usually) both AO1 and AO3 in what is effectively a short essay response. At AS level, questions will have equal amounts of AO1 and AO3 whereas at A level the proportions are different, usually a ratio of 3 AO1: 5 AO3. In some extended writing questions there is also an AO2 (application) component, in which case the marks for AS are: AO1 = 6 marks, AO2 = 2 marks, AO3 = 4 marks, and for A level: AO1 = 6 marks, AO2 = 4 marks, AO3 = 6 marks. There are four (and occasionally five) main criteria an examiner will be looking for in your answers.

Description (AO1) – have you described the material accurately and added appropriate detail? There are a number of ways in which you can add detail. These include expanding your description by going a bit deeper (i.e. giving more information rather than offering a superficial overview), providing an appropriate example to illustrate the point being made, or adding a study (which adds authority and evidence of wider reading).

Application (AO2) – sometimes extended writing questions include an AO2 component in the question, where you are required to include reference to a particular individual or scenario in your discussion. In a 16-mark question, for example, 4 of the 10 marks available for AO3 evaluation are 'diverted' to the AO2 component. Examiners assess how *effectively* you have used the psychological knowledge in your answer to explain the AO2 scenario.

Evaluation/discussion (AO3) – have you used your critical points *effectively*? Examiners will be assessing whether you have made the most of a critical point. Throughout this book we show you lots of ways to elaborate your evaluation, but a simple way is to *identify the point* (e.g. that there is research support), *elaborate the point* (e.g. justify it by providing the findings that back up your claim) and *draw a conclusion* (e.g. link back to the thing being evaluated, demonstrate how research support strengthens a theory or adds support to a research study).

Organisation – does your answer flow and are your arguments clear and presented in a logical manner? This is where planning pays off as you can organise a structure to your answer before you start writing. This is always more effective than just sticking stuff down as it occurs to you!

Specialist terminology – have you used the right psychological terms (giving evidence that you have actually understood what you have read or been taught) rather than presented your material in lay (i.e. non-specialist) language? This does not mean you have to write in an overly formal manner. Students often mistakenly believe that they have to use the sorts of words ('espoused' is a favourite) that they would never use in everyday life!

Extended writing questions (12 and 16-mark questions*)			(* 16-mark questions are A Level only)					
Level	8-mark question	12-mark question	16-mark question	Description	Evaluation/ discussion	Organisation	Specialist terminology	Application**
4	7–8	10–12	13–16	Accurate and well-detailed	Thorough and effective	Clear and coherent	Used effectively	Effective
3	5–6	7–9	9–12	Evident although occasional inaccuracies	Mostly effective	Mostly clear and organised	Mostly used effectively	Mostly effective
2	3–4	4–6	5–8	Mostly descriptive and lacking accuracy in places	Limited effectiveness	Lacks clarity and organisation in places	Used inappropriately on occasions	Limited effectiveness
1	1–2	1–3	1–4	Limited and many inaccuracies	Limited, poorly focused or absent	Poorly organised	Either absent or used inappropriately	Limited, poorly focused or absent
	0	0	0	No relevant content				

**Application criteria only when there is an AO2 component in the question. In a 12 mark question with application 4 marks are AO2, in a 16 mark question with application 6 marks are AO2.

How do examiners work out the right mark for an answer?

Levels and descriptors

Mark schemes are broken down into two, three or four levels (like the one above). Each of these levels has a descriptor, which describes what an answer for that level should look like.

Examiners must first decide on the right level for your response. To do this, they start at the lowest level to see whether the answer meets (or exceeds) the descriptor for that level. If it meets the criteria for the lowest level, the examiner moves up to the next level, and so on, until they have a match between the level descriptor and the answer.

Working out the actual mark

Of course answers are not always uniform (that would be too easy!) and often have some characteristics of one level and other characteristics that fit a different level. For example, the evaluation might be 'thorough and effective', but the description has 'occasional inaccuracies'. In such cases the examiner will work out which of the level descriptors best fits the answer, and then uses this variability to determine the final mark from the range of marks available for that level. If the answer is mainly level 4 but with some characteristics of level 3, then a mark within level 4 is awarded but at the lower end of the range.

IMPROVING EXAM PERFORMANCE: A FEW KEY PIECES OF ADVICE

What does the question require?

Throughout this book we try to prepare you for every conceivable question that might be thrown at you in an exam. However – and it is a big however – you have to play your part in this process. Questions make very specific requests, and examiners have marks available only for the specific requirements of the question. So, if a question asks you to describe the difference between two things, then that's what you must do in order to be awarded marks. You must not just describe the two things. Time spent reading questions carefully is time well spent, as it will stop you setting off on an answer that is not actually dealing with the question set. Being able to read questions accurately is a valuable skill, and one that can be usefully nurtured during your collaborative learning sessions (see 'Work with a friend', opposite).

To get top marks you should use specialist terms and write clearly and coherently – these are very important marking criteria.

Time management is crucial

Many students waste time by writing too much for questions that don't require it, and waste marks by not writing enough for questions that do. The marks that are available for each question (as well as the space provided) inform you about how much you need to write. Do not waste important time or marks by providing answers that are inappropriately long or short for the number of marks available.

You might think of about 25 words per mark, so for a 12-mark extended writing question you should write an answer which is about 300 words. You should allow about 15 minutes for a 12-mark answer and about 20 minutes for a 16-mark answer. We are often asked by students what they should do if they run out of time in an exam. The answer is simple – don't!

Don't panic

A moderate level of stress is good for performance, but too much can impair your ability to recall information and to use it effectively in the exam. A wise student learns to control their stress before the examination, and makes frequent use of stress management even during the revision stage. There are many excellent stress management techniques that are both free and portable (i.e. you can use them wherever you like). Use the internet to find one that works for you, and practise it regularly.

One interesting fact is that physical activity (stretching your arms or feet) reduces stress because the activity tells the body that the stressor has been dealt with and therefore the sympathetic nervous system can 'stand down', putting you in a more relaxed state.

Get yourself motivated People tend to do better when they are highly motivated. We have taught many mature students who all wished they had worked harder at school the first time around. You don't owe success to your teachers or your parents (although they would be delighted), you owe it to the person you will be ten years from now. Think what you would like to be doing in ten years, and what you need to get there, and let that thought prompt you into action now. It is always better to succeed at something you may not need later than to fail at something you will.

Work with your memory In an exam it is harder to access information learned by rote. When someone feels anxious it is easier for them to recall knowledge they understand well. Just reading or writing out notes may do little to help you create enduring memories or to understand the content. However, if you do something with your knowledge it will increase your understanding and make it more likely that material is accessible when you need it. Psychologists call this 'deep processing' as opposed to the 'shallow processing' that takes place when you read something without really thinking about it. Constructing spider-diagrams or mind-maps of the material, or even explaining it to someone else, involves deep processing and makes material more memorable.

Become multi-sensory

Why stick to using just one of your senses when revising? Visual learners learn best by seeing what they are learning, so make the most of text, diagrams, graphs, etc. By contrast, auditory learners learn best by listening (and talking), taking in material using their sense of hearing. You may associate more with one of these styles than the other, but actually we can make use of both these types of learning styles. As well as reading your notes and looking at pictures and diagrams, try listening to your notes and talking about topics with other people, and even performing some of the material, e.g. by role-playing a study.

Short bursts are best One of the problems with revision is that you can do too much of it (in one go, that is…). As you probably know all too well, your attention is prone to wander after a relatively short period of time. Research findings vary as to the optimum time to spend revising, but 30–45 minutes at a time appears to be the norm. What should you do when your attention begins to wander? As a rule, the greater the physiological change (i.e. going for a walk rather than surfing the internet), the more refreshed you will be when returning for your next 30–45 minute stint. There is another benefit to having frequent planned breaks – it increases the probability of subsequent recall.

Revisit regularly Have you ever noticed that if you don't use an icon on your computer for a long time, the cunning little blighter hides it? Your computer seems to take the decision that as you are not using it regularly, it can't be that important, so neatly files it away somewhere. Your brain works in a similar way; knowledge that is not used regularly becomes less immediately accessible. The trick, therefore, is to review what you have learned at regular intervals. Each time you review material, it will take less time, and it will surely pay dividends later on!

Work with a friend Although friends can be a distraction while you are trying to study, they can also be a very useful revision aid. Working together (what psychologists call 'collaborative learning') can aid understanding and make revision more interesting and more fun. Explaining something to someone else is a useful form of deep processing (see above), and by checking and discussing each other's answers to sample questions, you can practise your 'examiner skills' and therefore your understanding of what to put into an exam answer to earn the most marks.

PSYCHOLOGY

A brief history of the science of mind and behaviour

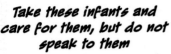

Take these infants and care for them, but do not speak to them

In 700 BC, King Psamtik I of Egypt carried out what was possibly the first psychology experiment. He gave two newborn babies to a shepherd with instructions that they should be cared for but nobody should speak to them.
Psamtik's hypothesis was that the first words they uttered would determine what was the root language of all humans.

TWO YEARS LATER...

Uh?

Βηκος

When one of the children cried "βηκος" (the Phrygian word for bread), Psamtik concluded that the Phrygians must be an older people than the Egyptians, and so Phrygian was the original language of all human beings.

Well, we've finally got the tablet, but now we'll have to wait until we've evolved enough to invent Facebook

The Descent of Man

In 1871, Charles Darwin put forward his ideas on human evolution, arguing that many human characteristics have their origins in our distant ancestral past.

From now on, Psychology will be an experimental science

INSTITUT FÜR PSYCHOLOGIE

In 1879, Wilhelm Wundt opened the first laboratory dedicated to psychology in Leipzig, Germany, marking the birth of experimental psychology.

The mind is like an iceberg. It's what goes on below the surface that is most important

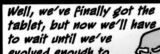

In the early 1900s, Sigmund Freud developed his theory of psychoanalysis, emphasising the importance of the unconscious mind in determining our behaviour.

Dinner time

Ding Ding

In 1927, Ivan Pavlov made the discovery that animals learn to respond to stimuli that predict significant events (such as the coming of food). He referred to this as classical conditioning.

I've got this guy trained now. Every time I press this lever, he gives me food

1938... Burrhus Skinner developed his theory of operant conditioning. The consequences of an action determine the likelihood of it happening again in the future.

Konrad Lorenz's research in Austria showed that geese would become attached on the first moving object they saw. 'Imprinting,' as he called it, would later form the basis for John Bowlby's theory of mother-infant attachment in humans.

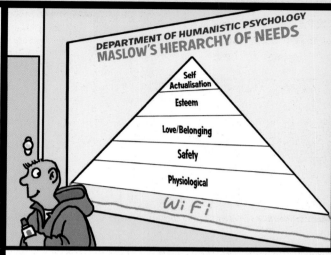

Not all psychologists accepted the view that human beings were at the mercy of forces outside of their control. Abraham Maslow believed that people were motivated by a desire for personal growth and fulfillment.

The development of computers and computer programming in the 1950s led to a new focus on how humans processed sensory information in the brain.

1960s social psychologist Stanley Milgram shocked the world with his discovery that people will deliver potentially fatal electric shocks when ordered to do so by an authority figure.

In the late 20th century advances in brain scanning techniques allowed researchers to investigate brain function directly by seeing inside the living brain.

Psychology continues to expand its horizons. Future directions for research include finding ways to overcome astronauts' feelings of isolation and homesickness during long spaceflights.

CHAPTER CONTENTS

SPECIFICATION CHECKLIST

- Types of conformity: internalisation, identification and compliance. Explanations for conformity: informational social influence and normative social influence, and variables affecting conformity including group size, unanimity and task difficulty as investigated by Asch.

- Conformity to social roles as investigated by Zimbardo.

- Explanations for obedience: agentic state and legitimacy of authority, and situational variables affecting obedience including proximity, location and uniform, as investigated by Milgram.

- Dispositional explanation for obedience: the Authoritarian Personality.

- Explanations of resistance to social influence, including social support and locus of control.

- Minority influence including reference to consistency, commitment and flexibility.

- The role of social influence processes in social change.

Social proof: the power of influence

Thinking of buying a psychology revision book, or choosing a new phone or booking a holiday (well, maybe after your A Levels)? You would probably consider checking what other people think about all the different options available. Studies suggest that over 80% of people read product reviews before making a purchase, and that reviews from other people are many times more trusted than the descriptions given by manufacturers, travel companies and so on. Product reviews are an example of what social psychologist Robert Cialdini calls *social proof*, one of six principles of influence identified by Cialdini after immersing himself in the dubious world of what he called 'compliance professionals' (sales people, fund raisers, etc.).

Social proof is a psychological phenomenon where people accept that the actions of others indicate the appropriate behaviour in a given situation. It allows us to make decisions quickly by focusing on the actions of people around us. When we see others, particularly large groups, doing something, we are likely to come to the conclusion that maybe we should be doing it too.

Milgram *et al.* (1969) designed a simple way to study the phenomenon of social proof. They used a busy street corner in New York, and placed a stooge there and told him to do nothing but stare at a spot high up on a tall building. They then counted how many passers by stopped and gazed up with the stooge or looked up as they passed by. They ran this a few times, each time increasing the number of stooges standing on the corner, noting the number of people who looked up or stopped and gazed with the stooges.

The data they collected was a clear demonstration of social proofing. When there was just one stooge gazing at the building, only 20% of passers by stopped and gazed with him or looked up as they passed. However, when there were five stooges all gazing up, this figure increased to 80%. After all, if five people are all looking at something, there must be something to look at!

This is one of those psychological studies that requires no equipment and can be a lot of fun. You could carry this out around your school or college campus or in your local town centre. As with the study described above, just keep increasing the number of stooges looking up towards the top of a tall building and have a (hidden) observer estimate the percentage of passers by that also look up. Does the percentage increase with the number of stooges? When you have thought about the implications of this finding you are ready to turn the page and learn more about conformity.

Types of conformity and explanations for conformity

Our social lives are characterised by many social influences, some of which we are aware of, and some of which we are not. An individual is said to **conform** if they choose a course of action that is favoured by the majority of other group members. People conform for many reasons, ranging from complete acceptance of the majority viewpoint (i.e. **internalisation**) at one extreme, to simply 'going along' with the crowd at the other (i.e. **compliance**). Two commonly cited explanations are **normative social influence**, when we 'follow the crowd' in order to be accepted, and **informational social influence**, when we accept the majority viewpoint because it is most likely to be right.

 APPLY YOUR KNOWLEDGE

Kane, Dean and Sam have started 'hanging out' with a gang of lads from the same estate. Kane and Dean are both 17 and Sam is 16, whereas the other boys in the group are 18–19. They spend their evenings smoking, drinking cider, daubing graffiti and more recently engaging in petty crime such as shoplifting and vandalism. The group is frequently in trouble with the police, something the older boys see as a 'badge of honour', in that it raises their status as being 'tough' and 'lawless'. The police are also seen to be 'always picking on' the group just because they come from a tough estate.

The three boys have different reasons for joining in with the actions of the group. Dean accepts the group's view that the police target them and so sees their behaviour as a way of 'hitting back'. Kane joins in because he doesn't want to be ridiculed for being immature by the older boys. Sam admires the older boys and wants people to think of him as a member of a tough group from a tough estate.

Which type of conformity is each boy showing? Explain why you came to that decision.

TYPES OF CONFORMITY

Kelman (1958) proposed three types of conformity:

Compliance
Individuals may go along with the group in order to gain their approval or avoid their disapproval. When exposed to the views or actions of the majority, individuals may engage in a process of social comparison, concentrating on what others say or do so that they can adjust their own actions to fit in with them. Fitting in is seen as desirable so this is what motivates conformity. Compliance does not result in any change in the person's underlying attitude, only in the views and behaviours they express in *public*.

Internalisation
Individuals may go along with the group because of an acceptance of their views. When exposed to the views of other members of a group, individuals are encouraged to engage in a validation process, examining their own beliefs to see if they or the others are right. Close examination of the group's position may convince the individual that they are wrong and the group is right. This is particularly likely if the group is generally trustworthy in their views and the individual has tended to go along with them on previous occasions. This can lead to acceptance of the group's point of view both publicly *and* privately.

Identification
In some instances, an individual might accept influence because they want to be associated with another person or group. By adopting the group's attitudes and behaviours, they feel more a part of it. **Identification** has elements of both compliance *and* internalisation, as the individual accepts the attitudes and behaviours they are adopting as right and true (internalisation), but the *purpose* of adopting them is to be accepted as a member of the group (compliance). For example, a child may start smoking because 'that's what cool kids do' and they want to be seen as a 'cool kid'.

What's the difference between them?
Each of these types of conformity has a particular set of motivating conditions that leads to a conforming response. For example, if an individual's prime motivation is to fit in with the rest of the group they may comply rather than internalise the group's position on a particular issue. Alternatively, if the primary motivation is to find the most appropriate way of responding in a particular situation, then internalising the group position may be seen as the most credible way of achieving this.

EXPLANATIONS FOR CONFORMITY

Normative social influence
It is possible to go along with the majority without really accepting their point of view. This type of conformity is usually referred to as 'compliance'. As humans are a social species, they have a fundamental need for social companionship and a fear of censure and rejection. It is this that forms the basis for normative social influence, i.e. to gain approval and acceptance, to avoid censure and disapproval or to achieve specific goals. An important condition for normative influence to occur is that the individual must believe they are under surveillance by the group. When this is the case, people tend to conform to the majority position in public but do not necessarily internalise this view as it does not carry over into private settings nor does it endure over time (Nail, 1986).

Informational social influence
Informational influence occurs when an individual accepts information from others as evidence about reality. As well as having a need to be accepted, human beings also have a need to feel confident that their perceptions and beliefs are correct. Initially, individuals may make objective tests against reality (i.e. check the facts), but if this is not possible they must rely on the opinions of others. Informational influence is more likely if the situation is ambiguous (i.e. the right course of action is not clear) or where others are experts (i.e. we believe that others have more knowledge than we have). As a result, the individual does not just comply in behaviour alone but also changes their behaviour in line with the group position. Because this involves changing both public *and* private attitudes and behaviour, this is an example of internalisation.

EVALUATION/DISCUSSION

Difficult to distinguish between compliance and internalisation

The relationship between compliance and internalisation is complicated because of difficulties in knowing when each is actually taking place.

For example, it is assumed that a person who publicly agrees with a majority yet disagrees with them in private must be demonstrating compliance rather than internalisation. However, it is also possible that acceptance of the group's views has occurred in public yet dissipates later when in private.

This could be because they have forgotten information given by the group or because they have received new information that changes their mind. This demonstrates the difficulty in determining what is, and what is not, simple compliance rather than internalisation.

Research support for normative influence

US research has supported the important role played by people's normative beliefs in shaping behaviours such as smoking and energy conservation.

Linkenbach and Perkins (2003) found that adolescents exposed to the simple message that the majority of their age peers did not smoke were subsequently less likely to take up smoking. Likewise, Schultz *et al.* (2008) found that hotel guests exposed to the normative message that 75% of guests reused their towels each day (an indication of energy conservation behaviour) reduced their own towel use by 25%.

These studies support the claim that people shape their behaviour out of a desire to fit in with their reference group, and as such demonstrate the power of normative influence.

Research support for informational influence

Studies have demonstrated how exposure to other people's beliefs and opinions can shape many aspects of social behaviour and beliefs.

Wittenbrink and Henley (1996) found that participants exposed to negative information about African Americans (which they were led to believe was the view of the majority) later reported more negative attitudes toward black individuals. Research has also shown how informational social influence can shape political opinion. In a study by Fein *et al.* (2007), participants saw what was supposedly the reaction of their fellow participants on screen during a presidential debate.

This information produced large shifts in their judgements of the candidates' performance, and shows the importance of informational influence in shaping social behaviour.

On most topic spreads in this book we have provided five points of evaluation/discussion. For 12 mark AS Level essays, two or three well-elaborated points are sufficient for a good answer. For 16 mark A Level essays, four or five well-elaborated points are ideal. We have used the AO3 Plus icon **(AO3 plus)** to indicate the 'extra' evaluation/discussion points for A Level students over and above those provided for AS students. However, regardless of whether you are an AS or A Level student, you are free to choose any of the points on the page when constructing your answer.

(AO3 plus) Normative influence may not be detected

Although normative influence undoubtedly has a powerful effect on the behaviour of the individual, it is possible that they do not actually recognise the behaviour of others as a causal factor in their own behaviour.

There is some support for this claim. Nolan *et al.* (2008) investigated whether people detected the influence of social norms on their energy conservation behaviour. When asked about what factors had influenced their own energy conservation, people believed that the behaviour of neighbours had the least impact on their own energy conservation, yet results showed that it had the strongest impact.

This suggests that people rely on beliefs about what should *motivate their behaviour, and so under-detect the impact of normative influence.*

(AO3 plus) Informational influence is moderated by type of task

A problem for the informational explanation of conformity is that features of the task moderate the impact of majority influence. For some judgements there are clear physical criteria for validation, but for other judgements, there may be no physical way of validating them.

For example, deciding whether Bristol is the most highly populated city in the South West of England can be determined through objective (i.e. physical) means such as consulting statistics, census records and so on. However, other judgements (e.g. deciding whether Bristol is the most fun city in the South West of England) cannot be made using objective criteria because such criteria do not exist. Consequently, these kinds of judgements must be made on the basis of social consensus (i.e. what other people, particularly experts, believe to be the case).

As a result, majorities should exert greater influence on issues of social *rather than* physical *reality, and this is precisely what research tends to show (Laughlin, 1999).*

▲ Normative influence has been used successfully to deter adolescents from taking up smoking, such as this poster from Evanston Township High School (ETHS) in the US.

KEY TERMS

Compliance occurs when an individual accepts influence because they hope to achieve a favourable reaction from those around them. An attitude or behaviour is adopted not because of its content, but because of the rewards or approval associated with its adoption.

Conformity is a form of social influence that results from exposure to the majority position and leads to compliance with that position. It is the tendency for people to adopt the behaviour, attitudes and values of other members of a reference group.

Identification A form of influence where an individual adopts an attitude or behaviour because they want to be associated with a particular person or group.

Informational social influence is a form of influence, which is the result of a desire to be right – looking to others as a way of gaining evidence about reality.

Internalisation occurs when an individual accepts influence because the content of the attitude or behaviour proposed is consistent with their own value system.

Normative social influence is a form of influence whereby an individual conforms with the expectations of the majority in order to gain approval or to avoid social disapproval.

CAN YOU? [No. 1.1]

1. Briefly explain what is meant by 'conformity'. (3 marks)
2. Briefly explain what is meant by 'compliance', 'internalisation' and 'identification'. (3 marks each)
3. Give an example of compliance, internalisation and identification. (2 marks each)
4. Explain normative social influence. (4 marks)
5. Explain informational social influence. (4 marks)
6. Outline and evaluate normative and informational influence explanations of conformity. (12 marks AS, 16 marks A)

Variables affecting conformity

Much of our understanding of conformity can be traced back to the pioneering work of Solomon Asch in the 1950s. During this time, Asch became famous for a series of studies that demonstrated the effects of social influence on conformity. Asch showed that people appeared willing to go against the compelling evidence of their senses in order to conform to a group consensus. This counter-intuitive finding has passed into psychological folklore as the 'Asch effect', a term used to describe the very human tendency for us sometimes to do as others do rather than what we feel is right.

KEY STUDY: ASCH (1956)

Asch asked student volunteers to take part in a visual discrimination task, although, unbeknown to these volunteers, all but one of the participants were really confederates (i.e. colleagues) of the investigator. The real purpose of the study was to see how the lone 'real' participant would react to the behaviour of the confederates.

Procedure

In total, 123 male US undergraduates were tested. Participants were seated around a table and asked to look at three lines of different lengths. They took turns to call out which of the three lines they thought was the same length as a 'standard' line (see below) with the real participant always answering second to last.

Standard line   Comparison lines

Although there was always a fairly obvious solution to this task, on 12 of the 18 trials (i.e. the 'critical' trials) the confederates were instructed to give the same incorrect answer. Asch was interested in whether the 'real' participants would stick to what they believed to be right, or cave in to the pressure of the majority and go along with its decision.

Findings

On the 12 critical trials, the average conformity rate was 33%, i.e. participants agreed with the incorrect response given by the other group members, on average, on one-third of the trials. Asch also discovered individual differences in conformity rates. One-quarter of the participants never conformed on any of the critical trials, half conformed on six or more of the critical trials and one in 20 of the participants conformed on all 12 of the critical trials.

To confirm that the stimulus lines were indeed unambiguous, Asch conducted a control condition without the distraction of confederates giving wrong answers. In this condition he found that participants made mistakes about 1% of the time, although this could not explain the relatively high levels of conformity in the main study.

When Asch interviewed his participants afterwards, he discovered that the majority of participants who conformed had continued privately to trust their own perceptions and judgements, but changed their public behaviour, giving incorrect answers to avoid disapproval from other group members (i.e. they showed compliance).

VARIABLES AFFECTING CONFORMITY

Asch carried out a number of variations of his original study to find out which variables had the most significant effects on the level of conformity shown by participants.

Group size

Asch found that there was very little conformity when the majority consisted of just one or two confederates. However, under the pressure of a majority of three confederates, the proportion of conforming responses jumped up to about 30%. Further increases in the size of the majority did not increase this level of conformity substantially, indicating that the size of the majority is important but only up to a point. Campbell and Fairey (1989) suggest that group size may have a different effect depending on the type of judgement being made and the motivation of the individual. Where there is no objectively correct answer (e.g. musical preferences) and the individual is concerned about 'fitting in', then the larger the majority the more likely they are to be swayed. However, when there *is* a correct response and the individual is concerned about being correct, then the views of just one or two others will usually be sufficient.

The unanimity of the majority

In Asch's original study, the confederates unanimously gave the same wrong answer. What would happen if this unanimity was disturbed? When the real participant was given the support of either another real participant or a confederate who had been instructed to give the right answers throughout, conformity levels dropped significantly, reducing the percentage of wrong answers from 33% to just 5.5%.

What would happen if the lone 'dissenter' gave an answer that was both different from the majority *and* different from the true answer? In this condition, conformity rates dropped to 9%, nearly as great a fall as when the dissenter provided support for the real participant by giving the same answer. This led Asch to conclude that it was breaking the group's unanimous position that was the major factor in conformity reduction.

The difficulty of the task

In one variation, Asch made the differences between the line lengths much smaller (so that the 'correct' answer was less obvious and the task much more difficult). Under these circumstances, the level of conformity increased. Lucas *et al.* (2006) investigated this relationship a little further. They found that the influence of task difficulty is moderated by the *self-efficacy* of the individual. When exposed to maths problems in an Asch-type task, high self-efficacy participants (i.e. participants who were confident in their own abilities) remained more independent than low self-efficacy participants, even under conditions of high task difficulty. This shows that situational differences (task difficulty) and individual differences (self-efficacy) are both important in determining conformity.

You may have noticed how some of the essay questions in the 'Can you' sections are worth 12 marks while others are worth 16 marks. This is because the 12-mark questions are for AS students and the 16-mark questions are for A Level students. The extra 4 marks are typically for the extra evaluation that A Level students are expected to provide, which is why we have used an AO3 plus icon on some evaluative points. Sometimes the extra marks may be AO2 and link to a scenario you have been given.

EVALUATION/DISCUSSION

Asch's research may be a 'child of its time'

It is possible that Asch's findings are unique because the research took place in a particular period of US history when conformity was more important.

In 1956, the US was in the grip of McCarthyism, a strong anti-Communist period when people were scared to go against the majority and so more likely to conform. Some years later, Perrin and Spencer (1980) attempted to repeat Asch's study in the UK. In their initial study they obtained only one conforming response out of a total of 396 trials where a majority unanimously gave the same wrong answer. However, in a subsequent study, where they used youths on probation as participants and probation officers as the confederates, they found similar levels of conformity to those found by Asch back in the 1950s.

This confirmed that conformity is more likely if the perceived costs of not conforming are high, which would have been the case during the McCarthy era in the US.

Problems with determining the effect of group size

Bond (2005) suggests a limitation of research in conformity is that studies have used only a limited range of majority sizes.

Asch had concluded that a majority size of three was a sufficient number for maximal influence and therefore most subsequent studies using the Asch procedure have used three as the majority size. Bond points out that no studies other than Asch have used a majority size greater than nine, and in other studies of conformity the range of majority sizes used is much narrower, typically between two and four.

This, suggests Bond, means we know very little about the effect of larger majority sizes on conformity levels.

Independent behaviour rather than conformity

We should remember that, in Asch's study, only one-third of the trials where the majority unanimously gave the same wrong answer produced a conforming response.

In other words, in two-thirds of these trials the participants resolutely stuck to their original judgement despite being faced with an overwhelming majority expressing a totally different view.

Asch believed that, rather than showing human beings to be overly conformist, his study had actually demonstrated a commendable tendency for participants to stick to what they believed to be the correct judgement, i.e. to show independent behaviour.

Unconvincing confederates?

A problem for the confederates in Asch's study is that it would have been difficult for them to act convincingly when giving the wrong answer, something that would pose serious problems for the validity of the study.

Mori and Arai (2010) overcame the confederate problem by using a technique where participants wore glasses with special polarising filters. Three participants in each group wore identical glasses and a fourth wore a different set with a different filter. This meant that each participant viewed the same stimuli but one participant saw them differently, causing them to judge that a different (to the rest of the group) comparison line matched the standard line. For female participants (although not male participants), the results closely matched those of the original Asch study.

This suggests that the confederates in the original study had *acted convincingly, reinforcing the validity of Asch's findings.*

Cultural differences in conformity

Research suggests that there are important cultural differences in conformity, and we might therefore expect different results dependent on the culture in which a study takes place.

Smith *et al.* (2006) analysed the results of Asch-type studies across a number of different cultures. The average conformity rate across the different cultures was 31.2%. What was interesting was that the average conformity rate for individualist cultures (e.g. in Europe and the US) was about 25%, whereas for collectivist cultures in Africa, Asia and South America it was much higher at 37%.

Markus and Kitayama (1991) suggest that the reason that a higher level of conformity arises in collectivist cultures is because it is viewed more favourably, a form of 'social glue' that binds communities together.

MEET THE RESEARCHER

Solomon Asch (1907–1996) was born in Warsaw and emigrated to the US as a teenager, studying psychology at Columbia University in New York. He influenced a generation of social psychologists including Stanley Milgram whose PhD he supervised.

Asch is probably best known for his studies of conformity in the 1950s and his name is synonymous with the topic to the extent that within psychology conformity is sometimes referred to as the *Asch effect*.

◀ In the Mori and Arai study, participants wore special polarising filters, which changed the perceived size of the comparison lines.

Research methods

Jenness (1932) asked students to guess how many beans there were in a jar. Then they were asked to discuss their estimates and, finally, asked individually to give their estimates again. Jenness found that estimates tended to converge to a group norm.

Some students conducted a similar study. They put 100 beans in a jar and then asked people to estimate the number of beans by writing their answer down on a form that some others had already filled in. For one group of participants, Group A, the previous answers on the form were high (mean estimate 120). For participants in Group B the answers on the form were low (mean estimate 80).

The findings are shown in the table below.

	Group A	Group B
Mean estimates for participants	115.6	92.7

1. What conclusion can you draw from these findings? (2 marks)
2. The students used the mean. What other measure of central tendency could they have used? (1 mark)
3. Give **one** strength of using the mean rather than the measure you identified in question 2. (2 marks)
4. Explain how the students would have calculated the mean.

LINK TO RESEARCH METHODS

Measures of central tendency on pages 212–213

CAN YOU?   No. 1.2

1. Outline what Asch did in his study of conformity and the findings of this study. (6 marks)
2. Explain the role of group size as a variable affecting conformity. (4 marks)
3. Explain the role of unanimity as a variable affecting conformity. (4 marks)
4. Explain the role of task difficulty as a variable affecting conformity. (4 marks)
5. Describe and evaluate research into conformity. (12 marks AS, 16 marks A)

Conformity to social roles

If 'ordinary' people were placed in a simulated prison environment and some of them were designated as guards and some prisoners, how would they behave in their new **social roles**? This was the question Philip Zimbardo, Craig Haney, Curtis Banks and Carlo Prescott set out to answer in the Stanford Prison Experiment (SPE). Zimbardo's study was set in the aftermath of the Attica Prison riots in New York, where nine hostages and 28 prisoners died following a protest over inhumane conditions in the prison. In contrast to Milgram's studies of obedience (see page 24), the aim of the SPE was to observe the interaction between the two groups in the *absence* of an obvious authority figure.

(see page 24)

KEY STUDY: THE STANFORD PRISON EXPERIMENT (HANEY *ET AL.*, 1973)

Procedure

A mock prison was set up in the basement of the psychology department at Stanford University in California, USA. Male student volunteers were psychologically and physically screened and the 24 most stable of these were randomly assigned to either play the role of 'prisoner' or 'guard'.

The prisoners were unexpectedly arrested at home and on entry to the 'prison' they were put through a delousing procedure, given a prison uniform and assigned an ID number. The guards referred to the prisoners only by these numbers throughout the study. Prisoners were allowed certain rights, including three meals and three supervised toilet trips a day and two visits per week.

Participants allocated the role of guard were given uniforms, clubs, whistles and wore reflective sunglasses (to prevent eye contact). Zimbardo himself took the role of Prison Superintendent. The study was planned to last two weeks.

Findings

Over the first few days of the study the guards grew increasingly tyrannical and abusive toward the prisoners. They woke prisoners in the night and forced them to clean the toilets with their bare hands and made them carry out other degrading activities. Some guards were so enthusiastic in their role that they volunteered to do extra hours without pay.

The participants appeared at times to forget that this was only a psychological study and that they were merely acting. Even when they were unaware of being watched, they still conformed to their role of prisoner or guard. When one prisoner had had enough he asked for 'parole' rather than asking to withdraw from the study.

Five prisoners had to be released early because of their extreme reactions (e.g. crying, rage and acute anxiety) – symptoms that had started to appear after just two days. The study was finally terminated after only six days, following the intervention of postgraduate student Christina Maslach (later to become Zimbardo's wife) who reminded the researchers that this was a psychological study and, as such, did not justify the abuse being meted out to the participants. This study demonstrated that both guards and prisoners conformed to their social roles. The guards became increasingly cruel and sadistic and the prisoners became increasingly passive and accepting of their plight.

▲ Over the course of the six days, guards became increasingly sadistic and prisoners increasingly passive.

Although Philip Zimbardo was the lead researcher in the SPE, the reference for the study has Craig Haney's name first. Confusing, but accurate!

Insider tip…

Some exam questions ask you to 'describe' or 'outline' a study, but don't specify what aspect (i.e. procedures or findings). When responding to such questions, it is better to focus mainly on the findings and a very brief outline of the procedures rather than lengthy descriptions of them.

OTHER RESEARCH: THE BBC PRISON STUDY (REICHER AND HASLAM, 2006)

Procedure

Like the Stanford Prison Experiment (SPE), the BBC study (so-called because it was broadcast as an ongoing documentary by the BBC) randomly assigned men to the role of guard or prisoner and examined their behaviour within a specially created 'prison'.

Fifteen male participants were divided into five groups of three people who were as closely matched as possible on key personality variables, and from each group of three, one person was randomly chosen to be a guard and the other two prisoners. The study was to run for eight days.

◄ The BBC study revealed a shift in the balance of power with prisoners challenging the authority of the guards.

Findings

The key finding of this study was that participants did not conform automatically to their assigned role as had happened in the SPE. Over the course of the study, the prisoners increasingly identified as a group and worked collectively to challenge the authority of the guards and establish a more egalitarian set of social relations within the prison. The guards also failed to identify with their role, which made them reluctant to impose their authority on the prisoners. This led to a shift of power and the collapse of the prisoner–guard system.

Conformity to roles is not automatic

Haslam and Reicher (2012) challenged Zimbardo's belief that the guards' drift into sadistic behaviour was an automatic consequence of them embracing their role.

They pointed out that, in the SPE, guard behaviour varied from being fully sadistic to, for a few, being 'good guards', who did not degrade or harass the prisoners, and even did small favours for them.

Haslam and Reicher argue that this shows that the guards chose how to behave, rather than blindly conforming to their social role, as suggested by Zimbardo.

The problem of demand characteristics

Banuazizi and Movahedi (1975) argued that the behaviour of participants in the SPE was more a consequence of demand characteristics (i.e. participants guessing how the experimenter wanted them to behave) than conformity to roles.

They presented some of the details of the SPE procedure to a large sample of students who had never heard of the study. The vast majority correctly guessed that the purpose of the experiment was to show that ordinary people assigned the role of guard or prisoner would act like real prisoners and guards, and they predicted that guards would act in a hostile, domineering way and the prisoners would react in a passive way.

This suggests that the behaviour of Zimbardo's guards and prisoners was not due to their response to a 'compelling prison environment', but rather it was a response to powerful demand characteristics in the experimental situation itself.

Were these studies ethical?

Zimbardo's study is often criticised for being unethical, despite the fact that it followed the guidelines of the Stanford University ethics committee that had approved it.

Despite this, Zimbardo acknowledges that perhaps the study should have been stopped earlier as so many of the participants were experiencing emotional distress. He attempted to make amends for this by carrying out debriefing sessions for several years afterwards and concluded that there were no lasting negative effects.

Recognising the potential for harm in studies such as this, Reicher and Haslam used the same basic set-up as Zimbardo, but took greater steps to minimise the potential harm to their participants. They created a situation that was harsh and testing, but not harmful.

A03 plus The SPE and its relevance to Abu Ghraib

Zimbardo argues that the conformity to social role effect can also be used to explain events in Abu Ghraib, a military prison in Iraq notorious for the torture and abuse of Iraqi prisoners by US soldiers in 2003 and 2004.

As was the case in the SPE, Zimbardo believed that the guards who committed the abuses were the victims of situational factors that made abuse more likely. These factors, such as lack of training, unrelenting boredom and no accountability to higher authority were present both in the SPE and at Abu Ghraib.

Zimbardo concludes that these factors, combined with an opportunity to misuse the power associated with the role of 'guard', led to the prisoner abuses in both situations.

A03 plus What did we learn from these studies?

Zimbardo's conclusion from the SPE was that people can quickly descend into tyrannical behaviour because they conform unthinkingly to their prescribed role without the need for specific orders.

The brutality of the guards in the SPE, claimed Zimbardo, was a natural consequence of being allocated the role of 'guard' and asserting the power associated with that role.

However, Reicher and Haslam reject this claim that group behaviour is necessarily mindless and tyrannical. By contrast, the results of their BBC prison study suggest that the way in which members of strong groups behave depends upon the norms and values associated with their specific social identity.

MEET THE RESEARCHER

Philip Zimbardo is one of the most distinguished living psychologists. He is best known for his controversial Stanford Prison Experiment that highlighted the ease with which ordinary college students could cross the line between good and evil when caught up in the matrix of situational forces. His current research looks at the psychology of heroism. He is interested in why some people become perpetrators of evil, while others act heroically on behalf of those who are in need.

KEY TERM

Social roles are the behaviours expected of an individual who occupies a given social position or status.

UPGRADE

You need to be aware of the specific content of the specification. Check this regularly throughout your studies and revision. Practise exam questions so you can quickly work out exactly what a question is asking.

The key features of any exam question are the command word, its specific requirements and the marks available.

For example, a question might read:

Briefly outline and evaluate the findings of **one** study of conformity to social roles. (4 marks)

- You first need to recognise that it is on 'conformity to social roles' and therefore Asch would not be the appropriate study.
- The question asks for 'findings'; therefore, material related to aims or procedures is not creditworthy.
- The command words 'briefly outline' and 'evaluate' tell you there should be two stages to your answer. 'Briefly outline' requires a brief description that shows some level of knowledge and understanding. 'Evaluate' means you have to say how useful, important or true these findings are, which could be through contrasting evidence, problems with applying it to real life, or potential implications of finding this out.
- Finally, there are 4 marks to be earned, meaning both 'parts' need more than simple identification. You need to add detail to show that you understand the findings and are able to judge how important they are.

 CAN YOU? No. 1.3

1. Outline Zimbardo's study of conformity to social roles and the findings of this study. (6 marks)
2. Outline how **one** study of conformity to social roles was carried out. (4 marks)
3. Outline the findings of **one** study of conformity to social roles. (4 marks)
4. Outline and evaluate Zimbardo's research into conformity to social roles. (12 marks AS, 16 marks A)

Situational variables affecting obedience

A more direct form of social influence where the individual has arguably less choice whether to behave in a particular way is **obedience to authority**. In this form of social influence, the individual is faced with the choice of whether to obey a direct order from a person with higher status, or whether to defy the order. Stanley Milgram's research demonstrated that ordinary people are astonishingly obedient even when asked to do something that goes against their own morality. Milgram's research appeared to suggest that it is not evil people who commit atrocities, such as those witnessed during the Holocaust, but ordinary people who are just obeying orders.

 APPLY YOUR KNOWLEDGE

In 1969, a US police department in California discontinued their traditional navy blue, paramilitary-style uniforms and adopted a non-traditional, more 'civilian'-style uniform hoping to improve police–community relations. After using the new-style uniform for eight years the police department decided that it did not command sufficient respect and so returned to a traditional-style uniform. The number of assaults on police officers, which had doubled after the initial uniform change, dropped steadily when they switched back to the traditional uniforms (Mauro, 1984).

Using your knowledge of research into social influence, suggest why, in this example, such changes in obedience might have been linked to the style of uniform worn by the police.

Percentage of fully obedient participants

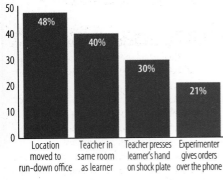

▲ Percentage of fully obedient participants in selected experimental variations.

KEY STUDY: MILGRAM (1963)

Procedure

Milgram's study involved 40 participants at a time over a series of conditions, each varying some aspect of the situation to calculate its effect on obedience. Participants were told it was a study of how punishment affects learning. There were two experimental confederates: an experimenter, and a 47-year-old man who was introduced as another volunteer participant. The two participants drew lots to see who would act as the 'teacher' and who the 'learner'. This was rigged so that the real participant was always the teacher and the 'fake' participant the learner.

The teacher was required to test the learner on his ability to remember word pairs. Every time he got one wrong the teacher had to administer increasingly strong electric shocks, starting at 15 volts, and then continuing up to the maximum of 450 volts in 15 volt increments.

In the *voice feedback* study, the learner, sitting in another room, gave mainly wrong answers and received his (fake) shocks in silence until they reached the 300 volt level (very strong shocks). At this point he pounded on the wall and then gave no response to the next question. He repeated this at 315 volts and from then on said/did nothing. If the 'teacher' asked to stop at any point, the experimenter had a series of 'prods' to repeat, such as saying, 'It is absolutely essential that you continue' or, 'You have no other choice, you must go on'.

Findings

Before the study, Milgram asked psychiatrists, college students and colleagues to predict how long participants would go before refusing to continue. Consistently these groups predicted that very few would go beyond 150 volts and only 1 in 1,000 would administer the full 450 volts.

However, contrary to these expectations, in the *voice feedback* study, 26 of the 40 participants (65%) continued to the maximum shock level, 450 volts. This was despite the shock generator being labelled 'Danger: severe shock' at 420 volts and 'XXX' at 450. In fact, all participants went to 300 volts with only five (12.5%) stopping there, the point at which the learner first objected (see above).

SITUATIONAL FACTORS IN OBEDIENCE

Proximity

In the *proximity* study, both teacher and learner were seated in the same room. Obedience levels fell to 40% as the teacher was now able to experience the learner's anguish more directly. In an even more extreme variation the teacher was required to force the learner's hand onto a shock plate. In this *touch proximity* condition, the obedience rate dropped even further to 30%. Milgram found the proximity of the authority figure also had an effect on obedience rates. In the *experimenter absent* study, after giving his instructions the experimenter left the room and gave subsequent orders over the telephone. The vast majority of participants now defied the experimenter, with only 21% continuing to the maximum shock level. Some even went as far as repeatedly giving the weakest shock level despite telling the experimenter they were following the correct procedure (see graph).

Location

The studies were conducted in the psychology laboratory at Yale University. Several participants remarked that the location of the study gave them confidence in the integrity of the people involved, and many indicated that they would not have shocked the learner if this study had been carried out elsewhere. What, then, would happen if the research were moved to a less prestigious location? To examine this possibility Milgram moved his study to a run-down office in Bridgeport, Connecticut, with no obvious affiliations with Yale. Obedience rates did drop slightly but not significantly, with 48% of participants delivering the 450 volt maximum shock.

The power of uniform

Research has shown that uniforms can have a powerful impact on obedience. They are easily recognisable and convey power and authority, which can become symbolised in the uniform itself.

Bushman (1988) carried out a study where a female researcher, dressed either in a 'police-style' uniform, as a business executive or as a beggar, stopped people in the street and told them to give change to a male researcher for an expired parking meter. When she was in the uniform, 72% of the people obeyed, whereas obedience rates were much lower when she was dressed as a business executive (48%) or as a beggar (52%). When interviewed afterwards, people claimed they had obeyed the woman in uniform because she appeared to have authority.

EVALUATION/DISCUSSION

Internal validity: a lack of realism

Orne and Holland (1968) claimed that participants in psychological studies have learned to distrust experimenters because they know that the true purpose of the study may be disguised.

Perry (2012) discovered that many of Milgram's participants had been sceptical at the time about whether the shocks were real. One of Milgram's research assistants, Taketo Murata, had divided the participants into what he called 'doubters' (those who believed the shocks were fake) and 'believers' (those who believed they were delivering real shocks to the learner). He found it was this latter group who were more likely to disobey the experimenter and give only low intensity shocks.

This finding challenges the validity of Milgram's study and suggests that when faced with the reality of destructive obedience, people are more likely to disobey an authority figure.

Historical validity: would the same thing happen today?

We might be tempted to dismiss the relevance of Milgram's study simply because it was carried out over 50 years ago. What would happen if the same studies were carried out today?

Blass (1999) carried out a statistical analysis of obedience studies carried out between 1961 and 1985. By carrying out a correlational analysis relating each study's year of publication and the amount of obedience it found, he discovered no relationship whatsoever, i.e. the later studies found no more or less obedience than the ones conducted earlier. A more recent study (Burger, 2009) found levels of obedience almost identical to those found by Milgram some 46 years earlier.

These findings suggest that Milgram's findings still appear to apply as much today as they did back in the early 1960s, i.e. they have 'historical validity'.

Proximity: Reserve Police Battalion 101

Mandel (1998) challenges the relevance of obedience research as an explanation of real-life atrocities, claiming that Milgram's conclusions about the situational determinants of obedience are not borne out by real-life events.

In 1942, the men of Reserve Police Battalion 101 received orders to carry out a mass killing of Jews in the town of Józefów, Poland. Their commanding officer, Major Wilhelm Trapp, made an offer to his men that anyone who 'didn't feel up to' this duty could be assigned other tasks. Despite the presence of factors shown by Milgram to increase defiance (e.g. close physical proximity to their victims and the presence of disobedient peers), only a small minority took up Trapp's offer. The vast majority carried out their orders without protest.

Mandel concludes that using 'obedience' as an explanation for these atrocities serves only as an alibi, masking the real reasons (e.g. antisemitism) behind such behaviours.

Location: high levels of obedience were not surprising

Fromm (1973) claims that, because Milgram's subjects know they were part of a scientific experiment, this made them more likely to obey than in real life.

In a laboratory setting, the experimenter acts as a representative of science, a prestigious institution in Western cultures. Because of this, Fromm suggested that the high degree of obedience in the Milgram experiment (65%) was less surprising than the 35% disobedience. In contrast to experiments that take place in scientific laboratories, real-life obedience to authority (particularly destructive obedience) is a lot more difficult and time-consuming to achieve. Genocides such as the one witnessed in Rwanda in 1994 required years of manipulation of the masses and a systematic dehumanisation of the target group.

As a result, we must be cautious about drawing broad generalisations from Milgram's study, believing that the majority of people would commit crimes of obedience in real life.

The power of uniform: research support

Durkin and Jeffery (2000) demonstrated that young children's understanding of police authority was dominated by visual cues, specifically the presence of a police uniform.

Using illustrated scenarios, they asked children aged 5-9 years to identify who was able to make an arrest. Options were: a policeman who had changed from his uniform into civilian clothes; a man with a different occupation who had put on a police uniform temporarily for reasons unconnected with police work; and a man in the uniform of another occupation. Children tended to select the man currently wearing the police uniform as being allowed to carry out an arrest. Younger children were more likely to select the non-policeman in police uniform than they were to select the policeman out of his uniform.

The findings suggest that children's initial perceptions of authority are dominated by superficial aspects of appearance, which are more easily accessible than socially conferred status.

Insider tip...

Although the term 'validity' is not on the AS spec, it is a very useful term to know and can be used as AO3.

KEY TERM

Obedience to authority Obedience refers to a type of social influence whereby somebody acts in response to a direct order from a figure with perceived authority. There is also the implication that the person receiving the order is made to respond in a way that they would not otherwise have done without the order.

▲ Members of Reserve Police Battalion 101 publicly humiliate a Jewish man.

CAN YOU? — No. 1.4

1. Outline what Milgram did in his study of obedience and the findings of this study. (6 marks)
2. Explain the role of proximity as a variable affecting obedience. (3 marks)
3. Explain the role of location as a variable affecting obedience. (3 marks)
4. Explain the role of uniform as a variable affecting obedience. (3 marks)
5. Outline and discuss research into obedience. (12 marks AS, 16 marks A)

Agentic state and legitimacy of authority

Milgram's research into obedience is often described as being 'counter-intuitive' in that the results go against what we might reasonably expect, given our knowledge of human behaviour. What Milgram seems to have demonstrated is the power of the situation in shaping behaviour, with moral constraints and compassion being sidelined when the individual is confronted by a powerful authority figure.

THE AGENTIC STATE

A common way of thinking for the obedient individual is to see themselves as not being responsible for their own actions. Instead, they attribute responsibility to someone else, particularly a figure of authority. Milgram referred to this process of shifting responsibility for one's actions onto someone else as 'agentic shift'. Agentic shift involves moving from an autonomous state, where a person 'sees himself or herself as responsible for their own actions', and into an **agentic state**, in which a person 'sees himself or herself as an agent for carrying out another person's wishes' (Milgram, 1974). In interviews carried out at the end of Milgram's study, when obedient participants were asked why they had continued to administer electric shocks, a typical reply was: 'I wouldn't have done it by myself. I was just doing what I was told.' The most far-reaching consequence of this appears to be that an individual feels responsible to the authority directing him or her but feels *no* responsibility for the actions that the authority dictates.

Self-image and the agentic state

One explanation for why people adopt an agentic state is the need to maintain a positive self-image. Tempted to do as requested and shock the learner, the participant may assess the consequences of this action for his or her self-image and refrain. However, once the participant has moved into the agentic state, this evaluative concern is no longer relevant. Because the action is no longer their responsibility, it no longer reflects their self-image. Actions performed under the agentic state are, from the participant's perspective, virtually guilt-free, however inhumane they might be.

Binding factors

Once a person has entered the agentic state, what keeps them in it? In all social situations, including experiments, there is a social etiquette that plays a part in regulating our behaviour. In order to break off the experiment, the participant must breach the commitment that he made to the experimenter. Thus, the subject fears that if he breaks off, he will appear arrogant and rude and so such behaviour is not taken lightly. These emotions, although they appear small in scope alongside the violence being done to the learner, nonetheless help bind the subject into obedience.

LEGITIMACY OF AUTHORITY

The first condition needed for a person to shift to the agentic state is the perception of a **legitimate authority**, i.e. someone who is perceived to be in a position of social control within a situation. Milgram (1974) believed that there is a shared expectation among people that many situations do ordinarily have a socially controlling figure. The *power* of a legitimate authority stems, therefore, not from any personal characteristics but from his or her perceived position in a social situation. In Milgram's study, the participant enters the laboratory with an expectation that someone will be in charge. The experimenter, upon first presenting himself, fills this role for them. He does this through a few introductory remarks, and as this and the experimenter's 'air of authority' fits the participant's expectation of encountering 'someone in charge', it is not challenged.

The definition of the situation

There is a tendency for people to accept definitions of a situation that are provided by a legitimate authority. Although it is the participant himself who performs the action (i.e. shocks the learner) he allows the authority figure to define its meaning. On the one hand, the apparent suffering of the learner convinces him that he should quit, but on the other, the experimenter, a legitimate authority to whom the subject feels some commitment, orders him to continue, reassuring the participant that the learner is, in fact, fine and not in any danger.

Legitimate authority requires an institution

If an authority figure's commands are of a potentially harmful or destructive form, then for them to be perceived as legitimate they must occur within some sort of institutional structure (e.g. a university, the military). It is clear from Milgram's study that this does not have to be a particularly reputable or distinguished institution. One variation of the study moved it from Yale University to a run-down building where the study was to be conducted by 'Research Associates of Bridgeport'. This was apparently a relatively unimpressive firm lacking in credentials, yet it still obtained relatively high levels of obedience. It is possible that it is the *category* of institution (i.e. a scientific laboratory), rather than its relative status within that category, that causes participants to obey. Participants may well consider one laboratory to be as competent as another, provided it is a *scientific* laboratory.

Following orders

Milgram's analysis of obedience in terms of agentic shift has been applied to many real-life atrocities, most notably the events of the Holocaust. However, Milgram believed that the definitive example of agentic shift could be found in the actions of American soldiers in 1968, in the village of My Lai, during the Vietnam War. Soldiers found a village full of non-combatants (old men, women, children), when they had been expecting Vietcong (North

▲ Lt William Calley – callous murderer or just obeying orders?

Vietnamese) fighters. Lt William Calley, the platoon commander, ordered his men to systematically murder the unarmed Vietnamese villagers. The men carried out Calley's command, and over the next few hours, over 500 villagers were killed. At his military trial, Calley did not accept his guilt, using the defence that he too had just been following the orders of *his* superior officer, Capt. Ernest Medina.

The agentic state explanation and real-life obedience

Milgram's claim that people shift back and forth between an autonomous state and an agentic state fails to explain the very gradual and irreversible transition that Lifton (1986) found in his study of German doctors working at Auschwitz.

Lifton found that these doctors had changed gradually and irreversibly from ordinary medical professionals, concerned only with the welfare of their patients, into men and women capable of carrying out vile and potentially lethal experiments on the helpless prisoners.

Staub (1989) suggests that rather than agentic shift being responsible for the transition found in many Holocaust perpetrators, it is the experience of carrying out acts of evil over a long time that changes the way in which individuals think and behave.

Agentic state or just plain cruel?

Although Milgram believed that the idea of the agentic state best explained his findings, he did concede other possibilities.

One common belief among social scientists is that he had detected signs of cruelty among his participants, who had used the situation to express their sadistic impulses. This belief was subsequently given substance by the Stanford Prison Experiment (see page 22), carried out by Zimbardo and colleagues (Haney *et al.*, 1973). Within just a few days, the guards inflicted rapidly escalating cruelty on increasingly submissive prisoners despite the fact there was no obvious authority figure instructing them to do so.

This suggests that, for some people, obedience might be explained in terms of agentic shift, but for others, 'obedient behaviour' may be due to some more fundamental desire to inflict harm on others.

▲ Guards in the SPE inflicted escalating levels of cruelty on the prisoners.

The legitimate authority explanation and real-life obedience

Although there are many positive consequences of obedience to legitimate authority (e.g. responding to a police officer during an emergency), it is also important to note that legitimacy can serve as the basis for justifying the harming of others.

If people authorise another person to make judgements for them about what is appropriate conduct, they no longer feel that their own moral values are relevant to their conduct. As a result, when directed by a legitimate authority figure to engage in immoral actions, people are alarmingly willing to do so.

A consequence of this is that people may readily engage in unquestioning obedience to authority, no matter how destructive and immoral are the actions called for.

The agentic state as loss of personal control

Fennis and Aarts (2012) claim that 'agentic shift' is more likely in any situation where the individual experiences a reduction in their sense of personal control.

Under such circumstances people may show an increased acceptance of external sources of control to compensate for this. Fennis and Aarts demonstrated that a reduction in personal control resulted not only in greater obedience to authority, but also in bystander apathy (i.e. the tendency to remain passive in the presence of unresponsive others when faced with an emergency), and greater compliance with behavioural requests.

They conclude that the process of agentic shift is not confined to obedience to authority, but may also extend to other forms of social influence where the individual feels 'less in control of' their actions.

Obedience in the cockpit – a test of legitimate authority

Tarnow (2000) provided support for the power of legitimate authority through a study of aviation accidents.

He studied data from a US National Transportation Safety Board (NTSB) review of all serious aircraft accidents in the US between 1978 and 1990 where a flight voice recorder (the 'black box') was available, and where flight crew actions were a contributing factor in the crash. As with Milgram's study, where the participant accepts the experimenter's definition of the situation, Tarnow found excessive dependence on the captain's authority and expertise, with sometimes tragic consequences.

The NTSB report found such 'lack of monitoring' errors in 19 of the 37 accidents investigated, providing a real-life demonstration of the power of legitimate authority to enforce obedience in those around them.

UPGRADE

Most of the material on this page is evaluation (AO3). Students often find it difficult to know what makes material truly evaluative rather than just descriptive. The difference can be quite subtle, but the important aspect is that it goes beyond simply saying what something is.

There are some key ways in which evaluation marks can be gained:

- Research evidence that supports the claims being made. It could be another study that found similar results or research that seems to show the theory or concept happening in real life.
- Evidence that 'challenges' what is being discussed, such as studies achieving different findings to previous ones.
- Real-life applications, for example showing the application as a concept or study to real-life events.
- Alternative explanations that might better account for the findings.

We have tried to include a good variety of evaluation on the right-hand side of each spread, but you can always do a bit of research and find your own if you are feeling adventurous. Include lead-in phrases to put your evaluation into context, e.g. 'There is research support for this explanation from…', or 'This explanation is challenged by…'. This will make it clear to the examiner that you are evaluating.

The secret to making your evaluation more discursive is to do more with it – elaborate. Try adding 'However', 'On the other hand', 'The xx theory would disagree with this' to your answers, creating a 'debate' or 'discussion' about how true something is. This becomes essential when the command word is 'Discuss' rather than 'Evaluate'.

Key command words that indicate AO3: 'discuss', 'evaluate', any question that refers to 'strengths', 'limitations' or 'criticisms'. As with AO1, 'explain' can be used here too.

KEY TERMS

Agentic state A person sees himself or herself as an agent for carrying out another person's wishes.

Legitimate authority A person who is perceived to be in a position of social control within a situation.

CAN YOU?   No. 1.5

1. Outline the role of the agentic state in obedience. (4 marks)
2. Outline the role of legitimacy of authority in obedience. (4 marks)
3. Outline and evaluate **two** explanations of obedience. (12 marks AS, 16 marks A)

The Authoritarian Personality

Milgram (1974) believed there was most probably a complex personality basis to obedience and disobedience. He noted that his obedience study created a conflict in participants who had a deeply rooted disposition not to harm someone else, yet the equally strong tendency to obey authority. The fact that some participants were driven more by the former and others by the latter led Milgram and other psychologists to explore the possible **dispositional** basis of obedience. They became interested in whether an individual's obedient behaviour emerged only under specific conditions or whether it responded to a specific personality pattern, most notably the Authoritarian Personality.

THE AUTHORITARIAN PERSONALITY

The F scale

The identification of a specific personality type – the **Authoritarian Personality** – provided a possible explanation for why some individuals require very little pressure in order to obey. The California **F scale** (the 'F' stood for 'Fascist') was used by Adorno *et al.* (1950) to measure the different components that made up the Authoritarian Personality. The F scale contained statements such as '*Obedience and respect for authority are the most important virtues children should learn*' and '*Rules are there for people to follow, not change*'. Agreeing with such items was indicative of an Authoritarian Personality. Individuals with this type of personality were rigid thinkers who obeyed authority, saw the world as black and white, and enforced strict adherence to social rules and hierarchies.

Adorno *et al.* also found that people who scored high on the F scale tended to have been raised by parents who used an authoritarian parenting style (including the use of physical punishment). Growing up within a particular social system means that people assume that this system is the expected norm. Therefore, if children happen to grow up in a particularly authoritarian family, with a strong emphasis on obedience, then they acquire these same authoritarian attitudes through a process of learning and imitation.

Right-wing authoritarianism

Robert Altemeyer (1981) refined the concept of the Authoritarian Personality by identifying a cluster of three of the original personality variables that he referred to as **right-wing authoritarianism** (RWA). According to Altemeyer, high-RWA people possess three important personality characteristics that predispose them to obedience:

- Conventionalism – an adherence to conventional norms and values.
- Authoritarian aggression – aggressive feelings toward people who violate these norms.
- Authoritarian submission – uncritical submission to legitimate authorities.

Altemeyer tested the relationship between RWA and obedience in an experiment where participants were ordered to give themselves increasing levels of shock when they made mistakes on a learning task. There was a significant correlation between RWA scores and the level of shocks that participants were willing to give themselves. Interestingly, there was also a large red button, above which was the warning – 'Do not push this button unless you are instructed to do so'. When the experiment was over, the experimenter ordered participants to push the button 'to administer an extra strong shock as a punishment for not trying' (Altemeyer, 1981). Participants' level of RWA appeared to be irrelevant for this instruction as the vast majority did as they were told without question!

KEY STUDY: ELMS AND MILGRAM (1966)

One of the major debates surrounding Milgram's study of obedience was whether participants' behaviour emerged only under specific situational conditions or whether it was dispositional, i.e. the result of a particular personality pattern. Research on obedience measures *actual* submission to authority, not just what a person says he or she is likely to do, and therefore allows researchers to study whether participants high in authoritarianism are more likely to obey an authority figure.

Procedure

Elms and Milgram carried out a follow-up study using participants who had previously taken part in one of Milgram's experiments two months before. They selected 20 'obedient' participants (those who had continued to the final shock level) and 20 'defiant' participants (those who had refused to continue at some point in the experiment). Each participant completed the MMPI scale (measuring a range of personality variables) and the California F scale to specifically measure their levels of authoritarianism. Participants were also asked a series of open-ended questions, including questions about their relationship with their parents during childhood and their attitude to the 'experimenter' (the authority figure) and the 'learner' during their participation in Milgram's original study.

Findings

The researchers found little difference between obedient and defiant participants on MMPI variables. However, they did find higher levels of authoritarianism among those participants classified as obedient, compared with those classified as defiant. They also found significant differences between obedient and defiant participants that were consistent with the idea of the Authoritarian Personality. For example, obedient participants reported being less close to their fathers during childhood, and were more likely to describe them in distinctly more negative terms. Obedient participants saw the authority figure in Milgram's study as clearly more admirable, and the learner as much less so. This was not the case among the defiant participants. These findings suggested to Elms and Milgram that the obedient group was higher on the trait of 'authoritarianism'.

The Cultural Revolution

The important role played by early socialisation is evident in a study of Communist Leader Mao Tse-tung's Cultural Revolution in 1960s China (Chan, 1985). Interviews with refugees of the revolution showed the highly authoritarian nature of their personality. Rather than the family being the primary source of this authoritarian socialisation, Chan believed that during the Cultural Revolution, the school took this role. Interestingly, once the individual was removed from the environment which encouraged such behaviour, the authoritarian side of their character diminished considerably.

▲ During the Chinese Cultural Revolution in the 1960s, schools became important sources of authoritarian socialisation.

EVALUATION/DISCUSSION

Research evidence for the authoritarianism/obedience link

Although several studies have found that authoritarian participants are more obedient (e.g. Elms and Milgram, 1966; Altemeyer, 1981), there has been a good deal of suspicion about whether these participants really believed they were giving electric shocks.

Dambrun and Vatiné (2010) overcame this problem by using an 'immersive virtual environment', where an actor taking the role of the learner was filmed, recorded and displayed on a computer screen. Participants were informed that the experiment was a simulation and that the shocks and the victim's reactions were not real, but simulated. Despite this, participants still tended to respond as if the situation was real, and there was a clear and significant correlation between participants' RWA scores (assessed before the experiment) and the maximum voltage shock administered to the victim.

In other words, participants who displayed higher levels of RWA were the ones who obeyed the most, confirming the link between authoritarianism and obedience.

The social context is more important

Although Milgram accepted that there might be a dispositional basis to obedience and disobedience, he did not believe the evidence for this was particularly strong.

Milgram showed that variations in the social context of the study (e.g. proximity of the victim, location, presence of disobedient peers) were the primary cause of differences in participants' levels of obedience, not variations in personality. He believed that the specific social situation participants found themselves in caused them to obey or resist regardless of their personalities.

Relying on an explanation of obedience based purely on authoritarianism lacks the flexibility to account for these variations (Milgram, 1974).

Differences between authoritarian and obedient participants

Elms and Milgram's research also presented some important differences in the characteristics of the Authoritarian Personality and the characteristics of obedient participants.

For example, when Elms and Milgram asked participants about their upbringing, many of the fully obedient participants reported having a very good relationship with their parents, rather than having grown up in the overly strict family environment associated with the Authoritarian Personality.

It also seems implausible, therefore, given the large number of participants who were fully obedient in Milgram's study, that the vast majority would have grown up in a harsh environment with a punitive father.

A03 plus Education may determine authoritarianism *and* obedience

Research (e.g. Middendorp and Meloen, 1990) has generally found that less-educated people are consistently more authoritarian than the well educated.

Milgram also found that participants with lower levels of education tended to be more obedient than those with higher levels of education.

This suggests that instead of authoritarianism causing obedience, lack of education could be responsible for both authoritarianism and obedience. As a result, any apparent causal relationship between authoritarianism and obedience may be more illusory than real.

A03 plus Left-wing views are associated with lower levels of obedience

Altemeyer's reformulation of the Authoritarian Personality in terms of 'right-wing authoritarianism' suggests that people who define themselves as on the right of the political spectrum would be more likely to obey authority. We might expect, therefore, that people who define themselves as more 'left-wing' would be characterised by lower levels of obedience.

There is some support for this distinction. Bègue *et al.* (2014) carried out a replication of Milgram's study as part of a fake game show, where contestants had to deliver (fake) electric shocks to other contestants. Subsequent interviews using the 'World Value Survey Questionnaire' revealed that the more participants defined themselves as on the left of the political spectrum, the lower the intensity of shocks they agreed to give to the other contestant.

This suggests that situational context (as studied by Milgram) does not exclude the possibility of individual differences as a determining influence in obedience.

CAN YOU? | No. 1.6

1. Briefly explain what is meant by the 'Authoritarian Personality'. (2 marks)
2. Explain the dispositional explanation for obedience. (4 marks)
3. Outline and evaluate **one** research study relating to the Authoritarian Personality explanation of obedience. (6 marks)
4. Outline and discuss the Authoritarian Personality explanation of obedience. (12 marks AS, 16 marks A)

Research methods

Adorno *et al.* investigated the Authoritarian Personality by using the F scale questionnaire to assess authoritarianism. This consisted of a set of statements (see text on the left) where participants were asked to indicate slight/moderate/strong support or slight/moderate/strong opposition.

Some participants were later interviewed about their parents' childrearing styles, e.g. they were asked about how strict their parents were and how much their parents lived by rules.

1. Does the F scale consist of open or closed questions? (1 mark)
2. The research found that people who were high on authoritarianism were also more obedient. Is this a positive or negative correlation? Explain your answer. (2 marks)
3. Sketch a graph to show the relationship you identified in question 2. Ensure that you label the axes carefully. (3 marks)
4. In the second part of the study the researchers decided to interview participants instead of using a questionnaire. Give **two** strengths of using an interview rather than a questionnaire in this study. (2 marks + 2 marks)
5. Suggest an open question that might have been used in the interviews. Explain why your question is an open question. (2 marks)

LINK TO RESEARCH METHODS

Questionnaires and interviews on pages 202–205
Correlation on pages 206–207

Note: The authoritarian personality explanation is an example of a 'dispositional explanation' of obedience so would be used to answer Q2 below.

KEY TERMS

Authoritarian Personality A distinct personality pattern characterised by strict adherence to conventional values and a belief in absolute obedience or submission to authority.

Dispositional Explanations of behaviours such as obedience emphasise them being caused by an individual's own personal characteristics rather than situational influences within the environment.

F scale Also known as the 'California F scale' or the 'Fascism scale', the F scale was developed in California in 1947 as a measure of authoritarian traits or tendencies.

Right-wing authoritarianism A cluster of personality variables (conventionalism, authority submission and authoritarian aggression) that are associated with a 'right-wing' attitude to life.

Resistance to social influence

The previous spreads have painted a somewhat pessimistic picture of human beings as slaves to situational or dispositional factors, but this need not be the case. Although the majority of people may conform or obey the demands of authority, there are always those who refuse to do so. Part of the reason for their resistance to social influence may lie with the social support provided by others. Standing firm against peer pressure or resisting the demands of a harmful authority figure is easier if you have an ally. Other explanations emphasise the importance of specific personality characteristics that provide an individual with the means of remaining independent in the face of pressure from those around them.

SOCIAL SUPPORT

Asch's research on conformity showed us how difficult it is to go against the crowd, not only because human beings have a strong need to be accepted by the group but also because they have a desire to act in the 'right' way.

Social support and resisting conformity

Asch (1956) found that the presence of **social support** enables an individual to resist conformity pressure from the majority. In one of the variations in his study, the introduction of an ally who also gave the right answer (and so appeared to resist the majority) caused conformity levels to drop sharply. The social support offered by the ally led to a reduction in conformity from 33% (with a unanimous majority) to just 5.5%.

The most important aspect of social support appears to be that it breaks the unanimous position of the majority. Supporters and dissenters are likely to be effective in reducing conformity because, by breaking the unanimity of the majority, they raise the possibility that there are other, equally legitimate, ways of thinking or responding. The presence of an ally provides the individual with an independent assessment of reality that makes them feel more confident in their decision and better able to stand up to the majority.

Social support and resisting obedience

It is often difficult to take a stand against authority because the obedient behaviour of others makes even a harmful action appear acceptable. However, their *disobedience* can change that perception. Research has shown that individuals are generally more confident in their ability to resist the temptation to obey if they can find an ally who is willing to join them in opposing the authority figure. Disobedient peers therefore act as role models on which the individual can model their own behaviour.

Individuals are able to use the defiance of peers as an opportunity to extricate themselves from having to cause any further harm to a victim as a result of their obedience. For example, in one of Milgram's variations, the participant was one of a team of three testing the learner. The other two were actually confederates who, one after another, refused to continue shocking the learner and withdrew. Their defiance had a liberating influence on the real participants, with only 10% continuing to the maximum 450V shock level.

CAN YOU?   No. 1.7

1. Explain the role of social support in resisting social influence. (6 marks)
2. Explain the role of locus of control in resisting social influence. (6 marks)
3. Outline and evaluate the role of social support and locus of control in resisting social influence. (12 marks AS, 16 marks A)

LOCUS OF CONTROL

The nature of locus of control

The term **locus of control** refers to a person's perception of personal control over their own behaviour. It is measured along a dimension of 'high internal' to 'high external', although most of us would be somewhere between the two extremes. A strong *internal* locus of control is associated with the belief that we can control events in our life. People with an *internal locus of control* believe that what happens to them is largely a consequence of their own ability and effort. They are more likely to display independence in thought and behaviour. People high in **internality** rely less on the opinions of others, which means they are better able to resist social influence.

People with an *external locus of control* tend to believe that what happens to them is determined by external factors, such as the influence of others or luck. They have a sense that things 'just happen to them' and are largely out of their control. People high in **externality** tend to approach events with a more passive and fatalistic attitude than internals, taking less personal responsibility for their actions and being less likely to display independent behaviour and more likely to accept the influence of others.

Internality and resistance to social influence

Locus of control research has uncovered a number of characteristics of internals that have relevance for resisting social influence. These include the following:

1. High internals are active seekers of information that is useful to them, and so are less likely to rely on the opinions of others, making them less vulnerable to social influence.
2. High internals tend to be more achievement-oriented and consequently more likely to become leaders rather than follow others. For example, Spector (1982) found that a relationship exists between locus of control and leadership style, with internals being more persuasive and goal-oriented than externals.
3. High internals are better able to resist coercion from others. For example, in a simulated prisoner-of-war camp situation, internals were better able to resist the attempts of an interrogator to gain information. The more intense the pressure, the greater the difference between the internal's performance and that of the external's (Hutchins and Estey, 1978).

KEY TERMS

Externality Individuals who tend to believe that their behaviour and experience is caused by events outside their control.

Internality Individuals who tend to believe that they are responsible for their behaviour and experience rather than external forces.

Locus of control People differ in their beliefs about whether the outcomes of their actions are dependent on what they do (internal locus of control) or on events outside their personal control (external locus of control).

Social support The perception that an individual has assistance available from other people, and that they are part of a supportive network.

Insider tip...

On the facing page we have included a number of evaluative (i.e. AO3) points that are appropriate to this topic. It is important, when writing AO3 points, that you make them truly evaluative. We have helped you to achieve this by breaking down each evaluation point into its three constituent parts – the critical point, evidence for (or elaboration of) the point, and a link back or conclusion about the point.

EVALUATION OF SOCIAL SUPPORT

The importance of response order

Allen and Levine (1969) studied whether the response position of the person providing social support made any difference to a participant resisting the majority.

In one condition, a confederate answered first, giving the right answer, while other confederates all gave the same wrong answer. The real participant always answered fifth (last). In the second condition, the confederate answered fourth, i.e. after the other confederates. Support was significantly more effective in position 1 than in position 4.

The researchers suggest that a correct first answer, in confirming the participant's own judgement, produces an initial commitment to the correct response that endures even though other group members disagree.

Research demonstrates the importance of social support in resisting social influence

Rees and Wallace (2015) showed that the social support provided by friends helped adolescents resist conformity pressures from the majority.

Individuals with a majority of friends who drank alcohol were significantly more likely to have engaged in drunkenness and binge drinking over the previous 12 months. However, they also found that individuals were able to resist pressures to drink alcohol when they had a friend or two who also resisted.

This is consistent with lab-based experiments on social influence and shows that the social support offered by non-drinking friends can decrease the odds of a non-drinker deciding to consume alcohol, even when faced with the conformity pressures of a drinking majority.

Social support in the real world: the Rosenstrasse protest

The Rosenstrasse protest is a stark illustration of Milgram's research in real life.

In 1943, a group of German women protested in the Rosenstrasse in Berlin, where the Gestapo (Nazi secret police) were holding 2,000 Jewish men, most of whom were married to non-Jewish partners or were the male children of these 'mixed' marriages. Despite the Gestapo threatening to open fire on them, the women's courage eventually prevailed and the Jews were set free.

Milgram found that the presence of disobedient peers gave the participant the confidence and courage to resist the authority's orders. Likewise, these women defied the authority of the Gestapo together, given courage by the collective action of their peers.

EVALUATION OF LOCUS OF CONTROL

Locus of control is related to normative but not informational influence

Spector (1983) measured locus of control and predisposition to normative and informational influence in 157 undergraduate students.

He found a significant correlation between locus of control and predisposition to normative social influence, with externals more likely to conform to this form of influence than internals. However, he found no such relationship for predisposition to informational social influence, with locus of control not appearing to be a significant factor in this type of conformity.

Spector concluded that externals would conform more than internals in situations of normative pressure but would not conform more in situations of informational pressure.

People are more external than they used to be

Research suggests a historical trend in locus of control, with young people becoming increasingly external.

A meta-analysis by Twenge *et al.* (2004) found that young Americans increasingly believed that their fate was determined more by luck and powerful others rather than their own actions. Researchers found that locus of control scores had become substantially more external in student and child samples between 1960 and 2002.

Twenge interprets this trend towards increasing externality in terms of the alienation experienced by young people and the tendency to explain misfortunes on outside forces.

Research support

Avtgis (1998) carried out a meta-analysis of studies of the relationship between locus of control and different forms of social influence, including conformity.

This showed a significant positive correlation for the relationship between scores of internality/ externality and scores on measures of persuasion, social influence and conformity.

The analysis showed that individuals who scored higher on external locus of control tend to be more easily persuaded, more easily influenced and more conforming than those who score as internal in terms of locus of control.

Research methods

Gamson *et al.* (1982) conducted a study on resisting obedience. Participants answered an advertisement to take part in a study supposedly run by a public relations firm, MHRC. Participants met in groups at a motel and were paid $10 for two hours' work. They were asked to consider the case of an employee, Mr C., who, it was claimed, had behaved immorally. It gradually became apparent that what the company wanted was some videotaped support for their views. At the end of the session each group was asked jointly to sign a form to allow the company to use the videotape.

Altogether 33 groups took part in this study and all but four of these groups refused to sign, i.e. they disobeyed authority. In all groups there were some people who wished to obey but the presence of dissenters led to group disobedience.

1. In fact the researchers intended to study a total of 80 groups but found that participants became highly emotionally involved and therefore they decided to stop. What ethical issue is raised here? (1 mark)
2. What sampling method was used in this study? (1 mark)
3. Explain **one** limitation of using this sampling method. (2 marks)
4. What percentage of the groups refused to sign the agreement? (2 marks)

LINK TO RESEARCH METHODS

Sampling methods on page 192
Percentages on page 211

Minority influence

Until the end of the 1960s, most research on social influence was focused on majority influence (conformity). Asch's research showed that people often ignored the evidence of their own senses to conform to the majority view. Influence was seen as flowing from the majority to the minority rather than the other way around. People's primary motivation appeared to be the need to be accepted and the fear of being rejected by the group. However, it is an inescapable fact that group opinion *does* change over time as new ideas are gradually accepted by the majority.

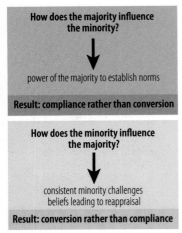

How does the majority influence the minority?

↓

power of the majority to establish norms

Result: compliance rather than conversion

How does the minority influence the majority?

↓

consistent minority challenges beliefs leading to reappraisal

Result: conversion rather than compliance

A naïve participant is simply someone who is unaware of the purpose of the research or the hypothesis being tested. The term is used here to describe a participant who is not one of the confederates.

MINORITY INFLUENCE AND BEHAVIOURAL STYLE

With majority influence, people identify with the majority and try to 'fit in' with their opinions without careful scrutiny of the message. **Minority influence**, in contrast, creates a *conversion* process whereby, provided the minority adopt a consistent and committed approach, people scrutinise the message itself. They want to understand *why* the minority hold this position. As a result, conversion to the minority position, when it occurs, tends to be deeper and longer lasting as people have internalised the minority's point of view. In order to bring about this conversion process, research suggests that minorities must adopt a particular behavioural style of being consistent, committed and flexible in their arguments.

Consistency

When people are first exposed to a minority with a differing view, they assume the minority is in error. However, if the minority adopt a **consistent** approach, others come to reassess the situation and consider the issue more carefully. After all, there must be a reason why the minority takes the position it does and is sufficiently confident to maintain it over time and with each other (Nemeth, 2010). Wood *et al.* (1994) carried out a meta-analysis of 97 studies of minority influence, and found that minorities who were perceived as being especially consistent in expressing their position were particularly influential. The importance of consistency is demonstrated in the Moscovici *et al.* key study on this page.

Commitment

It is difficult to dismiss a minority when it adopts an uncompromising and consistent commitment to its position. **Commitment** is important in the influence process because it suggests certainty, confidence and courage in the face of a hostile majority. Because joining a minority inevitably has greater cost for the individual than staying with the majority, the degree of commitment shown by minority group members is typically greater. This greater commitment may then persuade majority group members to take them seriously, or even convert to the minority position.

Flexibility

Mugny (1982) suggests that **flexibility** is more effective at changing majority opinion than rigidity of arguments. Because minorities are typically powerless compared to the majority, they must *negotiate* their position with the majority rather than try to enforce it. Mugny distinguished between rigid and flexible negotiating styles, arguing that a rigid minority that refuses to compromise risks being perceived as dogmatic, i.e. narrow-minded and refusing to consider that other opinions might also be justified. However, a minority that is *too* flexible and *too* prepared to compromise risks being seen as inconsistent. Neither approach is particularly effective at persuading the majority to shift to the minority's position, but, claims Mugny, some degree of flexibility is more effective than none at all.

KEY STUDY: MOSCOVICI *ET AL.* (1969)

Procedure

Each group comprised four naïve participants and a minority of two confederates. They were shown a series of blue slides that varied only in intensity and were asked to judge the colour of each slide. In the 'consistent' experimental condition, the two confederates repeatedly called the blue slides 'green', i.e. they said 'green' on every trial. In the 'inconsistent' condition, the confederates called the slides 'green' on two-thirds of the trials, and on the remaining one-third of trials called the slides 'blue'. In a control condition, comprising six naïve participants and no confederates, participants called the slides 'blue' throughout.

Findings

The findings showed that the consistent minority influenced the naïve participants to say 'green' on over 8% of the trials. The inconsistent minority exerted very little influence, and did not differ significantly from the control group. After the main study was over, participants were asked individually to sort 16 coloured discs into either 'blue' or 'green'. Three of these discs were unambiguously from the blue end of the colour spectrum and three were unambiguously from the green end. The remaining ten discs were ambiguous in that they might be considered either blue or green. To be able to do this, participants had to establish a threshold point where everything

one side of that point would then be judged 'blue', and everything the other side 'green'. Individuals who had been in the 'consistent' and 'inconsistent' minority conditions set their thresholds at different points, with the result that those in the consistent condition judged more of the chips to be green than those in the inconsistent condition. This effect was even greater for those participants who hadn't gone along with the minority during the experiment, suggesting that the initial influence was more at a *private* than a public level.

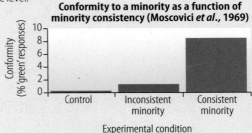

Conformity to a minority as a function of minority consistency (Moscovici *et al.*, 1969)

▲ Moscovici's research demonstrates that, although levels of conformity are nowhere near as great as with majority influence, a consistent minority is far more influential than an inconsistent one.

EVALUATION/DISCUSSION

Research support for flexibility

Nemeth and Brilmayer (1987) provided support for the role of flexibility in a simulated jury situation.

Group members discussed the amount of compensation to be paid to someone involved in a ski-lift accident. When a confederate put forward an alternative point of view and refused to change his position, this had no effect on other group members. A confederate who compromised, and therefore showed some degree of shift towards the majority, did exert an influence on the rest of the group. However, influence was only evident in those who shifted late in negotiations (showing flexibility) rather than those who shifted earlier (perceived as having 'caved in' to the majority).

This suggests that flexibility is only effective at changing majority opinion in certain circumstances.

The real 'value' of minority influence

Nemeth (2010) argues that dissent, in the form of minority opinion, 'opens' the mind.

As a result of exposure to a minority position, people search for information, consider more options, make better decisions, and are more creative. Dissenters liberate people to say what they believe and they stimulate divergent and creative thought even when they are wrong.

This view is supported by the work of Van Dyne and Saavedra (1996), who studied the role of dissent in work groups, finding that groups had improved decision quality when exposed to a minority perspective.

Do we really process the minority's message more?

Mackie (1987) argues that the views of the minority do not necessarily lead to greater processing, but rather it is the majority who are more likely to create greater message processing.

Why is this the case? We tend to believe that the majority of group members share similar beliefs to ours. If the majority express a different view from the one we hold, we must consider it carefully to understand why this is the case.

By contrast, people tend not to waste time trying to process why a minority's message is different; therefore it tends to be less, rather than more, influential.

 ### A 'tipping point' for commitment

Xie *et al.* (2011) discovered a 'tipping point' where the number of people holding a minority position becomes sufficient to change majority opinion.

They developed computer models of social networks, with 'individuals' free to 'chat' with each other across the networks. Each individual held a 'traditional' view, but the researchers also added some individuals representing an alternative point of view, which they expressed consistently. If the listener held the same opinion as the speaker, it reinforced the listener's belief. If the opinion was different, the listener considered it and moved on to talk to another individual. If that individual also held the new belief, the listener adopted it. After a while, opinion suddenly began to shift.

This study concluded that the percentage of committed opinion holders necessary to 'tip' the majority into accepting the minority position was just 10% (referred to as the snowball effect; see page 34).

 ### Minority influence in name only

Despite the evidence for higher quality decision-making, Nemeth (2010) claims it is still difficult to convince people of the value of dissent.

People accept the principle only on the surface, i.e. they *appear* tolerant, but quickly become irritated by a dissenting view that persists. They may also fear creating a lack of harmony within the group by welcoming dissent, or be made to fear repercussions, including being ridiculed by being associated with a 'deviant' point of view.

As a consequence, this means that the majority view persists and the opportunities for innovative thinking associated with minority influence are lost.

CAN YOU?

No. 1.8

1. Briefly explain what is meant by 'minority influence'. (2 marks)
2. Explain **one** criticism of the role of consistency in minority influence. (4 marks)
3. Explain **one** criticism of the role of commitment in minority influence. (4 marks)
4. Explain **one** criticism of the role of flexibility in minority influence. (4 marks)
5. Describe and evaluate research into minority influence. (12 marks AS, 16 marks A)

MEET THE RESEARCHER

Serge Moscovici (1928–2014) was born in Romania into a Jewish family. From an early age, Moscovici suffered the effects of anti-Semitic discrimination; in 1938, he was expelled from school on the basis of newly issued anti-Semitic legislation. In 1939 he joined the Communist Party (which was then illegal), although he later became disillusioned with communist politics. At the very start of the Cold War, he helped Jewish dissidents cross the border from Eastern Europe into the West, which was illegal. For this, he was tried in 1947 and eventually left Romania for good, arriving in France a year later. In Paris, helped by a refugee fund, he studied psychology at the Sorbonne. As one of the founding influences in European social psychology, his name is synonymous with the field of minority influence.

KEY TERMS

Commitment The degree to which members of a minority are dedicated to a particular cause or activity. The greater the perceived commitment, the greater the influence.

Consistency Minority influence is effective provided there is stability in the expressed position over time and agreement among different members of the minority.

Flexibility A willingness to be flexible and to compromise when expressing a position.

Minority influence A form of social influence where members of the majority group change their beliefs or behaviours as a result of their exposure to a persuasive minority.

 ## UPGRADE

The 'Can you?' section on the left gives you a flavour of some possible examination-style questions for this topic. However, you can also be asked other questions where you are required to 'apply your knowledge' to a novel scenario. We have a fair few of these scenarios dotted around this book, but of course the exact scenarios you might be presented with are almost impossible to predict. For this topic, for example, you might be presented with the following scenario:

'Simon and Maddy are two UKIP members in a rural area of Somerset. Because they have both studied psychology at university, they are asked how UKIP can exert a greater influence on voters in what has traditionally been a Tory safe seat.'

Using your knowledge of research into minority influence, explain how Simon and Maddy might use insights from this research to change the mind of the majority and increase the UKIP vote. (4 marks)

Try to think of your own scenarios and apply minority influence to these. The more you generate, the more comfortable you will be in applying the insights from this spread in an exam (should you need to).

Social influence processes in social change

Research into social influence does not just tell us how *individuals* change their beliefs and behaviours, but also how whole *societies* might change. If we look around us, we find evidence of social influence in many different types of social change, for example the actions of the suffragettes, the birth of trade unionism and the Paralympic movement. The power that persuasive groups possess in order to bring about **social change** is their ability to organise, educate and mobilise support for their cause. When individuals band together and form an organisation to focus their collective power, social change can be the result.

▶ The suffragettes were a classic example of social change through minority influence.

SOCIAL CHANGE THROUGH MINORITY INFLUENCE

If an individual is exposed to a persuasive argument under certain conditions, they may change their views to match those of the minority. Moscovici (1980) referred to this process as 'conversion', a necessary prerequisite for social change. Below we examine the stages in this process and illustrate each stage with an example from history – the suffragettes.

1. Drawing attention to an issue

Minorities can bring about social change by drawing the majority's attention to an issue. If their views are different to those held by the majority, this creates a conflict that they are motivated to reduce. The suffragettes used educational, political and militant tactics to draw attention to the fact that women were denied the same voting rights as men.

2. Cognitive conflict

The minority creates a conflict between what majority group members currently believe and the position advocated by the minority. This doesn't necessarily result in a move towards the minority position, but it does mean that majority group members think more deeply about the issues being challenged. The suffragettes created a conflict for majority group members between the existing status quo (only men allowed to vote) and the position advocated by the suffragettes (votes for women). Some people dealt with this conflict by moving towards the position advocated by the suffragettes, others simply dismissed it.

3. Consistency of position

Research on minority influence has established that minorities tend to be more influential in bringing about social change when they express their arguments consistently (over time and with each other). The suffragettes were consistent in their views, regardless of the attitudes of those around them. Protests and political lobbying that continued for years, plus the fact that women played a conspicuous role in WW1, eventually convinced society that some women were ready for the vote.

4. The augmentation principle

If a minority appears willing to suffer for their views, they are seen as more committed and so taken more seriously by others. Because the suffragettes were willing to risk imprisonment or even death from hunger strike, their influence became more powerful (i.e. it was *augmented*).

5. The snowball effect

Minority influence initially has a relatively small effect but this then spreads more widely as more and more people consider the issues being promoted, until it reaches a 'tipping point', at which point it leads to wide-scale social change. Universal suffrage (all adult citizens having the vote) was finally accepted by the majority of people in the UK.

SOCIAL CHANGE THROUGH MAJORITY INFLUENCE (CONFORMITY)

Research has consistently demonstrated that behavioural choices are often related to group norms, i.e. they are the subject of normative influence. The social norms approach (Perkins and Berkowitz, 1986) holds that if people perceive something to be the norm, they tend to alter their behaviour to fit that norm. For example, if university students think that heavy drinking is the norm, they'll drink more. If they think responsible drinking is the norm, then they'll drink less (i.e. they *conform*). Behaviour, therefore, is based more on what people *think* others believe and do (the 'perceived norm') than on their real beliefs and actions (the 'actual norm'). The gap between the perceived and actual norm is referred to as a 'misperception', and correcting this misperception is the basis for an approach to social change known as **social norms interventions**.

Social norms interventions

Social norms interventions typically start by identifying a widespread misperception relating to a specified risky behaviour within a target population. For example, young adults generally misperceive the frequency and quantity of alcohol typically consumed by their peers, and as a result develop norms that justify their own heavy drinking behaviour. Perception correction strategies can then be used in media campaigns, promotional material and through other routes. The aim of these strategies is to communicate to the target population the *actual* norm concerning that particular behaviour. By advertising these actual norms, researchers hope that recipients will moderate their own behaviour to bring it more in line with the behaviour of their peers.

An example: 'Most of Us® don't drink and drive'

This social norms intervention was designed to reduce drinking and driving among young adults (aged 21–34) in Montana, USA. This age group had been over-represented in alcohol-related crashes statewide. An initial survey found that while only 20.4% of Montana young adults reported having driven within one hour of consuming two or more drinks in the previous month, 92% of respondents believed that the majority of their peers had done so. By correcting this misperception with the simple message that 'MOST Montana Young Adults (4 out of 5) Don't Drink and Drive', the researchers found that the prevalence of reported driving after drinking was reduced by 13.7%, compared to counties that did not run the campaign. The correction of misperceptions about the 'norm' of driving after drinking led to positive changes in personal attitudes among the target population and a reduction in their reported frequency of risky behaviours.

MOST of Us® is a registered service mark of Montana State University

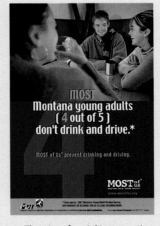

▲ The aim of social intervention strategies is to communicate to the target population what is the *actual* norm concerning a particular behaviour.

Social change through minority influence is very gradual

The role played by minority influence may be limited since minorities such as the suffragettes rarely bring about social change quickly.

Because there is a strong tendency for human beings to conform to the majority position, people are more likely to maintain the status quo rather than engage in social change.

This suggests, therefore, that the influence of a minority is frequently more latent than direct (i.e. it creates the potential for change rather than actual social change).

Being perceived as 'deviant' limits the influence of minorities

The potential for minorities to influence social change is often limited because they are seen as 'deviant' in the eyes of the majority.

Members of the majority may avoid aligning themselves with the minority position because they do not want to be seen as deviant themselves. The message of the minority would then have very little impact because the focus of the majority's attention would be the source of the message (i.e. the deviant minority) rather than the message itself.

In trying to bring about social change, therefore, minorities face the double challenge of avoiding being portrayed as deviants and also making people directly embrace their position.

The social norms approach doesn't always work

While social norms interventions have shown positive results in a number of different settings (e.g. reducing drink-driving, heavy drinking among students and teenage smoking), they also have their limitations.

DeJong *et al.* (2009) tested the effectiveness of social norms marketing campaigns to drive down alcohol use among students across 14 different college sites. Despite receiving normative information that corrected their misperceptions of subjective drinking norms, students in the social norms condition did not report lower self-reported alcohol consumption as a result of the campaign.

It appears, therefore, that not all social norms interventions are able to produce social change.

Social norms and the 'boomerang effect'

Schultz *et al.* (2007) suggest an unwelcome problem with social norms interventions. Although they are typically aimed at individuals whose behaviour is less desirable than the norm, those whose behaviour is more desirable than the norm will also receive the message.

For those individuals who already engage in the constructive behaviour being advocated (e.g. drink less than the norm, use less energy than the norm and so on), a normative message can also be a spur to increasing these aspects of their behaviour to be more in line with the norm.

Schultz et al. refer to this as the boomerang effect, where a social norms campaign might be effective in getting heavy energy users to use less electricity, but can also cause those who use less than the norm to increase their usage!

Overcoming the deviant minority problem: *The Communist Manifesto*

Minorities have the particular problem of avoiding being portrayed as deviants in order to persuade the majority to embrace their position.

The birth of communism owes much to the careful way in which an influential minority overcame the 'deviant' problem. To avoid being portrayed as deviants, early communists made it clear in their *Communist Manifesto* (Marx and Engels, 1848) that they were really part of the majority (i.e. the 'proletariat', or working class) and that the struggle was actually with the 'owners of the means of production', i.e. the 'bourgeoisie'.

By avoiding being portrayed as deviants, they were able to stand as equals to the majority, creating the impression that they had the potential to overthrow the powerful majority and create social change.

The case for animal rights

Supporters of animal rights believe that animals have an inherent worth, something over and above their usefulness to humans. They believe that all living beings, not just humans, have the right to exist without pain and suffering. The animal rights movement challenges the traditional view that non-human animals exist solely for human use, for example as food or as subjects for testing and research. Supporters of the animal rights movement believe that this view of animals as 'renewable resources' is morally wrong, as it denies non-humans the rights that we take for granted for ourselves. Any form of discrimination, they argue, is morally unacceptable, regardless of whether it is based on race, gender or species.

Using your knowledge of social influence research, suggest how animal rights campaigners might change majority attitudes and behaviours concerning the use of non-human animals in testing and research.

Social change occurs when a society or section of society adopts a new belief or way of behaving which then becomes widely accepted as the norm.

Social norms interventions attempt to correct misperceptions of the normative behaviour of peers in an attempt to change the risky behaviour of a target population.

1. Explain how social influence can lead to social change. (6 marks)
2. With reference to **one or more** examples, explain how social influence has led to social change. (6 marks)
3. Using insights from social influence research, explain how psychologists might bring about social change in healthy eating habits. (6 marks)
4. Outline and discuss the role of social influence processes in social change. (12 marks AS, 16 marks A)

We have identified here the key points of the topics on the AQA specification covered in this chapter, i.e. the bare minimum that you need to know. You may want to fill in further details to elaborate and personalise this material.

TYPES OF CONFORMITY AND EXPLANATIONS FOR CONFORMITY

TYPES OF CONFORMITY

- Compliance – conforming to gain approval.
- Internalisation – conforming because of an acceptance of their views.
- Identification – accepting influence because of a desire to be associated with a group.
- Identification has elements of compliance *and* internalisation.

EXPLANATIONS FOR CONFORMITY

- Normative social influence – conformity based on the desire for approval.
- More likely to occur when individual believes they are under surveillance by the group.
- Informational social influence – based on an acceptance of information from others as evidence about reality.
- More likely if the situation is ambiguous or where others are experts.

EVALUATION/DISCUSSION

- Difficulties distinguishing between compliance and internalisation.
- Research support for normative influence, e.g. smoking take-up (Linkenbach and Perkins).
- Research support for informational influence, e.g. attitudes about African Americans (Wittenbrink and Henley).
- **A03 plus** People underestimate the impact of normative influence on their behaviour (Nolan *et al.*).
- **A03 plus** Informational influence is moderated by type of task (Laughlin).

VARIABLES AFFECTING CONFORMITY

KEY STUDY (ASCH, 1956)

- Procedure – participants viewed lines of different lengths and compared them to a standard line.
- Group contained confederates with participants answering second to last.
- Confederates gave same wrong answer on 12 out of 18 trials.
- Findings – conformity rate was approx 33%.
- Without confederates, participants made mistakes 1% of the time.
- Participants conformed to avoid disapproval.

VARIABLES AFFECTING CONFORMITY

- Group size – increased to 30% with majority of three.
- Campbell and Fairey – group size has different effect depending on type of judgement and motivation.
- Unanimity of the majority – with one dissenter giving the right answer, conformity 5.5%.
- Dissenter giving different wrong answer, conformity 9%.
- Difficulty of the task – if correct answer less obvious, conformity was higher.
- Lucas *et al.* – influence of task difficulty moderated by individual's self-efficacy.

EVALUATION/DISCUSSION

- Asch's research a 'child of its time' (Perrin and Spencer).
- We know very little about the effects of larger majority sizes on conformity levels.
- Independent behaviour rather than conformity – participants maintained their independence on two-thirds of trials.
- **A03 plus** Unconvincing confederates – Mori and Arai overcame this problem. Similar results to Asch.
- **A03 plus** Cultural differences in conformity – Smith *et al.* found conformity rates higher in collectivist cultures.

CONFORMITY TO SOCIAL ROLES

KEY STUDY: THE STANFORD PRISON EXPERIMENT

- Procedure – male volunteers assigned roles of either prisoners or guards.
- Prisoners referred to by numbers only, guards given uniforms and power to make rules.
- Findings – guards became tyrannical and abusive with the prisoners.
- Prisoners conformed to their role with some showing extreme reactions of crying and rage.

BBC PRISON STUDY (REICHER AND HASLAM)

- Procedure – male volunteers, matched on social and clinical measures, assigned roles of prisoners or guards.
- Findings – unlike SPE, neither guards nor prisoners conformed to their assigned role.
- Prisoners worked collectively to challenge authority of the guards, resulting in power shift.

EVALUATION/DISCUSSION

- Conformity to roles is not automatic – Haslam and Reicher argue the guards *chose* how to behave, rather than blindly conforming to their social role.
- Demand characteristics – Banuazizi and Movahedi argue that participants' behaviour in the SPE was a response to powerful demand characteristics.
- Were these studies ethical? Zimbardo's study followed ethical guidelines but participants still suffered. Greater steps to minimise potential harm to participants in the BBC study.
- **A03 plus** The SPE and its relevance to Abu Ghraib – similarities between the SPE and prisoner abuses at Abu Ghraib.
- **A03 plus** What did we learn? Zimbardo claims unthinking conformity can lead to a drift into tyranny – disputed by Reicher and Haslam.

SITUATIONAL VARIABLES AFFECTING OBEDIENCE

KEY STUDY: MILGRAM (1963)
- Procedure – 40 volunteer participants in each condition.
- Real participant acted as 'teacher', confederate as 'learner'.
- Teacher administered increasing shock levels up to 450v.
- Findings – in *voice feedback* condition, 65% went to maximum 450V.
- All participants went to 300V level.

SITUATIONAL FACTORS IN OBEDIENCE
- Proximity – obedience levels decreased with increasing proximity.
- Location – obedience levels dropped to 48% in lower-status setting.
- The power of uniform – people more likely to obey someone in a uniform (Bushman).

EVALUATION/DISCUSSION
- Internal validity – Orne and Holland claim many participants saw through the deception.
- Historical validity – Milgram's findings still as relevant today. No relationship between year of study and obedience levels found (Blass).
- Proximity – Reserve Police Battalion 101.
- (A03 plus) Location – high levels of obedience not surprising.
- (A03 plus) The power of uniform – research support.

AGENTIC STATE AND LEGITIMACY OF AUTHORITY

THE AGENTIC STATE
- Person acts as an agent to carry out another person's wishes.
- Binding factors operate to maintain obedience, e.g. social etiquette.
- Demonstrated in actions at My Lai.

LEGITIMACY OF AUTHORITY
- Person must perceive an individual in a position of social control.
- People accept definitions of a situation offered by legitimate authority figure.
- Legitimate commands arise from institutions, e.g. a university or the military.

EVALUATION/DISCUSSION
- The agentic state does not explain gradual transitions found in Nazi doctors.
- Agentic state or cruelty? Obedient behaviour may be due to a desire to inflict harm on others.
- Agentic shift is a common response when a person loses self-control (Fennis and Aarts).
- (A03 plus) Legitimacy can serve as the basis for justifying harm to others.
- (A03 plus) Tarnow provides support for power of legitimate authority in aircraft cockpits.

THE AUTHORITARIAN PERSONALITY

THE AUTHORITARIAN PERSONALITY
- People scoring high on F scale raised within authoritarian family background (Adorno *et al.*).
- RWA – conventionalism, authoritarian submission, authoritarian aggression (Altemeyer).

KEY STUDY: ELMS AND MILGRAM (1966)
- Procedure – 20 'obedient' participants and 20 'defiant' participants.
- Completed MMPI and F scale, and asked open-ended questions.
- Findings – little difference between obedient and defiant participants on MMPI.
- Higher levels of authoritarianism in obedient participants.
- Obedient participants reported being less close to fathers.

EVALUATION/DISCUSSION
- Research evidence – correlation between RWA scores and maximum voltage shock (Dambrun and Vatiné).
- Social context explanations are more flexible.
- Differences – many fully obedient participants had *good* relationship with their parents.
- (A03 plus) Education may determine authoritarianism *and* obedience (Middendorp and Meloen).
- (A03 plus) Left-wing views associated with lower levels of obedience (Bègue *et al.*).

RESISTANCE TO SOCIAL INFLUENCE

SOCIAL SUPPORT
- Presence of social support enables individual to resist conformity (Asch).
- Social support breaks unanimity and provides an independent assessment of reality.
- Disobedient peers act as role models.
- Obedience rates dropped to 10% when two confederates defied experimenter (Milgram).

LOCUS OF CONTROL
- Internal LOC = greater independence and less reliance on the opinions of others.
- External LOC = more passive attitude and greater acceptance of the influence of others.
- High internals less vulnerable to influence and better able to resist coercion (Hutchins and Estey).

EVALUATION OF SOCIAL SUPPORT
- Social support in conformity studies more effective when it was from *first* responder in group.
- Research demonstrates importance of social support in resisting pressure to drink (Rees and Wallace).
- (A03 plus) The Rosenstrasse protest showed power of social support.

EVALUATION OF LOCUS OF CONTROL
- Locus of control related to normative but not informational influence (Spector).
- Young people far more external than in 1960s (Twenge *et al.*).
- (A03 plus) Research support – people high in externality more easily persuaded and more likely to conform (Avtgis).

MINORITY INFLUENCE

MINORITY INFLUENCE AND BEHAVIOURAL STYLE
- Minority influence effective with a consistent, committed and flexible style.
- Wood *et al.* – minorities who were especially consistent were most influential.
- Commitment important as it suggests certainty and confidence.
- Flexibility more effective at changing opinion than rigid arguments.

KEY STUDY: MOSCOVICI *ET AL.* (1969)
- Procedure – groups of four naïve participants and two confederates.
- Shown blue slides varying in intensity but confederates called them green.
- Group 1 confederates answered consistently, Group 2 confederates answered inconsistently.
- Findings – consistent minority influenced naïve participants to say green on 8% of trials.
- Inconsistent minority exerted very little influence.

EVALUATION/DISCUSSION
- Research support for flexibility (Nemeth and Brilmayer).
- The real value of minority influence is that it 'opens the mind' (Nemeth).
- Mackie argues that it is the *majority* rather than the minority that processes information more.
- (A03 plus) Tipping point for commitment – percentage of committed opinion holders necessary to 'tip' the majority was 10% (Xie *et al.*).
- (A03 plus) Minority influence in name only – difficult to convince people of the value of dissent.

SOCIAL INFLUENCE PROCESSES IN SOCIAL CHANGE

SOCIAL CHANGE THROUGH MINORITY INFLUENCE
- Drawing attention to an issue.
- Minority creates a conflict between majority position and minority position.
- Minorities more influential when they express their views consistently.
- Augmentation principle – minorities more influential if they suffer for their views.
- The snowball effect – an initial small effect spreads more widely until it reaches a 'tipping point'.

SOCIAL CHANGE THROUGH MAJORITY INFLUENCE
- If people perceive something as the norm, they alter their behaviour to fit that norm.
- Correcting misperceptions about 'actual' norms using social norms interventions.
- E.g. 'Most of us don't drink and drive' campaign.
- Resulted in a drop of drink driving by 13.7%.

EVALUATION/DISCUSSION
- Social change through minority influence is gradual.
- Being perceived as 'deviant' limits the influence of minorities.
- Social norms interventions have their limitations – not all have led to social change, e.g. DeJong *et al.*
- (A03 plus) Social norms and the boomerang effect, e.g. Schultz *et al.* with electricity usage.
- (A03 plus) *The Communist Manifesto* – overcame issues that typically limit the influence of minorities.

The exam questions on social influence will be varied but there will be some short answer questions (AO1), including some multiple choice questions, some questions that ask you to apply your knowledge (AO2) and possibly an extended writing question (AO1 + AO3). Some questions may involve research methods and maths skills. We have provided a selection of these different kinds of questions here.

AS AND A LEVEL QUESTIONS

0 1 Which **one** of the following is a dispositional factor affecting obedience?

A location
B personality
C proximity
D uniform

[1 mark]

0 2 Which **two** of the following are variables affecting conformity investigated by Asch?

A agentic state
B locus of control
C task difficulty
D unanimity

[2 marks]

0 3 (i) Identify **one** factor that increases obedience. [1 mark]

(ii) Identify **one** factor that decreases obedience. [1 mark]

0 4 Explain **one** difference between compliance and internalisation with reference to conformity. [2 marks]

0 5 Using an example, explain what is meant by identification in relation to conformity. [3 marks]

0 6 State what is meant by unanimity and outline its effect on conformity. [3 marks]

0 7 Outline the findings of Asch's research into group size on conformity. [3 marks]

0 8 Choose **one** of the following and outline its impact on minority social influence.

• commitment
• consistency
• flexibility

[3 marks]

0 9 Describe Milgram's research into obedience. [6 marks]

1 0 Explain the difference between normative social influence and informational social influence as explanations of conformity. [4 marks]

1 1 Explain how **both** agentic state and legitimacy of authority have an effect on obedience. [6 marks]

1 2 Describe **one** study in which conformity to social roles was investigated. [4 marks]

1 3 Read the item below and then answer the questions that follow.

A psychologist wanted to investigate the effect of gender on obedience. She carried out a field experiment over two days where she sent a confederate out onto the streets of a busy city. The confederates were instructed to approach passers-by and tell them they had to cross to the other side of the street. On the first day, a female confederate was used, and on the second day, a male confederate was used. On each day, the psychologist recorded the number of passers-by who followed the command and crossed to the other side of the street.

(i) Outline **one** strength of using a field experiment for this study. [2 marks]

(ii) Briefly explain what sampling method was used in this study. [2 marks]

(iii) Identify the independent variable and the dependent variable in this study. [2 marks]

(iv) Identify **one** possible extraneous variable in this study and outline how it could affect the results. [3 marks]

1 4   Discuss the role of social influence processes in social change.   **[8 marks]**

1 5   Describe and evaluate **two** explanations of resistance to social influence.   **[12 marks]**

1 6   Read the item below and then answer the questions that follow.

> Bhavna believes it is right to be a vegetarian having thought carefully about the views on the websites she has visited.
>
> Keegan pretends that he is a vegetarian to fit in with the new friends he has met at college.
>
> Zoe is a vegetarian because her friends say she looks healthier as a result of her new diet.

     (i)   Name the person who demonstrates the process of compliance.   **[1 mark]**

     (ii)   Name the person who demonstrates the process of internalisation.   **[1 mark]**

1 7   Describe and evaluate research into conformity.   **[12 marks]**

1 8   Read the item below and then answer the questions that follow.

> Martha had been doing a difficult maths question in class but thought she had come up with the right solution. The teacher went around the class and asked some of the students to say out loud their answer to the question before he gave the right answer. The three students before Martha gave the same answer but it was different from hers. Although Martha was quite confident the others were wrong, she decided to say the same as them. When the teacher went over the question, Martha found out that her own answer was correct but now she felt too embarrassed to tell the teacher this.

     (i)   Explain how Martha's behaviour demonstrates the process of compliance.   **[2 marks]**

     (ii)   Explain why Martha's answer might have been different if the teacher had asked only one other student for their answer before Martha's.   **[3 marks]**

1 9   'Obedience has much more to do with the situation we are in rather than the kind of person we are.'

Describe and evaluate how the Authoritarian Personality can be used to explain obedience.   **[12 marks]**

2 0   Read the item below and then answer the question that follows.

> Nadia is passionate about a charity that supports children living in developing countries. However, most of her classmates want to raise money for an animal charity. The class is due to vote for the class charity at the end of the week.

Using your knowledge of minority social influence, explain **two** ways in which Nadia could try to persuade her classmates to vote for her charity.   **[6 marks]**

2 1   Describe and evaluate Asch's research into variables affecting conformity.   **[12 marks]**

2 2   Read the item below and then answer the questions that follow.

> A psychologist carried out a covert participant observation to investigate the process of conformity in criminal gangs. He managed to join a criminal gang by going undercover. After three months in the gang he left to write up his research findings.

     (i)   Identify the sample in this study.   **[1 mark]**

     (ii)   Outline **one** strength and **one** limitation of using a covert participant observation in this study.   **[4 marks]**

     (iii)   Explain **one** ethical issue raised by this study.   **[3 marks]**

A LEVEL ONLY QUESTIONS

2 3   Discuss how far situational factors can be used to explain obedience.   **[16 marks]**

2 4   Describe and evaluate research into normative social influence **and/or** informational social influence.   **[16 marks]**

2 5   Discuss the effect of **at least two** variables on conformity.   **[16 marks]**

2 6   Discuss explanations of resistance to social influence.   **[16 marks]**

We've provided answers by two students to some of the questions from pages 38–39 here, together with comments from an examiner about how well they've each done. **Green** comments show what the student has done well. **Orange** comments indicate areas for improvement.

---

10 Explain the difference between normative social influence and informational social influence as explanations of conformity. *(4 marks)*

Ciaran's answer

Normative social influence is when people go along with the rest of the group because they want to be accepted and liked by the group. Informational social influence is when people go along with the group because they think other group members know more than they do about the task and so, because they want to do the right thing, they just follow what everybody else in the group is doing.

✓ An accurate description of NSI.

✓ A good description of ISI.

! No differences are explained, thus missing the whole point of the question.

Examiner's comments

Ciaran has simply stated what each of these is without explaining any differences between them. *2/4 marks*

✓ An accurate description of NSI.

✓ Maisie draws a distinction between the two: different reasons for conforming.

Maisie's answer

When an individual conforms to normative social influence they go along with the majority because they don't want to be ridiculed for disagreeing with the rest of the group. The reason for conformity to informational social influence is different, because it is based not on the need to be accepted, but the desire to be right. If the majority are seen as experts or if the task is difficult, then the individual is more likely to conform to their views. In addition, normative influence leads to compliance only, with private attitude unchanged, whereas informational influence leads to internalisation of the majority's views, so agreement in public and private.

✓ Maisie has added a second difference: the outcome of conforming.

Examiner's comments

This is a much better way of approaching the question as it is focused on outlining where the two explanations are different rather than simply what they are. *4/4 marks*

AS essay

19 'Obedience has much more to do with the situation we are in rather than the kind of person we are.' Discuss the Authoritarian Personality as a way of explaining obedience to authority. *(12 marks)*

✓ A good, focused start with some clear and accurate AO1.

Maisie's answer

People with an Authoritarian Personality tend to believe in conventional values, the importance of social rules and obedience/submission to authority. Adorno used the F scale to investigate the Authoritarian Personality and found that people who were likely to agree with statements such as 'obedience and respect for authority are the most important virtues children should learn' were likely to have an Authoritarian Personality. This is because they grew up with a strict family background that had a strong emphasis on children doing as they are told.

Elms and Milgram carried out a study to investigate whether there was a relationship between the Authoritarian Personality and obedience. They found that participants who had been obedient in Milgram's obedience to authority study scored higher on the F scale. Research by Altemeyer identified three parts of the Authoritarian Personality that were particularly associated with obedience, including submission to authority. This research seems to go against the statement above and shows that personality can be used to explain why people obey.

However, others suggest that the situation is more important than personality. Even Milgram himself showed that the situation was key and could be more important than dispositional ones. For example, in his research he found that factors such as proximity to the victim, legitimacy of authority and whether there were other non-obedient models around were more important than personality.

✓ Some accurate and detailed elaboration.

✓ A good use of accurate research which shows depth of knowledge.

✓ A clear link back to the question that makes the discussion relevant and effective.

✓ An effective way to create AO3/discussion and is in line with the statement made in the question so it shows that Maisie is focused.

Even in the Elms and Milgram study, some of the characteristics of an Authoritarian Personality, such as growing up in a harsh family environment, were not found to be true of many of the obedient participants. This casts doubt on the fact that an Authoritarian Personality could be the cause of their obedience.

There is a suggestion that other factors, such as level of education, could be more important than Authoritarian Personality in determining the likelihood of a person obeying authority. A study by Middendorp and Meloen found that people who were less well educated were more likely to have an Authoritarian Personality than well-educated people and were also more likely to show high levels of obedience. This suggests that education might determine level of authoritarianism and the tendency to obey. The evidence seems to suggest that Authoritarian Personality is certainly a factor in obedience but it is likely to be a combination of both situational and dispositional factors, such as personality. *(388 words)*

> This is a very good evaluation point

Examiner's comments
Clear and detailed knowledge of what Authoritarian Personality is. There is an excellent use of research evidence as evaluation, and overall discussion was mainly effective. There are some good links back to the question, helping Maisie ensure that she stayed focused on the question at hand. **Level 4 essay: this answer is likely to get 11 marks out of 12.**

> Another good use of research that is concise and relevant.

> A strong conclusion that doesn't simply repeat things already stated earlier in the answer and goes on to discuss the merits of both Authoritarian Personality and situational factors.

A Level essay
26 Discuss explanations of resistance to social influence. *(16 marks)*

> **Exam tip…**
> If a question asks you to 'discuss' something, you should go beyond merely stating strengths and/or limitations. Try to engage with the AO3 material you are using, e.g. by offering counterpoints, implications, applications and so on.

> A good focused start to the essay.

> Good use of research.

Ciaran's answer
Social support is important in resisting conformity. Asch found that the presence of another person who resisted the majority had an effect on the overall conformity rates. These dropped from 33% to 5.5% if a confederate also gave the right answer. The presence of another person who resisted the majority meant that the individual felt more confident in their decision and better able to stand up to the majority. This was supported by Allen and Levine, who showed that social support helped people resist the majority even when it was not particularly valid, showing that breaking the unanimity of the group was the most important factor in helping the individual resist conformity.

Social support has also been shown to be effective in helping people resist obedience. Milgram suggested that the presence of disobedient confederates acted as role models and made it more likely that the real participant would also resist. In his study, the presence of two disobedient peers reduced the percentage of participants who were fully obedient to just 10%. This explanation is supported by real-life events during the Second World War. During the Rosenstrasse protest, German women used the social support provided by other women to defy the orders of the Gestapo and continue to demand the release of their husbands and sons. This demonstrates a degree of external validity for the social support explanation.

People are better able to resist social influence if they have an internal locus of control, i.e. they believe that what happens to them is largely a consequence of their own ability and effort rather than the influence of other people. For example, research by Hutchins and Estey (1978) showed that high internals were more able to resist coercion from others in a simulated interrogation exercise. People with an external locus of control, on the other hand, tend to accept that what happens to them is determined by external factors, and therefore are more susceptible to social influence. Avtgis (1998) found support for the influence of locus of control. In a meta-analysis of social influence studies, he found that there was a significant relationship between locus of control scores and resistance to social influence across many different types of influence.

However, there are some limitations to the influence of locus of control. For example, Spector (1983) found that an internal locus of control was important in resisting normative social influence, but did not appear to be a significant factor in resisting informational social influence. *(411 words)*

> Elaboration of the previous point.

> Development of the explanation is positive.

> Good reference to real-life example (AO3) which is then related back to the explanation.

> This explanation follows a similar pattern of description of how people resist (AO1) and then use of research to back it up (mainly AO3).

> ! This point could be elaborated further and/or linked back to the question explicitly. 'This research suggests that…'

> ! A good contradiction that develops the discussion further. More of that would push the essay up to the top level.

Examiner's comments
Ciaran's answer is clear and organised and includes good detail. He clearly has good knowledge and understanding and the use of research is good. Discussion is mostly effective but to get into the top band Ciaran would need to broaden his discussion, for example by making more explicit comparisons to other explanations or including more contradictory evidence in order to make the answer more discursive. **Top of level 3 essay: this answer is likely to get 12 marks out of 16.**

Memory

CONTENTS OF CHAPTER

SPECIFICATION

- The multi-store model of memory: sensory register, short-term memory and long-term memory. Features of each store: coding, capacity and duration.

- Types of long-term memory: episodic, semantic, procedural.

- The working memory model: central executive, phonological loop, visuo-spatial sketchpad and episodic buffer. Features of the model: coding and capacity.

- Explanations for forgetting: proactive and retroactive interference and retrieval failure due to absence of clues.

- Factors affecting the accuracy of eyewitness testimony: misleading information, including leading questions and post-event discussion; anxiety.

- Improving the accuracy of eyewitness testimony, including the use of the cognitive interview.

TRY THIS

NOW THAT IS INTERESTING

Humans have evolved to be pretty good at remembering things. It appears, however, that we need to be *interested* in something in order to remember it well – the more interested we are, the better motivated we are to remember it. For example, Chase and Simon (1973) showed that expert chess players were much better at recalling chess positions than were novice players. Similarly, Morris *et al.* (1981) found that football enthusiasts could recall scores better than people with little or no interest in football. This particular relationship is fairly easy to test – simply get some people, test their knowledge about (and therefore interest in…) football using the test below, and then ask them to read through the football scores. These scores are randomly chosen from the 2013–14 season – you could choose a different day if you don't like the result for your team! Likewise you may have to change some of the questions if Tottenham sack their manager or Chelsea's owner changes. About 30 minutes or so later, give your participants the same list of matches, but this time with the scores removed. Their task is to fill in the scores. You might give 2 marks for a completely correct score and just 1 mark if the result is right (e.g. Liverpool winning) although the score was wrong (e.g. 2–0).

FOOTBALL KNOWLEDGE TEST

1. What country does Chelsea's owner come from?
2. Who is manager of Tottenham Hotspur?
3. Which British club plays at 'The Stadium of Light'?
4. What was the name of the Liverpool goalkeeper whose heroics helped them to win the Champions League final in 2005?
5. How many substitutes can be used on one team during a Premier League match?
6. What colour shirts do Everton wear?
7. For what Spanish club did David Beckham play until his transfer in 2007?
8. Which team has the nickname 'The Canaries'?
9. England's 1966 World Cup winning captain Bobby Moore played for which club side?
10. Who is Motty?

Premier League scores for 13 May 2018

Burnley	**1–2**	AFC Bournemouth
Crystal Palace	**2–0**	West Bromwich Albion
Huddersfield Town	**0–1**	Arsenal
Liverpool	**4–0**	Brighton & Hove Albion
Manchester United	**1–0**	Watford
Newcastle United	**3–0**	Chelsea
Southampton	**0–1**	Manchester City
Swansea City	**1–2**	Stoke City
Tottenham Hotspur	**5–4**	Leicester City
West Ham United	**3–1**	Everton

When you have tested a few people and worked out their scores for the two tests, you can correlate them (see page 206 to read about correlation) to see if people who score higher on the football knowledge test also score higher on their recall of the scores. There should be a lesson in this for your own study of psychology – if you haven't worked out what that is, maybe you just aren't interested enough…!

Short- and long-term memory

Your memory for events in the present or immediate past (e.g. trying to remember an order of drinks at the bar) is referred to as your **short-term memory** (or STM). Your memory for events that have happened in the more distant past (such as remembering this distinction between STM and LTM in an exam) is referred to as your **long-term memory** (or LTM).

STM and LTM are often distinguished in terms of their **capacity**, **duration** and **coding**.

CAPACITY

Capacity concerns how much data can be held in a memory store. STM is a limited capacity store whereas LTM has a potentially infinite capacity.

The capacity of STM

The capacity of STM can be assessed using digit span (see 'Try this' above). In one of the earliest studies in psychology, Joseph Jacobs (1887) used this technique to assess STM capacity. He found that the average span for digits was 9.3 items and 7.3 for letters. Why was it easier to recall digits? Jacobs suggests that it may be because there are only nine digits whereas there are 26 letters.

The magic number 7 ± 2

George Miller (1956) wrote a memorable article called *The magic number seven plus or minus two*, in which he reviewed psychological research and concluded that the span of immediate memory is about seven items – sometimes a bit more, sometimes a bit less. He noted that people can count seven dots flashed onto a screen but not many more (see 'Try this' at the top of the facing page). The same is true if you are asked to recall musical notes, letters and even words. Miller also found that people can recall five words as well as they can recall five letters – we chunk things together and can then remember more.

EVALUATION/DISCUSSION

The capacity of STM may be even more limited

One criticism of the research investigating STM is that Miller's original findings have not been replicated.

Cowan (2001) reviewed a variety of studies on the capacity of STM and concluded that STM is likely to be limited to about four chunks. Research on the capacity of STM for visual information (rather than verbal stimuli) also found that four items was about the limit (e.g. Vogel *et al.*, 2001). This means that the lower end of Miller's range is more appropriate (i.e. 7 – 2 which is 5).

This suggests that STM may not be as extensive as was thought.

The size of the chunk matters

It seems that the size of the chunk affects how many chunks you can remember.

Simon (1974) found that people had a shorter memory span for larger chunks, such as eight-word phrases, than smaller chunks, such as one-syllable words.

This continues to support the view that STM has a limited capacity and refines our understanding.

 Individual differences

The capacity of STM is not the same for everyone.

Jacobs also found that recall (digit span) increased steadily with age; eight year olds could remember an average of 6.6 digits whereas the mean for 19 year olds was 8.6 digits. This age increase might be due to changes in brain capacity, and/or to the development of strategies such as chunking.

This suggests that the capacity of STM is not fixed and individual differences may play a role.

TRY THIS

Cover all of the columns except the first and say the digits, then shut your eyes and recall them. Were you right? (Of course you were.) Now try it with five digits. Keep going until you don't get them right.

How many digits could you recall correctly? This is the capacity of your immediate or short-term memory. The technique for assessing this is called the digit span technique.

2	4	7	3	4	8
4	5	4	5	1	1
8	6	5	6	3	6
1	2	8	4	6	3
	9	2	8	5	6
		4	7	8	5
			5	9	9
				3	1
					2

DURATION

LTM potentially lasts forever but STM doesn't last very long – it has a short duration, unless you repeat the items over and over again.

The duration of STM

Lloyd Peterson and Margaret Peterson (1959) studied the duration of STM, using 24 students. Each participant was tested over eight trials. On each trial a participant was given a consonant syllable and a three-digit number (e.g. THX 512). They were asked to recall the consonant syllable after a retention interval of 3, 6, 9, 12, 15 or 18 seconds. During the retention interval they had to count backwards from their three-digit number.

Participants, on average, were 90% correct over 3 seconds, 20% correct after 9 seconds and only 2% correct after 18 seconds. This suggests that STM has a very short duration – less than 18 seconds – as long as verbal rehearsal is prevented.

The duration of LTM

Harry Bahrick *et al.* (1975) tested 400 people of various ages (17–74) on their memory of classmates. A photo-recognition test consisted of 50 photos, some from the participant's high-school yearbook. In a free-recall test participants were asked to list the names they could remember of those in their graduating class.

Participants who were tested within 15 years of graduation were about 90% accurate in identifying faces. After 48 years, this declined to about 70% for photo recognition. Free recall was about 60% accurate after 15 years, dropping to 30% after 48 years.

EVALUATION/DISCUSSION

Testing STM was artificial

Another criticism of research investigating STM is that it is artificial.

Trying to memorise consonant syllables does not truly reflect most everyday memory activities where what we are trying to remember is meaningful. However, we do sometimes try to remember fairly meaningless things, such as groups of numbers (phone numbers) or letters (postcodes).

This means that, although the task was artificial, the study does have some relevance to everyday life.

STM results may be due to displacement

A criticism of the Petersons' study is that it did not actually measure what it set out to measure.

In the Petersons' study participants were counting the numbers in their STM and this may displace or 'overwrite' the syllables to be remembered. Reitman (1974) used auditory tones instead of numbers so that displacement wouldn't occur (sounds don't interfere with verbal rehearsal) and found that the duration of STM was longer.

This suggests that forgetting in the Petersons' study was due to displacement rather than decay.

Cover up the picture below. How many dots were there? The capacity of STM is probably fewer than nine items, which would predict that you wouldn't get the answer right because there were 12 dots. If there were five dots you would probably have coped.

KEY TERMS

Capacity This is a measure of how much can be held in memory. It is represented in terms of bits of information, such as number of digits.

Coding (also 'encoding') The way information is changed so that it can be stored in memory. Information enters the brain via the senses (e.g. eyes and ears). It is then stored in various forms, such as visual codes (like a picture), acoustic codes (sounds) or semantic codes (the meaning of the experience).

Duration A measure of how long a memory lasts before it is no longer available.

Long-term memory (LTM) Your memory for events that have happened in the past. This lasts anywhere from 2 minutes to 100 years. LTM has potentially unlimited duration and capacity and tends to be coded semantically.

Short-term memory (STM) Your memory for immediate events. STMs are measured in seconds and minutes rather than hours and days, i.e. a short duration. They disappear unless they are rehearsed. STM also has a limited capacity of about four items or chunks and tends to be coded acoustically. This type of memory is sometimes referred to as working memory.

CODING

Information that we store has to be 'written' in memory in some form – it is described as a 'code' in which it is held in the form of sounds (acoustic), images (visual) or meaning (semantic).

Acoustic and semantic coding

- The following words are acoustically similar but semantically different: cat, cab, can, cad, cap, mad, max, mat, man, map.
- The following words are the opposite – semantically similar but acoustically different: great, large, big, huge, broad, long, tall, fat, wide, high.

Alan Baddeley (1966a and 1966b) used word lists like those above to test the effects of acoustic and semantic similarity on STM and LTM. He found that participants had difficulty remembering acoustically similar words in STM but not in LTM, whereas semantically similar words posed little problem for STMs but led to muddled LTMs.

This suggests that STM is largely encoded acoustically whereas LTM is largely encoded semantically.

EVALUATION/DISCUSSION

STM may not be exclusively acoustic

Some experiments have shown that visual codes are also used in STM.

For example, Brandimote et al. (1992) found that participants used visual coding in STM if they were given a visual task (pictures) and prevented from doing any verbal rehearsal in the retention interval (they had to say 'la la la') before performing a visual recall task. Normally we 'translate' visual images into verbal codes in STM but, as verbal rehearsal was prevented, participants used visual codes. Other research has shown that STM sometimes uses a semantic code (Wickens et al., 1976).

This suggests that STM is not exclusively acoustic.

LTM may not be exclusively semantic

In general LTM appears to be semantic but not always.

Frost (1972) showed that long-term recall was related to visual as well as semantic categories, and Nelson and Rothbart (1972) found evidence of acoustic coding in LTM.

Therefore it seems that coding in LTM is not simply semantic but can vary according to circumstances.

A03 plus Baddeley may not have tested LTM

Baddeley's methodology has been criticised.

In the study by Baddeley, STM was tested by asking participants to recall a word list immediately after hearing it. LTM was tested by waiting 20 minutes. It is questionable as to whether this is really testing LTM.

This casts doubt on the validity of Baddeley's research because he wasn't testing LTM after all.

Research methods

A Russian psychologist, Bluma Zeigarnik, challenged the rather neat idea of STM versus LTM memories. Maybe it isn't so simple. For example, in a restaurant a waiter remembers who ordered what for more than five minutes but forgets it as soon as the orders are served. Zeigarnik (1927) tested this in a lab by asking participants to do about 20 little tasks, such as solving puzzles and stringing beads. On some occasions participants were interrupted halfway through the task. The interesting thing was that participants were about twice as likely to remember the tasks during which they'd been interrupted than those they completed. This suggests that we forget things when the 'I have completed this task' switch is flicked, but otherwise it continues in our longer-term memories.

1. Explain why this might be considered to be a repeated measures experiment. (2 marks)
2. Identify the dependent variable in this study. (1 mark)
3. This study is a laboratory experiment. Give **one** strength and **one** limitation of this kind of research in the context of this study. (2 marks + 2 marks)
4. If you were going to conduct this study, identify **two** things that participants would need to know beforehand in order to provide informed consent. (2 marks)

LINK TO RESEARCH METHODS

Repeated measures on page 184
Laboratory experiments on pages 186–187
Informed consent on page 194

KAREN FITZPATRICK "Fitzy" Pet peeve: Braces Hobby: Sports Activities: Chorus, Cheerleading, Hall Monitor, Hockey, Basketball

CARA FLANAGAN "Clara-Belle" Pet peeve: Riding bike to school on cold mornings Hobby: Sports Activities: Hockey, Basketball, Journalism, Junior Red Cross

ELIZABETH FOGLESONG "Betsy" Pet peeve: School lunches Hobby: Talking on the telephone Activities: Hockey, Yearbook, Cafeteria monitor, Chorus, Swimming

◀ Bahrick et al.'s study (see facing page) demonstrated the considerable duration of LTM by asking people of various ages to put names to faces from their high-school yearbook. Forty-eight years on, people were about 70% accurate.

And just to prove that, here's a copy of Cara's high-school yearbook circa 1962 – good old Karen and Betsy.

CAN YOU? No. 2.1

1. Explain what is meant by the terms 'duration', 'capacity' and 'coding' in relation to memory. (2 marks each)
2. Describe and evaluate research that has investigated capacity in STM. (8 marks)
3. Describe and evaluate research that has investigated duration in STM and/or LTM. (10 marks)
4. Describe and evaluate research that has investigated coding in memory. (8 marks)

The multi-store model of memory

In psychology, a 'model' of something should never be taken as an exact copy of the thing being described, but as a representation of it – like a map of the London Underground. A model of memory provides us with what is essentially an analogy of how memory works. Describing memory in terms of 'stores' or 'loops' makes our understanding more concrete, and simply conveys an approximate idea of how a particular psychologist has attempted to understand and explain the available evidence.

On this spread and the next we will be looking at two models – the **multi-store model** (MSM) and the working memory model (WMM). They are not alternative models – the WMM is an expansion of the original concept of a short-term store.

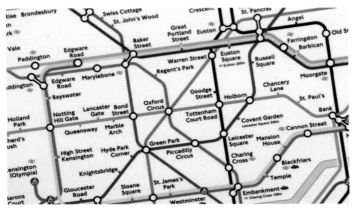

▲ The map of the London Underground – it's a model, not an exact copy. It represents the system in a way that helps us appreciate how it works and where it goes. Of course direction, scale, etc. must be distorted somewhat to make it all fit neatly on the page.

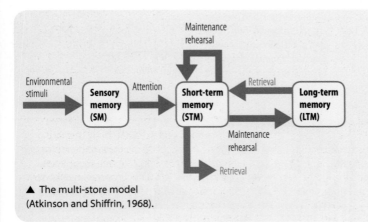

▲ The multi-store model (Atkinson and Shiffrin, 1968).

MEET THE RESEARCHER

Richard Atkinson (pictured) and Richard Shiffrin met at Indiana University, USA (where the Petersons also worked). Atkinson later moved to Stanford but continued to collaborate with Shiffrin as well as being a co-author on one of the best-known psychology textbooks of all time – so famous that it is now called Atkinson and Hilgard's *Introduction to Psychology*. Atkinson has received a long list of honours, but perhaps one of the more special ones was to have a mountain in Antarctica named after him.

DESCRIPTION OF THE MULTI-STORE MODEL

The MSM was first described by Richard Atkinson and Richard Shiffrin in 1968. It is illustrated in the diagram on the left. It has been called the 'modal model' because it was, for a long time, the most usually used model of memory.

It is called 'multi-store' because it consists of three memory stores, linked to each other by the processes that enable transfer of information from one store to the next.

Sensory register

The **sensory register** is the place where information is held at each of the senses – the eyes, ears, nose, fingers, tongue, etc., and the corresponding areas of the brain. The capacity of these registers is very large. The sensory registers are constantly receiving information, but most of this receives no attention and remains in the sensory register for a very brief duration (milliseconds).

Attention

If a person's attention is focused on one of the sensory stores, then the data is transferred to short-term memory (STM). Attention is the first step in remembering something.

Short-term memory

Information is held in STM so it can be used for immediate tasks, such as working on a maths problem or remembering the directions to a friend's house.

STM has a limited duration – it is in a 'fragile' state and will disappear (decay) relatively quickly if it isn't rehearsed. When you try to remember things for a test, what do you do? Possibly you repeat the things you want to remember over and over again – this is called maintenance rehearsal, which is largely verbal (and therefore sometimes called *verbal rehearsal*).

Information will also disappear from STM if new information enters STM, pushing out (or displacing) the original information. This happens because STM has a limited capacity.

Maintenance rehearsal

Repetition keeps information in STM but eventually such repetition will create a long-term memory (LTM). Atkinson and Shiffrin proposed a direct relationship between rehearsal in STM and the strength of the LTM – the more the information is rehearsed, the better it is remembered. This again is called maintenance rehearsal.

Long-term memory

LTM is potentially unlimited in duration and capacity. You may feel that there are many things you once knew but have forgotten, but the evidence suggests that either you actually had never really made the memory permanent or it is there, you just can't find it! As you continue through this chapter you will learn more about such 'forgetting'.

Retrieval

The process of getting information from LTM involves the information passing back through STM. It is then available for use.

Have you ever had the experience of vaguely hearing someone say something and then hearing them say 'DID YOU HEAR ME???'? At which point you say 'What?' but simultaneously you 'hear' what was said. This is because the words are still in your sensory register.

EVALUATION/DISCUSSION

Supporting evidence

Controlled lab studies on capacity, duration and coding (described on the previous spread) support the existence of a separate short- and long-term store, which is the basis of the MSM.

Studies using brain scanning techniques have also demonstrated that there is a difference between STM and LTM. For example, Beardsley (1997) found that the prefrontal cortex is active during STM but not LTM tasks. Squire *et al.* (1992) also used brain scanning and found the hippocampus is active when LTM is engaged.

This evidence provides strong support for the MSM.

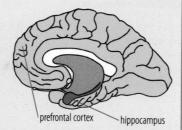

prefrontal cortex   hippocampus

▲ Locations for STM and LTM.

Case studies

Psychologists have also shown that different areas of the brain are involved in STM and LTM from their study of individuals with brain damage.

One case involved a man referred to as HM (Scoville and Milner, 1957). His brain damage was caused by an operation to remove the hippocampus from both sides of his brain to reduce the severe epilepsy he had suffered. HM's personality and intellect remained intact but he could not form new LTMs, although he could remember things from before the surgery.

This provides support for the MSM's notion of separate stores, as HM was unable to transfer information from his STM to LTM, but was able to retrieve information from before his surgery (i.e. from his LTM).

The multi-store model is too simple

The MSM suggests that both STM and LTM are single 'unitary' stores. However, research does not support this.

The working memory model and its supporting research (see next spread) shows that working memory (STM) is divided into a number of qualitatively different stores, i.e. it isn't just a difference in terms of capacity and duration, but in the *kind* of memory stored there. The same is true for LTM. Research shows there are a number of qualitatively different kinds of LTM (see pages 50–51) and each behaves differently. For example, maintenance rehearsal can explain long-term storage in semantic memory (memory for knowledge about the world) but doesn't explain long-term episodic memories (memories for things that you experienced).

This suggests that the MSM may be overly simplistic.

Long-term memory involves more than maintenance rehearsal

The MSM has been criticised for its emphasis on maintenance rehearsal.

Craik and Lockhart (1972) suggested that enduring memories are created by the *processing* that you do, rather than through maintenance rehearsal. Things that are processed more deeply are more memorable just because of the way they are processed. Craik and Tulving (1975) gave participants a list of nouns (e.g. 'shark') and asked a question that involved shallow or deep processing – asked whether a word was printed in capital letters (shallow processing) or asked whether the word fitted in a sentence (deep processing). The participants remembered more words in the task involving deep processing rather than shallow processing.

This suggests that the process of rehearsal does not full explain the process of creating long-term memories. 'Deep' or elaborative processing is also a key part of the process.

How separate are STM and LTM?

The multi-store model suggests that STM is involved *before* LTM. This claim has been questioned by other researchers.

Logie (1999) pointed out that STM actually *relies* on LTM and therefore cannot come 'first'. Consider the following list of letters: AQABBCITVIBM. In order to chunk this you need to recall the meaningful groups of letters and such meanings are stored in LTM. Ruchkin *et al.* (2003) demonstrated this by asking participants to recall a set of words and pseudo-words (words designed to sound like real words but with no meaning). They found that there was much more brain activity when real words were processed compared to pseudo-words, indicating the involvement of other areas of the brain than just STM.

This research suggests that STM is actually just a part of LTM and not a separate store.

UPGRADE

Descriptive questions such as 'Outline the multi-store model of memory' for 6 marks should be a gift for the well-prepared student, but questions like this can cause problems when selecting what to cram into an answer that is likely to be only about 150 words – there are far more than 150 words to choose from.

The number of points given is important but so is the quality and depth of each point. Ten superficial points will only get you to the limited level in terms of marks so clarity and detail is key. You could start by drawing a rough diagram of the MSM which would help your recall and then go on to describe each store and transfer between stores. That is five things to describe, so with about 30 words for each aspect you would have your 150 words.

Of course, it pays to be flexible, so it is a good idea to practise outlining the multi-store model in fewer words should there be only 3 or 4 marks offered for this question. The important lesson is that although you can't predict the actual questions, you can make sure that you are suitably prepared for whatever comes your way on the day!

Insider tip...

Students often lose marks on extended writing questions on the MSM because they don't provide enough descriptive detail. For example, they might say STM has a limited capacity but don't specify that this is counted in seconds and minutes rather than hours, and there is evidence that it might last up to 90 seconds.

Having said that – don't forget that the descriptive content is, at most, only half your marks on such questions.

KEY TERMS

Multi-store model An explanation of memory based on three separate memory stores, and how information is transferred between these stores.

Sensory register This is the information at the senses – information collected by your eyes, ears, nose, fingers and so on. Information is retained for a very brief period by the sensory registers. We are only able to hold accurate images of sensory information momentarily (less than half a second). The capacity of sensory memory is very large, such as all the cells on the retina of the eye. The method of coding depends on the sense organ involved, e.g. visual for the eyes or acoustic for the ears.

CAN YOU?   No. 2.2

1. Outline the multi-store model of memory. (6 marks)
2. Explain **one** criticism of the multi-store model of memory. (4 marks)
3. Discuss the multi-store model of memory. Refer to research evidence in your answer. (12 marks AS, 16 marks A)

The working memory model

On the previous spread we considered the multi-store model of memory. Now we will consider one alternative model – the **working memory model** (WMM). The working memory model addresses one aspect of memory – short-term or immediate memory.

It is concerned with the memory that you use when you are working on a complex task which requires you to store information as you go along. For example, if you are calculating a complex sum such as $21 + 12 + 52$, you add 21 and 12 and hold that answer in working memory before adding the final number. Or, when reading a sentence, you store the individual words in working memory while determining the sentence's meaning.

MEET THE RESEARCHER

Alan Baddeley has carried out a great deal of research on human memory. On page 45 we looked at his classic study on encoding in short- and long-term memory. His continued research on memory led him to formulate the working memory model, with colleague Graham Hitch. Baddeley continues to research and refine this model.
In addition to conducting research, Baddeley (2004) has also written many books, including a very readable one called *Your Memory: A User's Guide*.

KEY TERMS

Central executive Monitors and coordinates all other mental functions in working memory.

Episodic buffer Receives input from many sources, temporarily stores this information, and then integrates it in order to construct a mental episode of what is being experienced.

Phonological loop Codes speech sounds in working memory, typically involving maintenance rehearsal (repeating the words over and over again). This is why this component of working memory is referred to as a 'loop'.

Visuo-spatial sketchpad Codes visual information in terms of separate objects as well as the arrangement of these objects in one's visual field.

Working memory model An explanation of the memory used when working on a task. Each store is qualitatively different.

DESCRIPTION OF THE WORKING MEMORY MODEL (WMM)

Baddeley and Hitch (1974) felt that STM was not just one store, but a number of different stores. Why did they think this?

- If you do two things at the same time (dual task performance) and they are both visual tasks, you perform them less well than if you do them separately.
- If you do two things at the same time and one is visual whereas the other involves sound, then there is no interference. You do them as well simultaneously as you would do them separately.

This suggests that there is one store for visual processing and a separate store for processing sounds. This formed the basis of the WMM where 'slave systems' are organised by a **central executive** (CE).

Central executive

The function of the CE is to direct attention to particular tasks, determining at any time how the brain's '*resources*' are allocated to tasks. The 'resources' are the three slave systems listed below. Data arrive from the senses or from long-term memory. The CE has a very limited capacity; in other words it can't attend to too many things at once and has no capacity for storing data.

Phonological loop

This too has a limited capacity. The **phonological loop** (PL) deals with auditory information and preserves the order of information. Baddeley (1986) further subdivided this loop into:

- The phonological store which holds the words you hear, like an inner ear.
- An articulatory process which is used for words that are heard or seen. These words are silently repeated (looped), like an inner voice. This is a form of maintenance rehearsal.

Visuo-spatial sketchpad

The **visuo-spatial sketchpad** (VSS) is used when you have to plan a spatial task (like getting from one room to another, or counting the number of windows in your house). Visual and/or spatial information is temporarily stored here. Visual information is what things look like. Spatial information is the physical relationship between things.

Logie (1995) suggested that the visuo-spatial sketchpad can be divided into:

- A visual cache which stores information about visual items, e.g. form and colour.
- An inner scribe which stores the arrangement of objects in the visual field.

Episodic buffer

Baddeley (2000) added the **episodic buffer** because he realised the model needed a general store. The phonological loop and visuo-spatial sketchpad deal with processing and temporary storage of *specific* kinds of information. The central executive has no storage capacity; so there was nowhere to hold information that relates to both visual *and* acoustic information. The episodic buffer is an extra storage system that has, in common with all working memory units, limited capacity.

The episodic buffer integrates information from the central executive, the phonological loop and the visuo-spatial sketchpad. It also maintains a sense of time sequencing – basically recording events (episodes) that are happening. The episodic buffer sends information to LTM.

The **central executive** functions like the people in the control tower at an airport. There are only a few people there and they focus their attention on the most important tasks, such as planes that are taking off and landing. However, if a problem arises in relation to a routine task (such as baggage falling off a truck) they are ready to take control – they keep an eye on everything that is going on and deal with the tasks requiring attention.

'**Phonological**' relates to sound. 'Phono' is like phone – a telephone carries sound.
You are undoubtedly familiar with the effects of the phonological loop – if you are watching your favourite TV show and your mother tries to speak to you, you find it difficult to listen to both at the same time. This is because of the limited capacity of the phonological loop.

Top sportspeople rely on efficient **visuo-spatial processing** in working memory. For example, Wayne Gretzky (probably the greatest ice hockey player ever) scored a goal on one occasion by hitting the puck so it bounced off the goalie's back and into the goal. He was able to visualise the spatial relationship between objects even when the objects were in motion.

Central executive

Episodic buffer

Phonological loop
Subdivided into phonological store (inner ear) and articulatory process (inner voice)

Long-term memory

Visuo-spatial sketchpad

Added to the model to explain why some patients with amnesia can remember passages from a book when tested fairly immediately despite having no long-term recall.

▲ The working memory model.

Dual task performance

The main reason for developing the WMM was to account for dual task performance, described on the facing page. Hitch and Baddeley (1976) supported the existence of the central executive in one such study.

Task 1 occupied the central executive (e.g. participants were given a statement 'B is followed by A' and shown two letters such as 'AB' and asked to say true or false). Task 2 either involved the articulatory loop (e.g. asked to say 'the the the' repeatedly) or involved both the central executive and the articulatory loop (saying random digits). Task 1 was slower when Task 2 involved both the central executive and the articulatory loop.

This demonstrates the dual task performance effect and shows that the central executive is one of the components of working memory.

Evidence from brain-damaged patients

Studies of individuals with brain damage also support the WMM.

Shallice and Warrington (1970) studied a man called KF whose short-term forgetting of auditory information was much greater than that of visual stimuli. In addition his auditory problems were limited to verbal material such as letters and digits but not meaningful sounds (such as a phone ringing). Thus his brain damage seemed to be restricted to the phonological loop. Another patient, SC, had generally good learning abilities with the exception of being unable to learn word pairs that were presented out loud. This suggests damage to the phonological loop (Trojano and Grossi, 1995). Another patient, LH, who had been involved in a road accident, performed better on spatial tasks than those involving visual imagery (Farah *et al.*, 1988).

This supports the idea of separate visual and spatial systems, as suggested by the WMM.

Problems with using case studies

There are a number of problems with using evidence from case studies of individuals who have suffered serious brain damage.

First of all, the process of brain injury is traumatic, which may in itself change behaviour so that a person performs worse on certain tasks. Second, such individuals may have other difficulties such as difficulties paying attention and therefore underperform on certain tasks. Finally case studies are of unique individuals and cannot be generalised to the population.

This is an issue for the WMM as some of the key research that supports the WMM comes from case studies.

A03 plus Evidence for the phonological loop and articulatory process

A strength of the WMM lies in the phonological loop and its explanation of the word-length effect – the fact that people cope better with short words than long words in working memory (STM).

It seems that the phonological loop holds the amount of information that you can say in 2 seconds (Baddeley *et al.*, 1975). This makes it hard to remember a list of long words such as 'association' and 'representative' compared to shorter words like 'harm' and 'twice'. The longer words can't be rehearsed on the phonological loop because they don't fit. However, the word-length effect disappears if a person is given an articulatory suppression task, for example if you are asked to say 'the the the…' while reading the words. This repetitive task ties up the articulatory process and means you can't rehearse the shorter words more quickly than the longer ones, so the word-length effect disappears.

This is evidence for the articulatory process – a key component of the WMM.

A03 plus The central executive

Some psychologists feel the concept of the central executive is too vague and doesn't really explain anything.

All it appears to do is allocate resources and essentially be the same as 'attention'. Critics also feel that the notion of a single central executive is wrong and that there are probably several components. Eslinger and Damasio (1985) studied EVR, who had had a cerebral tumour removed. He performed well on tests requiring reasoning, which suggested that his central executive was intact. However, he had poor decision-making skills (he would spend hours trying to decide where to eat, for example), which suggests that in fact his central executive was not wholly intact.

In summary the account offered of the central executive is unsatisfactory because it is probably more complex than Baddeley and Hitch originally suggested.

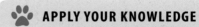

▲ Mental rotation test – are the figures 1a and 1b the same except for their orientation? What about 2a and 2b? Doing this test is an example of the visual sketchpad in action.

🐾 APPLY YOUR KNOWLEDGE

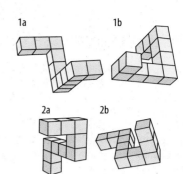

Megan is a university student studying psychology. During seminars she often plays the computer game *Sims* on her laptop, while at the same time listening to what her lecturer is saying. She explains to her lecturer that she can still concentrate on what he is saying while she plays the game. However, she notices that when her friend Jesse starts chatting to her during seminars (which she does a lot), she loses track of what her lecturer is saying.

Using your knowledge of the working memory model, explain why Megan is able to concentrate on what her lecturer is saying in one situation but not in the other.

Insider tip…

If you are asked to describe a research study you should always include some information on the procedures (what the researchers did) and some information on the results/conclusions of the study – unless otherwise directed. For example, a question might ask you to describe how a research study investigated working memory, in which case only the procedures would be creditworthy.

CAN YOU? No. 2.3

1. Outline the working memory model. (6 marks)
2. Describe **one** research study that supports the working memory model. (4 marks)
3. Explain **one** criticism of the working memory model. (4 marks)
4. Discuss the working memory model. Include strengths and limitations in your answer. (12 marks AS, 16 marks A)

Types of long-term memory

One of the key criticisms of the multi-store model is that it is too simple because it describes both short-term memory (working memory) and long-term memory as unitary stores.

The working memory model explained how short-term memory can be divided into qualitatively different sub-systems: the phonological loop for sounds and visuo-spatial sketchpad for visual and spatial tasks, plus the divisions within these sub-systems.

It is now time to look at how long-term memory can be separated into qualitatively different types: **episodic**, **semantic** and **procedural memory**.

Research methods

Automatic performance (procedural memory) has been studied in relation to something called social facilitation – how the presence of other people can make performing some tasks easier.

Norman Triplett (1897) showed that when people work together (coact) they perform faster than when working individually. Further studies of this phenomenon have shown that this is only true for dominant (well-learned, automatic) skills, i.e. procedural memories.

Michaels *et al.* (1982) watched pool players and recorded the number of successful shots and compared this to when they were playing alone. Players who are 'watched' should do better.

1. Identify the independent and dependent variables in this study. (2 marks)
2. Write a suitable directional hypothesis for this study. (2 marks)
3. This study used a repeated measures design. Explain how you might test the same hypothesis using an independent groups design. (3 marks)
4. Give **one** strength and **one** limitation of using an independent groups design rather than a repeated measures design for this hypothesis. (3 marks + 3 marks)
5. Identify **one** suitable sampling method and explain how you would use this method in this study. (3 marks)

LINK TO RESEARCH METHODS

Hypothesis and variables on page 179
Experimental design on page 184
Sampling on page 192

▲ An episodic memory she'd rather forget – perhaps her procedural memory wasn't so automatic after all.

KEY TERMS

Episodic memory Personal memories of events, such as what you did yesterday or a teacher you liked. This kind of memory includes contextual details plus emotional tone.

Procedural memory Memory for how to do things, for example riding a bicycle or learning how to read. Such memories are automatic as the result of repeated practice.

Semantic memory Shared memories for facts and knowledge. These memories may be concrete, such as knowing that ice is made of water, or abstract, such as mathematical knowledge.

DESCRIPTION OF DIFFERENT TYPES OF LONG-TERM MEMORY

Long-term memory (LTM) is divided into two main types: explicit (or declarative) memory and implicit (or procedural) memory. This is a distinction between knowing *that* and knowing *how*. Within these two broad categories are key types of memory which are the focus of your study. Episodic and semantic memories are examples of knowing that – explicit/declarative memories. Procedural memories are knowing how.

Each of the three different types of memory has unique characteristics.

Episodic memory

Episodic memories are about knowing *that*. The term 'episodic' comes from the word 'episode' – an event or a group of events occurring as part of a larger sequence. This kind of memory is concerned with your personal experiences, with your recollection of your first day at school, a family holiday, playing with friends and so on. You may recall the time and place of such events as well as who was there.

You also may recall the context surrounding the event such as what happened just before or after, or why you were there. Finally, you may also recall associated emotions that you felt at the time.

So, episodic memories have three elements: specific details of the event, the context and the emotion.

Semantic memory

Semantic memories are also about knowing *that*, but instead of knowing that your first day at school was scary you also know that people of a certain age go to school and that $2+2=4$ and that the capital of England is London. The latter three examples are semantic memories – knowledge about the world which is shared by everyone rather than the personal kind of knowledge that is classed as episodic memories.

Semantic memories may relate to things, such as the functions of objects, may relate to what behaviour is appropriate, such as social customs, but also may relate to abstract concepts, such as mathematics and language.

Semantic memories generally begin as episodic memories because we acquire knowledge based on personal experiences. There is a gradual transition from episodic to semantic memory where the memory slowly loses its association to particular events, so that the information can be generalised as a semantic memory. Sometimes, however, people continue to have a strong recollection of when and where they learned a particular fact.

Procedural memory

Procedural memory is concerned with skills, such as knowing how to tie a shoelace, knowing how to dive into a swimming pool or knowing how to read. It is about remembering how to do something rather than knowing the rules of what to do (knowing how to behave towards others is a semantic memory, as distinct from behaving nicely towards others which is procedural).

Procedural memories are typically acquired through repetition and practice. Unlike episodic and semantic memory, this kind of memory is implicit. We are less aware of these memories because they have become automatic. Often, if you try to think too much about such procedural memories it prevents you acting them out – try riding a bicycle while really thinking about what you are doing: you may lose your balance. This attention to the step-by-step procedure disrupts the well-learned, automatic performance.

It is important that procedural memories are automatic so we can focus our attention on other tasks while performing these everyday skills.

EVALUATION/DISCUSSION

Evidence from brain scans

The distinction made between the three kinds of LTM is supported by brain scan research.

Episodic memory is associated with the hippocampus and other parts of the temporal lobe where the hippocampus is located, as well as with activity in the frontal lobe. Semantic memory also relies on the temporal lobe. Procedural memory activation is associated with the cerebellum, which is involved in the control of fine motor skills as well as the motor cortex. The basal ganglia and limbic system are also involved in this kind of learning.

Brain scans therefore indicate that the three types of memory are found in different parts of the brain and so are separate.

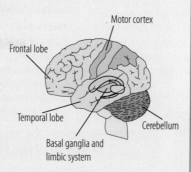

▲ Locations for different types of LTM.

Distinguishing procedural and declarative memories

Evidence from case studies offers further support for different types of LTM.

The case study of HM was described on page 47. We noted that his ability to form new LTMs was affected by the destruction of his hippocampus (parts of his temporal lobes were also destroyed) but he retained his pre-existing LTMs. In fact this is a bit of a simplification. After the surgery, HM could still form new procedural memories but not episodic or semantic memories. For example, he was able to learn how to draw a figure by looking at its reflection in a mirror, a skill called mirror-drawing (Corkin, 2002). This is a procedural memory. However, he had no memory *that* he had learned this (an episodic/semantic memory).

This supports the distinction between procedural and declarative memories, and hence the existence of multiple types of LTM.

Problems with evidence from patients with brain damage

It is difficult to reach a firm conclusion by studying brain-damaged patients.

Problems with evidence from brain-damaged patients were considered on page 49 and they apply here too. In addition, the difficulty with studies of amnesiacs, including HM, is that it is difficult to be certain of the exact parts of the brain that have been affected until a patient has died. Most studies are conducted with living patients. Damage to a particular area of the brain does not necessarily mean that area is responsible for a particular behaviour – it may be acting as a relay station. Malfunction of the relay station would impair performance.

This means we cannot establish a causal relationship between a particular brain region and type of LTM.

A03 plus Distinguishing episodic and semantic memories

Further support for different types of LTM comes from studies of patients with Alzheimer's.

Researchers have sought to examine the relationship between episodic and semantic memories by studying patients with Alzheimer's disease and found some patients who retain the ability to form new semantic memories but not episodic memories (Hodges and Patterson, 2007). This is a single dissociation, i.e. a separation between two abilities. A second dissociation was found by Irish *et al.* (2011) in Alzheimer's patients who have the reverse – poor semantic memories but generally intact episodic memories.

This double dissociation suggests that episodic and semantic memories are separate, and that episodic memories may be a gateway to semantic memory, but it is possible for semantic memories to form separately.

A03 plus Priming and a fourth kind of LTM

The possibility that other types of LTM may exist raises questions about existing theories.

For example, priming describes how implicit memories influence the responses a person makes to a stimulus. If a person is given a list of words including the word 'yellow' and is later asked to name a fruit, they are more likely to answer 'banana' than if not primed. This is a kind of implicit memory because the answers are automatic and unconscious. Research has shown that priming is controlled by a brain system separate from the temporal system that supports explicit memory (semantic and episodic memories). This has led to the suggestion that there is a fourth kind of LTM, the perceptual-representation system (PRS) memory related to priming, supported by Spiers *et al.* (2001).

This suggests that other types of LTM may exist and the original theory of LTM may be too simplistic.

I remember when I was revising for my A levels – I was not happy!

Episodic knowledge

I know many theories and studies in psychology.

Long-term memory

Semantic knowledge

In an exam you have to write longhand, but I know how to type much faster on a computer.

Procedural knowledge

▲ Types of long-term memory.

CAN YOU? No. 2.4

1. Explain what is meant by 'episodic memory'. (3 marks)
2. Explain what is meant by 'semantic memory'. (3 marks)
3. Explain what is meant by 'procedural memory'. (3 marks)
4. Explain evidence to support the distinction between episodic and procedural memory. (6 marks)
5. Describe and evaluate types of long-term memory. (12 marks AS, 16 marks A)

Explanations for forgetting: Interference

The concept of *forgetting* has a number of meanings in psychology, but generally is taken to refer to a person's loss of the ability to recall or recognise something that they have previously learned. Forgetting in short- or long-term memory is often explained in terms of trace decay – the suggestion that the memory code created in the brain to store an item has disappeared. In the twentieth century there was a second, very popular explanation for forgetting – **interference** theory.

▲ Consider the following: you are used to opening a particular drawer to get a knife. Your mother decides to re-organise the kitchen and puts the knives in a different drawer. However, every time you go to get a knife you go to the old drawer. An old memory is continuing to interfere with new learning. This is proactive interference ('pro' is going forwards).

After many months you have got used to the new arrangement. Your mother decides it was a bad idea and changes them back to the original scheme. Now what happens? You continue to go to the second location. The newer memory interferes with past learning. This is retroactive interference ('retro' is going backwards).

Paired associate testing

A common way to test RI and PI is using word pairs that have something in common – paired associates.

- First participants are required to learn words from List A paired with List B (e.g. cat + tree).
- Second they are asked to learn words from List A paired with List C (e.g. cat + stone).
- Finally each participant is given the first word of the pair and asked to recall the word from List C (proactive interference) or List B (retroactive interference). A control condition only learns list A–B to see what recall will occur when there is no interference.

You might try this yourself to test RI and PI. Which causes more forgetting, RI or PI?

List A	List B	List C
Cat	Tree	Stone
Candle	Whale	Cloth
Book	Fork	Jail
Plant	Tank	Claw
Water	Market	Gold
Track	Lemon	Kettle
Dish	Cane	Swamp
Flask	Picture	Mast
Cigar	Jelly	Nail
Animal	Nurse	Pencil

DESCRIPTION OF INTERFERENCE THEORY

Retroactive interference

Georg Müller (one of the founders of psychology) and his student (Müller and Pilzecker, 1900) were the first to identify **retroactive interference (RI)** effects. They gave participants a list of nonsense syllables to learn for 6 minutes and then, after a retention interval, asked participants to recall the lists. Performance was less good if participants had been given an intervening task between initial learning and recall (they were shown three landscape paintings and asked to describe them).

The intervening task produced RI because the later task (describing pictures) interfered with what had previously been learned.

Proactive interference

Benton Underwood (1957) showed that **proactive interference (PI)** could be equally significant. He analysed the findings from a number of studies and concluded that when participants have to learn a series of word lists they do not learn the lists of words encountered later on in the sequence as well as lists of words encountered earlier on.

Overall, Underwood found that, if participants memorised 10 or more lists, then, after 24 hours, they remembered about 20% of what they learned. If they only learned one list recall was over 70%. These results can be seen in the graph on the right.

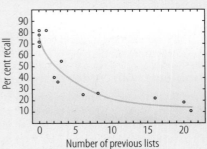

▲ Recall as a function of number of lists learned. The more lists a participant has to learn, the worse their overall recall. This is explained by proactive interference because each list makes it harder to learn subsequent lists.

Similarity of test materials

In another early study McGeoch and McDonald (1931) experimented with the effects of similarity of materials. They gave participants a list of 10 adjectives (List A). Once these were learned there was then a resting interval of 10 minutes during which they learned List B, followed by recall.

If List B was a list of synonyms of List A, recall was poor (12%); if List B was nonsense syllabus this had less effect (26% recall); if List B was numbers this had the least effect (37% recall). This shows that interference is strongest the more similar the items are. Only interference, rather than decay, can explain such effects.

A real-world study

Baddeley and Hitch (1977) investigated interference effects in an everyday setting of rugby players recalling the names of the teams they had played against over a rugby season. Some players played in all of the games in the season whereas others missed some games because of injury. The time interval from start to end of the season was the same for all players but the number of intervening games was different for each player because of missed games.

If decay theory is correct then all players should recall a similar percentage of the games played because time alone should cause forgetting. If interference theory is correct then those players who played most games should forget proportionally more because of interference – which is what Baddeley and Hitch found, demonstrating the effect of interference in everyday life.

Research is quite artificial

One issue with the evidence offered in support of both pro- and retroactive interference concerns the methodology of the studies.

Most of this research has often used rather artificial lists of words and/or nonsense syllables. Thus the findings may not relate to everyday uses of memory, which tends not to involve word lists. In addition, participants may lack motivation to remember the links in such studies, and this may allow interference effects to appear stronger than they really are.

This means that the research is low in ecological validity, although the counterargument is that interference effects have been observed in everyday situations, as described on the facing page.

Interference only explains some situations of forgetting

Another criticism of research into interference is that, while interference effects do occur in everyday life, they don't occur that often.

Rather special conditions are required for interference to lead to forgetting – the two memories need to be quite similar. For this reason interference is considered a relatively unimportant explanation for everyday forgetting. Anderson (2000) concluded that there is no doubt that interference plays a role in forgetting, but how much forgetting can be attributed to interference remains unclear.

This means that other theories are needed to provide a complete explanation of forgetting.

Accessibility versus availability

Researchers have often questioned whether interference effects actually cause a memory to disappear or whether interference effects are just temporary.

Ceraso (1967) found that, if memory was tested again after 24 hours, recognition (accessibility) showed considerable spontaneous recovery, whereas recall (availability) remained the same. This suggests that interference occurs because memories are temporarily not accessible rather than having actually been lost (unavailable). The study by Tulving and Psotka, described on the next spread, also supports this finding.

This research supports the view that interference affects availability rather than accessibility.

Real-world application to advertising

There is a considerable body of research on the effects of interference when people are exposed to adverts from competing brands within a short time period.

For example, Danaher *et al.* (2008) found that both recall and recognition of an advertiser's message were impaired when participants were exposed to two advertisements for competing brands within a week. They suggest that one strategy might be to enhance the memory trace by running multiple exposures to an advertisement on one day rather than spread these out over a week. This results in reduced interference from competitors' advertisements.

This shows how interference research can help advertisers maximise the effectiveness of their campaigns and target their spending most effectively.

Individual differences

There is evidence that some people are less affected by proactive interference than others.

Kane and Engle (2000) demonstrated that individuals with a greater working memory (WM) span were less susceptible to proactive interference. The researchers tested this by giving participants three word lists to learn. Those participants with low working memory spans showed greater proactive interference when recalling the second and third lists than did participants with higher spans. A further test suggested that having a greater working memory span meant having greater resources to consciously control processing and counteract the effects of proactive interference.

This highlights the role that individual differences play in how people are affected by interference.

▶ 'This amnesia of yours … can you remember how long you've had it?'

⬆ UPGRADE

'Explain what is meant by the terms 'proactive interference' and 'retroactive interference'.' (2 marks + 2 marks)

Students commonly make one of two mistakes with 2-mark questions – either they write too little and only get 1 mark, or they write too much and waste valuable time. So, the secret is writing just enough so that an examiner will look at your response and be able to see that what you have written is enough to edge your answer up to 2 marks.

For example, you may write 'Proactive interference is when past learning makes learning something in the future more difficult'. Now, this is perfectly accurate, but ask yourself, what would a 1-mark answer look like if not like this? Make life easier for the examiner and provide that extra little bit of information so they can be confident you have done something over and above the 1-mark answer. For example, 'Proactive interference is when past learning makes learning something in the future more difficult. This is because the original memory for something interferes with the formation of new memories associated with it.' Now you have explained the term as well. An alternative way to get the second mark is to give an appropriate example.

Insider tip…

It is easy to mix up proactive and retroactive interference. Whenever there is a topic where such mix-ups are likely, you need to establish an aid for your memory (aide memoire) – have some little picture (like the one on the right) or phrase you can jot down when you get in the exam to make sure your don't muddle them up.

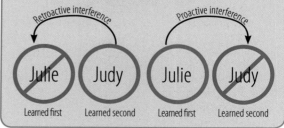

CAN YOU? No. 2.5

1. Briefly explain what is meant by the terms 'proactive interference' and 'retroactive interference'. (2 marks + 2 marks)
2. Describe **one** study that demonstrated that interference may cause forgetting. (6 marks)
3. Describe and evaluate **one** explanation for forgetting. (12 marks AS, 16 marks A)

Explanations for forgetting: Retrieval failure

Earlier in this chapter you have read that the duration of long-term memory (LTM) is effectively unlimited, so why do we appear to lose information once we have submitted it to LTM? It is possible that the information was never stored there in the first place, or the actual memory trace has disappeared, or it is there (available) but is just not accessible. If you are given a reminder (a **cue**) then you may suddenly be able to bring it to mind.

Consider the following example: you have forgotten the name of the psychologist who researched the capacity of short-term memory, but if I give you a clue that his name started with M, you might remember it was Miller.

▶ Retrieval cues are used in advertisements where the advertiser wants you to recall the message at the moment you are actually making a purchase. The image cues the recollection of the message.

▲ Have you had the experience of looking at a photo from your younger days or visiting a place where you grew up – and all sorts of memories came flooding back? That's an example of context dependent recall.

Another example, in the reverse direction, is going on holiday. The unfamiliar environment means that you have more chance to rest and leave the cares of the world behind – there are no cues to remind you.

DESCRIPTION OF RETRIEVAL FAILURE

Forgetting in LTM is mainly due to **retrieval failure** (lack of accessibility rather than availability). This is the failure to find an item of information because you have insufficient clues or cues.

The encoding specificity principle

Endel Tulving and Donald Thomson (1973) proposed that memory is most effective if information that was present at encoding is also available at the time of retrieval. The encoding specificity principle further states that a cue doesn't have to be exactly right but the closer the cue is to the original item, the more useful it will be.

Tulving and Pearlstone (1966) demonstrated the value of retrieval cues in a study where participants had to learn 48 words belonging to 12 categories. Each word was presented as category + word, e.g. fruit–apple, fruit–orange. There were two different recall conditions. Participants either had to recall as many words as they could (free recall) or they were given cues in the form of the category names (cued recall). In the free recall condition 40% of words were recalled on average, whereas in the cued-recall condition participants recalled 60% of the words.

This is evidence of cues that have been explicitly or implicitly encoded at the time of learning and have a meaningful link to the learning material. There is another type of cue which is not related to the learning material in any meaningful way. Whenever any information is learned, we also often remember where we were (environmental context) or how we felt (the emotional state at the time). This information is encoded to varying degrees along with the material learned. It is sometimes the case that being reminded of a particular place or mood can act as a trigger (or cue) to help access a memory.

Context-dependent forgetting

One example of context-dependent forgetting is a study by Ethel Abernethy (1940). She arranged for a group of students to be tested before a certain course began. They were then tested each week. Some students were tested in their teaching room by their usual instructor, whereas others were tested by a different instructor. Others were tested in a different room either by their usual instructor or by a different one. Therefore there were four experimental conditions in this study. Those tested by the same instructor in the same room performed best. Presumably familiar things (room and instructor) acted as memory cues. Abernethy also found that superior students were least affected by the changes and inferior students the most.

A study by Godden and Baddeley (1975) investigated the effect of contextual cues. The researchers recruited scuba divers as participants and arranged for them to learn a set of words either on land or underwater. Subsequently, they were tested either on land or underwater, so there were again four experimental conditions. The results again showed that highest recall occurred when the initial context matched the recall environment, e.g. learning on land and recalling on land.

State-dependent forgetting

The mental state you are in at the time of learning can also act as a cue – state-dependent forgetting. Goodwin et al. (1969) asked male volunteers to remember a list of words when they were either drunk or sober (those in the drunk condition imbibed about three times the UK drink driving limit). The participants were asked to recall the lists after 24 hours when some were sober but others had to get drunk again (for experimental purposes). The recall scores are shown in the graph on the right, suggesting that information learned when drunk is more available when in the same state later.

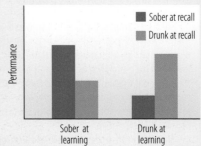

▲ Findings from Goodwin et al.'s study.

There is a lot of research support

The wealth of research evidence that has documented the importance of retrieval cues on memory is a real strength of this explanation of forgetting.

Such research includes lab, field and natural experiments as well as anecdotal evidence. For example, Tulving and Pearlstone (1966), in a lab experiment, demonstrated the power of retrieval clues, while a field experiment by Abernethy (1940) demonstrated the importance of context-dependent learning among a group of students studying a course.

Because much of the evidence has relevance to everyday memory experiences, the evidence has high ecological validity.

Real-world application

An obvious application of this research is to use it to improve recall when you need to, for example when you are taking exams.

Abernethy's research suggests that you ought to revise in the room where you will be taking the exams. This may be unrealistic, but you could use imagination to achieve this. Smith (1979) showed that just thinking of the room where you did the original learning (mental reinstatement) was as effective as actually being in the same room at the time of retrieval. Another application of retrieval cues is in the cognitive interview, which you will learn about on page 60 of this chapter.

This shows how research into retrieval failure can suggest strategies for improving recall in real-world situations, such as taking exams or giving eyewitness testimony.

Retrieval cues do not always work

Having said you could use cues to improve your exam performance, the reality is that this is not very effective (sorry).

The issue is that the information you are learning is related to a lot more than just the cues. In most of the research on context effects, participants learn word lists but when you are learning, for example, about Milgram's research into obedience, you are learning about complex associations that are less easily triggered by single cues. This has been called the *outshining hypothesis*: a cue's effectiveness is reduced by the presence of better cues. According to Smith and Vela (2001) context effects are largely eliminated when learning meaningful material.

This suggests that while the use of retrieval cues can explain instances of everyday forgetting, they don't explain everything.

 The danger of circularity

A limitation is that the relationship between encoding cues and later retrieval is a correlation rather than a cause.

Nairne (2002) calls this the 'myth of the encoding-retrieval match'. Baddeley (1997) made a similar criticism, pointing out that the encoding specificity principle is impossible to test because it is circular. If a stimulus leads to the retrieval of a memory then it must have been encoded in memory. If it does not lead to retrieval of a memory then, according to the encoding specificity principle, it can't have been encoded in memory. But it is impossible to test for an item that hasn't been encoded in memory, so this cannot be proved.

According to this criticism, therefore, the cues do not cause *retrieval, they are just* associated *with retrieval.*

 Retrieval failure explains interference effects

A strength of the retrieval failure explanation is its ability to explain interference effects.

Tulving and Psotka (1971) demonstrated that apparent interference effects are actually due to the absence of cues. Participants were given 6 different word lists to learn, each consisting of 24 words divided into 6 different categories (such as kinds of tree). Participants were then asked to list the words with no cues (free recall) or after being given the category names as cues (cued recall). The more lists a participant had to learn the worse their performance became – evidence of retroactive interference. However, when participants were given cued recall, the effects of interference disappeared – they remembered about 70% of the words regardless of how many lists they had been given.

This shows that information is there (available) but cannot be retrieved and therefore retrieval failure is a more important explanation of forgetting than interference.

▲ Smells often act as powerful retrieval cues.

This was demonstrated in a study by Aggleton and Waskett (1999). Participants were all people who had visited the Jorvik Viking Centre in York, where smells are very much a feature of the display of Viking life. Their museum visits were 6–7 years prior to the study. A memory test asked questions about the museum and was accompanied by some of the smells of the museum or, for a control group, there were no smells. The smelly group did best on the test.

Is this an example of state- or context-dependent forgetting?

 APPLY YOUR KNOWLEDGE

Maggie is studying psychology, and has been reading around the subject because she enjoys it so much. Recently she has been reading about something called 'reminiscence therapy' where therapists use photographs, music and postcards to jog the memories of elderly adults. She thinks this would be great to help her grandmother remember when she was Maggie's age. Maggie's gran has been on her own since 1968, when her husband died quite suddenly, so she and Maggie have always been close. After consulting with her mum about what her gran's teenage and early adult years were like, Maggie makes a tape of some music of the 1960s that her gran would have listened to and takes round a film of *West Side Story* that they can watch together.

To Maggie's surprise, her gran becomes quite emotional listening to the music, and is particularly upset when watching the film. Maggie is at a loss to explain why her gran is reacting in this way, so heads back to her textbook to read up on memory.

Using the material on this spread, explain why you think Maggie's gran would have reacted in the way that she did when presented with these memories of her younger years.

CAN YOU?   No. 2.6

1. Briefly explain how the lack of cues may lead to retrieval failure. (3 marks)
2. Describe **one** study that demonstrated how the absence of cues may lead to retrieval failure. (6 marks)
3. Describe and evaluate how retrieval failure due to the absence of cues leads to forgetting. (12 marks AS, 16 marks A)

Accuracy of eyewitness testimony: Misleading information

Eyewitnesses (or earwitnesses) frequently play a critical role in criminal investigations, yet there is good reason to suspect that their testimony may not be reliable. The importance of this issue is highlighted by the Innocence Project (*www.innocenceproject.org*) who claim that 72% of convictions overturned by DNA testing involved **eyewitness testimony** (EWT) that was not accurate.

There are various reasons why eyewitness testimony may not be accurate. One of these concerns anxiety, which is explored on the next spread. On this spread we look at the effect of **misleading information** that may affect what you remember and/or recall about an event. There are two examples of this: **leading questions** and **post-event discussion**.

▲ How fast were the cars going when they hit each other?

LEADING QUESTIONS

Key study: Loftus and Palmer (1974)

Experiment 1: procedure
Forty-five students were shown seven films of different traffic accidents. After each film the participants were given a questionnaire which asked them to describe the accident and then answer a series of specific questions about it. There was one *critical question*: 'About how fast were the cars going when they hit each other?' One group of participants was given this question. The other four groups were given the verbs *smashed*, *collided*, *bumped* or *contacted* in place of the word *hit*. This critical question was a leading question because it suggested the answer that a participant might give.

Findings
The findings are shown in the table on the right, which demonstrate that leading questions affect the response given by participants.

Experiment 2: procedure
The leading question may bias a participant's response or may actually cause information to be altered before it is stored.

To test this, a new set of participants was divided into three groups and shown a film of a car accident lasting 1 minute, and again asked questions about speed. The participants were then asked to return one week later when they were asked a series of 10 questions about the accident, including another critical question, 'Did you see any broken glass?' There was no broken glass in the film but, presumably, those who thought the car was travelling faster might be more likely to think that there would be broken glass.

Findings
The findings (in the second table on the right) show that the leading question did change the actual memory a participant had for the event.

Verb	Mean speed estimate
smashed	40.8
collided	39.3
bumped	38.1
hit	34.0
contacted	31.8

▲ Speed estimates for the different verbs.

	Verb condition		
	Smashed	Hit	Control
Yes	16	7	6
No	34	43	44

▲ 'Yes' and 'No' responses to the question about broken glass.

POST-EVENT DISCUSSION

The memory of an event may also be altered or contaminated through discussing events with others and/or being questioned multiple times.

Conformity effect
Co-witnesses may reach a consensus view of what actually happened. This was investigated by Fiona Gabbert and colleagues (2003). Participants were in pairs where each partner watched a different video of the same event so that they each viewed unique items. Pairs in one condition were encouraged to discuss the event before each partner individually recalled the event they watched. A very high number of witnesses (71%) who had discussed the event went on to mistakenly recall items acquired during the discussion.

Repeat interviewing
Each time an eyewitness is interviewed there is the possibility that comments from the interviewer will become incorporated into their recollection of events. It is also the case that an interviewer may use leading questions and thus alter the individual's memory for events. This is especially the case when children are being interviewed about a crime (LaRooy *et al.*, 2005).

What is eyewitness testimony?
Psychologists tend to use the term 'eyewitness memory' instead of 'testimony' when carrying out research to test the accuracy of eyewitness testimony.

Eyewitness memory goes through three stages:

1. The witness encodes into LTM details of the event and the persons involved. Encoding may be only partial and distorted, particularly as most crimes happen very quickly, frequently at night, and sometimes accompanied by rapid, complex and often violent action.
2. The witness retains the information for a period of time. Memories may be lost or modified during retention (most forgetting takes place within the first few minutes of a retention interval) and other activities between encoding and retrieval may interfere with the memory itself.
3. The witness retrieves the memory from storage. The presence or absence of appropriate retrieval cues or the nature of the questioning may significantly affect the accuracy of what is recalled.

MEET THE RESEARCHER

Elizabeth Loftus is Distinguished Professor at the University of California, Irvine. Her experiments have revealed how memories can be changed by things that we are told after the event. The legal field has been a significant application of her memory research.

Real-life conformity effect
The Oklahoma bombing was an infamous crime in the US in 1995. One witness claimed to have seen the murderer, Timothy McVeigh, with an accomplice. Initially no other witnesses could describe this person but later they too claimed to recall this person.

Eventually the first witness realised that their recollection was wrong. Why did the other two witnesses make the same mistake? The first confident witness unintentionally influenced them, leading them too to believe there was a second man.

Eyewitness testimony The evidence provided in court by a person who witnessed a crime, with a view to identifying the perpetrator of the crime.

Leading question A question that, either by its form or content, suggests to the witness what answer is desired or leads him or her to the desired answer.

Misleading information Supplying information that may lead a witness' memory for a crime to be altered.

Post-event discussion A conversation between co-witnesses or an interviewer and an eyewitness after a crime has taken place which may contaminate a witness' memory for the event.

▶ Elizabeth Loftus investigated leading questions by asking people the question 'Do you get headaches frequently?' People who were asked this question reported an average of 2.2 headaches per week whereas those who were asked 'Do you get headaches occasionally, and if so, how often?' reported an average of 0.7 headaches. The way the question was asked had a significant effect on the answer given. Try it out yourself.

EVALUATION/DISCUSSION

Supporting evidence

There has been considerable support for research on the effect of misleading information.

For example, Loftus conducted a memorable study involving a cut-out of Bugs Bunny (Braun *et al.*, 2002). College students who had visited Disneyland as children were asked to evaluate advertising material about Disneyland containing misleading information about Bugs Bunny (not a Disney character) or Ariel (not introduced at the time of their childhood). Participants assigned to the Bugs or Ariel groups were more likely to report having shaken hands with these characters than the control group (no misleading information).

This shows how powerful misleading information can be in creating an inaccurate (false) memory.

EWT in real life

Loftus' research suggested that EWT was generally inaccurate and hence unreliable, but other researchers have criticised her research for its lack of ecological validity.

Lab experiments such as those carried out by Loftus may not represent real life because people don't take the experiment seriously and/or they are not emotionally aroused in the way that they would be in a real accident. Foster *et al.* (1994) found that if participants thought they were watching a real-life robbery, and also thought that their responses would influence the trial, their identification of a robber was more accurate. Yuille and Cutshall (1986) also found that witnesses to an armed robbery in Canada gave very accurate reports of the crime four months after the event despite initially being given two misleading questions.

This suggests that misleading information may have less influence on real-life EWT than Loftus' research suggests.

Real-world application

A strength of research investigating EWT is its application to the criminal justice system, which relies heavily on eyewitness identification for investigating and prosecuting crimes.

Psychological research has been used to warn the justice system of problems with eyewitness identification evidence. Recent DNA exoneration cases have confirmed the warnings of eyewitness identification researchers by showing that mistaken eyewitness identification was the largest single factor contributing to the conviction of these innocent people (Wells and Olson, 2003).

This demonstrates the important role of EWT research in helping ensure that innocent people are not convicted of crimes they did not commit on the basis of faulty EWT.

Individual differences

A criticism of research investigating EWT concerns individual differences of witnesses.

An eyewitness typically acquires information from two sources, from observing the event itself and from subsequent suggestions (misleading information). A number of studies (e.g. Schacter *et al.*, 1991) have found that, compared to younger subjects, elderly people have difficulty remembering the source of their information, even though their memory for the information itself is unimpaired. As a result, they become more prone to the effect of misleading information when giving testimony.

This suggests that individual differences, age in particular, are an important factor when assessing the reliability of EWT.

It may be response bias

The possibility of a response bias is another criticism of Loftus and Palmer's research into EWT.

Loftus and Palmer found that leading questions changed the original memory. However, Bekerian and Bowers (1983) replicated a study by Loftus *et al.* (1978) and found that participants are not susceptible to misleading information if questions are presented in the same order as the original data (Loftus had presented the questions in random order). This suggests that the order of questions had a significant effect and therefore memory change was due to response bias not storage.

This provides an alternative explanation to Loftus and Palmer and highlights the importance of question order in police interviews.

 UPGRADE

Sometimes on these spreads we use research studies as description only (i.e. AO1), but at other times we use research as evaluation or as part of our discussion (i.e. AO3). We have separated these by putting the AO1 studies on the left-hand side of each spread and those intended as AO3 evaluation on the right-hand side. However, a study by itself is not AO3, but what you *do* with the study is what transforms mere description into effective evaluation.

If we take the essay question on this spread as an example, we can see that the instruction to 'Discuss research…' requires more than simply describing studies and then hoping the examiner will be kind enough to count some of them as AO3. Assuming your AO1 material would be the Loftus and Palmer study or one of the other studies on the left-hand page, you can then use the research on the right-hand page to build a critical argument. To do this you need to introduce the research with a contextualising phrase such as 'There is considerable research support for the effect of misleading information, e.g. Loftus…' or 'Not all researchers agree with this conclusion, e.g. Foster *et al.*…' Other Upgrade features in this book will offer further advice on how to make your evaluation more effective.

CAN YOU? No. 2.7

1. Explain what is meant by a 'leading question'. Use an example in your answer. (3 marks)
2. Explain how post-event discussion might create inaccuracy in eyewitness testimony. (3 marks)
3. Describe **one** research study related to the effect of misleading information on eyewitness testimony. (5 marks)
4. Discuss research on the effect of misleading information on eyewitness testimony. (12 marks AS, 16 marks A)

Accuracy of eyewitness testimony: Anxiety

On the previous spread we looked at evidence related to the accuracy of eyewitness testimony (EWT) and considered one factor which may influence accuracy – the role of misleading information. There are a number of other factors that influence the accuracy of EWT, **anxiety** being perhaps the most significant.

People often become anxious when they are in stressful situations, and this anxiety tends to be accompanied by physiological arousal (e.g. a pounding heart and rapid, shallow breathing). Because of this, much of the research in this area is focused on the effects of physiological arousal because that can be measured.

▲ Weapon focus. Does it reduce the accuracy of eyewitness testimony?

EFFECTS OF ANXIETY

Anxiety has a negative effect on accuracy

Stress (and anxiety) has a negative effect on memory as well as performance generally. We saw on page 50 that automatic skills are not affected by stress/physiological arousal but performance on complicated cognitive tasks is reduced by stress.

Key study: Johnson and Scott (1976)

A different account of why anxiety might reduce the accuracy of EWT is the weapon focus effect – the view that a weapon in a criminal's hand distracts attention (because of the anxiety it creates) from other features and therefore reduces the accuracy of identification.

Procedure

To test this effect Johnson and Scott (1976) asked participants to sit in a waiting room where they heard an argument in an adjoining room and then saw a man run through the room carrying either a pen covered in grease (low anxiety condition) or a knife covered in blood (high anxiety, 'weapon focus' condition). Participants were later asked to identify the man from a set of photographs.

Findings

The findings supported the idea of the weapon focus effect. Mean accuracy was 49% in identifying the man in the pen condition, compared with 33% accuracy in the knife condition.

Loftus et al. (1987) showed that anxiety does focus attention on central features of a crime (e.g. the weapon). The researchers monitored eyewitnesses' eye movements and found that the presence of a weapon caused attention to be physically drawn towards the weapon itself and away from other things such as the person's face.

Anxiety has a positive effect on accuracy

There is an alternative argument that says high anxiety/arousal creates more enduring and accurate memories. For example, there is an evolutionary argument that suggests it would be adaptive to remember events that are emotionally important so that you could identify similar situations in the future and recall how to respond – such as what you did last time when you escaped from a lion.

Christianson and Hubinette (1993) found evidence of enhanced recall when they questioned 58 real witnesses to bank robberies in Sweden. The witnesses were either victims (bank teller) or bystanders (employee or customer), i.e. high and low anxiety respectively. The interviews were conducted 4–15 months after the robberies.

The researchers found that all witnesses showed generally good memories for details of the robbery itself (better than 75% accurate recall). Those witnesses who were most anxious (the victims) had the best recall of all. This study generally shows that anxiety does not reduce accuracy of recall.

Christianson (1992), in a review of research, concluded that memory for negative emotional events is better than for neutral events, at least for the central details.

Resolving the contradiction

Kenneth Deffenbacher (1983) reviewed 21 studies of the effects of anxiety on eyewitness memory. He found that 10 of these studies had results that linked higher arousal levels to increased eyewitness accuracy while 11 of them showed the opposite.

Deffenbacher suggested that the Yerkes–Dodson effect (see left) can account for this apparent inconsistency. According to this principle there would be occasions when anxiety/arousal is only moderate and then eyewitness accuracy would be enhanced. When anxiety/arousal is too extreme then accuracy will be reduced.

▲ Yerkes–Dodson effect. The observation that arousal has a negative effect on performance (such as memory recall) when it is very low or very high, but moderate levels are actually beneficial. This is described as an inverted U-shape curve.

(Graph: Performance on vertical axis, Arousal on horizontal axis with low, medium, high labels, showing an inverted U-shape curve.)

EVALUATION/DISCUSSION

Weapon focus may not be caused by anxiety

A criticism of the weapon focus effect comes from Pickel (1998), who proposed that the reduced accuracy of identification could be due to surprise rather than anxiety.

To test this she arranged for participants to watch a thief enter a hairdressing salon carrying scissors (high threat, low surprise), handgun (high threat, high surprise), wallet (low threat, low surprise) or a whole raw chicken (low threat, high surprise). Identification was least accurate in the high surprise conditions rather than high threat.

This supports the view that the weapon focus effect is related to surprise rather than anxiety.

Real life versus lab studies

One of the strengths of the study by Christianson and Hubinette was that it was a study of anxiety in the context of a real crime.

It may well be the case that lab studies do not create the real levels of anxiety experienced by a real eyewitness during an actual crime. Deffenbacher *et al.* (2004) agree with this but found, from a review of 34 studies, that lab studies in general demonstrate that anxiety leads to *reduced* accuracy and that real-life studies are associated with an even greater loss in accuracy.

These findings are at odds with the result from Christianson and Hubinette, but suggest that the results from lab studies are valid, as they are supported by most real-life studies.

No simple conclusion

Critics of the weapon focus effect have suggested that the violence of a crime may affect the accuracy of recall.

The study by Christianson and Hubinette concerned a violent real-life crime. Many other studies of anxiety and accuracy of identification, even the real-life ones, did not involve violence. Like Christianson and Hubinette, Halford and Milne (2005) found that victims of violent crimes were more accurate in their recall of crime scene information than victims of non-violent crimes.

This shows that there is no simple rule about the effect of anxiety on accuracy of eyewitness testimony.

 A03 plus Individual differences

It has been suggested that one key extraneous variable in many studies of anxiety is emotional sensitivity.

In a study by Bothwell *et al.* (1987) participants were tested for personality characteristics and were labelled as either 'neurotic' (tend to become anxious quickly) or 'stable' (less emotionally sensitive). It was found that the 'stable' participants showed rising levels of accuracy as stress levels increased, whereas the opposite was true for neurotics – their accuracy levels decreased as stress increased. Deffenbacher *et al.* (2004) point out that the modest effect sizes shown in many studies of anxiety may be the result of averaging out low accuracy and high accuracy scores of sensitive and non-sensitive participants respectively.

These studies suggest that individual differences may indeed play an important role in the accuracy of EWT.

 A03 plus An alternative model

Fazey and Hardy (1988) suggested a more complex relationship between anxiety and performance than the Yerkes–Dodson model.

Their catastrophe theory predicts that when physiological arousal increases beyond the optimum level, the inverted-U hypothesis predicts a gradual decrease in performance. However, Fazey and Hardy observed that in fact there is sometimes a catastrophic decline, which they suggest is due to increased mental anxiety (worry) – the inverted U only describes increases in physiological anxiety (see diagram on right).

This therefore suggests an alternative model, one that Deffenbacher et al. (2004) believe fits better with research findings, especially those of real-life eyewitnesses.

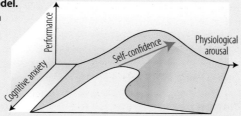

▲ At the back of the graph you can see the inverted U (Yerkes–Dodson effect) – as arousal increases performance rises to an optimal point and then decreases. However, as cognitive anxiety increases (closer to the viewer), performance falls off a cliff after the optimal point and even arousal drops slightly. This is catastrophe theory.

Insider tip…

The reason that anxiety may affect recall is because of the physiological arousal associated with anxiety – but take care to make this link rather than discussing the effects of arousal. It is also important to focus on the effects on recall rather than performance generally. That may seem obvious but many students forget to make the links when composing exam answers.

CAN YOU? No. 2.8

1. Explain how anxiety might affect the accuracy of eyewitness testimony. (4 marks)
2. Describe **one** research study related to the effect of anxiety on eyewitness testimony. (5 marks)
3. Discuss research on the effect of anxiety on eyewitness testimony. (12 marks AS, 16 marks A)

Improving the accuracy of eyewitness testimony: The cognitive interview

Although much of the research on eyewitness testimony (EWT) has highlighted its fallibility, research has also looked at ways in which the accuracy of EWT can be improved. On this spread we take a look at the **cognitive interview** (CI). This is a procedure designed for use in police interviews that involve witnesses. There were two main influences behind the development of the CI. The first was the need to improve the effectiveness of police interviewers when questioning witnesses. The second was to apply the results of psychological research to this area, particularly the work of Elizabeth Loftus, whose research had already dispelled the myth that eyewitness memory operates like a video camera.

KEY TERM

Cognitive interview A police technique for interviewing witnesses to a crime, which encourages them to recreate the original context of the crime in order to increase the accessibility of stored information. Because our memory is made up of a network of associations rather than of discrete events, memories are accessed using multiple retrieval strategies.

The standard police interview

Fisher and Geiselman (1992) identified what is wrong with the techniques usually used by policemen when interviewing witnesses. The standard interview revolves around the interviewer rather than the witness. The interviewer does most of the talking, often asking specific questions that require forced choice answers such as 'Was the criminal black or white?'. Questions are often predetermined following a written checklist. Witnesses are discouraged from adding extra information. The interviewer may unconsciously ask leading questions to confirm his/her beliefs about the crime. Discussions during such interviews may contaminate a witness' memory so that what they recall later is inaccurate.

Such practices tend to increase the amount of inaccurate information collected in the interview. Aside from the obvious problem of leading questions, such predetermined practices encourage witnesses to withhold information, give abbreviated answers and provide answers they are unsure of. The standard techniques disrupt the natural process of searching through memory, thereby making memory retrieval inefficient.

DESCRIPTION OF THE COGNITIVE INTERVIEW

Geiselman *et al.* (1984) developed an interviewing technique, the cognitive interview (CI), which was based on proven psychological principles concerning effective memory recall. The original cognitive interview technique is characterised by the following four distinct components.

1. Mental reinstatement of original context

One of the principal techniques of the CI is where the interviewer encourages the interviewee to mentally recreate both the physical and psychological environment of the original incident. The interviewer may say:

I would like you to try to think back to the day the event happened. Think about that day ... what had you been doing ... what was the weather like ... try and get a picture of it in your mind. Think of all the objects that were there ... think about the colours. How did you feel at the time? When you are ready tell me everything that you can remember, in your own time. (Adapted from Dando and Milne, 2009)

The aim is to make memories accessible. People often cannot access memories that are there. They need appropriate contextual and emotional cues to retrieve memories.

2. Report everything

The interviewer encourages the reporting of every single detail of the event without editing anything out, even though it may seem irrelevant. Witnesses should not leave anything out even if they believe it to be insignificant or irrelevant. For example the interviewer might say:

Some people hold back information because they are not quite sure that it is important or you may think that I already know this information. Please do not leave anything out. I am interested in absolutely everything that you remember, anything that pops into your head. Even partial memories and things you think may not be important. Please just tell me it all. (Adapted from Dando and Milne, 2009)

Memories are interconnected with one another so that recollection of one item may then cue a whole lot of other memories. In addition the recollection of small details may eventually be pieced together from many different witnesses to form a clearer picture of the event.

3. Change order

The interviewer may try alternative ways through the timeline of the incident, for example by reversing the order in which events occurred. The rationale behind this is that our recollections are influenced by schemas. For example, if you think about when you went to a restaurant a few weeks ago your recollection will be influenced by your general expectations (schema) of what is likely to happen at a restaurant – someone seats you at your table, a waitress takes your order, etc. If you have to recall the events starting from the end of the event backwards this prevents your pre-existing schema influencing what you recall. The interviewer might say:

I would like to try something which sometimes helps people to remember more. I would like you to tell me what happened backwards. I know it sounds hard but I am going to help you. To start, what is the very last thing that you remember happening ... what happened before that ... what happened just before that? (Adapted from Dando and Milne, 2009)

4. Change perspective

The interviewee is asked to recall the incident from multiple perspectives, for example by imagining how it would have appeared to other witnesses present at the time. This is again done to disrupt the effect that schemas have on recall. For example:

Try to recall the incident from the perspective of another person involved in the incident. Think about where he/she was and isolate everything that you can remember about them, as if they are in a spotlight. Describe what he/she would have seen. (Adapted from Dando and Milne, 2009)

This approach was suggested by the research by Anderson and Pichert, described on the facing page.

Research into the effectiveness of the cognitive interview

A strength of the cognitive interview is the amount of supporting research.

A meta-analysis of 53 studies found, on average, an increase of 34% in the amount of correct information generated in the CI compared with standard interviewing techniques (Köhnken *et al.*, 1999) although most of these studies involved volunteer witnesses (usually college students) tested in a lab (such studies may not reflect real-world practices). However, the effectiveness of the CI may be due more to some individual elements rather than the whole thing. Milne and Bull (2002) found that when participants were interviewed using a combination of the 'report everything' and 'mental reinstatement' components of the CI, their recall was significantly higher than when using just one individual component or the control condition (being instructed simply to 'try again').

This suggests that overall the CI is an effective technique for increasing the accessibility of stored information.

Quality may suffer

A criticism of the CI is that its effectiveness has largely been in terms of quantity of information, rather than quality.

The procedure is designed to enhance the *quantity* (the amount) of correct recall without compromising the *quality* (the amount of correct recall as a percentage of total recall) of that information. Köhnken *et al.* (1999) found an 81% increase of correct information but also a 61% increase of incorrect information (false positives) when the enhanced CI was compared to a standard interview.

This means that police need to treat all information collected from CIs with caution. It does not guarantee accuracy.

Problems with using the CI in practice

Another criticism of the CI is the amount of time and training needed to implement it.

From their interviews with police, Kebbell and Wagstaff report a problem with the CI in practice. Police officers suggest that this technique requires more time than is often available and that instead they prefer to use deliberate strategies aimed to limit an eyewitness report to the minimum amount of information that the officers feel is necessary. In addition, the CI requires special training and many forces have not been able to provide more than a few hours (Kebbell and Wagstaff, 1996).

These limitations have meant that the use of the CI in police interviews has not been widespread.

Comparisons are difficult

One of the problems with evaluating the effectiveness of the CI when it is used in the real world is that it is not really just one 'procedure', but a collection of related techniques.

For example, Thames Valley Police use a version that does not include the 'changing perspectives' component. Other police forces that describe themselves as using the CI technique have tended to use only the 'reinstate context' and 'report everything' components of the CI (Kebbell and Wagstaff, 1996).

This means that it is hard to establish the overall effectiveness of the technique when using all components.

Individual differences

The CI may be particularly useful when interviewing older witnesses.

Negative stereotypes about older adults' 'declining' memory can make such witnesses overly cautious about reporting information. However, the CI may overcome such difficulties, because it stresses the importance of reporting any detail regardless of its perceived insignificance. Mello and Fisher (1996) compared older (mean age 72) and younger (mean age 22) adults' memory of a filmed simulated crime using either a CI or a standard police interview (SI). The CI produced more information than the SI but, significantly, the strength of the CI over the SI was greater for the older than for the young participants.

This suggests that individual differences matter and that the CI is more effective when interviewing older people in comparison to younger people.

▲ Use of the cognitive interview in practice led to the realisation that officers often lacked the necessary social skills to use the cognitive techniques effectively, for example using inappropriate language and constantly interrupting the witness (Fisher *et al.*, 1987). The ECI was therefore developed to add social and communication skills to the training of interviewers.

Research methods

Anderson and Pichert (1978) conducted a study that showed the benefits of recalling an incident from different perspectives. They did this by asking participants to read a story about two boys playing hooky from school.

Participants were randomly allocated to one of two recall conditions: some participants were asked to imagine they were a prospective house buyer recalling the details while other participants were asked to recall the details from the perspective of a burglar.

The kind of details recalled varied depending on which perspective they took. Furthermore, when participants were asked to recall the story again, this time from the other perspective, they recalled new information.

1. Explain how participants might have been randomly allocated to the two experimental conditions. (2 marks)
2. The participants were not told the true aims of the study beforehand. Explain why this is an ethical issue and suggest how the researchers may have dealt with this issue. (2 marks + 2 marks)
3. Before conducting this study the researchers conducted a pilot study. Explain the purpose of conducting a pilot study. (2 marks)
4. Explain why the findings of this study support the idea of asking eyewitnesses to consider a crime from different perspectives. (3 marks)

LINK TO RESEARCH METHODS

Random allocation on page 184
Ethical issues on pages 194–497
Pilot study on page 183

CAN YOU? No. 2.9

1. Identify and briefly explain **two** techniques used in the cognitive interview. (3 marks + 3 marks)
2. Explain how a cognitive interview differs from a standard interview. (4 marks)
3. Discuss the use of the cognitive interview as a means of improving the accuracy of memory. (12 marks AS, 16 marks A)

We have identified here the key points of this topic on the AQA specification covered in this chapter, i.e. the bare minimum that you need to know. You may want to fill in further details to elaborate and personalise this material.

SHORT- AND LONG-TERM MEMORY

CAPACITY

- Jacobs – digit span 9.3 for digits, 7.3 for letters.
- Miller – people remember about 7 items and 7 chunks.

EVALUATION/DISCUSSION

- Cowan – 4 chunks probably the limit. Same for visual information (Vogel *et al.*).
- Simon – larger chunks means fewer recalled.
- **A03 plus** Jacobs – 19-year-olds have longer digit span than 8-year-olds.

DURATION

- Peterson and Peterson – used consonant syllables, prevented verbal rehearsal. STM lasted 18 seconds.
- Bahrick *et al.* – after 48 years participants were 70% accurate in face recognition of classmates and 30% for names.

EVALUATION/DISCUSSION

- Consonant syllables not meaningful but some memory activities do involve such stimuli.
- Reitman – auditory tones to avoid displacement, led to longer duration of STM.

CODING

- Baddeley – difficulty remembering acoustically similar words in STM but not in LTM, reverse for semantically similar words.

EVALUATION/DISCUSSION

- STM not always acoustic – Brandimote *et al.* (can be visual), Wickens *et al.* (can be semantic).
- LTM not always semantic – Frost (can be visual), Nelson and Rothbart (can be acoustic).
- **A03 plus** In Baddeley's study LTM was tested by waiting 20 minutes, not really LTM.

THE MULTI-STORE MODEL OF MEMORY (MSM)

DESCRIPTION

- Sensory register – large capacity, very short duration (milliseconds).
- Attention transfers information from sensory register to STM.
- STM – limited capacity (5 items/chunks) so information decays, limited duration (a few minutes) unless rehearsed.
- Maintenance rehearsal eventually creates a LTM.
- LTM – potentially unlimited capacity and duration, forgetting may be due to lack of accessibility.
- Retrieval from LTM goes through STM.

EVALUATION/DISCUSSION

- Support from Jacobs, Miller, Peterson and Peterson, Bahrick, Baddeley, and also brain scans show STM → prefrontal cortex (Beardsley), LTM → hippocampus (Squire *et al.*).
- Case studies – HM, loss of hippocampus → no new LTMs (Scoville and Milner).
- Too simple – STM and LTM subdivided, e.g. components of working memory and LTM subtypes.
- **A03 plus** More than maintenance rehearsal – elaborative processing (Craik and Lockhart).
- **A03 plus** STM not independent of LTM – different brain activity for words and pseudo-words (Ruchkin *et al.*).

THE WORKING MEMORY MODEL (WMM)

DESCRIPTION

- Central executive (CE) acts as 'attention', allocates tasks to slave systems, no storage.
- Phonological loop (PL) preserves order of auditory information.
  - Phonological store holds the words for the PL, inner ear.
  - Articulatory process performs maintenance rehearsal for PL, inner voice.
- Visuo-spatial sketchpad (VSS) for planning and processing visual and/or spatial tasks.
  - Visual cache for form and colour.
  - Inner scribe for spatial relations.
- Episodic buffer records events (episodes) as they happen, links to LTM.

EVALUATION/DISCUSSION

- Hitch and Baddeley – participants slower when doing dual tasks (CE + CE and articulatory loop). Demonstrates CE.
- Brain-damaged patients – KF – damage to PL, problems with verbal material (words not sounds) (Shallice and Warrington). SC – damage to PL, unable to learn word pairs presented out loud (Trojano and Grossi). LH – damage to spatial system (Farah *et al.*).
- Case studies limited, e.g. trauma itself may cause problems, individuals not typical and not generalisable.
- **A03 plus** Word-length effect – longer words can't be rehearsed (supports phonological loop), articulatory suppression task cancels out word-length effect (supports articulatory process).
- **A03 plus** CE doesn't explain anything and more complex than currently represented, evidence from EVR (Eslinger and Damasio).

TYPES OF LTM

DESCRIPTION
- Episodic memories – personal memories for events forming a sequence.
- They include details of context and emotion.
- Semantic memories – knowledge shared by everyone, abstract and concrete.
- They are acquired via episodic memories.
- Procedural memories – knowing how to do something.
- They become automatic through repetition and are disrupted if you think about them.

EVALUATION/DISCUSSION
- Brain scans – episodic memory → frontal and temporal lobe (including hippocampus). Semantic memory → temporal lobe. Procedural memory → cerebellum, basal ganglia and limbic system.
- Procedural vs. declarative memories – HM formed new procedural memories but not semantic and episodic ones.
- Brain damage evidence unreliable – can't be certain that causal part of brain identified.
- (A03 plus) Episodic vs. semantic memories can form independently, double dissociation demonstrated in Alzheimer's patients (Hodges and Patterson, Irish et al.).
- (A03 plus) Priming and fourth LTM – perceptual-representation system may be a kind of implicit memory related to priming.

EXPLANATIONS FOR FORGETTING

INTERFERENCE

DESCRIPTION
- Retroactive interference – new interferes with old.
- Müller and Pilzecker – recall was less good if there was an intervening task (describing paintings).
- Proactive interference – old interferes with new.
- Underwood – analysed many studies, the more lists learned the lower percentage of recall.
- McGeoch and McDonald – learn list of words + list of synonyms → 12% recall, learn list of words + list of digits → 37% recall. Similarity matters.
- Baddeley and Hitch – rugby players who played fewer games had better recall of teams played against (less interference).

EVALUATION/DISCUSSION
- Artificial research – words and nonsense syllables, and low motivation. Doesn't represent everyday memory.
- Only explains some situations of forgetting, where two sets of stimuli are quite similar.
- Accessible not available – suggested by spontaneous recovery of recognition memory after interference (Ceraso).
- (A03 plus) Real-world application – competing advertisements reduce their effect because of interference, better to show three in one day (Danaher et al.).
- (A03 plus) Individual differences – people with greater working memory span less susceptible to proactive interference (Kane and Eagle).

RETRIEVAL FAILURE

DESCRIPTION
- Encoding specificity principle – material present at encoding is present at retrieval (Tulving and Thomson).
- Tulving and Pearlstone – category + word learned. Free recall was 40%, cued recall was 60%.
- Some cues are not meaningfully linked at encoding but also act as cues.
- Context-dependent forgetting: Abernethy – recall best with same instructor in same room.
- Context-dependent forgetting: Baddeley and Godden – recall best when initial context (land or water) matched recall environment.
- State-dependent forgetting: Goodwin et al. – recall best when initial state (drunk or sober) matched state at recall.

EVALUATION/DISCUSSION
- Research support, e.g. Tulving and Pearlstone (lab experiment), Abernethy (field experiment).
- Real-world application – to revising and the cognitive interview.
- Retrieval cues don't always work – not useful when learning meaningful material (Smith and Vela).
- (A03 plus) Encoding specificity is circular – it is not a causal relationship (Nairne) and cannot be tested (Baddeley).
- (A03 plus) Retrieval failure can explain interference effects – thus is the more important explanation of forgetting.

ACCURACY OF EYEWITNESS TESTIMONY

MISLEADING INFORMATION

DESCRIPTION
- Leading questions suggest the desired answer.
- Loftus and Palmer – critical question containing hit, smashed, collided, bumped or contacted, speed estimates highest with the verb smashed.
- Loftus and Palmer – the verb altered the actual memory of the event; participants more likely to report broken glass.
- Post-event discussion may contaminate eyewitness memory of an event.
- Conformity effect – participants' recollection influenced by discussion with others (Gabbert et al.).
- Repeat interviewing – especially problematic with child witnesses (LeRooy et al.).

EVALUATION/DISCUSSION
- Supporting evidence – misleading information (Bugs Bunny) altered participant recall (Braun et al.).
- EWT in real-life may be more accurate – lab studies not taken seriously.
  Foster et al. – film of supposed robbery, high accuracy.
  Yuille and Cutshall – witnesses to real crime fed misleading information but still accurate recall.
- Real-world application – mistaken EWT largest factor in conviction of innocent people (Wells and Olson).
- (A03 plus) Individual differences – misinformation effect in older people, thus more susceptible to misleading information.
- (A03 plus) Response bias – recalling events in original order led to recovery of recall so memory not altered (Bekerian and Bowers).

ANXIETY

DESCRIPTION
- Stress (physiological arousal) reduces performance on complicated cognitive tasks.
- Johnson and Scott – weapon focus effect reduces accuracy of face identification.
- Loftus et al. – monitored eye movements during weapon exposure, focus was on a weapon.
- Evolutionary argument – it is adaptive to remember stress-inducing events.
- Christianson and Hubinette – high-anxiety victims (bank tellers) remember most accurately.
- Deffenbacher et al. – Yerkes–Dodson effect explains high accuracy at moderate levels of anxiety and low accuracy when anxiety is high (or low).

EVALUATION/DISCUSSION
- May not be anxiety – weapon focus effect due to surprise (Pickel).
- Real-life studies show even less accuracy than lab studies (Deffenbacher et al.), lab findings underestimate effects of anxiety.
- No simple conclusion – victims of violent crime more accurate than those of non-violent crimes (Halford and Milne).
- (A03 plus) Individual differences – neurotic participants become less accurate with increasing anxiety, opposite for emotionally more stable participants (Bothwell et al.).
- (A03 plus) Catastrophe model (Fazey and Hardy) better than inverted U (Deffenbacher et al.).

THE COGNITIVE INTERVIEW

DESCRIPTION
- Based on psychological research:
  1. Mental reinstatement of original context – physical and psychological, cued recall.
  2. Report everything – even seemingly insignificant details, may cue recall.
  3. Change order – reduces effect of schemas.
  4. Change perspective – disrupts schemas, supported by Anderson and Pichert's study (burglar and house buyer perspective).

EVALUATION/DISCUSSION
- Effectiveness – review of 53 studies found 34% more information from (Köhnken et al.), most due to 'report everything' and 'mental reinstatement' components (Milne and Bull).
- Quality may suffer – 81% increase in correct recall but 61% false positives (Köhnken et al.).
- CI in practice – police dislike because time consuming and inadequate training.
- (A03 plus) Comparisons difficult – police forces use different versions of CI.
- (A03 plus) Individual differences – older adults' memories helped more by the CI than younger adults (Mello and Fisher).

The exam questions on memory will be varied but there will be some short answer questions (AO1), including some multiple choice questions, some questions that ask you to apply your knowledge (AO2) and possibly an extended writing question (AO1 + AO3). Some questions may involve research methods and maths skills. We have provided a selection of these different kinds of questions here.

AS AND A LEVEL QUESTIONS

0 1   Briefly outline **one** difference between short-term memory and long-term memory.   **[2 marks]**

0 2   Which of the following describes the phonological loop? Choose **one** answer only.

    A   a component of working memory that controls other sub-systems
    B   a component of working memory that deals with auditory data
    C   a component of working memory that directs attention
    D   a component of working memory which registers the distance of objects   **[1 mark]**

0 3   In terms of the multi-store model, give:

    (i)   the duration of the sensory register.   **[1 mark]**
    (ii)   the duration of the short-term memory.   **[1 mark]**

0 4   **(i)** Briefly outline the proactive interference explanation of forgetting.   **[3 marks]**
    (ii) Explain **one** criticism of the proactive interference explanation of forgetting.   **[3 marks]**

0 5   Explain how leading questions can affect the accuracy of eyewitness testimony.   **[4 marks]**

0 6   Read the item below and then answer the question that follows.

> Mika witnessed two masked men making their getaway from a bank they had just robbed. He was out shopping at the time. He has some memory of what they were wearing, what they shouted at each other, how they assaulted a passer-by, and the vehicle they sped off in.

Briefly outline what is meant by cognitive interview. Explain how police officers could use this to improve the accuracy of Mika's testimony.   **[5 marks]**

0 7   Evaluate the use of the cognitive interview as a technique for improving the accuracy of eyewitness testimonies.   **[4 marks]**

0 8   Briefly outline and evaluate how **one** research study into eyewitness testimony was carried out.   **[5 marks]**

0 9   Briefly outline the retrieval failure explanation in forgetting and give **one** evaluation point.   **[5 marks]**

1 0   Read the item below and then answer the question that follows.

> Two students were having the following conversation:
>
> Amy: It's really embarrassing. I keep forgetting my Art teacher's new married name and still call her Miss Short instead. I think she is getting annoyed with me.
>
> Dylan: I am going to have the opposite problem I think. I really can't remember the name of my Maths teacher and she is due back from maternity leave next week. My mind goes blank and I can only remember the name of the teacher that has been covering for her.

Using your knowledge of interference as an explanation of forgetting, explain why Amy and Dylan cannot easily recall their teachers' names.   **[5 marks]**

1 1   Read the item below and then answer the questions that follow.

> A psychologist wanted to test the effect of cues on memory. To do this, she divided her 20 participants into two groups. Ten participants read a passage wearing fragrance A and ten participants read the same passage whilst wearing fragrance B. One week later, both groups were asked to recall the passage. All participants now had to wear fragrance A during the test. Results were as predicted – participants who wore the same fragrance for both the reading and the test recalled significantly more than the participants who wore a different fragrance.

(i)   Identify the independent variable in this study.   **[1 mark]**

(ii)   Identify both the research method and research design that the psychologist used.   **[2 marks]**

(iii) Outline **one** strength and **one** limitation of using this experimental design in this study.   **[4 marks]**

1 2   Briefly discuss the effect of anxiety on the accuracy of eyewitness testimony.   **[4 marks]**

1 3   Read the item below and then answer the questions that follow.

> •   Fred forgot his lines in the school play because he did not rehearse them enough.
> •   Dana forgot most of what her teacher had dictated as he said too many words in one go.
> •   Eliza forgot most of what she learnt in her last lesson because she did not find it very interesting.
> •   Kalim forgot most of what he had revised for the test because he was in a strange room.

(i)   Name the student whose forgetting is associated with absence of cues.   **[1 mark]**

(ii)   Name the student whose forgetting is associated with the capacity of memory.   **[1 mark]**

(iii) Name the student whose forgetting is associated with the duration of memory.   **[1 mark]**

1 4   Describe and evaluate research into **at least one** factor affecting the accuracy of eyewitness testimony.   **[12 marks]**

1 5   Describe and evaluate the multi-store model of memory.   **[12 marks]**

1 6   Describe and evaluate the working memory model.   **[12 marks]**

1 7   Discuss **either** interference **or** retrieval failure as an explanation of forgetting.   **[12 marks]**

A LEVEL ONLY QUESTIONS

1 8   Read the item below and then answer the questions that follow.

> Psychologists sometimes study memory through case studies of people with severe memory loss. For example, in one famous case, a man developed a disease that stopped most of his long-term memory from functioning but his short-term memory was still intact. A psychologist studied him for many years through interviews and observations and used this to describe the type of information that the man could recall and could not recall.

(i)   Identify **one** feature of a case study and state how it is demonstrated by the example in the item.   **[2 marks]**

(ii)   Case studies tend to provide qualitative data. Outline what is meant by qualitative data with reference to the case study in the source.   **[2 marks]**

1 9   Discuss at least **two** factors that can affect the accuracy of eyewitness testimony.   **[16 marks]**

2 0   Discuss the multi-store model of memory. Refer to **at least one** other explanation of memory as part of your discussion.   **[16 marks]**

2 1   Discuss the working memory model.   **[16 marks]**

2 2   Outline and evaluate research (theories and/or studies) into **at least one** explanation of forgetting.   **[16 marks]**

* Case studies (in question 18) are on the A Level specification for research methods but not on the AS-only specification.

We've provided answers by two students to some of the questions from pages 64–65 here, together with comments from an examiner about how well they've each done. **Green** comments show what the student has done well. **Orange** comments indicate areas for improvement.

01 Outline **one** difference between short-term memory and long-term memory. *(2 marks)*

Maisie's answer
One difference is that short-term memory has a short capacity and long-term memory has a large capacity.

Correct difference identified.

Examiner's comments
The answer is accurate but too brief to gain the second mark. *1/2 marks*

Valid difference identified.

Clear distinction.

Detail provided.

Ciaran's answer
One difference is capacity. STM can hold around 7 items whereas LTM is potentially unlimited.

Examiner's comments
Brief, but accurate, detail given for both and as it is only a 2-mark question it is enough to gain full marks. *2/2 marks*

07 Read the item below and then answer the question that follows.

> Mika witnessed two masked men making their getaway from a bank they had just robbed. He was out shopping at the time. He has some memory of what they were wearing, what they shouted at each other, how they assaulted a passer-by, and the vehicle they sped off in.

Briefly outline what is meant by cognitive interview. Explain how police officers could use this to improve the accuracy of Mika's testimony. *(5 marks)*

Exam tip…
The 5 marks for this question would be likely to be split: AO1 2 marks, AO2 3 marks, so for questions such as this make sure you get the balance right in your answer.

Maisie's answer
The cognitive interview consists of four components that aim to increase both the quantity and quality of information collected from an eyewitness. The four stages are report everything, reinstate the context, change order and change perspective.

Report everything means saying every single thing you can think of even if it seems irrelevant. Reinstate the context means thinking of the physical and psychological things around the event in case that jogs your memory. Change order and change perspective interrupt your schema for the events.

These ideas are all based on psychological research about memory, for example retrieval cues are an explanation of forgetting. People have the memories in their minds but they can't access them. But if they are given the right cues the memories can be accessed. Cues can relate to context and also to mood. This might help Mika remember what he saw.

Examiner's comments
Maisie's answer shows sound knowledge and understanding of the key features of the cognitive interview but is limited to AO1. *2/5 marks*

(!) This still doesn't explain *how* it will improve accuracy.

(!) This reference is not enough to gain AO2 marks, which means the answer is almost entirely AO1. This means that Maisie will get the AO1 marks but none of the AO2 marks. When a question includes a scenario, make sure you spend most of your time applying your knowledge (description) to the scenario by, for example, selecting quotes from the scenario and linking them to your description.

Ciaran's answer
Cognitive interview is a technique which aims to recreate the original context of the crime and is based on 4 main components. The police could ask Mika to pretend he was back in the original environment at the shopping centre and say things like 'what was the weather like that day?'. He should try to remember what shops were around him and what he could hear and smell.

Next the police should ask him to tell them about the whole incident and include everything, even if Mika didn't think it would be relevant.

Good, crisp start identifying what a cognitive interview is.

Ciaran covers the same features as Maisie in his response but does so in a way that applies it to the scenario and the case of Mika each time. Excellent AO2 skills.

Then they could 'change the order' and ask Mika to recall the crime but to start at the end and work backwards. So they would say 'What do you remember about the car speeding off? What happened just before that?' Trying to recall things this way prevents expectations creating memories that didn't actually happen because you are going backwards.

A fourth thing to do is change perspective where Mika should imagine he was one of the masked men and try to report the incident from this perspective.

> Clear AO2 application again.

Examiner's comments
Ciaran's answer covers the AO1 needed but also relates it to the item and the case of Mika, demonstrating that he can apply what he has learned to a novel situation. **5/5 marks**

A Level essay

20 Discuss **at least two** factors that can affect the accuracy of eyewitness testimony.
(16 marks)

Exam tip...
This would be split: AO1 6 marks, AO3 10 marks.

Ciaran's answer

One factor that affects the accuracy of EWT is misleading information such as leading questions. Policemen or lawyers may not realise that the way they frame a question often subtly suggests the expected answer. But more importantly it affects the way a person stores the information. Loftus illustrated this in her study of a car accident. The way people were asked about the speed of a car (how fast were the cars travelling when they hit each other) affected the answer a participant gave and later made them more likely to believe there had been broken glass — the leading question shaped their memory of the event.

This study has been supported by many other lab studies but not by real-life studies. It could be that, in a lab, people are more careless because their answers to questions don't matter very much. One study of an armed robbery in Canada found that witnesses gave accurate recall four months later, despite having been given some misleading information when first interviewed. Another study found that, if participants thought they were watching a real-life robbery, and also thought that their responses would influence the trial, their identification of a robber was more accurate.

A second key factor in the accuracy of EWT is anxiety. There is one argument that suggests anxiety creates physiological arousal and therefore you pay less attention to events around you and remember less. This is the case in the weapon focus effect where people focus on the weapon because of their fear and then can't identify the criminal's face. In fact a study by Pickel showed that this effect is more likely to be caused by surprise rather than anxiety — though it is still an explanation for the inaccuracy of EWT in some circumstances.

There are instances of heightened accuracy when witnesses are anxious but in general it leads to reduced accuracy. Christianson and Hubinette looked at real-life robberies and found good recall and Christianson reviewed a number of studies and concluded that memory for negative emotional events is better than for neutral events at least for the central details. However, Deffenbacher looked more recently at a wider range of studies and claims that anxiety leads to reduced accuracy and that real-life studies are associated with an even greater loss in accuracy. (382 words)

> Factor clearly highlighted.

> Add detail here – more examples of the 'way' it was asked.

> Expand this by saying *why* this is positive before going on to the 'real-life' studies that might contradict it.

> The reason for this could be explained here – in a lab, the consequences can't affect someone's freedom, for example.

> More details of these studies would help elaborate the evaluation.

> An effective use of research. It is most effective if it is linked back to the factor. 'This evidence shows…'.

> These two points could be made more clearly. Make the first point then add the evidence and then contradict it with the second.

> The end of the essay shows elaboration and better discussion. A conclusion could help pull the discussion together.

> Second factor clearly highlighted.

> Anxiety discussed more thoroughly than leading questions.

> Good use of research as both AO1 and AO3.

Examiner's comments
There is clear evidence of knowledge of two factors and evaluation is apparent and mostly effective. Ciaran also evaluates the methodology used in the studies; however, this will only get credit if it directly relates to the factors – if not, the evaluation is not related to the question which is a common mistake. *Level 3 essay: this answer is likely to get 10 marks out of 16.*

Exam tip...
You would only get this as a 16 mark essay if you are doing the full A level and the demands are obviously higher. It could, however, also be asked as a 12-mark question for those doing AS, in which case this would be a very good answer likely to get into the top band.

Attachment

CONTENTS OF CHAPTER

SPECIFICATION CHECKLIST

- Caregiver–infant interactions in humans: reciprocity and interactional synchrony.

- Stages of attachment identified by Schaffer.

- Multiple attachments and the role of the father.

- Animal studies of attachment: Lorenz and Harlow.

- Explanations of attachment: learning theory and Bowlby's monotropic theory. The concepts of a critical period and an internal working model.

- Ainsworth's 'Strange Situation'. Types of attachment: secure, insecure-avoidant and insecure-resistant.

- Cultural variations in attachment, including van IJzendoorn.

- Bowlby's theory of maternal deprivation.

- Romanian orphan studies: effects of institutionalisation.

- The influence of early attachment on childhood and adult relationships, including the role of an internal working model.

TRY THIS

Babyface hypothesis

Which face would you select as the most attractive?
Psychologists have conducted studies using faces such as those above. They do this to investigate the *babyface hypothesis*. Have you ever noticed that most young mammals have the same distinctive facial features (big eyes, large forehead, squashed up nose)? We have been cooing over babies and 'aaahing' over young animals for thousands of years. If you haven't noticed this similarity, Walt Disney certainly did! These features act as a trigger for parenting behaviour, which is necessary for a young animal's survival. They elicit our desire to look after and care for babies.

However, the effect doesn't end there. Since we have an innate tendency to find babyface features appealing, this spills over into the way we judge adult faces. This is called the *babyface overgeneralisation hypothesis*. People all over the world rate adult faces with an element of 'babyfaceness' as the most attractive (Langlois and Roggmann, 1990), and also describe people with baby-like faces as being socially, physically and intellectually weak (Zebrowitz, 1997).

Understanding the faces above
The faces above were created by 'morphing' an adult woman's face with an average child's face (formed by averaging four child photos). The first photo is 50% child/50% adult, the second photo is 30% child, the third photo is 20% child and the final one is 0% child/100% adult.

In a study using sets of faces similar to those above, only a few participants (9.5%) rated the totally adult face as being most attractive. Most of the participants preferred female faces that displayed between 10–50% childlike proportions (Gründl, 2007).

Caregiver–infant interactions

Infancy is the period of a child's life before speech begins. The Latin word *infans* means 'without speech'. This is usually taken to refer to the child's first year of life, although some psychologists include a child's second year.

One of the key interactions between caregivers and infants is their non-verbal communication, i.e. communicating without words and sometimes without sound. Such interactions may form the basis of attachment between an infant and caregiver. It is the manner in which each responds to the other that determines the formation of attachment – the more sensitive each is to the other's signals, the deeper the relationship.

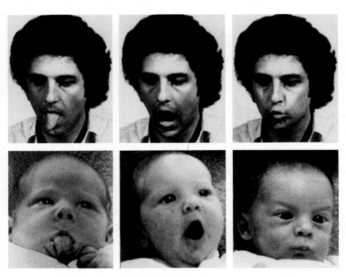

▲ Photographs from the study by Meltzoff and Moore, showing infant imitation of adult facial expressions – tongue protrusion, mouth opening and lip protrusion. Imitation of a hand gesture was also tested (opening the hand).

Observational research

The study by Meltzoff and Moore was a controlled observation. They selected four different stimuli (three different faces plus a hand gesture) and observed the behaviour of infants in response.

To record observations an observer watched videotapes of the infant's behaviour in real time, slow motion and frame by frame if necessary. This video was then judged by independent observers who had no knowledge of what the infant had just seen. Each observer was asked to note all instances of infant tongue protrusions and head movements using these behavioural categories:

- *Mouth opening* = abrupt jaw drop opening the mouth across entire extent of lips.
- *Termination of mouth opening* = return of lips to their closed resting position (lips closed and touching across entire extent or there might be a small crack).
- *Tongue protrusion* = clear forward thrust of tongue such that the tongue tip crossed the back edge of the lower lip.
- *Termination of tongue protrusion* = retraction of tip of tongue behind the back edge of the lower lip.

Each observer scored the tapes twice so that both intra-observer and inter-observer reliability could be calculated. All scores were greater than .92.

Reciprocity

Research in the 1970s (e.g. Jaffe *et al.*, 1973) demonstrated that infants coordinated their actions with **caregivers** in a kind of conversation. From birth babies move in a rhythm when interacting with an adult almost as if they were taking turns, as people do when having a conversation – one person leans forwards and speaks and then it is the other person's turn. This is an example of **reciprocity**.

Brazelton (1979) suggested that this basic rhythm is an important precursor to later communications. The regularity of an infant's signals allows a caregiver to anticipate the infant's behaviour and respond appropriately. This sensitivity to infant behaviour lays the foundation for later **attachment** between caregiver and infant.

Interactional synchrony

Psychologists have also described a slightly different kind of interaction between infants and caregivers called **interactional synchrony**. Andrew Meltzoff and Keith Moore (1977) conducted the first systematic study of interactional synchrony and found that infants as young as two to three weeks old imitated specific facial and hand gestures (see illustration left). The study was conducted using an adult model who displayed one of three facial expressions or hand movements where the fingers moved in a sequence. A dummy was placed in the infant's mouth during the initial display to prevent any response. Following the display the dummy was removed and the child's expression was filmed on a video. They found that there was an association between the infant behaviour and that of the adult model.

In a later study Meltzoff and Moore (1983) demonstrated the same synchrony with infants only three days old. The fact that infants as young as this were displaying the behaviour would appear to rule out the possibility that the imitation behaviours are learned, i.e. the behavioural response must be innate.

Real or pseudo-imitation?

Meltzoff and Moore proposed that this imitation is intentional (i.e. the infant is deliberately copying what the other person is doing). By contrast, the renowned psychologist Jean Piaget (1962) believed that true imitation only developed towards the end of the first year and anything before this was a kind of 'response training' – what the infant is doing is repeating a behaviour that was rewarded (i.e. the result of operant conditioning). For example an infant might happen to stick its tongue out after seeing a caregiver do this. The consequence would be that the caregiver smiles, which is experienced as rewarding, encouraging the infant to repeat the same behaviour next time. Thus, in Piaget's view, what the infant would be doing was just pseudo-imitation; the infant had not consciously translated what they see into a matching movement.

Evidence to support Meltzoff and Moore's view was presented in a study by Murray and Trevarthen (1985). In this study two-month-old infants first interacted via a video monitor with their mother in real time. In the next part of the study the video monitor played a tape of the mother so that the image on screen was not responding to the infant's facial and bodily gestures. The result was one of acute distress. The infants tried to attract their mothers' interest but, gaining no response, turned away. This shows that the infant is actively eliciting a response rather than displaying a response that has been rewarded. This shows that the infant is an active and intentional partner in the mother–infant interaction.

This further supports the notion that such behaviours are innate rather than learned.

Attachment is an emotional bond between two people. It is a two-way process that endures over time. It leads to certain behaviours such as clinging and proximity-seeking, and serves the function of protecting an infant.

Caregiver Any person who is providing care for a child, such as a parent, grandparent, sibling, other family member, childminder and so on.

Interactional synchrony When two people interact they tend to mirror what the other is doing in terms of their facial and body movements. This includes imitating emotions as well as behaviours. This is described as a synchrony – when two (or more) things move in the same pattern.

Reciprocity Responding to the action of another with a similar action, where the actions of one partner elicit a response from the other partner. The responses are not necessarily similar as in interactional synchrony.

▲ Interactional synchrony is often described as a 'dance' between caregiver and infant. In fact the same 'dance' can be seen when any pair of individuals are interacting.

EVALUATION/DISCUSSION

Problems with testing infant behaviour

There is reason to have some doubt about the findings of research on the facing page because of the difficulties in reliably testing infant behaviour.

Infants' mouths are in fairly constant motion and the expressions that are tested occur frequently (tongue sticking out, yawning, smiling). This makes it difficult to distinguish between general activity and specific imitated behaviours. To overcome these problems Meltzoff and Moore measured infant responses by filming infants and then asking an observer (who had no idea what behaviour was being imitated) to judge the infants' behaviour from the video.

This research highlights the difficulties in testing infant behaviour, but also suggests one way of increasing the internal validity of the data.

Failure to replicate

Other studies have failed to replicate the findings of studies on the facing page.

For example, a study by Koepke *et al.* (1983) failed to replicate Meltzoff and Moore's findings; Meltzoff and Moore counterargued that the research by Koepke *et al.* failed because it was less carefully controlled. Marian *et al.* (1996) replicated the study by Murray and Trevarthen and found that infants couldn't distinguish live from videotaped interactions with their mothers, which suggests that the infants are actually not responding to the adult. Marian *et al.* acknowledge that the failure to replicate may lie with the procedure.

Therefore, the earlier studies' findings were not replicated in later studies, although differences in methodology may account for this.

Intentionality supported

Another method used to test the intentionality of infant behaviour is to observe how they respond to inanimate objects.

Abravanel and DeYong (1991) observed infant behaviour when 'interacting' with two objects, one simulating tongue movements and the other mouth opening/closing. They found that infants of median age 5 and 12 weeks made little response to the objects.

This suggests that infants do not just imitate anything they see – it is a specific social response to other humans.

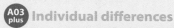 Individual differences

An important feature of interactional synchrony is that there is some variation between infants.

Isabella *et al.* (1989) found that more strongly attached infant–caregiver pairs showed greater interactional synchrony. Heimann (1989) showed that infants who demonstrate a lot of imitation from birth onwards have a better quality of relationship at three months. However, it isn't clear whether the imitation is a cause or an effect of this early synchrony.

This research therefore shows that there are significant individual differences but doesn't indicate the cause of the differences.

 The value of the research

The importance of this imitative behaviour is that it forms the basis for social development.

Meltzoff (2005) has developed a 'like me' hypothesis of infant development based on his research on interactional synchrony. He proposes that first there is the connection between what the infant sees and their imitation of this. Second, infants associate their own acts and their own underlying mental states. Third, infants project their own internal experiences onto others performing similar acts. As a result infants begin to acquire an understanding of what other people are thinking and feeling – a so-called 'Theory of Mind', which is fundamental for conducting social relationships.

Therefore, a strength of this research is that it explains how children begin to understand what others think and feel, and thus are able to conduct relationships.

 UPGRADE

Essays are where most differentiation occurs between students. Some questions are definitely more challenging than others: the content is perhaps more complex, or the question has more specific requirements that you need to add into the mix. However, there are some common tips that apply to all or most essays. We'll start with the very first stage – reading the question.

- Read the essay question carefully. Identify the key phrase or concept that will be central to your answer. For example, an essay on infant–caregiver interactions should focus on this specific aspect of attachment rather than presenting a more general account of attachment theory.
- Remember to make regular references to the key phrase/concept during your answer to make sure all points are relevant (it is easy to get side-tracked).
- Reread the question to identify any other requirements such as:
  – Is there a source to refer to?
  – Do you need to compare with another theory/explanation?
  – Do you have to make reference to evidence or a specified number of studies?

In question 4 in the 'Can You?' box below, there is a requirement to refer to reciprocity and interactional synchrony. Failure to include in your answer any information specified in the question will limit the number of marks an examiner can give you.

CAN YOU? | No. 3.1

1. Briefly explain what is meant by the term 'interactional synchrony' in caregiver–infant interactions. (2 marks)
2. Briefly explain what is meant by the term 'reciprocity' in the context of caregiver–infant interactions. (2 marks)
3. Outline **one** study of infant–caregiver interactions. (4 marks)
4. Discuss infant–caregiver interactions. Refer to reciprocity and interactional synchrony in your answer. (12 marks AS, 16 marks A)

The development of attachment

The focus of this chapter is on 'attachment'. We all have attachments – to our parents, friends, lovers, cats… John Bowlby proposed that all of these attachments are linked back to your very first love – your relationship with your mother (or mother-substitute). It is through this special relationship, according to Bowlby, that each of us learns about how to conduct and be in a relationship.

On the previous spread we looked at the beginnings of attachment – reciprocal and synchronous communications between infant and caregiver. We now look at how attachment 'proper' develops.

KEY TERMS

Multiple attachment Having more than one attachment figure.

Primary attachment figure The person who has formed the closest bond with a child, demonstrated by the intensity of the relationship. This is usually a child's biological mother, but other people can fulfil the role – an adoptive mother, a father, grandmother and so on. Throughout this chapter when we say 'mother' we are referring to the person who fulfils the role of primary attachment figure.

Separation anxiety The distress shown by an infant when separated from his/her caregiver. This is not necessarily the child's biological mother.

Stranger anxiety The distress shown by an infant when approached or picked up by someone who is unfamiliar.

Research methods

Schaffer and Emerson (1964) conducted a study on the development of attachments. Sixty infants from mainly working-class homes in Glasgow were studied. At the start of the investigation the infants ranged from 5 to 23 weeks of age. They were studied until the age of one year.

The mothers were visited every four weeks. At each visit each mother reported their infant's response to separation in seven everyday situations (such as being left alone in a room, or with other people). The mother was also asked to describe the intensity of any protest (for instance a full-blooded cry, or a whimper) which was then rated on a four-point scale. Finally the mother was asked to say to whom the protest was directed.

Stranger anxiety was also measured by assessing the infant's response to the interviewer at each visit.

1. The graph shows data from this study. Describe **two** conclusions you could draw from this graph. (4 marks)

2. Identify **one** piece of quantitative data collected in this study and explain why it is quantitative. (2 marks)

3. How was strength of attachment measured in this study? (2 marks)

4. Data was reported by the mothers. Explain **one** limitation of this method of data collection. (2 marks)

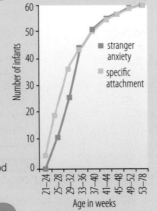

LINK TO RESEARCH METHODS

Graphs on page 214
Quantitative data on page 216

STAGES OF ATTACHMENT

In the 1960s, Rudolph Schaffer and Peggy Emerson conducted a landmark study on attachment (see Research Methods activity on left). They used the findings from this study to construct a description of how attachment develops.

Stage 1: indiscriminate attachments

From birth until about two months infants produce similar responses to all objects, whether they are animate or inanimate. Towards the end of this period, infants are beginning to show a greater preference for social stimuli, such as a smiling face, and to be more content when they are with people. During this period of time reciprocity and interactional synchrony play a role in establishing the infant's relationships with others.

Stage 2: the beginnings of attachment

Around the age of four months infants become more social. They prefer human company to inanimate objects and can distinguish between familiar and unfamiliar people. However, they are still relatively easily comforted by anyone, and do not yet show anxiety with strangers (called **stranger anxiety**). The most distinctive feature of this phase is their general sociability (enjoyment of being with people).

Stage 3: discriminate attachment

By seven months old most infants begin to show a distinctly different sort of protest when one particular person puts them down (called **separation anxiety**). Equally, they show especial joy at reunion with that person and are most comforted by this person. They are said to have formed a specific attachment to one person, their **primary attachment figure**.

Around the same time, the infant also begins to display stranger anxiety, another sign of a specific attachment having formed.

Schaffer and Emerson found that primary attachments were not always formed with the person who spent most time with the child. They observed that intensely attached infants had mothers who responded quickly and sensitively to their 'signals' and who offered their child the most interaction. Infants who were poorly attached had mothers who failed to interact. Thus, they concluded that it is quality of the relationship, not quantity, that mattered most in the formation of attachment.

In 65% of the children the first specific attachment was to the mother, and in a further 30% the mother was the first joint object of attachment. Fathers were rarely the first sole object of attachment (3%), but 27% of them were the joint first object.

Stage 4: multiple attachments

Very soon after the main attachment is formed, the infant also develops a wider circle of **multiple attachments** depending on how many consistent relationships he/she has. Specifically, Schaffer and Emerson found that, within one month of first becoming attached, 29% of the infants had multiple attachments to someone else – to their other parent, grandparents, siblings, other relatives, friends and/or neighbours. These are called secondary attachments. Infants also display separation anxiety in these relationships.

Within six months this had risen to 78%. In other words, by the age of about one year the majority of infants had developed multiple attachments, with one-third of the infants having formed five or more secondary attachments, such as their father, grandparent or older sibling.

Primary attachment figures and caregivers

*Psychologists use the word **caregiver** to refer to the person who has a role in looking after a child. This is not the same as the person to whom a child is most intensely attached – that person is called the primary attachment figure. This is the person a child responds to most intensely at separation.*

EVALUATION/DISCUSSION

Unreliable data

The data collected by Schaffer and Emerson may be unreliable.

This is because it was based on mothers' reports of their infants. Some mothers might have been less sensitive to their infants' protests and therefore less likely to report them.

This would create a systematic bias which would challenge the validity of the data.

Biased sample

The sample was biased in a number of ways.

First, it was from a working-class population and thus the findings may apply to that social group and not others. Second, the sample was from the 1960s. Parental care of children has changed considerably since that time. More women go out to work so many children are cared for outside the home, or fathers stay at home and become the main carer. Research shows that the number of dads who choose to stay at home and care for their children and families has quadrupled over the past 25 years (Cohn *et al.*, 2014).

Therefore, if a similar study to that of Schaffer and Emerson was conducted today, the findings might well be different.

Challenging monotropy

One of the central discussions relating to multiple attachment is whether all attachments are equivalent or whether one or two have some special significance.

Bowlby's view was that an infant forms one special emotional relationship (see monotropy on page 78). Subsidiary to this are many other secondary attachments which are important as an emotional safety net or to meet other needs. For example, fathers may offer a special kind of care (see right) and relationships with siblings are important in learning how to negotiate with peers. By contrast, Rutter (1995) has argued that all attachment figures are equivalent, with all attachments being integrated to produce an infant's attachment type. This is a topic we will return to later when discussing Bowlby's theory.

This suggests that Bowlby may have been wrong about the idea of a hierarchy of attachments.

Cultural variations

There are important differences between cultures in terms of the way people relate to each other.

In individualist cultures (such as Britain and the US), each person in the society is primarily concerned with their own needs or the needs of their immediate family group. In contrast collectivist cultures are more focused on the needs of the group rather than the individuals, with people sharing many things, such as possessions and childcare. It follows that we would expect multiple attachment to be more common in collectivist societies. Research supports this. For example, Sagi *et al.* (1994) compared attachments in infants raised in communal environments (Israeli kibbutzim) with infants raised in family-based sleeping arrangements. In a kibbutz children spend their time in a community children's home cared for by a *metapelet*; this includes night-time. Closeness of attachment with mothers was almost twice as common in family-based arrangements than in the communal environment.

This suggests that the stage model presented on the facing page applies specifically to individualist cultures.

Stage theories

One difficulty with 'stage theories' is that they suggest development is inflexible.

A stage theory, such as the one on the facing page, proposes that there is a fixed order for development. For example, it suggests that, normally, single attachments must come before multiple attachments. In some situations and cultures multiple attachments may come first.

The use of stage theories, therefore, may be problematic if they become a standard by which families are judged and lead to them being classed as abnormal.

THE ROLE OF THE FATHER

Primary attachment figures

Schaffer and Emerson found that fathers were far less likely to be primary attachment figures than mothers. This may be because they spend less time with their infants. In any case, Lamb (1997) reported that studies have shown little relationship between father accessibility (amount of time) and infant–father attachment.

It is possible that most men are just not psychologically equipped to form an intense attachment because they lack the emotional sensitivity that women offer. This may be due to biological or social factors. The female hormone oestrogen underlies caring behaviour so women, generally, are more oriented towards interpersonal goals than men. In terms of cultural expectations there continue to be sex stereotypes that affect male behaviour, such as it thought of as rather feminine to be sensitive to the needs of others.

There is evidence that men are indeed less sensitive to infant cues than mothers (e.g. Heermann *et al.*, 1994). However, Frodi *et al.* (1978) showed videotapes of infants crying and found no differences in the *physiological* responses of men and women.

Nevertheless, men do form secure attachments with their children, as is the case in single (male) parent families. Research has found that in two-parent families where the father is the primary caregiver, both parents often share the role of primary attachment figure (Frank *et al.*, 1997). So, men *can* be primary attachment figures but biological and social factors may discourage this.

Secondary attachments

Fathers have a role to play as important secondary attachment figures. Research has consistently highlighted the fact that fathers are more playful, physically active and generally better at providing challenging situations for their children. A father is an exciting playmate whereas mothers are more conventional and tend to read stories to their children (Geiger, 1996).

It may be that a *lack* of sensitivity from fathers can be seen as positive because it fosters problem-solving by making greater communicative and cognitive demands on children (White and Woollett, 1992).

CAN YOU?   No. 3.2

1. Briefly explain what is meant by the term 'multiple attachments'. (2 marks)
2. Describe **one** study that investigated the development of attachments. (6 marks)
3. Outline the role of the father in the development of attachment. (6 marks)
4. Describe and evaluate the stages of attachment identified by Schaffer and Emerson. (12 marks AS, 16 marks A)

Animal studies of attachment

At the same time as early attachment research was underway, such as the study by Schaffer and Emerson, a number of important animal studies took place which had a profound effect on the development of our understanding of human attachment. On this spread we will look at some of these studies. You will see, as you continue to read through this chapter, how the findings from these studies shaped understanding of attachment.

▲ Konrad Lorenz going for a swim followed by his goslings.

▲ Orphan monkeys spent most time with a 'cloth-covered mother', visiting the 'mother' with the feeding bottle for food. This suggests that attachment is related to contact comfort and not food.

LORENZ'S RESEARCH

Konrad Lorenz was an ethologist, studying animal behaviour under relatively natural conditions – though his research did involve some manipulation.

Key study: Lorenz (1935)

Procedure Lorenz (1935) took a clutch of gosling eggs and divided them into two groups. One group was left with their natural mother while the other eggs were placed in an incubator. When the incubator eggs hatched the first living (moving) thing they saw was Lorenz and they soon started following him around.

To test this effect of **imprinting** Lorenz marked the two groups to distinguish them and placed them together; they had become imprinted on him. Both Lorenz and their natural mother were present.

Findings The goslings quickly divided themselves up, one following their natural mother and the other group following Lorenz. Lorenz's brood showed no recognition of their natural mother. Lorenz noted that this process of imprinting is restricted to a very definite period of the young animal's life, called a critical period. If a young animal is not exposed to a moving object during this early critical period the animal will not imprint. This suggests animals can imprint on a persistently present moving object seen within its first two days. Imprinting is a process similar to attachment in that it binds a young animal to a caregiver in a special relationship.

Lorenz did observe that imprinting to humans does not occur in some animals, for example curlews will not imprint on a human.

Long-lasting effects

Lorenz (1952) noted several features of imprinting, for example that the process is irreversible and long lasting. Lorenz described how one of the geese who imprinted on him, called Martina, used to sleep on his bed every night.

Lorenz also noted that this early imprinting had an effect on later mate preferences, called sexual imprinting. Animals (especially birds) will choose to mate with the same kind of object upon which they were imprinted.

HARLOW'S RESEARCH

Harry Harlow (1959) conducted landmark research on attachment. He called his research report *The Origins of Love* and sought to demonstrate that mother love (attachment) was not based on the feeding bond between mother and infant as predicted by learning theory (described on the next spread).

Key study: Harlow (1959)

Procedure Harlow created two wire mothers each with a different 'head' (see picture on left). One wire mother additionally was wrapped in soft cloth. Eight infant rhesus monkeys were studied for a period of 165 days. For four of the monkeys the milk bottle was on the cloth-covered mother and on the plain wire 'mother' for the other four monkeys. During that time measurements were made of the amount of time each infant spent with the two different 'mothers'. Observations were also made of the monkey infants' responses when frightened by, for example, a mechanical teddy bear.

Findings All eight monkeys spent most of their time with the cloth-covered mother whether or not this mother had the feeding bottle. Those monkeys who fed from the wire mother only spent a short amount of time getting milk and then returned to the cloth-covered mother.

When frightened, all monkeys clung to the cloth-covered mother, and when playing with new objects the monkeys often kept one foot on the cloth-covered mother seemingly for reassurance.

These findings suggest that infants do not develop an attachment to the person who feeds them but to the person offering contact comfort.

Long-lasting effects

Harlow (1959) continued to study his rhesus monkeys as they grew up and noted many consequences of their early attachment experiences. He reported that the motherless monkeys, even those who did have contact comfort, developed abnormally. They were socially abnormal – they froze or fled when approached by other monkeys. And they were sexually abnormal – they did not show normal mating behaviour and did not cradle their own babies.

Like Lorenz, Harlow also found that there was a critical period for these effects.

If the motherless monkeys spent time with their monkey 'peers' they seemed to recover but only if this happened before they were three months old. Having more than six months with only a wire mother was something they did not appear able to recover from.

EVALUATION OF LORENZ'S RESEARCH

Research support for imprinting

A number of other studies have demonstrated imprinting in animals.

For example, Guiton (1966) demonstrated that leghorn chicks, exposed to yellow rubber gloves while being fed during their first few weeks, became imprinted on the gloves. This supports the view that young animals are not born with a predisposition to imprint on a specific type of object but probably on any moving thing that is present during the critical window of development. Guiton also found that the male chickens later tried to mate with the gloves, showing that early imprinting is linked to later reproductive behaviour.

Therefore, Guiton's findings provide clear support for Lorenz's original research and conclusions.

Criticisms of imprinting

There is some dispute over the characteristics of imprinting.

For many years the accepted view of imprinting was that it was an irreversible process, whereby the object encountered was somehow stamped permanently on the nervous system. Now, it is understood that imprinting is a more 'plastic and forgiving mechanism' (Hoffman, 1996). For example, Guiton (1966) found that he could reverse the imprinting in chickens that had initially tried to mate with the rubber gloves. He found that, later, after spending time with their own species, they were able to engage in normal sexual behaviour with other chickens.

This suggests that imprinting may not, after all, be so very different from any other kind of learning. Learning can also take place rapidly, with little conscious effort, and is also fairly reversible.

EVALUATION OF HARLOW'S RESEARCH

Confounding variable

One criticism that has been made of Harlow's study is that the two stimulus objects varied in more ways than being cloth-covered or not.

The two heads were also different, which acted as a confounding variable because it varied systematically with the independent variable ('mother' being cloth-covered or not). It is possible that the reason the infant monkeys preferred one 'mother' to the other was because the cloth-covered mother had a more attractive head.

Therefore, the conclusions of this study lack internal validity.

Generalising animal studies to human behaviour

The ultimate aim of animal studies is to be able to generalise the conclusions to human behaviour.

However, humans differ in important ways – perhaps most importantly because much more of their behaviour is governed by conscious decisions. Nevertheless, a number of studies have found that the observations made of animal attachment behaviour are mirrored in studies of humans. For example, Harlow's research is supported by Schaffer and Emerson's findings (on the previous spread) that infants were not most attached to the person who fed them.

This demonstrates that, while animal studies can act as a useful pointer in understanding human behaviour, we should always seek confirmation by looking at research with humans.

Ethics of Harlow's study

A study such as Harlow's could not be done with humans, but there is also the question of whether it should be done with monkeys.

The study created lasting emotional harm as the monkeys later found it difficult to form relationships with their peers. On the other hand, the experiment can be justified in terms of the significant effect it has had on our understanding of the processes of attachment, and the research derived from this study has been used to offer better care for human (and primate) infants.

Therefore, it could be argued that the benefits outweigh the costs to the animals involved in the study. Such criticisms do not challenge the findings of the research but are important in monitoring what counts as good science.

 UPGRADE

On page 71 we looked at reading essay questions effectively. Now let's look at planning your response.

Investing a bit of time deciding and organising what you are going to write is an important part of the process. Some students see this as a 'waste of time' but your brain can work faster than your hand and you might find you are thinking of your next point before you have finished writing the one you are on. This can lead to incomplete points and can affect the flow of the answer.

- Think about the material you have that is relevant to the question and how you will use it to cover the requirements of the question.
- Split up how much time you will spend on each required 'part'.
- Really good essay plans might have a numbering system which shows that you have thought about the order in which information will be presented. Remember, order and logic are important parts of any essay – giving it the coherency that an examiner is looking for to award high marks.
- Go back to the plan as you write your essay to make sure you are on track and to add other points that you think of.

There is no need to cross out your plan – simply label it as such.

CAN YOU? No. 3.3

1. Outline **one** animal study of attachment. In your answer include what the researcher(s) did and what they found. (6 marks)
2. Describe Lorenz's research related to attachment. (4 marks)
3. Outline what animal studies have shown about attachment. (4 marks)
4. Describe and evaluate animal studies of attachment. (12 marks AS, 16 marks A)

Explanations of attachment: Learning theory

There are many different approaches to understanding behaviour, which you will learn about in Chapter 5. One of the major approaches is the learning approach which proposes that certain behaviours are innate, such as crying when you feel pain, but beyond such simple stimulus-response associations, learning theorists (behaviourists) claim that behaviour is learned through experience.

Learning theory dominated psychology in the first half of the twentieth century, so in the 1940s and 1950s their theory of attachment was the key explanation. They used the principles of conditioning to explain how an infant becomes attached to a mother figure. Note that the word 'conditioning' essentially means 'learning'.

The learning theory explanation has been called the 'cupboard love theory' of attachment because it suggests that attachment is based on provision of food alone.

KEY TERMS

Classical conditioning Learning through association. A neutral stimulus is consistently paired with an unconditioned stimulus so that it eventually takes on the properties of this stimulus and is able to produce a conditioned response.

Learning theory The name given to a group of explanations (classical and operant conditioning), which explain behaviour in terms of learning rather than any inborn tendencies or higher order thinking.

Operant conditioning Learning through reinforcement.

Social learning theory Learning through observing others and imitating behaviours that are rewarded.

Before conditioning

Food (UCS) ⟶ pleasure (UCR)

Mother (NS) ⟶ no response

During conditioning

NS and UCS paired

After conditioning

NS is now CS ⟶ pleasure (CR)

LEARNING THEORY OF ATTACHMENT

Learning theory proposes that all behaviour is learned rather than inborn. When children are born they are 'blank slates' and everything they become can be explained in terms of the experiences they have.

Learning theory is put forward by behaviourists who prefer to focus their explanations solely on behaviour – what people do rather than what may or may not be going on in their minds. Behaviourists suggest that all behaviour (including attachment) is learned either through **classical** or **operant conditioning**.

Classical conditioning

Classical conditioning was first investigated by Ivan Pavlov (see page 126). The process begins with an innate stimulus-response. In the case of attachment this innate stimulus is food which produces the innate (unlearned) response of pleasure. Food is an unconditioned stimulus (UCS) and pleasure is an unconditioned response (UCR) – 'unconditioned' means it is not learned.

During an infant's early weeks and months certain things become associated with food because they are present at the time when the infant is fed. This might include the infant's mother, the chair that she sits in to feed her infant or some sounds that might always be present. All of these things are called neutral stimuli (NS).

If any neutral stimulus is regularly and consistently associated with a UCS it takes on the properties of the UCS and will produce the same response. So the NS now becomes a learned or conditioned stimulus (CS) and produces a conditioned response (CR). In this case the person who feeds the infant moves from being an NS to being a CS. Just seeing this person gives the infant a feeling of pleasure (a CR). Learning theorists called this newly formed stimulus-response 'mother love'.

Operant conditioning

Operant conditioning was first investigated by B.F. Skinner (see page 126). John Dollard and Neal Miller (1950) offered an explanation of attachment based on operant conditioning and drive reduction theory. A 'drive' is something that motivates behaviour. When an animal is uncomfortable this creates a drive to reduce that discomfort. In the case of a hungry infant there is a drive to reduce the accompanying discomfort.

When the infant is fed, the drive is reduced and this produces a feeling of pleasure. This is rewarding – called negative reinforcement (escape from something unpleasant). The behaviour that led to being fed is more likely to be repeated in the future because it was rewarding. Food becomes a primary reinforcer because it supplies the reward, i.e. it reinforces the behaviour that avoided discomfort.

Through the process of classical conditioning the person who supplies the food is associated with avoiding discomfort and becomes a secondary reinforcer, and a source of reward in his/her own right. Attachment occurs because the child seeks the person who can supply the reward.

Social learning theory

Social learning theory is a further development of learning theory by Albert Bandura (see page 128). Dale Hay and Jo Vespo (1988) suggested that modelling could be used to explain attachment behaviours. They proposed that children observe their parents' affectionate behaviour and imitate this. Parents would also deliberately instruct their children about how to behave in relationships and reward appropriate attachment behaviours such as giving kisses and hugs.

Learning theory is based on animal studies

A criticism of learning theory is that it is largely based on studies with non-human animals, such as Skinner's research with pigeons.

Behaviourists believe that humans are actually no different from other animals in terms of how they learn. Our behaviour patterns are constructed from the same basic building blocks of stimulus and response and therefore, they argue, it is legitimate to generalise from animal studies to human behaviour. However, not all human behaviour can be explained by conditioning, especially a complex behaviour such as attachment. Non-behaviourists argue that attachment involves innate predispositions and mental activity that could not be explained by conditioning.

Therefore, behaviourist explanations may lack validity because they present an oversimplified version of human behaviour.

Attachment is not based on food

The main limitation of learning theory as an explanation for attachment is that it suggests that food is the key element in the formation of attachment.

There is strong evidence to show that feeding has nothing to do with attachment. Famously, the study conducted by Harlow (1959), described on the previous spread, showed that infant rhesus monkeys were most 'attached' to the wire mother that provided contact comfort, not food. Although Harlow's study was with animals, it is supported by Schaffer and Emerson's research (see page 72).

These research studies therefore suggest that the learning explanation is oversimplified and ignores other important factors such as contact comfort.

Learning theory has some explanatory power

One strength of learning theory is it can explain some aspects of attachment.

Infants *do* learn through association and reinforcement, but food may not be the main reinforcer. It may be that attention and responsiveness from a caregiver are important rewards that assist in the formation of attachment. Such reinforcers were not part of the learning theory account. It may also be that responsiveness is something that infants imitate and thus learn about how to conduct relationships (see page 70).

Learning theory may not provide a complete explanation of attachment but it still has some value.

 Drive reduction theory is limited

Drive reduction theory was very popular in the 1940s, but it is no longer used by psychologists for a number of reasons.

For example, it only can explain a limited number of behaviours – there are many things that people do that have nothing to do with reducing discomfort; in fact there are some things that people do that *increase* discomfort, such as bungee jumping. Furthermore, the theory does not adequately explain how secondary reinforcers work. Secondary reinforcers do not directly reduce discomfort yet they are reinforcing. For example, money is a secondary reinforcer. In itself it does not reduce discomfort, but it is nevertheless reinforcing (we are motivated to do things when offered money).

These limitations go some way to explain the rejection of drive reduction theory.

 An alternative explanation

One of the main reasons that learning theory was rejected as an account of attachment is that a better theory appeared.

Bowlby's theory (which you are about to study) has many strengths compared to learning theory. First of all it can explain *why* attachments form, whereas learning theory can only explain *how* they might form. For example, it can explain Schaffer and Emerson's findings that infants are not always most strongly attached to the person who feeds them. Learning theory also offers no explanation of the strengths of attachment. According to Bowlby's theories the strengths include protection from harm and thus increased chances of survival.

In this way Bowlby's theory offers a more complete explanation of attachment than learning theory.

APPLY YOUR KNOWLEDGE

Michelle had a baby, Josh, about six months ago but has now returned to her job as a teacher for three days a week. While she works, her mother, who is retired, looks after Josh. Michelle is a good mother in that she takes good care of little Josh, but she also has lessons to prepare and marking to do, so doesn't manage the sort of 'quality time' with Josh that her mother is able to provide.

Although Josh is thriving physically, and seems happy enough, Michelle has noticed he is often reluctant to leave her mother when it is time for her to pick him up after work. Josh will often cry when she tries to put him in the car and his granny is the only person who seems to be able to comfort him. Michelle is starting to worry that she is doing something wrong and can't understand why he is behaving like this.

Using the material on this spread, explain why Josh behaves in the way he does.

▲ Animals soon learn to associate the sound of the fridge door opening with food. That's classical conditioning.

Insider tip...

When asked the question 'Describe and evaluate the learning theory explanation of attachment', you will receive no credit if you just describe learning theory (i.e. the processes of classical and operant conditioning).

You must apply the principles of conditioning to the development of attachment. Students often fail to do this and just write about Pavlov's research with dogs or Skinner's studies of pigeons – and get no marks.

CAN YOU? No. 3.4

1. Explain the development of attachments using learning theory. (4 marks)
2. Explain **one** criticism of the learning theory explanation of attachment. (4 marks)
3. Describe and evaluate the learning theory explanation of attachment. (12 marks AS, 16 marks A)

Explanations of attachment: Bowlby's theory

John Bowlby worked as a psychiatrist in London, treating emotionally disturbed children. He observed that a number of the children he treated had experienced early separations from their families which led him to propose his first theory, the theory of maternal deprivation (1951). In this theory he proposed that children deprived of an early, strong attachment may suffer permanent long-term emotional maladjustment. We will look in more detail at this theory later in this chapter.

Bowlby's maternal deprivation theory led Bowlby to think further about the nature and function of the attachment bond. The research by Lorenz and Harlow in the 1950s had a profound influence on Bowlby's subsequent theory of attachment. He first published an article on the theory of attachment in 1958; a fuller version appeared in 1969.

◀ Who's got a babyface then?

The features of a young animal's face elicit caregiving from adults – we find large eyes, a little nose and chin, and high forehead ever so cute. This is an innately determined preference to ensure we care for our young.

KEY TERMS

Continuity hypothesis The idea that emotionally secure infants go on to be emotionally secure, trusting and socially confident adults.

Critical period A biologically determined period of time, during which certain characteristics can develop. Outside of this time window such development will not be possible.

Internal working model A mental model of the world which enables individuals to predict and control their environment. In the case of attachment the model relates to a person's expectations about relationships.

Monotropy (monotropic) The idea that the one relationship that the infant has with his/her primary attachment figure is of special significance in emotional development.

Social releaser A social behaviour or characteristic that elicits caregiving and leads to attachment.

The evolutionary perspective

The main principle of Bowlby's theory is that strong attachment and the consequences of such attachment are adaptive.

The notion of adaptiveness is based on Darwin's Theory of Evolution which states that any genetically determined behaviour that enhances an individual's survival (and reproduction) will be naturally selected. This happens in the same way that a farmer might breed certain animals because the animals possess desirable characteristics (e.g. a high milk yield in cows). In nature, there is no person doing the selecting – it is simply that some traits (or the genes for the traits) become automatically selected because possessors are more likely to survive, reproduce and pass on these traits.

Bowlby introduced one of the key concepts of the evolutionary approach – the environment of evolutionary adaptedness (EEA). This is the environment to which any species is adapted and the selective pressures that existed at that time. For humans our most recent period of evolutionary change was about two million years ago when humans moved from a forest life to the developing savannahs in Africa. Bowlby argued that there would have been a strong selective pressure for close attachment between an infant and its mother at this time.

BOWLBY'S MONOTROPIC ATTACHMENT THEORY (1969)

Why attachment forms

Lorenz's research on imprinting led Bowlby to assume that a similar process was operating in humans. Attachment behaviour evolved because it serves an important survival function – an infant who is not attached is less well protected. Our distant infant ancestors would have been in danger if they did not remain close to an adult.

It is important that attachments are formed in two directions – parents must also be attached to their infants in order to ensure that they are cared for and survive. It is only the parents who look after their offspring that are likely to produce subsequent generations.

How attachment forms

Bowlby's theory also explains *how* attachment occurs.

Critical period Babies have an innate drive to become attached. Innate (biological) behaviours usually have a special time period – a **critical period** – for development (e.g. babies learn to walk at about 11 months). The critical period for attachment is around three to six months. Infants who do not have the opportunity to form an attachment during this time seem to have difficulty forming attachments later on.

During this critical period, what determines who an infant will attach to? For learning theorists food was the important factor. Bowlby proposed that attachment is determined by sensitivity. His views were influenced by Mary Ainsworth (see next spread) whose observations of mothers led her to suggest that the infants who seemed most strongly attached were the ones whose mothers were more responsive, more cooperative and more accessible than less closely attached infants. This was something we have already discussed when considering the importance of reciprocity and interactional synchrony.

Social releasers are important during this time to ensure that attachments develop from parent to infant. Bowlby suggested one important mechanism in this process are **social releasers**, such as smiling and having a 'babyface', all of which elicit caregiving. These social releasers are innate mechanisms that explain how attachments *to* infants are formed.

Monotropy Bowlby proposed that infants have one special emotional bond (**monotropy**) – the primary attachment relationship. This individual is often the infant's biological mother but not always. Infants also form many secondary attachments that provide an important emotional safety net and are important for healthy psychological and social development (see discussion on page 73).

The consequences of attachment

The importance of monotropy is that an infant has one special relationship and forms a mental representation of this relationship called an **internal working model**. This model has several consequences: (1) in the short term it gives the child insight into the caregiver's behaviour and enables the child to influence the caregiver's behaviour, so that a true partnership can be formed; (2) in the long term it acts as a template for all future relationships because it generates expectations about what intimate, loving relationships are like.

The continuity hypothesis proposes that individuals who are strongly attached in infancy continue to be socially and emotionally competent whereas infants who are not strongly attached have more social and emotional difficulties in childhood and adulthood. In other words, there is continuity from infancy to adulthood in terms of emotional type.

Attachment is adaptive

Attachment is clearly important in emotional development, but the question is whether it is critical for survival.

Bowlby suggested that attachments develop when the infant is older than three months. This is very late as a mechanism to protect infants. In our distant ancestors it might have been vital for infants to become attached as soon as they are born – after all, young monkeys cling tenaciously to their mother's fur. The age of attachment may be linked to features of a species' life. Human infants don't need to cling on – mothers can carry their babies. However, when human infants start crawling (from around six months), attachment is vital and that is when attachments develop in humans.

This therefore supports Bowlby's view that attachment is adaptive.

A sensitive period rather than 'critical'

According to Bowlby it should not be possible to form attachments beyond the important critical period between three and six months.

Psychologists have studied children who fail to form attachments during this period. Evidence from Rutter *et al.* (which we review on page 86) shows that Bowlby's claim is true to an extent. It appears less likely that attachments will form after this period, but it is not impossible. The developmental window is one where children are maximally receptive to the formation of certain characteristics or behaviour, but nevertheless such developments can take place outside this window.

For this reason researchers now prefer to use the term 'sensitive period' rather than 'critical period'.

Multiple attachment versus monotropy

The multiple attachment model proposes all attachments are simply integrated into one single internal working model.

This appears to contradict Bowlby's idea of monotropy. However, the two models may not be so very different. Secondary attachments, in Bowlby's theory, *do* contribute to social development, but healthy development requires one central person 'higher' than all the others in a hierarchy. Research on infant–father attachment, for example, suggests a key role for fathers as secondary attachments and in social development (Grossmann and Grossmann, 1991). Prior and Glaser (2006) conclude, from a review of research, that the evidence still points to the hierarchical model.

This therefore supports Bowlby's concept of monotropy.

 Continuity hypothesis

According to Bowlby's theory, one outcome of attachment is the effect it has on subsequent relationships.

This has been tested by the Minnesota parent–child study (Sroufe *et al.*, 2005). This study followed participants from infancy to late adolescence and found continuity between early attachment and later emotional/social behaviour. Individuals who were classified as securely attached in infancy were highest rated for social competence later in childhood, were less isolated and more popular, and more empathetic.

This supports the **continuity hypothesis** *because there is a link between early and later attachments.*

 An alternative explanation

The temperament hypothesis (Kagan, 1984) proposes that an infant's innate emotional personality (called their 'temperament') may explain attachment behaviour.

Infants with an 'easy' temperament are more likely to become strongly attached because it is easier to interact with them whereas those who are 'difficult' tend to be insecurely attached. There is research support for this – Belsky and Rovine (1987) found that infants between one and three days old who had signs of behavioural instability (i.e. were more temperamentally 'difficult') were later judged to be more likely to have developed an insecure attachment. Bowlby's theory suggested that attachment type is due to the primary attachment figure's sensitivity, whereas Kagan's view is that attachment can be explained in terms of infant behaviours.

However, it may be that there is an interaction between the two, a suggestion proposed by Belsky and Rovine and supported by research that found mothers' perceptions of their infant's temperament influenced the mother's responsiveness (Spangler, 1990).

MEET THE RESEARCHER

John Bowlby (1907–1990) was born into an upper-middle-class family and raised mainly by a nanny. His son, Sir Richard Bowlby, explains how this led to his father's interest in attachment:

The origin of my father's motivation for working on the conundrum of the parent–child attachment bond probably stems from a traumatic childhood. His father, my grandfather, was a successful surgeon who lived in a large London townhouse with his wife and six children. The children, as was normal for the time, were raised by nannies. The children only saw their mother for one hour each day, and even then the children went to see her all together, so there wasn't exactly individual quality time. My father grew to love his nanny called Minnie, and I have little doubt that she was his surrogate primary attachment figure, but when he was four years old Minnie left the family. He lost his 'mother figure', and his primary attachment bond was broken. He was then sent away to boarding school when he was eight years old, causing further trauma. I think one thing that saved him was that he did have those four years of secure attachment with Minnie. (Personal communication)

Research methods

The Minnesota parent–child project (see left) began in 1975 and the mother–child pairs continue to be studied. Over this time the mothers' and children's behaviour has been assessed using questionnaires and observations. For example, the mothers and children were videotaped while playing for a period of 10–15 minutes at home. The mothers were aware they were being videotaped. Two observers analysed the recordings.

1. This is a naturalistic observation. Explain **one** strength of using this method to investigate behaviour. (2 marks)
2. Explain in what way this observation was overt and give **one** limitation of using this method. (3 marks)
3. Explain why the researchers chose to videotape the observation. (2 marks)
4. Explain why they arranged to have two observers to analyse the videotapes. (2 marks)
5. Identify **two** behavioural categories that might have been used in this observation. (2 marks)
6. Describe how event sampling could be used in this study. (3 marks)
7. Explain why event sampling might be preferable to time sampling. (2 marks)
8. Identify **one** ethical issue in this study and explain how it could be dealt with. (3 marks)

LINK TO RESEARCH METHODS

Observation on pages 198–201
Ethical issues on pages 194–197

CAN YOU? No. 3.5

1. Briefly explain what the term 'monotropic' means. (2 marks)
2. Outline Bowlby's monotropic theory of attachment. (4 marks)
3. Briefly outline **one** research study that supports Bowlby's theory of attachment. (3 marks)
4. Discuss Bowlby's monotropic theory of attachment. (12 marks AS, 16 marks A)

Ainsworth's Strange Situation: Types of attachment

Mary Ainsworth had a considerable influence on John Bowlby's views on attachment, and provided him with important evidence for his theory. For example, Ainsworth provided Bowlby with the concept of the attachment figure as a *secure base* from which an infant can explore the world, and pointed to the importance of *maternal sensitivity* in the development of mother–infant attachment patterns.

Bowlby focused on the universality of attachments, whereas Ainsworth was particularly interested in individual differences – the different attachment types that infants formed with their caregivers. These types or *styles* of attachment are seen as patterns of thinking, feeling and behaving in interpersonal situations. Ainsworth's method of assessing attachment type continues to be the standard test used in a great number of studies of attachment.

Episodes (about 3 minutes' duration)		Behaviour assessed
1	Parent and infant play.	–
2	Parent sits while infant plays.	Use of parent as secure base
3	Stranger enters and talks to parent.	Stranger anxiety
4	Parent leaves, infant plays, stranger offers comfort if needed.	Separation anxiety
5	Parent returns, greets infant, offers comfort if needed; stranger leaves.	Reunion behaviour
6	Parent leaves, infant alone.	Separation anxiety
7	Stranger enters and offers comfort.	Stranger anxiety
8	Parent returns, greets infant, offers comfort.	Reunion behaviour

▲ The Strange Situation is a research technique used to assess an infant's attachment type. It is conducted in an observation laboratory with video cameras so as to record the behaviour of mothers and their children. The laboratory contains two easy chairs, a low table and a set of toys.

	Secure attachment (Type B)	Insecure-avoidant (Type A)	Insecure-resistant (Type C)
Willingness to explore	High	High	Low
Stranger anxiety	Moderate	Low	High
Separation anxiety	Some easy to soothe	Indifferent	Distressed
Behaviour at reunion with caregiver	Enthusiastic	Avoids contact	Seeks and rejects
Percentage of infants in this category	66%	22%	12%

KEY STUDY: THE STRANGE SITUATION

Ainsworth *et al.* (1971, 1978) devised the **Strange Situation** to be able to systematically test the nature of attachment. The aim was to see how infants (aged between 9 and 18 months) behave under conditions of mild stress and also novelty.

Procedure

The research room is a novel environment, a 9 × 9 foot space often marked off into 16 squares to help in recording the infant's movements.

The procedure consists of eight episodes, each designed to highlight certain behaviours as shown in the table on the left. The key feature of these episodes is that the caregiver and stranger alternately stay with the infant or leave. This enables observation of the infant's response to:

- separation from the caregiver (separation anxiety)
- reunion with the caregiver (reunion behaviour)
- response to a stranger (stranger anxiety)
- the novel environment, which aims to encourage exploration and thus tests the *secure base* concept.

Data is typically collected by a group of observers using a video recorder or one-way mirror. They may record what the infant is doing every 15 seconds using the following behavioural categories: (1) proximity and contact-seeking behaviours, (2) contact-maintaining behaviours, (3) proximity and interaction-avoiding behaviours, (4) contact and interaction-resisting behaviours, and (5) search behaviours. Each item is also scored for intensity on a scale of 1 to 7.

Findings

Ainsworth *et al.* combined the data from several studies, to make a total of 106 middle-class infants observed in the Strange Situation. They noted similarities and differences in the ways that infants behaved. In terms of similarity, for example, it was noted that exploratory behaviours declined in all infants from episode 2 onwards, whereas the amount of crying increased.

In terms of differences, Ainsworth *et al.* found three main patterns of behaviour in the infants observed, i.e. there seemed to be consistent clusters of behaviours which added up to three qualitatively different types of attachment (originally called A, B and C to avoid any descriptive labels). The characteristics of the main attachment types, with respect to the Strange Situation, are described below and summarised in the table on the left.

- The **secure attachment** type B refers to those who have harmonious and cooperative interactions with their caregiver. They are not likely to cry if the caregiver leaves the room and show some distress when left with a stranger. When feeling anxious they seek close bodily contact with their caregiver and are easily soothed, but they may be reluctant to leave their caregiver's side prematurely. They seek and are comfortable with social interaction and intimacy. The securely attached infant uses the caregiver as a secure base from which to explore and thus is able to function independently.
- The **insecure-avoidant** type A is characterised as children who tend to *avoid* social interaction and intimacy with others. In the Strange Situation such children show little response to separation and do not seek the proximity of their caregiver on reunion. If the infant is picked up he/she shows little or no tendency to cling or resist being put down. Such children are happy to explore with or without the presence of their caregiver. They are also characterised by high levels of anxiousness.
- The **insecure-resistant** type C both seeks and *resists* intimacy and social interaction. Such children respond to separation from their caregiver with immediate and intense distress, and behave similarly towards strangers. On reunion, such children display conflicting desires for and against contact; they may angrily resist being picked up while also trying other means to maintain proximity.

> **Insider tip…**
>
> *There is a lot of information here about the Strange Situation which is intended to enhance your understanding. You may be asked other questions about the Strange Situation, such as evaluation questions.*

Other types of attachment

Subsequent research has found that Ainsworth *et al.*'s analysis overlooked a fourth type of attachment.

Main and Solomon (1986) analysed over 200 Strange Situation videotapes and proposed the insecure-disorganised type D, characterised by a lack of consistent patterns of social behaviour. In other words, some infants don't have a consistent type of attachment and lack a coherent strategy for dealing with the stress of separation. For example, they show very strong attachment behaviour which is suddenly followed by avoidance or looking fearful towards their caregiver. Van IJzendoorn *et al.* (1999) further supported this with a meta-analysis of nearly 80 studies in the US. They found 62% secure, 15% insecure-avoidant, 9% insecure-resistant and 15% insecure-disorganised.

This suggests that Ainsworth's original conclusions were oversimplified and do not account for all attachment behaviours.

Observations had high reliability

In observational studies such as Ainsworth's, the reliability of observations is important.

The measurements are confirmed as meaningful if there is agreement amongst observers – called inter-observer reliability, which is determined by comparing the ratings made by a panel of experienced judges. Ainsworth *et al.* (1978) found almost perfect agreement when rating exploratory behaviour – they found .94 agreement between raters (1.00 would be perfect).

This points to a strength of the Strange Situation, namely that the observations can be accepted as being reliable.

Real-world application

Another strength of the Strange Situation is that intervention strategies can be developed to tackle situations where disordered patterns of attachment develop between infant and caregiver.

For example, the *Circle of Security Project* (Cooper *et al.*, 2005) teaches caregivers to better understand their infants' signals of distress and to increase their understanding of what it feels like to experience anxiety. The project showed a decrease in the number of caregivers classified as disordered (from 60% to 15%) and an increase in infants classed as securely attached (from 32% to 40%).

This supports the research on attachment types because such research can be used to improve children's lives.

Low internal validity

One criticism of the Strange Situation centres on whether it does actually measure the attachment type of a child, or whether it merely measures the quality of one particular relationship.

Main and Weston (1981) found that children behaved differently depending on which parent they were with. This suggests that the classification of an attachment type may not be valid because what we are measuring is one relationship rather than a personal characteristic lodged in the individual. However, according to Bowlby's view of monotropy, the attachment *type* is largely related to the one special relationship. Main (1999) tested a group of children and reassessed them at age nine using the AAI (adult attachment interview), finding that attachment type seemed to be chiefly influenced by the mother.

This supports Bowlby's concept of monotropy and the internal validity of the Strange Situation (i.e. it was measuring what it intended to measure).

Maternal reflective functioning

Ainsworth's suggestion that secure attachment was linked to maternal sensitivity has been criticised by later researchers.

Some studies (e.g. Raval *et al.*, 2001) have actually found rather low correlations between measures of maternal sensitivity and the strength of attachment. Slade *et al.* (2005) found a greater role for *maternal reflective functioning*. 'Reflective functioning' is the ability to understand what someone else is thinking and feeling.

This suggests that maternal reflective thinking rather than sensitivity may be the central mechanism in establishing attachment type.

MEET THE RESEARCHER

Mary Salter Ainsworth (1913–1999) was an American who studied in Canada where she joined the Women's Army Corp during the Second World War. Later she moved to London to work with John Bowlby investigating the effects of separation on young children. She subsequently studied mothers and children in Uganda before returning to the US in the 1970s to work at Johns Hopkins University, which is where she conducted her landmark research on the Strange Situation.

KEY TERMS

Insecure-avoidant A type of attachment which describes those children who tend to *avoid* social interaction and intimacy with others.

Insecure-resistant A type of attachment which describes those infants who both seek and *reject* intimacy and social interaction, i.e. resist.

Secure attachment This is a strong and contented attachment of an infant to his or her caregiver, which develops as a result of sensitive responding by the caregiver to the infant's needs. Securely attached infants are comfortable with social interaction and intimacy. Secure attachment is related to healthy subsequent cognitive and emotional development.

Strange Situation A controlled observation designed to test attachment security.

APPLY YOUR KNOWLEDGE

On this spread you have learned about Ainsworth's 'Strange Situation', a technique by which researchers can identify the attachment type of an individual child.

- When his mother leaves the room, Tom doesn't show a lot of emotion and he ignores her when she returns.
- Kenny is a little perturbed when his mother leaves the room, but he doesn't cry. When she returns, he lets her pick him up and soothe him.
- Kenny's sister Yasmin can show the same response to separation as her brother, but sometimes she ignores her mother on her return.
- Tilda seems happy enough to continue playing while her mother is out of the room and is likely to be comforted by a stranger in the room.
- Larry doesn't explore much when his mother leaves and seems wary of the stranger in the room. When his mother returns Larry seems angry with her for leaving him.
- When her mother returns, Anna is pleased to see her and is easily comforted. Anna soon resumes her exploration of the room, and plays happily once more.

Above are some examples of infant behaviour in the stages of the Strange Situation. For each one, identify the attachment type that behaviour is suggesting.

CAN YOU? No. 3.6

1. Identify and briefly explain **one** type of attachment. (2 marks)
2. Outline the Strange Situation procedure. (4 marks)
3. Explain **one** limitation of using the Strange Situation to investigate attachment. (3 marks)
4. Describe and evaluate the Strange Situation. (12 marks AS, 16 marks A)

Cultural variations in attachment

Culture is an issue of central importance in Bowlby's theory because the theory suggests that attachment evolved to provide the biological function of protection for the infant, thus enhancing survival. If attachment is a biological and innate process, secure attachment should be the optimal form for all humans regardless of **cultural variations**. If, however, such attachments are found in particular cultures and not others, this suggests that attachment is not innately determined but is related to different childrearing methods used in different cultures. There may be a middle ground – the view that there is some variation between cultures, related to specific cultural childrearing practices, but with some common ground, e.g. the dominance of secure attachment.

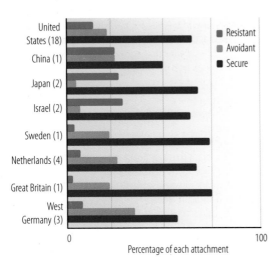

▲ The findings from the study by van IJzendoorn and Kroonenberg (1988).

KEY TERM

Cultural variations The ways that different groups of people vary in terms of their social practices, and the effects these practices have on development and behaviour.

*The term **culture** refers to all the rules, customs, morals and ways of interacting that bind together members of a society or some other collection of people.*

We learn all these rules, customs, etc. through the process of socialisation so that we are able to interact appropriately with the other members of our culture.

The term 'culture' doesn't necessarily equate to the term 'country' or even the term 'society', as many different groups, each with their own rules and customs, may coexist within a country like the UK.

The term 'subculture' is usually used to refer to a group within a country that, although it shares many of the dominant cultural characteristics of that country, may also have some special, different characteristics.

*One of the key dimensions on which cultures differ is the individualist–collectivist one. Western cultures such as ours and American culture are classed as **individualist** cultures which value independence and the importance of the individual.*

*By contrast, some other cultures are described as **collectivist**, emphasising the importance of the group or collective. Such cultures are characterised by the extent to which things are shared – groups live and work together sharing tasks, belongings and childrearing. They value interdependence, i.e. they aspire to be dependent on each other rather than function as self-determining individuals. Japan and Israel are examples of collectivist societies.*

STUDIES OF CULTURAL VARIATIONS

Key study: van IJzendoorn and Kroonenberg (1988)

Procedure Van IJzendoorn and Kroonenberg conducted a meta-analysis of the findings from 32 studies of attachment behaviour. Altogether the studies examined over 2,000 Strange Situation classifications in eight different countries. Van IJzendoorn and Kroonenberg were interested to see whether there would be evidence that *inter*-cultural differences did exist, i.e. differences between different countries/cultures. They were also interested to find out whether there were *intra*-cultural differences – differences in the findings from studies conducted *within* the same culture.

Findings The graph on the left shows the data from this study. With reference to variation *between* cultures/countries, van IJzendoorn and Kroonenberg found that the differences were small. Secure attachment was the most common classification in every country. Insecure-avoidant attachment was the next most common in every country except Israel and Japan (two countries classed as collectivist at that time – see text bottom left). With reference to variation *within* cultures, they found that this was *1.5 times* greater than the variation between cultures.

The conclusion to be drawn from this meta-analysis is that the global pattern across cultures appears to be similar to that found in the US. Secure attachment is the 'norm' – it is the most common form of attachment in all countries. This supports the idea that secure attachment is 'best' for healthy social and emotional development. These cultural similarities support the view that attachment is an innate and biological process.

Cultural similarities

Other studies support van IJzendoorn and Kroonenberg's main finding. For example, Tronick *et al.* (1992) studied an African tribe, the Efe, from Zaire who live in extended family groups. The infants were looked after and even breastfed by different women but usually they slept with their own mother at night. Despite such differences in childrearing practices the infants, at six months, still showed one primary attachment.

Cultural differences

Grossmann and Grossmann (1991) found higher levels of insecure attachment amongst German infants than in other cultures. This may be due to different childrearing practices. German culture involves keeping some interpersonal distance between parents and children, so infants do not engage in proximity-seeking behaviours in the Strange Situation and thus appear to be insecurely attached.

Takahashi (1990) used the Strange Situation to study 60 middle-class Japanese infants and their mothers and found similar rates of secure attachment to those found by Ainsworth *et al*. However, the Japanese infants showed no evidence of insecure-avoidant attachment and high rates of insecure-resistant attachment (32%). The Japanese infants were particularly distressed on being left alone; in fact their response was so extreme that for 90% of the infants the study was stopped at this point.

This cultural variation might again be accounted for in terms of different childcare practices. In Japan infants rarely experience separation from their mothers, which would explain why they were more distressed in the Strange Situation than their American counterparts. This would make them *appear* to be insecurely attached.

Conclusion

These studies suggest that, despite the fact that there are cultural variations in infant care arrangements, the strongest attachments are still formed with the infant's mother.

The research also shows, however, that there are differences in the patterns of attachment that can be related to differences in cultural attitudes and practices.

Similarities may be due to global culture

According to Bowlby's theory of attachment the reason for universal similarities in how attachments form is because attachment is an innate mechanism, unmodified by culture.

Van IJzendoorn and Kroonenberg carried out a meta-analysis of 32 studies and concluded that at least some cultural similarities might be explained by the effects of mass media (e.g. TV and books), which spread ideas about parenting so, as a result, children all over the world are exposed to similar influences.

This means that cultural similarities may not be due to innate biological influences but are because of our increasingly global culture.

Countries rather than cultures

An issue with the conclusions drawn by van IJzendoorn and Kroonenberg is that they actually were not comparing cultures but *countries*.

For example, they compared Japan with the US. Within each country there are many different subcultures, each of which may have different childcare practices. One study of attachment in Tokyo (an urban setting) found similar distributions of attachment types to the Western studies, whereas a more rural sample found an over-representation of insecure-resistant individuals (van IJzendoorn and Sagi, 2001). Indeed, van IJzendoorn and Kroonenberg found more variation *within* cultures than between cultures, presumably because the data was collected on different *subcultures* within each country.

This suggests that great caution needs to be exercised when using the term 'cultural variations' and especially when assessing whether an individual sample is representative of a particular culture.

Cross-cultural research

A particular issue for research conducted in different countries is the 'tools' that are used and whether they are valid.

Observational methods such as the Strange Situation are related to the cultural assumptions of the 'designer'. In the case of the Strange Situation (designed by an American) it is assumed that willingness to explore is a sign of secure attachment. However, in some cultures this is not the case. In traditional Japanese culture, dependence rather than independence would be the sign of secure attachment. The Japanese children may *appear* to be insecurely attached according to Western criteria, whereas they are securely attached by Japanese standards. (The term 'imposed etic' is used to describe the use of a technique designed in one culture but imposed on another.)

This means that research using the Strange Situation may lack validity in other cultures.

 Culture bias

Rothbaum *et al.* (2000) argued that it isn't just the methods used in attachment research that are not relevant to other cultures, but also the theory because it is so rooted in American culture.

Rothbaum *et al.* looked in particular at the contrasts between American (Western) and Japanese culture. For example, the continuity hypothesis does not have the same meaning in both cultures. Bowlby and Ainsworth proposed that infants who are more securely attached go on to develop into more socially and emotionally competent children and adults. However, this competence is defined in terms of individuation – being able to explore, being independent and able to regulate one's own emotions. In Japan the opposite is true; competence is represented by the inhibition of emotional expression (not showing feelings) and being group-oriented rather than self-oriented.

Therefore, the high levels of insecure-resistant attachment found in Japanese children may be explained by cultural bias in attachment theory.

A03 plus **Indigenous theories of attachment**

The solution may lie in producing explanations of attachment rooted in individual cultures ('indigenous theories').

Rothbaum *et al.* suggest that there may be a small set of universal principles, such as the need for protection, but in general, childcare practices should be related to cultural values. However, Posada and Jacobs (2001) note that there is actually a lot of evidence that supports the universality of attachment from many different countries: China, Colombia, Germany, Israel, Japan and Norway. They also point out that the issue is not whether sensitivity leads to independence, but simply that sensitivity is linked to secure attachment however that secure attachment is manifested.

Therefore, Prior and Glaser (2006) conclude that expressions of maternal sensitivity and manifestations of secure-base behaviour may vary across cultures but the core concepts are universal.

▲ Childrearing practices vary across different cultures. For example, in some cultures infants are cared for by many relatives, whereas in others infants spend most time with their mother alone.

The Japanese encourage a dependent relationship (or 'sense of oneness') between mother and child. Doi (1973) called this amae (pronounced 'a-mah-yeh'). Doi claims that this is a natural tendency that is discouraged in Western cultures.

🌀 Research methods

The key study by van IJzendoorn and Kroonenberg was a meta-analysis.

1. Explain what a meta-analysis involves. (2 marks)
2. From the point of view of the study by van IJzendoorn and Kroonenberg, explain **one** strength and **one** limitation of using a meta-analysis to study cultural variations in attachment. (2 marks + 2 marks)
3. In a meta-analysis is primary or secondary data being used? (1 mark)
4. Explain why studies that compare the effects of childrearing practices on attachment could be regarded as a kind of natural experiment. (2 marks)

The research described on this page used the Strange Situation first designed by Ainsworth.

1. Ainsworth found that about 66% of infants in her American sample were securely attached. What fraction is this? (1 mark)
2. Ainsworth suggested that there was a positive correlation between maternal sensitivity and the closeness of attachment between an infant and mother. Explain what positive correlation means in this context. (2 marks)
3. Explain why this research cannot show that maternal sensitivity causes close attachment. (2 marks)

LINK TO RESEARCH METHODS

Meta-analysis on page 208
Natural experiment on page 188
Correlation on page 206

CAN YOU?   No. 3.7

1. Describe research by van IJzendoorn on cultural variations in attachment. (6 marks)
2. Explain **one** criticism of research on cultural variations in attachment. (4 marks)
3. Discuss research on cultural variations in attachment. Refer to evidence in your answer. (12 marks AS, 16 marks A)

Bowlby's theory of maternal deprivation

We're going back in time to look at Bowlby's first theory – on page 78 you learned about his theory of attachment. Prior to that he produced a theory of maternal **deprivation**. In this original theory Bowlby's focus was on the consequences of deprivation of maternal care rather than the benefits of maternal attachment.

Background

In the 1930s and 1940s a number of psychologists studied children who had experienced prolonged separations from their families. They observed that such children were often profoundly disturbed and lagged behind in intellectual development. For example, Spitz and Wolf (1946) observed that 100 'normal' children who were placed in an institution became severely depressed within a few months.

Skodak and Skeels (1949) also studied children placed in institutions. They found that these children scored poorly on intelligence tests. However, when the same children were transferred to a different institution where some inmates gave the children emotional care, the IQ scores improved by almost 30 points.

▲ Mothering can be done by fathers.

	Separations from mother before the age of two		Total
	Frequent	**None**	
Affectionless thieves	12 (86%)	2 (14%)	14
Other thieves	5 (17%)	25 (83%)	30
All thieves	17 (39%)	27 (61%)	44
Control participants	2 (4%)	42 (96%)	44

⬍ Findings from Bowlby's 44 juvenile thieves study.

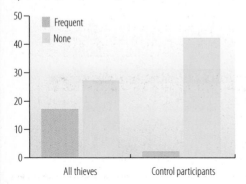

Deprivation To be deprived is to lose something. In the context of child development deprivation refers to the loss of emotional care that is normally provided by a primary caregiver.

THEORY OF MATERNAL DEPRIVATION

John Bowlby (1951, 1953) proposed that prolonged emotional deprivation would have long-term consequences in terms of emotional development. We will consider three important strands of this theory.

The value of maternal care

The findings from Bowlby's 44 thieves study (see below), as well as the findings from other research (see left), came as quite a surprise because no one had really considered the long-term importance that the effects of separation had on infants and children. It was assumed that a good standard of food and physical care was the key importance of good care. If children were separated from their caregivers then all that was necessary was to maintain this standard.

By contrast, Bowlby believed that it wasn't enough to make sure that a child was well-fed and kept safe and warm. He believed that infants and children needed a 'warm, intimate and continuous relationship' with a mother (or permanent mother-substitute) to ensure continuing normal mental health. He famously said that 'mother-love in infancy and childhood is as important for mental health as are vitamins and proteins for physical health' (Bowlby 1953, page 240).

Critical period

Bowlby believed that a young child who is denied such care because of frequent and/or prolonged separations may become emotionally disturbed. However, there are several important 'ifs'. This only applies to a critical period in development – separation will only have this effect *if* this happens before the age of about two and a half years, and *if* there is no substitute mother-person available. Bowlby also felt there was a continuing risk up until the age of five years.

So, the point to note is that potential damage can be avoided if suitable substitute emotional care is provided by a mother-substitute (who could be male or female). In other words, separation need not necessarily result in deprivation, and it is deprivation that has the potential to cause long-term harm.

Long-term consequences

Bowlby suggested that the long-term consequence of deprivation was emotional maladjustment or even mental health problems such as depression. He demonstrated this in his key study.

Key study: 44 juvenile thieves

Procedure Bowlby (1944) analysed the case histories of a number of his patients in the Child Guidance Clinic in London where he worked. All the children attending the clinic were emotionally maladjusted. He studied 88 of these children – half had been caught stealing (the 44 'thieves') and the other half were a control group. Bowlby suggested that some of the 'thieves' were affectionless psychopaths – they lacked normal signs of affection, shame or sense of responsibility. Such characteristics enabled them to be 'thieves' – they could steal from others because it didn't matter to them.

Findings Bowlby found that those individuals diagnosed as affectionless thieves had experienced frequent early separations from their mothers. The figures in the table show that 86% of the affectionless thieves (12 out of 14) experienced frequent separations compared with 17% (5 out of 30) of the other thieves.

Furthermore almost none of the control participants experienced early separations whereas 39% of all the thieves had experienced early separations. These early separations often consisted of continual or repeated stays in foster homes or hospitals, when the children were scarcely visited by their families.

These findings suggest that early separations are linked to affectionless psychopathy. In other words lack of continuous care may well cause emotional maladjustment or even mental disorder.

Physical and emotional separation

When discussing deprivation, people assume that it is *physical* separation that is the cause, but it may also be related to *emotional* separation.

For example, a mother who is depressed may be physically present, yet unable to provide suitable emotional care, thus depriving her children of that care. Marian Radke-Yarrow *et al.* (1985) studied mothers who were severely depressed and found that 55% of their children (mean age 32 months) were insecurely attached, compared with 29% in the non-depressed group.

This shows that emotional separation can also lead to deprivation.

Support for long-term effects

One way to consider the effects of maternal deprivation is in terms of *vulnerability*.

Experiencing early maternal deprivation does not always result in negative outcomes, but it does appear to create an increased likelihood that this will happen. This was illustrated in a classic study by Antonia Bifulco *et al.* (1992) of women who had experienced separation from their mothers either because of maternal death or temporary separation of more than a year. Bifulco found that about 25% later experienced depression or an anxiety disorder, compared with 15% who had no experience of separation. The mental health problems were much greater in those women whose loss occurred before the age of six.

This supports Bowlby's notion of a critical period, suggesting that early childhood deprivation can lead to later vulnerability for depression and anxiety disorders.

Real-world application

Bowlby's study and theory had an enormous, positive impact on post-war thinking about childrearing and also on how children were looked after in hospitals.

Before Bowlby's research, children were separated from parents when they spent time in hospital. Visiting was discouraged or even forbidden. One of Bowlby's colleagues, James Robertson (1952), filmed a two-year-old girl called Laura during the eight-day period she was in hospital. She is seen to be frequently distressed and begs to go home.

Bowlby and Robertson's work led to a major social change in the way that children were cared for in hospital.

Individual differences

Research has shown that not all children are affected by emotional disruption in the same way.

Barrett (1997) reviewed various studies on separation and concluded that securely attached children may sometimes cope reasonably well, whereas insecurely attached children become especially distressed. A similar conclusion was drawn from another study by Bowlby (Bowlby *et al.*, 1956) of 60 children under the age of four being treated for TB (tuberculosis). During a prolonged stay in hospital, the children were visited only once a week and so probably experienced prolonged early disruption of attachment. When assessed in adolescence, some children in the TB group were more maladjusted (63%) than the 'normal' children, but there were no significant differences between them and their 'normal' peers in terms of intellectual development.

Bowlby et al. suggest that those children who coped better may have been more securely attached and thus more resilient, supporting the idea that individual differences may be an important factor when examining the effects of deprivation.

Deprivation versus privation

Michael Rutter (1981), in his book *Maternal Deprivation Reassessed*, criticised Bowlby's view of deprivation.

Rutter claimed that Bowlby did not make clear whether the child's attachment bond had formed but been broken, or had never formed in the first place. Rutter's view of deprivation was that the latter (the *lack* of an attachment bond) would have potentially far more serious consequences for the child than the former (the *loss* of an attachment bond). He therefore used the term 'privation' to refer to situations where the child fails to develop an attachment bond with one caregiver, and deprivation to refer to situations where a bond does develop, but through prolonged or traumatic separations is disrupted or lost.

This lack of clarity in Bowlby's definition of deprivation may therefore negatively affect the validity of research findings.

▲ Laura was filmed while she was in hospital for eight days. Her obvious struggle to control her feelings was hard to watch and ultimately these films changed the minds of the medical profession about the harm being done by emotional deprivation while a young child is in hospital.

⬆ UPGRADE

In essay questions such as question 3 in the 'Can you?' box below, students can spend lots of time describing and evaluating studies without making this relevant to the *theory*. For example, in an essay on the *theory* of maternal deprivation, Bowlby's study of 44 thieves could be used as AO1 if it is given as an example of some of the principles of the theory, or could be used as AO3 if presented as supporting evidence for the theory. In both cases the emphasis should be on the findings rather than the actual procedural details.

So, you need to think carefully about what the study shows and how this offers a critical point that is relevant to the question, e.g. *'Bowlby's claim that deprivation has the potential to cause long-term harm is supported by his study of 44 juvenile thieves. He found that individuals diagnosed as affectionless thieves had experienced frequent early separations from their mothers. This finding suggests that lack of continuous care may well cause emotional maladjustment.'*

Insider tip...

Many students find it difficult to distinguish between Bowlby's theory of maternal deprivation and his theory of attachment. Writing about the wrong one will significantly reduce marks so use the lists below to guide your focus.

- *The theory of attachment focuses on the benefits of attachment, e.g. protection for the infant and the templates for later relationships.*
- *Maternal deprivation focuses on the consequences of emotional separation, e.g. affectionless psychopathy.*

CAN YOU? No. 3.8

1. Explain what is meant by 'maternal deprivation'. (4 marks)
2. Outline research into maternal deprivation. (6 marks)
3. Describe and evaluate Bowlby's theory of maternal deprivation. (12 marks AS, 16 marks A)

An 'institution' is a place dedicated to a particular task, such as looking after children awaiting adoption, or caring for the mentally ill, or looking after patients in hospital. An institution is a place where people live for a period of time as opposed to day care or outpatient care where people go home every day. In the past such institutions had fairly strict regimes and offered little emotional care. Many institutions today strive to avoid this, especially where children are involved. This means that psychologists are no longer able to study deprivation – because their research had reduced the problem. However, in some countries limited resources mean that it is still not possible to offer very much emotional care in institutions.

Romanian orphans

Events in Romania offered psychologists a chance to study separation and deprivation. In 1966 the Romanian government, under the dictator Nicolae Ceauşescu, tried to boost the population of Romania by encouraging parents to have large families and also banning abortion. The consequence was that many babies could not be cared for by their families.

When the regime collapsed in 1989 the Western world became aware of the plight of the orphans in institutional care in Romania. There were more than 100,000 orphans in 600 state-run orphanages. The children spent their days alone in cribs with very little stimulation – cognitive or emotional. They were malnourished and uncared for. Many were adopted by Western families.

ROMANIAN ORPHANS

Key study: Rutter and Sonuga-Barke (2010)

Procedure Michael Rutter and Edmund Sonuga-Barke have led the study of a group of Romanian orphans since the early 1990s – the study is called 'ERA', which stands for 'English and Romanian adoptees'. The study includes 165 Romanian children who spent their early lives in Romanian institutions and thus suffered from the effects of **institutionalisation**. Of this group, 111 were adopted before the age of two years and a further 54 by the age of four.

The adoptees have been tested at regular intervals (ages 4, 6, 11 and 15) to assess their physical, cognitive and social development. Information has also been gathered in interviews with parents and teachers. Their progress has been compared to a control group of 52 British children adopted in the UK before the age of six months.

Findings At the time of adoption the Romanian orphans lagged behind their British counterparts on all measures of physical, cognitive and social development. They were smaller, weighed less and were classified as mentally retarded. By the age of four, some of the children had caught up with their British counterparts. This was true for almost all of the Romanian children adopted before the age of six months.

Subsequent follow-ups have confirmed that significant deficits remain in a substantial minority of individuals who had experienced institutional care to beyond the age of six months. Many of those orphans adopted after six months showed disinhibited attachments and had problems with peer relationships.

This suggests that long-term consequences may be less severe than was once thought *if* children have the opportunity to form attachments. However, when children do not form attachments (i.e. continuing failure of attachment) then the consequences are likely to be severe.

Other studies of Romanian orphans

Romanian orphans were also adopted in other parts of the world. Le Mare and Audet (2006) have reported the findings from a longitudinal study of 36 Romanian orphans adopted to families in Canada. The dependent variables in this study have been physical growth and health. The adopted orphans were physically smaller than a matched control group at age four and a half years, but this difference had disappeared by ten and a half years. The same was true for physical health. This suggests that recovery is possible from the effects of institutionalisation on physical development.

In a Romanian-based study, Zeanah et al. (2005) compared 136 Romanian children who had, on average, spent 90% of their lives in an institution, to a control group of Romanian children who had never been in an institution. The children were aged 12–31 months and were assessed in the Strange Situation. The institutionalised children showed signs of disinhibited attachment (see below).

Effects of institutionalisation

There are a number of well-documented effects of institutionalisation, including:

- Physical underdevelopment – children in institutional care are usually physically small; research has shown (e.g. Gardner, 1972) that lack of emotional care rather than poor nourishment is the cause of what has been called deprivation dwarfism.
- Intellectual underfunctioning – cognitive development is also affected by emotional deprivation (see Skodak and Skeels on previous spread).
- Disinhibited attachment – a form of insecure attachment where children do not discriminate between people they choose as attachment figures. Such children will treat near-strangers with inappropriate familiarity (overfriendliness) and may be attention seeking.
- Poor parenting – Harlow (page 74) showed that monkeys raised with a surrogate mother went on to become poor parents. This is supported in a study by Quinton et al. (1984) who compared a group of 50 women who had been reared in institutions (children's homes) with a control group of 50 women reared at home. When the women were in their 20s it was found that the ex-institutional women were experiencing extreme difficulties acting as parents. For example, more of the ex-institutional women had children who had spent time in care.

Institutionalisation The effect of institutional care. The term can be applied widely to the effects of an institution but our concern focuses specifically on how time spent in an institution such as an orphanage can affect the development of children. The possible effects include social, mental and physical underdevelopment. Some of these effects may be irreversible.

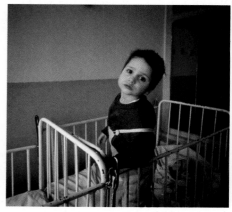

▲ A Romanian orphan with nowhere to go except his cot.

EVALUATION/DISCUSSION

Individual differences

It may not be true that all children who experience institutionalisation are unable to recover.

Research shows that some children are not as strongly affected as others, i.e. there are individual differences. Rutter has suggested that it might be that some of the children received special attention in the institution, perhaps because they smiled more, and this might have enabled them to cope better. Bowlby *et al.*'s study (previous spread) also shows that individual differences matter.

This means that it is not possible to conclude that institutionalisation inevitably leads to an inability to form attachments.

Real-life application

The research into institutionalisation can be applied to improving the lives of children placed in such care.

The early research by Bowlby and Robertson (previous spread) changed the way that children were looked after in hospital. The research on this spread points specifically to the importance of early adoption. In the past, mothers who were going to give a baby up for adoption were encouraged to nurse the baby for a significant period of time. By the time the baby was adopted the sensitive period for attachment may have passed, making it difficult to form secure attachments with a new mother.

The result has been that most babies are now adopted within the first week of birth and research shows that adoptive mothers and children are just as securely attached as non-adoptive families (Singer et al., 1985).

Value of longitudinal studies

A strength of the studies reviewed on this spread is that they followed the lives of children over many years.

Such longitudinal studies take a lot of time, which means a lot of planning and waiting for results, but the benefits are large. Without such studies we may mistakenly conclude that there are major effects due to early institutional care, whereas some of these studies show that the effects may disappear after sufficient time and with suitable high-quality care.

This research, taken together with the consideration of individual differences, shows that it is wrong to assume that institutionalisation inevitably causes negative effects.

(A03 plus) Deprivation is only one factor

A limitation of this research is that inevitably there were confounding variables.

The Romanian orphans were faced with much more than emotional deprivation. The physical conditions were appalling, and this impacted their health. The lack of cognitive stimulation would also affect their development. It is also the case that, for many institutionalised children, poor care in infancy is followed by poor subsequent care, such as living in poverty, parental disharmony and so on (Turner and Lloyd, 1995).

This means that it is likely that the effects of institutional care go beyond emotional deprivation.

(A03 plus) The effects may just be due to slower development

It may be that the effects of institutionalisation do disappear over time if children have good-quality emotional care.

One of the findings from the Romanian study was that at the last assessment, at age 11, a lower number of children had disinhibited attachment. Therefore ex-institutional children may simply need more time than normal to learn how to cope with relationships. This is further supported by Le Mare and Audet's finding that physical underdevelopment had improved by age 11, thus suggesting that development does continue in these children.

This is a criticism of the research, which implies that the effects are permanent, whereas this may not be true.

🐾 APPLY YOUR KNOWLEDGE

In the West African country of Sierra Leone, endemic disease has had a devastating effect on people already struggling with poverty and the aftermath of civil war. The fear and stigma associated with diseases like Ebola, for example, has meant that many orphaned children are abandoned by their families and communities.

Moved by news stories about an epidemic in Sierra Leone, Hayley and Silas decide to adopt an orphan and give her the chance of a new life in the UK. They have been in touch with an adoption agency in Sierra Leone and have been offered a five-year-old girl called Claudetta, who has been in an orphanage in Freetown since her mother died two years before and her father abandoned her.

Based on the insights offered on this spread, what advice might Hayley and Silas be offered about their forthcoming adoption?

CAN YOU? No. 3.9

1. Outline **one** study of Romanian orphans. Include details of what the researcher(s) did and what they found. (6 marks)
2. Outline the effects of institutionalisation on the development of attachment. (2 marks)
3. Discuss research related to the effects of institutionalisation. (12 marks AS, 16 marks A)

The influence of early attachment

The final part of this chapter looks at the consequences of early attachment. One of the key issues in Bowlby's theory of attachment (page 78) was that early attachments have lifelong consequences. He proposed that the quality of an infant's primary attachment would have a positive correlation with the quality of later attachments. The key to this correlation is the internal working model which is acquired through interactions with the child's primary attachment figure and then applied to subsequent relationships with friends, boyfriends and girlfriends, long-term partners and eventually their own children.

On this spread we will review and expand on the research already described in this chapter.

▲ Some people believe that love lasts forever – are they the securely attached ones?

Statements about the internal working model

Data from Hazan and Shaver's study. The table shows what percentage of each attachment type endorsed each statement.

Statements about the internal working model	Avoidant	Resistant	Secure
The kind of head-over-heels love depicted in novels and movies doesn't exist.	25	28	13
Intense romantic love is common at the beginning of a relationship but rarely lasts forever.	41	34	28
Romantic feelings wax and wane over the course of a relationship, but at times they can be as intense as they were at the start of a relationship.	60	75	79
In some relationships, romantic love really lasts, it doesn't fade with time.	41	46	59
Most of us could love many different people equally well; there is no 'one true love' which is 'meant to be'.	39	36	40
It's easy to fall in love. I feel myself beginning to fall in love often.	4	20	9
find someone you can	66	56	43

THE INFLUENCE OF EARLY ATTACHMENT

The role of the internal working model

Bowlby's concept of the **internal working model** is similar to a schema. A schema is basically a concept plus a bit more. For example you can now define imprinting. That's the basic concept, but you also know how imprinting happens and why it happens (or you should). That's the schema.

The internal working model is like this. An infant learns about a relationship from experience – the infant learns what relationships are and how partners in a relationship behave towards each other. It is 'an "operable" model of self and attachment partner, based on their joint attachment history' (Bretherton and Mulholland 1999, page 89). It is 'operable' because it is used to predict the behaviour of other people in the future.

Key study: Hazan and Shaver

Cindy Hazan and Philip Shaver (1987) designed a study to test the internal working model.

Procedure Hazan and Shaver placed a 'Love Quiz' in the *Rocky Mountain News* (an American small-town publication). The quiz asked questions about current attachment experiences and about attachment history to identify current and childhood attachment types. The questionnaire also asked questions about attitudes towards love, an assessment of the internal working model.

They analysed 620 responses, 205 from men and 415 from women, from a fair cross-section of the population.

Findings When analysing self-report of attachment history they found that the prevalence of attachment styles was similar to that found in infancy – 56% were classified as secure, 25% as avoidant and 19% are resistant.

They also found a positive correlation between attachment type and love experiences. Securely attached adults described their love experiences as happy, friendly and trusting; they emphasised being able to accept and support their partner despite faults. These relationships were more enduring – 10 years on average compared to five and six years for resistant and avoidant participants respectively.

Finally, they found a relationship between the conception of love (the internal working model) and attachment type – securely attached individuals tended to have a positive internal working model. See table on left.

Behaviours influenced by the internal working model

Childhood friendships The Minnesota child–parent study mentioned on page 79 found continuity between early attachment and later emotional/social behaviour. Individuals who were classified as securely attached in infancy were highest rated for social competence later in childhood, were less isolated and more popular, and more empathetic. This can be explained in terms of the internal working model because securely attached infants have higher expectations that others are friendly and trusting, and this would enable easier relationships with others.

Poor parenting Harlow's research with monkeys also demonstrated a link between poor attachment and later difficulties with parenting. On the previous spread we reported a study by Quinton *et al.* which showed that the same is true in humans. The lack of an internal working model means that individuals lack a reference point to subsequently form relationships with their own children.

Romantic relationships The study by Hazan and Shaver (above) demonstrated a link between early attachment type and later relationships. Individuals who were securely attached had longer-lasting romantic relationships.

Mental health The lack of an attachment during the critical period in development would result in a lack of an internal working model. Children with attachment disorder have no preferred attachment figure, an inability to interact and relate to others that is evident before the age of five, and experience of severe neglect or frequent change of caregivers. For some time a condition called attachment disorder has been recognised but it has recently been classed as a distinct psychiatric condition and included in the DSM (see page 98).

Research is correlational

The research linking the internal working model/early attachment with later relationship experiences is correlational rather than experimental.

Therefore we can't claim that the relationship between early attachment and, for example, later love styles is one of cause and effect. It is possible that both attachment style and later love styles are caused by something different – such as innate temperament (see Kagan's temperament hypothesis on page 79). An infant's temperament affects the way a parent responds and thus may be a determining factor in infant attachment type. The individual's temperament may explain their issues (good or bad) with relationships later in life.

This means that researchers cannot claim that the internal working model determines later relationships. In this case temperament is an intervening variable.

Retrospective classification

A criticism of studies of early attachment (e.g. Hazan and Shaver) is that they rely on retrospective classification.

When adults are asked questions about their early lives in order to assess infant attachment, their recollections are likely to be flawed. This is because our memories of the past are not always accurate. However, longitudinal studies also support Hazan and Shaver's findings. For example, an ongoing longitudinal study (Simpson *et al.*, 2007) found that participants who were securely attached as infants were rated as having higher social competence as children, were closer to their friends at age 16, and were more expressive and emotionally attached to their romantic partners in early adulthood.

These longitudinal studies support the view that attachment type does predict relationships in adult life and may offer a more accurate representation of early attachment influences.

Overly determinist

Another criticism of attachment research is that it is overly determinist.

For example, the research by Hazan and Shaver suggests that very early experiences have a fixed effect on later adult relationships: children who are insecurely attached at one year of age are doomed to experience emotionally unsatisfactory relationships as adults. This is fortunately not the case as researchers have found plenty of instances where participants were experiencing happy adult relationships *despite* not having been securely attached as infants.

As Simpson et al. (2007) conclude, the research does not suggest that 'an individual's past unalterably determines the future course of his/her relationships'.

 Low correlations

Not all research has found a strong positive correlation between early attachment and later relationships.

Fraley (2002) conducted a review of 27 samples where infants were assessed in infancy and later reassessed (ranging from one month to 20 years later). He found correlations ranging from .50 to as low as .10. Fraley suggested that one reason for low correlations may be because insecure-resistant attachment is more unstable. Such low correlations would pull down the overall correlations.

Nevertheless, such low correlations pose a significant challenge to attachment research, as they do not suggest that attachment type is very stable.

 An alternative explanation

Feeney (1999) argues that adult attachment patterns may be properties of the relationship rather than the individual.

The argument presented on this spread is that early relationships cause later attachment types. An alternative explanation is that adult relationships are guided by a self-verification process – the tendency to seek others who confirm your expectations of relationships. Therefore it is the adult secure relationship that is causing the adult attachment type, rather than vice versa.

This means that another explanation may account for the findings of early attachment research.

KEY TERM

Internal working model A mental model of the world which enables individuals to predict and control their environment. In the case of attachment the model relates to a person's expectations about relationships.

 UPGRADE

In other Upgrade features in this chapter we have emphasised the importance of careful construction of responses to essay questions. The same advice applies to shorter questions, i.e. read the question carefully, making a note of any specific requirements, plan your response accordingly and use the right material in the right way.

For example, let's look at question 3 in the 'Can you?' box below, one of the lower tariff questions on this spread. The command word in this question is *Evaluate*, so no description is required and would not gain marks. Evaluate is a broad term – see some examples of appropriate material on this page. The next word is *research*, which could refer to either studies and/or theoretical insights. The specific requirements of the question are to evaluate research in two areas, the influence of early attachment on *childhood* relationships and the influence of early attachment on *adult* relationships.

Planning your response should be straightforward if you have read the question carefully. The last decision is to decide *how many* evaluative points to include. Given the need for your answer to be 'well explained' (AQA criterion) to hit the top mark band, two points at 50 words each would be ideal for a 4-mark answer.

▲ The Child is father of the Man – William Wordsworth.

CAN YOU? No. 3.10

1. Explain the role of the internal working model in the development of later relationships. (4 marks)
2. Outline **one** study of the influence of early attachment on childhood and adult relationships. (6 marks)
3. Evaluate research on the influence of early attachment on childhood and adult relationships. (4 marks)
4. Describe and evaluate the influence of early attachment on childhood and adult relationships. In your answer make reference to the role of the internal working model. (12 marks AS, 16 marks A)

We have identified here the key points of the topics on the AQA specification covered in this chapter, i.e. the bare minimum that you need to know. You may want to fill in further details to elaborate and personalise this material.

CAREGIVER–INFANT INTERACTIONS

DESCRIPTION

- Reciprocity – taking turns as in a conversation (e.g. Jaffe et al.).
- Brazelton – mother anticipates infant signals, basis of attachment.
- Interactional synchrony – coordinated behaviour.
- Meltzoff and Moore – 3-day-old babies imitate mothers.
- Piaget – behaviour is pseudo-imitation (operant conditioning).
- Murray and Trevarthen – infant distress if no response, supports innateness.

EVALUATION/DISCUSSION

- Problems testing infant behaviour as they are in constant motion.
- Failure to replicate Meltzoff and Moore, e.g. Marian et al. (live vs taped interactions).
- Intentionality supported – no response to inanimate object (Anravanel and DeYong).
- **A03 plus** Individual differences – security of attachment associated with interactional synchrony (Isabella et al.).
- **A03 plus** 'Like me' hypothesis (Meltzoff) – interactional synchrony leads to Theory of Mind.

THE DEVELOPMENT OF ATTACHMENT

DESCRIPTION

- Schaffer and Emerson studied 60 infants and mothers from Glasgow.
- Stage 1: indiscriminate attachments.
- Stage 2: beginnings of attachment.
- Stage 3: specific attachment.
- Stage 4: multiple attachments.
- The role of the father – changing social practices: increased exposure might lead to primary attachments.
- Biological factors – women have hormones which encourage caringness.
- Nevertheless men are primary attachment figures or share this role (Frank et al.).
- Secondary attachment – fathers more playful (Geiger); problem-solving (White and Woollett).

EVALUATION/DISCUSSION

- Unreliable data – mothers of less securely attached infants would be less sensitive and possibly less accurate in their reports, a systematic bias.
- Biased sample – working-class population from 1960s, results may not generalise.
- Challenging monotropy – Rutter argued that all relationships equivalent.
- **A03 plus** Cultural variations – infants raised in collectivist environment showed less maternal attachment than in individualist/family-based homes (Sagi et al.)
- **A03 plus** Stage theories of development – may be too inflexible.

ANIMAL STUDIES OF ATTACHMENT

LORENZ'S RESEARCH

DESCRIPTION

- Lorenz: procedure – goose eggs incubated so first living thing they saw was their natural mother or Lorenz.
- Findings – goslings imprinted on Lorenz and followed him.
- Critical period – imprinting doesn't happen later.
- Long-lasting effects – irreversible and related to mate choice (sexual imprinting).

EVALUATION/DISCUSSION

- Research support – imprinting on yellow rubber gloves (Guiton et al.).
- Criticisms of imprinting – may not be irreversible and may be little more than just learning.

HARLOW'S RESEARCH

DESCRIPTION

- Harlow: procedure – wire 'mothers', one cloth covered. Feeding bottle attached to one or other.
- Findings – monkeys spent most time with cloth-covered 'mother', whether or not feeding bottle attached.
- Critical period – attachments must be formed before six months.
- Long-lasting effects – all motherless monkeys were abnormal socially and sexually.

EVALUATION/DISCUSSION

- Confounding variable – wire mother faces different, varied systematically with independent variable.
- Generalising to humans may not be justified but findings confirmed, e.g. Schaffer and Emerson.
- **A03 plus** Ethics – benefits may outweigh costs, but does not challenge findings.

EXPLANATIONS OF ATTACHMENT

LEARNING THEORY

DESCRIPTION

- Learning theory (behaviourism): all behaviours are learned rather than inherited.
- Classical conditioning – new conditioned response learned through association between a neutral stimulus (mother) and an unconditioned stimulus (food).
- Operant conditioning – the reduction of discomfort created by hunger is rewarding so food becomes a primary reinforcer, associated with mother who becomes secondary reinforcer.
- Social learning – children model parents' attachment behaviours (Hay and Vespo).

EVALUATION/DISCUSSION

- Animal studies – lack external validity because simplified view of human attachment.
- Attachment is not based on food – Harlow showed it was contact comfort; supported by Schaffer and Emerson.
- Learning theory can explain some aspects of attachment – attention and responsiveness are rewards.
- **A03 plus** Drive reduction theory is limited – reducing discomfort does not explain secondary reinforcers.
- **A03 plus** Alternative explanation – Bowlby's theory.

BOWLBY'S THEORY

DESCRIPTION

- Bowlby's attachment theory (1969): critical period – attachments form around 3–6 months, afterwards this becomes increasingly difficult.
- Primary attachment figure – determined by caregiver sensitivity (Ainsworth).
- Social releasers elicit caregiving and ensure attachment from parent to infant.
- Monotropy – primary attachment has special emotional role, secondary attachments provide safety net.
- Internal working model – acts as template for future relationships, creating continuity (continuity hypothesis).

EVALUATION/DISCUSSION

- Attachment is adaptive – human infants form attachments when they start to be mobile.
- A sensitive period rather than a critical one (Rutter et al.).
- Multiple attachments – Bowlby's views are not contradictory because secondary attachments contribute to one single internal working model.
- **A03 plus** Continuity hypothesis – securely attached infants later classed as more empathetic and more popular (Sroufe et al.).
- **A03 plus** Temperament hypothesis – Kagan suggested that innate emotional personality determines attachment.

AINSWORTH'S STRANGE SITUATION: TYPES OF ATTACHMENT

DESCRIPTION

- Ainsworth *et al.* – a systematic test of attachment to one caregiver, situation of mild stress and novelty.
- Procedure – observations every 15 seconds of behaviours, e.g. contact-seeking or contact-avoidance.
- Behaviours assessed – separation anxiety, reunion behaviour, stranger anxiety, secure base.
- Findings: types of attachment: secure (65% type B), insecure-avoidant (22% type A), insecure-resistant (12% type C).

EVALUATION/DISCUSSION

- Other types of attachment – disorganised (type D) (Main and Solomon).
- High reliability – inter-observer reliability > .94.
- Real-world application – Circle of Security Project.
- **A03 plus** Low internal validity – children behave differently depending on which parent (Main and Solomon), though attachment type may be related to primary attachment figure.
- **A03 plus** Maternal reflexive functioning may explain attachment better than sensitivity (Raval *et al.*).

CULTURAL VARIATIONS IN ATTACHMENT

DESCRIPTION

- Key study: van IJzendoorn and Kroonenberg – meta-analysis of 32 studies using the Strange Situation, from 8 countries.
- Findings – secure attachment was the norm in all countries, greater variation within countries than between them.
- Cultural similarities – Efe infants (Tronick *et al.*).
- Cultural differences – more insecure attachment in German sample (Grossmann and Grossmann).
- Cultural differences – no avoidant attachment in Japan sample (Takahashi).

EVALUATION/DISCUSSION

- Similarities may be due to global culture (van IJzendoorn and Kronenberg).
- Results relate to countries yet within countries there are cultural differences, e.g. rural versus urban Japanese (van IJzendoorn and Sagi).
- Cross-cultural research – uses tools developed in one country in a different setting where it has a different meaning (imposed etic).
- **A03 plus** Culture bias – Rothbaum argues that attachment theory generally has a Western bias.
- **A03 plus** Indigenous theories – may be the solution, though Posada and Jacobs suggest that there are universal attachment behaviours.

BOWLBY'S THEORY OF MATERNAL DEPRIVATION

DESCRIPTION

- Value of maternal care – children need a warm, intimate and continuous relationship with a mother or mother-substitute.
- Critical period – frequent and/or prolonged separations from a mother will have negative effects if they occur before the age of $2\frac{1}{2}$ (critical period) or up to age 5 (sensitive period) if there is no mother-substitute.
- Long-term consequences – include emotional maladjustment or mental disorder such as depression.
- Key study: 44 juvenile thieves.
- Findings – 86% of affectionless thieves had frequent separations before 2 compared with 17% of other thieves and just 2% of the control group.

EVALUATION/DISCUSSION

- Emotional rather than physical separation is harmful (Radke-Yarrow).
- Support for long-term effects – women who experienced early separation more likely to experience depression later in life (Bifulco *et al.*).
- Real-world application – films of Laura brought about social change (Bowlby and Robertson).
- **A03 plus** Individual differences – some children more resilient, e.g. securely attached children in TB hospital (Bowlby *et al.*).
- **A03 plus** Deprivation versus privation – loss of care (deprivation) may not have as serious consequences as total lack of attachment (privation) (Rutter).

ROMANIAN ORPHAN STUDIES: EFFECTS OF INSTITUTIONALISATION

DESCRIPTION

- Key study: Rutter *et al.* (ERA) – 165 Romanian orphans, physical, cognitive and social development tested at regular intervals.
- Findings – at age 11 those children adopted before 6 months showed good recovery, older adoptions associated with disinhibited attachment.
- Canadian study (Le Mare and Audet) – Romanian orphans physically smaller at adoption but recovered by age $10\frac{1}{2}$.
- Romanian study (Zeanah *et al.*) – institutionalised Romanian orphans compared to control group more likely to display disinhibited attachment.
- Effects of insitutionalisation – physical underdevelopment (deprivation dwarfism, Gardner), intellectual underfunctioning (Skodak and Skeels), disinhibited attachment, poor parenting (Quinton *et al.*).

EVALUATION/DISCUSSION

- Individual differences – some children appear to recover despite no apparent attachments within sensitive period.
- Real-life application – adoption should be as early as possible and then infants securely attached (Singer *et al.*).
- Longitudinal studies – show that some changes take a while to become apparent, current studies show some recovery possible.
- **A03 plus** Deprivation is only one factor – most institutionalised children experience multiple 'risks', thus maternal deprivation should not be over-exaggerated (Turner and Lloyd).
- **A03 plus** The effects may just be due to slower development – the fact that children do appear to recover in time suggests that the effects simply slow down development (LeMare and Audet).

THE INFLUENCE OF EARLY ATTACHMENT

DESCRIPTION

- Internal working model – model of self and attachment partner based on their joint attachment history which generates expectations about current and future relationships.
- Key study: Hazan and Shaver – placed 'Love Quiz' in newspaper and analysed 620 responses.
- Findings: positive relationship between attachment type (childhood and current one) and love experiences/attitudes (internal working model).
- Behaviours influenced by internal working model – childhood friendships (Minnesota child–parent study), poor parenting (Quinton *et al.*), romantic relationships (Hazan and Shaver) and mental health (attachment disorder).

EVALUATION/DISCUSSION

- Correlational research – internal working model may not cause later relationship experiences, temperament may be intervening variable.
- Retrospective classification – childhood attachment type based on memory of childhood which may be inaccurate, though support from longitudinal study (Simpson *et al.*).
- Overly determinist – past attachment experiences do not always determine the course of future relationships (Simpson *et al.*).
- **A03 plus** Low correlations – a meta-analysis of studies suggest correlations between early attachments and later relationships may be as low as .10 (Fraley).
- **A03 plus** Alternative explanation – adult relationships guided by self-verification (Feeney).

The exam questions on attachment will be varied but there will be some short answer questions (AO1), including some multiple choice questions, some questions that ask you to apply your knowledge (AO2) and possibly an extended writing question (AO1 + AO3). Some questions may involve research methods and maths skills. We have provided a selection of these different kinds of questions here.

AS AND A LEVEL QUESTIONS

0 1 Below are stages of attachment. Choose **one** stage when answering the questions that follow.

  A Infants show a preference for certain people but accept care from anyone.
  B Infants show a preference for people over objects.
  C Infants show extreme anxiety when separated from certain special people.

  (i) Identify the first stage of attachment.   [1 mark]

  (ii) Identify the final stage of attachment.   [1 mark]

0 2 Read the item and then answer the question that follows.

> Suzanna is a young woman who has been in an intimate relationship for two years. She describes herself as a clingy and obsessive partner who can get extremely jealous.

  Choose the type of attachment that Suzanna is most likely to have shown as an infant.

  A insecure-avoidant   **B** insecure-resistant   **C** secure   [1 mark]

0 3 Name two of the countries studied by van IJzendoorn in his research into cultural variations in attachment.   [2 marks]

0 4 Give **two** features of the concept of the critical period.   [2 marks]

0 5 Read the item below and then answer the question that follows.

> Tanya and Tina were discussing their marriages. Tanya suggested that she was far too needy and jealous and put that down to the type of attachment she had with her parents as a child. Tina said that her marriage was loveless and pointless. She decided it was because her father had walked out of the family home when she was just three years old and had never returned.

  Describe and evaluate research into the influence of early attachment on childhood and adult relationships. Refer to Tanya's and Tina's experiences as part of your answer.   [12 marks]

0 6 Explain what Bowlby meant by an internal working model in relation to attachment.   [3 marks]

0 7 Outline the procedure used in **one** animal study where Lorenz investigated attachment.   [2 marks]

0 8 Distinguish between insecure-avoidant and insecure-resistant attachment.   [3 marks]

0 9 Outline how a psychologist might investigate the attachment type of an infant.   [3 marks]

1 0 Read the item below and then answer the questions that follow.

> Hania is three years old and has strong bonds with both of her parents and her grandparents too.
>
> Toby is four months old and likes attention but shows no preference for any person in particular.
>
> Lola is five years old and shows little distress when her parents leave her and hardly responds when they return.
>
> Victor is two years old and only has one strong bond and that is with his mother.

  (i) Name the child who demonstrates a monotropic attachment.   [1 mark]
  (ii) Name the child who demonstrates an indiscriminate attachment.   [1 mark]
  (iii) Name the child who demonstrates an insecure-avoidant attachment.   [1 mark]

1 1 Describe the findings of Ainsworth's research into the Strange Situation. [3 marks]

1 2 Outline **two** limitations of using the Strange Situation to measure attachment. [4 marks]

1 3 Explain how reciprocity and interactional synchrony are involved in caregiver–infant interactions. [4 marks]

1 4 Evaluate learning theory as an explanation of attachment. [4 marks]

1 5 Explain what Romanian orphan studies have shown about the effects of institutionalisation. [6 marks]

1 6 Read the item below and then answer the questions that follow.

> A psychologist wanted to investigate the role that fathers played in the development of attachment by observing a sample of 20 fathers interacting with one-year-old children. The observations took place within the home. The psychologist decided to use overt non-participant observations for the research.

　(i) Outline **one** strength and **one** limitation of using an overt observation for this investigation. [4 marks]

　(ii) Outline **one** strength and **one** limitation of using a non-participant observation for this investigation. [4 marks]

1 7 Outline and briefly evaluate Bowlby's theory of maternal deprivation. [6 marks]

1 8 Briefly discuss the findings of **one** of Harlow's animal studies on attachment. [6 marks]

1 9 Discuss the role of the father in the development of attachments. [8 marks]

2 0 Read the item below and then answer the questions that follow.

> Freddie was raised by his mother – a single parent – for the first three years of his life. He had developed a strong bond with her but, after experiencing a nervous breakdown, Freddie's mother abandoned him and he is now in the care of social services.

　(i) Explain why this is an example of maternal deprivation. [3 marks]

　(ii) Using Bowlby's theory, outline **two** ways in which Freddie may be affected by the maternal deprivation. [4 marks]

2 1 Discuss animal studies carried out on attachment by **both** Lorenz and Harlow. [12 marks]

2 2 Discuss Bowlby's monotropic theory of attachment. [12 marks]

2 3 Read the item below and then answer the questions that follow.

> A researcher carried out cross-cultural research to compare the attachment types across two countries: Germany and Japan. He interviewed parents in both countries and asked to describe their interactions with their young children. From this, he categorised their attachment as secure, insecure-avoidant or insecure-resistant. The results from the study are shown on the right.

Distribution of attachment types in Germany
Distribution of attachment types in Japan

■ Insecure-resistant
■ Insecure-avoidant
■ Secure

Germany: 9%, 51%, 40%
Japan: 30%, 4%, 66%

　(i) Calculate the percentage difference in secure attachments between Germany and Japan. [1 mark]

　(ii) Explain **one** limitation of using the interview method to categorise the attachment type. [2 mark]

　(iii) Briefly discuss what this study has shown us about attachment types in different cultures. [5 marks]

A LEVEL ONLY QUESTIONS

2 4 Discuss the use of animal studies for investigating attachment. [16 marks]

2 5 Discuss Bowlby's monotropic theory of attachment. Use learning theory as part of your discussion. [16 marks]

2 6 Discuss the extent to which early attachment influences childhood and adult relationships. [16 marks]

We've provided answers by two students to some of the questions on pages 92–93 here, together with comments from an examiner about how well they've each done. **Green** comments show what the student has done well. **Orange** comments indicate areas for improvement.

---

06 Explain what Bowlby meant by an 'internal working model' in relation to attachment. *(3 marks)*

> This is not actually explained.

> The opening statement is vague.

Ciaran's answer

Bowlby wrote about the internal working model (IWM) to describe something that babies learn from their mothers. They use this model as they go through life to create expectations about other relationships. It will affect their other relationships. There is evidence to show that this is true, such as Hazan and Shaver's study.

> This is potentially accurate but not well explained.

> There are no marks for evaluation here.

Examiner's comments

All the points here are underdeveloped or muddled. The examiner could not be sure that Ciaran really understands what the IWM is. *1/3 marks*

> ✓ This is a better start with a clearer view of what the IWM is.

> ✓ Accurately outlines what it is, how it develops and its purpose.

Maisie's answer

The internal working model is basically a schema of relationships. It is created through the early relationship with the infant's primary attachment figure. The kind of relationship that is experienced creates future expectations which mould the way a person behaves with friends, partners and their own children.

Examiner's comments

3/3 marks

AS essay

21 Discuss animal studies carried out on attachment by **both** Lorenz and Harlow. *(12 marks)*

Exam tip…

This question asks for 'discussion' – it is important to know that discussion requires both description and evaluation in equal measure in an AS essay, but also the evaluation should seek to be a discussion where you present contrasting points.

> ✓ Accurate and snappy start.

Maisie's answer

Lorenz conducted research on imprinting with geese. He incubated half of a batch of eggs and when they hatched the first thing they saw was Lorenz. To demonstrate that the goslings had imprinted on him he put his goslings together with the others who had seen their actual mother first to see if they would all follow their true mother. Lorenz's goslings went to him and generally followed him around everywhere. This shows that imprinting is innate but the thing that is imprinted on is learned. It happens in a short window after hatching and Bowlby said attachment was similar in that it has a 'critical period'.

> An attempt at discussion but not elaborated as far as it could be.

Lorenz also observed birds as they got older and noticed that early imprinting was related to mating behaviour later, suggesting that attachment is biological and determined rather than learned. However, other research has found that this is reversible.

> A discussion point that is not elaborated. Follow this up with more detail or 'this suggests that…'

Harlow conducted a very influential study that showed that the learning theory of attachment was wrong. He did the study by having two wire 'mothers'. One had a feeding bottle attached and the other was covered in cloth. Sometimes the feeding bottle was on the cloth monkey but other times it was on the wire only mother. Either way the infant monkeys spent almost all their time with the cloth-covered one, especially when scared, which shows that contact comfort mattered more than feeding. In a later study he showed that even the monkeys with the cloth-covered mother grew up to be poor parents, they were damaged emotionally.

> Again, an attempt at discussion although how the study showed learning theory to be wrong is not fully explained and remains implicit.

> ✓ Good, concise description of the key points of the study and what they mean.

The trouble with using animal research to understand human behaviour is that animals and humans are very different, but monkeys are at least more similar than geese. Another criticism of this research is that it wasn't ethical because the monkeys were maladjusted for the rest of their lives. There was a confounding variable in Harlow's study because the two wire monkeys had different faces. (316 words)

> ✓ Some accurate discussion points that are developed more than earlier ones; although more could be added.

> Maisie could go on to explain why this is a confounding variable.

Examiner's comments

Knowledge is accurate with some detail and with concise reference to the methods and findings. More focus on developing discussion is needed as it currently lacks effectiveness. *Bottom of Level 3: this answer is likely to get 7 marks out of 12.*

A Level essay

26 Discuss the extent to which early attachment influences childhood and adult relationships. *(16 marks)*

Exam tip…

When asked a question about 'the extent' of something it is really asking you how true something is or 'how far' one things affects another. So here, how true is it that early attachments affect later relationships and how far does that influence go? Do they completely dictate the later relationships or is it just one of many factors that can have an impact?

> The explanation of the internal working model and why it impacts on later relationships could be made clearer, for example by including specific behaviours that might be expected from the different attachment types. This will make the study that follows more effective.

> A clear and concise use of research.

> It would help to have a sentence to explain what this means in terms of the essay (extent of impact). 'Therefore, this suggests that…'

Ciaran's answer

Early attachment has an important effect on childhood and adult relationships. The reason for this link is the internal working model. A person develops this internal working model in infancy as a reflection of the relationship with their primary attachment figure. If this is a secure attachment it leads to the expectation that all relationships will be like this. If it is insecure this similarly predicts that's what future relationships will be like. It creates an expectation about future relationships.

One study that investigated this was by Sroufe et al. They followed a group of children from infancy through their school years. They found that children who were measured as securely attached in infancy were rated as the highest for social competency and were more popular whereas this was less true for insecurely attached children. One strength of this study is that it was longitudinal which meant that it started in infancy so that attachment type was not retrospectively assessed.

Another important study was by Hazan and Shaver. They placed a quiz in a newspaper and analysed the results from over 600 people. They found that people assessed as being secure in infancy described their adult love relationships as being happy and secure, whereas those people who had insecure attachments in infancy had less success and much shorter adult relationships on average — it was 10 years for securely attached adults and 5 or 6 years for insecurely attached. The problem with this study is the infant attachment type had to be retrospectively assessed which isn't very reliable.

Other research has also shown a link between early attachment type and later relationships by looking at mothers and their own children. Quinton et al. found that women who had been in institutions as children and therefore not formed attachments early in life later had more difficulties as parents. I have already pointed out the issue of when attachment type was assessed but there is furthermore the question of how valid that assessment is. The Strange Situation is often used and has been criticised for lacking validity particularly for some cultural groups.

Another issue is that the research is just correlational. Therefore it is wrong to jump to the conclusion that attachment type is the cause of these later behaviours. It could be that temperament is an intervening variable. Innate temperament may cause initial attachment type and may cause the later relationship issues. For example a child who has a sociable temperament and is easy to get on with will form a secure attachment early in life and this would also explain their later successes in relationships.

By suggesting this is a causal relationship, there may be a negative effect on people who have difficult early lives, for example in an institution, who may feel there is no point trying because they will never be good parents or have a good marriage, so this research is socially irresponsible. (485 words)

> Although this is a valid comment about the study, it needs to be linked back to the question and used to discuss the 'extent' of the impact of early attachment to gain credit.

> Accurate and well detailed description of research. Adding a comment such as 'This shows that the extent to which early attachment…' will help make the discussion more effective too.

> Again, as the question is not asking for evaluation of the study, this needs to be related back to the question to help discuss the extent to which early attachment affects future relationships.

> To help discussion, elaborate these points. 'This shows that…'.

> This point is not explicitly linked to the question. Make it clear to the examiner why you are making each point.

> Good development of the point, increasing its effectiveness.

> A good point (it could be explained a little more and might have flowed a little better after Quinton et al.'s research).

> A good comment to build on, which is focused on discussing the 'extent'. This is the kind of comment that should be present with earlier points to help make sure the answer fully engages with the question asked.

> Attempts to discuss the issue throughout the essay rather than just leaving it until the end.

Examiner's comments

Ciaran demonstrates a good knowledge of the topic, with only minor omissions, and is able to draw on a number of studies. The answer is mostly clear and organised. The AO1 is generally well detailed but needs to be related back to the question more and focused on the extent to which early attachment influences later relationships. The discussion needs the same focus as it lacks effectiveness without it.
Level 3 essay: this answer is likely to get 10 marks out of 16.

Psychopathology

CONTENTS OF CHAPTER

SPECIFICATION CHECKLIST

- Definitions of abnormality, including deviation from social norms, failure to function adequately, statistical infrequency and deviation from ideal mental health.

- The behavioural, emotional and cognitive characteristics of phobias, depression and obsessive-compulsive disorder (OCD).

- The behavioural approach to explaining and treating phobias: the two-process model, including classical and operant conditioning; systematic desensitisation, including relaxation and use of hierarchy; flooding.

- The cognitive approach to explaining and treating depression: Beck's negative triad and Ellis' ABC model; cognitive behaviour therapy (CBT), including challenging irrational thoughts.

- The biological approach to explaining and treating OCD: genetic and neural explanations; drug therapy.

TRY THIS

Who needs treatment?
Make two copies of the table on the right.

In table 1, think about each individual case below and consider, on a scale of 1 to 5, is this person's behaviour abnormal?

In table 2, think about each individual case below and consider, on a scale of 1 to 5, does this person need treatment for his/her problems?

Finally, consider: why do we need to decide what is abnormal?

Case history	1	2	3	4	5
A					
B					
C					
D					
E					
F					
G					
H					
I					
J					
K					
L					

1 = strongly agree
2 = moderately agree
3 = neither agree nor disagree
4 = moderately disagree
5 = strongly disagree

Case histories

A. Mr Smith has always lived in an isolated cottage. He has six dogs which he looks after. He never goes out of the cottage unless absolutely necessary, and has no friends or visitors.

B. Mrs Patel is intensely afraid of heights. She has left a job because it was on the fifth floor, and refuses to visit her daughter who lives in Austria because of the mountains.

C. Mrs Jarvis, who was born in Jamaica, is a follower of the Pentecostal Church and believes that on occasions she is possessed by spirits which make her 'speak in tongues'.

D. Mr Jones was arrested for shoplifting two weeks ago. He blamed the tablets (Valium) that he has been taking for the last five years but had recently discontinued.

E. Mr Khan is a successful executive who has just been told by his GP that he has high blood pressure.

F. Ben is a street musician who recently dropped out of art school. He likes to 'perform' using a variety of vegetables and dead fish!

G. Mrs Lee is a housewife who spends nearly every day at home keeping the house 'spick and span'. Her husband returned home from night work early one night last week and found her dusting at 2 am.

H. Nadia is 22 years old and a dancer. Although she weighs only six stone she is continually dieting.

I. Bob is a loner who keeps himself to himself because he believes that the Social Security snoopers are out to kill him. Although unemployed, he refuses to seek any welfare benefits.

J. Sue is a six-year-old girl who is extremely shy and seldom speaks. She becomes very upset if her parents alter her playroom furniture.

K. Joe is nine years old and wets the bed about five times a week. His parents' marriage broke up when he was five.

Definitions of abnormality

Psychopathology is the scientific study of psychological disorders ('pathology' is the study of disease). In the case of physical disorders, doctors identify certain signs and symptoms to determine when someone is ill. In the case of psychological disorders, the issue is how do we identify when someone is 'ill' – in what way does their behaviour differ from what is normal, i.e. is it abnormal?

All of you probably have some idea about what constitutes abnormality, regardless of whether or not you could put this clearly into words. This may be acceptable among non-experts, but such unstated definitions would not be acceptable among health professionals. If definitions remain unstated, it means that they cannot be challenged, that alternative explanations are ignored, and that we don't develop our scientific understanding of abnormal behaviour.

As will become evident, no single definition is adequate on its own, although each captures some aspect of what we might expect from a true definition of the term. Consequently, abnormality is usually determined by the presence of several of the characteristics we discuss on this spread and the following spread.

KEY TERMS

Cultural relativism The view that behaviour cannot be judged properly unless it is viewed in the context of the culture in which it originates.

Deviation from social norms Abnormal behaviour is seen as a deviation from unstated rules about how one 'ought' to behave. Anything that violates these rules is considered abnormal.

DSM (*Diagnostic and Statistical Manual of Mental Disorders*) A list of mental disorders that is used to diagnose mental disorders. For each disorder a list of clinical characteristics is given, i.e. the symptoms that should be looked for.

Statistical infrequency Abnormality is defined as those behaviours that are extremely rare, i.e. any behaviour that is found in very few people is regarded as abnormal.

Research methods

The graph below shows the number of births per annum in England and Wales by age of mother. The red line on the graph indicates a normal distribution. In a normal distribution, most people (the 'normals') are in the central group, clustered around the mean, and fewer people (the 'abnormals') are at either extreme.

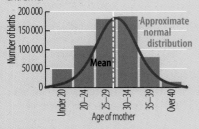

1. The graph is actually not quite a normal distribution. There are more people to the left of the mean. Is this a positive or negative skew? (2 marks)
2. Identify the modal age group in the graph above. (1 mark)
3. Do you think the mean would be a smaller or larger number than this modal group? (1 mark)
4. In the text we describe collecting data about fear of dogs. Explain why it would be preferable to use a rating scale of 1 to 10 rather than 1 to 5. (2 marks)
5. A researcher asked 100 people to rate their fear of dogs on a rating scale of 1 to 10. She found the data was normally distributed. Sketch a graph to show what the frequency distribution is likely to look like. Carefully label your graph. (3 marks)

LINK TO RESEARCH METHODS

Distributions on page 215
Descriptive statistics on page 212
Graphs on page 214

STATISTICAL INFREQUENCY

Probably the most obvious way to define abnormality is in terms of **statistical infrequency**. You are no doubt familiar with the idea of mean, median and mode – these are descriptive *statistics*. They are used as a way to represent the *typical* value in any set of data.

We define many aspects of what is normal by referring to typical values. Statistics inform us about things such as what age is most typical for women (and men) to have their first baby, the average shoe size for 10-year-old children, how many people read daily newspapers and which papers they read, and so on.

If we can define what is most common or normal, then we also have an idea of what is not common, i.e. abnormal. For example, it is not the norm (i.e. it is abnormal) to have your first baby when you are over 40 or under 20, as you can see from the graph on the left.

Example

Consider a characteristic such as fear of dogs. You can ask everyone in your class to say how fearful they are of dogs on a rating scale of 1 to 10 where 1 is no fear at all and 10 is panic. We would expect most people to give us a figure of 4, 5, 6 or 7 – their ratings would cluster around the middle. There would be a few people either end of the scale. The frequency distribution should look something like the graph on the left – approximately a normal distribution. The abnormal ratings are those at either end because they are not the 'norm'.

DEVIATION FROM SOCIAL NORMS

In our first definition we referred to *statistical* norms; we now turn to *social* norms. These norms are created by a group of people and thus are 'social'. In any society there are standards of acceptable behaviour that are set by the social group, and adhered to by those socialised into that group. Anyone who behaves differently ('deviates') from these socially created norms is classed as abnormal, i.e. **deviation from social norms**.

These standards are often in place for good reasons. An example of a social norm is politeness. Politeness oils the wheels of interpersonal relations. People who are rude or surly are considered to be behaving in a socially deviant way because others find it difficult to interact with them.

Some rules about unacceptable behaviour are implicit whereas others are policed by laws. For example, not laughing at a funeral is an implicit social rule whereas causing a disorder in public is both a deviation from social norms and against the law.

Example

In the past, homosexuality was classified as abnormal and regarded as a mental disorder. It was also against the law in the UK (but not nowadays). This judgement was based on social deviation – it was a judgement made by society at that time. Other forms of sexual behaviour continue to be classified as abnormal, such as paedophilia and voyeurism. The reason that such behaviours are judged as abnormal is because they deviate from social norms of what is acceptable.

EVALUATION OF STATISTICAL INFREQUENCY

Some abnormal behaviours are desirable

The main issue is that there are many abnormal behaviours that are actually quite desirable.

For example, very few people have an IQ over 150 but this abnormality is desirable not undesirable. Equally, there are some 'normal' behaviours that are undesirable. Experiencing depression, for example, is relatively common.

Therefore, using statistical infrequency to define abnormality means that we are unable to distinguish between desirable and undesirable behaviours.

The cut-off point is subjective

The fact that cut-off points are subjectively determined is a limitation.

If abnormality is defined in terms of statistical infrequency, we need to decide where to separate normality from abnormality. For example, one of the symptoms of depression is 'difficulty sleeping'. Some people might think abnormal sleep is less than 6 hours a night on average, others might think the cut-off should be 5 hours.

Such disagreements mean it is difficult to define abnormality in terms of statistical infrequency.

Statistical infrequency is sometimes appropriate

In some situations it is appropriate to use a statistical criterion to define abnormality.

For example, intellectual disability is defined in terms of the normal distribution using the concept of standard deviation to establish a cut-off point for abnormality. Any individual whose IQ is more than two standard deviations below the mean is judged as having a mental disorder – however, such a diagnosis is only made in conjunction with failure to function adequately.

This suggests that statistical infrequency is only one of a number of tools.

Ⓐ Level Cultural relativism

An issue is that behaviours that are statistically infrequent in one culture may be statistically more frequent in another.

For example, one of the symptoms of schizophrenia is claiming to hear voices. However, this is an experience that is common in some cultures.

What this means in practice is that there are no universal standards or rules for labelling a behaviour as abnormal.

EVALUATION OF DEVIATION FROM SOCIAL NORMS

Susceptible to abuse

What is socially acceptable now may not have been socially acceptable 50 years ago.

For example, today homosexuality is acceptable in most countries in the world, but in the past it was included under sexual and gender identity disorders in the DSM. Similarly, 50 years ago in Russia, anyone who disagreed with the state ran the risk of being regarded as insane and placed in a mental institution. In fact, Thomas Szasz (1974) claimed that the concept of mental illness was simply a way to exclude nonconformists from society.

Therefore, if we define abnormality in terms of deviation from social norms, there is a real danger of creating definitions based on prevailing social morals and attitudes.

Deviance is related to context and degree

Another limitation is that judgements on deviance are often related to the context of a behaviour.

For example, a person on a beach wearing next to nothing is regarded as normal, whereas the same outfit in the classroom or at a formal gathering would be regarded as abnormal and possibly an indication of a mental disorder. Shouting loudly and persistently is deviant behaviour but not evidence of mental disturbance unless it is excessive – and even then it might not be a mental disorder.

This means that social deviance on its own cannot offer a complete definition of abnormality, because it is inevitably related to both context and degree.

There are some strengths

On the positive side, this definition does distinguish between desirable and undesirable behaviour, a feature that was absent from the statistical infrequency model.

The social deviancy model also takes into account the effect that behaviour has on others. Deviance is defined in terms of transgression of social rules and (ideally) social rules are established in order to help people live together. According to this definition, abnormal behaviour is behaviour that damages others.

This definition, therefore, offers a practical and useful way of identifying undesirable and potentially damaging behaviour, which may alert others to the need to secure help for the person concerned.

Ⓐ Level Cultural relativism

Attempting to define abnormality in terms of social norms is obviously bound by culture because social norms are defined by the culture.

Classification systems, such as the **DSM**, are almost entirely based on the social norms of the dominant culture in the West (white and middle class), and yet the same criteria are applied to people from different subcultures living in the West. **Cultural relativism** is now acknowledged in the most recent revision to the DSM in 2013 (DSM-V), which makes reference to cultural contexts in many areas of diagnosis. For example, in the section on panic attacks a note is made that uncontrollable crying may be a symptom in some cultures, whereas difficulty breathing may be a primary symptom in other cultures.

This shows that it is possible to address this issue by including cultural differences in diagnostic systems.

▶ As touch, taste, sight, smell and hearing boarded the chartered flight to Havana, Professor Fitzherbert knew in his heart that he had lost more than good friends. In fact, he had finally lost his senses.

CAN YOU?   No. 4.1

1. Explain how statistical infrequency can be used to define abnormality. (3 marks)
2. Explain how deviation from social norms can be used to define abnormality. (3 marks)
3. Outline **one** limitation of defining abnormality in terms of statistical deviation. (3 marks)
4. Describe and evaluate **two** definitions of abnormality. (12 marks AS, 16 marks A)

On the previous spread we discussed two of the four definitions of abnormality identified in the specification. Both definitions discussed have serious limitations. To some extent these limitations can be overcome by using more than one definition. For example, in terms of intellectual disability a judgement of abnormality was based on statistical infrequency plus failure to function adequately (one of the definitions explored on this spread).

This means that, in the end, we are not looking at four separate definitions but at being able to define abnormality using elements from each of the four definitions.

KEY TERMS

Deviation from ideal mental health Abnormality is defined in terms of mental *health*, behaviours that are associated with competence and happiness. Ideal mental health would include a positive attitude towards the self, resistance to stress and an accurate perception of reality.

Failure to function adequately People are judged on their ability to go about daily life. If they can't do this and are also experiencing distress (or others are distressed by their behaviour) then it is considered a sign of abnormality.

MEET THE RESEARCHER

Marie Jahoda (1907–2001) was born in Vienna, Austria, to a Jewish family, and fled to the US at the start of the Second World War. She later settled in the UK and worked at the University of Sussex, where she developed the first department of social psychology in Britain. Throughout her career she focused on issues such as nationalism, antisemitism, and the impact of poverty and unemployment.

 APPLY YOUR KNOWLEDGE

Robert was an eight-year-old boy who had always been very reluctant to go to school. In the morning, he got up early and paced up and down, or sat in a corner occasionally rushing to the toilet to be sick. When it was time to go to school, he had to be pushed out of the house, though often his tears and complaints of feeling unwell led his mother to relent and allow him to stay at home. It didn't matter greatly as he was unlikely to get much out of school in the state he was in.

If Robert did go to school there was some solace in the fact that his mother would visit the school at playtime bringing milk and cookies. She came because that was part of the 'deal' about going to school, but also because she would otherwise worry about Robert.

Robert surprisingly got on quite well with the other children and was well liked, despite crying on the way to school and often acting like a baby. He was good at athletics and quite bright. He did not like being away from home for anything – he did not go to play at friends' houses. However, it wasn't just being away from home that caused the problem, Robert was simply terrified of school. (Oltmanns *et al.*, 1999)

Is Robert's behaviour normal or abnormal? How does it fit the definitions of abnormality on these two pages?

FAILURE TO FUNCTION ADEQUATELY

From an individual's point of view, abnormality can be judged in terms of not being able to cope with everyday living, i.e. a **failure to function adequately**. So the 'functioning' refers to just going about day-to-day life, such as eating regularly, washing clothes, getting up to go out to a job or some activity, being able to communicate with others, having some control over your life and so on.

Not functioning adequately causes distress and suffering for the individual, and/or may cause distress for others. It is important to include 'distress to others', because, in the case of some mental disorders, the individual may not be distressed at all. People with schizophrenia generally lack awareness that anything is wrong but their behaviour (hallucinations, believing that they are being persecuted) may well be distressing to others.

There may be situations where a person is not coping with everyday life in a 'normal' way – for example, a person may be content living in unwashed clothes and not having a regular job. If this doesn't cause distress to self or others then a judgement of abnormality is inappropriate.

Example

The DSM includes an assessment of ability to function called WHODAS (World Health Organization Disability Assessment; which is available online). This considers six areas: understanding and communicating, getting around, self-care, getting along with people, life activities and participation in society. Individuals rate each item on a scale of 1 to 5 and are given an overall score out of 180. Therefore an assessment of abnormality using the DSM would include a quantitative measure of functioning.

DEVIATION FROM IDEAL MENTAL HEALTH

Marie Jahoda (1958) pointed out that we define physical illness in part by looking at the *absence* of signs of physical health. Physical health is indicated by having correct body temperature, normal skin colour, normal blood pressure, etc., so the absence of these indicates illness. Jahoda suggested we should do the same for mental illness.

Jahoda conducted a review of what others had written about good mental health. These are the characteristics that enable an individual to feel happy (free of distress) and behave competently. She identified six categories that were commonly referred to:

- *Self-attitudes*: having high self-esteem and a strong sense of identity.
- *Personal growth* and self-actualisation: the extent to which an individual develops their full capabilities.
- *Integration*, such as being able to cope with stressful situations.
- *Autonomy*: being independent and self-regulating.
- Having an *accurate perception of reality*.
- *Mastery of the environment*: including the ability to love, function at work and in interpersonal relationships, adjust to new situations and solve problems.

This **deviation from ideal mental health** definition proposes that the *absence* of these criteria indicates abnormality, and potential mental disorder.

Note that there is some overlap between the criteria here and those for failure to function adequately – for example, in both definitions not being able to cope with stressful situations is a sign of abnormality.

EVALUATION OF FAILURE TO FUNCTION ADEQUATELY

Who judges?

Who is the person who decides if someone is failing to function adequately?

If a person is experiencing personal distress, for example is unable to get to work or eat regular meals, they may recognise that this is undesirable and may feel distressed and seek help. On the other hand, the individual may be quite content with the situation and/or simply unaware that they are not coping. It is others who are uncomfortable and judge the behaviour as abnormal. For example, some schizophrenics are potentially dangerous, as in the case of someone like Peter Sutcliffe, the Yorkshire Ripper.

▲ Peter Sutcliffe, a serial killer, known as the Yorkshire Ripper, who terrorised the women of Yorkshire and was arrested in 1983. Some mentally ill people like Sutcliffe might behave violently under the delusion that they are defending themselves or others from evil, i.e. functioning adequately.

Therefore, the limitation of this approach is that the judgement depends on who is making the decision, i.e. it is subjective.

The behaviour may be functional

Another limitation is that some apparently dysfunctional behaviour can actually be adaptive and functional for the individual.

For example, some mental disorders, such as eating disorders or depression, may lead to extra attention for the individual. Such attention is rewarding and thus quite functional rather than dysfunctional. For example, transvestitism is classed as a mental disorder but individuals are likely to regard it as perfectly functional.

This failure to distinguish between functional and dysfunctional behaviours means that this definition is incomplete.

Subjective experience recognised

On the positive side, this definition of abnormality does recognise the subjective experience of the patient.

It allows us to view mental disorder from the point of view of the person experiencing it. In addition, 'failure to function' is also relatively easy to judge objectively because we can list behaviours (can dress self, can prepare meals – as in WHODAS) and thus judge abnormality objectively.

This definition of abnormality therefore has a certain sensitivity and practicality.

Cultural relativism

An important issue is that failure to function adequately is limited by being culturally relative.

Definitions of adequate functioning are related to cultural ideas of how one's life should be lived. The 'failure to function' criterion is likely to result in different diagnoses when applied to people from different cultures, because the standard of one culture is being used to measure another. This may explain, for example, why lower-class and non-white patients (whose lifestyles differ from the dominant culture) are more often diagnosed with mental disorders.

This means that the use of this model is limited by its cultural relativism.

EVALUATION OF IDEAL MENTAL HEALTH

Unrealistic criteria

One of the major criticisms of this definition is that, according to ideal mental health criteria, most of us are abnormal!

Jahoda presented them as ideal criteria and they certainly are. We also have to ask how many need to be lacking before a person would be judged as abnormal. Furthermore, the criteria are quite difficult to measure. For example, how easy is it to assess capacity for personal growth or environmental mastery?

This means that this approach may be an interesting concept but not really useable when it comes to identifying abnormality.

Equates mental and physical health

Another limitation of this definition is that it tries to apply the principles of physical health to mental health.

In general, physical illnesses have physical causes such as a virus or bacterial infection, and as a result this makes them relatively easy to detect and diagnose. It is possible that some mental disorders also have physical causes (e.g. brain injury or drug abuse) but many do not. They are the consequence of life experiences.

Therefore, it is unlikely that we could diagnose mental abnormality in the same way that we can diagnose physical abnormality.

It is a positive approach

This definition focuses on the positives rather than the negatives.

It offers an alternative perspective on mental disorder that focuses on the 'ideal' – what is desirable rather than what is undesirable. Even though Jahoda's ideas were never really taken up by mental health professionals, the ideas have had some influence and are in accord with the 'positive psychology' movement (see the humanistic approach on page 136).

A strength of this approach, therefore, lies in its positive outlook and its influence on humanistic approaches.

Cultural relativism

Many of Jahoda's mental health criteria are culture-bound.

For example, the goal of self-actualisation (reaching one's full potential) is relevant to members of individualist cultures but not collectivist cultures where people promote the needs of the group not themselves. If we apply Jahoda's criteria to people from collectivist cultures or even non-middle-class social groups, we will most probably find a higher incidence of abnormality.

This limits the usefulness of this definition to certain cultural groups.

Insider tip…

Students often get confused between the four definitions and include characteristics of one definition when explaining a different one. To avoid this it is worth spending time understanding the similarities and differences between the four definitions, because you won't get credit in an exam question if your description is not specific to the definition named.

CAN YOU? No. 4.2

1. Explain how failure to function adequately can be used to define abnormality. (3 marks)
2. Two criteria for ideal mental health are high self-esteem and a strong sense of identity. Identify and describe **two** other criteria of ideal mental health. (3 marks + 3 marks)
3. Outline **two** limitations of the ideal mental health definition of abnormality. (4 marks)
4. Describe and evaluate **two or more** definitions of abnormality. (12 marks AS, 16 marks A)

Mental disorders

The current edition of DSM (DSM-V) was published in 2013 and lists about 300 mental disorders. The first edition of this manual, DSM-I, was published in 1952 with 106 disorders. There is an alternative diagnostic system, ICD (*International Statistical Classification of Diseases and Related Health Problems*), dating back to the nineteenth century. This is about to be published in its eleventh edition. Psychiatrists in the UK use ICD.

Three of the most common mental disorders are **phobias**, **depression** and **obsessive-compulsive disorder (OCD)**. Your study of psychopathology focuses on these three disorders, looking at explanations of them and treatments for them. We begin by looking at the key features of each disorder in terms of behavioural, emotional and cognitive characteristics.

Statistics

According to the mental health charity Mind (www.mind.org.uk), one in four people in the UK experience a mental health problem each year. In 2009, the following rates were reported in the UK population:

- phobias 2.6%
- depression 2.6%
- OCD 1.3%.

This means that, in any group of 100 people, you would expect that about three would have a clinical phobia, about three of them would be experiencing clinical depression, one or two would have OCD and a further 18 would have some other mental disorder such as an eating disorder. The term 'clinical' means that it is a diagnosed condition, as distinct from a more casual use of the terms – all of us experience feelings of depression or phobia or even obsessions (for example avoiding the cracks in the pavement) but these are not *clinical* disorders. In a clinical disorder a condition will significantly affect a person's day-to-day life over an extended period of time.

PHOBIAS

Phobic disorders are included in diagnostic manuals (DSM and ICD) within the category of 'anxiety disorders', a group of mental disorders that share the primary symptom of extreme anxiety. Phobic disorders, or phobias, are instances of irrational fears that produce a conscious avoidance of the feared object or situation. This includes agoraphobia (fear of being trapped in a public place where escape is difficult), social phobia (anxiety related to social situations, such as talking to a group of people) and specific phobias (fears about specific objects, such as spiders or snakes, or specific situations, such as heights or the dark).

Emotional characteristics

The primary emotional characteristic of a phobia is fear that is marked and persistent, and is likely to be excessive and unreasonable. Coupled with fear are feelings of anxiety and panic. These emotions are cued by the presence or anticipation of a specific object or situation (e.g. spiders, flying, heights, seeing blood) and are out of proportion to the actual danger posed.

Behavioural characteristics

One obvious behavioural characteristic of phobias is avoidance. When a person with a phobia is faced with the object or situation that creates fear the immediate response is to try to avoid it. For example a person with a phobia of spiders avoids being near them; a person with a phobia about social situations avoids being in groups of people.

However, there is also the opposite behavioural response, which is to freeze or even faint. The stress response is often described as fight or flight (see page 154) – but it is actually fight, flight or freeze. 'Freezing' is an adaptive response because a predator may think the prey is dead.

Avoidance in the feared situation interferes significantly with the person's normal routine, occupation, social activities or relationships, and there is marked distress about having the phobia. This distinguishes phobias from more everyday fears that do not interfere with normal day-to-day living.

Cognitive characteristics

Cognitive characteristics relate to thought processes. In the case of phobias, a defining characteristic is the irrational nature of the person's thinking and the resistance to rational arguments. For example, a person with a fear of flying is not helped by arguments that flying is actually the safest form of transport.

A further defining characteristic is that the person recognises that their fear is excessive or unreasonable, although this feature may be absent in children. This characteristic distinguishes between a phobia and a delusional mental illness (such as schizophrenia) where the individual is not aware of the unreasonableness of their behaviour.

DEPRESSION

Depression is classified as a mood disorder. DSM-V distinguishes between major depressive disorder and persistent depressive disorder which is longer term and/or recurring.

Emotional characteristics

A formal diagnosis of 'major depressive disorder' requires the presence of at least five symptoms and must include either sadness or loss of interest and pleasure in normal activities.

Sadness is the most common description people give of their depressed state, along with feeling empty. Associated with this, people may feel worthless, hopeless and/or experience low self-esteem – all negative emotions.

Loss of interest and pleasure in usual hobbies and activities is associated with feelings of despair and lack of control.

Anger is also associated with depression – anger directed towards others or turned inwards on the self. Depression may arise from feelings of being hurt and wishing to retaliate.

Behavioural characteristics

In most patients there is a shift in activity level – either reduced or increased. Many depressed individuals experience reduced energy, a sense of tiredness and a wish to sleep all of the time. However, some become increasingly agitated and restless, and may pace around a room, wring their hands or tear at their skin.

Sleep may be affected; some people sleep much more whereas others find it difficult to sleep and experience insomnia.

Appetite may also be affected; again there is a variation in this where some people have a reduced appetite whereas others eat considerably more than usual.

Cognitive characteristics

The negative emotions related to depression are associated with negative *thoughts*, such as a negative self-concept (negative self-beliefs) as well as guilt, a sense of worthlessness and so on.

Depressed people often have a negative view of the world and expect things to turn out badly rather than well. In fact, as you will discover later in this chapter, this is one of the explanations for depression – people have negative expectations about their lives and relationships and the world generally. Such expectations can be self-fulfilling; for example, if you believe that you are going to fail an exam, that belief may reduce the effort you make and/or increase your anxiety and thus you will fail, confirming your negative self-beliefs.

In general such negative thoughts are irrational; i.e. they do not accurately reflect reality.

Depression A mood disorder where an individual feels sad and/or lacks interest in their usual activities. Further characteristics include irrational negative thoughts, raised or lowered activity levels and difficulties with concentration, sleep and eating.

Obsessive-compulsive disorder (OCD) An anxiety disorder where anxiety arises from both obsessions (persistent thoughts) and compulsions (behaviours that are repeated over and over again). Compulsions are a response to obsessions and the person believes the compulsions will reduce anxiety.

Phobias A group of mental disorders characterised by high levels of anxiety in response to a particular stimulus or group of stimuli. The anxiety interferes with normal living.

OCD

Obsessive-compulsive disorder (OCD) is also classed as an anxiety disorder. The disorder typically begins in young adult life and has two main components – obsessions and compulsions. Obsessions are persistent *thoughts* and compulsions are repetitive *behaviours*.

Emotional characteristics

Both the obsessions and compulsions are a source of considerable anxiety and distress.

Sufferers are aware that their behaviour is excessive and this causes feelings of embarrassment and shame.

A common obsession concerns germs which gives rise to feelings of disgust.

Cognitive characteristics

Obsessions are recurrent, intrusive thoughts or impulses that are perceived as inappropriate or forbidden. They may be frightening and/or embarrassing so that the person doesn't want to share them with others.

Common obsessional themes include ideas (e.g. that germs are everywhere), doubts (e.g. the worry that something important has been overlooked), impulses (e.g. to shout out obscenities) or images (e.g. fleeting sexual images).

These thoughts, impulses or images are not simply excessive worries about everyday problems. They are seen as uncontrollable, which creates anxiety. The person recognises that the obsessional thoughts or impulses are a product of their own mind (rather than thoughts inserted by someone else as is typical of schizophrenia).

At some point during the course of the disorder, the person does recognise that the obsessions or compulsions are excessive or unreasonable.

Behavioural characteristics

Compulsive behaviours are performed to reduce the anxiety created by obsessions. They are repetitive and unconcealed, such as hand washing or checking. They may be mental acts such as praying or counting.

Patients feel they must perform these actions, i.e. they are compelled to perform these actions otherwise something dreadful might happen. This creates anxiety.

The behaviours are not connected in a realistic way with what they are designed to neutralise or prevent and are clearly excessive. Some patients only experience compulsive behaviours with no particular obsessions, for example, they compulsively avoid certain objects..

▲ One OCD patient described his experience of OCD as being like living in an Escher print – you just go round and round. 'You've just parked the car. You hop out, grab your bag, and head towards the gym. But wait. Did you lock the car? You head back to make sure you did. Yup, it's locked, problem solved.' But a person with OCD doesn't stop there. 'I went and checked the car, but did I really check it? I'm looking at my hand turning the key in the lock, but is that perception really clear enough? Did I hear the click, or do I just remember hearing the click, or did I hear the click last time I checked this?' (Katz, 2008).

🔍 Research methods

Research into mental disorder often involves case studies. For example:

Jane is 18 years old. A few months ago she started to feel lonely a lot of the time and reported that she often found herself sobbing for no reason at all. Her parents are going through a divorce and she says that life at home is just awful. She can't get enthusiastic about anything and even going shopping feels overwhelming. Her friends describe her as 'outgoing' and 'bubbly' but she doesn't feel like that now and finds it difficult to even go out with her friends. She has no energy and no interest in anything.

1. The data in this case study was collected using a questionnaire, asking Jane to describe her current feelings, what her friends thought of her and so on. What are the strengths of using a questionnaire rather than an interview to collect this information? (3 marks)

2. The questions used were all open questions. Explain why open questions are likely to produce qualitative data. (2 marks)

3. Identify **two** ethical issues that would be important when conducting a case study and explain how the researcher might have dealt with these issues. (3 marks + 3 marks)

LINK TO RESEARCH METHODS

Self-report on pages 202–203
Qualitative data on page 216
Ethical issues on page 194–195

CAN YOU? No. 4.3

1. Outline the behavioural characteristics of phobias. (3 marks)
2. Outline the emotional characteristics of depression. (3 marks)
3. Identify **one** behavioural and **one** cognitive characteristic of OCD. (2 marks)
4. Outline the emotional characteristics of phobias and OCD. (4 marks)

The behavioural approach to explaining phobias

The behavioural approach in general is explained (and evaluated) on pages 126–129. In essence the approach suggests that all behaviour is *learned*, as distinct from being inherited. For that reason it is sometimes called *learning* theory. Behaviourists use the word 'conditioning' to mean 'learning', so something that is unconditioned is unlearned and something that is conditioned has been learned.

On this spread we apply behaviourist principles to understanding how people develop phobias. The focus is on the two-process model but a brief mention is also made of social learning of phobias, another learning theory explanation.

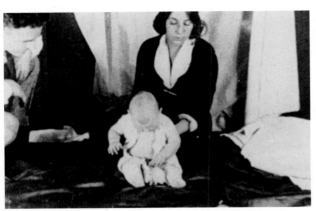

▲ Conditioning fear in Little Albert, a clip from the filmed study.

Little Albert

John B. Watson is known as the father of behaviourism. Together with Rosalie Rayner (1920) he conducted one of the classic studies in psychology. They sought to demonstrate that emotional responses could be learned through classical conditioning. Their 'subject' was an 11-month-old boy called 'Little Albert'. At the beginning of the study Little Albert showed no fear response to white furry objects: a white rat, a white rabbit and white cotton wool, i.e. they were neutral stimuli.

Watson and Rayner created a conditioned response to these previously neutral objects. To do this they used a steel bar that was four feet long. When Albert reached out for the rat they struck the bar with a hammer behind Albert's head to startle him. They repeated this three times, and did the same a week later. After this, when they showed Albert the furry rat and other furry white objects, he began to cry. They had conditioned a fear response to furry white objects in Little Albert.

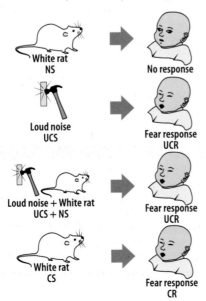

White rat
NS → No response

Loud noise
UCS → Fear response
UCR

Loud noise + White rat
UCS + NS → Fear response
UCR

White rat
CS → Fear response
CR

THE TWO-PROCESS MODEL

Orval Hobart Mowrer (1947) proposed the **two-process model** to explain how phobias are learned. The first stage is **classical conditioning** and then, in a second stage, **operant conditioning** occurs. Both processes are needed to explain why phobias begin in the first place and then also continue.

Classical conditioning: initiation

A phobia is acquired through association – the association between a neutral stimulus (NS), such as a white furry rat, and a loud noise results in a new stimulus response being learned, as demonstrated by Little Albert (see left).

In this case the original unconditioned stimulus (UCS) was a loud noise, and the original unconditioned response (UCR) was fear. By pairing the loud noise with the furry object, the furry object acquired the same properties as the UCS and produced the response of fear, now called a conditioned response (CR) because this is a learned response. The furry object is now a conditioned stimulus (CS). When Albert saw a white furry rat he cried, presumably because the object was now associated with fear.

The same process can explain, for example, why someone develops a fear of dogs after being bitten:
- Being bitten (UCS) creates fear (UCR).
- Dog (NS) associated with being bitten (UCS).
- Dog (now CS) produces fear response (now CR).

The same steps can explain how a person might develop a fear of social situations after having a panic attack in such a situation.

Little Albert's phobia generalised to other furry white objects. Little Albert showed anxiety when exposed to a non-white rabbit, a fur coat and Watson wearing a Santa Claus beard.

Operant conditioning: maintenance

Through classical conditioning a phobia is acquired. However, this does not explain why individuals continue to feel fearful, nor does it explain why individuals *avoid* the feared object.

The next step involves operant conditioning – the likelihood of a behaviour being repeated is increased if the outcome is rewarding. In the case of a phobia, the avoidance of (or escape from) the phobic stimulus reduces fear and is thus reinforcing. This is an example of negative reinforcement (escaping from an unpleasant situation). The individual avoids the anxiety created by, for example, the dog or social situation by avoiding them entirely.

Social learning

Social learning theory is not part of the two-process model but it is a neo-behaviourist explanation, i.e. the fear seems reduced.

Phobias may also be acquired through modelling the behaviour of others. For example, seeing a parent respond to a spider with extreme fear may lead a child to acquire a similar behaviour because the behaviour appears rewarding, i.e. the fearful person gets attention.

EVALUATION/DISCUSSION

The importance of classical conditioning

The two-process model is supported by research asking people about their phobias.

People with phobias often do recall a specific incident when their phobia appeared, for example being bitten by a dog or experiencing a panic attack in a social situation (Sue *et al.*, 1994). However, not everyone who has a phobia can recall such an incident. It is possible that such traumatic incidents did happen, but have since been forgotten (Öst, 1987). Sue *et al.* suggest that different phobias may be the result of different processes. For example, agoraphobics were most likely to explain their disorder in terms of a specific incident, whereas arachnophobics (people who are scared of spiders) were most likely to cite modelling as the cause.

This demonstrates the role of classical conditioning in developing phobias, but other processes may be involved in their maintenance.

Incomplete explanation

If a neutral stimulus becomes associated with a fearful experience the result should be a phobia, but this doesn't always happen.

Research has found, for example, that not everyone who is bitten by a dog develops a phobia of dogs (Di Nardo *et al.*, 1988). This could be explained by the diathesis-stress model. This proposes that we inherit a genetic vulnerability for developing mental disorders. However, a disorder will only manifest itself if triggered by a life event, such as being bitten by a dog.

This suggests that a dog bite would only lead to a phobia in those people with such a vulnerability. Therefore, the behavioural explanation is incomplete on its own.

Support for social learning

An experiment by Bandura and Rosenthal (1966) supported the social learning explanation.

In the experiment a model acted as if he was in pain every time a buzzer sounded. Later on, those participants who had observed this showed an emotional reaction to the buzzer, demonstrating an acquired 'fear' response.

This demonstrates that modelling the behaviour of others can lead to the acquisition of phobias.

Biological preparedness

The fact that phobias do not always develop after a traumatic incident may be explained in terms of biological preparedness.

Martin Seligman (1970) argued that animals, including humans, are genetically programmed to rapidly learn an association between potentially life-threatening stimuli and fear. These stimuli are referred to as ancient fears – things that would have been dangerous in our evolutionary past (such as snakes, heights, strangers). It would have been adaptive to rapidly learn to avoid such stimuli. This would explain why people are much less likely to develop fears of modern objects such as toasters and cars that are much more of a threat than spiders. Such items were not a danger in our evolutionary past.

This suggests that the behavioural approach cannot explain all phobias.

The two-process model ignores cognitive factors

Another limitation of the two-process model is that there are cognitive aspects to phobias that cannot be explained in a traditionally behaviourist framework.

An alternative explanation is the cognitive approach, which proposes that phobias may develop as the consequence of irrational thinking. For example, a person in a lift may think: 'I could become trapped in here and suffocate' (an irrational thought). Such thoughts create extreme anxiety and may trigger a phobia.

The value of this alternative explanation is that it leads to cognitive therapies such as CBT (described on page 110) that may, in some situations, be more successful than behaviourist treatments (described on the next page). For example, social phobia responds better to CBT (Engels et al., 1993).

KEY TERMS

Classical conditioning Learning through association. A neutral stimulus is consistently paired with an unconditioned stimulus so that it eventually takes on the properties of this stimulus and is able to produce a conditioned response.

Operant conditioning Learning through reinforcement or punishment. If a behaviour is followed by a desirable consequence then that behaviour is more likely to occur again in the future.

Two-process model A theory that explains the two processes that lead to the development of phobias – they begin through classical conditioning and are maintained through operant conditioning.

 UPGRADE

To produce a Grade A answer to an essay question you need to be 'selective'. Deciding what material to include or leave out relies on knowing what is important and what is less important for any given question. This can be based on the marks available or it could be linked to the content of the question itself.

If we use the essay below (question 4 in the 'Can you?' box) as an example, an important point when choosing the AO1 material for your answer is that you avoid writing lengthy descriptions of classical and operant conditioning. These are only relevant when being applied to phobias. Description of Skinner and Pavlov would not be useful.

Focus on the basic principles of the two-process model on the facing page. This information can be used as the basis for the descriptive component of your answer. However, don't try to memorise this. Instead, select the key words for each component and write these down on a prompt card. Close your book and try to recreate your answer using just your key words. Time yourself – the descriptive part of a 12 mark question should take up 6–8 minutes. Keep doing this until you feel confident that you can remember the material and reproduce it in the exam.

Insider tip...

In an exam question on phobias you must avoid a general description of the behavioural approach – your answer must be related specifically to phobias.

CAN YOU? No. 4.4

1. Outline the two-process model as an explanation of phobias. (4 marks)
2. Explain how classical conditioning can be used to explain the development of phobias. (3 marks)
3. Give **one** criticism of the two-process model. (3 marks)
4. Describe and evaluate the behavioural approach to explaining phobias. (12 marks AS, 16 marks A)

The behavioural approach to treating phobias

The two therapies discussed on this spread, **systematic desensitisation** and **flooding**, involve counterconditioning, whereby a fear response to an object or situation is replaced with a relaxation response. This is a form of classical conditioning.

The conditioning is achieved either through a slow process of gradual exposure or one single intense exposure. The treatment is complete when the patient can relax in the presence of their most feared stimulus.

FLOODING

This is an alternative method that is used to treat phobias. Instead of introducing the phobic object in a gradual progression using a hierarchy (as in systematic desensitisation), the person with a phobia is immersed in the experience in one long session, experiencing their phobia at its worst. The session continues until the patient's anxiety has disappeared.

For example, a person who is afraid of clowns is placed in a room full of clowns, or a person who is afraid of spiders has to sit with a large hairy spider on their hand. The person with the phobia remains in position until they have become calm.

The procedure can be conducted *in vivo* (actual exposure) or virtual reality can be used.

Rationale

A person's fear response (and the release of adrenaline underlying this) has a time limit. As adrenaline levels naturally decrease, a new stimulus–response link can be learned – the feared stimulus is now associated with a non-anxious response.

KEY TERMS

Flooding A form of behavioural therapy used to treat phobias and other anxiety disorders. A client is exposed to (or imagines) an extreme form of the threatening situation under relaxed conditions until the anxiety reaction is extinguished.

Systematic desensitisation A form of behavioural therapy used to treat phobias and other anxiety disorders. A client is gradually exposed to (or imagines) the threatening situation under relaxed conditions until the anxiety reaction is extinguished.

SYSTEMATIC DESENSITISATION (SD)

One of the reasons that phobias may persist is that phobics avoid the phobic stimulus and therefore there is no opportunity to learn that their feared stimulus is not so fearful after all. Joseph Wolpe (1958) developed a technique where phobics were introduced to the feared stimulus gradually.

Counterconditioning

The basis of the therapy is counterconditioning because the patient is taught a new association that runs *counter* to the original association. The patient is taught, through classical conditioning, to associate the phobic stimulus with a new response, i.e. relaxation instead of fear. In this way their anxiety (related to sensitivity) is reduced – they are desensitised.

Wolpe also called this 'reciprocal inhibition' because the response of relaxation inhibits the response of anxiety.

Relaxation

The first thing that the therapist does is teach the patient relaxation techniques. Relaxation can be achieved by the patient focusing on their breathing and taking slow, deep breaths. When we are anxious we breathe quickly, so slowing this down helps us to relax. Being mindful of 'here and now' can help, as well as focusing on a particular object or visualising a peaceful scene. Progressive muscle relaxation is also used where one muscle at a time is relaxed.

Desensitisation hierarchy

SD works by gradually introducing the person to the feared situation one step at a time so it is not as overwhelming. At each stage the patient practises relaxation so the situation becomes more familiar, less overwhelming and their anxiety diminishes.

The diagram below shows how the therapy proceeds through gradual steps that are determined at the beginning of therapy when the patient and therapist work out a hierarchy from least to most fearful stimuli.

HOW DOES IT WORK?

▼ Problem: patient is terrified whenever she sees a spider.

▼ Result: after SD, patient has overcome her fear of spiders and feels relaxed in their presence.

Systematic desensitisation

Step 1: Patient is taught how to relax their muscles completely. (A relaxed state is incompatible with anxiety.)

Step 2: Therapist and patient together construct a desensitisation hierarchy – a series of imagined scenes, each one causing a little more anxiety than the previous one.

Step 3: Patient gradually works his/her way through desensitisation hierarchy, visualising each anxiety-evoking event while engaging in the competing relaxation response.

Step 4: Once the patient has mastered one step in the hierarchy (i.e. they can remain relaxed while imagining it), they are ready to move onto the next.

Step 5: Patient eventually masters the feared situation that caused them to seek help in the first place.

Flooding

Step 1: Patient is taught how to relax their muscles completely.

Step 2: Patient masters the feared situation that caused them to seek help in the first place. This is accomplished in one long session.

EVALUATION OF SD

Effectiveness

Research has found that SD is successful for a range of phobias.

For example, McGrath *et al.* (1990) reported that about 75% of patients with phobias respond to SD. The key to success appears to lie with actual contact with the feared stimulus, so *in vivo* techniques are more successful than ones just using pictures or imagining the feared stimulus (*in vitro*) (Choy *et al.*, 2007). Often a number of different exposure techniques are involved – *in vivo*, *in vitro* and also modelling, where the patient watches someone else who is coping well with the feared stimulus (Comer, 2002).

This demonstrates the effectiveness of SD, but also the value of using a range of different exposure techniques.

Not appropriate for all phobias

SD may not be effective against all phobias.

Öhman *et al.* (1975) suggest that SD may not be as effective in treating phobias that have an underlying evolutionary survival component (e.g. fear of the dark, fear of heights or fear of dangerous animals), than in treating phobias which have been acquired as a result of personal experience.

This suggests that SD can only be used effectively in tackling some phobias.

EVALUATION OF FLOODING

Effectiveness

Flooding can be an effective treatment for those who stick with it and it is relatively quick (compared to CBT).

For example, Choy *et al.* (see above) reported that both SD and flooding were effective but flooding was the more effective of the two at treating phobias. On the other hand, another review (Craske *et al.*, 2008) concluded that SD and flooding were equally effective in the treatment of phobias.

This shows that flooding is an effective therapy, albeit just one of several options.

Individual differences

Flooding is not for every patient (or indeed for every therapist).

It can be a highly traumatic procedure. Patients are obviously made aware of this beforehand but, even then, they may quit during the treatment, which reduces the ultimate effectiveness of the therapy for some people.

Individual differences in responding to flooding therefore limit the effectiveness of the therapy.

EVALUATION OF BEHAVIOURAL THERAPIES IN GENERAL

Strengths of behavioural therapies

Behavioural therapies for dealing with phobias are generally relatively faster, cheaper and require less effort on the patient's part than other psychotherapies.

For example, CBT (discussed on page 110) requires a willingness for people to think deeply about their mental problems, which is not true for behavioural therapies. This lack of 'thinking' means that the technique is also useful for people who lack insight into their motivations or emotions, such as children or patients with learning difficulties. A further strength of behavioural therapy is that it can be self-administered – a method that has proved successful with, for example, social phobia (Humphrey, 1973).

These benefits were confirmed in the study described in 'Research methods' (below), which also found that self-administered therapy was as effective as therapist-guided therapy.

Relaxation may not be necessary

It may be that the success of both SD and flooding is more to do with exposure to the feared situation than relaxation.

It might also be that the expectation of being able to cope with the feared stimulus is most important. For example, Klein *et al.* (1983) compared SD with supportive psychotherapy for patients with either social or specific phobias. They found no difference in effectiveness, suggesting that the 'active ingredient' in SD or flooding may simply be the generation of hopeful expectancies that the phobia can be overcome.

This suggests that cognitive factors are more important than the behavioural approach generally acknowledges.

Symptom substitution

Behavioural therapies may not work with certain phobias because the symptoms are only the tip of the iceberg.

If the symptoms are removed the cause still remains, and the symptoms will simply resurface, possibly in another form (known as symptom substitution). For example, according to the psychodynamic approach phobias develop because of projection. Freud (1909) recorded the case of Little Hans who developed a phobia of horses. The boy's actual problem was an intense envy of his father, but he could not express this directly and his anxiety was projected onto the horse. The phobia was cured when he accepted his feelings about his father.

This demonstrates the importance of treating the underlying causes of a phobia rather than just the symptoms.

Research methods

The randomised control trial (RCT) is the gold standard for clinical research (and progressively other areas of research). In an RCT individuals are randomly allocated to receive one of the treatments under study. This is important in order to eliminate confounding variables – for example certain personality variables might vary systematically with the choice of treatment.

In one such study Tarik Al-Kubaisy and colleagues (1992) recruited 99 phobic patients who were allocated to one of three treatment groups:

Group 1: systematic desensitisation working with a therapist.
Group 2: self-administered systematic desensitisation.
Group 3: relaxation only, self-administered.

The study found that relaxation on its own was least effective but the other groups fared equally well, suggesting that there is little benefit from having guided therapy.

1. Explain how they might have randomly allocated participants to conditions. (2 marks)
2. The dependent variable was improvement. Suggest **one** way this might have been operationalised. (2 marks)
3. Explain the difference between confounding variables and extraneous variables. (2 marks)
4. Personality variables might act as a confounding variable. Explain why. (2 marks)
5. Identify a possible extraneous variable in this study. (1 mark)

LINK TO RESEARCH METHODS

Operationalisation on page 178
Confounding and extraneous variables on page 180

CAN YOU?   No. 4.5

1. Outline how systematic desensitisation is used in the treatment of phobias. (6 marks)
2. Outline how flooding is used in the treatment of phobias. (6 marks)
3. Explain **one** strength of flooding as compared to systematic desensitisation in the treatment of phobias.
4. Describe and evaluate the behavioural approach to the treatment of phobias. (12 marks AS, 16 marks A)

The cognitive approach to explaining depression

The cognitive approach in general is explained (and evaluated) on pages 130–131. The emphasis of the cognitive approach is on how thinking shapes our behaviour – quite the opposite of the behavioural approach where the concept of the mind is banished from any explanations.

In terms of understanding abnormality, cognitive psychologists are most concerned with how *irrational* thinking leads to a mental disorder. Since depression is very much characterised by negative irrational thinking, cognitive explanations are particularly appropriate.

There are two examples of the cognitive approach to explaining depression, both developed by Americans in the 1960s at the beginning of the cognitive revolution in psychology.

MEET THE RESEARCHERs

Albert Ellis (1913–2007) held open audiences demonstrating his ABC approach until his death at the age of 93 in 2007. Every Friday night there were lively sessions with audience volunteers at the Albert Ellis Institute in New York for only $5.00, including coffee and cookies!

Like many psychologists, Ellis became interested in an area of behaviour that was personally challenging. His own experiences of unhappiness (for example his parents divorced when he was 12) led him to develop ways to help others. Initially he trained as a psychoanalyst, but gradually became disillusioned with the Freudian approach and developed his own methods.

Aaron Beck (1921–) also trained as a psychoanalyst but found, through his research with depressed clients, that psychodynamic explanations were inadequate and that he could better explain his clients' experiences in terms of negative thoughts. This led to his being one of the first to develop a cognitive therapy. He now runs the Beck Institute for Cognitive Therapy and Research in Philadelphia, USA, with his daughter, Dr Judith Beck.

KEY TERMS

ABC model A cognitive approach to understanding mental disorder, focusing on the effect of irrational beliefs on emotions.

Negative triad A cognitive approach to understanding depression, focusing on how negative expectations (schema) about the self, world and future lead to depression.

Schema A cognitive framework that helps organise and interpret information in the brain. A schema helps an individual to make sense of new information.

ELLIS' ABC MODEL (1962)

Albert Ellis proposed that the key to mental disorders such as depression lay in irrational beliefs. In his **ABC model**:

- **A** refers to an activating event (e.g. you get fired at work).
- **B** is the belief, which may be rational or irrational (e.g. 'The company was overstaffed' or 'I was sacked because they've always had it in for me').
- **C** is the consequence – rational beliefs lead to healthy emotions (e.g. acceptance) whereas irrational beliefs lead to unhealthy emotions (e.g. depression).

Musturbatory thinking

The source of irrational beliefs lies in musturbatory thinking – thinking that certain ideas or assumptions *must* be true in order for an individual to be happy. Ellis identified the three most important irrational beliefs.

- *I must* be approved of or accepted by people I find important.
- *I must* do well or very well, or I am worthless.
- The world *must* give me happiness, or I will die.

Other irrational assumptions include: 'others *must* treat me fairly and give me what I need' and 'people *must* live up to my expectations or it is terrible!'

An individual who holds such assumptions is bound to be, at the very least, disappointed; at worst, depressed. An individual who fails an exam becomes depressed not because they have failed the exam but because they hold an irrational belief regarding that failure (e.g. 'I must always do well so failing the exam means I am stupid'). Such 'musts' need to be challenged in order for mental healthiness to prevail.

BECK'S NEGATIVE TRIAD (1967)

Aaron Beck also developed a cognitive explanation for mental disorder but one that focused specifically on depression. Beck believed that depressed individuals feel as they do because their thinking is biased towards negative interpretations of the world and they lack a perceived sense of control.

Negative schema

Depressed people have acquired a negative **schema** during childhood – a tendency to adopt a negative view of the world. This may be caused by a variety of factors, including parental and/or peer rejection and criticisms by teachers. These negative schemas (e.g. expecting to fail) are activated whenever the person encounters a new situation (e.g. an exam) that resembles the original conditions in which these schemas were learned.

Negative schemas lead to systematic *cognitive biases* in thinking. For example, individuals over-generalise, drawing a sweeping conclusion regarding self-worth on the basis of one small piece of negative feedback.

The negative triad

Negative schemas and cognitive biases maintain what Beck calls the **negative triad**, a pessimistic and irrational view of three key elements in a person's belief system:

- The self; for example: 'I am just plain undesirable, what is there to like? I'm unattractive and seem to bore everyone.'
- The world (life experiences); for example: 'I can understand why people don't like me. They would all prefer someone else's company. Even my boyfriend left me.'
- The future; for example: 'I am always going to be on my own, there is nothing that is going to change this.'

▲ The negative triad.

EVALUATION/DISCUSSION

Support for the role of irrational thinking

The view that depression is linked to irrational thinking is supported by research.

Hammen and Krantz (1976) found that depressed participants made more errors in logic when asked to interpret written material than did non-depressed participants. Bates *et al.* (1999) found that depressed participants who were given negative automatic-thought statements became more and more depressed.

This research supports the view that negative thinking leads to depression, although this link does not mean that negative thoughts cause *depression. Instead, negative thinking may develop* because of *their depression.*

Blames the client rather than situational factors

The cognitive approach suggests that it is the client who is responsible for their disorder.

This placing of emphasis on the client is a good thing because it gives the client the power to change the way things are. (Note that the cognitive approach refers to a 'client' rather than a 'patient'.) However, this stance has limitations. It may lead the client or therapist to overlook situational factors, for example not considering how life events or family problems may have contributed to the mental disorder.

The strength of the cognitive approach therefore lies in its focus on the client's mind and recovery, but other aspects of the client's environment and life may also need to be considered.

Practical applications in therapy

One evaluation point for any theory is the consideration of whether it can be usefully applied.

The cognitive explanations presented here have both been applied to CBT, as you will see on the next spread. CBT is consistently found to be the best treatment for depression, especially when used in conjunction with drug treatments (e.g. Cuijpers *et al.*, 2013).

The usefulness of CBT as a therapy supports the effectiveness of the cognitive approach – if depression is alleviated by challenging irrational thinking, then this suggests such thoughts had a role in the depression in the first place.

Irrational beliefs may be realistic

A limitation of the cognitive approach is that not all irrational beliefs are 'irrational', they may simply *seem* irrational.

In fact, Alloy and Abramson (1979) suggest that depressive realists tend to see things for what they are (with normal people tending to view the world through rose-coloured glasses). They found that depressed people gave more accurate estimates of the likelihood of a disaster than 'normal' controls, and called this the *sadder but wiser* effect.

These doubts about whether irrational thinking really is irrational raise questions about the value of the cognitive approach.

Alternative explanations

The biological approach to understanding mental disorder suggests that genes and neurotransmitters may cause depression.

For example research supports the role of low levels of the neurotransmitter serotonin in depressed people and has also found that a gene related to this is 10 times more common in people with depression (Zhang *et al.*, 2005). The success of drug therapies for treating depression suggests that neurotransmitters do play an important role (see page 115). At the very least a diathesis-stress approach might be advisable, suggesting that individuals with a genetic vulnerability for depression are more prone to the effects of living in a negative environment, which then leads to negative irrational thinking.

The existence of alternative approaches and (effective) therapies suggest that depression can't be explained by the cognitive approach alone.

Insider tip…

If you do use an alternative explanation as evaluation it is important to avoid too much description. The key strategy is to consider the relative strengths and/or limitations of the alternative approach – only then is it worth AO3 marks.

APPLY YOUR KNOWLEDGE

Millie left school after her GCSEs and has lived at home with her parents ever since. She has had no luck getting a job and has now more or less given up looking as she is convinced that she must be unemployable. As if that weren't bad enough, one evening she overhears her parents arguing over money and her father storms out, slamming the door. She sits and cries in her room, telling herself that its all her fault because she isn't contributing. Her friends have all moved on, she has no job and no future and now this. Sometimes she wishes she could just disappear forever.

From your knowledge of Ellis' and Beck's views on depression, outline how each of these psychologists would explain the way that Mille is feeling.

▲ 'Beauty is in the eye of the beholder'. This sums up the cognitive approach – there is no 'reality', what matters is the way you think about reality.

CAN YOU?   No. 4.6

1. Outline Ellis' ABC model as an explanation for depression. (4 marks)
2. Outline Beck's negative triad as an explanation for depression. (4 marks)
3. Give **one** criticism of Ellis' ABC model as an explanation of depression. (3 marks)
4. Describe and evaluate the cognitive approach to explaining depression. (12 marks AS, 16 marks A)

The cognitive approach to treating depression

The explanations presented on the previous spread each form the basis for a form of psychotherapy generically referred to as **cognitive-behavioural therapy (CBT)**. CBT started life as cognitive therapy, based on the view that the way we feel is partly dependent on the way we *think* about events (i.e. cognition) and then treatment involves identifying this irrational thinking.

Cognitive therapy grew into cognitive-behavioural therapy because, once irrational cognitions are identified, coping strategies need to be developed (i.e. *behavioural* change).

On the previous spread we considered two cognitive approaches to explaining depression. Both Ellis and Beck developed a form of therapy based on their theoretical ideas. We will follow Ellis' version of CBT here.

KEY TERMS

Cognitive-behavioural therapy (CBT)
A combination of cognitive therapy (a way of changing maladaptive thoughts and beliefs) and behavioural therapy (a way of changing behaviour in response to these thoughts and beliefs).

Irrational thoughts Rational thinking is flexible and realistic, where beliefs are based on fact and logic. Irrational thinking is rigid and unrealistic and lacks internal consistency.

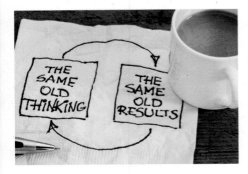

CAN YOU?   No. 4.7

1. Explain how cognitive-behavioural therapy is used in the treatment of depression. (4 marks)
2. Explain how challenging irrational thoughts can work as a treatment of depression. (3 marks)
3. Give **one** criticism of cognitive-behavioural therapy as a treatment of depression. (3 marks)
4. Describe and evaluate the cognitive approach to treating depression. (12 marks AS, 16 marks A)

COGNITIVE-BEHAVIOUR THERAPY (CBT)

In the 1950s, Albert Ellis was one of the first psychologists to develop a form of CBT. He first called it 'rational therapy' to emphasise the fact that, as he saw it, psychological problems occur as a result of **irrational thinking** – individuals frequently develop self-defeating habits because of faulty beliefs about themselves and the world around them. The aim of therapy is to turn these *irrational* thoughts into rational ones.

Ellis renamed his therapy 'rational *emotive* therapy' (RET) because the therapy focuses on resolving emotional problems, and, even later, he renamed it *rational emotional behaviour therapy* (REBT) because the therapy also resolves behavioural problems.

Challenging irrational thoughts

Ellis extended his ABC model (see previous spread) to ABCDEF where:
- **D** refers to **D**isputing irrational thoughts and beliefs.
- **E** stands for the **E**ffects of disputing and **E**ffective attitude to life.
- **F** is the new **F**eelings (emotions) that are produced.

The key issue to remember is that it is not the activating events that cause unproductive consequences – it is the beliefs that lead to the self-defeating consequences. REBT therefore focuses on challenging or disputing the irrational thoughts/beliefs and replacing them with effective, rational beliefs. For example:
- *Logical disputing* – self-defeating beliefs do not follow logically from the information available (e.g. 'Does thinking in this way make sense?').
- *Empirical disputing* – self-defeating beliefs may not be consistent with reality (e.g. 'Where is the proof that this belief is accurate?').
- *Pragmatic disputing* – emphasises the lack of usefulness of self-defeating beliefs (e.g. 'How is this belief likely to help me?').

Effective disputing changes self-defeating beliefs into more rational beliefs. The client can move from *catastrophising* ('No one will ever like me') to more rational interpretations of events ('My friend was probably thinking about something else and didn't even see me'). This in turn helps the client to feel better, and eventually become more self-accepting.

Homework

Clients are often asked to complete assignments between therapy sessions. This might include asking a person out on a date when they had been afraid to do so before for fear of rejection, looking for a new job, asking friends to tell them what they really think about the person and so on. Such homework is vital in testing irrational beliefs against reality and putting new rational beliefs into practice.

Behavioural activation

CBT often involves a specific focus on encouraging depressed clients to become more active and engage in pleasurable activities. This is based on the common-sense idea that being active leads to rewards that act as an antidote to depression.

A characteristic of many depressed people is that they no longer participate in activities that they previously enjoyed. In CBT, therapist and client identify potentially pleasurable activities and anticipate and deal with any cognitive obstacles (e.g. 'I won't be able to achieve that').

Unconditional positive regard

Ellis (1994) came to recognise that an important ingredient in successful therapy was convincing the client of their value as a human being. If the client feels worthless, they will be less willing to consider changing their beliefs and behaviour. However, if the therapist provides respect and appreciation regardless of what the client does and says (i.e. *unconditional positive regard*), this will facilitate a change in beliefs and attitudes.

EVALUATION/DISCUSSION

Research support

Ellis (1957) claimed a 90% success rate for REBT, taking an average of 27 sessions to complete the treatment – impressive research support for his therapy.

REBT, and CBT in general, have done well in outcome studies of depression (i.e. studies designed to measure the outcome of treatment). For example, a review by Cuijpers *et al.* (2013) of 75 studies found that CBT was superior to no treatment. However, Ellis recognised that the therapy was not always effective, and suggested that this could be because some clients did not put their revised beliefs into action (Ellis, 2001). Therapist competence also appears to explain a significant amount of the variation in CBT outcomes (Kuyken and Tsivrikos, 2009).

This suggests that REBT is effective, but other factors relating to both client and therapist may limit its effectiveness.

Individual differences

CBT appears to be more suitable for some individuals than others.

For example, CBT appears to be less suitable for people who have high levels of irrational beliefs that are both rigid and resistant to change (Elkin *et al.*, 1985). CBT also appears to be less suitable in situations where high levels of stress in the individual reflect realistic stressors in the person's life that therapy cannot resolve (Simons *et al.*, 1995). Ellis also explained a possible lack of success in terms of suitability – some people simply do not want the direct sort of advice that CBT practitioners tend to dispense; they prefer to share their worries with a therapist without getting involved in the cognitive effort associated with recovery (Ellis, 2001).

A limitation of CBT, therefore, is the fact that individual differences affect its effectiveness.

Support for behavioural activation

The belief that changing behaviour can go some way to alleviating depression is supported by a study on the beneficial effects of exercise.

Babyak *et al.* (2000) studied 156 adult volunteers diagnosed with major depressive disorder. They were randomly assigned to a four-month course of aerobic exercise, drug treatment (an antidepressant drug) or a combination of the two. Clients in all three groups exhibited significant improvement at the end of the four months. Six months after the end of the study, those in the exercise group had significantly lower relapse rates than those in the medication group.

This shows that a change in behaviour (i.e. physical activity) can indeed be beneficial in treating depression.

 Alternative treatments

Other treatments are available. Indeed, the most popular treatment for depression is the use of antidepressants such as SSRIs (see page 114).

Drug therapies have the strength of requiring less effort on the part of the client (note that Ellis required 27 sessions of REBT, which is a lot of commitment). They can also be used in conjunction with a psychotherapy such as CBT. This may be useful because a distressed client may be unable to focus on the demands of CBT and the drug treatment could enable them to cope better. The review by Cuijpers *et al.* (above) found that CBT was especially effective if it was used in conjunction with drug therapy.

This suggests that using both CBT and drugs might be the best option.

 The 'Dodo Bird effect'

All methods of treatment for mental disorder may be equally effective.

Rosenzweig (1936) named the 'Dodo Bird effect' after the Dodo bird in Lewis Carroll's *Alice in Wonderland*, who decided that everyone should win. Research does tend to find fairly small differences in success rates, for example Luborsky *et al.* (1975, 2002) reviewed over 100 different studies that compared different therapies and found that there were only small differences. Rosenzweig argued that the lack of difference was because there were so many common factors in the various different psychotherapies, such as being able to talk to a sympathetic person (which may enhance self-esteem) and having an opportunity to express one's thoughts (Sloane *et al.*, 1975).

These commonalities, therefore, might explain the lack of difference in the effectiveness of different therapies.

CBT and sports

Many sportsmen and women unwittingly respond to stress with irrational thinking that greatly hinders their performance. They are under tremendous pressure to win and any failure is met by increased future pressure.

Turner (2014) suggests that the principles of REBT should be used more often by sports teams and has found that 9 or 10 sessions can help sportspeople to exchange their irrational beliefs for rational ones. For example, the belief that you 'must win' should be abandoned. Tennis player Rafa Nadal said, after losing in the first round at Wimbledon in 2013, 'It's tough … but life continues … it's not a tragedy, it's sport'. Such rational thinking in response to a negative event leads to mental healthiness and success. Nadal went on to win the US Open that year.

 UPGRADE

In most of the Upgrade features in this book we have given you advice about what to do in order to gain high marks. However, it is also worth knowing what *not* to do to avoid losing marks. Common errors include:

Not adequately focusing on the content of a question or essay title.
If a question is on the *treatment* of depression, don't spend too much time explaining the disorder.

Spending too long on an introduction.
It is best to simply get straight on with the answer rather than wasting time telling the examiner what you are about to do.

Not considering the marks available.
Sometimes students write more than is needed or, conversely, do not write enough. It is easy to spend 10 minutes writing about something you know well, but if the question is worth only 2 or 3 marks then you are *not using time effectively*. Aim to allocate around *1 minute per mark* for the questions.

'Forgetting' the need to *discuss*.
For example, in an 8-mark question about 'discussing cognitive treatments of depression' students may spend most of the time doing a really comprehensive description of the treatment. As they come to the end of the answer, they add a quick evaluation point.

They will get a maximum of 4 marks for the description (AO1) no matter how much is written. A short, underdeveloped evaluation (AO3) point will not get much credit, so make sure you balance your answer appropriately and make your evaluation 'discursive' if required by the question.

The biological approach to explaining OCD

In this chapter we have considered explanations for phobias and depression – and in both cases the explanations described have been psychological ones. Psychologists also put forward biological explanations and on this spread our focus will be on biological explanations of obsessive-compulsive disorder (OCD).

The biological approach in general is explained (and evaluated) on pages 132–133. The emphasis of the biological approach is on how the physical elements of our body may be used to understand behaviour. This includes genes which are present in every cell of the body, providing instructions for physical and psychological characteristics. Biological explanations also concern the brain and neurotransmitters in the brain. So we will consider genetic and neural (brain) explanations.

KEY TERMS

Concordance rate A measure of genetic similarity. In a sample of, for example, 100 twin pairs, one twin of each pair has a phobic disorder. The number of times their other twin also shows the illness determines the concordance rate, so if 40 have phobic disorder, then the concordance rate is 40%.

Dopamine One of the key neurotransmitters in the brain, with effects on motivation and 'drive'.

Gene A part of the chromosome of an organism that carries information in the form of DNA.

Neurotransmitter Chemical substances that play an important part in the workings of the nervous system by transmitting nerve impulses across a synapse.

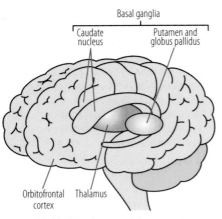

Basal ganglia
Caudate nucleus
Putamen and globus pallidus
Orbitofrontal cortex
Thalamus

▲ The worry circuit.
The OFC sends 'worry' signals to the thalamus. These are normally suppressed by the caudate nucleus but, if damaged, then the thalamus is alerted and confirms the 'worry' to the OFC, creating a worry circuit.

GENETIC EXPLANATIONS

A popular explanation for mental disorders is that they are inherited. This would mean that individuals inherited specific **genes** from their parents that are related to the onset of OCD.

The COMT gene

The COMT gene may contribute to OCD. It is called the COMT gene because it is involved in the production of *catechol-O-methyltransferase*, or COMT for short. In turn, COMT regulates the production of the **neurotransmitter dopamine** that has been implicated in OCD (see neural explanations below). All genes come in different forms (alleles) and one form of the COMT gene has been found to be more common in OCD patients than people without the disorder. This variation produces lower activity of the COMT gene and higher levels of dopamine (Tükel *et al.*, 2013).

The SERT gene

Another possible candidate gene is the SERT gene (also called 5-HTT) which affects the transport of the serotonin, creating lower levels of this neurotransmitter. These lower levels are also implicated in OCD. One study found a mutation of this gene in two unrelated families where six of the seven family members had OCD (Ozaki *et al.*, 2003).

Diathesis-stress

The idea of a simple link between one gene and a complex disorder like OCD is unlikely. Something as simple as eye colour may have one gene that determines it but the same is not true for complex behaviours. Genes such as the SERT gene are also implicated in a number of other disorders such as depression and post-traumatic stress disorder.

What this suggests is that each individual gene only creates a vulnerability (a diathesis) for OCD as well as other conditions, such as depression. Other factors ('stressors') affect what condition develops or indeed whether any mental illness develops. Therefore some people could possess the COMT or SERT gene variations but suffer no ill effects.

NEURAL EXPLANATIONS

As we have seen there is a link between genetic factors and abnormal levels of certain neurotransmitters. It is also true that genetic factors affect certain brain circuits that may be abnormal.

Abnormal levels of neurotransmitters

Dopamine levels are thought to be abnormally high in people with OCD. This is based on animal studies – high doses of drugs that enhance levels of dopamine induce stereotyped movements resembling the compulsive behaviours found in OCD patients (Szechtman *et al.*, 1998).

In contrast with dopamine, it is lower levels of serotonin that are associated with OCD. This conclusion is based on the fact that antidepressant drugs that increase serotonin activity have been shown to reduce OCD symptoms (Pigott *et al.*, 1990), whereas antidepressants that have less effect on serotonin do not reduce OCD symptoms (Jenicke, 1992).

Abnormal brain circuits

Several areas in the frontal lobes of the brain are thought to be abnormal in people with OCD. The caudate nucleus (located in the basal ganglia) normally suppresses signals from the orbitofrontal cortex (OFC). In turn, the OFC sends signals to the thalamus about things that are worrying, such as a potential germ hazard. When the caudate nucleus is damaged, it fails to suppress minor 'worry' signals and the thalamus is alerted, which in turn sends signals back to the OFC, acting as a *worry circuit*.

This is supported by PET scans of patients with OCD, taken while their symptoms are active (e.g. when a person with a germ obsession holds a dirty cloth). Such scans show heightened activity in the OFC.

Serotonin and dopamine are linked to these regions of the frontal lobes. Comer (1998) reports that serotonin plays a key role in the operation of the OFC and the caudate nuclei, and it would therefore appear that abnormal levels of serotonin might cause these areas to malfunction.

Dopamine is also linked to this system, as it is the main neurotransmitter of the basal ganglia. High levels of dopamine lead to overactivity of this region (Sukel, 2007).

EVALUATION/DISCUSSION

Family and twin studies

Evidence for the genetic basis of OCD comes from studies of first-degree relatives (parents or siblings) and twin studies.

Nestadt *et al.* (2000) identified 80 patients with OCD and 343 of their first-degree relatives and compared them with 73 control patients without mental illness and 300 of their relatives. They found that people with a first-degree relative with OCD had a five-times greater risk of having the illness themselves at some time in their lives, compared to the general population. A meta-analysis of 14 twin studies of OCD found that, on average, identical (monozygotic, MZ) twins were more than twice as likely to develop OCD if their co-twin had the disorder than was the case for non-identical (dizygotic, DZ) twins (Billett *et al.*, 1998).

*This evidence points to a clear genetic basis for OCD, but the fact that the **concordance rates** are never 100% means that environmental factors must play a role too (the diathesis-stress model).*

Tourette's syndrome and other disorders

Evidence of the role of genes in OCD comes from studies of people with other disorders.

Pauls and Leckman (1986) studied patients with Tourette's syndrome and their families, and concluded that OCD is one form of expression of the same gene that determines Tourette's. The obsessional behaviour of OCD and Tourette's patients is also found in children with autism, who display stereotyped behaviours and rituals as well as compulsions. In addition, obsessive behaviour is typical of anorexia nervosa, and is one of the characteristics distinguishing individuals with anorexia from individuals with bulimia. Furthermore, it is reported that two out of every three patients with OCD also experience at least one episode of depression (Rasmussen and Eisen, 1992).

This all supports the view that there is not one specific gene or genes unique to OCD, but they merely act as a predisposing factor towards obsessive-type behaviour.

Research support for genes and OFC

Many studies demonstrate the genetic link to abnormal levels of neurotransmitters.

For example, Menzies *et al.* (2007) used MRI to produce images of brain activity in OCD patients and their immediate family members without OCD (a sibling, parent or child) and also a group of unrelated healthy people. OCD patients and their close relatives had reduced grey matter in key regions of the brain, including the OFC.

This supports the view that anatomical differences are inherited and these may lead to OCD in certain individuals. Menzies et al. concluded that, in the future, brain scans may be used to detect OCD risk.

Real-world application

The mapping of the human genome has led to the hope that specific genes could be linked to particular mental and physical disorders.

For example, it might be that where one or the other parent-to-be has the COMT gene, the mother's fertilised eggs could be screened, thus giving the parents the choice of whether to abort those eggs with the gene. Alternatively gene therapy may produce a means of turning certain genes 'off' so that a disorder is not expressed. Both raise important ethical issues, not least that the same genes may have other benefits. Furthermore this presumes that there is a relatively simple relationship between a disorder, such as OCD, and genes, which may well not be the case.

Applying biological therapies (such as gene therapy) is therefore more complex and controversial than it may at first appear.

Alternative explanations

The biological approach faces strong competition from psychological explanations.

The two-process model can be applied to OCD. Initial learning occurs when a neutral stimulus (such as dirt) is associated with anxiety. This association is maintained because the anxiety-provoking stimulus is avoided. Thus an obsession is formed and then a link is learned with compulsive behaviours (such as hand-washing) that appear to reduce the anxiety. Such explanations are supported by the success of a treatment for OCD called exposure and response prevention (ERP) which is fairly similar to systematic desensitisation. Patients have to experience their feared stimulus and at the same time are prevented from performing their compulsive behaviour. Studies have reported high success rates, for example Albucher *et al.* (1998) report that between 60 and 90% of adults with OCD have improved considerably using ERP.

This suggests that OCD may have psychological causes as well as, or instead of, biological causes.

▲ One of the most common obsessions for OCD patients relates to fear of contamination. The actual symptoms are often shaped by the patient's culture of origin. For example, a patient from a Western country may have a contamination obsession that is focused on germs, whereas a patient from India may fear contamination by touching a person from a lower social caste.

⬆ UPGRADE

Continuing the theme (from page 111) of what students tend to do wrong when answering exam questions, here are some more common errors:

Not spending enough time thinking about or planning an answer to a question.

This is particularly important when a question leaves you with a number of choices e.g. which genetic (or neural) explanation of OCD to outline, which criticism of genetic explanations to give, which AO1 and AO3 points to include in an essay question? Spending time prior to your exam, thinking about these choices, will make your actual exam performance that much more sleek and effective.

Not structuring answers, especially essay responses.

Weak essays tend to follow an illogical structure, leaving the examiner having to make links between concepts, ideas and issues themselves. Some essays are also very pedestrian – running through a series of descriptive features (with little coherency) and a list of evaluation points (with little expansion). It is well worth spending a little time organising your answer and planning how it develops so it all makes sense.

Not always explaining points fully enough.

This is especially the case with evaluation points. Students often start a point without 'seeing it through'. The use of connectives such as 'because' and 'therefore' would help with this, or simply asking yourself 'so what?' To add depth to discussion, you should work harder to 'exhaust' a point.

CAN YOU? No. 4.8

1. Outline genetic explanations for OCD. (4 marks)
2. Outline neural explanations for OCD. (4 marks)
3. Give **one** criticism of the genetic explanations for OCD. (3 marks)
4. Describe and evaluate the biological approach to explaining OCD. (12 marks AS, 16 marks A)

The biological approach to treating OCD

There are a number of biological treatments used with OCD patients, including deep brain stimulation, a fairly new technique holding some promise. However, for many patients drugs remain an easy and accessible means of dealing with their obsessions and compulsions. According to Gava *et al.* (2007), drug therapy is currently the most commonly used treatment for OCD.

'Biological' refers to processes in the body, whereas 'psychological' refers to processes in the mind.

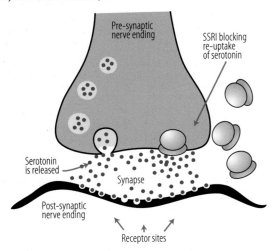

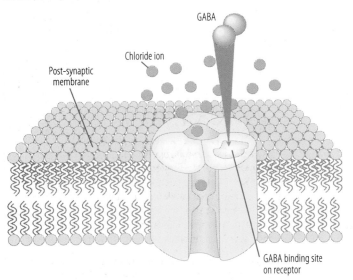

▲ SSRIs block the re-uptake of serotonin at the pre-synaptic membrane, increasing serotonin concentration at receptor sites on the post-synaptic membrane.

▲ There are GABA receptors on the ends of receiving some neurons at a synapse. When GABA is released from one neuron it travels across the synaptic gap where it locks onto one of these receptors and increases the flow of chloride ions into the neuron, thus slowing down the receiving neuron's activity and 'quietening down' the neuron and nervous system generally.

KEY TERMS

GABA (gamma-aminobutyric acid) A neurotransmitter that regulates excitement in the nervous system, thus acting as a natural form of anxiety reducer.

Noradrenaline A neurotransmitter found mainly in areas of the brain that are involved in governing autonomic nervous system activity, e.g. blood pressure or heart rate.

Serotonin A neurotransmitter implicated in many different behaviours and physiological processes, including aggression, eating behaviour, sleep and depression.

DRUG THERAPY

Antidepressants: SSRIs

The most commonly used drugs for OCD as well as depression are antidepressants. Low levels of the neurotransmitter **serotonin** are associated with depression as well as OCD, so drugs to increase levels of serotonin are used with both mental disorders. Low levels of serotonin are implicated in the 'worry circuit' described on the previous spread, so increasing levels of serotonin may therefore normalise this circuit.

Antidepressants are used to reduce the anxiety associated with OCD. Selective serotonin re-uptake inhibitors (SSRIs) are currently the preferred drug for treating anxiety disorders (Choy and Schneier, 2008). SSRIs, with brand names such as *Zoloft*, *Paxil* and *Prozac*, increase levels of the neurotransmitter serotonin, which regulates mood and anxiety.

The diagram on the left illustrates how they work. Serotonin is released into a synapse from one nerve (neuron). It targets receptor cells on the receiving neuron at receptor sites and, afterwards, is re-absorbed by the initial neuron sending the message. In order to increase levels of serotonin at the synapse, and increase stimulation to the receiving neuron, this re-absorption (re-uptake) is inhibited.

Antidepressants: tricyclics

The tricyclic *clomipramine* (brand name *Anafranil*) was the first antidepressant to be used for OCD and today is primarily used in the treatment of OCD rather than depression. Tricyclics block the transporter mechanism that re-absorbs both serotonin and **noradrenaline** into the pre-synaptic cell after it has fired. As a result, more of these neurotransmitters are left in the synapse, prolonging their activity, and easing transmission of the next impulse.

Tricyclics have the advantage of targeting more than one neurotransmitter. However, they have greater side effects so are used as a second-line treatment for patients where SSRIs are not effective.

Anti-anxiety drugs

Benzodiazepines (BZs) are commonly used to reduce anxiety. They are manufactured under various trade names, such as *Librium*, *Xanax*, *Valium* and *Diazepam*. BZs slow down the activity of the central nervous system by enhancing the activity of the neurotransmitter **GABA (gamma-aminobutyric acid)**, a neurotransmitter that, when released, has a general quietening effect on many of the neurons in the brain.

It does this by reacting with special sites (called GABA receptors) on the outside of receiving neurons. When GABA locks into these receptors it opens a channel that increases the flow of *chloride ions* into the neuron. *Chloride ions* make it harder for the neuron to be stimulated by other neurotransmitters, thus slowing down its activity and making the person feel more relaxed.

Other drugs

Recent research has found that D-Cycloserine has an effect on reducing anxiety and thus may be an effective treatment for OCD, particularly when used in conjunction with psychotherapy. D-Cycloserine is an antibiotic used in the treatment of tuberculosis. It also appears to enhance the transmission of GABA and thus reduce anxiety (Kushner *et al.*, 2007).

EVALUATION/DISCUSSION

Effectiveness

There is considerable evidence for the effectiveness of drug treatments.

Typically a randomised control trial is used to compare the effectiveness of the drug versus a placebo (a substance that has no pharmacological value but controls for the belief that the pill you are taking will affect you). Soomro *et al.* (2008) reviewed 17 studies of the use of SSRIs with OCD patients and found them to be more effective than placebos in reducing the symptoms of OCD up to three months after treatment. One of the issues regarding the evaluation of treatment is that most studies are only of three to four months' duration (Koran *et al.*, 2007).

Therefore, while drug treatments have been shown to be effective in the short term, the lack of long-term data is a limitation.

Drug therapies are preferred to other treatments

One of the great appeals of using drug therapy is that it requires little input from the user in terms of effort and time.

In contrast, therapies such as CBT require the patient to attend regular meetings and put considerable thought into tackling their problems. Drug therapies are also cheaper for the health service because they require little monitoring and cost much less than psychological treatments. Furthermore, patients may benefit simply from talking with a doctor during consultations (see the 'Dodo Bird effect' on page 111).

These benefits means that drug therapies are more economical for the health service than psychological therapies.

Side effects

All drugs have side effects, some more severe than others.

For example, nausea, headache and insomnia are common side effects of SSRIs (Soomro *et al.*, 2008). Although not necessarily severe, they are often are enough to make a patient stop taking the drug. Tricyclic antidepressants tend to have more side effects (such as hallucinations and irregular heartbeat) than SSRIs and so are only used in cases where SSRIs are not effective. The possible side effects of BZs include increased aggressiveness and long-term impairment of memory. There are also problems with addiction, so the recommendation is that BZ use should be limited to a maximum of four weeks (Ashton, 1997).

These side effects, and the possibility of addiction, therefore limit the usefulness of drugs as treatments for OCD.

Not a lasting cure

An issue with drug treatments is that they are not a lasting cure for people with OCD.

Maina *et al.* (2001) found that patients relapse within a few weeks if medication is stopped. Koran *et al.* (2007), in a comprehensive review of treatments for OCD sponsored by the American Psychiatric Association (APA), suggested that, although drug therapy may be more commonly used, psychotherapies such as CBT should be tried first.

This suggests that, while drug therapy may require little effort and also may be relatively effective in the short term, it does not provide a lasting cure.

Publication bias

Turner *et al.* (2008) claim that there is evidence of a publication bias towards studies that show a positive outcome of antidepressant treatment, thus exaggerating the benefits of antidepressant drugs.

The authors found that, not only were positive results more likely to be published, but studies that were not positive were often published in a way that conveyed a positive outcome. Drug companies have a strong interest in the continuing success of psychotherapeutic drugs and much of the research is funded by these companies.

As Turner et al. suggest, such selective publication can lead doctors to make inappropriate treatment decisions that may not be in the best interest of their patients.

◀ Leonardo di Caprio played one of the richest men in the world, Howard Hughes, in the film *The Aviator*. This is ironic, as both men have suffered from OCD. Howard Hughes developed various obsessions, including a fear of germs, which meant that he used tissues to pick things up or open doors. He also became obsessed with the film *Ice Station Zebra* and is said to have watched it over 150 times. In addition to OCD he suffered from social phobia and towards the end of his life disappeared from public view.

Di Caprio says he has to force himself not to step on every piece of squashed chewing gum when walking down a pavement, and fights urges to walk through a doorway several times, because he doesn't want the condition taking over his life.

🐾 APPLY YOUR KNOWLEDGE

As a psychology student you are asked by a local GP's surgery to put together a single page information sheet about the treatment of OCD. You are asked to explain the different drug treatments available for this disorder in a clear and non-technical manner. You are also asked to include something about the effectiveness of these treatments and any side-effects that patients might encounter.

Have a go at writing this information sheet. You should write about 150 words outlining the different drug treatments and how they work (in clear and non-technical language remember). You should also write another 150 words explaining the effectiveness of drug treatments for OCD and any possible side effects.

You might (if you have easy access to the internet) take a look at the NHS guidance on these treatments at https://www.nhs.uk/conditions/obsessive-compulsive-disorder-ocd/treatment/

CAN YOU? No. 4.9

1. Outline the use of drug therapy in treating OCD. (4 marks)
2. Give **one** criticism of the biological approach to treating OCD. (3 marks)
3. Describe and evaluate the biological approach to treating OCD. (12 marks AS, 16 marks A)

End-of-chapter review > CHAPTER SUMMARY

We have identified here the key points of the topics on the AQA specification covered in this chapter, i.e. the bare minimum that you need to know. You may want to fill in further details to elaborate and personalise this material.

DEFINITIONS OF ABNORMALITY

STATISTICAL INFREQUENCY
- Statistics describe typical values.
- A frequency graph of behaviours tends to show a normal distribution.
- The extreme ends define what is not the norm, i.e. abnormal.

EVALUATION/DISCUSSION
- Some behaviour is desirable – can't distinguish desirable from undesirable abnormal behaviour.
- Cut-off point is subjective – important for deciding who gets treatment.
- Sometimes appropriate – e.g. for intellectual disability defined as less than two standard deviations below mean IQ.
- (A Level) Cultural relativism – statistical frequency is relative to the reference population.

DEVIATION FROM SOCIAL NORMS
- Norms defined by a group of people ('society').
- Standards of what is acceptable.
- May be implicit or defined by law.

EVALUATION/DISCUSSION
- Susceptible to abuse – varies with changing attitudes/morals, can be used to incarcerate those who are nonconformists.
- Related to context and degree – e.g. shouting is normal in some places and in moderation.
- Strengths – distinguishes desirable from undesirable behaviour, and considers effect on others.
- (A Level) Cultural relativism – social norms of dominant culture used as basis for DSM, imposed on other cultural groups.

FAILURE TO FUNCTION ADEQUATELY
- Being unable to manage everyday life, e.g. eating regularly.
- Lack of functioning is abnormal if it causes distress to self and/or others.
- WHODAS used to provide a quantitative measure of functioning.

EVALUATION/DISCUSSION
- Who judges – distress may be judged subjectively.
- Behaviour may be functional – e.g. depression may be rewarding for the individual.
- Subjective experience recognised – can be measured objectively.
- (A Level) Cultural relativism – standards of everyday life vary between cultures, non-traditional lifestyles may be judged as inadequate.

DEVIATION FROM IDEAL MENTAL HEALTH
- Jahoda identified characteristics commonly used when describing competent people.
- For example: high self-esteem, self-actualisation, autonomy, accurate perception of reality, mastery of the environment.

EVALUATION/DISCUSSION
- Unrealistic criteria – may not be useable because too ideal.
- Equates mental and physical health – whereas mental disorders tend not to have physical causes.
- Positive approach – a general part of the humanistic approach.
- (A Level) Culture-bound criteria, e.g. self-actualisation not relevant to collectivist cultures.

MENTAL DISORDERS

PHOBIAS
- Emotional: excessive fear, anxiety and/or panic cued by a specific object or situation.
- Behavioural: avoidance, faint or freeze. Interferes with everyday life.
- Cognitive: not helped by rational argument, unreasonableness of the behaviour recognised.

DEPRESSION
- Emotional: negative emotions – sadness, loss of interest and sometimes anger.
- Behavioural: reduced or increased activity related to energy levels, sleep and/or eating.
- Cognitive: irrational, negative thoughts and self-beliefs that are self-fulfilling.

OCD
- Emotional: anxiety and distress, and awareness that this is excessive, leading to shame.
- Cognitive: recurrent, intrusive, uncontrollable thoughts (obsessions), more than everyday worries.
- Behavioural: compulsive behaviours to reduce obsessive thoughts, not connected in a realistic way.

THE BEHAVIOURAL APPROACH

EXPLAINING PHOBIAS

THE TWO-PROCESS MODEL
- Classical conditioning – phobia acquired through association between NS and UCR; NS becomes CS, producing fear.
- Little Albert (Watson and Rayner) – developed fear of white rat which generalised to other white furry objects.
- Operant conditioning – phobia maintained through negative reinforcement (avoidance of fear).
- Social learning – phobic behaviour of others modelled.

EVALUATION/DISCUSSION
- Classical conditioning – people often report a specific incident but not always, may only apply to some types of phobia (Sue et al.).
- Incomplete explanation – not everyone bitten by a dog develops a phobia (di Nardo et al.), may depend on having a genetic vulnerability for phobias.
- Social learning – fear response acquired through observing reaction to a buzzer (Bandura and Rosenthal).
- (A Level) Biological preparedness – phobias more likely with ancient fears, conditioning alone can't explain all phobias (Seligman).
- (A Level) Two-process model ignores cognitive factors – irrational thinking may explain social phobias, for example, which are more successfully treated with cognitive methods (Engels et al.).

TREATING PHOBIAS

SYSTEMATIC DESENSITISATION (SD)
- Counterconditioning – phobic stimulus associated with new response of relaxation.
- Reciprocal inhibition – the relaxation inhibits the anxiety (Wolpe).
- Relaxation – deep breathing, focus on peaceful scene, progressive muscle relaxation.
- Desensitisation hierarchy – from least to most fearful, relaxation practised at every step.

EVALUATION/DISCUSSION
- Effectiveness – 75% success (McGrath et al.), in vivo techniques may work better or a combination (Comer).
- Not for all phobias – works less well for 'ancient fears' (Öhman et al.).

THE COGNITIVE APPROACH

EXPLAINING DEPRESSION

ELLIS' ABC MODEL (1962)
- Activating event leads to rational or irrational belief, which then leads to consequences.
- Mustabatory thinking (e.g. I must be liked) – causes disappointment and depression.

BECK'S NEGATIVE TRIAD (1967)
- Negative schema – develops in childhood (e.g. parental rejection), leads to cognitive biases.
- Negative triad – irrational and negative view of self, the world and the future.

EVALUATION/DISCUSSION
- Support for role of irrational thinking – depressed people make more errors in logic (Hammen and Krantz); however, irrational thinking may not *cause* depression.
- Blames the client and ignores situational factors – recovery may depend on recognising environmental factors.
- Practical applications to CBT – supports the role of irrational thoughts in depression.
- (A Level) Irrational beliefs may be realistic – depressed people may be realists, 'sadder but wiser' (Alloy and Abrahamson).
- (A Level) Alternative explanation – genes may cause low levels of serotonin, predisposing people to develop depression.

TREATING DEPRESSION

COGNITIVE-BEHAVIOURAL THERAPY (CBT)
- Ellis' ABCDEF model.
- D for disputing irrational beliefs, e.g. logical, empirical, pragmatic.
- E and F for Effects of disputing and Feelings that are produced.
- Homework – trying out new behaviours to test irrational beliefs.
- Behavioural activation – encouraging re-engagement with pleasurable activities.
- Unconditional positive regard – reduces sense of worthlessness (Ellis).

EVALUATION/DISCUSSION
- Research support – generally successful, Ellis estimated 90% success over 27 sessions. May depend on therapist competence (Kuyken and Tsivrikos).
- Individual differences – CBT not suitable for those with rigid irrational beliefs, those whose stressors cannot be changed and those who don't want direct advice.
- Behavioural activation – depressed clients in an exercise group had lower relapse after 6 months (Babyak et al.).
- (A Level) Alternative treatments – drug therapy is much easier in time and effort, and can be used with CBT.
- (A Level) 'Dodo Bird effect' – all treatments equally effective because they share features, e.g. talking to a sympathetic person (Rosenzweig).

FLOODING
- One long session with the most fearful stimulus.
- Continues until anxiety subsides and a new stimulus-response link is learned.
- Can be *in vivo* or virtual reality.

EVALUATION OF FLOODING
- Effectiveness – research suggests it may be more effective than SD and quicker (Choy et al.).
- Individual differences – traumatic and, if patients quit, then has failed as a treatment.

EVALUATION OF BEHAVIOURAL THERAPIES
- Strengths – behavioural therapies are fast and require less effort than CBT, can be self-administered.
- (A Level) Relaxation may not be necessary – creating a new expectation of coping may matter more (Klein et al.).
- (A Level) Symptom substitution – a phobia may be a symptom of an underlying problem (e.g. Little Hans).

THE BIOLOGICAL APPROACH

EXPLAINING OCD

GENETIC EXPLANATIONS
- COMPT gene – one allele more common in OCD, creates high levels of dopamine (Tükel et al.).
- SERT gene – one allele more common in a family with OCD, creates low levels of serotonin (Ozaki et al.).
- Diathesis-stress – same genes linked to other disorders or no disorder at all, therefore genes create a vulnerability.

NEURAL EXPLANATIONS
- Dopamine levels high in OCD – linked to compulsive behaviours in animal studies (Szechtman et al.).
- Serotonin levels low in OCD – antidepressants that increase serotonin most effective (Jenicke).
- Worry circuit – damaged caudate nucleus doesn't suppress worry signals from OFC to thalamus.
- Serotonin and dopamine linked to activity in these parts of the frontal lobe (e.g. Sukel).

EVALUATION/DISCUSSION
- Family and twin studies – 5 times greater risk of OCD if relative has OCD (Nestadt et al.), twice as likely to have OCD if MZ twins (Billett et al.), but concordance rates never 100%.
- Tourette's, anorexia, autism and depression linked – genes not unique to OCD.
- Research support for genes and OFC – OCD patients and family members (genetic link) more likely to have reduced grey matter in OFC (Menzies et al.).
- (A Level) Real-world application – genes may be blocked or modified, genetic explanations lull people into thinking there are simple solutions.
- (A Level) Alternative explanations – relevance of two-process model supported by success of SD-like therapy called ERP (Albucher et al.).

TREATING OCD

DRUG THERAPY
- Antidepressants increase serotonin.
- SSRIs – prevent re-uptake of serotonin by pre-synaptic neuron.
- Tricyclics – block re-uptake of noradrenaline and serotonin but have more severe side effects, so are second choice treatment.
- Anti-anxiety drugs – BZs enhance GABA, a neurotransmitter that slows down the nervous system.
- D-Cycloserine – reduces anxiety (Kushner et al.).

EVALUATION/DISCUSSION
- Effectiveness – SSRIs better than placebo over short term (Soomro et al.).
- Drug therapies are preferred – less time and less effort than CBT, and may benefit from interaction with caring doctor.
- Side effects – not so severe with SSRIs (e.g. insomnia), more severe with tricyclics (e.g. hallucinations) and BZs (e.g. addiction).
- (A Level) Not a lasting cure – patients relapse when treatment stops (Maina et al.), CBT may be preferable (Koran et al.).
- (A Level) Publication bias – more studies with positive results published which may bias doctor preferences (Turner et al.).

The exam questions on psychopathology will be varied but there will be some short answer questions (AO1), including some multiple choice questions, some questions that ask you to apply your knowledge (AO2) and possibly an extended writing question (AO1 + AO3). Some questions may involve research methods and maths skills. We have provided a selection of these different kinds of questions here.

AS AND A LEVEL QUESTIONS

0 1   Which **one** of the following is not a definition of abnormality?   **[1 mark]**

    A   deviation from ideal mental health

    B   deviation from social norms

    C   failure to function adequately

    D   statistical frequency

0 2   **(i)**   Outline **one** definition of abnormality.   **[2 marks]**

    (ii)   Briefly explain **one** limitation of this definition of abnormality.   **[2 marks]**

0 3   Outline **two** limitations of using drug therapy to treat obsessive-compulsive disorder.   **[4 marks]**

0 4   Briefly describe the genetic explanation of obsessive-compulsive disorder. Give **one**
criticism of the explanation.   **[6 marks]**

0 5   Which **two** of the following are **cognitive** characteristics of depression?   **[1 mark]**

    A   inability to concentrate

    B   loss of pleasure

    C   negative view of the world

    D   sleeplessness

0 6   Distinguish between the behavioural and cognitive characteristics of obsessive-compulsive disorder.   **[2 marks]**

0 7   Identify the three viewpoints in Beck's negative triad.   **[3 marks]**

0 8   Identify **one** emotional characteristic of:

    (i)   depression

    (ii)   obsessive-compulsive disorder

    (iii)   phobias   **[3 marks]**

0 9   Using an example, outline how deviation from social norms is used to define abnormality.   **[3 marks]**

1 0   Briefly evaluate **one or more** neural explanations of obsessive-compulsive disorder.   **[4 marks]**

1 1   Read the item below and then answer the question that follows.

> Martina has a phobia of spiders. She is not even able to be in the same room as a spider without suffering high levels of anxiety.

    Explain how either flooding or systematic desensitisation could be used to treat Martina's phobia.   **[6 marks]**

1 2   Explain how **both** classical and operant conditioning can be involved in the development of phobias.   **[6 marks]**

1 3   Discuss statistical infrequency and failure to function adequately as definitions of abnormality.   **[12 marks]**

1 4   Read the item below and then answer the question that follows.

> Ewan has just been diagnosed with depression having felt overwhelmed with despair for the last 12 weeks. His doctor suggested that the cause of this was the fact that Ewan's long-term partner walked out on him three months ago. When this happened, Ewan convinced himself that he would never find himself another boyfriend.

Using Ellis' ABC model, explain why Ewan is suffering from depression.   **[6 marks]**

1 5   Evaluate Ellis's ABC model as an explanation of depression.   **[6 marks]**

1 6   Read the item and then answer the question that follows.

> Thomas has a phobia of clowns. He relates this to a scary experience he had as a child. He was at the circus when a clown jumped up from the row behind Thomas and startled him so much that his parents had to leave before the show ended. Thomas was so disturbed that he has not even been able to look at a picture of a clown since, let alone go anywhere near one.

Describe and evaluate the two-process model as an explanation of phobias. Refer to the example of Thomas as part of your answer.   **[12 marks]**

1 7   Discuss the use of drug therapy as a treatment for obsessive-compulsive disorder.   **[12 marks]**

1 8   Read the item below and then answer the questions that follow.

> Claire is one of a small number of people that fear travelling in a car.
> Deepak has low self-esteem and an inaccurate perception of reality.
> Rebecca often swears loudly in the presence of people that she does not know.
> Theo is so depressed that, most days, he does not have the motivation to wash or get dressed.

(i)   Name the person whose abnormal behaviour demonstrates deviation from ideal mental health.   **[1 mark]**

(ii)   Name the person whose abnormal behaviour demonstrates failure to function adequately.   **[1 mark]**

(iii)   Name the person whose abnormal behaviour demonstrates statistical infrequency.   **[1 mark]**

> **Exam tip...**
> *Once you identify the correct person, try writing down why you think they demonstrate the named definitions. After that, you could further test yourself by trying to find ways that each person might be linked to the other definitions.*

A LEVEL ONLY QUESTIONS

1 9   Read the item below and then answer the question that follows.

> Diana is suffering from clinical depression. She feels extremely sad and full of despair because she believes that life has nothing to offer her. She is especially depressed by work. Diana thinks that most of her colleagues do not really like her. In her view, she is no longer good at a job that she used to do so well.

Discuss the use of cognitive behavioural therapy as a treatment for depression. Refer to the case of Diana as part of your discussion.   **[16 marks]**

2 0   Discuss the ways in which psychologists have attempted to define abnormality.   **[16 marks]**

2 1   Discuss **two or more** treatments for abnormal behaviours.   **[16 marks]**

2 2   Discuss the use of systematic desensitisation and flooding in the treatment of phobias.   **[16 marks]**

End-of-chapter review

We've provided answers by two students to some of the questions from pages 118–119 here, together with comments from an examiner about how well they've each done. **Green** comments show what the student has done well. **Orange** comments indicate areas for improvement.

---

9 Using an example, outline how deviation from social norms is used to define abnormality. *(3 marks)*

Maisie's answer

Deviation from social norms provides an explanation for abnormality that says people are abnormal because they are different to the social norms. For example, a person walks down the main street wearing no clothes which is not acceptable behaviour and then other people would judge them as abnormal. The trouble is that such judgements rely on context because the same behaviour would not be abnormal in some other places.

The definition is limited as Maisie has simply replaced 'deviation' with 'different'.

The example is OK but is not used effectively alongside the definition.

There are no marks for evaluation here as the question does not ask for it.

Examiner's comments

The outline of the definition is quite weak and vague. *1/3 marks*

This is good as students often simply outline what social norms are without ever explicitly saying why they would be classed as abnormal in this definition.

Ciaran's answer

According to this, people are abnormal if their behaviour is different to what their society regards as acceptable behaviour. A norm is what is most typical of people and these are social norms which means that 'typical' is defined by a group of people like a cultural group or a smaller social group. Context is important in making this judgement, as is degree — sometimes doing a little bit is regarded as acceptable, such as shouting.

Examiner's comments

The outline is clear and accurate, but could be more concise. However, the example does not gain credit and would need a clearer link to what makes it abnormal to get the final mark. *2/3 marks*

The example given is based on what is normal, rather than what is abnormal, and is too brief. A more detailed example could be that in Britain it is a norm to use manners in many situations so if someone doesn't, it appears abnormal.

---

10 Briefly evaluate **one or more** neural explanations of obsessive-compulsive disorder. *(4 marks)*

The evaluation point is identified at the start and reinforced at the end.

This point could be elaborated with the idea of drug fallacy and would be useful to do in a longer question.

Maisie's answer

One strength of neural explanations for OCD is that they can be translated into drug treatments. For example, if serotonin levels are low in patients with OCD then it makes sense that they should be given drugs that increase levels of serotonin. The success of such treatments indicates that this explanation is correct.

However, a problem with this is that people with depression also have low levels of serotonin, which means that this explanation for OCD isn't specific to OCD. It may not be an explanation of OCD at all but may apply to people who have OCD and depression.

Examiner's comments

Two good, developed points that highlight both good and bad aspects of the explanation. *4/4 marks*

A well-developed point that is a good length for a 4-mark answer.

There is clearly a link between genetics and neurotransmitter levels but the question specifically asks for neural explanations rather than any other.

Description rather than evaluation.

Ciaran's answer

Neural explanations of OCD relate to abnormal levels of neurotransmitters or abnormal brain circuits. In both cases the cause of such abnormality is likely to be genetic. Therefore evidence for a genetic basis for OCD would support the role of neurotransmitters. There is evidence that supports this in a study of people with OCD.

Brain scans were done on some of their close family members who didn't have OCD — the scans showed that the genetic relatives also had reduced grey matter in the OFC compared to people from families where there was no OCD. This suggests that some people do inherit the brain abnormalities. The study was done by Menzies.

The evaluation is centred around there being evidence to support the neural explanation but it is not used effectively.

Examiner's comments

This is very different to Maisie's answer as, despite writing more, Ciaran doesn't get straight to the point and his answer is not clearly expressed or structured. This wouldn't get beyond Level 1. *1/4 marks*

This becomes more relevant to neural now that the research has been linked to the explanation.

21 Discuss **two or more** treatments for abnormal behaviours. *(16 marks)*

Maisie's answer

One treatment for abnormality is drug therapy, which is based on the idea that there are irregularities in neurotransmitter levels. SSRIs are antidepressants used for depression and OCD. They work on the basis that low levels of serotonin are disrupting normal functioning. The SSRIs work on increasing serotonin concentration at receptor sites on the post-synaptic neuron by blocking the re-uptake by the pre-synaptic neuron and therefore bringing things back to usual levels.

Drug therapies have advantages as they work relatively quickly, especially in comparison to psychological therapies like cognitive behavioural therapy (CBT). This is particularly useful in acute cases of mental ill health. However, SSRIs take up to 4-6 weeks to be fully effective in improving the symptoms despite them having an impact on serotonin levels much sooner. However, this highlights an issue of explaining why there is a delay in improvement.

There is considerable evidence that drug treatments are effective. Soomro et al. carried out a meta-analysis of 17 studies into the effectiveness of SSRIs compared to groups that were given a placebo and found SSRIs to be more effective than the placebo in reducing OCD symptoms. This suggests that they are an effective treatment for OCD.

However, this only looked at the short term impact (3 months after treatment) so it is difficult to know how long lasting the treatment was. A negative of drug therapy is the potential side effects. Soomro et al. found that nausea, headaches and insomnia were common side effects of SSRIs and can often be bad enough for the patient to stop taking the drug, which means the drug therapy will be ineffective.

A second therapy is CBT with one example being REBT, which is based on Ellis' ABC model. It claims that depression is caused by irrational cognitive reactions to a life event and it works by identifying and challenging irrational and maladaptive thoughts that lead to unwanted behaviours. This 'dispute' (D) is essential in changing the thoughts. The client then learns how to deal with the situations in a more rational and adaptive fashion, enabling them to overcome the unwanted behaviours. This can include 'homework tasks' where the patient adapts certain behaviours to test the irrational beliefs against reality. This leads to E — effects of dispute and eventually F, which relates to the new feelings and emotions.

A major strength of CBT is that the client is able to transfer the skills of more rational thinking to future situations, which can mean that CBT is potentially longer lasting than drugs as it focuses on changing the cause rather than masking symptoms.

However, CBT will only work if the client is motivated to work on changing their irrational beliefs, which means that it is not always effective, particularly for severely depressed clients. A further limitation of CBT is that the success of the treatment is very much reliant on the ability of the therapist; the more capable the therapist is the better the client will do, meaning the CBT itself may be secondary.

Rosenzweig argued that all methods of treatments for mental disorder were pretty much equally effective. Research has backed this up, such as Luborsky et al. who reviewed over 100 studies into treatment effectiveness and found only very small differences. It has been suggested the opportunity for patients to express themselves, experience an increase in self-esteem and have a chance to speak to someone who is supportive, interested and empathetic is what is key to successful treatment, regardless of the 'approach'.
(581 words)

✓ As this is for an A Level essay, there is an expectation that detail will be better than that in an AS essay. Maisie has elaborated her AO1.

✓ A good way to develop discussion is to compare theories.

✓ The point regarding how quickly they work is used as a positive, a comparison, and is further elaborated with a counterpoint.

✓ A good, effective use of research which focuses on key aspects and is also made relevant to the question explicitly.

✓ By using both positive and negatives here, Maisie is showing a clear and effective discussion.

✓ Good, comprehensive description of CBT.

✓ Another good point that shows development in the discussion.

✓ A strong conclusion that adds something new to the essay and very good use of research.

Examiner's comments

Knowledge of both treatments is accurate and well detailed. There is thorough and effective discussion throughout with a good use of research – all the criteria required for a Level 4 response. *Level 4 essay – this answer is likely to get full marks: 16/16.*

Approaches in psychology

CONTENTS OF CHAPTER

A LEVEL ONLY ZONE (vertical label)

SPECIFICATION CHECKLIST

- Origins of psychology: Wundt, introspection and the emergence of psychology as a science.

The basic assumptions of the following approaches:

- Learning approaches: the behaviourist approach, including classical conditioning and Pavlov's research, operant conditioning, types of reinforcement and Skinner's research; social learning theory including imitation, identification, modelling, vicarious reinforcement, the role of meditational processes and Bandura's research.

- The cognitive approach: the study of internal mental processes, the role of schemas, the use of theoretical and computer models to explain and make inferences about mental processes. The emergence of cognitive neuroscience.

- The biological approach: the influence of genes, biological structures and neurochemistry on behaviour. Genotype and phenotype, genetic basis of behaviour, evolution and behaviour.

A LEVEL ONLY ZONE (vertical label)

- The psychodynamic approach: the role of the unconscious, the structure of personality, id, ego and superego, defence mechanisms including repression, denial and displacement, psychosexual stages.

- Humanistic psychology: free will, self-actualisation and Maslow's hierarchy of needs, focus on the self, congruence, the role of conditions of worth. The influence on counselling psychology.

- Comparison of approaches.

Approaches to amusement parks

A few summers ago I (Mike) paid a visit to Tivoli Gardens, the famous amusement park in Copenhagen, Denmark. The park opened in 1843 and is the second oldest amusement park in the world. It features the world's second tallest carousel at 80 metres high (The Star Flyer – pictured above) and Vertigo, a looping plane ride where the rider is able to control the plane him or herself. This one seemed to draw the loudest screams, so must have been the scariest. I watched while a seemingly never-ending line of people threaded their way onto all sorts of horrifying contraptions that swung them around ancient towers, dropped them from great heights, turned them upside down at frighteningly high speeds and generally did the sorts of things that logically we should avoid at all costs.

So, why do some people (like me…) stare upwards at these monstrosities with a sense of absolute dread, whereas others can't wait to be twirled, dropped, rotated and generally scared witless? Perhaps psychology has the answer, so try doing this activity in two parts.

TRY THIS

Part 1 (Before reading this chapter.) Why do *you* think some people love these rides and other people hate them?

Part 2 (After reading this chapter.) Now you are more psychologically informed, how would the different approaches explain this difference?

The origins of psychology

The success of the natural sciences had a significant influence on the emergence of psychology, particularly because the scientific methods used by sciences such as biology and chemistry were regarded as the only reliable methods for discovering reliable knowledge about the world. Therefore, in order to be accepted and to flourish as a subject in its own right, psychology had to adopt the methods of the natural sciences. This was not a straightforward process, as there was a long-standing belief that the human psyche was not amenable to scientific investigation. Despite this, the scene was set for a dramatic evolution in our understanding of the human condition, and, towards the end of the nineteenth century, scientific psychology was finally born.

◖ Research methods

Introspection was used in a study of gambling behaviour (Griffiths, 1994). The study investigated the thought processes of people who gambled regularly versus non-regular gamblers, proposing that the thought processes of regular gamblers would be more irrational. To assess irrational thinking the participants were asked to 'think aloud' while playing a fruit machine. In order to do this the participants were given a list of instructions, such as:

- Say everything that goes through your mind. Do not censor any thoughts even if they seem irrelevant to you.
- Keep talking as continuously as possible, even if your ideas are not clearly structured.
- Do not hesitate to use fragmented sentences if necessary.
- Do not try to justify your thoughts.

The study found that gamblers used more irrational verbalisations.

1. Explain how the dependent variable in this study has been operationalised. (1 mark)
2. Write a suitable hypothesis for this study. (2 marks)
3. State whether your hypothesis is directional or non-directional and explain why you chose this kind of hypothesis. (2 marks)
4. Explain why this study would be considered to be a quasi-experiment using self-report. (3 marks)
5. Explain in what way the procedures of this study were standardised. (2 marks)

LINK TO RESEARCH METHODS ➤

Hypotheses on pages 179, 182
Experiments on page 188
Standardisation on page 178

WILHELM WUNDT (1832–1920)

Wundt was the first person to call himself a psychologist, believing that all aspects of nature, including the human mind, could be studied scientifically. His approach paved the way for the acceptance of psychology as a distinct science in its own right, and experimental psychology as the preferred method of studying human behaviour. In his laboratory in Leipzig, Germany, he studied only those aspects of behaviour that could be strictly controlled under experimental conditions. These included the study of reaction time (how long it takes people to respond to various stimuli) and various aspects of sensation and perception.

Wundt's aim was to study the *structure* of the human mind, and he believed that the best way to do this was to break down behaviours such as sensation and perception into their basic elements. Because of this, his approach was referred to as structuralism and the technique he used as **introspection**. Although Wundt originally believed that *all* aspects of human experience could be investigated experimentally, he eventually came to realise that higher mental processes, such as learning, language and emotions, could not be studied in this strict controlled manner. These topics could instead be described in terms of general trends in behaviour among groups of people. He referred to this latter field as *Völkerpsychologie* (cultural psychology).

Introspection

Introspection, from the Latin meaning 'looking into', is the process by which a person gains knowledge about his or her own mental and emotional states. Just as our perceptual ability enables us to observe and make sense of the outer world, our introspective ability enables us to observe our inner world.

Wundt claimed that, with sufficient training, mental processes such as memory and perception could be observed systematically as they occurred using introspection. For example, observers might be shown an object and asked to reflect upon *how* they were perceiving it. This information could then be used to gain insight into the nature of the mental processes involved in perception, reaction time, etc. For example, in Wundt's studies of perception, participants would be presented with carefully controlled stimuli (e.g. visual images or auditory tones). They would then be asked to provide a description of the inner processes they were experiencing as they looked at the image or listened to the tone. This made it possible to compare different participants' reports in response to the same stimuli, and so establish general theories about perception and other mental processes.

THE EMERGENCE OF PSYCHOLOGY AS A SCIENCE

We might ask 'What is the glue that holds psychology together as a discipline?' This is most probably its reliance on a philosophical view known as **empiricism**. Empiricists believe that knowledge comes from observation and experience alone (rather than being innate). When empirical methods were first applied to the study of human beings by Wundt and his followers, psychology began to emerge as a distinct entity. This new 'scientific' approach to psychology was based on two major assumptions. First, all behaviour is seen as being *caused* (the assumption of determinism). Second, if behaviour is determined, then it should be possible to *predict* how human beings would behave in different conditions (the assumption of predictability). The technique used to explore these assumptions became known as the scientific method.

The scientific method in psychology

The **scientific method** refers to the use of investigative methods that are objective, systematic and replicable. It is objective in that researchers do not let preconceived ideas or biases influence the collection of their data, and systematic in that observations or experiments are carried out in an orderly way. Measurement and recording of empirical data are carried out accurately and with due consideration for the possible influence of other factors on the results obtained. It is replicable in that observations can be repeated by other researchers to determine whether the same results are obtained. If results are not replicable, then they are not reliable and cannot be accepted as being universally true. The research process is not restricted to empirical observation alone, but also necessitates the use of reason to explain the results of these observations. The development of scientific theories and the constant testing and refining of these theories through further observation completes the scientific cycle (see the diagram on the facing page).

EVALUATION/DISCUSSION

Wundt's methods were unreliable

A criticism of Wundt's structuralist approach, mainly from behaviourists, was that this approach relied primarily on 'nonobservable' responses.

Although participants could report on their conscious experiences, the processes themselves (e.g. memory, perception) were considered to be unobservable constructions. Wundt's approach ultimately failed because of the lack of reliability of his methods. Introspective 'experimental' results were not reliably reproducible by other researchers in other laboratories.

In contrast, the early behaviourists such as Pavlov and Thorndike were already achieving reliably reproducible results and discovering explanatory principles that could be easily generalised to all human beings.

A scientific approach tests assumptions about behaviour

Because of its reliance on objective and systematic methods of observation, knowledge acquired using the scientific method is more than just the passive acceptance of theories about behaviour.

This means that scientific methods are able to establish the causes of behaviour through the use of methods that are both empirical and replicable.

A consequence of this is that if scientific theories no longer fit the facts, they can be refined or abandoned, meaning that scientific knowledge is self-corrective.

A scientific approach is not always appropriate

Not all psychologists share the view that all human behaviour can, or should, be explored by the use of scientific methods.

If human behaviour is not subject to the laws and regularities implied by scientific methods, then predictions become impossible and these methods are inappropriate. Likewise, much of the subject matter of psychology is unobservable, therefore cannot be measured with any degree of accuracy.

A consequence of this is that much of psychological knowledge is inferential, i.e. there is a gap between the actual data obtained in research investigations and the theories put forward to explain this data.

Introspection is not particularly accurate

Nisbett and Wilson (1977) claim that we have very little knowledge of the causes of, and processes underlying, our behaviour and attitudes.

Nisbett and Wilson found this problem was particularly acute in the study of implicit attitudes, i.e. attitudes or stereotypes that are unknown to us. For example, a person may be implicitly racist, which influences the way they react to members of a different ethnic group.

Because such attitudes exist outside of conscious awareness, self-reports through introspection would not uncover them. This challenges the value of introspective reports in exploring the roots of our behaviour.

Introspection is still useful in scientific psychology

Despite the fact that introspection rapidly fell out of favour as a research tool, it has not been *entirely* abandoned by psychologists, and in recent years it has made something of a comeback.

Csikszentmihalyi and Hunter (2003) used introspective methods as a way of making 'happiness' a measurable phenomenon. They gave a group of teenagers beepers that went off during random times throughout the day, requiring them to write down their thoughts and feelings in the moment before the beep. Most of the entries indicated that the teens were unhappy rather than happy, but when their energies were focused on a challenging task, they tended to be more upbeat.

Introspection therefore offers researchers a way of understanding more clearly the momentary conditions that affect happiness, and as such may help them to improve the quality of our lives.

MEET THE RESEARCHER

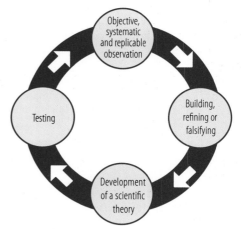

Wilhelm Wundt
In 1873 Wundt published the first book on psychology – *Principles of Physiological Psychology*. This book established psychology as a unique branch of science with its own subject matter and its own methods. He was the first person in history to be called a 'psychologist'. Wundt was certainly prolific as a writer. If you were to read his works at the rate of 60 pages a day, it would take you two and a half years to finish them!

KEY TERMS

Empiricism The belief that all knowledge is derived from sensory experience. It is generally characterised by the use of the scientific method in psychology.

Introspection The process by which a person gains knowledge about his or her own mental and emotional states as a result of the examination or observation of their conscious thoughts and feelings.

Scientific method Refers to the use of investigative methods that are objective, systematic and replicable, and the formulation, testing and modification of hypotheses based on these methods.

▲ The scientific cycle.

(scientific cycle diagram: Objective, systematic and replicable observation → Building, refining or falsifying → Development of a scientific theory → Testing)

CAN YOU? No. 5.1

1. Explain Wundt's contribution to the development of psychology. (4 marks)
2. Outline **one** criticism of Wundt's contribution to psychology. (3 marks)
3. Explain what is meant by 'introspection'. (4 marks)
4. Briefly outline **two** criticisms of introspection as a method of investigation. (2 marks each)
5. Explain the emergence of psychology as a science. (6 marks)
6. Outline **one** strength and **one** limitation of the scientific approach in psychology. (3 marks each)

125

The behaviourist approach

The **behaviourist** approach rejected the vagueness of introspection, focusing instead on *observable* events, i.e. stimuli and responses, and the conditions under which learning would be most likely to occur. Because of the focus on learning, this approach is sometimes referred to as 'learning theory'. Behaviourists believed that much of human behaviour could be explained in terms of a basic form of learning known as *conditioning*, which involves the formation of learned associations between stimuli in the environment and an organism's responses. On this spread we look at two influential forms of conditioning – Pavlov's research on **classical conditioning** and Skinner's research on **operant conditioning**.

Don't be confused by the words 'positive' and 'negative' in this context. 'Positive' means adding something, and 'negative' means taking something away. Both positive and negative reinforcement increase the frequency of a behaviour.

CLASSICAL CONDITIONING

All animals (including humans) are born with a number of natural reflexes such as the reflex action of salivation when food is placed in the mouth. These reflexes are made up of a *stimulus* (such as food) and its naturally associated response (in this case, salivation). When other stimuli are consistently associated with this stimulus, and predict its arrival, then eventually they too trigger the same response and the animal is described as having been 'classically conditioned'.

Pavlov's research

Russian physiologist Ivan Pavlov is normally credited with discovering the process of classical conditioning (Pavlov, 1927). He was investigating the salivary reflex in dogs when he noticed that the animals not only salivated when food was placed in their mouths, but also reacted to stimuli that coincided with the presentation of food, such as the presence of a food bowl or the person who fed them. This led him to explore the conditions under which this type of learning was most likely to occur.

The natural stimulus in any reflex is referred to as the unconditioned stimulus (UCS) and the natural response to this stimulus is the unconditioned response (UCR). During the acquisition phase, a neutral stimulus (NS), which does not elicit the UCR, is presented shortly before the UCS. After many pairings of NS + UCS, this changes and the NS is now able to produce the same response *in the absence of the UCS*. The NS is now referred to as a conditioned stimulus (CS) and the response it produces is called a conditioned response (CR). Ringing a bell shortly before presenting food to a hungry animal will eventually (after many pairings of NS and UCS) mean that the bell on its own will be sufficient to produce the response of salivation (CR).

Other important features

- *Timing* – if the NS cannot be used to predict the UCS (e.g. if it occurs after the UCS or the time interval between the two is too great), then conditioning does not take place.
- *Extinction* – Pavlov discovered that, unlike the UCR, the CR does not become permanently established as a response. After a few presentations of the CS in the absence of the UCS, it loses its ability to produce the CR.
- *Spontaneous recovery* – following extinction, if the CS and UCS are then paired together once again, the link between them is made much more quickly.
- *Stimulus generalisation* – Pavlov discovered that once an animal has been conditioned, they will also respond to other stimuli that are similar to the CS.

BEFORE CONDITIONING

UCS   UCR

Neutral stimulus   No salivation

UCS automatically produces UCR. Neutral stimulus does not produce salivation

DURING CONDITIONING

UCS paired with neutral stimulus   UCR

UCS is paired with neutral stimulus. UCS produces UCR.

AFTER CONDITIONING

CS   CR

Neutral stimulus is now the conditioned stimulus. It produces CR, salivation, which is similar to the UCR produced by the food.

OPERANT CONDITIONING

The basic idea behind Skinner's theory of operant conditioning (Skinner, 1938) is that organisms spontaneously produce different behaviours, and these behaviours produce *consequences* for that organism, some of which may be positive (i.e. desirable) and some negative (i.e. undesirable). Whether or not an organism repeats a particular behaviour depends on the nature of these consequences, i.e. it is *reinforced*.

▲ Skinner developed a special cage (called a 'Skinner box') in order to investigate operant conditioning in rats. The rat moves around the cage, and when it accidentally presses the lever, a food pellet (the reinforcer) falls into the cage. In no time at all the hungry rat begins pressing the lever in order to obtain food. If the food pellets stop, the rat presses the lever a few more times and then abandons it (*extinction*).

Types of reinforcement

Reinforcement means just what the word implies, i.e. something in the environment that strengthens (or reinforces) a particular behaviour and so makes it more likely to recur. There are two main types of reinforcer, positive and negative reinforcers. Although they both make it more likely that a behaviour will recur, they do this in different ways.

Positive reinforcement occurs when behaviour produces a consequence that is satisfying or pleasant for the organism; for example, food to a hungry animal or praise given to a child after they do something particularly well are both effective positive reinforcers.

Negative reinforcers work because they remove something aversive (unpleasant) and so restore the organism to its 'pre-aversive' state. For example, the act of hitting the 'off' button on an alarm clock allows a person to escape from the unpleasant ringing and restores the restful pre-alarm state.

Other important features

- Schedules of reinforcement – although a *continuous* reinforcement schedule (e.g. reinforcing a rat every time it presses a lever) is most effective in establishing a particular response, a partial reinforcement schedule (e.g. reinforcing every third lever press or every 10 minutes) is more effective in maintaining that response and avoiding extinction.
- **Punishment** – refers to the circumstance whereby a behaviour is followed by a consequence that is undesirable or unpleasant for the organism. Reinforcement increases the likelihood of a behaviour recurring, whereas punishment decreases it. As with reinforcement, punishment can also be positive (i.e. adding something unpleasant as a consequence, such as slapping a naughty child) or negative (i.e. taking away something pleasant such as 'grounding' a naughty teenager).

EVALUATION/DISCUSSION

Classical conditioning has been applied to therapy

Classical conditioning has been applied in the development of treatments for the reduction of anxiety associated with various phobias.

Systematic desensitisation is a therapy based on classical conditioning (see page 106). It works by eliminating the learned anxious response (the CR) that is associated with a feared object or situation (the CS). It is then possible to eliminate one learned response (anxiety) by replacing it with another (relaxation) so the patient is no longer anxious in the presence of the feared object or situation.

This classical conditioning-based approach has been found to be effective for a range of phobias such as fear of spiders (arachnophobia) and fear of flying (aerophobia).

Classical conditioning is only appropriate for some learning

Because different species face different challenges to survive, some relationships between CS and UCS are more difficult (and others easier) to establish.

Seligman (1970) proposed the concept of preparedness to explain this. Animals are *prepared* to learn associations that are significant in terms of their survival needs (e.g. associating the smell of meat with the presence of food), yet *unprepared* to learn associations that are not significant in this respect (e.g. associating the sound of a bell with food).

This suggests that classical conditioning may be more appropriate in the learning of specific types of association (i.e. those important to survival), something that is linked to a species' evolutionary history.

Operant conditioning based on experimental work

A particular strength of Skinner's research was his reliance on the experimental method, using controlled conditions to discover a possible causal relationship between variables.

Skinner's reliance on the Skinner box was a good example of this approach in practice. By manipulating the consequences of behaviour (the independent variable), he was able to accurately measure the effects on the rat's behaviour (the dependent variable).

This allowed him to establish a cause-and-effect relationship between the consequences of a behaviour (i.e. positive or negative) and the future frequency of its occurrence.

Over-reliance on non-human animals in research

Skinner's research has received some criticism because his experiments involved the study of non-human animals rather than humans.

Critics claim that his reliance on rats and pigeons means that Skinner's studies can tell us little about human behaviour. They claim that, unlike non-human animals, human beings have free will rather than having their behaviour determined by positive and negative reinforcement.

However, Skinner argued that free will is merely an illusion and what we believe are behaviours chosen through free will are actually the product of external influences that 'guide' our behaviour on a daily basis.

A limited perspective on behaviour

Behaviourists have been accused of ignoring other levels of explanation such as those that emphasise the importance of cognitive factors or emotional states.

Treating human beings as a product of their conditioning alone means that we ignore the evidence for the role of these other factors in shaping behaviour. However, Skinner rejected this claim, arguing that these internal states are scientifically untestable.

Skinner argued that even complex behaviours, such as our interactions with the opposite sex or pathological behaviour, could be better understood by studying the reinforcement history of the individual.

MEET THE RESEARCHER

Burrhus Skinner

While the US military were working on their first missile guidance systems, psychologist Burrhus Skinner (1904–1990) had an unusual idea – pigeons could be trained to guide anti-ship missiles to their targets. The project, known as 'Project Pelican', involved three pigeons in separate compartments in the nose cone of a 'Pelican' missile. Each compartment had a lens, and using operant conditioning, the pigeons were trained to peck at the target projected on it in order to keep the missiles on target. This idea was taken seriously enough for the military to adapt some missiles to accommodate the pigeons before they eventually decided that electronics was a better bet for the future.

⬆ UPGRADE

Questions requiring AO3 are looking for *elaboration*, which means you need to explain and develop any point that you make. Shorter questions such as 'Briefly outline one strength of the behaviourist approach. (2 marks)' do not need much detail and doing more than one point will not get you extra credit. In contrast, consider the question: 'Evaluate the behaviourist approach. (6 marks)'. This question requires you to go deeper in your evaluation but you are not restricted to just the one point.

Here's what you could do to answer this question: start by **identifying a strength** of the approach – such as 'There is research to support the behaviourist approach'. Elaborate that by **giving an example** of a study without going into much detail. Say why this is a strength of the approach. Next you could comment on the fact that behaviourists often use a **scientific approach** (such as experiments) and say why this is a strength (i.e. it can establish a causal relationship between two variables and the research is replicable). You could further elaborate this by bringing in **other research** that backs up or goes against it, or by highlighting a potential problem of the methods used.

Try this elaboration process for one of the other evaluation points of the behaviourist approach.

KEY TERMS

Behaviourist People who believe that human behaviour can be explained in terms of conditioning, without the need to consider thoughts or feelings.

Classical conditioning When a neutral stimulus is consistently paired with an unconditioned stimulus so that it eventually takes on the properties of this stimulus and is able to produce a conditioned response.

Operant conditioning Learning through reinforcement or punishment. If a behaviour is followed by a desirable consequence then that behaviour is more likely to occur again in the future.

Punishment Involves the application of an unpleasant consequence following a behaviour, with the result that the behaviour is less likely to occur again in the future.

Reinforcement Anything that strengthens a response and increases the likelihood that it will occur again in the future.

CAN YOU?   No. 5.2

1. Briefly explain what is meant by 'classical' and 'operant conditioning'. (2 marks each)
2. Outline the main findings of Pavlov's research. (4 marks)
3. Explain what is meant by 'positive' and 'negative reinforcement' in operant conditioning. (3 marks each)
4. Outline the main findings of Skinner's research. (4 marks)
5. Outline **one** strength and **one** limitation of the behaviourist approach. (6 marks)
6. Discuss the behaviourist approach in psychology. (12 marks AS, 16 marks A)

Social learning theory

Albert Bandura believed that new patterns of behaviour could be acquired not only through direct experience, but also by observing one's own behaviour and the behaviour of others. Unlike operant conditioning, where the role of reinforcement is simply to strengthen a response by providing immediate consequences, Bandura believed that reinforcement could also serve an informative function for the individual. During the course of learning, people not only perform responses; they also observe the different consequences of their own and others' behaviour. On the basis of this feedback, they develop hypotheses about the types of behaviour most likely to succeed in a given situation. These hypotheses then serve as guides for their future behaviour. Bandura referred to this approach as **social learning theory**.

Insider tip…

A common pitfall when answering questions in this area is that students provide descriptions of a study when a question has actually asked about the theory. Make sure you use appropriate material to answer the specific question set.

◀ The Bobo doll.

Social learning theory is nowadays known as 'social cognitive theory' to acknowledge the importance of mediational processes in social learning.

The term 'identification' is used in a slightly different way here than it was on page 18. However, both uses of the term stress either a desire to be part of, or a recognition of similarity between, the individual and others.

SOCIAL LEARNING THEORY (BANDURA, 1986)

Modelling

In order for social learning to take place, someone must carry out (or 'model') the attitude or behaviour to be learned. Individuals that perform this role are referred to as **models**. There are different types of model. A *live* model might be a parent, a teacher at school or a member of a peer group. A *symbolic* model would be someone portrayed in the media, for example a character on TV. These models provide examples of behaviour that can be observed by the individual and later reproduced by them in a process known as **imitation**.

Imitation

Although a certain amount of learning takes place through direct reinforcement, much of what a child learns is acquired through imitation of attitudes and behaviour that are modelled by parents and significant others. Research on imitation has shown that, unlike the relatively slow learning that takes place with conditioning, when a model is provided, whole patterns of behaviour can be rapidly acquired. The key determinants of whether a behaviour is imitated are (i) the characteristics of the model, (ii) the observer's perceived ability to perform that behaviour and (iii) the observed consequences of the behaviour.

Identification

Identification refers to the extent to which an individual relates to a model and feels that he or she is similar to that person. In order to identify with a model, observers must feel that he or she is similar enough to them that they would be likely to experience the same outcomes in that situation. Research (e.g. Shutts *et al.*, 2010) suggests that children are more likely to identify with, and preferentially learn from, models who are similar to them, particularly same-sex models. Identification with a model means that the individual is more likely to imitate their behaviour, meaning that social learning is more likely to be effective.

Vicarious reinforcement

Bandura and Walters (1963) noted that children who observed a model rewarded for aggressive behaviour were much more likely to imitate that behaviour than children who had observed a model punished for the same behaviour. Bandura called this **vicarious reinforcement** – i.e. individuals learn about the likely consequences of an action, and then adjust their subsequent behaviour accordingly. The concept of vicarious reinforcement suggests that individuals do not need to experience rewards or punishments directly in order to learn. Instead they can observe the consequences experienced by a model and then make judgements as to the likelihood of experiencing these outcomes themselves.

The role of mediational processes

Social learning differs from other learning approaches in that it places special importance on internal **mediational processes**. Bandura (1986) claimed that, in order for social learning to take place, the observer must form mental representations of the behaviour displayed by the model and the probable consequences of that behaviour in terms of expectancies of future outcomes. When appropriate opportunities arise in the future, the individual might display the learned behaviour *provided* that the expectation of positive consequences is greater than the expectation of negative consequences.

KEY STUDY: BANDURA *ET AL.* (1961)

Procedures

Bandura *et al.* (1961) carried out an experiment involving children who observed aggressive or non-aggressive adult models and were then tested for imitative learning in the absence of the model. Half the children were exposed to adult models interacting aggressively with a life-sized Bobo doll and half exposed to non-aggressive models.

The aggressive model displayed distinctive physically aggressive acts towards the doll, e.g. striking it with a mallet, accompanied by verbal aggression such as saying 'POW'. Following exposure to the model, children were frustrated by being shown attractive toys which they were not allowed to play with. They were then taken to a room where, among other toys, there was a Bobo doll.

Findings

Children who observed the aggressive model reproduced a good deal of physically and verbally aggressive behaviour resembling that of the model. Children who observed the non-aggressive model exhibited virtually no aggression toward the Bobo doll.

About one-third of the children who observed the aggressive model repeated the model's verbal responses while none of the children who had observed the non-aggressive model made verbally aggressive remarks.

In a follow-up to this study, Bandura and Walters found that children who saw the model being rewarded for aggressive acts were more likely to show a high level of aggression in their own play.

EVALUATION/DISCUSSION

Social learning theory has useful applications

The principles of social learning have been usefully applied to increase our understanding of many areas of human behaviour, including criminal behaviour.

Akers (1998) suggests that the probability of someone engaging in criminal behaviour increases when they are exposed to models who commit criminal behaviour, identify with these models and develop the expectation of positive consequences for their own criminal behaviour.

Ulrich (2003) supports the importance of social learning in this process in a review of the literature, finding that the strongest cause of violent behaviour in adolescence was association with delinquent peer groups, where violence was both modelled and rewarded.

Research support for identification

According to social learning theory, observing a model similar to the self should lead to more learning than observing a dissimilar model.

Fox and Bailenson (2009) found evidence for this using computer generated 'virtual' humans engaging in exercise or merely loitering. The models looked either similar or dissimilar to the individual participants. Participants who viewed their virtual model exercising engaged in more exercise in the 24 hours following the experiment than participants who viewed their virtual model merely loitering or a dissimilar model exercising.

They concluded that greater identification with a model leads to more learning because it is easier to visualise the self in the place of the model, so the observer feels as if he or she is having the same experience.

A problem of establishing causality

A major criticism of social learning theory explanations of deviant behaviour relates to its claim that increased associations with deviant peers increases the likelihood that an individual will adopt the same values and behaviours.

Siegel and McCormick (2006) suggest that young people who possess deviant attitudes and values (e.g. low self-control) would seek out peers with similar attitudes and behaviours, as they are more fun to be with than their less reckless counterparts.

The cause of delinquency, therefore, may not be social learning as a result of exposure to deviant role models, but the possession of deviant attitudes prior to contact with deviant peers.

A problem of complexity

In focusing exclusively on the processes of social learning, advocates of this approach disregard other potential influences on behaviour.

For example, in explaining the development of gender role behaviour, social learning theorists would emphasise the importance of gender-specific modelling. In real life, however, a child is exposed to many different influences, all of them interacting in complex ways. These include genetic predispositions, media portrayals, locus of control and so on.

This presents a serious problem for social learning researchers. If virtually anything can have an influence on a specific behaviour, it becomes very difficult to show that one particular thing (social learning) is the main causal influence.

The importance of identification in social learning

Media attempts to change health-related behaviours have shown that models similar to the target audience are more likely to bring about identification and greater social learning.

To achieve this, health campaigns have tried to match characters that model the desired behaviour with the target audience in terms of physical characteristics, attitudes and behaviours. Greater identification with the model is then expected to influence modelling behaviour. Andsager *et al.* (2006) found that perceived similarity to a model in an anti-alcohol advertisement was positively related to the message's effectiveness.

Based on this finding, the researchers suggest that some of a message's potency may be lost if the individual finds it difficult to identify with a given model.

MEET THE RESEARCHER

Albert Bandura was born in 1925, in Northern Canada. He was educated in a small local school before enrolling as a biological sciences major at the University of British Columbia. While working nights to make ends meet, he found himself arriving at university much earlier than his classes started. To pass the time, he began taking 'filler classes' during these early morning hours, which led him to stumble upon psychology. 'One morning, I was wasting time in the library. I thumbed through a course catalogue attempting to find a filler course to occupy the early time slot. I noticed a course in psychology. It sparked my interest and I found my career.' He still continues to research and teach at Stanford University, at over 90 years of age!

KEY TERMS

Identification is a form of influence where an individual adopts an attitude or behaviour because they want to be associated with a particular person or group.

Imitation The action of using someone or something as a model and copying their behaviour.

Mediational processes refer to the internal mental processes that exist between environmental stimuli and the response made by an individual to those stimuli.

Modelling A form of learning where individuals learn a particular behaviour by observing another individual performing that behaviour.

Social learning theory Learning through observing others and imitating behaviours that are rewarded.

Vicarious reinforcement Learning that is not a result of direct reinforcement of behaviour, but through observing someone else being reinforced for that behaviour.

APPLY YOUR KNOWLEDGE

Jack and Jess are two 10-year-old children. Their mother has noticed that Jack has a tendency to be disruptive and badly behaved after watching television programmes with a violent theme. She is shocked when she discovers that he has been caught fighting at school and the teacher asks whether he has been watching a lot of violent TV. Jack's mum is puzzled because Jess watches the same programmes but doesn't appear to be as affected by them.

Social learning theory has been used as a possible explanation of how and why children learn aggressive behaviour as a result of their exposure to violence on TV.

Using what you have learned from this spread, explain Jack's behaviour and suggest why Jess does not behave in the same way after watching violent programmes on TV.

CAN YOU?   No. 5.3

1. Briefly explain what is meant by 'imitation', 'identification', 'modelling', 'vicarious reinforcement' and the role of 'mediational processes'. (2 marks each)
2. Outline the main findings of Bandura's research into social learning. (4 marks)
3. Discuss the social learning approach in psychology. (12 marks AS, 16 marks A)

The cognitive approach

Cognitive psychology focuses on how people perceive, store, manipulate and interpret information; studying processes like perception, memory, thinking and problem solving. Unlike behaviourists, cognitive psychologists believe it is necessary to look at internal mental processes in order to understand behaviour. Much of cognitive psychology uses an information processing model, whereby information received through the senses is processed by various systems in the brain. Because the information processing approach was first used to describe the way in which computers processed information, what goes on in the human brain is often explained using computing metaphors such as 'encoding', 'processing' and 'retrieval'.

THE STUDY OF INTERNAL MENTAL PROCESSES

The cognitive approach studies information processing, i.e. ways in which we extract, store and retrieve information that helps to guide our behaviour. Many different kinds of mental processes contribute to information processing. These include selecting important information (attention), using it to solve problems (thinking), storing it in memory and retrieving it as and when it is needed. The cognitive approach recognises that these mental processes cannot be studied directly but must be studied indirectly by **inferring** what goes on as a result of measuring behaviour. This enables cognitive psychologists to develop theories about the mental processes that led to the observed behaviour.

The role of schemas

A **schema** (plural *schemas* or *schemata*) is a cognitive framework that helps organise and interpret information in the brain. For example, schemas for specific events are based on expectations of how to behave in different situations (such as in a restaurant or a classroom) or in different roles (e.g. as a guard in a mock prison – see page 22). Schemas are useful to us because they allow us to take shortcuts when interpreting the huge amount of information we have to deal with on a daily basis. However, schemas also cause us to exclude anything that does not conform to our established ideas about the world, focusing instead on things that confirm our pre-existing beliefs and ideas. Schemas help us fill in the gaps in the absence of full information about a person, event or thing. For example, if we classify food as 'foreign' or someone we sit next to on the bus as 'old', our schemas will tell us what to expect and we act accordingly, regardless of how tasty the food or stimulating our companion might really be. A consequence of this is that we may develop stereotypes that are difficult to disconfirm, even when faced with new and conflicting information.

The role of theoretical and computer models

Theoretical models In cognitive psychology, models such as the multi-store model of memory or the working memory model are simplified representations based on current research evidence. Models are often pictorial in nature, represented by boxes and arrows that indicate cause and effect or the stages of a particular mental process. Models such as the working memory model are often incomplete and informal and are frequently changed, updated and refined. For example, the working memory model was first proposed by Baddeley and Hitch in 1974. Their initial model consisted of three main sections with a fourth (the episodic buffer) added by Baddeley in 2000.

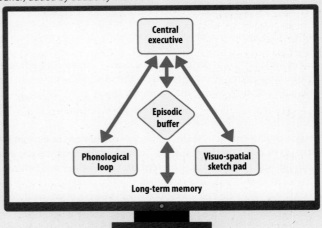

Computer models The development of computers and computer programming led to a focus on the way in which sensory information is 'coded' as it passes through the system. Using a computer analogy, information is inputted through the senses, encoded into memory and then combined with previously stored information to complete a task. A computer model of memory is a good example. Information stored on the hard disk is like long-term memory and RAM (random access memory) corresponds to working memory (see page 48). The idea of working memory as a temporary workspace fits the computer model nicely as, like working memory, RAM is cleared and reset when the task being carried out is finished.

THE EMERGENCE OF COGNITIVE NEUROSCIENCE

The rapid advances in ways of studying the brain in the latter part of the twentieth century has meant that neuroscientists are now able to study the living brain, giving them detailed information about the brain structures involved in different kinds of mental processing (**cognitive neuroscience**). The use of non-invasive neuroimaging techniques such as positron emission tomography (PET) and functional magnetic resonance imaging (fMRI) helps psychologists to understand how the brain supports different cognitive activities and emotions by showing what parts of the brain become active in specific circumstances. For example, Burnett *et al.* (2009) found that when people feel guilty, several brain regions are active, including the medial prefrontal cortex, an area associated with social emotions.

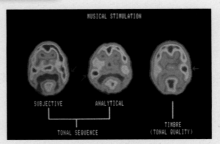

▲ Neuroimaging techniques such as PET scans help psychologists by showing what parts of the brain become active in specific circumstances.

Cognitive neuroscientists study many different aspects of human cognition, including the neural processes underlying memory, attention, perception and awareness. They are also interested in social cognition, the brain regions involved when we interact with others, and how impairments in these regions may characterise different psychological conditions.

EVALUATION/DISCUSSION

The cognitive approach has many applications

A strength of the cognitive approach is that it has been applied in many other areas of psychology.

In social psychology, research in *social* cognition has helped psychologists better understand how we interpret the actions of others, and the cognitive approach to psychopathology has been used to explain how much of the dysfunctional behaviour shown by people can be traced back to faulty thinking processes.

These insights have led to the successful treatment, using cognitive-based interventions, of people suffering from disorders such as depression and OCD.

The cognitive approach is scientific

Cognitive psychologists' emphasis on scientific methods is a particular strength of this approach.

The use of the experimental method provides researchers with a rigorous method for collecting and evaluating evidence in order to reach accurate conclusions about how the mind works.

This means that conclusions about how the mind works are based on far more than common sense and introspection, as these can give a misleading picture of mental processes, many of which are not consciously accessible.

Computer models have limited explanatory powers

The cognitive approach uses computer models to explain human information processing.

For example, terms such as 'encoding', 'storage' and 'retrieval' are borrowed directly from the field of computing. However, there is an important difference between the sort of information processing that takes place within a computer program and the information processing that takes place within the human mind. Computers do not make mistakes, nor do they ignore available information or forget anything that has been stored on their hard drives.

Humans, on the other hand, do all of these things, which limits the appropriateness of explaining human thought and behaviour using computer models.

The cognitive approach ignores emotion and motivation

A problem for the cognitive approach is that, although it can tell us *how* different cognitive processes take place, it fails to tell us *why* they do.

In other words, the role of emotion and motivation has largely been ignored by this approach. This is not surprising given that approaches that focus on the motivational processes in behaviour (e.g. Freud; see page 134) largely ignore the cognitive processes involved in behaviour.

The lack of focus on motivational states may be explained by the over-dependence on information processing analogies, as motivation is clearly irrelevant to a computer, but not to a human being.

Studies may lack ecological validity

Many studies of cognitive psychology tend to use tasks that have little in common with participants' natural everyday experiences.

For example, experiments in memory use artificial test materials that are relatively meaningless in everyday life (e.g. random word lists or digits) rather than being based on the way in which memory is used in everyday life (e.g. why people forget appointments or repress early childhood memories).

As a result, it is unlikely that we would be able to generalise these findings to real-life situations. Therefore, much of the research in cognitive psychology might be criticised as lacking ecological validity, i.e. it fails to reflect the behaviours that occur in real-life settings.

▲ Cognitive psychology research may not always reflect real-life situations.

 UPGRADE

Students often lose marks or waste valuable time in the exam because they do not consider the marks available when constructing their answers to questions. Sometimes students write more than is needed for the marks available or, conversely, do not write enough. For example, a question that asks you to . . .

Briefly explain what is meant by the terms 'internal mental processes' and 'schema'. (4 marks)

. . . should make you realise that the explanation of each term is worth just 2 marks. Having these 2 marks assigned to each term means that you might *define* each term (for the first mark) and then elaborate it (perhaps through an example) for the second mark. Putting in extra and unnecessary detail would not get you any more than the 2 marks available. Likewise, a question that asks for *two* strengths (or *two* limitations) for 6 marks warrants a *little more* elaboration because there are more marks available.

For questions worth 5 marks or less, practise writing answers that take 'a mark a minute'. That will keep you from writing too much and losing time that you should be spending on answering higher tariff questions.

KEY TERMS

Cognitive Relates to mental processes such as perception, memory and reasoning.

Cognitive neuroscience An area of psychology dedicated to the underlying neural bases of cognitive functions.

Computer model Refers to the process of using computer analogies as a representation of human cognition.

Inference/inferring means reaching a logical conclusion on the basis of evidence and reasoning.

Schema A cognitive framework that helps to organise and interpret information in the brain. Schemas help an individual to make sense of new information.

Theoretical models In cognitive psychology, models are simplified, usually pictorial, representations of a particular mental process based on current research evidence.

CAN YOU? No. 5.4

1. Briefly explain what is meant by 'internal mental processes', 'schema', 'theoretical and computer models', and 'cognitive neuroscience'. (3 marks each)
2. Outline the use of theoretical and computer models as an explanation of mental processes. (3 marks each)
3. Using examples from research, explain the emergence of cognitive neuroscience. (4 marks)
4. Outline **two** strengths of the cognitive approach in psychology. (6 marks)
5. Outline **two** limitations of the cognitive approach in psychology. (6 marks)
6. Discuss the cognitive approach in psychology. (12 marks AS, 16 marks A)

The biological approach

The **biological approach** views human beings as biological organisms and so provides biological explanations of all aspects of psychological functioning. Biological psychologists are particularly interested in the genetic basis of behaviour, showing how some characteristics can be passed from generation to generation through the genes. Biological researchers have also studied the important role that chemical changes in the nervous system (**neurochemistry**) and hormonal changes play. More recently, psychologists have become interested in how Charles Darwin's ideas about biological **evolution** might apply to human behaviour, allowing us to understand the original adaptive significance of behaviours such as mate selection or aggression.

BIOLOGICAL INFLUENCES ON BEHAVIOUR

The influence of genes on behaviour

Genes: the mechanisms of heredity
Heredity is the passing of characteristics from one generation to the next through the **genes**, and is the reason why offspring 'take after' their parents in terms of psychological characteristics. Genes carry the instructions for a particular characteristic (such as intelligence or temperament), but how this characteristic develops depends partly on the interaction of the gene with other genes, and partly on the influence of the environment. The extent to which a psychological characteristic is determined by genes or environment is called the nature–nurture debate.

Genotype and phenotype
There is an important difference between the **genotype** – the genetic code that is 'written' in the DNA of an individual's cells – and the **phenotype**, which is the physical appearance that results from this inherited information. Whilst we might expect a direct relationship between the two, this is not always the case. For example, in the case of eye colour, someone may inherit a recessive gene for blue eyes, but this will not be expressed if they have also inherited a dominant gene for brown eyes from the other parent. In this case, we cannot determine the *genotype* (one blue eyes gene, one brown eyes gene) from just observing the *phenotype* (i.e. brown eyes).

The genetic basis of behaviour
Each individual possesses a unique combination of genetic instructions, therefore we differ from each other in terms of personality, intelligence, abilities and so on. The term heritability refers to the amount of variability in a trait within a population that can be attributed to genetic differences between individuals within that population. The more that a trait is influenced by genetic factors, the greater its heritability. For example, studies of identical twins have suggested that the variation in individual intelligence – what makes one person more intelligent than another – could be 60–80% due to genes.

The influence of biological structures on behaviour

Neurons and the nervous system
The nervous system is comprised of several connected systems.
- The central nervous system (CNS) comprises the brain and spinal cord.
- The peripheral nervous system (PNS) comprises the somatic and autonomic nervous systems.

The nervous system carries messages from one part of the body to another using individual nerve cells known as neurons. Neurons transmit nerve impulses in the form of electrical signals. Many aspects of behaviour are under neuronal control, including breathing, eating and sexual behaviour.

The brain
The largest part of the brain is the cerebrum, making up about 85% of the total mass of the brain. The outer surface of the cerebrum is called the cerebral cortex, which is responsible for many of the 'higher-order' functions such as thought and language. The cerebrum is divided into two halves (known as hemispheres), with each hemisphere further divided into four different parts (known as lobes):

The influence of neurochemistry on behaviour

Neurotransmitters
When a nerve impulse reaches the end of one neuron, a chemical called a neurotransmitter is released. It travels from one neuron to the next across a junction called the synapse. There are many different types of neurotransmitter, some of which trigger the receiving neuron to send an impulse and some stop it from doing so. Those neurotransmitters that trigger nerve impulses in the receiving neuron and stimulate the brain into action are called *excitatory* neurotransmitters. Those that inhibit nerve impulses in order to calm the brain and balance mood are called *inhibitory* neurotransmitters (see page 151). Dopamine is an excitatory neurotransmitter that is associated with our 'drive' or motivation. Serotonin is an inhibitory transmitter, adequate amounts of which are necessary to maintain a stable mood. For example, Crockett *et al.* (2008) found that when serotonin levels are low people tend to display increased aggression.

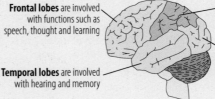

Frontal lobes are involved with functions such as speech, thought and learning

Temporal lobes are involved with hearing and memory

Parietal lobes process sensory information such as touch, temperature and pain

Occipital lobes process visual information

Hormones
Hormones are chemicals that are produced by endocrine glands such as the pituitary gland, which together make up the endocrine system. In response to a signal from the brain, hormones are secreted directly into the bloodstream by the endocrine glands, where they travel to their 'target cells' and exert their influence by stimulating receptors on the surface of or inside cells. The presence of a hormone causes a physiological reaction in the cell, altering its activity (see page 152). For example, Carré *et al.* (2006) studied a Canadian ice hockey team over the course of a season. They found evidence of a surge in levels of the hormone testosterone whenever the team played in their home stadium, suggesting the hormone energised the players to defend their home territory.

Evolution and behaviour

Charles Darwin argued that, over time, organisms become adapted to their environment through biological evolution. This refers to the changes that take place in the characteristics of a population over time. The mechanism behind biological evolution is **natural selection**. Individuals within a species differ from each other in terms of their physical characteristics and in their behaviour, and at least some of this variation is inherited. Because individuals must compete with each other for access to resources (mates, food, etc.), those who survive this competition and go on to reproduce will tend to have behaviours that are more likely to lead to survival and reproductive success than those who do not.

These behaviours will be passed on to offspring and will become more widespread in the population; through the process of natural selection, successive generations will develop behaviours that are even more likely to lead to survival and reproductive success. Buss (1989) studied 37 different cultures and found universal similarities in human mate preferences. Women desired mates with resources (to provide for offspring) whilst men desired young, physically attractive women (an indication of their fertility and reproductive value).

EVALUATION/DISCUSSION

The importance of the scientific method

The biological approach uses the scientific method, particularly the experimental method, as its main method of investigation.

Experimental studies take place in highly controlled environments so that other researchers are able to replicate research studies under the same experimental conditions, adding to the validity of the original findings if they can be reproduced. The use of sophisticated imaging and recording techniques has increased the precision and objectivity of experimental research in this area.

As a result, these techniques have contributed to the scientific validity of the biological approach.

Applications of the biological approach

A strength of the biological approach is that it provides clear predictions, e.g. about the effects of neurotransmitters on behaviour or the influence of biological rhythms on behaviour.

This has led to significant applications of biological research in the real world. Research into the role of neurochemical imbalance in depression has led to the development of effective drug treatments.

Likewise, research into circadian rhythms and their effect on psychological well-being (see page 164) has led to significant improvements in the working conditions of shift workers.

This further demonstrates the value of adopting a biological approach to the study of human behaviour.

The biological approach is reductionist

The biological approach is criticised for its belief that complex behaviour can be broken down into the action of genes, neurochemicals and hormones.

For example, many explanations of mental disorders are reductionist because genes or neurochemical imbalances are believed to be the main cause of these disorders.

However, whilst a reductionist approach lends itself to scientific investigation, we cannot fully understand a behaviour without also taking account of the other factors that influence it. These include cognitive, emotional and cultural factors, all of which have a significant influence on behaviour.

Problems for evolutionary explanations

Because human behaviours can evolve through either genetic *or* cultural routes, a biologically based evolutionary explanation may have limited explanatory power.

Critics of such explanations claim that many established patterns of human behaviour have purely cultural origins with no obvious survival value. For example, in many cultures, such as in China and parts of India, the sex ratio at birth is strongly biased in favour of males. This cultural preference for sons has resulted in sex-selective abortion or the withholding of resources from daughters. Unlike behaviours shaped by biological evolution, which change very gradually over many generations, behaviours shaped by cultural evolution can change more rapidly.

In China, a consequence of the more rapid change possible through cultural evolution is that there has been a change in public attitudes toward girls and a reduction in the widespread cultural preference for sons.

A03 plus The dangers of genetic explanations

Recent research suggesting a genetic basis for criminal behaviour has led to concerns about how this information might be used.

Critics claim this may lead to genetic screening of the population to identify this genetic susceptibility and subsequent discrimination against those with a predisposition for criminality. This also creates the danger that genes might then be used as convenient explanations for complicated human behaviour, despite the fact that the connection between genes and complex behaviour such as criminality is far from straightforward.

However, there may be positive consequences of such research. If individuals discover that they have a genetic predisposition for criminality or a mental disorder such as schizophrenia, this gives them the opportunity to avoid environmental situations likely to trigger this predisposition, or to develop coping skills that would protect them from its influence.

KEY TERMS

Biological approach Views humans as biological organisms and so provides biological explanations for all aspects of psychological functioning.

Evolution Refers to the change over successive generations of the genetic make-up of a particular population. The central proposition of an evolutionary perspective is that the genotype of a population is changeable rather than fixed, and that this change is likely to be caused by the process of natural selection.

Gene A part of the chromosome of an organism that carries information in the form of DNA.

Genotype The genetic make-up of an individual. The genotype is a collection of inherited genetic material that is passed from generation to generation.

Natural selection The process by which inherited characteristics that enhance an individual's reproductive success (or 'fitness') are passed on to the next generation, and so become more widespread in the population over time.

Neurochemistry The study of chemical and neural processes associated with the nervous system.

Phenotype The observable characteristics of an individual. This is a consequence of the interaction of the genotype with the environment.

APPLY YOUR KNOWLEDGE

Criminal behaviour may be all in the genes
Turning to crime may be a consequence of our genes according to a recent study. Researchers in the US found that men and women who had been adopted as children were over four times more likely to get into trouble with the police if one of their biological parents had a criminal record. The fact that biological parents had an influence on their children's behaviour despite having no input in their upbringing appears to show a significant genetic influence.

1   With reference to the report above, explain the relationship between genetics and criminal behaviour.
2   What limitations can you think of for genetic explanations of criminal behaviour?

CAN YOU?   No. 5.5

1. Briefly explain what is meant by the terms 'genotype' and 'phenotype'. (2 marks + 2 marks)
2. Outline the influence of genes on behaviour. (4 marks)
3. Outline the influence of biological structures and neurochemistry on behaviour. (4 marks + 4 marks)
4. Explain the difference between genotype and phenotype. (3 marks)
5. Outline the relationship between evolution and behaviour. (4 marks)
6. Outline **two** strengths and **two** limitations of the biological approach in psychology. (3 marks for each)
7. Discuss the biological approach in psychology. (12 marks AS, 16 marks A)

The psychodynamic approach

The term **psychodynamic** describes any theory that emphasises change and development in the individual. It is also used to describe theories where drive is a central concept in this development. Both of these uses of the term stress the importance of change, i.e. the person is seen as dynamic, or constantly changing as they develop. Although there are a number of theories that fit this psychodynamic profile, they all emphasise unconscious motives and desires, as well as the importance of early childhood experiences in shaping personality. The best known of the psychodynamic theories is Freudian **psychoanalysis**.

> Although the idea of defence mechanisms is attributed to Sigmund Freud, much of the development of this idea was done by his daughter, Anna Freud, in her 1936 book *The Ego and the Mechanisms of Defence*.

FREUD'S THEORY OF PSYCHOANALYSIS

Sigmund Freud believed that behaviour was determined more by psychological factors than by biological factors or environmental reinforcement. He assumed that people are born with basic instincts and needs and that behaviour is in large part controlled by the **unconscious** mind.

The role of the unconscious

Freud believed in the existence of a part of the mind that was inaccessible to conscious thought. He referred to this as the unconscious mind. He used the metaphor of an iceberg to describe the mind, the tip of the iceberg (representing the conscious mind) being visible, but the much larger part (representing the unconscious) being hidden under water. Freud believed that most of our everyday actions and behaviours are not controlled consciously but are the product of the unconscious mind, which reveals itself in slips of the tongue (or 'Freudian slips'), in creativity and in neurotic symptoms. The unconscious, he believed, extended its influence into every part of our waking (and sleeping) lives. Freud believed the mind actively prevents traumatic memories from the unconscious from reaching conscious awareness. These memories might cause anxiety; therefore the mind uses **defence mechanisms** (see below) to prevent the person becoming aware of them.

The structure of personality

Freud divided the mind into three structures – the id, the ego and the superego – each of which demands gratification, but is frequently in conflict with the other parts.

The id The id operates solely in the unconscious. It contains the libido, the biological energy created by the reproductive instincts. The id operates according to the *pleasure principle*, i.e. it demands immediate gratification regardless of circumstances. For example, if a person is hungry, the id demands that they eat there and then.

The ego The ego mediates between the impulsive demands of the id and the reality of the external world (the reality principle). For example, it may delay gratifying the id until there is a more appropriate opportunity to satisfy its demands. It must also compromise between the impulsive demands of the id and the moralistic demands of the superego.

The superego This is divided into the conscience and the ego-ideal. The conscience is the internalisation of societal rules. It determines which behaviours are permissible and causes feelings of guilt when rules are broken. The ego-ideal is what a person strives towards, and is most probably determined by parental standards of good behaviour.

▶ The ego mediates between the demands of the id and the demands of the superego.

Defence mechanisms

If an individual is faced with a situation that they are unable to deal with rationally, their defence mechanisms may be triggered. These tend to operate unconsciously and work by distorting reality so that anxiety is reduced. By using defence mechanisms the individual stops themselves becoming aware of any unpleasant thoughts and feelings associated with the traumatic situation.

Examples of defence mechanisms

Repression refers to the unconscious blocking of unacceptable thoughts and impulses. Rather than staying quietly in the unconscious, these repressed thoughts and impulses continue to influence behaviour without the individual being aware of the reasons behind their behaviour. For example, a child who is abused by a parent may have no recollection of these events, but has trouble forming relationships.

Denial is the refusal to accept reality so as to avoid having to deal with any painful feelings that might be associated with that event. The person acts as if the traumatic event had not happened, something that those around them find to be quite bizarre. For example, an alcoholic will often deny they have a drinking problem even after being arrested several times for being drunk and disorderly.

Displacement involves the redirecting of thoughts or feelings (usually hostile) in situations where the person feels unable to express them in the presence of the person they *should* be directed towards. Instead, they may 'take it out' on a helpless victim or object. This gives their hostile feelings a route for expression, even though they are misapplied to an innocent person or object.

Psychosexual stages

Freud believed that personality developed through a sequence of five stages. These are referred to as *psychosexual* stages to emphasise that the most important driving force in development is the need to express sexual energy (libido). Freud believed that the individual experiences tension due to the build up of this sexual energy and that pleasure comes from its discharge. At each stage this energy is expressed in different ways and through different parts of the body.

Stage	Approx age	Description of stage
Oral	0–2 years	The mouth is the focal point of sensation and is the way in which the child expresses early sexual energy (e.g. through sucking and biting).
Anal	2–3 years	The beginnings of ego development, as the child becomes aware of the demands of reality and the need to conform to the demands of others. The major issue at this stage is toilet training as the child learns to control the expulsion of bodily waste.
Phallic	3–6 years	Sexual energy is now focused on the genitals. The major conflict of this stage is the **Oedipus complex** in which the male child unconsciously wishes to possess their mother and get rid of their father. As a result of this desire, boys experience castration anxiety (punishment from the father), and in an attempt to resolve this problem, the child identifies with their father.
Latent	6–12 years	The child develops their mastery of the world around them. During this stage, the conflicts and issues of the previous stages are repressed with the consequence that children are unable to remember much of their early years.
Genital	12+	The culmination of psychosexual development and the fixing of sexual energy in the genitals. This eventually directs us towards sexual intercourse and the beginnings of adult life.

EVALUATION/DISCUSSION

A pioneering approach to understanding human behaviour

The development of psychoanalysis as an explanation of human behaviour represented a dramatic shift in psychological thinking.

It suggested new methodological procedures for gathering evidence (case studies) and the development of the approach was based on observations of behaviour rather than relying on introspection (see page 124). From these observations, Freud and his followers were the first to demonstrate the potential of *psychological*, rather than biological, treatments for disorders such as depression and anxiety.

This approach has led to successful treatments; for example, de Maat et al.'s (2009) large-scale review of psychotherapy studies concluded that psychoanalysis produced significant improvements in symptoms that were maintained in the years after treatment.

Scientific support for the psychoanalytic approach

Critics of psychoanalysis often claim there is no scientific evidence for psychoanalysis and that its claims are not testable or falsifiable.

However, many of the claims of psychoanalysis *have* been tested and many have been confirmed using scientific methodology. Fisher and Greenberg (1996) summarised 2,500 of these studies, concluding that experimental studies of psychoanalysis 'compare well with studies relevant to any other major area of psychology'.

Fisher and Greenberg's support for the existence of unconscious motivation in human behaviour and for the defence mechanisms of repression, denial and displacement adds scientific credibility to psychoanalytic explanations of human behaviour.

Psychoanalysis is a gender-biased approach

Freud's views of women and female sexuality were less well developed than his views on male sexuality.

Despite the fact that his theories were focused on sexual development, Freud seemed content to remain ignorant of female sexuality and how it may differ from male sexuality. This led psychoanalysts such as Karen Horney, who broke away from Freudian theory, to criticise his work, particularly his views on women and their development.

Dismissing women and their sexuality in such a way is problematic, not only because Freud treated many female patients, but also because his theories are still so influential today.

Psychoanalysis is a culture-biased approach

Sue and Sue (2008) argue that psychoanalysis has little relevance for people from non-Western cultures.

Psychoanalysts believe that mental disorders are the result of traumatic memories being 'locked' in the unconscious, and that freeing them through therapy gives the individual the chance to deal with them in the supportive therapeutic environment. However, they claim that many cultural groups do not value insight in the same way that Western cultures do. In China, for example, a person who is depressed or anxious avoids thoughts that cause distress rather than being willing to discuss them openly.

This contrasts with the Western belief that open discussion and insight are always helpful in therapy.

Psychoanalysis: a comprehensive theory

One of the main strengths of psychoanalysis is the comprehensive nature of the theory.

As well as its therapeutic applications, psychoanalysis can be used to explain many other aspects of human behaviour outside of the realm of psychology. For example, psychoanalysis has been used as a form of literary criticism. Works of literature such as Shakespeare's play *Hamlet* have repressed messages hidden beneath the surface of the text – many aspects of Hamlet's psyche are seen as a projection of Shakespeare's own mind.

As a result, we are able to interpret these works using psychoanalytic concepts, delving into the mind of the author or the fictional character and so enrich our understanding of their psychological state.

 Research methods

Some psychology students conducted a study to test whether people with an anal personality were more careful with their money. They did this by constructing a questionnaire to assess personality type based on Freud's ideas that too much or too little pleasure during any psychosexual stage would result in a fixation on that stage and would result in certain personality types. One particular prediction is that 'anal-retentives', people who are treated harshly at this stage, are stingy.

The questionnaire also asked people to say how much money they typically withdrew when they went to a cash machine. The students then correlated personality score (a high score indicated a strong anal-retentive character) with amount of money withdrawn.

1. Were the students expecting to find a negative or positive correlation? Explain your answer. (2 marks)
2. Identify an appropriate sampling method that the students might use in their study and explain your choice. (2 marks)
3. Describe how the students might carry out a pilot study before undertaking the full study. (3 marks)
4. The students designed their own questionnaire. Identify and explain **three** considerations that are important when designing a questionnaire. (3 marks)

> **LINK TO RESEARCH METHODS**
>
> Correlation on pages 206–207
> Sampling methods on pages 192–193
> Pilot studies on page 183
> Questionnaire design on pages 204–205

KEY TERMS

Defence mechanisms Unconscious strategies that protect our conscious mind from anxiety. Defence mechanisms involve a distortion of reality in some way, so that we are better able to cope with a situation.

Psychoanalysis A term used to describe the personality theory and therapy associated with Sigmund Freud.

Psychodynamic Refers to any theory that emphasises change and development in the individual, particularly those theories where 'drive' is a central concept in development. The best known psychodynamic theory is Freudian psychoanalysis.

Unconscious That part of the human mind that contains repressed ideas and memories, as well as primitive desires and impulses that have never been allowed to enter the conscious mind.

CAN YOU?   No. 5.6

1. Explain the role of the unconscious. (3 marks)
2. Outline the structure of personality from a psychodynamic perspective. (4 marks)
3. Outline what is meant by the terms 'id', 'ego' and 'superego'. (2 marks each)
4. Explain the defence mechanisms of 'repression', 'denial' and 'displacement'. (3 marks each)
5. Outline **two** strengths and **two** limitations of the psychodynamic approach in psychology. (3 marks each)
6. Discuss the psychodynamic approach in psychology. (16 marks)

A LEVEL ONLY ZONE

Humanistic psychology

Humanistic psychology differs from most other approaches in psychology by focusing on conscious experience rather than on behaviour, on personal responsibility and **free will** rather than on determinism, and on discussion of experience rather than on use of the experimental method. Developed by Carl Rogers and Abraham Maslow in the 1950s, humanistic psychology is concerned with topics that are meaningful to human beings, and emphasises the importance of the individual's striving towards personal growth and fulfilment.

BASIC ASSUMPTIONS OF HUMANISTIC PSYCHOLOGY

Free will

Unlike most other approaches, humanistic theories emphasise that people have full conscious control over their own destiny, i.e. they have free will. This is not to say that we are free to do anything at all, as we are subject to many other forces, including biological and societal influences. However, humanistic psychologists believe that human beings are able to make significant personal choices within the constraints imposed by these other forces.

Maslow's theory (Maslow, 1943)

Unlike the psychoanalysts, Maslow was not interested in what went *wrong* with people, but rather he was interested in finding out what could go *right* with them. His hierarchy of needs emphasised the importance of personal growth and fulfilment and opened the door for later movements in psychology, such as positive psychology and happiness.

Hierarchy of needs

Although Maslow did not include the visual idea of a 'pyramid' (see bottom of page) in his original theory, the **hierarchy of needs** is usually represented in this way. The most basic, physiological needs are represented at the bottom of the pyramid and the most advanced needs at the top. Each level must be fulfilled before a person can move up to a higher need. Maslow believed that the more basic the need, the more powerfully it is experienced and the more difficult it is to ignore.

Self-actualisation

Maslow found that most of those who attained this level shared certain characteristics. They tended to be creative, accepting of other people and had an accurate perception of the world around them. Maslow believed that such individuals experienced **self-actualisation** in the form of *peak experiences*. These are moments of extreme inspiration and ecstasy during which they felt able to leave behind all doubts, fears and inhibitions.

Focus on the self

The **self** (or self-concept) refers to how we perceive ourselves as a person. Rogers (1951) claimed that people have two basic needs: positive regard from other people and a feeling of self-worth (i.e. what we *think* about ourselves). Feelings of self-worth develop in childhood and are formed as a result of the child's interactions with parents. Further interactions with significant others (friends, spouse, etc.) also influence the person's feelings of self-worth. Rogers believed that how we think about ourselves, and our feelings of self-worth, are important in determining our psychological health. The closer our self-concept and our ideal self (i.e. who we feel we should be or would like to be) are to each other, the greater our feelings of self-worth and the greater our psychological health.

Congruence

When there is similarity between a person's ideal self and how they perceive themselves to be in real life, a state of **congruence** exists. However, if there is a difference between the self and ideal self, the person experiences a state of incongruence. The closer our self-image and ideal self are to each other, the greater the congruence and the higher our feelings of self-worth. It is rare for a complete state of congruence to exist, with most people experiencing some degree of incongruence. Because most people prefer to see themselves in ways that are consistent with their self-image, they may use defence mechanisms in order to feel less threatened by inconsistencies between how they would like to be and how they really are.

Conditions of worth

Although other people may help the process of self-actualisation, Rogers (1959) believed that more often they hinder it. The love and acceptance given by others may be unconditional (unconditional positive regard), when a person is accepted for who they are or what they do, or conditional, when they are accepted only if they do what others want them to do. When people experience conditional positive regard they develop **conditions of worth**. These are the conditions that they perceive significant others (e.g. parents or a spouse) put upon them, and which they believe have to be in place if they are to be accepted by others and see themselves positively. An individual may experience a sense of self-acceptance only if they meet the expectations that others have set as conditions of acceptance.

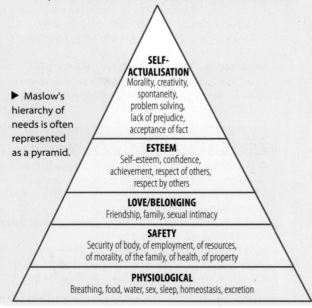

▶ Maslow's hierarchy of needs is often represented as a pyramid.

SELF-ACTUALISATION
Morality, creativity, spontaneity, problem solving, lack of prejudice, acceptance of fact

ESTEEM
Self-esteem, confidence, achievement, respect of others, respect by others

LOVE/BELONGING
Friendship, family, sexual intimacy

SAFETY
Security of body, of employment, of resources, of morality, of the family, of health, of property

PHYSIOLOGICAL
Breathing, food, water, sex, sleep, homeostasis, excretion

The influence on counselling psychology

Rogers (1959) claimed that an individual's psychological problems were a direct result of their conditions of worth and the *conditional* positive regard they receive from other people. He believed that, with counselling, people would be able to solve their own problems in constructive ways, and move towards becoming a more fully functioning person. Instead of acting in a directive way, humanistic therapists regard themselves as 'guides' or 'facilitators' to help people understand themselves and to find ways to enable their potential for self-actualisation.

Therapists provide empathy and unconditional positive regard, expressing their acceptance and understanding, regardless of the feelings and attitudes the client expresses. By doing this, a therapist is able to offer an appropriately supportive environment to help dissolve the client's conditions of worth. This results in the client moving towards being more authentic and more true to self, i.e. able to behave in a way that is true to the person they are, rather than the person others want them to be.

EVALUATION/DISCUSSION

Links to economic development

Research suggests that Maslow's hierarchy may have relevance on a much larger stage than individual growth.

Hagerty (1999) looked at the relationship between economic growth and measures of Maslow's levels in 88 countries over a 34-year period. Countries in the early stages of economic development were characterised by lower level needs (e.g. *physiological* needs such as access to food and *safety* needs).

As would be predicted by Maslow's model, it was only in the advanced stages of economic development that self-actualisation *became important (e.g. using levels of educational enrolment as a measure of people's desire to better themselves).*

Research support for conditions of worth

Research with adolescents has shown evidence consistent with Rogers' view.

Individuals who experience conditional positive regard are likely to display more 'false self behaviour' – doing things to meet others' expectations even when they clash with their own values. Harter *et al.* (1996) discovered that teenagers who feel that they have to fulfil certain conditions in order to gain their parents' approval frequently end up not liking themselves.

Consistent with Rogers' predictions, adolescents who created a 'false self', pretending to be the kind of person his or her parents would love, were more likely to develop depression and a tendency to lose touch with their true self.

Humanistic research methods do not establish causality

Evaluating the humanistic approach scientifically is difficult because most of the evidence used to support this approach fails to establish a causal relationship between variables.

Rogers in particular was an advocate of non-experimental research methods, arguing that the requirements of experimental methods make it impossible to verify the results of counselling. Most psychologists would argue that, without experimental evidence, evaluation of a therapy, or the theory that underlies it, becomes very difficult.

Although some studies have shown personal growth as a result of receiving humanistic counselling, these do not show that the therapy caused the changes, a fundamental requirement of scientific psychology.

The humanistic approach is unrealistic

Humanistic psychology represents an overly idealised and unrealistic view of human nature.

Critics argue that people are not as inherently good and 'growth oriented' as humanistic theorists suggest, and the approach does not adequately recognise people's capacity for pessimism and self-destructive behaviour. The view that personality development is directed only by an innate potential for growth is seen as an oversimplification, as is the humanistic assumption that all problems arise from blocked self-actualisation.

This suggests that encouraging people to focus on their own self-development rather than on situational forces may be neither realistic nor appropriate in modern society.

Cultural differences in the hierarchy of needs

In a later development to his theory Maslow did acknowledge that, for some people, needs may appear in a different order or may even be absent altogether.

This is borne out by cross-cultural evidence. For example, a study carried out in China (Nevis, 1983) found that belongingness needs were seen as more fundamental than physiological needs and that self-actualisation was defined more in terms of contributions to the community than in terms of individual development.

Consistent with this view, many studies have confirmed that Europeans and Americans focus more on personal identity in defining their self-concept, whereas Chinese, Japanese and Koreans define self-concept more in terms of social relationships.

MEET THE RESEARCHER

Abraham Maslow (1908–1970) was born in a New York slum, the child of immigrant Russian Jews. As a child he was the victim of anti-Semitism. Despite having an IQ of 195 he still flunked some of his undergraduate courses as he found it difficult to focus on anything that didn't interest him. Described as shy and incredibly humble, Maslow eventually became an intellectual whose influence stretched far beyond academic psychology, into the world of business and popular culture.

KEY TERMS

Conditions of worth Conditions imposed on an individual's behaviour and development that are considered necessary to earn positive regard from significant others.

Congruence If there is similarity between a person's ideal self and self-image, a state of congruence exists. A difference represents a state of incongruence.

Free will The ability to act at one's own discretion, i.e. to choose how to behave without being influenced by external forces.

Hierarchy of needs The motivational theory proposed by Abraham Maslow, often displayed as a pyramid. The most basic needs are at the bottom and higher needs at the top.

Humanistic Refers to the belief that human beings are born with the desire to grow, create and to love, and have the power to direct their own lives.

Self Our personal identity, used synonymously with the terms 'self-image' and 'self-concept'.

Self-actualisation A term used in different ways. Rogers used it as the drive to realise one's true potential. Maslow used it to describe the final stage of his hierarchy of needs.

APPLY YOUR KNOWLEDGE

Entrepeneurs like Chip Conley, the founder of *Joie de Vivre Hospitality*, attribute much of their success to psychologist Abraham Maslow's hierarchy of needs. By applying this theory to his business, particularly to staff and customers, Conley was able to build a successful business empire and set out to teach others how to do the same thing.

Imagine you have started a new company selling hot tubs in the North of England. You have a staff of 20 and a potential customer base of millions.

How could you utilise Maslow's hierarchy of needs model to make your staff happier and your customer base more likely to buy one of your expensive hot tubs?

CAN YOU?   No. 5.7

1. Briefly explain what is meant by the terms 'free will', 'self-actualisation', 'congruence' and 'conditions of worth'. (2 marks each)
2. Outline Maslow's hierarchy of needs. (4 marks)
3. Explain the influence of humanistic psychology on counselling psychology. (4 marks)
4. Outline **one** strength and **one** limitation of humanistic psychology. (3 marks each)
5. Discuss the humanistic approach in psychology. (16 marks)

Comparison of approaches

The six approaches we have covered in this chapter are very different, but also have some notable similarities in the assumptions they make about human behaviour. In this final spread we examine where each approach stands with regards three central issues in psychology, **determinism**, **nature–nurture**, and the importance of the **scientific method**.

DETERMINISM: THE CAUSES OF BEHAVIOUR

Determinism refers to the belief that behaviour is determined by forces other than the individual's will to do something. Many of the approaches covered in this chapter represent a determinist view, because they suggest that our behaviour is determined by, for example, biology, early experience or rewards. Free will is used to refer to the alternative end of the spectrum, where the individual is seen as being capable of self-determination. As with most debates in psychology, the answer usually lies somewhere in between – our behaviour is probably a mixture of the two extremes.

APPROACH	Behaviour is determined by ...
Behaviourist	... the consequences of our behaviour (i.e. our reinforcement history), which determines the likelihood of a behaviour reoccurring. Behaviourists such as Skinner emphasise the importance of external forces in the environment (e.g. rewards and punishments) in shaping our behaviour (environmental determinism).
Social learning	... observations of others (vicarious learning) and so behaviour is largely a product of our experience (i.e. it is *determined*). However, although the learning process provides the 'tools' to conduct a particular behaviour, it is up to the individual how and when to apply these tools (i.e. *free will*).
Cognitive	... our own thought processes, which determine our behaviour. Therefore the individual has some degree of control over his or her behaviour.
Biological	... physiological (e.g. neurochemical and hormonal) factors and/or inherited (genetic) factors, both of which are outside of our control.
Psychodynamic	... unconscious factors, which are largely unknown to us and therefore beyond our conscious control. Freud believed that even trivial phenomena such as Freudian slips (e.g. calling someone by the wrong name) are caused by unconscious factors operating within the individual's motivational system.
Humanistic	... our own free will. Humanistic psychologists such as Abraham Maslow and Carl Rogers believed that people exercise choice in their behaviour, rather than being at the mercy of outside forces such as biological predispositions or reinforcement history.

NATURE AND NURTURE: THE ROLE OF INNATE AND EXPERIENTIAL FACTORS

Human behaviour is either the product of a person's genes and biology (nature) or what they experience as a result of interacting with the environment (nurture). It is rare that behaviour is entirely one or the other alone. More usually, the question of 'nature or nurture' lies in looking at the way in which nature and nurture interact.

APPROACH	The origin of behaviour is ...
Behaviourist	... *nurture*, as it is a consequence of our interactions with the environment and the consequences of our behaviour within that environment.
Social learning	... primarily *nurture* in that people learn as a result of observing others. However, it is generally assumed that the capacity to learn from an observation of others has some adaptive value, therefore is likely to be innate (i.e. *nature*).
Cognitive	... both *nature* and *nurture*, as thought processes may be a product of innate factors or our experiences. We all share the same means of cognitive processing (*nature*), but problems may arise when people develop irrational thoughts and beliefs as a result of their experiences (*nurture*).
Biological	... primarily *nature*. Biological systems such as the CNS and the endocrine system are the product of innate factors (*nature*). However, experience may modify these systems, e.g. Maguire *et al.*'s study (2000) of London taxi drivers, which found structural changes in the brain as a result of having to learn to navigate London's complex road layout (see page 161).
Psychodynamic	... both *nature* and *nurture*. The psychodynamic approach focuses on the *nature* side of human behaviour in the unconscious forces (e.g. the demands of the id) and conflicts that we must all deal with. However, how we cope with these is in a large way a product of our upbringing (i.e. *nurture*).
Humanistic	... both *nature* and *nurture*. The humanistic approach makes various assumptions about human nature, e.g. our drive to self-actualise (*nature*). However, it also acknowledges the problems in achieving self-actualisation that arise from our experiences and upbringing, e.g. our experience of conditional positive regard and conditions of worth (*nurture*).

PSYCHOLOGY AS SCIENCE

Psychology is often defined as the 'science of behaviour', and psychologists have adopted the scientific method as the most appropriate way of studying human behaviour. However, because psychology lies at the intersection of many other different disciplines, such as biology, philosophy and sociology, the application of scientific methods is not universal across the subject. For example, psychologists who are allied with biology may adopt the methods associated with the natural sciences, whereas psychologists who are more allied with philosophy or sociology may not always see scientific methodology as appropriate to their areas of interest.

APPROACH	Its commitment to the scientific method is . . .
Behaviourist	. . . *positive*, as the behavioural approach is highly objective and experimentally based. By focusing only on responses that can be accurately measured, it aligns itself with the rigour of the scientific method more than most other approaches. This also allows for a high degree of replication, which is an important part of the scientific process.
Social learning	. . . *positive*, as its research investigations are reliable and allow inferences about cause and effect to be drawn. However, this does mean that research (e.g. Bandura's Bobo doll studies) tends to be carried out in rather artificial settings, so can lack validity in terms of real-life behaviour.
Cognitive	. . . *positive* to a degree, as most propositions can be easily tested. However, because mental processes are largely unobservable, a great deal of inference is necessary to develop models of cognitive processing.
Biological	. . . *positive*, as it lends itself to experimental study. For example, the influence of neurotransmitters in a behaviour can be investigated by administrating drugs which change the levels of a particular neurotransmitter in the brain and then measuring any change in that behaviour.
Psychodynamic	. . . *mixed*. Although some aspects of this approach are open to scientific investigation, there tends to be much greater reliance on case studies and subjective interpretation.
Humanistic	. . . *largely negative*. Humanistic psychologists argue that scientific research methods are derived from and suited for the natural sciences, but are not appropriate for studying the complexities of human consciousness and experience.

KEY TERMS

Determinism Behaviour is determined by external or internal factors acting upon the individual.

Nature Behaviour is seen to be a product of innate (biological or genetic) factors.

Nurture Behaviour is a product of environmental influences.

Science A systematic approach to creating knowledge. The method used to gain scientific knowledge is referred to as the scientific method.

CAN YOU?   No. 5.8

1. Using every combination of the six approaches covered in this chapter, outline **one** similarity and **one** difference between each combination (2 marks each).

   For example: Psychodynamic vs Social learning
   Cognitive vs Biological
   Humanistic vs Behavioural
   Biological vs Psychodynamic

AN OVERVIEW

APPROACH	Basic assumptions
Behaviourist	• External forces in the environment shape our behaviour (i.e. it is determined). • Explanations of behaviour emphasise the role of nurture more than nature. • Behaviourism aligns itself strongly with the scientific method.
Social learning	• Behaviour is learned as a result of the observations of others (i.e. it is determined). • Explanations of behaviour emphasise the role of nurture more than nature. • Social learning aligns itself with the scientific method but research can lack validity.
Cognitive	• Thought processes determine behaviour (i.e. some degree of control over behaviour). • Explanations of behaviour emphasise the role of nature *and* nurture. • Cognitive psychology aligns itself with the scientific method despite some inference.
Biological	• Physiological and/or inherited factors determine behaviour. • Explanations of behaviour emphasise the role of nature more than nurture. • Biological psychology aligns itself strongly with the scientific method.
Psychodynamic	• Unconscious factors beyond our conscious control determine behaviour. • Explanations of behaviour emphasise the role of nature *and* nurture. • Psychodynamic psychology does not really align itself with the scientific method.
Humanistic	• Behaviour is under our conscious control (i.e. we have free will). • Explanations of behaviour emphasise the role of nature *and* nurture. • Humanistic psychology mostly rejects the use of the scientific method.

 UPGRADE

This spread focuses on a 'comparison' of the different approaches, so the main skill to acquire is to be able to explain *similarities* and *differences* between the approaches. This is quite a challenging thing to do, although the comparison tables on this spread should make it easier. You could:

1. State the way in which they are similar, e.g. both the behaviourist approach and the biological approach see human behaviour as being determined by factors that are largely out of the person's control.

2. Elaborate this similarity by pointing out how it applies to the approaches concerned, e.g. behaviourists see an individual's behaviour as being a product of their reinforcement history, and biological psychologists focus on the determining influences of genetics and brain chemistry.

Explaining differences can be achieved in a similar way, which is where the word 'whereas' comes in handy. For example, psychodynamic and humanistic approaches differ in their focus on determinism or free will. Psychodynamic theorists believe that behaviour is determined by unconscious forces beyond our conscious control, whereas humanistic psychologists believe that we are free to choose how to act.

End-of-chapter review ⟩ CHAPTER SUMMARY

We have identified here the key points of the topics on the AQA specification covered in this chapter, i.e. the bare minimum that you need to know. You may want to fill in further details to elaborate and personalise this material.

THE ORIGINS OF PSYCHOLOGY

WILHELM WUNDT
- Established experimental psychology as a science.
- Involves breaking down behaviours into basic elements.
- Introspection was the chosen method of study.
- Worked by asking individuals to engage in a task and then reflect the mental processes they were performing.
- Used to establish general theories about mental processes.

THE EMERGENCE OF PSYCHOLOGY AS A SCIENCE
- Scientific psychology uses empirical methods.
- Assumptions of determinism and predictability.
- The scientific method refers to the use of methods that are objective, systematic and replicable.
- Replication means results might be accepted as true.
- Scientific method also includes development of theories that can explain results and constant testing and refining.

EVALUATION/DISCUSSION
- Wundt's methods were unreliable (relied on 'nonobservable' responses).
- Scientific approach tests assumptions about behaviour by establishing causality and correcting theories.
- Not all psychologists believe human behaviour can be explored using scientific methods – much is unobservable and relies on inferences from data.
- **A03 plus** Introspection not particularly accurate (e.g. Nisbett and Wilson).
- **A03 plus** Introspection still useful in psychology (e.g. Csikszentmihalyi and Hunter).

THE BEHAVIOURIST APPROACH

CLASSICAL CONDITIONING
- Associated with Pavlov.
- Involves pairing of NS with UCS so that eventually NS becomes CS, capable of eliciting a CR.
- NS + UCS = UCR.
- After many pairings NS (CS) + CR.
- Timing – NS must be *shortly* before UCS.
- Extinction – CS loses its ability to produce CR after a few trials if no reinforcement.
- Spontaneous recovery – CS + UCS paired again, link made much more quickly.
- Stimulus generalisation – CR also to stimuli that are similar to CS.

EVALUATION/DISCUSSION
- Classical conditioning has been applied to therapy, e.g. in treatment of phobias.
- Classical conditioning only appropriate for some forms of learning, e.g. concept of preparedness (Seligman).
- Operant conditioning based on experimental work – allows establishment of cause-effect relationships.

OPERANT CONDITIONING
- Likelihood of repeating behaviour depends on its consequences.
- Positive *and* negative reinforcement increases the likelihood of a behaviour occurring.
- Pleasant consequences = positive reinforcement.
- Removal of unpleasant stimulus = negative reinforcement.
- Continuous reinforcement effective for establishing a behaviour, partial reinforcement for maintaining it.
- Adding unpleasant consequence, or removing pleasant stimulus = punishment.

- **A03 plus** Operant conditioning over-reliance on non-human animals in research, ignores possibility of free will.
- **A03 plus** Limited perspective – behaviourist explanations ignore the role played by cognitive and emotional factors.

SOCIAL LEARNING THEORY

SOCIAL LEARNING THEORY (BANDURA, 1986)
- New patterns of behaviour acquired as a result of the observation of others.
- Models provide examples of behaviour that can be observed and imitated.
- Key determinants: (i) characteristics of the model; (ii) observer's ability to perform the behaviour; (iii) its observed consequences.
- Identification with a model based on perceived similarity.
- Vicarious reinforcement – individuals learn about the likely consequences of behaviour by observing others.
- Individuals must form mental representations of the behaviour and its probable consequences.

KEY STUDY (BANDURA *ET AL.*, 1961)
- Procedure: children observed aggressive or non-aggressive models interacting with Bobo doll.
- The aggressive model displayed distinctive physical and verbal aggressive acts toward the doll.
- Children then allowed to interact with the Bobo doll.
- Findings: children who observed the aggressive model imitated their aggression.
- Children who observed the non-aggressive model showed little aggression.

EVALUATION/DISCUSSION
- SLT has useful applications – offers a way of understanding criminal behaviour (Ulrich).
- Research support for identification – learning more effective from similar than dissimilar model (Fox and Bailenson).
- Problem of causality – criticism of view of criminal behaviour due to exposure to deviant models (Siegel and McCormick).

- **A03 plus** Problem of complexity – advocates of SLT disregard other potential influences on behaviour.
- **A03 plus** Identification has been shown to be important in social learning (e.g. Andsager study on health campaigns).

THE COGNITIVE APPROACH

THE STUDY OF INTERNAL MENTAL PROCESSES
- Mental processes cannot be studied directly so must be inferred.
- Schemas help organise and interpret information.
- Schemas fill in gaps in the absence of full information.
- Theoretical models are simplified representations based on current evidence.
- Computer models of mental processes – analogies of information processing where information is inputted through the senses, encoded into memory, etc.

THE EMERGENCE OF COGNITIVE NEUROSCIENCE
- The emergence of cognitive neuroscience, e.g. use of neuroimaging techniques to study the brain.
- Burnett *et al.*, when people feel guilt, medial prefrontal cortex is active.

EVALUATION/DISCUSSION
- Cognitive approach has applications, e.g. cognitive approach to psychopathology.
- Cognitive approach is scientific, i.e. it uses the scientific method.
- Computer models – there are many differences between computer processing and human processing, e.g. computers do not make mistakes.
- **(A03 plus)** The cognitive approach ignores emotion and motivation – irrelevant to a computer but not to a human.
- **(A03 plus)** Studies may lack ecological validity – most research uses tasks that are relatively meaningless in real-life settings.

THE BIOLOGICAL APPROACH

BIOLOGICAL INFLUENCES ON BEHAVIOUR
- Genes carry the instructions for a particular characteristic from one generation to the next.
- Relative role of genes or environment = nature–nurture debate.
- Genotype is the genetic code written in individual's DNA.
- Phenotype is physical manifestation of this inherited information.
- Heritability = the amount of variability in a trait within a population attributed to genetic differences.
- The nervous system = central and peripheral nervous systems.
- The largest part of the brain is the cerebrum, divided into four lobes.
- Neurotransmitters enable nerve impulses to cross the synapse.
- Excitatory and inhibitory neurotransmitters stimulate or inhibit a receiving nerve cell.
- Serotonin is an inhibitory neurotransmitter.
- Hormones – produced by endocrine cells and stimulate target cells.
- Evolution and behaviour – through natural selection.

EVALUATION/DISCUSSION
- Biological approach uses the scientific method – makes replication easier.
- Biological approach provides clear predictions, which can be tested.
- Biological approach is reductionist.
- **(A03 plus)** Evolutionary explanations stress importance of biological evolution, but ignores possibility of *cultural* evolution.
- **(A03 plus)** Identifying a genetic basis for behaviour may lead to discrimination of the basis of a particular genotype.

A LEVEL ONLY ZONE

THE PSYCHODYNAMIC APPROACH

FREUD'S THEORY OF PSYCHOANALYSIS
- Unconscious mind controls many of our everyday activities.
- Defence mechanisms prevent traumatic memories from the unconscious from reaching conscious awareness.
- The id, ego and superego.
- Id operates according to the pleasure principle.
- Ego mediates between the demands of the id and demands of reality.
- Superego divided into conscience and ego-ideal.
- Defence mechanisms operate unconsciously, distorting reality to reduce anxiety.
- Repression – the unconscious blocking of unacceptable thoughts.
- Denial – the refusal to accept reality.
- Displacement – redirecting of thoughts and feelings from original target onto an innocent object.
- Psychosexual stages – oral, anal, phallic, latent, genital.

EVALUATION/DISCUSSION
- Pioneering approach – Freud the first to demonstrate the potential of psychological treatments for disorders.
- Scientific support – Fisher and Greenberg found support for many psychoanalytic claims.
- Psychoanalysis is gender biased – based on male rather than female sexuality.
- Psychoanalysis is culture biased – little relevance for people from non-Western cultures.
- Psychoanalysis is a comprehensive theory, including use as a form of literary criticism.

HUMANISTIC PSYCHOLOGY

BASIC ASSUMPTIONS OF THE HUMANISTIC APPROACH
- Stresses the importance of free will and conscious control over our own destiny.
- Maslow interested in what could go right rather than what could go wrong.
- Hierarchy of needs – most basic needs at the bottom, higher needs at the top.
- People reaching self-actualisation experience it through peak experiences. Rogers used term to describe 'fully functioning person'.
- Feelings of self-worth develop in childhood as a result of interactions with parents.
- State of congruence exists when similarity between person's ideal self and how they perceive themselves to be.
- Conditions of worth arise when people experience conditional rather than unconditional positive regard.
- Problems a product of person's conditions of worth. Therapist provides unconditional positive regard to help person self-actualise.

EVALUATION/DISCUSSION
- Maslow's hierarchy linked to economic development (e.g. Hagerty).
- Research support for conditions of worth, e.g. Harter *et al.*.
- Humanistic research methods produce data that is mostly correlational.
- The humanistic approach represents an overly idealised and unrealistic view of human nature.
- Cross-cultural evidence that in some cultures needs appear in a different order (Nevis).

COMPARISON OF APPROACHES

DETERMINISM: THE CAUSES OF BEHAVIOUR
- Behaviourist – our reinforcement history.
- Social learning – observation of others.
- Cognitive – our own thought processes.
- Biological – physiological and/or genetic factors.
- Psychodynamic – unconscious factors.
- Humanistic – our own free will.

NATURE AND NURTURE: THE ORIGINS OF BEHAVIOUR
- Behaviourist – nurture (interactions with the environment).
- Social learning – primarily nurture (observing others).
- Cognitive – both nature and nurture (innate factors or our own experiences).
- Biological – primarily nature (innate factors although can be modified by experience).
- Psychodynamic – both nature and nurture (unconscious forces *and* upbringing).
- Humanistic – both nature and nurture (drive to self-actualise *and* conditions of worth).

PSYCHOLOGY AS SCIENCE
- Behaviourist – positive (highly objective and experimentally based).
- Social learning – positive (inferences about cause and effect can be drawn).
- Cognitive – positive to a degree (propositions can be tested, but a good deal of inference is necessary).
- Biological – positive (lends itself to experimental study).
- Psychodynamic – mixed (some aspects open to scientific investigation but greater reliance on case studies).
- Humanistic – largely negative (scientific methods seen as inappropriate for human experience).

The exam questions on approaches in psychology will be varied but there will be some short answer questions (AO1), including some multiple choice questions, some questions that ask you to apply your knowledge (AO2) and possibly an extended writing question (AO1 + AO3). Some questions may involve research methods and maths skills. We have provided a selection of these different kinds of questions here.

AS AND A LEVEL QUESTIONS

0 1 Which of the following terms best matches the statements below? Choose **one** term that matches each statement. Use each letter once only.

  A phenotype
  B identification
  C introspection
  D reinforcement
  E genotype

  (i) The process of observing our inner world through analysing thoughts.   **[1 mark]**

  (ii) The process that results in a response being strengthened.   **[1 mark]**

  (iii) The process of relating to a model who we see as similar to ourselves.   **[1 mark]**

  (iv) The genetic make-up of an individual.   **[1 mark]**

0 2 Outline what is meant by cognitive neuroscience.   **[2 marks]**

0 3 Using an example, outline **one** type of reinforcement used in learning theories.   **[3 marks]**

0 4 Read the item below and then answer the question that follows.

> Petra has just started university. She has decided to approach other students who dress similarly to her as she assumes that they will be 'into' the same kinds of things as her. Petra understands that many other people must feel like her, and this is why she does not get upset if other people have awkward conversations with her.

Outline what is meant by a schema. Make reference to Petra's experiences as part of your response.   **[4 marks]**

0 5 Outline the role of meditational processes in social learning.   **[3 marks]**

0 6 Read the item below and then answer the question that follows.

> Both of Oliver's parents were very intelligent so there is a good chance that he had inherited the potential to be as intelligent as them. However, his parents died when he was very young, and he has been brought up by his aunt, who has five other children. Now that Oliver has just started school, he appears to be behind his year group and needs extra help with phonics.

Distinguish between the concepts of genotype and phenotype. Make reference to the case of Oliver as part of your answer.   **[4 marks]**

0 7 Using an example, outline how neurochemistry can influence behaviour.   **[3 marks]**

0 8 Distinguish between classical and operant conditioning.   **[3 marks]**

0 9 Explain how computer models are used to make inferences about mental processes.   **[4 marks]**

1 0   Describe and briefly evaluate the influence of evolution on behaviour.   **[6 marks]**

1 1   Describe and evaluate Skinner's research into operant conditioning.   **[12 marks]**

1 2   Discuss the biological approach in psychology.   **[12 marks]**

1 3   Read the item below and then answer the question that follows.

> Rory looks up to his older sister Rosie and tries to copy many of the things that he sees her doing. Rory is particularly keen to be as sporty as Rosie as he sees that their parents give her lots of praise and attention for this. Rosie is also aware that Rory pays a lot of attention to what she does. This is why she is always careful to play fair when she knows that he is watching.

With reference to social learning theory, explain Rory's sporty behaviour.   **[6 marks]**

A LEVEL ONLY QUESTIONS

1 4   Name **two** psychosexual stages.   **[2 marks]**

1 5   Choose **one** of the following defence mechanisms.

- Repression
- Displacement
- Denial

Using an example, outline how it is used according to the psychodynamic approach.   **[3 marks]**

1 6   Describe the influence of humanistic psychology on counselling.   **[8 marks]**

1 7   Outline what is meant by self-actualisation in humanistic psychology.   **[2 marks]**

1 8   Explain the role of conditions of worth in the development of self.   **[3 marks]**

1 9   Read the item below and then answer the questions that follow.

> Sometimes Veronica cannot control her urge to just eat everything that is in her treat drawer. When she does do it, she feels extremely guilty and often forces herself to be sick afterwards. However, most of the time, Veronica deals with her urge by making sure that her treat drawer is not too full.

(i) State what is meant by the following structures of personality, according to the psychodynamic approach.
- Id   **[1 mark]**
- Ego   **[1 mark]**
- Superego   **[1 mark]**

(ii) For each structure of personality, briefly state how it is shown in the case of Veronica.   **[3 marks]**

2 0   Discuss the biological approach in psychology. Refer to **at least one** other approach in your discussion.   **[16 marks]**

2 1   Discuss the humanistic approach in psychology.   **[16 marks]**

2 2   Outline and discuss the cognitive approach. Refer to cognitive neuroscience in your answer.   **[16 marks]**

2 3   Discuss both the psychodynamic approach and the humanistic approach. Include a comparison of the approaches as part of your discussion.   **[16 marks]**

We've provided answers by two students to some of the questions from pages 142–143 here, together with comments from an examiner about how well they've each done. **Green** comments show what the student has done well. **Orange** comments indicate areas for improvement.

---

10 Describe and briefly evaluate the influence of evolution on behaviour. *(6 marks)*

✓ Clear link to the question.

Ciaran's answer

Evolutionary explanations of behaviour emphasise the role of natural selection in behaviours linked to survival and reproductive success. Evolutionary explanations of reproductive behaviour claim that males and females select mates that have certain characteristics because this makes it more likely that their offspring will survive and reproduce and so these characteristics become more widespread in the population.

A problem for evolutionary explanations of behaviour is that behaviour such as mate choice is just as likely to be determined by cultural factors such as media messages. Unlike explanations of behaviour based on cultural factors, it is difficult to subject evolutionary explanations to scientific testing in the same way, nor control for all the other factors that might influence the behaviour in question.

! More of a focus on the process than the influence it has.

✓ A good evaluation point, but it could be developed with an example or further elaboration.

Examiner's comments

After a positive start, the answer lacks detail in relation to the influence on behaviour. There is some development of the evaluation points but it doesn't go far enough. *3/6 marks*

AS essay

12 Discuss the biological approach in psychology. *(12 marks)*

✓ 'Assumptions' of the approach are included, giving a clear and accurate beginning.

Maisie's answer

The biological approach argues that there is a biological basis to all behaviour. For example an imbalance of neurotransmitters, such as serotonin, has been shown to be important in lots of different behaviours, such as aggression. Crockett et al. found that low levels of serotonin increased aggressive behaviour. An imbalance has also been found with many mental disorders, such as increased dopamine linked to schizophrenia and low serotonin also linked to increased depression. Scientific evidence like this adds to the approach and suggests that the explanations are valid.

Genetic factors influence behaviour too, with characteristics such as intelligence, personality and eye colour being passed down from one generation to the next (heredity). This genetic material is our genotype, whereas phenotype is the consequence of the genotype interacting with the environment. The biological approach also states that different parts of the brain have different functions, such as the hippocampus being linked to our memory.

There has been lots of research to back the approach up, such as twin studies and Buss's study into human mate preferences. Buss's study showed that there were universal similarities across 37 cultures. This suggests that at least parts of the biological approach are correct.

Another strength is that it uses the scientific method to test its predictions, allowing there to be more replicability to check the findings. To test a neurochemical explanation of depression, for example, drugs that alter the levels of neurotransmitters in the brain can be given to one group and a placebo given to a control group. If the first group has a reduction in their symptoms and the control group doesn't, then this suggests that their depression has a neurochemical cause. This has also led to important applications using biological (drug) treatments in the treatment of depression. These have gone on to be effective in treating the disorder, and have led to real-life improvements for many people.

The biological approach also has limitations, for example it is accused of being reductionist. This means that it reduces behaviour down into its smallest units, such as genes, and other possible influences, such as conditioning or internal mental processes, are ignored. This can be a problem

✓ Good elaboration of the point. It is linked back to the approach well and used as AO3 by saying the research adds to the explanation.

✓ Some excellent knowledge demonstrated in this section with detail – all AO1.

✓ Accurate detail and an effective, concise use of research.

✓ Excellent link back to the approach, which shows that Maisie understands what the question is asking.

! A decent example of the scientific method but a little generic.

! A good point but could be elaborated further.

✓ A good point that is elaborated.

when there is evidence to show that things like conditioning can be linked to our behaviour, again using a scientific method. It looks more likely that the biological explanations of our behaviour are a significant part of the answer but other factors need to be included as well. (409 words)

✓ A good attempt at a conclusion. which could be more detailed but given the time limit and the length of this essay, it is not needed.

A Level essay

23 Discuss both the psychodynamic approach and the humanistic approach. Include a comparison of the approaches as part of your discussion. *(16 marks)*

Ciaran's answer

✓ Concisely written and although there is a lot more that could be written, you don't want to spend too long on AO1 and leave yourself without enough time for AO3.

Freud's psychoanalytic theory claimed that much of our behaviour was not under conscious control but was influenced by the unconscious mind. The id lies within the unconscious mind and is driven by the need to express sexual energy (libido). The ego must deal with the demands of the id within the constraints imposed by reality. The superego is the moralistic part of personality. It contains the conscience and the ego ideal which is what a person strives towards and is largely a product of parental influence. Freud believed that the child went through five psychosexual stages, each of which expresses libido in different ways.

✓ Some elaboration of this point. It could be made a little more specific, countered with a problem with the research or a confirmation point such as 'this suggests that….'

There is some support for Freud's claims. For example, Fisher and Greenberg looked at over 2,000 studies that had tested Freudian claims. They found support for a number of these, including the role played by unconscious motivation in behaviour. A problem for this approach is the claim that it is gender biased. Freud concentrated on males only, and his theory is largely a theory of male development.

! A valid criticism but limited development. No real examples and no explanation of how that will affect the approach itself, for example, outlining how the gender bias may limit how effective the explanation is.

The humanistic approach focuses more on positive development in humans, and so has a strong emphasis on conscious experience and self-actualisation. Maslow's self-actualisation theory represents development in the form of a pyramid, with the basic 'deficit' needs at the bottom, and the higher 'growth' needs at the top. The highest of these is self-actualisation. People who achieve self-actualisation tend to be more creative than those motivated by lower level needs. Rogers' humanistic theory stresses the importance of self-worth in development. If there is congruence between our ideal self and our actual self, then we experience greater feelings of self-worth and so higher levels of psychological health.

! This would be a good point to use to make comparisons. It would help the flow of the essay and mean less writing, as the point about conscious experience is already being made.
'Unlike the psychodynamic approach, the humanistic approach emphasises conscious experience rather than unconscious drives'.

! Only support for one of these is highlighted here though. It would help to explain support for both.

There is research support for both of these humanistic theories. Hagerty (1999) found evidence that the economic development of different countries was linked to Maslow's levels. Countries in the early stages of economic development were more concerned with lower levels, e.g. physiological needs such as access to food. Countries in more advanced stages of economic development were concerned with higher level needs such as education and female emancipation. A problem for the humanistic approach is that it doesn't lend itself to experimental testing and relies too much on case studies, which do not give researchers the opportunity to establish cause and effect relationships.

✓ Good use of research.

! There are a number of limitations, such as the approach being unrealistic, that could be added here.

✓ A good attempt to develop the point. It could be elaborated further by saying 'This is a problem because...'

There are some differences between the psychodynamic and humanistic approaches. The humanistic approach believes that people have free will rather than the psychodynamic belief that people are at the mercy of forces that are out of their conscious control. There are some similarities between the two approaches. Both have based their theories on individual case studies rather than using the scientific method. (442 words)

✓ A good comparison point. Try to think of ways that this could be developed further.

✓ Given the time constraints, there is some accurate and generally well detailed description.

! Accurate comparison – however it could be elaborated and it would be better to have some comparison throughout the essay.

CHAPTER

6 Biopsychology

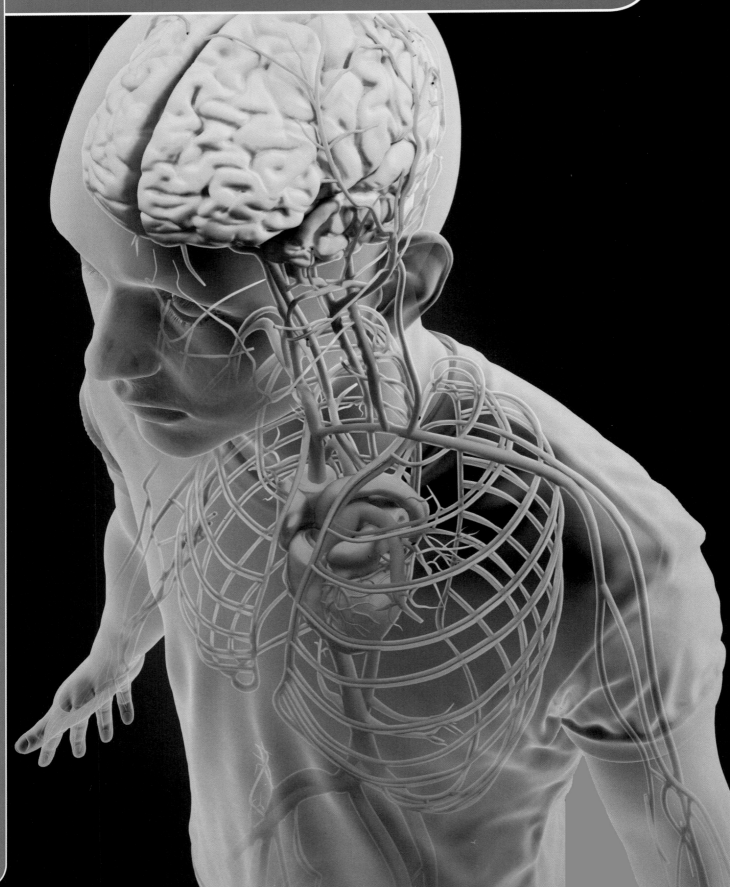

CONTENTS OF CHAPTER

A LEVEL ONLY ZONE

SPECIFICATION CHECKLIST

AS and A Level

- The divisions of the nervous system: central and peripheral (somatic and autonomic).

- The structure and function of sensory, relay and motor neurons. The process of synaptic transmission, including reference to neurotransmitters, excitation and inhibition.

- The function of the endocrine system: glands and hormones.

- The fight-or-flight response including the role of adrenaline.

A Level only

- Localisation of function in the brain and hemispheric lateralisation: motor, somatosensory, visual, auditory and language centres; Broca's and Wernicke's areas, split-brain research. Plasticity and functional recovery after trauma.

- Ways of studying the brain: scanning techniques, including functional magnetic resonance imaging (fMRI); electroencephalogram (EEGs) and event-related potentials (ERPs); post-mortem examinations.

- Biological rhythms: circadian, infradian and ultradian and the difference between these rhythms. The effect of endogenous pacemakers and exogenous zeitgebers.

Ever wondered how fast a nerve impulse travels?

A nerve impulse is an electrical signal that travels along an axon. The speed of nerve impulses varies enormously in different types of neuron, with the fastest travelling at around 250 mph – faster than a Formula 1 racing car.

TRY THIS

Okay, let's try a little experiment to measure how fast a nerve impulse travels down the length of one arm. To do this you will need a group of people, 10 people minimum, but as many as you have available. Stand one person behind the other and have them rest their right hand on the right shoulder of the person in front. At a predetermined signal from the 'experimenter' (whoever has the stopwatch), the first person squeezes the shoulder of the person in front, who, when they feel it, squeezes the shoulder of the person in front of them and so on. When the final person feels their shoulder squeezed they shout 'STOP' and the stopwatch is stopped. Given that an arm is approximately one metre in length, you should be able to work out how many metres per second the impulse travelled. For example, for 25 people, that's 25 metres, which might take about five seconds or so. That's a speed of about five metres per second. Try that a few times and then take an average speed.

Now stand in a circle facing outwards with each person holding hands with the person standing each side of them. This time at the signal to start, the first person squeezes the hand of the person on their left, who, when they feel it, squeezes the hand of the person on their left and so on, until the starting person feels their right hand being squeezed and they shout 'STOP'. What do you predict the time will be? You should find it is a fair bit longer as the impulse must now travel through two arms, and so two metres. Again, calculate the average speed. With practice you may be able to get it up to 10–15 metres per second, which is about right for a nerve impulse of this type, or to put it another way, about 30 mph. That's quite quick, but quite a bit slower than electricity, which speeds down a wire at about 186,000 miles per second!

The nervous system

The human nervous system is a complex network of nerve cells that carry messages to and from the brain and spinal cord to different parts of the body and so helps all the parts of the body to communicate with each other. Controlling the nervous system is the brain, the powerhouse of the body, even though it only makes up about 2% of the body's weight. This organ has many billions of neural cross-connections. The brain oversees the workings of the body, while its higher functions provide us with consciousness and makes us who we are.

DIVISIONS OF THE NERVOUS SYSTEM

The human nervous system is divided into the **central nervous system (CNS)** and **peripheral nervous system**, with each of these further divided into different components, each with a different function but all working together. Let's begin by looking at these different divisions and their component parts (see below).

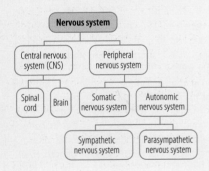

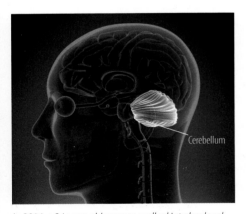

In 2014, a 24-year-old woman walked into her local emergency room in Shandong Province, China, with symptoms of vertigo (loss of balance and nausea) but ended up receiving a surprising diagnosis – her entire cerebellum was missing! However, the New Scientist *reports, the missing cerebellum had resulted in only mild to moderate motor deficiency, as other parts of her brain had filled in for it.*

THE CENTRAL NERVOUS SYSTEM

The CNS, comprising the **brain** and **spinal cord**, has two main functions: the control of behaviour and the regulation of the body's physiological processes. In order to do this, the brain must be able to receive information from the sensory receptors (eyes, ears, skin, etc.) and be able to send messages to the muscles and glands of the body. This involves the spinal cord, a collection of nerve cells that are attached to the brain and run the length of the spinal column.

The spinal cord

The main function of the spinal cord is to relay information between the brain and the rest of the body. This allows the brain to monitor and regulate bodily processes, such as digestion and breathing, and to coordinate voluntary movements. The spinal cord is connected to different parts of the body by pairs of spinal nerves, which connect with specific muscles and glands. For example, spinal nerves which branch off from the thoracic region of the spinal cord, carry messages to and from the chest and parts of the abdomen. The spinal cord also contains circuits of nerve cells that enable us to perform some simple reflexes without the direct involvement of the brain, for example pulling your hand away from something that is hot. If the spinal cord is damaged, areas supplied by spinal nerves below the damaged site will be cut off from the brain and will stop functioning.

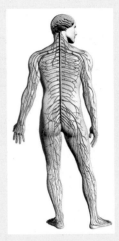

▲ The central nervous system is the brain and spinal column. The peripheral nervous system comprises the nerves leading to and from the CNS.

The brain

The brain can be divided into four main areas – the cerebrum, cerebellum, diencephalon and brain stem.

The cerebrum is the largest part of the brain, and is further divided into four different lobes, each of which has a different primary function (see page 132). For example, the frontal lobe is involved in thought and the production of speech, and the occipital lobe (at the back of the cerebrum) is involved in the processing of visual images. The cerebrum is split down the middle into two halves called cerebral hemispheres. Each hemisphere is specialised for particular behaviours, and the two halves communicate with each other through the corpus callosum (see page 158).

The cerebellum sits beneath the back of the cerebrum. It is involved in controlling a person's motor skills and balance, coordinating the muscles to allow precise movements. Abnormalities of this area can result in a number of problems, including speech and motor problems and epilepsy.

The diencephalon lies beneath the cerebrum and on top of the brain stem (see diagram on the right). Within this area are two important structures, the thalamus and the hypothalamus. The thalamus acts as a relay station for nerve impulses coming from the senses, routing them to the appropriate part of the brain where they can be processed. The hypothalamus has a number of important functions, including the regulation of body temperature, hunger and thirst. It also acts as the link between the endocrine system (see page 152) and the nervous system, controlling the release of hormones from the pituitary gland.

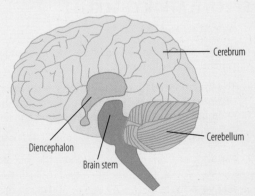

The brain stem is responsible for regulating the automatic functions that are essential for life. These include breathing, heartbeat and swallowing. Motor and sensory neurons travel through the brain stem, allowing impulses to pass between the brain and the spinal cord.

THE PERIPHERAL NERVOUS SYSTEM

All the nerves *outside* the CNS make up the peripheral nervous system. This function of this part of the nervous system is to relay nerve impulses from the CNS (the brain and spinal cord) to the rest of the body and from the body back to the CNS. There are two main divisions of the peripheral nervous system, the **somatic nervous system** and the **autonomic nervous system (ANS)**.

The somatic nervous system

The somatic system is made up of 12 pairs of cranial nerves (nerves that emerge directly from the underside of the brain) and 31 pairs of spinal nerves (nerves that emerge from the spinal cord). These nerves have both sensory neurons and motor neurons. Sensory neurons relay messages *to* the CNS, and motor neurons relay information *from* the CNS to other areas of the body. We'll learn more about these different types of neuron on the next spread. The somatic system is also involved in reflex actions without the involvement of the CNS, which allows the reflex to occur very quickly.

The autonomic nervous system

When you type on a keyboard or take a drink you are performing voluntary actions and are conscious of what you are doing. However, the body also carries out some actions *without* your conscious awareness. For example, your heart beats and your intestines digest food without you being consciously aware of this happening. Involuntary actions such as these are regulated by the ANS. This system is necessary because vital bodily functions such as heartbeat and digestion would not work so efficiently if you had to think about them. The ANS has two parts: the sympathetic and the parasympathetic. Both of these divisions tend to regulate the same organs but have opposite effects. This is because of the neurotransmitters associated with each division. Generally, the sympathetic division uses the neurotransmitter noradrenaline, which has stimulating effects, and the parasympathetic division uses acetylcholine, which has inhibiting effects.

The sympathetic nervous system

The sympathetic nervous system (SNS) is primarily involved in responses that help us to deal with emergencies (fight or flight; see page 154), such as increasing heart rate and blood pressure and dilating blood vessels in the muscles. Neurons from the SNS travel to virtually every organ and gland within the body, preparing the body for the rapid action necessary when the individual is under threat. For example, the SNS causes the body to release stored energy, pupils to dilate and hair to stand on end. It slows bodily processes that are less important in emergencies, such as digestion and urination.

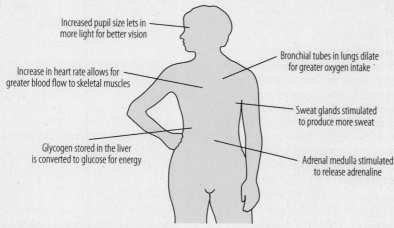

Increased pupil size lets in more light for better vision

Increase in heart rate allows for greater blood flow to skeletal muscles

Glycogen stored in the liver is converted to glucose for energy

Bronchial tubes in lungs dilate for greater oxygen intake

Sweat glands stimulated to produce more sweat

Adrenal medulla stimulated to release adrenaline

▲ Effect of SNS activation on the body.

The parasympathetic nervous system

If we think of the SNS as pushing an individual into action when faced with an emergency, then the parasympathetic nervous system (PNS) relaxes them again once the emergency has passed. Whereas the SNS causes the heart to beat faster and blood pressure to increase, the PNS slows the heartbeat down and reduces blood pressure. Another benefit is that digestion (inhibited when the SNS is aroused) begins again under PNS influence. Because the PNS is involved with energy conservation and digestion, it is sometimes referred to as the body's rest and digest system.

🐾 APPLY YOUR KNOWLEDGE

On your way home from a day relaxing with friends you are chased by a neighbour's dog. You are forced to run to escape the dog.

When you get home you slump down on the sofa and switch on *Shaun the Sheep* on the TV. Gradually you feel yourself relaxing as your body returns to normal. Maybe tomorrow you'll take the bus home!

Try to explain this sequence of events using your knowledge of the sympathetic and parasympathetic nervous systems.

KEY TERMS

Autonomic nervous system (ANS) Governs the brain's involuntary activities (e.g. stress, heartbeat) and is self-regulating (i.e. autonomous). It is divided into the sympathetic branch (fight or flight) and the parasympathetic branch (rest and digest).

Brain That part of the central nervous system that is responsible for coordinating sensation, intellectual and nervous activity.

Central nervous system (CNS) Comprises the brain and spinal cord. It receives information from the senses and controls the body's responses.

Peripheral nervous system The part of the nervous system that is outside the brain and spinal cord.

Somatic nervous system The part of the peripheral nervous system responsible for carrying sensory and motor information to and from the central nervous system.

Spinal cord A bundle of nerve fibres enclosed within the spinal column and which connects nearly all parts of the body with the brain.

CAN YOU?   No. 6.1

1. Outline the role of the central nervous system. (4 marks)
2. Identify the **two** divisions of the autonomic nervous system. (2 marks)
3. Identify the **two** components of the central nervous system. (2 marks)
4. Outline the role of the somatic nervous system. (4 marks)
5. Outline the role of the autonomic nervous system. (4 marks)

Neurons and synaptic transmission

What we think of as our mental life involves the activities of the nervous system, especially the brain. Most of the brain is made up of cells called glial cells and astrocytes. Among these cells are neurons – specialised cells whose function is to move electrical impulses to and from the central nervous system. The average human brain contains somewhere in the region of 100 billion neurons and, on average, each neuron is connected to 1,000 other neurons. This creates highly complex neural networks that give the brain its impressive processing capabilities.

The action potential

Neurons must transmit information both within the neuron and from one neuron to the next. The dendrites of neurons receive information from sensory receptors or other neurons. This information is then passed down to the cell body and on to the axon. Once the information has arrived at the axon, it travels down its length in the form of an electrical signal known as an action potential.

Research methods

Here are some facts and questions about neurons.

1. One neuron may be as narrow as 0.004 centimetres in diameter. Express this in standard form. (2 marks)
2. The mean number of neurons in the human brain is 100,000,000,000 (100 billion). Express this in standard form. (2 marks)
3. The longest neuron in the body is about 1 metre in length. What fraction is this of the body length of a person who is 2 metres tall? (2 marks)
4. The rate of neuron growth during foetal development in utero is 250,000 neurons per minute. Estimate how many neurons grow every hour. (2 marks)
5. Your brain makes up only about 2% of body mass, but uses 10 times as much of the oxygen. What fraction of your body's requirements of oxygen are used by the brain? (2 marks)
6. What percentage of your body's oxygen is used by the brain? (2 marks)

THE STRUCTURE AND FUNCTION OF NEURONS

Neurons are cells that are specialised to carry neural information throughout the body. Neurons can be one of three types: sensory neurons, relay neurons or motor neurons. Neurons typically consist of a cell body, dendrites and an axon. Dendrites at one end of the neuron receive signals from other neurons or from sensory receptors. Dendrites are connected to the cell body, the control centre of the neuron. From the cell body, the impulse is carried along the axon, where it terminates at the axon terminal. In many nerves, including those in the brain and spinal cord, there is an insulating layer that forms around the axon – the myelin sheath. This allows nerve impulses to transmit more rapidly along the axon. If the myelin sheath is damaged, impulses slow down. The length of a neuron can vary from a few millimetres up to one metre.

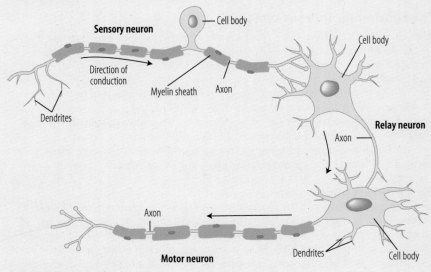

▲ Three types of neuron.

Sensory neurons

Sensory neurons carry nerve impulses *from* sensory receptors (e.g. receptors for vision, taste, touch) *to* the spinal cord and the brain. Sensory receptors are found in various locations in the body, for example in the eyes, ears, tongue and skin. Sensory neurons convert information from these sensory receptors into neural impulses. When these impulses reach the brain, they are translated into sensations of, for example, visual input, heat, pain, etc., so that the organism can react appropriately.

Not all sensory information travels as far as the brain, with some neurons terminating in the spinal cord. This allows reflex actions to occur quickly without the delay of sending impulses to the brain.

Relay neurons

Most neurons are neither sensory nor motor, but lie somewhere between the sensory input and the motor output. Relay neurons allow sensory and motor neurons to communicate with each other. These **relay neurons** (or interneurons) lie wholly within the brain and spinal cord.

Motor neurons

The term **motor neuron** refers to neurons located in the PNS that project their axons outside the PNS and directly or indirectly control muscles. Motor neurons form **synapses** with muscles and control their contractions. When stimulated, the motor neuron releases **neurotransmitters** that bind to receptors on the muscle and triggers a response which leads to muscle movement. When the axon of a motor neuron fires, the muscle with which it has formed synapses with contracts. The strength of the muscle contraction depends on the rate of firing of the axons of motor neurons that control it. Muscle relaxation is caused by inhibition of the motor neuron.

LINK TO RESEARCH METHODS

Mathematical skills on page 210

SYNAPTIC TRANSMISSION

Once an action potential has arrived at the terminal button at the end of the axon, it needs to be transferred to another neuron or to tissue. To achieve this, it must cross a gap between the presynaptic neuron and the postsynaptic neuron. This area is known as the synapse – which includes the end of the presynaptic neuron, the membrane of the postsynaptic neuron and the gap in between. The physical gap between the pre- and postsynaptic cell membranes is known as the synaptic gap. At the end of the axon of the nerve cell are a number of sacs known as synaptic vesicles. These vesicles contain the chemical messengers that assist in the transfer of the impulse, the neurotransmitters. As the action potential reaches the synaptic vesicles, it causes them to release their contents through a process called exocytosis.

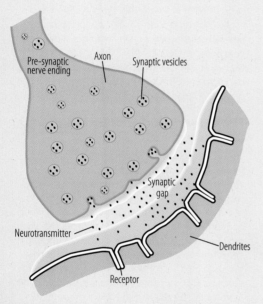

▲ The synapse.

The released neurotransmitter diffuses across the gap between the pre- and the postsynaptic cell, where it binds to specialised receptors on the surface of the cell that recognise it and are activated by that particular neurotransmitter. Once they have been activated, the receptor molecules produce either excitatory or inhibitory effects (see right) on the postsynaptic neuron.

This whole process of **synaptic transmission** takes only a fraction of a second, with the effects terminated at most synapses by a process called 're-uptake'. The neurotransmitter is taken up again by the presynaptic neuron, where it is stored and made available for later release (a sort of recycling programme). How quickly the presynaptic neuron takes back the neurotransmitter from the synaptic cleft determines how prolonged its effects will be. The quicker it is taken back, the shorter the effects on the postsynaptic neuron. Some antidepressant drugs prolong the action of the neurotransmitter by inhibiting this re-uptake process, leaving the neurotransmitter in the synapse for longer. Neurotransmitters can also be 'turned off' after they have stimulated the postsynaptic neuron. This takes place through the action of enzymes produced by the body, which make the neurotransmitters ineffective.

EXCITATORY AND INHIBITORY NEUROTRANSMITTERS

Neurotransmitters are the chemical messengers that carry signals across the synaptic gap to the receptor site on the postsynaptic cell. Neurotransmitters can be classified as either excitatory or inhibitory in their action. Excitatory neurotransmitters such as acetylcholine and noradrenaline are the nervous system's 'on switches'. These increase the likelihood that an excitatory signal is sent to the postsynaptic cell, which is then more likely to fire. Inhibitory neurotransmitters, such as serotonin and GABA, are the nervous system's 'off switches', in that they decrease the likelihood of that neuron firing. Inhibitory neurotransmitters are generally responsible for calming the mind and body, inducing sleep, and filtering out unnecessary excitatory signals.

An excitatory neurotransmitter binding with a postsynaptic receptor causes an electrical change in the membrane of that cell, resulting in an excitatory post-synaptic potential (EPSP), meaning that the postsynaptic cell is more likely to fire. An inhibitory neurotransmitter binding with a postsynaptic receptor results in an inhibitory postsynaptic potential (IPSP), making it less likely that the cell will fire.

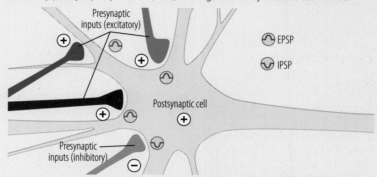

▲ The likelihood of a cell firing is determined by the summation of EPSPs and IPSPs.

A nerve cell can receive both EPSPs *and* IPSPs at the same time. The likelihood of the cell firing is therefore determined by adding up the excitatory and the inhibitory synaptic input. The net result of this calculation (known as summation) determines whether or not the cell fires. The strength of an EPSP can be increased in two ways. In *spatial* summation, a large number of EPSPs are generated at many different synapses on the same postsynaptic neuron at the same time. In *temporal* summation, a large number of EPSPs are generated at the same synapse by a series of high-frequency action potentials on the presynaptic neuron. The rate at which a particular cell fires is determined by what goes on in the synapses. If excitatory synapses are more active, the cell fires at a high rate. If inhibitory synapses are more active, the cell fires at a much lower rate, if at all.

KEY TERMS

Motor neurons form synapses with muscles and control their contractions.
Neurotransmitter Chemical substances that play an important part in the workings of the nervous system by transmitting nerve impulses across a synapse.
Relay neurons These neurons are the most common type of neuron in the CNS. They allow sensory and motor neurons to communicate with each other.
Sensory neurons carry nerve impulses from sensory receptors to the spinal cord and the brain.
Synapse The conjunction of the end of the axon of one neuron and the dendrite or cell body of another.
Synaptic transmission refers to the process by which a nerve impulse passes across the synaptic cleft from one neuron (the presynaptic neuron) to another (the postsynaptic neuron).

CAN YOU?   No. 6.2

1. Briefly explain what is meant by 'sensory', 'relay' and 'motor neurons'. (2 marks each)
2. Explain the nature of synaptic transmission. (5 marks)
3. Briefly explain what is meant by 'excitation' and 'inhibition' in synaptic transmission. (2 marks each)
4. Explain the role of excitatory and inhibitory neurotransmitters. (3 marks each)

The endocrine system

The work of the nervous system is supplemented by a second system in the body, the **endocrine system**. This is a network of glands throughout the body that manufacture and secrete chemical messengers known as hormones. The endocrine and nervous systems work very closely together to regulate the physiological processes of the human body. However, instead of using nerves to transmit information, the endocrine system uses blood vessels to deliver hormones to their target sites in the body.

GLANDS AND HORMONES

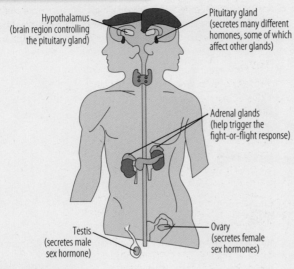

Hypothalamus (brain region controlling the pituitary gland)

Pituitary gland (secretes many different hormones, some of which affect other glands)

Adrenal glands (help trigger the fight-or-flight response)

Testis (secretes male sex hormone)

Ovary (secretes female sex hormones)

▲ The endocrine system.

Endocrine glands

Endocrine glands produce and secrete hormones, chemical substances that regulate the activity of cells or organs in the body. The major glands of the endocrine system include the pituitary gland, adrenal glands and the reproductive organs (ovaries and testes). Each gland in the endocrine system produces different hormones, which regulate the activity of organs and tissues in the body.

The endocrine system is regulated by feedback similar to how a thermostat regulates temperature in a room. For example, a signal is sent from the hypothalamus to the pituitary gland in the form of a 'releasing hormone'. This causes the pituitary to secrete a 'stimulating hormone' into the bloodstream. This hormone then signals the target gland (e.g. the adrenal glands) to secrete *its* hormone. As levels of this hormone rises in the bloodstream, the hypothalamus shuts down secretion of the releasing hormone and the pituitary gland shuts down secretion of the stimulating hormone. This slows down secretion of the target gland's hormone, resulting in stable concentrations of hormones circulating in the bloodstream.

Hormones

Hormones are chemicals that circulate in the bloodstream and are carried to target sites throughout the body. The word 'hormone' comes from the Greek word *hormao* meaning 'I excite', which refers to the fact that each hormone 'excites' or stimulates a particular part of the body.

Although hormones come into contact with most cells in the body, a given hormone usually affects only a limited number of cells, known as target cells. Target cells respond to a particular hormone because they have receptors for that hormone. Cells that do not have such a receptor cannot be influenced directly by that hormone. When enough receptor sites are stimulated by hormones, this results in a physiological reaction in the target cell. Timing of hormone release is critical for normal functioning, as are the levels of hormones released. Too much or too little at the wrong time can result in dysfunction of bodily systems. For example, too high a level of cortisol can lead to Cushing's syndrome, characterised by high blood pressure and depression. The most common cause of excess cortisol is a tumour in the pituitary gland which makes too much of a hormone called adrenocorticotrophic hormone (ACTH) which stimulates the adrenal glands to make too much cortisol.

PITUITARY GLAND

The **pituitary gland** produces **hormones** whose primary function is to influence the release of hormones from other glands, and in so doing regulate many of the body's functions. The pituitary is controlled by the hypothalamus, a region of the brain just above the pituitary gland. The hypothalamus receives information from many sources about the basic functions of the body, then uses this information to help regulate these functions. One of the ways it does this involves controlling the pituitary gland.

As the 'master gland', the pituitary produces hormones that travel in the bloodstream to their specific target. These hormones either directly cause changes in physiological processes in the body or stimulate other glands to produce other hormones. High levels of hormones produced in other endocrine glands can stop the hypothalamus and pituitary releasing more of their own hormones. This is called negative feedback, and prevents hormone levels from rising too high.

Hormones produced by the pituitary gland

The pituitary gland has two main parts: the anterior (front) pituitary and the posterior (back) pituitary. These two parts release different hormones, which target different parts of the body. The two sections of the pituitary gland produce a number of different hormones, which act on different target glands or cells. For example, the *anterior* pituitary releases ACTH as a response to stress. ACTH stimulates the adrenal glands to produce cortisol. The anterior pituitary also produces two hormones important in the control of reproductive functioning and sexual characteristics – luteinising hormone (LH) and follicle-stimulating hormone (FSH). In females these hormones stimulate the ovaries to produce oestrogen and progesterone, and in males they stimulate the testes to produce testosterone and sperm. The *posterior* pituitary releases oxytocin, which stimulates contraction of the uterus during childbirth, and is important for mother–infant bonding. Recent research using mice has found that oxytocin is indispensable for healthy maintenance and repair, and that it declines with age (Elabd *et al.*, 2014).

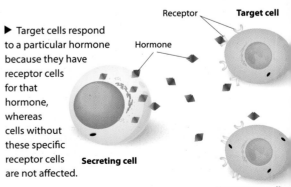

Receptor

Target cell

Hormone

▶ Target cells respond to a particular hormone because they have receptor cells for that hormone, whereas cells without these specific receptor cells are not affected.

Secreting cell

Not a target cell (no receptors for that specific hormone)

THE ADRENAL GLANDS

The two adrenal glands sit on top of the kidneys. The name 'adrenal' relates to their location (*ad* – near or at; *renes* – kidneys). Each adrenal gland is made up of two distinct parts. The outer part of each gland is called the adrenal cortex and the inner region is known as the adrenal medulla. The adrenal cortex and the adrenal medulla have very different functions. One of the main distinctions between them is that the hormones released by the adrenal cortex are necessary for life; those released by the adrenal medulla are not.

Hormones produced by the adrenal glands

The adrenal cortex (the outer part of the adrenal gland) produces cortisol, which regulates or supports a variety of important bodily functions including cardiovascular and anti-inflammatory functions. Cortisol production is increased in response to stress. If the cortisol level is low, the individual has low blood pressure, poor immune function and an inability to deal with stress. The adrenal cortex also produces aldosterone, which is responsible for maintaining blood volume and blood pressure. The adrenal medulla (the inner part of the adrenal gland) releases adrenaline and noradrenaline, hormones that prepare the body for fight or flight (see page 154). Adrenaline helps the body respond to a stressful situation, for example by increasing heart rate and blood flow to the muscles and brain and helping with the conversion of glycogen to glucose to provide energy. Noradrenaline constricts the blood vessels, causing blood pressure to increase.

UPGRADE

When answering exam questions it is important to learn the skill of précis – to give a summary or the main points of something. We have emphasised the need for elaboration with AO3 but you also need to be able to reduce material to fit a specific question, giving your answer more focus. This is something students can struggle to do for AO1 material.

Let's take Q1 in the 'Can you?' box on the right as an example:

'Outline **one or more** functions of the endocrine system.' (6 marks)

- Begin by outlining the overall function of the endocrine system (to regulate the activity of cells or organs within the body).
- Then move on to illustrate this by looking at the specific functions of perhaps two of the glands that make up the system. For example, the pituitary gland's primary function is to influence the release of hormones from other glands.
- You might link this to other functions such as that the anterior pituitary releases growth hormones to stimulate growth and ACTH in response to stress, which in turn stimulates the adrenal glands to produce cortisol.

You need to practise choosing the right material so you can answer questions accurately in the time you have. For Q3 on the right; you would only need 2 marks worth of information for each part of the question, so you wouldn't need to start with any 'general' information about the system. The lesson from all this is to go straight into answering the question and to practise your précis!

There is a lot of information on these two pages. This gives you a good overview of the endocrine system and hormones. This is more than you need when answering questions such as those in the 'Can you?' box on the right, so you need to be selective when choosing content to answer these questions.

Ovaries

The two ovaries are part of the female reproductive system. Ovaries are responsible for the production of eggs and for the hormones oestrogen and progesterone. Progesterone, which is more important in the post-ovulation phase of the menstrual cycle, has also been found to be associated with heightened sensitivity to social cues that indicate the presence of social opportunity (e.g. recruiting allies) or threat (e.g. from outsiders) that would be significant in the case of pregnancy (Maner and Miller, 2014).

Testes

The testes are the male reproductive glands that produce the hormone testosterone. Testosterone causes the development of male characteristics such as growth of facial hair, deepening of the voice and the growth spurt that takes place during puberty. Testosterone production is controlled by the hypothalamus and pituitary gland. The hypothalamus instructs the pituitary gland on how much testosterone to produce, and the pituitary gland passes this message on to the testes. Testosterone also plays a role in sex drive, sperm production and maintenance of muscle strength, and is associated with overall health and well-being in men. Testosterone is not exclusively a male hormone. Women also have testosterone, but in smaller amounts.

As well as playing an important reproductive role in preparing the womb for pregnancy, there is also evidence that oestrogen, administered in the form of hormone replacement therapy, might lead to a reduction in the long-term risk of Alzheimer's disease (Maki and Henderson, 2012).

KEY TERMS

Endocrine glands Special groups of cells within the endocrine system, whose function is to produce and secrete hormones.

Endocrine system A network of glands throughout the body that manufacture and secrete chemical messengers known as hormones.

Hormones The body's chemical messengers. They travel through the bloodstream, influencing many different processes including mood, the stress response and bonding between mother and newborn baby.

Pituitary gland The 'master gland', whose primary function is to influence the release of hormones from other glands.

CAN YOU? No. 6.3

1. Outline **one or more** functions of the endocrine system. (6 marks)
2. Explain the relationship between endocrine glands and hormones. (4 marks)
3. Outline the role of **one** endocrine gland and of **one** hormone that it produces. (4 marks)

The fight-or-flight response

When a person experiences a threatening or stressful situation, their body reacts in specific ways. The heart beats faster, their breathing becomes more rapid and their muscles tense. These reactions to stressful situations are known collectively as the **fight-or-flight response**. This response evolved as a survival mechanism, enabling animals and humans to react quickly to life-threatening situations. The bodily changes associated with 'fight or flight' allow an individual to fight off the threat or flee to safety. Unfortunately, the fight-or-flight response is also activated in conditions that are not life-threatening, and where fighting or running away is not particularly helpful.

The **amygdala** associates sensory signals with emotions such as anger or fear and sends a 'distress signal' to the hypothalamus.

The **hypothalamus**, in response to continued threat, releases CRH into the bloodstream.

The **pituitary gland** releases ACTH into the bloodstream, and from there to its target sites.

The **SNS** prepares the body for the rapid action associated with fight or flight.

The **PNS** dampens down the stress response when the threat has passed.

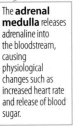

The **adrenal medulla** releases adrenaline into the bloodstream, causing physiological changes such as increased heart rate and release of blood sugar.

The **adrenal cortex** releases stress hormones, including cortisol, in response to stress.

The **feedback system**. Cortisol levels are monitored so that CRH and ACTH production is inhibited if cortisol is too high.

▲ The fight-or-flight response

These changes happen so quickly that people usually aren't aware of them. In fact, this response is so efficient that the amygdala and hypothalamus start responding even before the brain has a chance to fully process what is happening. This is why people are able to jump out of the path of an oncoming car before they have the chance to think about what they are doing.

THE FIGHT-OR-FLIGHT RESPONSE TO STRESS

The amygdala and hypothalamus

When an individual is faced with a threat, an area of the brain called the amygdala is mobilised. The amygdala associates sensory signals (what we see, hear or smell) with emotions associated with fight or flight, such as fear or anger. The amygdala then sends a distress signal to the hypothalamus, which functions like a command centre in the brain, communicating with the rest of the body through the sympathetic nervous system. The body's response to stressors involves two major systems, one for *acute* (i.e. sudden) stressors such as personal attack, and the second for *chronic* (i.e. ongoing) stressors such as a stressful job.

Response to acute (sudden) stressors

The sympathetic nervous system
When the sympathetic nervous system (SNS) is triggered, it begins the process of preparing the body for the rapid action necessary for fight or flight. The SNS sends a signal through to the adrenal medulla, which responds by releasing the hormone adrenaline into the bloodstream.

Adrenaline
As adrenaline circulates through the body, it causes a number of physiological changes. The heart beats faster, pushing blood to the muscles, heart and other vital organs, and blood pressure increases. Breathing becomes more rapid in order to take in as much oxygen as possible with each breath. Adrenaline also triggers the release of blood sugar (glucose) and fats, which flood into the bloodstream, supplying energy to parts of the body associated with the fight-or-flight response.

The parasympathetic nervous system
When the threat has passed, the parasympathetic branch of the autonomic nervous system (ANS) dampens down the stress response. Whereas the sympathetic branch causes the heart to beat faster and blood pressure to increase, the parasympathetic branch slows down the heartbeat again and reduces blood pressure. Another benefit of parasympathetic action is that digestion (inhibited when the SNS is aroused) begins again.

Response to chronic (ongoing) stressors

If the brain continues to perceive something as threatening, the second system kicks in. As the initial surge of adrenaline subsides, the hypothalamus activates a stress response system called the **HPA axis**. This consists of the hypothalamus, the pituitary gland and the adrenal glands.

'H' – The hypothalamus
The HPA axis relies on a series of hormonal signals to keep the SNS working. In response to continued threat, the hypothalamus releases a chemical messenger, *corticotrophin-releasing hormone* (CRH), which is released into the bloodstream in response to the stressor.

'P' – The pituitary gland
On arrival at the pituitary gland, CRH causes the pituitary to produce and release *adrenocorticotrophic hormone* (ACTH). From the pituitary, ACTH is transported in the bloodstream to its target site in the adrenal glands.

'A' – The adrenal glands
ACTH stimulates the adrenal cortex to release various stress-related hormones, including cortisol. Cortisol is responsible for several effects in the body that are important in the fight-or-flight response. Some of these are positive (e.g. a quick burst of energy and a lower sensitivity to pain) whereas others are negative (e.g. impaired cognitive performance and a lowered immune response).

Feedback
This system is also very efficient at regulating itself. Both the hypothalamus and pituitary gland have special receptors that monitor circulating cortisol levels. If these rise above normal, they initiate a reduction in CRH and ACTH levels, thus bringing cortisol levels back to normal.

EVALUATION: FIGHT OR FLIGHT

The 'tend and befriend' response

Taylor *et al.* (2000) suggest that, for females, behavioural responses to stress are more characterised by a pattern of tend and befriend than fight or flight.

This involves protecting themselves and their young through nurturing behaviours (tending) and forming protective alliances with other women (befriending). Women may have a different system for coping with stress because their responses evolved in the context of being the primary caregiver of their children. Fleeing at any sign of danger would put a female's offspring at risk.

This finding, explained in terms of the higher levels of the hormone oxytocin in females, suggests that previous research, which has mainly focused on males, has obscured patterns of stress response in females.

Negative consequences of the fight-or-flight response

The physiological responses associated with fight or flight may be adaptive for a stress response that requires energetic behavioural responses. However, the stressors of modern life rarely require such levels of physical activity.

The problem for modern humans arises when the stress response is repeatedly activated. For example, the increased blood pressure that is characteristic of SNS activation can lead to physical damage in blood vessels and eventually to heart disease.

As a consequence, although cortisol may assist the body in fighting a viral infection, too much cortisol suppresses the immune response, shutting down the very process that fights infection and increasing the likelihood of stress-related illness.

'Fight or flight' does not tell the whole story

Gray (1988) argues that the first phase of reaction to a threat is not to fight or flee, but to avoid confrontation.

He suggests that, prior to responding with attacking or running away, most animals (including humans) typically display the 'freeze response'. This initial freeze response is essentially a 'stop, look and listen' response, where the animal is hyper-vigilant, alert to the slightest sign of danger.

The adaptive advantages of this response for humans are that 'freezing' focuses attention and makes them look for new information in order to make the best response for that particular threat.

Positive rather than 'fight or flight' behaviours

Von Dawans *et al.* (2012) challenge the classic view that, under stress, men respond only with 'fight or flight', whereas women are more prone to 'tend and befriend'.

▲ Acute stress, such as that experienced in the terrorist attacks on New York in 2001, can lead to greater cooperative and friendly behaviour.

Von Dawans *et al.*'s study found that acute stress can actually lead to greater cooperative and friendly behaviour, in both men and women. This could explain the human connection that happens during times of crises such as the 9/11 terrorist attacks in New York.

One reason why stress may lead to greater cooperative behaviour is because human beings are fundamentally social animals and it is the protective nature of human social relationships that has allowed our species to thrive.

A genetic basis to sex differences in the fight-or-flight response

Lee and Harley (2012) have found evidence of a genetic basis for gender differences in the fight-or-flight response.

The *SRY* gene, found exclusively on the male Y chromosome, directs male development, promoting aggression and resulting in the fight-or-flight response to stress. The *SRY* gene may prime males to respond to stress in this way by the release of stress hormones such as adrenaline and through increased blood flow to organs involved in the fight-or-flight response.

In contrast, the absence of the SRY *gene in females (who do not have a Y chromosome) may prevent this response to stress, leading instead to 'tend and befriend' behaviours.*

APPLY YOUR KNOWLEDGE

Consider these two stressful situations:

1. In an episode of the BBC series *The Apprentice*, one of the contestants publicly criticises one of his teammates, blaming him personally for the team's failure to successfully complete a task. As everyone's eyes turn on him, the accused contestant feels his face going red, his muscles tensing and his anger rising. He turns on his accuser, trying to contain the almost overwhelming urge to hit him.

2. Another contestant has to pitch a sales presentation to executives from a major department store. She starts hesitantly, then, as she sees the faces of the executives looking back at her, she stops mid-sentence. Her mouth goes dry and she just stands there, shaking uncontrollably and staring at her audience, wishing she could just get out of there.

Using your knowledge of the fight-or-flight response, explain what is going on in each of these examples and why the two contestants are behaving in the way that they are.

Insider tip...

Question 3 in the 'Can you?' box below asks you to 'Outline the role of adrenaline in the fight-or-flight response'. Your material for this question should be restricted to the role of the SNS on the opposite page. Although adrenaline does have a role in the regulation of the HPA axis, it is not considered a core component of this response to stress.

CAN YOU? No. 6.4

1. Explain what is meant by the term 'fight-or-flight response'. (3 marks)
2. Outline the fight-or-flight response. (6 marks)
3. Outline the role of adrenaline in the fight-or-flight response. (3 marks)
4. Discuss the fight-or-flight r[...] AS, 16 marks A)

Localisation of function

Localisation of function refers to the principle that specific functions (language, memory, hearing, etc.) have specific locations within the brain. The early nineteenth century witnessed a growth of interest in the localisation of functions in the brain. Franz Gall's theory of phrenology (the study of the structure of the skull to determine a person's character and capacity) was undoubtedly influential but was quickly discredited. Shortly after, using animal experimentation, Pierre Flourens was able to demonstrate that the main divisions of the brain were responsible for largely different functions. Since Gall and Flourens' day, the techniques have grown considerably more sophisticated, as has our understanding of the functional organisation of the human brain.

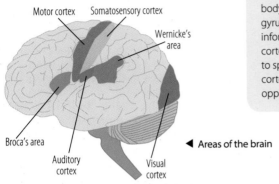

◀ Areas of the brain

MOTOR AND SOMATOSENSORY AREAS

The motor cortex

The **motor cortex** is responsible for the generation of voluntary motor movements. It is located in the frontal lobe of the brain, along a bumpy region known as the precentral gyrus. Both hemispheres of the brain have a motor cortex, with the motor cortex on one side of the brain controlling the muscles on the opposite side of the body. Different parts of the motor cortex exert control over different parts of the body. These regions are arranged logically next to one another, e.g. the region that controls the actions of the foot is next to the region that controls the leg and so on.

The somatosensory cortex

The **somatosensory cortex** detects sensory events arising from different regions of the body. It is located in the parietal lobe of the brain, along a region known as the postcentral gyrus. The postcentral gyrus is the area of the cortex dedicated to the processing of sensory information related to touch. Using sensory information from the skin, the somatosensory cortex produces sensations of touch, pressure, pain and temperature, which it then localises to specific body regions. As with the motor cortex, both hemispheres have a somatosensory cortex, with the cortex on one side of the brain receiving sensory information from the opposite side of the body.

VISUAL AND AUDITORY CENTRES

Visual centres

The primary visual centre in the brain is located in the visual cortex, in the occipital lobe of the brain. However, visual processing actually begins in the retina, at the back of the eye, where light enters and strikes the photoreceptors (rods and cones). Nerve impulses from the retina are then transmitted to the brain via the optic nerve. Some nerve impulses from the retina travel to areas of the brain involved in the coordination of circadian rhythms (see page 164), but the majority terminate in an area of the brain called the thalamus, which acts as a relay station, passing this information on to the visual cortex.

The visual cortex spans both hemispheres, with the right hemisphere receiving its input from the left-hand side of the visual field, while the visual cortex in the left hemisphere receives its input from the right-hand side of the visual field. The visual cortex contains several different areas, with each of these areas processing different types of visual information, such as colour, shape or movement.

Auditory centres

The auditory centre in the brain is concerned with hearing. Most of this area lies within the temporal lobes on both sides of the brain, where we find the auditory cortex. The auditory pathways begin in the cochlea in the inner ear, where sound waves are converted to nerve impulses, which travel via the auditory nerve to the auditory cortex in the brain.

On the journey from the cochlea to the brain, the first stop is the brain stem. Within the brain stem a basic decoding takes place, for example the duration and intensity of a sound. The next stop is in the thalamus, which acts as a relay station and also carries out further processing of the auditory stimulus.

The last stop in this journey is the auditory cortex. Although the sound has already been largely decoded by this stage, in the auditory ˙tex it is recognised and may result in an appropriate response.

LANGUAGE CENTRES

Broca's area

This area is named after Paul Broca, the French neurosurgeon who treated a patient who he referred to as 'Tan' because that was the only syllable this particular patient could express. Tan had an unusual disorder. Although he had been able to understand spoken language, he was unable to speak, nor express his thoughts in writing.

Subsequently, Broca studied eight other patients, all of whom had similar language deficits, along with lesions in their left frontal hemisphere. Patients with damage to these areas in the right hemisphere did not have the same language problems. This led him to identify the existence of a 'language centre' in the posterior portion of the frontal lobe of the left hemisphere (Broca, 1865). This area is believed to be critical for speech production. However, neuroscientists have found evidence of activity in **Broca's area** when people perform cognitive tasks that have nothing to do with language. Fedorenko *et al.* (2012) discovered two regions of Broca's area, one selectively involved in language, the other involved in responding to many demanding cognitive tasks (such as performing maths problems).

Wernicke's area

Shortly after Broca had discovered a 'speech production' area in the brain, Carl Wernicke, a German neurologist, discovered another area of the brain that was involved in *understanding* language. This area, named **Wernicke's area**, was in the posterior portion of the left temporal lobe. Whereas Broca's patients could understand language but not speak, patients with a lesion in Wernicke's area could speak but were unable to *understand* language.

Wernicke proposed that language involves separate motor and sensory regions located in different cortical regions. The motor region, located in Broca's area, is close to the area that controls the mouth, tongue and vocal cords. The sensory region, located in Wernicke's area, is close to regions of the brain responsible for auditory and visual input. Input from these regions is thought to be transferred to Wernicke's area where it is recognised as language and associated with meaning. There is a neural loop known as the arcuate fasciculus running between Broca's area and Wernicke's area. At one end lies Broca's area, responsible for the production of language, and at the other lies Wernicke's area, responsible for the processing of spoken language.

Challenges to localisation: equipotentiality

Not all researchers agree with the view that cognitive functions are localised in the brain.

A conflicting view is the equipotentiality theory (Lashley, 1930). Lashley believed that basic motor and sensory functions were localised, but that higher mental functions were not. He claimed that intact areas of the cortex could take over responsibility for specific cognitive functions following injury to the area normally responsible for that function. According to this point of view, the effects of damage to the brain would be determined by the *extent* rather than the location of the damage.

This view has received some support from the discovery that humans were able to regain some of their cognitive abilities following damage to specific areas of the brain (see page 160).

Communication may be more important than localisation

Research suggests that what might be more important is how brain areas communicate with each other, rather than which specific brain regions control a particular cognitive process.

Wernicke claimed that although different regions of the brain had different specialist functions, they are interdependent in the sense that in order to work they must interact with each other. For example, in 1892 a neurologist, Joseph Dejerine, described a case in which the loss of an ability to read resulted from damage to the connection between the visual cortex and Wernicke's area.

This suggests that complex behaviours such as language, reading and movement are built up gradually as a stimulus enters the brain, then moves through different structures before a response is produced. Damage to the connection between any two points in this process results in impairments that resemble damage to the localised brain region associated with a specific function.

Support for language centres from aphasia studies

Evidence for the different functions of Broca's and Wernicke's areas in language production and understanding comes from the discovery that damage to these different areas results in different types of aphasia.

Expressive aphasia (also known as Broca's aphasia) is an impaired ability to produce language. In most cases, this is caused by brain damage in Broca's area. Receptive aphasia (also known as Wernicke's aphasia) is an impaired ability to understand language, an inability to extract meaning from spoken or written words. This form of aphasia is usually the result of damage (e.g. from a stroke) in Wernicke's area.

This demonstrates the important role played by these brain regions in different aspects of language.

There are individual differences in language areas

The pattern of activation observed in response to various language activities can vary from individual to individual.

Bavelier *et al.* (1997) found considerable variability in patterns of activation across different individuals when reading. They observed activity in the right temporal lobe as well as in the left frontal, temporal and occipital lobes. Other studies have found significant gender differences in the size of the brain areas associated with language. For example, Harasty *et al.* (1997) found that women have proportionally larger Broca's and Wernicke's areas than men.

These anatomical differences may well explain the superior language skills often found in females.

Language production may not be confined to Broca's area alone

Dronkers *et al.* (2007) re-examined the preserved brains of two of Broca's patients, Louis Leborgne (Tan) and Lazare Lelong. They used modern high-resolution brain MRI imaging in order to identify the extent of any lesions in more detail.

The MRI findings revealed that other areas besides Broca's area could also have contributed to the patients' reduced speech abilities. This finding is significant because although lesions to Broca's area alone can cause temporary speech disruption, they do not usually result in severe disruption of spoken language.

This study suggests that language and cognition are far more complicated than once thought and involve networks of brain regions rather than being localised to specific areas.

 UPGRADE

Other Upgrade features have considered how to tackle the higher scoring questions, i.e. how to add detail or elaborate evaluation. However, many of the questions you will face in biopsychology will be relatively short, low tariff questions that require you, for example, to identify a particular brain area or to outline its function.

These questions are not to be taken lightly as, if you know your stuff, they are a quick and easy way of gaining valuable marks. So, after reading this spread, close your book and draw a rough side view of the brain (a sagittal view if you want to be technical). On your drawing of the brain, identify the location of the sensory cortex, the motor cortex, the visual and auditory centres, Broca's area and Wernicke's area. Now write about 50 words (equivalent to a 3 mark question) for each on its role within the brain.

Finally, open your book again and see how you did. Keep repeating this exercise until you're confident you can do it under exam conditions.

KEY TERMS

Broca's area An area in the frontal lobe of the brain, usually in the left hemisphere, related to speech production.

Localisation of function Refers to the belief that specific areas of the brain are associated with specific cognitive processes.

Motor cortex A region of the brain responsible for the generation of voluntary motor movements.

Somatosensory cortex A region of the brain that processes input from sensory receptors in the body that are sensitive to touch.

Wernicke's area An area in the temporal lobe of the brain important in the comprehension of language.

CAN YOU? No. 6.5

1. Briefly explain what is meant by the term 'localisation of function'. (2 marks)
2. Outline the nature of the motor centre in the brain. (3 marks)
3. Outline the role of the somatosensory centre in the brain. (3 marks)
4. Outline the role of the visual centre in the brain. (3 marks)
5. Outline the role of the auditory centre in the brain. (3 marks)
6. Explain the role of Broca's and Wernicke's areas. (3 marks each)
7. Discuss localisation of function in the human brain. (16 marks)

Lateralisation and split-brain research

The idea that the different hemispheres of the brain might have different specialisations can be traced back to Marc Dax, a French country doctor. In the early 1800s, Dax treated a significant number of patients who had lost the power of speech as a result of brain damage. He observed that in every case there had been damage in the left hemisphere but none of these patients had experienced right-hemisphere damage. This suggested to Dax that language was located in the left hemisphere; something that would be subsequently investigated experimentally in **split-brain research**. These split-brain patients had received surgery to isolate the two hemispheres from each other, something that enabled psychologists to study each hemisphere independently.

HEMISPHERIC LATERALISATION

The term brain lateralisation refers to the fact that the two halves of the human brain are not exactly alike. Each hemisphere has functional specialisations, i.e. neural mechanisms for some functions (such as language) are localised primarily in one half of the brain. For example, research has found that the left hemisphere is dominant for language and speech, whereas the right excels at visual-motor tasks. In 1861, Paul Broca established that damage in a particular area of the left brain hemisphere led to language deficits, yet damage to the same area of the right hemisphere did not have the same consequence (see page 157).

However, this raises an important question: if language is located in the left hemisphere, how can we talk about things that are experienced in the right hemisphere (e.g. face recognition)? The answer is that the two hemispheres are connected. This allows information received by one hemisphere to be sent to the other hemisphere through connecting bundles of nerve fibres such as the corpus callosum.

The chance to investigate the different abilities of the two hemispheres came about when, in a treatment for severe epilepsy, surgeons cut the bundle of nerve fibres that formed the corpus callosum. The aim of this procedure was to prevent the violent electrical activity that accompanies epileptic seizures crossing from one hemisphere to the other. Patients who underwent this form of surgery are often referred to as 'split-brain' patients.

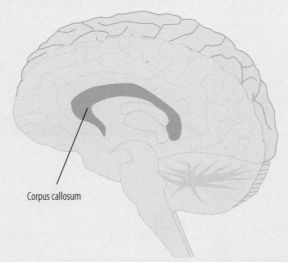

Corpus callosum

▲ The corpus callosum allows the two hemispheres to communicate with each other.

SPLIT-BRAIN RESEARCH

Sperry and Gazzaniga's research

Roger Sperry and Michael Gazzaniga (1967) were the first to study the capabilities of split-brain patients. To test the capabilities of the separated hemispheres, they were able to send visual information to just one hemisphere at a time in order to study what is known as **hemispheric lateralisation**.

Sperry and Gazzaniga took advantage of the fact that information from the left visual field goes to the right hemisphere and information from the right visual field goes to the left hemisphere. Because the corpus callosum is cut in split-brain patients, the information presented to one hemisphere has no way of travelling to the other hemisphere and can be processed only in the hemisphere that received it. In a typical study, the split-brain patient would fixate on a dot in the centre of a screen while information was presented to either the left or right visual field. They would then be asked to make responses with either their left hand (controlled by the right hemisphere) or their right hand (controlled by the left hemisphere), or verbally (which is controlled by the left hemisphere), without being able to see what their hands were doing.

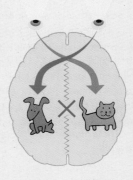

For example, if the patient was flashed a picture of a dog to the right visual field and asked what they had seen, they would answer 'dog'. However, if a picture of a cat was flashed to the left visual field the patient would say that he or she sees nothing. Why is this the case? The information from the left visual field is processed by the right hemisphere (as can be seen in the picture), but as it has no language centre, cannot respond verbally. The left hemisphere, which does have a language centre, does not receive information about seeing the picture of a cat, therefore cannot say that it has seen it.

What have we learned from split-brain research?

Work with split-brain patients has discovered a number of differences between the two hemispheres, e.g. that the left hemisphere is responsible for speech and language, and the right hemisphere specialises in visual–spatial processing and facial recognition. However, split-brain research has not shown that the brain is organised into discrete regions with specific sections responsible for specific tasks. Instead it suggests that the connectivity between the different regions is as important as the operation of the different parts.

EVALUATION OF LATERALISATION

Related to increased neural capacity

The main strength of hemispheric lateralisation appears to be that it increases neural processing capacity.

By using only one hemisphere to engage in a particular task (e.g. language or mathematical ability), this would leave the other hemisphere free to engage in another function. However, despite this assumption, very little empirical evidence has been provided to show that lateralisation confers any advantage to the functioning of the brain in humans. However, Rogers *et al.* (2004) found that, in the domestic chicken, brain lateralisation is associated with an enhanced ability to perform two tasks simultaneously – finding food and being vigilant for predators.

This finding does provide some evidence that brain lateralisation enhances brain efficiency in cognitive tasks that demand the simultaneous but different use of both hemispheres.

Lateralisation and immune system functioning

There are a number of disadvantages associated with hemispheric lateralisation.

For example, architects and the mathematically gifted tend to have superior right-hemispheric skills but are also much more likely to be left-handed and to suffer higher rates of allergies and problems with the immune system. Tonnessen *et al.* (1993) found a small but significant relationship between handedness and immune system disorders, suggesting that the same genetic processes that lead to lateralisation may also affect the development of the immune system.

Morfit and Weekes (2001) lent support to this suggestion, finding that left-handers had a higher incidence of immune system disorders in their immediate families than did right-handers.

Lateralisation changes with age

Lateralisation of function appears not to stay exactly the same throughout an individual's lifetime, but changes with normal ageing.

Lateralised patterns found in younger individuals tend to switch to bilateral patterns in healthy older adults. For example, Szaflarski *et al.* (2006) found that language became more lateralised to the left hemisphere with increasing age in children and adolescents, but after the age of 25, lateralisation decreased with each decade of life.

It is difficult to know why this is the case, but one possibility is that using the extra processing resources of the other hemisphere may in some way compensate for age-related declines in function.

KEY TERMS

Hemispheric lateralisation refers to the fact that some mental processes in the brain are mainly specialised to either the left or right hemisphere.

Split-brain research Research that studies individuals who have been subjected to the surgical separation of the two hemispheres of the brain as a result of severing the corpus callosum.

CAN YOU? No. 6.6

1. Briefly explain what is meant by the terms 'lateralisation' and 'split-brain research'. (2 marks each)
2. Explain the nature of lateralisation in the brain. (6 marks)
3. Outline the findings of split-brain research. (6 marks)
4. Discuss research into lateralisation and/or the split brain. (16 marks)

EVALUATION OF SPLIT-BRAIN RESEARCH

Language may not be restricted to the left hemisphere

Gazzaniga (1998) suggests that some of the early discoveries from split-brain research have been disconfirmed by more recent discoveries.

Damage to the left hemisphere was found to be far more detrimental to language function than was damage to the right. However, case studies have demonstrated that this was not necessarily the case. One patient, known as J.W., developed the capacity to speak out of the right hemisphere, with the result that he can now speak about information presented to the left or to the right brain (Turk *et al.*, 2002).

This challenges the claim that the right hemisphere is unable to handle even the most rudimentary language.

Limitations of split-brain research

The split-brain procedure is rarely carried out nowadays, and Andrewes (2001) points out that many studies are presented with as few as three participants or even just the one single participant.

Andrewes claims that, in some cases, conclusions have been drawn from individuals who either have a confounding physical disorder that made the split-brain procedure necessary, or have had a less complete sectioning of the two hemispheres than was originally believed.

As a result, patients who have had this procedure without these confounding factors are rarely encountered in sufficient numbers to be useful for research.

Research methods

It is possible to demonstrate right and left field advantages in normal individuals (without split brains). The way to do this is to present two words on a computer screen for less than 100 milliseconds each. One word is presented to the right and one to the left. Participants should show a preference for reporting the word on the right because that is processed by the left hemisphere. Some students tested this by showing 20 word pairs to each participant and recording how many times the word on the left or right was reported first. Their results are shown below.

Participant	1	2	3	4	5	6	7	8	9	10
Word on left	13	9	10	8	5	11	9	10	12	4
Word on right	7	11	10	12	15	9	11	10	8	16

1. Write a suitable hypothesis for this study. (2 marks)
2. The students used the Sign Test to determine if their result was significant. Explain why it would be appropriate to use this test with this data. (2 marks)
3. The statistic for the Sign Test is S. Calculate the value of S for this data. (3 marks)
4. With reference to the hypothesis you wrote for question 1, state whether you would use a one- or a two-tailed test when determining significance. (1 mark)

LINK TO RESEARCH METHODS

Hypothesis on pages 178 and 182
Sign Test on pages 218–219

Plasticity and functional recovery of the brain

Brain plasticity refers to the brain's ability to change and adapt as a result of experience. This ability to change plays an important role in brain development and behaviour. Researchers used to believe that changes in the brain only took place during infancy and childhood, but more recent research has demonstrated that the brain continues to create new neural pathways and alter existing ones to adapt to new experiences as a result of learning. The brain also appears to show evidence of **functional receovery**, moving functions from a damaged area of the brain after trauma to other undamaged areas.

PLASTICITY

In recent years, it has become clear not only that neuronal organisation is changed as a result of experience, but also that there any many different *types* of experience that can do this. Factors that are now known to affect neuronal structure and function include life experience, video games and even meditation.

Plasticity as a result of life experience

As people gain new experiences, nerve pathways that are used frequently develop stronger connections, whereas neurons that are rarely or never used eventually die. By developing new connections and pruning away weak ones, the brain is able to constantly adapt to a changing environment. However, there is also a natural decline in cognitive functioning with age that can be attributed to changes in the brain. This has led researchers to look for ways in which new connections can be made to reverse this effect. For example, Boyke *et al.* (2008) found evidence of brain plasticity in 60 year olds taught a new skill – juggling. They found increases in grey matter in the visual cortex, although when practising stopped, these changes were reversed.

Playing video games

Playing video games makes many different complex cognitive and motor demands. Kühn *et al.* (2014) compared a control group with a video game training group that was trained for two months for at least 30 min per day on the game *Super Mario*. They found a significant increase in grey matter in various brain areas including the cortex, hippocampus and cerebellum. This increase was not evident in the control group that did not play *Super Mario*. The researchers concluded that video game training had resulted in new synaptic connections in brain areas involved in spatial navigation, strategic planning, working memory and motor performance – skills that were important in playing the game successfully.

Meditation

Researchers working with Tibetan monks have been able to demonstrate that meditation can change the inner workings of the brain. Davidson *et al.* (2004) compared eight practitioners of Tibetan meditation with 10 student volunteers with no previous meditation experience. Both groups were fitted with electrical sensors and asked to meditate for short periods. The electrodes picked up much greater activation of gamma waves (important because they coordinate neuron activity) in the monks. The students showed only a slight increase in gamma wave activity while meditating. The researchers concluded that meditation not only changes the workings of the brain in the short term, but may also produce permanent changes, based on the fact that the monks had far more gamma wave activity than the control group even *before* they started meditating.

FUNCTIONAL RECOVERY AFTER TRAUMA

In the 1960s, researchers studied cases in which stroke victims were able to regain functioning. They discovered that when brain cells are damaged or destroyed, as they are during a stroke, the brain re-wires itself over time so that some level of function can be regained. Although parts of the brain may be damaged or even destroyed as a result of trauma, other parts appear able to take over the functions that were lost. Neurons next to damaged brain areas can form new circuits that resume some of the lost function.

Mechanisms for recovery

Regenerative developments in brain function arise from the brain's plasticity, its ability to change structurally and functionally following trauma. Two ways in which the brain is able to do this are neuronal unmasking and stem cells.

Neuronal unmasking

Wall (1977) first identified what he called 'dormant synapses' in the brain. These are synaptic connections that exist anatomically but their function is blocked. Under normal conditions these synapses may be ineffective because the rate of neural input to them is too low for them to be activated. However, increasing the rate of input to these synapses, as would happen when a surrounding brain area becomes damaged, can then open (or 'unmask') these dormant synapses. The unmasking of dormant synapses can open connections to regions of the brain that are not normally activated, creating a lateral spread of activation which, in time, gives way to the development of new structures.

Stem cells

Stem cells are unspecialised cells that have the potential to give rise to different cell types that carry out different functions, including taking on the characteristics of nerve cells. There are a number of views on how stem cells might work to provide treatments for brain damage caused by injury or neurodegenerative disorders. The first view is that stem cells implanted into the brain would directly replace dead or dying cells. A second possibility is that transplanted stem cells secrete growth factors that somehow 'rescue' the injured cells. A third possibility is that transplanted cells form a neural network, which links an uninjured brain site, where new stem cells are made, with the damaged region of the brain.

◀ Davidson *et al.*'s research with Tibetan monks suggests that regular meditation can produce changes in the working of the brain, increasing the efficiency with which information is processed.

EVALUATION OF PLASTICITY

Research support from animal studies

Kempermann et al. (1998) suggested that an enriched environment could alter the number of neurons in the brain.

They found evidence of an increased number of new neurons in the brains of rats housed in complex environments compared to rats housed in laboratory cages. In particular, the rats housed in the complex environment showed an increase in neurons in the hippocampus, a part of the brain associated with the formation of new memories and the ability to navigate from one location to another.

This shows clear evidence of the brain's ability to change as a result of experience, i.e. it demonstrates plasticity.

Research support from human studies

Maguire et al. (2000), in a study of London taxi drivers, discovered that changes in the brain could be detected as a result of their extensive experience of spatial navigation.

Using an MRI scanner, the researchers calculated the amount of grey matter in the brains of taxi drivers and a set of control participants. The posterior hippocampi of taxi drivers were significantly larger relative to those of control participants and posterior hippocampal volume was positively correlated with the amount of time they had spent as a taxi driver.

This not only shows that hippocampal volume was greater in those individuals with job-related experience of spatial navigation, but also that the highest levels of plasticity were evident in those with more extensive experience.

 UPGRADE

Questions such as question 4 in the 'Can you?' box on the right can be quite intimidating, particularly as they can be worth 16 marks so have quite an impact on your overall mark for the paper. There are a few things to consider in questions like this so it pays to do a bit of planning before you start your answer.

The command word in this question is 'Discuss', which tells you that, in addition to the AO1 description of evidence for plasticity and/or functional recovery, you need a more 'discursive' form of AO3 evaluation. This might include pointing out that functional recovery reduces with age as well as the role of 'cognitive reserve' in this process. Remember that whatever AO3 points you choose, they should be elaborated in order to be effective in your discussion.

You should be mindful of the marks for each skill (6 AO1 and 10 AO3 here) and adapt your answer to reflect that. The final decision you need to make is how to handle the 'and/or' invitation. Trying to cover both in sufficient detail and with thorough evaluation can be tricky, so the general rule is, if you can do a good job on just one of the choices, go for the 'or' option. If you can't, go for the 'and' option. However, in this case it is probably better to go for the 'and' option to have enough discussion points for your AO3.

EVALUATION OF FUNCTIONAL RECOVERY AFTER TRAUMA

Research support from animal studies

Tajiri et al. (2013) provided evidence for the role of stem cells in recovery from brain injury.

They randomly assigned rats with traumatic brain injury to one of two groups. One group received transplants of stem cells into the region of the brain affected by traumatic injury. The control group received a solution infused into the brain containing no stem cells. Three months later, the brains of the stem cell rats showed clear development of neuron-like cells in the area of injury. This was accompanied by a solid stream of stem cells migrating to the brain's site of injury.

This development of new neuronal cells was not evident in the control group, supporting the important role played by stem cells in recovery from brain injury.

Age differences in functional recovery

It is a commonly accepted view that functional plasticity reduces with age (Huttenlocher, 2002).

According to this view, the only option following traumatic brain injury beyond childhood is to develop compensatory behavioural strategies to work around the deficit (such as seeking social support or developing strategies to deal with cognitive deficits). However, studies have suggested that even abilities commonly thought to be fixed in childhood can still be modified in adults with intense retraining.

Despite these indications of adult plasticity, Elbert et al. (2001) conclude that the capacity for neural reorganisation is much greater in children than in adults, as demonstrated by the extended practice that adults require in order to produce changes.

Educational attainment and functional recovery

Schneider et al. (2014) found that patients with the equivalent of a college education are seven times more likely than those who didn't finish high school to be disability-free one year after a moderate to severe traumatic brain injury.

They carried out a retrospective study based on data from the US Traumatic Brain Injury Systems Database. Of the 769 patients studied, 214 had achieved disability-free recovery (DFR) after one year. Of these, 39.2% of patients with 16 or more years of education had achieved DFR, as had 30.8% of those with 12–15 years of education, and just 9.7% of those with less than 12 years of education achieved DFR after one year.

The researchers concluded that 'cognitive reserve' (associated with greater educational attainment) was an important factor in neural adaptation during recovery from traumatic brain injury.

KEY TERMS

Brain plasticity refers to the brain's ability to modify its own structure and function as a result of experience.

Functional recovery refers to the recovery of abilities and mental processes that have been compromised as a result of brain injury or disease.

CAN YOU? No. 6.7

1. Briefly explain what is meant by the term 'plasticity of the brain'. (2 marks)
2. Outline evidence for plasticity in the brain. (6 marks)
3. Outline evidence for functional recovery after trauma. (6 marks)
4. Discuss the evidence for plasticity and/or functional recovery after trauma. (16 marks)

Ways of studying the brain

The brain is the main focus of neuroscience. Studying the brain gives us important insights into the underlying foundations of our behaviour and mental processes. A variety of methods are used by research scientists in order to study the functions of different areas of the brain. Some involve scanning the living brain, looking for patterns of electrical activity associated with the performance of particular tasks. Other methods involve studying sections of a deceased brain to investigate anatomical reasons for behaviour observed while the patient was alive.

POST-MORTEM EXAMINATIONS

Post-mortem examinations are used to establish the underlying neurobiology of a particular behaviour. For example, researchers may study a person who displays behaviour while they are alive that suggests possible underlying brain damage. Subsequently, when the person dies, the researchers can examine their brains to look for abnormalities that might explain that behaviour and which are not found in control individuals. An early example of this technique was Broca's work with his patient, Tan (see page 157), who displayed speech problems when alive and was subsequently found to have a lesion in the area of the brain that is now known as 'Broca's area'; an area important for speech production.

Post-mortem studies have also made it possible to identify some of the brain structures involved in memory. Jacopo Annese's post-mortem of Henry Molailson (HM) confirmed that HM's inability to store new memories was linked to lesions in the hippocampus (Annese *et al.*, 2014). The use of post-mortem studies has also been used to establish a link between psychiatric disorders, such as schizophrenia and depression, and underlying brain abnormalities. For example, post-mortem studies have found evidence of reduced numbers of glial cells in the frontal cortex of patients with depression (Cotter *et al.*, 2001).

◄ Post-mortem examinations help to establish the underlying neurobiology of a particular behaviour

SCANNING TECHNIQUES

Functional magnetic resonance imaging

Functional magnetic resonance imaging (fMRI) is a technique for measuring changes in brain activity while a person performs a task. It does this by measuring changes in blood flow in particular areas of the brain, which indicates increased neural activity in those areas. If a particular area of the brain becomes more active, there is an increased demand for oxygen in that area. The brain responds to this extra demand by increasing blood flow, delivering oxygen in the red blood cells. As a result of these changes in blood flow, researchers are able to produce maps showing which areas of the brain are involved in a particular mental activity.

For example, a participant might be asked to alternate between periods of doing a particular task (e.g. looking at a visual stimulus for 30 seconds) and a control state (e.g. 30 seconds with their eyes closed). The resulting fMRI data can then be used to identify the brain areas where there is a matching pattern of change. As a result of this data it can be concluded that these areas have been activated by the stimulus in question.

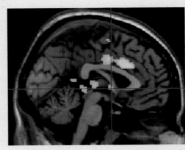

▲ fMRI measures changes in blood flow while a participant performs tasks, so we can learn about the brain regions involved in the performance of these tasks.

Electroencephalogram

An **electroencephalogram (EEG)** measures electrical activity in the brain. Electrodes placed on the scalp detect small electrical charges resulting from the activity of brain cells. When electrical signals from the different electrodes are graphed over a period of time, the resulting representation is called an EEG.

EEG data can be used to detect various types of brain disorder (such as epilepsy) or to diagnose other disorders that influence brain activity (such as Alzheimer's disease). For example, EEG readings of patients with epilepsy show spikes of electrical activity. EEG patterns in patients with brain disease and brain injury show overall slowing of electrical activity.

The four basic EEG patterns are alpha waves, beta waves, delta waves and theta waves. When a person is awake but relaxed, rhythmical alpha waves are recorded. When the person is physiologically aroused, their EEG pattern shows low amplitude and fast frequency beta waves. Beta waves are also found in REM sleep when the eyes move rapidly back and forth. Delta and theta waves occur during sleep. As the person moves from light to deep sleep the occurrence of alpha waves decreases and are replaced first by lower frequency theta waves and then by delta waves.

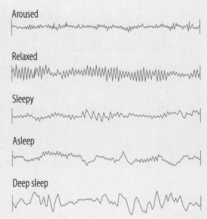

Event-related potentials

Event-related potentials (ERPs) are very small voltage changes in the brain that are triggered by specific events or stimuli, such as cognitive processing of a specific stimulus. ERPs are difficult to pick out from all the other electrical activity being generated within the brain at a given time. To establish a specific response to a target stimulus requires many presentations of the stimulus and these responses are then averaged together. Any extraneous neural activity that is not related to the specific stimulus will not occur consistently, whereas activity linked to the stimulus will. This has the effect of cancelling out the background neural 'noise', making the specific response to the stimulus in question stand out more clearly.

ERPs can be divided into two categories. Waves occurring within the first 100 milliseconds after presentation of the stimulus are termed 'sensory' ERPs as they reflect an initial response to the physical characteristics of the stimulus. ERPs generated *after* the first 100 milliseconds reflect the manner in which the subject evaluates the stimulus and are termed 'cognitive' ERPs as they demonstrate information processing.

	Strengths	Limitations
fMRI	✓ fMRI is noninvasive (i.e. it does not involve the insertion of instruments into the body), nor does it expose the brain to potentially harmful radiation, as is the case with some other scanning techniques used in the study of the brain. ✓ fMRI offers a more objective and reliable measure of psychological processes than is possible with verbal reports. It is useful as a way of investigating psychological phenomena that people would not be capable of providing in verbal reports.	✗ Because fMRI measures changes in blood flow in the brain, then it is not a *direct* measure of neural activity in particular brain areas. This means it is not a truly quantitative measure of mental activity in these brain areas. ✗ Critics argue that fMRI overlooks the networked nature of brain activity, as it focuses only on localised activity in the brain. They claim that it is *communication* among the different regions that is most critical to mental function.
EEG	✓ One strength of the EEG technique is that it provides a recording of the brain's activity in real time rather than a still image of the passive brain. This means that the researcher can accurately measure a particular task or activity with the brain activity associated with it. ✓ An EEG is useful in clinical diagnosis, e.g. by recording the abnormal neural activity associated with epilepsy. Epileptic seizures are caused by disturbed brain activity, which means that the normal EEG reading suddenly changes. This helps diagnose whether someone experiencing seizures has epilepsy.	✗ Because an EEG can only detect the activity in superficial regions of the brain, it cannot reveal what is going on in the deeper regions such as the hypothalamus or hippocampus. Electrodes can be implanted in non-humans to achieve this, but it is not ethically permissible to do this with humans because this would be too invasive. ✗ Electrical activity can be picked up by several neighbouring electrodes, therefore the EEG signal is not useful for pinpointing the exact source of an activity. As a result, it does not allow researchers to distinguish between activities originating in different but closely adjacent locations in the brain.
ERP	✓ Because ERPs provide a continuous measure of processing in response to a particular stimulus, it makes it possible to determine how processing is affected by a specific experimental manipulation, for example during presentation of different visual stimuli. ✓ An ERP can measure the processing of stimuli even in the absence of a behavioural response. ERP recordings make it possible to monitor 'covertly' the processing of a particular stimulus without requiring the person to respond to them.	✗ Because ERPs are so small and difficult to pick out from other electrical activity in the brain, it requires a large number of trials to gain meaningful data. This places limitations on the types of question that ERP readings can realistically answer. ✗ A limitation of the ERP technique is that only sufficiently strong voltage changes generated across the scalp are recordable. Important electrical activities occurring deep in the brain are not recorded, meaning that the generation of ERPs tends to be restricted to the neocortex.
Post-mortem examinations	✓ Post-mortem studies allow for a more detailed examination of anatomical and neurochemical aspects of the brain than would be possible with the sole use of non-invasive scanning techniques such as fMRI and EEG. For example, it enables researchers to examine deeper regions of the brain such as the hypothalamus and hippocampus. ✓ Harrison (2000) claims that post-mortem studies have played a central part in our understanding of the origins of schizophrenia. He suggests that as a direct result of post-mortem examinations, researchers have discovered structural abnormalities of the brain and found evidence of changes in neurotransmitter systems, both of which are associated with the disorder.	✗ Because people die in a variety of circumstances and at varying stages of disease, these factors can influence the post-mortem brain. Similarly, the length of time between death and the post-mortem (post-mortem delay), drug treatments and age at death are possible confounding influences of any difference between cases and controls. ✗ This approach is limited because it is retrospective as the person is already dead. As a result, the researcher is unable to follow up on anything that arises from the post-mortem concerning a possible relationship between brain abnormalities and cognitive functioning.

Research methods

One of the most famous case studies is mentioned on this spread, that of HM. This case study is also discussed on page 47 in relation to models of memory.

1. Discuss the strengths of using a case such as HM to increase our understanding of the brain. (4 marks)
2. Discuss the limitations of using a case such as HM to increase our understanding of the brain. (4 marks)
3. HM's behaviour during his lifetime was also studied to provide insights into the relationship between brain and behaviour. What research techniques are psychologists likely to have used as part of this case study? Explain how they might have used these techniques with HM. (4 marks)
4. Many case studies are longitudinal. Explain what this means. (2 marks)
5. Identify **one** ethical issue with the use of HM's brain after death and explain how this issue might have been dealt with. (3 marks)

LINK TO RESEARCH METHODS

Case studies on pages 208–209
Ethical issues on pages 194–195

KEY TERMS

Electroencephalogram (EEG) A method of recording changes in the electrical activity of the brain using electrodes attached to the scalp.

Event-related potential (ERP) A technique that takes raw EEG data and uses it to investigate cognitive processing of a specific event. It achieves this by taking multiple readings and averaging them in order to filter out all brain activity that is not related to the appearance of the stimulus.

Functional magnetic resonance imaging (fMRI) A technique for measuring brain activity. It works by detecting changes in blood oxygenation and flow that indicate increased neural activity.

Post-mortem examinations Ways of examining the brains of people who have shown particular psychological abnormalities prior to their death in an attempt to establish the possible neurobiological cause for this behaviour.

CAN YOU?
No. 6.8

1. Outline the nature of functional magnetic resonance imaging (fMRI) as a way of studying the brain. (3 marks)
2. Outline **one** strength and **one** limitation of functional magnetic resonance imaging (fMRI). (3 marks each)
3. Outline the nature of electroencephalograms (EEGs) as a way of studying the brain. (3 marks)
4. Outline **one** strength and **one** limitation of electroencephalograms (EEGs). (3 marks each)
5. Outline the nature of event-related potentials (ERPs) as a way of studying the brain. (3 marks)
6. Outline **one** strength and **one** limitation of electroencephalograms (EEGs). (3 marks each)
7. Outline the nature of post-mortem examinations as a way of studying the brain. (3 marks)
8. Outline **one** strength and **one** limitation of post-mortem examinations. (3 marks each)
9. Outline **two** strengths of functional resonance imaging (fMRI). (6 marks)

Circadian rhythms

Biological rhythms are cyclical changes in the way that biological systems behave. These rhythms have evolved because the environment in which organisms live has cyclic changes, day/night, summer/winter and so on. The most important of these rhythms are the **circadian rhythms**, i.e. any cycle that lasts about 24 hours. In fact, the word 'circadian' comes from the Latin 'circa' (about) plus 'dies' (a day). Nearly all organisms possess a biological representation of the 24-hour day. These circadian rhythms (often referred to as the body clock) optimise an organism's physiology and behaviour to best meet the varying demands of the day/night cycle.

> **Insider tip…**
>
> *Exam questions tend to be very specific in their requirements, so make sure you have a good understanding of the different types of biological rhythms so that you use the right material for the right question!*

A case study

Evidence for a 'free-running' circadian rhythm comes from a series of studies conducted by the French cave explorer, Michel Siffre. On several occasions Siffre has subjected himself to long periods of time living underground in order to study his own circadian rhythms. While living underground he had no external cues to guide his rhythms – no daylight, no clocks or radio. He simply woke, ate and slept when he felt it was appropriate to do so. The only thing influencing his behaviour was his internal body clock, i.e. his 'free-running' circadian rhythms.

After his first underground stay of 61 days in the southern Alps in 1962, he resurfaced on 17 September believing the date was really 20 August! On the second occasion, he spent six months in a cave in Texas. His natural circadian rhythm settled down to just over 24 hours, but with some dramatic variations. On his final underground stay in 1999, he was interested in the effects of ageing on circadian rhythms (by this time he was 60 years old). He found that his body clock ticked more slowly compared to when he was a young man, sometimes stretching his circadian rhythms to 48 hours.

▲ Michel Siffre.

THE NATURE OF CIRCADIAN RHYTHMS

Our circadian rhythms are driven by our body clocks, found in all of the cells of the body, and synchronised by the master circadian pacemaker, the suprachiasmatic nuclei (SCN), found in the hypothalamus. This pacemaker must constantly be reset so that our bodies are in synchrony with the outside world. Light provides the primary input to this system, setting the body clock to the correct time in a process termed photoentrainment. In mammals, light-sensitive cells within the eye act as brightness detectors, sending messages about environmental light levels direct to the SCN. The SCN then uses this information to coordinate the activity of the entire circadian system. The most familiar of the circadian rhythms subject to this entrainment process is the **sleep–wake cycle**.

The sleep–wake cycle

The circadian rhythm not only dictates when we should be sleeping, but also when we should be awake. Light and darkness are the external signals that determine when we feel the need to sleep and when to wake up. The circadian rhythm also dips and rises at different times of the day, so our strongest sleep drive usually occurs in two 'dips', between 2–4 am and between 1–3 pm (the 'post-lunch dip'). The sleepiness we experience during these circadian dips is less intense if we have had sufficient sleep, and more intense when we are sleep deprived.

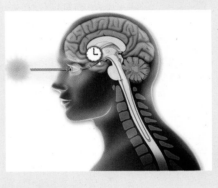

Sleep and wakefulness are not determined by the circadian rhythm alone, but are also under homeostatic control. When we have been awake for a long period of time, homeostasis tells us that the need for sleep is increasing because of the amount of energy used up during wakefulness. This homeostatic drive for sleep increases gradually throughout the day, reaching its maximum in the late evening when most people fall asleep.

Therefore, the circadian system keeps us awake as long as there is daylight, prompting us to sleep as it becomes dark. The homeostatic system tends to make us sleepier as time goes on throughout the waking period, regardless of whether it is night or day. The internal circadian 'clock' is described as 'free-running', i.e. it will maintain a cycle of about 24–25 hours, even in the absence of external cues. The circadian system is, however, intolerant of any major alterations in sleep and wake schedules (e.g. through jet travel, shift work), because this causes the biological clock (and the internal physiological systems that are dependent on this) to become completely out of balance.

Other circadian rhythms

Core body temperature

Core body temperature is one of the best indicators of the circadian rhythm. It is at its lowest (about 36 °C) at about 4:30 am and at its highest (about 38 °C) at about 6 pm. During the normal circadian rhythm, sleep occurs when the core temperature begins to drop, and body temperature starts to rise during the last hours of sleep, promoting a feeling of alertness in the morning. A small drop in body temperature also occurs in most people between 2 pm and 4 pm, which may explain why many people feel sleepy in the early afternoon.

Hormone production

Hormone release follows a circadian rhythm. For example, the production and release of melatonin from the pineal gland in the brain follows a circadian rhythm, with peak levels occurring during the hours of darkness. By activating chemical receptors in the brain, melatonin encourages feelings of sleep. When it is dark, more melatonin is produced, and when it is light again, the production of melatonin drops and the person wakes.

EVALUATION/DISCUSSION

Research support for the importance of light

Hughes (1977) tested the circadian hormone release in four participants stationed at the British Antarctic Station.

In February, at the end of the Antarctic summer, cortisol levels followed the familiar pattern, reaching their highest point as the participants awoke, and their lowest point as the participants retired to bed. However, after three months of continuous darkness, this pattern had changed, with the peak levels of cortisol now being at noon rather than as the men awoke.

This suggests that the extremes of daylight found in polar regions of the world may be responsible for variations in circadian hormone release. However, other research using scientific communities in the Arctic, who would be subject to similar prolonged winter darkness, found no such disruption of cortisol release patterns.

▲ The extreme variations in daylight found in Antarctica present a considerable challenge for physiological processes that are dependent on circadian rhythms.

Individual differences

Research suggests there are individual differences in circadian rhythms.

One is the cycle length; research has found that circadian cycles can vary from 13 to 65 hours (Czeisler *et al.*, 1999). The other type of individual difference relates to cycle onset – individuals appear to be innately different in terms of when their circadian rhythms reach their peak.

This, according to Duffy et al. (2001), would explain why some people prefer to rise early and go to bed early (about 6 am and 10 pm), whereas others prefer to wake and go to bed later (10 am and 1 am).

Research methodology

Early research studies of circadian rhythms suffered from an important flaw when estimating the 'free-running' cycle of the human circadian rhythm.

In most studies, participants were isolated from variables that might affect their circadian rhythms, such as clocks, radios and daylight. However, they were not isolated from artificial light because it was believed that dim artificial light, in contrast to daylight, would not affect their circadian rhythms.

Research suggests that this may not be true. Czeisler et al. (1999) altered participants' circadian rhythms down to 22 hours and up to 28 hours by using dim artificial lighting alone, suggesting that these early studies may have been confounded by the presence of artificial light.

Chronotherapeutics

One real-world application of circadian rhythms is chronotherapeutics – the study of how timing affects drug treatments.

The specific time that patients take their medication is very important as it can have a significant impact on treatment success. It is essential that the right concentration of a drug is released in the target area of the body at the time that the drug is most needed. For example, the risk of heart attack is greatest during the early morning hours after awakening.

As a result, chronotherapeutic medications have been developed with a novel drug delivery system. These medications can be administered before the person goes to sleep at 10 pm, but the actual drug is not released until the vulnerable period of 6 am to noon (Evans and Marain, 1996).

Temperature may be more important than light in setting circadian rhythms

Buhr et al. (2010) believe that it is temperature that actually controls our body clock rather than light.

Although light may be the trigger, the SCN transforms information about light levels into neural messages that set the body's temperature. Body temperature fluctuates on a 24-hour circadian rhythm and even small changes in body temperature can send a powerful signal to our body clocks. Buhr *et al.* found that these fluctuations in temperature set the timing of cells in the body, and therefore cause tissues and organs to become active or inactive.

This suggests that temperature may be more important than light in setting circadian rhythms.

🐾 APPLY YOUR KNOWLEDGE

Your friend Shelby lives in Chicago in the US, and is flying over to the UK for an important job interview. She has only flown short distances within the US before, and is concerned about the possibility of jet lag and how that might affect her performance at her interview. As you have studied circadian rhythms, you feel you should be able to help her.

What advice can you give Shelby about how her circadian rhythms will be out of sync after a seven-hour flight from Chicago to London? What steps could she take to minimise the negative effects of jet lag due to this desynchronisation of her circadian rhythms?

KEY TERMS

Circadian rhythm A pattern of behaviour that occurs or recurs approximately every 24 hours, and which is set and reset by environmental light levels.

Sleep–wake cycle refers to alternating states of sleep and waking that are dependent on the 24-hour circadian cycle.

CAN YOU?   No. 6.9

1. Briefly explain what is meant by the term 'circadian rhythm'? (2 marks)
2. Give **one** example of a circadian rhythm. (2 marks)
3. Outline the nature of circadian rhythms. (6 marks)
4. Outline **one** research study that has investigated circadian rhythms. (4 marks)
5. Discuss circadian rhythms. (16 marks)

Ultradian and infradian rhythms

The circadian rhythm isn't the only biological rhythm – there are two other important rhythms that determine human behaviour. **Ultradian rhythms** span a period of less than one day. An example is the 90-minute Basic Rest Activity Cycle (BRAC) that characterises both our waking and sleeping hours. **Infradian rhythms** span a period longer than one day. An example is the monthly menstrual cycle in women, although in humans there is even evidence for an annual infradian rhythm in some behaviours.

ULTRADIAN RHYTHMS

In humans, daily cycles of wakefulness and sleep follow a circadian rhythm. However, within the sleep portion of this cycle another type of rhythm exists – an ultradian rhythm. A biological rhythm is referred to as ultradian if its period is shorter than 24 hours. In humans, a classic example of such a rhythm would be the five stages that make up a typical night's sleep (see below).

Sleep stages

The ultradian rhythm found in human sleep follows a pattern of alternating REM (rapid eye movement) and NREM (non-rapid eye movement) sleep, which consists of stages one through to four. This cycle repeats itself about every 90–100 minutes throughout the night, with different stages having different durations (see right). A complete cycle consists of a progression through the four stages of NREM sleep before entering a final stage of REM sleep, then the whole cycle starts all over again.

Most of what we know about these different stages of sleep comes from recording the electrical activities of the brain, with each stage showing a distinct EEG pattern. As the person enters deep sleep, their brainwaves slow and their breathing and heart rate decreases. During the fifth stage (REM sleep), the EEG pattern resembles that of an awake person, and it is in this stage that most dreaming occurs.

Stage 1	Stage 2	Stage 3	Stage 4	Stage 5
4–5% Light sleep. Muscle activity slows down. Occasional muscle twitching.	45–55% Breathing pattern and heart rate slows. Slight decrease in body temperature.	4–6% Deep sleep begins. Brain begins to generate slow delta waves.	12–15% Very deep sleep. Rhythmic breathing. Limited muscle activity. Brain produces delta waves.	20–25% Rapid eye movement. Brainwaves speed up and dreaming occurs. Muscles relax and heart rate increases. Breathing is rapid and shallow.

The Basic Rest Activity Cycle

Kleitman (1969) referred to the 90-minute cycle found during sleep as the Basic Rest Activity Cycle, or BRAC. However, Kleitman also suggested that this 90-minute ultradian rhythm continues during the day, even when we are awake. The difference is that during the day, rather than moving through sleep stages, we move progressively from a state of alertness into a state of physiological fatigue approximately every 90 minutes. Research suggests that the human mind can focus for a period of about 90 minutes, and towards the end of these 90 minutes the body begins to run out of resources, resulting in loss of concentration, fatigue and hunger. The operation of the BRAC in wakefulness is not as obvious as it is in sleep but, argued Kleitman, everyday observations provide evidence of its existence. For example, the familiar 10:30 am coffee break allows workers to divide the 9 am to noon morning session into two 90-minute phases. This pattern is repeated in the afternoon, with cat-naps more likely in mid-afternoon.

INFRADIAN RHYTHMS

Infradian rhythms are rhythms that have a duration greater than 24 hours, i.e. longer than circadian rhythms. They may be cycles lasting days, weeks, months or may even be annual. Infradian rhythms include the female menstrual cycle in humans (monthly cycles) and the organisation of human activities into weeks (weekly cycles).

Weekly rhythms

The grouping of seven days into a unit called a week is common in most areas of the world, and there are obvious (and sometimes less obvious) differences in human behaviour that conform to this weekly cycle. For example, although male testosterone levels are elevated at weekends and young couples report more sexual activity at weekends than on weekdays, the frequency of births at weekends is *lower* than on weekdays. It is tempting to look for underlying biological cycles that would dictate these differences. For example, Halberg *et al.* (2002) reported seven-day rhythms of blood pressure and heart rate in humans, but the evidence for weekly infradian rhythms in humans remains sketchy at best.

Monthly rhythms: the human menstrual cycle

A woman's reproductive cycle is known as a menstrual cycle because it lasts about one month (*mensis* is Latin for month). There are considerable variations in the length of this cycle, with some women experiencing a relatively short 23-day cycle whereas others have a cycle as long as 36 days (Refinetti, 2006). The average appears to be around 28 days. The menstrual cycle is regulated by hormones, which either promote ovulation or stimulate the uterus for fertilisation. Ovulation occurs roughly halfway through the menstrual cycle, when oestrogen levels peak, and usually lasts for 16 to 32 hours. After the ovulatory phase, progesterone levels increase in preparation for the possible implantation of an embryo in the uterus.

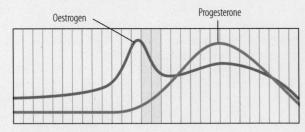

▲ Sex hormone cycle.

Annual rhythms

In most animals, annual rhythms are related to the seasons (e.g. migration as a response to lower temperatures and decreased food sources in winter), but in humans the calendar year appears to influence behaviour regardless of changes in temperature. Research suggests a seasonal variation in mood in humans, especially in women (Magnusson, 2000), with some people becoming severely depressed during the winter months (seasonal affective disorder). The winter is also associated with an increase in heart attacks, which varies seasonally and peaks in winter. In fact, there is a robust annual rhythm in human deaths, with most deaths occurring in January (Trudeau, 1997).

Individual differences in sleep stages

Differences in the sleep patterns of individuals are usually attributed to differences in non-biological factors (e.g. sleep hygiene) but a study by Tucker *et al.* (2007) suggests that these differences are in large part biologically determined and may even be genetic in origin.

Participants were studied over 11 consecutive days and nights in a strictly controlled laboratory environment. The researchers assessed sleep duration, time to fall asleep and the amount of time in each sleep stage. They found large individual differences in each of these characteristics, which showed up consistently across the 8 nights. For deep sleep (stages 3 and 4), the individual differences were particularly significant.

This meant that differences between participants were not driven by circumstances, but were at least partially biologically determined.

Research support for the BRAC

Ericsson *et al.* (2006) provide research support for the BRAC in a study of elite performers.

They studied a group of elite violinists and found that, among this group, practice sessions were usually limited to a duration of no more than 90 minutes at a time, with practice systematically distributed during the day in these 90-minute segments. This supported Kleitman's claim that fatigue was a characteristic of the end of the BRAC cycle. Ericsson's analysis also indicated that the violinists frequently napped to recover from practice, with the very best violinists napping more than their teachers.

Consistent with the predictions of the BRAC, Ericsson discovered the same pattern among other musicians, athletes, chess players and writers.

The menstrual cycle – the role of exogenous cues

The menstrual cycle is normally governed by an endogenous system – the release of hormones by the pituitary gland. However, it can also be controlled by exogenous cues.

When several women of childbearing age live together and do not take oral contraceptives, their menstrual cycles tend to synchronise. In one study, daily samples of sweat were collected from one group of women and rubbed onto the upper lips of women in a second group. The groups were kept separate yet their menstrual cycles became synchronised with their 'odour donor' (Russell *et al.*, 1980).

This suggests that the synchronisation of menstrual cycles can be affected by pheromones, which act in a similar way to hormones, but have an effect on the bodies of people close by rather than the body of the person producing them.

The menstrual cycle influences mate choice

Research by Penton-Voak *et al.* (1999) suggests that human mate choice varies across the menstrual cycle, an infradian rhythm, with different preferences at different stages of the cycle.

They found that women generally expressed a preference for 'slightly feminised' male faces when picking a partner for a long-term relationship. However, when in the ovulatory phase of their menstrual cycle, women showed a preference for more masculinised faces.

This study appears to demonstrate a preference for kindness and cooperation in long-term mates, but a preference for males with 'good genes' for short-term liaisons so that these genes might be passed on to their offspring.

Belief in lunar rhythms

Despite empirical evidence to the contrary, the belief in an infradian rhythm based on the phases of the moon remains strong.

For example, many midwives still believe that more babies are born during a full moon than during a new moon, but the statistics show that this is a purely subjective association (Arliss *et al.*, 2005). Likewise, surveys of workers in the mental health professions have shown a persistent belief that the full moon can alter behaviour (Vance, 1995), yet study after study has failed to find any consistent association between the moon and human psychopathology.

Occasional studies have found correlations between the phase of the moon and various aspects of human behaviour, but there is no evidence of a causal relationship (Foster and Roenneberg, 2008).

 Research methods

There are many examples of ultradian rhythms such as your heart rate, appetite and even blinking. A study by Bentivoglio *et al.* (1997) recorded blinking rates in 150 male and female participants when at rest, reading or talking freely. The participants were all doctors, nurses or students at a university or friends or relatives.

1. The graph below shows the distribution of blinking when participants were at rest. What kind of distribution is this? (2 marks)
2. Based on the graph estimate the value of the mode, median and mean blinking rates when participants were at rest. (3 marks)
3. Identify the sampling method used in the sample and explain whether or not the sample characteristics might bias the results of the study. (3 marks)
4. Some participants were excluded from the study. Identify **two** characteristics of people who should not be included in the study. (2 marks)

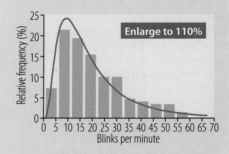

LINK TO RESEARCH METHODS

Distributions on page 215
Sampling on pages 192–193

KEY TERMS

Infradian rhythms Rhythms that have a duration of over 24 hours, and may be weekly, monthly or even annually.

Ultradian rhythms Cycles that last less than 24 hours, such as the cycle of sleep stages that occur throughout the night.

CAN YOU? No. 6.10

1. Briefly explain what is meant by the terms 'infradian rhythm' and 'ultradian rhythm'. (2 marks each)
2. Give **one** example of an infradian rhythm and **one** example of an ultradian rhythm. (2 marks)
3. Discuss infradian and/or ultradian rhythms. (16 marks)

A LEVEL ONLY ZONE

Endogenous pacemakers and exogenous zeitgebers

On the previous two spreads we looked at different types of biological rhythm. These biological rhythms must be constantly fine tuned in order to stay in tune with the external world. In order to achieve this we have **endogenous pacemakers**, sometimes referred to as 'biological clocks', and **exogenous** (or external) **zeitgebers**, which reset this clock every day to maintain its coordination with the external world. On this spread we take a look at how these two important processes work.

ENDOGENOUS PACEMAKERS

The term 'endogenous' refers to anything whose origins are within the organism. These pacemakers are most probably the products of inherited genetic mechanisms and allow us to keep pace with changing cycles in the environment. The most important pacemaker in human beings is the suprachiasmatic nucleus.

The suprachiasmatic nucleus

In mammals, the main endogenous pacemaker is a tiny cluster of nerve cells called the suprachiasmatic nucleus (SCN), which lies in the hypothalamus. The SCN plays an important role in generating the body's circadian rhythm. It acts as the 'master clock', with links to other brain regions that control sleep and arousal, and has control over other biological clocks throughout the body. Neurons within the SCN spontaneously synchronise with each other, so that their target neurons in sites elsewhere in the body receive correctly time-coordinated signals. These peripheral clocks can maintain a circadian rhythm, but not for very long, which is why they must be controlled by the SCN.

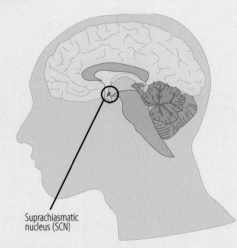

Suprachiasmatic nucleus (SCN)

▲ The suprachiasmatic nucleus (SCN) is located in the hypothalamus of the brain. The SCN sends signals throughout the body in response to dark and light.

This is possible because of the SCN's built-in circadian rhythm, which only needs resetting when external light levels change. The SCN receives information about light levels via the optic nerve. This happens even when our eyes are shut, because light penetrates the eyelids. If our biological clock is running slow (e.g. the sun rises earlier than on the previous day), then morning light automatically adjusts the clock, putting its rhythm in step with the world outside. The SCN also regulates the manufacture and secretion of melatonin in the pineal gland via an interconnecting neural pathway.

The pineal gland

The SCN sends signals to the pineal gland, directing it to increase production and secretion of the hormone melatonin at night and to decrease it as light levels increase in the morning. Melatonin induces sleep by inhibiting the brain mechanisms that promote wakefulness. The pineal and the SCN function jointly as endogenous pacemakers in the brain. The sensitivity of the pineal gland and the SCN to light, and the role of melatonin in controlling sleep and activity, mean that, despite the endogenous nature of these clocks, their activity must be synchronised with the light–dark rhythm of the world outside.

KEY TERMS

Endogenous pacemakers Mechanisms within the body that govern the internal, biological bodily rhythms.

Exogenous zeitgeber An environmental cue, such as light, that helps to regulate the biological clock in an organism.

EXOGENOUS ZEITGEBERS

The term 'exogenous' refers to anything whose origins are outside the organism. The term 'zeitgeber' comes from the German words *zeit* and *geber*, meaning 'time giver'. Exogenous zeitgebers are environmental events that are responsible for entraining the biological clock of an organism. The most important zeitgeber for most animals is light.

Light

Receptors in the SCN are sensitive to changes in light levels during the day and use this information to synchronise the activity of the body's organs and glands. Light resets the internal biological clock each day, keeping it on a 24-hour cycle. Rods and cones in the retina of the eye detect light to form visual images. However, there is a third type of light-detecting cell in the retina that gauges overall brightness to help reset the internal biological clock. A protein called melanopsin, which is sensitive to natural light, is critical in this system. A small number of retinal cells contain melanopsin and carry signals to the SCN to set the daily body cycle.

Social cues

Social stimuli, such as mealtimes and social activities, may also have a role as zeitgebers. Aschoff *et al.* (1971) showed that individuals are able to compensate for the absence of zeitgebers such as natural light by responding to social zeitgebers instead.

One of the earliest studies on jet lag (Klein and Wegmann, 1974) found that the circadian rhythms of air travelers adjusted more quickly if they went outside more at their destination. This was thought to be because they were exposed to the social cues of their new time zone, which acted as a zeitgeber.

Likewise, the circadian rhythms of blind people were thought to be no different to sighted people as both groups were exposed to the same social cues. We now know that both examples can better be explained in terms of light exposure acting as a zeitgeber. The sleep–wake cycle of most blind people is still influenced by light during the day, even though they have no visual perception. This is because connections exist between the eye and the SCN that do not involve those parts of the visual system on which the perception of light depends.

EVALUATION OF ENDOGENOUS PACEMAKERS

The role of the SCN

The importance of the SCN as an endogenous pacemaker was demonstrated in Morgan's study of hamsters.

Morgan (1995) bred a strain of hamsters so that they had abnormal circadian rhythms of 20 hours rather than 24 hours. SCN neurons from these abnormal hamsters were then transplanted into the brains of normal hamsters. These normal hamsters then displayed the same abnormal circadian rhythm of 20 hours, showing that the transplanted SCN had imposed its pattern onto the recipients' brains. Morgan then transplanted SCN neurons from normal hamsters into the brains of the abnormal hamsters. Rather than maintaining their abnormal circadian rhythm, the recipient hamsters then changed to a circadian pattern of 24 hours.

This confirms the importance of the SCN in setting circadian rhythms.

▲ Studies with hamsters have shown that abnormal SCNs means abnormal circadian rhythms.

Dangers of disrupted rhythms

Touitou *et al.* (2017) argue that exposure to artificial light at night results in a disruption of the circadian system, which has adverse effects on health.

For example, Touitou's research has shown that teenagers spend increasing amounts of time on electronic media at night. The LED bulbs of these devices are enriched with a blue light component very active on the circadian clock, which leads to suppression of melatonin secretion and circadian disruption. As a result, adolescent sleep becomes irregular, shortened and delayed.

In the long run, this combination of sleep deprivation and circadian disruption is detrimental to health, as shown by the many studies that have found increased rates of cardiovascular disorders and mood disorders such as depression.

 UPGRADE

A common type of question throughout the A Level specification is the 'application'-type question. This is where you are asked to take what you have learned and apply it to a 'new' situation.

Let's imagine the following question:

Alex has just started a new job, which requires her to work the night shift every other week. When she is working the night shift she finds that she has difficulty sleeping during the day and feels she is less alert during the shift itself.

Using your knowledge of endogenous pacemakers and exogenous zeitgebers, explain Alex's experiences. (4 marks)

The mark scheme for this question would be split into two bands. For the top band, you would need to display a clear and accurate knowledge of the role of endogenous pacemakers and exogenous zeitgebers in the sleep-wake cycle (the psychology bit). You would also need to use this material appropriately to explain Alex's experiences (the application bit).

The psychology bit doesn't have to be that detailed (this is only a 4-mark question, remember), just 'clear and accurate'. However, it must be used 'appropriately' to explain why Alex is having difficulty sleeping during the day and has alertness problems during the night shift.

These two requirements are interlinked and you are being tested on your ability to use what you already know to explain this situation. If you do not apply it to the scenario then your marks will be limited to a maximum of 2 marks. For more advice on answering AO2 application questions, see 'Problem Corner' p233–4.

EVALUATION OF EXOGENOUS ZEITGEBERS

Support for the role of melanopsin

The important role played by melanopsin in setting the circadian rhythm is demonstrated in studies of blind people.

Some blind people are still able to reliably entrain their circadian rhythm in response to light despite a total lack of image-forming visual perception (i.e. non-functioning rods and cones). Skene and Arendt (2007) estimate that the vast majority of blind subjects who still have some light perception have normally entrained circadian rhythms.

This suggests that the pathway from retinal cells containing melanopsin to the SCN is still intact. As further evidence for the importance of this pathway in setting the biological clock, people without light perception show abnormal circadian entrainment.

Using light exposure to avoid jet lag

An application of research on exogenous zeitgebers comes from Burgess *et al.* (2003), who found that exposure to bright light prior to an east–west flight decreased the time needed to readjust to local time on arrival.

Volunteers participated in one of three treatments (continuous bright light, intermittent bright light, dim light), each of which shifted their sleep–wake cycle back by 1 hour a day over 3 days. Participants exposed to continuous bright light shifted their circadian rhythm by 2.1 hours over the course of the study. Those exposed to intermittent bright light shifted their rhythm by 1.5 hours, and a third group exposed to dim light shifted theirs by just 0.6 hours. As a result, participants in the first treatment group felt sleepier 2 hours earlier in the evening and woke 2 hours earlier in the morning.

This suggests that light exposure prior to a flight would allow travellers to arrive with their circadian rhythms already partially re-entrained to local time.

▲ Exposure to bright light prior to air travel may help travellers to adjust to local daylight conditions more easily.

The role of artificial light as a zeitgeber

Vetter *et al.* (2011) demonstrated the importance of light in the regulation of the sleep–wake and activity–rest patterns of two groups of volunteer participants over a five-week study period.

One group remained in normal 'warm' artificial light over the five weeks while the other group experienced artificial 'blue-enriched' light that had a spectral composition close to daylight. All participants kept a daily sleep log and wore devices that measured their movement over each 24-hour period. Participants working under the warmer light synchronised their circadian rhythms each day with the natural light of dawn. Over the course of the study, sunrise advanced by 42 minutes. The participants who were exposed to blue-enriched light did not show the same 42-minute adjustment and instead synchronised their rhythms to office hours.

The results confirm that light is the dominant zeitgeber for the SCN and that its effectiveness depends on its spectral composition.

CAN YOU?   No. 6.11

1. Briefly explain what is meant by the terms 'endogenous pacemaker' and 'exogenous zeitgeber'. (2 marks each)
2. Outline the effect of endogenous pacemakers on the sleep–wake cycle. (6 marks)
3. Outline the effect of exogenous zeitgebers on the sleep–wake cycle. (6 marks)
4. Discuss the effect of endogenous pacemakers and exogenous zeitgebers on the sleep–wake cycle. (16 marks)

End-of-chapter review — CHAPTER SUMMARY

THE NERVOUS SYSTEM

DIVISIONS OF THE NERVOUS SYSTEM
- Nervous system divided into CNS and PNS.
- CNS: brain and spinal cord.
- CNS controls behaviour and regulates physiological processes.

THE CENTRAL NERVOUS SYSTEM

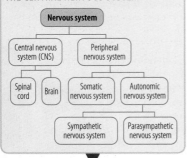

THE PERIPHERAL NERVOUS SYSTEM
- PNS: somatic and autonomic nervous systems (ANS).
- Somatic NS – sensory and motor neurons.
- ANS: sympathetic and parasympathetic (Broca, 1865).
- Sympathetic NS involved in 'fight or flight'.
- Parasympathetic NS involved in 'rest and digest'.

THE ENDOCRINE SYSTEM

GLANDS AND HORMONES
- Endocrine glands produce hormones.
- Hypothalamus sends releasing hormone to pituitary gland.
- Pituitary gland secretes releasing hormone into bloodstream.
- Hormones stimulate receptors in target cells.

PITUITARY GLAND
- Pituitary controls other endocrine glands.
- Releases hormones that influence other glands to release hormones.
- Anterior pituitary releases ACTH.
- Posterior pituitary releases oxytocin.

THE ADRENAL GLANDS
- Adrenal cortex produces cortisol in response to stress.
- Adrenal medulla releases adrenaline and noradrenaline to prepare for fight or flight.

OVARIES AND TESTES
- Ovaries part of female reproductive system.
- Release oestrogen and progesterone.
- Testes part of male reproductive system.
- Release testosterone.
- Other glands: thyroid gland, parathyroid glands and the pancreas.

NEURONS AND SYNAPTIC TRANSMISSION

STRUCTURE AND FUNCTION OF NEURONS
- Neurons: cell body, dendrites and axon.
- Sensory neurons carry impulses from sensory receptors to CNS.
- Motor neurons form synapses with muscles.
- Relay neurons allow sensory and motor neurons to communicate.

SYNAPTIC TRANSMISSION
- Nerve impulses cross synaptic cleft.
- Synaptic vesicles release neurotransmitters.
- These stimulate receptors on postsynaptic neuron.
- Produce excitatory or inhibitory effects.
- Excitatory effect produces new action potential.

EXCITATORY AND INHIBITORY NEUROTRANSMITTERS
- Excitatory neurotransmitters cause EPSPs (increase likelihood of cell firing).
- Inhibitory neurotransmitters cause IPSPs (decrease likelihood of cell firing).
- Summation of EPSPs and IPSPs determines whether cell fires.
- Summation can be spatial or temporal.

THE FIGHT-OR-FLIGHT RESPONSE

THE FIGHT-OR-FLIGHT RESPONSE TO STRESS
- Amygdala sends distress signal to hypothalamus.
- Hypothalamus releases CRH.
- SNS prepares body for fight or flight.
- Pituitary releases ACTH.
- Adrenal medulla releases adrenaline.
- Adrenal cortex releases stress hormones.
- Parasympathetic NS dampens stress response.
- Feedback system for cortisol levels.
- SNS responds to acute stressors by release of adrenaline.
- HPA: hypothalamus, pituitary gland, adrenal glands.

EVALUATION/DISCUSSION
- Tend and befriend response in females.
- Fight or flight has some negative consequences, e.g. heart disease.
- Does not tell the whole story – 'freezing' precedes both fight and flight.
- **A03 plus** Positive behaviours (e.g. cooperation) also common response to stress.
- **A03 plus** Genetic basis (SRY gene) to sex differences in fight-or-flight response (Lee and Harley).

A LEVEL ONLY ZONE

LOCALISATION OF FUNCTION

MOTOR AND SOMATOSENSORY AREAS
- Motor cortex responsible for voluntary motor movements.
- Different body regions are arranged disproportionately along motor cortex.
- Somatosensory cortex detects sensory events.
- Area of sensory cortex correlates with amount of sensory input from each area.

VISUAL AND AUDITORY CENTRES
- Visual cortex in the occipital lobe.
- Right hemisphere input from left visual field, left hemisphere from right visual field.
- Auditory area in auditory cortex in temporal lobe.

LANGUAGE CENTRES
- Broca's area in frontal lobe in left hemisphere.
- Involved in speech production.
- Wernicke's area in temporal lobe of left hemisphere.
- Involved in understanding of language.
- Arcuate fasciculus lies between the two areas.

EVALUATION/DISCUSSION
- Localisation challenged by equipotentiality theory.
- Communication between brain areas may be more important than localisation.
- Support for language centres from studies of aphasia, e.g. Broca's area.
- Individual differences in language areas, e.g. gender (Bavelier et al.).
- Language production not confined to Broca's area alone (Dronkers et al.).

LATERALISATION AND SPLIT-BRAIN RESEARCH

HEMISPHERIC LATERALISATION
- Two hemispheres have functional specialisations.
- Left hemisphere dominant for language and speech.
- Right hemisphere for visual-motor tasks.
- Hemispheres connected by the corpus callosum.

EVALUATION/DISCUSSION
- Increased neural capacity – supported by research with other species, e.g. chickens (Rogers et al.)
- Lateralisation and immune system functioning – left-handers had higher incidence of immune system disorders (Morfit and Weekes).
- Lateralisation increases with age (Szaflarski et al.).

SPLIT-BRAIN RESEARCH
- Sperry and Gazzaniga studied split-brain patients.
- Stimuli presented to one hemisphere and participants asked to respond.
- Stimuli presented to right hemisphere did not produce a verbal response.
- Conclusion was that left hemisphere is responsible for language.

EVALUATION/DISCUSSION
- Language may not be restricted to the left hemisphere (Turk et al.).
- Limitations – conclusions drawn from studies with very few participants, who may have a confounding physical disorder or less complete sectioning of the two hemispheres.

PLASTICITY AND FUNCTIONAL RECOVERY OF THE BRAIN

PLASTICITY
- Brain adapts by developing new connections and pruning weak ones.
- Boyke *et al.* – increases in grey matter after juggling.
- Kühn *et al.* – increases in grey matter after game play.
- Increase in gamma waves after meditation (Davidson *et al.*).

EVIDENCE FOR PLASTICITY
- Evidence from animal studies – enriched environment led to increase in neurons in rats (Kempermann *et al.*).
- Evidence from human studies – taxi drivers had increased hippocampal volume as a result of extensive experience of spatial navigation (Maguire *et al.*).

FUNCTIONAL RECOVERY AFTER TRAUMA
- Brain forms new circuits to compensate for injury.
- Neuronal unmasking – dormant synapses 'unlocked'.
- Stem cells implanted may directly replace dead brain cells.
- Stem cells may secrete growth factors that rescue dying cells.
- Transplanted cells may form a neural network to migrate stem cells to injury site.

EVALUATION FOR FUNCTIONAL RECOVERY AFTER TRAUMA
- Evidence from animal studies (Tajiri *et al.*).
- Age differences – capacity for neural reorganisation greater in children (Elbert *et al.*).
- Educational attainment and functional recovery – seven times higher in college educated individuals (Schneider *et al.*).

WAYS OF STUDYING THE BRAIN

SCANNING TECHNIQUES
- fMRI – measures changes in brain activity while performing a task.
- EEG – measures electrical activity in the brain through electrodes.
- Detects brain disorders through representation of electrical activity patterns.
- ERPs – small voltage changes in the brain triggered by specific stimuli.
- Many presentations needed to distinguish from background 'noise'.
- Sensory ERPs represent initial response to physical characteristics of stimulus, cognitive ERPs represent further information processing.

POST-MORTEM EXAMINATIONS
- Establish underlying neurobiology of a behaviour.
- Used to check for brain damage to explain a pre-death disorder.
- Annese confirmed role of hippocampus in memory using post-mortem.

EVALUATION (STRENGTHS)
- fMRI: Strength 1 – non-invasive and non-harmful.
- Strength 2 – more objective and reliable than verbal reports.
- EEG: Strength 1 – measure of brain activity in real time.
- Strength 2 – useful in clinical diagnosis, e.g. epilepsy.
- ERP: Strength 1 – useful for studying effects of specific experimental manipulation.
- Strength 2 – can measure in the absence of a behavioural response.
- Post-mortem examinations: Strength 1 – allow for more detailed examination than scanning.
- Strength 2 – have played a central part in understanding origins of schizophrenia.

EVALUATION (LIMITATIONS)
- fMRI: Limitation 1 – not a direct measure of neural activity.
- Limitation 2 – ignores communication *between* different regions.
- EEG: Limitation 1 – cannot measure activity in deeper brain regions.
- Limitation 2 – does not distinguish between activities originating in adjacent brain areas.
- ERP: Limitation 1 – requires many trials to gain meaningful data.
- Limitation 2 – generation of ERPs restricted to the neocortex.
- Post-mortem examinations: Limitation 1 – many confounding variables.
- Limitation 2 – no opportunity for follow-up.

CIRCADIAN RHYTHMS

THE NATURE OF CIRCADIAN RHYTHMS
- Circadian rhythms last 24 hours.
- Master circadian pacemaker is SCN.
- SCN is reset daily by light.
- Sleep–wake cycle is on a circadian cycle.
- Sleep and wakefulness also under homeostatic control.
- Case study – Michel Siffre.
- Core body temperature varies with a circadian rhythm.
- Hormone production follows circadian cycle.

EVALUATION/DISCUSSION
- Importance of light – tested in Antarctic (Hughes).
- Individual differences – cycle length varies between 13 and 65 hours (Czeisler *et al.*).
- Research methodology – early studies did not isolate participants from artificial light.
- Chronotherapeutics – development of 'circadian cycle friendly' medications.
- Temperature more important than light in setting circadian rhythms (Buhr *et al.*).

ULTRADIAN AND INFRADIAN RHYTHMS

ULTRADIAN RHYTHMS
- Ultradian rhythms less than 24 hours, e.g. cycles of sleep.
- The cycle repeats itself every 90 minutes.
- BRAC – 90-minute cycle continues throughout the day.

INFRADIAN RHYTHMS
- Infradian rhythms more than 24 hours.
- Male testosterone levels show a weekly cycle.
- Menstrual cycle has monthly rhythm but with considerable variations (Refinetti).
- Annual rhythms – seasonal variation in mood (Magnusson).

EVALUATION/DISCUSSION
- Individual differences in sleep stages, e.g. sleep duration (Czeisler *et al.*, 1999).
- Research support for the BRAC (e.g. Ericsson *et al.*).
- The menstrual cycle and exogenous cues.
- Human mate choice varies across the menstrual cycle (Penton-Voak *et al.*).
- Belief in lunar rhythms – no evidence to support infradian rhythm based on phases of the moon.

ENDOGENOUS PACEMAKERS AND EXOGENOUS ZEITGEBERS

ENDOGENOUS PACEMAKERS
- Origins *within* the organism.
- SCN the 'master' biological clock.
- SCN controls other biological clocks in the body.
- SCN resets itself when light levels change.
- Pineal gland – secretes melatonin as light levels decrease.

EVALUATION/DISCUSSION
- The role of the SCN – demonstrated in hamster studies (Morgan, 1995).
- Disruption of circadian rhythms through use of electronic media is detrimental to health (Touitou *et al.*)

EXOGENOUS ZEITGEBERS
- Origins *outside* the organism.
- Light resets internal biological clock each day.
- Melanopsin sensitive to natural light and signals to SCN to reset daily cycle.
- Social cues act as zeitgebers (Klein and Wegmann).
- Sleep–wake cycle of blind people still influenced by light even without visual perception.

EVALUATION/DISCUSSION
- Support for role of melanopsin – blind subjects who have some light perception have normally entrained circadian rhythms (Skene and Arendt).
- Light exposure may avoid jet lag (Burgess *et al.*).
- Role of artificial light as a zeitgeber (Vetter *et al.*).

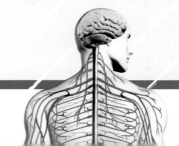

End-of-chapter review

EXAM QUESTION BANK ON BIOPSYCHOLOGY TOPICS

The exam questions on approaches in psychology will be varied but there will be some short answer questions (AO1), including some multiple choice questions, some questions that ask you to apply your knowledge (AO2) and possibly an extended writing question (AO1 + AO3). Some questions may involve research methods and maths skills. We have provided a selection of these different kinds of questions here.

AS AND A LEVEL QUESTIONS

0 1 Which **one** of the following divisions of the nervous system is made of the brain and spinal cord?

A autonomic nervous system
B central nervous system
C peripheral nervous system
D somatic nervous system **[1 mark]**

0 2 Distinguish between the function of a motor neuron and the function of a sensory neuron. **[2 marks]**

0 3 Using an example, outline the function of neurotransmitters in synaptic transmission. **[3 marks]**

0 4 Using an example, outline the function of the endocrine system in the human body. **[4 marks]**

0 5 Describe the structure and function of a relay neuron. **[4 marks]**

0 6 Explain the processes of excitation and inhibition in synaptic transmission. **[6 marks]**

0 7 Outline the 'fight-or-flight' response. **[3 marks]**

0 8 Read the item below and then answer the question that follows.

> Fraser and Seth were walking down a dark alleyway one evening when they became aware of a gang of youths who were running up behind them. Both of the boys experienced their heart rates increasing, felt sweaty, and Fraser even began to feel nauseous. Fraser's next reaction was to start running and he carried on down the alleyway while Seth turned to face the youths, his fists clenched and held up in front of him. Seth then saw that the youths were friends from school and began to laugh. Not long after this, his heart rate and breathing began to slow down.

With reference to both the 'fight-or-flight' response and the autonomic nervous system, explain the experiences of Fraser and Seth. **[8 marks]**

A LEVEL ONLY QUESTIONS

0 9 Outline the difference between infradian and ultradian rhythms. **[2 marks]**

1 0 Evaluate the use of post-mortem examinations as a way of studying the brain. **[4 marks]**

1 1 With reference to the sleep–wake cycle, distinguish between endogenous pacemakers and exogenous zeitgebers. **[4 marks]**

1 2 Explain what is meant by 'hemispheric lateralisation'. **[3 marks]**

1 3   Which of the following areas of the brain is being defined in each of the examples below? Choose one area of the brain that matches each function. Use each letter once only.

   A Broca's area

   B Motor area

   C Somatosensory area

   D Wernicke's area

   (i) Area of the brain responsible for the production of speech.

   (ii) Area of the brain responsible for comprehension of speech.

   (iii) Area of the brain responsible for processing inputs from touch.   **[3 marks]**

1 4   Which of the following biological rhythms is being illustrated in each of the examples below? Choose one rhythm that matches each example. Use each letter once only.

   A circadian rhythm

   B infradian rhythm

   C ultradian rhythm

   (i) The female menstrual cycle

   (ii) The sleep–wake cycle   **[2 marks]**

1 5   Outline the findings of research into functional recovery after trauma.   **[4 marks]**

1 6   Describe and evaluate ways of investigating localisation of function in the brain.   **[16 marks]**

1 7   Briefly discuss the evidence for plasticity in the brain.   **[6 marks]**

1 8   Discuss the use of functional magnetic resonance imaging as a way of studying the brain. Refer to other scanning techniques as part of your discussion.   **[16 marks]**

1 9   Read the item below and then answer the questions that follow.

> • Person W is unable to recognise simple everyday objects.
> • Person X is insensitive to pain on certain parts of his body.
> • Person Y has a very limited vocabulary and so repeats the same phrase.
> • Person Z has significant problems making sense of what others are saying.

   (i) Identify the person who is likely to have damage to his visual cortex.   **[1 mark]**

   (ii) Identify the person who is likely to have damage to his Broca's area.   **[1 mark]**

2 0   Read the item below and answer the question that follows.

> Kim was a passenger on a plane flight where she travelled from one side of the world to the other. When she landed and was in the airport, she felt very disorientated. For the rest of the day she was alert at times that she would normally be tired and vice versa.

Using your knowledge of endogenous pacemakers and exogenous zeitgebers, explain Kim's experiences.   **[4 marks]**

We've provided answers by two students to some of the questions from pages 172–173 here, together with comments from an examiner about how well they've each done. **Green** comments show what the student has done well. **Orange** comments indicate areas for improvement.

---

04 Using an example, outline the function of the endocrine system in the human body. *(4 marks)*

Maisie's answer

The endocrine system is a network of endocrine glands of which the pituitary is the main controlling gland. The main function of the endocrine system is to regulate physiological processes through the release of hormones. The endocrine system manufactures and secretes a range of different hormones that travel via the bloodstream to receptors in different parts of the body. For example, in the adrenal glands, the adrenal cortex produces cortisol in response to stress and the adrenal medulla releases adrenaline andnoradrenaline, which prepares the body for fight or flight.

> Main function explained broadly.

> Good, detailed elaboration.

> More specific function with good detail.

Examiner's comments

Maisie's answer covers the function of the endocrine system in broad terms first, then in specific detail. She uses technical language appropriately and has a clear focus on the question. *4/4 marks*

Ciaran's answer

> The description is quite vague.

The function of the endocrine system is to produce hormones. The different glands that make up the endocrine system produce different hormones, and these influence different parts of the body by travelling through the bloodstream to different parts of the body. An example of an endocrine gland is the pituitary gland in the brain. This is known as the master gland because it controls the other glands in the endocrine system.

> A good, specific example but it highlights what that gland does rather than the function of the system overall.

Examiner's comments

This is a fairly basic answer, which gives very little detail and limited explanation of the actual function. *1/4 marks*

---

11 With reference to the sleep–wake cycle, distinguish between endogenous pacemakers and exogenous zeitgebers. *(4 marks)*

> Clear distinction between the two.

Maisie's answer

> Clear and accurate detail.

The main endogenous pacemaker is the suprachiasmatic nucleus, which receives light from the eyes and uses this information to coordinate all the other body clocks within the body. Whereas endogenous pacemakers are a part of the individual's own body, exogenous zeitgebers are part of the environment, and these include daylight and social cues (such as mealtimes). Endogenous pacemakers and zeitgebers form part of the process to control the individual's circadian rhythms. Exposure to daylight resets the body clock each day to keep the body's circadian rhythm in step with the day and night cycle in the environment.

> Accurate reference to the sleep–wake cycle with explanation.

Examiner's comments

Excellent answer, which gets full marks. More detail than would be needed for 4 marks as 2 marks are for distinguishing between and 2 marks for reference/application to the sleep–wake cycle. *4/4 marks*

Ciaran's answer

Endogenous pacemakers are found within the body. The main endogenous pacemaker is the body clock or suprachiasmatic nucleus. Exogenous zeitgebers are found outside the body. The main exogenous zeitgeber is light, which resets the body clock every day so that the body is synchronised with the outside world.

> Distinction made between them, although not as neatly as in Maisie's answer.

> The reference to the sleep–wake cycle is ok but a touch limited.

Examiner's comments

A good answer that makes an implicit distinction between endogenous pacemakers and exogenous zeitgebers and reference to the sleep–wake cycle. However, it is slightly limited in detail. *3/4 marks*

18 Discuss the use of functional magnetic resonance imaging as a way of studying the brain. Refer to other scanning techniques as part of your discussion. *(16 marks)*

Ciaran's answer

fMRI is a way of measuring brain activity while a person does a task. It works by measuring neural activity in different areas of the brain through blood flow. When someone is taking part in a task the blood flow increases and this is thought to show an increase in neural activity in that area as oxygen is needed to support the increased neural activity in that area. Researchers are then able to produce a map of the brain showing areas that are more active when a person engages in different tasks. For example, someone might be asked to do a task, such as looking at a visual stimulus for 30 seconds, then asked to close their eyes for 30 seconds. The pattern that the fMRI shows will suggest that those parts of the brain are activated by that type of stimulus.

> Clear and detailed explanation that is well elaborated. The use of an example task illustrates the point clearly.

One benefit of using fMRIs is that it is non-invasive, unlike PET scans, and is not thought to be dangerous as it does not expose the brain to dangerous radiation as is the case with PET scans. A further strength of this is that this means it is safe to test participants repeatedly if there is a need to. Obviously this is not the case with PET scans. The resolution is better for fMRIs as well, and the technology is improving all the time.

> A good evaluation point with comparison to PET scans.

However, measuring neural activity by recording changes in blood flow means researchers do not study brain activity directly but must infer changes in neural activity by recording these changes in blood flow. A scanning method that can overcome this is event-related potentials (ERPs). These record voltage changes in the brain that are triggered by specific stimuli, making it possible to work out how neural processing is affected by particular events. However, ERPs are very small and difficult to pick out against the background of neural activity in the brain. Also, like fMRIs, ERPs are restricted to recording activity in the cortex, rather than in deeper areas of the brain, therefore both are limited in their ability to record activity in the whole brain.

> Good elaboration of the previous points, making the AO3 more effective.

> The question asks for reference to scanning techniques (plural) and Ciaran has done that by using PET scans and ERPs.

> Further positive elaboration that brings the point back to fMRIs.

The problem that fMRI scans can only show what is happening on the surface of the brain and cannot record what is going on much deeper could be resolved by doing a post-mortem. Post-mortems are able to offer a far more detailed examination of brain physiology than is possible with noninvasive methods such as fMRI. However, it is necessary for the person to be dead and so this is retrospective whereas fMRIs are carried out when the individual is alive, so anything interesting that is found can be followed up on.

> Although post-mortems are not a scanning technique, this is a good comparison with a further method. There is clear elaboration again, increasing the effectiveness of the discussion.

With post-mortems, the reason for death, the stage of disease they were at and the length of time between death and the post-mortem could all be confounding influences on findings from the examinations. fMRIs don't suffer from these particular problems, which is another reason why they are superior to post-mortems.

One further strength of fMRI scans is that they are an objective way of measuring what is happening in the brain. Early methods such as introspection relied on verbal reports, so fMRI means that reports of neural processing are far less subjective and therefore far more accurate. (537 words)

> Although this is a general point about scanning, it is certainly relevant to fMRIs and there are many specific points made earlier.

> A good, clear comparison with another scanning method using a number of points.

Examiner's comments

An excellent answer with clear and detailed AO1. The AO3 is effective and elaborated and the overall structure is excellent. *Level 4 essay – potentially full marks: 16/16.*

CONTENTS OF CHAPTER

SPECIFICATION CHECKLIST

- Experimental method. Types of experiment, laboratory and field experiments; natural and quasi-experiments.

- Observational techniques. Types of observation: naturalistic and controlled observation; covert and overt observation; participant and non-participant observation.

- Self-report techniques. Questionnaires; interviews, structured and unstructured.

- Correlations. Analysis of the relationship between co-variables. The difference between correlations and experiments.

Scientific processes

- Aims: stating aims, the difference between aims and hypotheses.

- Hypotheses: directional and non-directional.

- Sampling: the difference between population and sample; sampling techniques including: random, systematic, stratified, opportunity and volunteer; implications of sampling techniques, including bias and generalisation.

- Pilot studies and the aims of piloting.

- Experimental designs: repeated measures, independent groups, matched pairs.

- Observational design: behavioural categories; event sampling; time sampling.

- Questionnaire construction, including use of open and closed questions; design of interviews.

- Variables: manipulation and control of variables, including independent, dependent, extraneous, confounding; operationalisation of variables.

- Control: random allocation and counterbalancing, randomisation and standardisation.

- Demand characteristics and investigator effects.

- Ethics, including the role of the British Psychological Society's code of ethics; ethical issues in the design and conduct of psychological studies; dealing with ethical issues in research.

- The role of peer review in the scientific process.

- The implications of psychological research for the economy.

Data handling and analysis

- Quantitative and qualitative data; the distinction between qualitative and quantitative data collection techniques.

- Primary and secondary data, including meta-analysis.

- Descriptive statistics: measures of central tendency – mean, median, mode; calculation of mean, median and mode; measures of dispersion; range and standard deviation; calculation of range; calculation of percentages; positive, negative and zero correlations.

- Presentation and display of quantitative data: graphs, tables, scattergrams, bar charts.

- Distributions: normal and skewed distributions; characteristics of normal and skewed distributions.

- Introduction to statistical testing; the sign test.

The experimental method

Your study of psychology should be fun(!) and relevant to your life. So a good way to begin understanding the research process is to investigate something about human behaviour that interests you. However, before you get too excited, you can't study anything that would be unethical!

Psychologists use a number of different methods and techniques to conduct research and that's what this chapter focuses on. Many people think it is all experiments – in fact people quite often use the phrase 'They conducted an experiment on…,' when they actually mean 'They conducted an investigation on…' An experiment has some very specific rules and this is where we are going to begin our exploration of research methods.

Whenever you conduct research, you must always carefully consider **ethical issues** and related matters.
- Never use anyone under the age of 16 as a participant (or in fact any people who may be described as 'vulnerable' in any way).
- Always obtain **informed consent** from all participants – tell your participants what they will be expected to do and allow them to refuse to take part.
- **Debrief** your participants after the study to tell them of any deception and to allow them to withdraw their data if they object, on reflection, to having taken part. Before beginning any study, consult with others on the 'script' you will use for the informed consent and the debrief.

Observations of everyday life

You might think up your own idea but here is one possibility. Many students do their homework in front of the TV. Cara's daughter thinks she does it just as well in front of the TV as when working at a desk with no distractions. As you might imagine, Cara doesn't think this is true.

Research aim

To investigate whether people work just as well with the TV on, or whether their work will suffer as a result.
1. Work with a small group of other students and discuss the following questions:
   - How could you find out whether people can work just as well with the TV on as in a quiet room?
   - What will you need to measure?
   - Will you have two different conditions? What will you change across the two conditions?
   - How many participants will you need? Will everyone take part in both conditions, or will you have two groups of participants?
   - What will you expect to find?
   - What will the participants do?
   - What do you need to control?
2. When you have worked out what you will do, join with another group and explain your ideas to each other. The other group may ask useful questions that will help you refine your ideas.
3. Conduct your study. You may be able to do this in class or each member of your group could go away and collect some data.
4. Pool the data collected by your group and prepare a poster to present your results and conclusions.

KEY TERMS

Aims A statement of what the researcher(s) intend to find out in a research study.

Debriefing A post-research interview designed to inform participants of the true nature of the study and to restore them to the state they were in at the start of the study. It may also be used to gain useful feedback about the procedures in the study. Debriefing is not an ethical issue; it is a means of dealing with ethical issues.

Ethical issues concern questions of right and wrong. They arise in research where there are conflicting sets of values between researchers and participants concerning the goals, procedures or outcomes of a research study.

Experiment A research method where causal conclusions can be drawn because an independent variable has been deliberately manipulated to observe the causal effect on the dependent variable.

Extraneous variables do not vary systematically with the IV and therefore do not act as an alternative IV but may have an effect on the dependent variable. They are nuisance variables that muddy the waters and make it more difficult to detect a significant effect.

Hypothesis A precise and testable statement about the assumed relationship between variables. Operationalisation is a key part of making the statement testable.

Independent variable (IV) Some event that is directly manipulated by an experimenter in order to test its effect on another variable – the **dependent variable (DV)**.

Informed consent Participants must be given comprehensive information concerning the nature and purpose of the research and their role in it, in order that they can make an informed decision about whether to participate.

Operationalise Ensuring that variables are in a form that can be easily tested. A concept such as 'educational attainment' needs to be specified more clearly if we are going to investigate it. For example it might be operationalised as 'GCSE grade in Maths'.

Standardised procedures A set of procedures that are the same for all participants in order to be able to repeat the study. This includes standardised instructions – the instructions given to participants to tell them how to perform the task.

ABOUT EXPERIMENTS

You have just done what psychologists do – conducted a systematic study of human behaviour. You followed the scientific method: observe → state expectations → design a study → see if your expectations were correct.

Psychologists use special words to identify aspects of the research process. We have already used some of the terms in this book, and most of them are probably familiar to you from using them in science classes.

- **Question**: *What will you measure?* This is called the **dependent variable (DV)**. When you decided exactly what you would measure, you **operationalised** the DV – it isn't enough just to get people to do 'some work' – you should have made sure that all participants were doing the same task and would have specified what that task was (such as a memory test).

- **Question**: *What are your two conditions?* This is called the **independent variable (IV)**. There are often two conditions of the IV – in this case having the TV on or having the TV off.

In order to conduct an experiment we need to compare one condition (studying with the TV on) with another condition – studying with the TV off. These two conditions are described as different *levels* of the IV. A good study and good hypothesis should always include the two (or more) levels of the IV. If we don't have these different conditions or levels, we have no basis for comparison. So the hypothesis might be:

Students who do a memory task with the TV on produce work which gets fewer marks than those who do the same task without the TV on.

- **Question**: *What will you expect to find?* This is your **hypothesis**, a statement of what you believe to be true. Your hypothesis might have been something like:

Students who do a memory task with the TV on produce work which gets fewer marks.

This is different to the **aims** of the experiment – the aims would be to investigate the effect of TV on the work a student produces. Aims are intentions or possibly a research question ('Does noise affect the quality of work?') whereas a hypothesis is a statement of the relationship between the independent and dependent variable.

- **Question**: *What will the participants do?* You worked out a set of **standardised procedures**. It is important to make sure that each participant did exactly the same thing in each condition, otherwise the results might vary because of changes in procedure rather than because of the IV. Such identical procedures are described as 'standardised'.

- **Question**: *What do you need to control?* You will have tried to control some **extraneous variables** such as time of day (people might do better on a test in the morning than in the afternoon, so all participants should do the test at about the same time of day).

This study you just did is an **experiment**. The main characteristic of an experiment is that there is an IV which is deliberately changed (TV on or not) to see if this has any effect on the DV (quality of work). This permits us to draw *causal conclusions* – we can make a statement about whether having the TV on or off *causes* a change in quality of the work that is done because we can compare the effect of the two levels of the IV.

▶ Ivy Deevy.

Many students find it difficult to remember which is the IV and which is the DV – think of the silly woman. The thing that comes first (Ivy) is the IV which leads to a change in the DV (Deevy).

🐾 APPLY YOUR KNOWLEDGE

Four experiments are described below. For each experiment, answer the following questions:
1. Identify the IV and DV (including both levels of the IV). (2 marks)
2. Explain how you could operationalise the IV and DV. (2 marks)
3. Identify **one** possible extraneous variable. (1 mark)

Study A In order to study the effects of sleep deprivation, students are asked to limit their sleep to five hours a night for three nights and then sleep normally for the next night. Each day the students' cognitive abilities are assessed using a memory test.

Study B Participants volunteer to take part in a study. They are told the study is about public speaking but the real aim is to see how people respond to encouragement by others. Some participants speak in front of a group of people who smile at them, while others talk to a group who appear disinterested.

Study C Marathon runners are assessed on how much sleep they have the night before and the night after a race to see what the effects of exercise are on sleep.

Study D A teacher is doing a psychology course and decides to try a little experiment with her class of eight-year-olds. She gives half the class a test in the morning, and half of them do the same test in the afternoon to see if time of day affects their performance.

CAN YOU? No. 7.1

1. Identify the key features of an experiment. (2 marks)
2. Briefly explain the difference between the aims of a study and a hypothesis. (2 marks)
3. Explain what is meant by 'operationalisation'. (3 marks)
4. Explain why standardisation is important in research procedures. (2 marks)

Control of variables

Invariably, studies in psychology involve a trade-off between **control** and realism. The greatest control can be achieved in a laboratory. However, it is debatable to what extent findings from the laboratory can be generalised to other environments, especially the less controlled environments in which everyday life is lived.

Some psychologists argue that we can only discover things about behaviour if we uncover cause-and-effect relationships in highly controlled laboratory experiments.

Others argue that studies in the natural environment are the only real option for psychologists who are interested in how life is actually lived.

KEY TERMS

Confounding variable A variable under study that is not the IV but which varies systematically with the IV. Changes in the dependent variable may be due to the confounding variable rather than the IV, and therefore the outcome is meaningless. To 'confound' means to cause confusion.

Control Refers to the extent to which any variable is held constant or regulated by a researcher.

External validity The degree to which a research finding can be generalised: to other settings (**ecological validity**); to other groups of people (**population validity**); over time (**historical validity**).

Extraneous variables do not vary systematically with the IV and therefore do not act as an alternative IV but may have an effect on the dependent variable. They are nuisance variables that muddy the waters and make it more difficult to detect a significant effect.

Internal validity The degree to which an observed effect was due to the experimental manipulation rather than other factors such as confounding/extraneous variables.

Mundane realism Refers to how a study mirrors the real world. The research environment is realistic to the degree to which experiences encountered in the research environment will occur in the real world.

Validity Refers to whether an observed effect is a genuine one.

CONTROL

Confounding variables

Consider our experiment on the previous spread: A class of psychology students conducted the study with the aim of finding out whether participants could do their homework effectively while in front of the TV. The independent variable (IV) was whether the TV was on or not. The dependent variable (DV) was the participants' score on the memory test. If TV is a distraction, the 'TV off' group should do better on the test.

But consider this: suppose it happened that all the participants in the 'TV off' condition did the memory test in the morning and all the participants in the 'TV on' condition did the memory test in the afternoon.

People (generally) are more alert in the morning and this might mean that it was the time of day rather than the lack of noise that caused the change in the IV. Time of day may then be regarded as a **confounding variable**.

The experimenter may claim that the IV caused a change in the DV but in fact this may not be the case – changes in the DV may actually be caused by a confounding variable(s). *Consequently the experimenter may not have actually tested what he (or she) intended to test.* Instead, the influence of a different variable has been tested.

The experimenter must be careful to control any possible confounding variable(s). In this case participants in both conditions should do the test at the same time of day.

Extraneous variables

Some students will have better memories than others. It is unlikely that all the people with better memories would end up in the 'TV off' group. If they did, this would act as a confounding variable, but it is more likely that this variation is a nuisance variable because we can never be sure that people with good (or bad) memories are distributed evenly across the two conditions. The extraneous variable of memory ability just makes it more difficult to detect an effect because other factors have an influence.

These nuisance variables are called **extraneous variables**. They also should be controlled if possible because they may affect the DV but not in a systematic way. They are 'extra'.

REALISM

The aim of any psychological study is to provide information about how people behave in 'real life' – the everyday settings in which life is lived. If the set-up of a study is too artificial or contrived then the participants will not act as they would normally.

For example, the study by Loftus and Palmer (see page 56) investigated eyewitness testimony by showing participants a film of a car accident and asking questions about the speed of a car. But how realistic is this? Is watching the film the same as seeing a real accident?

Many things affect the *realism* of a psychological study. The term **mundane realism** refers to how an experiment mirrors the real world. 'Mundane' means 'of the world' – commonplace, ordinary. So lack of mundane realism means something is not like everyday experience. Watching a car accident on film lacks mundane realism because it is not like everyday experience, and this means that the results of the study may not be very useful in terms of understanding behaviour in the real world.

Generalisation

The point of realism in psychological research is to be able to *generalise* the results beyond the particular unique research setting – in particular to be able to understand behaviour in everyday life (the 'real world').

- If the *materials* used in the study are contrived (such as film clips) then the behaviour observed may lack realism.
- If the *environment* in which a study is conducted is contrived, and especially if participants are aware they are being studied, the participants' behaviour may lack realism.
- Even if the environment and materials are 'natural' or real (i.e. high realism) a study can still lack generalisability. For example, if all the participants in a study are American university students, it may not be reasonable to generalise the findings to the behaviour of all people because Americans (and students) have unique characteristics that may set them apart in some way from other people.

The question psychologists are always asking themselves is: 'To what extent can I generalise these findings to everyday life?'

Insider tip...

*Types of **validity** are named only in the full A Level specification, so you won't be asked questions about them in an AS exam – but they are still important concepts to use.*

The term **validity** refers to how true or legitimate something is as an explanation of behaviour. It involves the issues of control, realism and generalisability.

Students often believe that validity is about 'being correct'. This is both right and wrong. It is right because a researcher seeks to find out whether their hypothesis is true, i.e. correct, but it is wrong if you think that being correct means finding out that the predicted expectations have been confirmed. Validity is not about confirming your expectations.

Validity can be separated into **internal validity** and **external validity**. Internal validity is about control and realism. External validity is about being able to generalise from research participants to other people and situations.

Internal validity

Internal validity concerns what goes on inside a study. It is concerned with things such as:

- Whether the IV produced the change in the DV (or did something else affect the DV, such as a confounding variable?).
- Whether the researcher tested what she or he intended to test. For example, if you want to find out whether watching TV affects the quality of homework, you cannot be certain you are testing 'watching the TV' by just having the TV on (the person may not be watching it).
- Whether the study possessed (or lacked) mundane realism.

To gain high internal validity researchers must design the research carefully, controlling confounding and extraneous variables, and ensuring that they are testing what they intended to test.

External validity

External validity is affected by internal validity – you cannot generalise the results of a study that was low in internal validity because the results have no real meaning for the behaviour in question. External validity also concerns:

- The place where the research was conducted (**ecological validity**). It may not be appropriate to generalise from the research setting to other settings, most importantly to everyday life.
- The people who are studied (**population validity**). If a research study involved just students or all men or only Americans, etc. then it may not be appropriate to generalise the findings to all people.
- The historical period (**historical validity**). If a study was conducted in the 1950s it may not be appropriate to generalise the findings to people today because many other factors affect behaviour now.

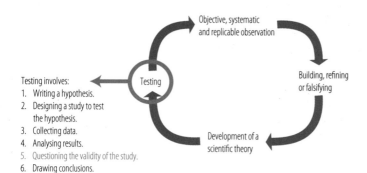

Testing involves:
1. Writing a hypothesis.
2. Designing a study to test the hypothesis.
3. Collecting data.
4. Analysing results.
5. Questioning the validity of the study.
6. Drawing conclusions.

Testing

Objective, systematic and replicable observation

Building, refining or falsifying

Development of a scientific theory

▲ The scientific cycle.

 UPGRADE

Learning about research methods is a bit like learning a foreign language. When you learn a foreign language you have to learn a new set of words and, more especially, you have to learn what they mean. One of the best ways to do this is to *speak* the language.

The same is true for research methods. Don't hold back, don't be scared – use the words. Talk the talk.

To help you learn the language you could create your own **Research Methods Vocabulary Book** to record all the terms used, their meanings and their strengths and limitations.

You can include a copy of the specification for research methods in your book – we have listed this on pages 170 and 210 – and tick off each term when you have recorded the details and again when you feel you understand it.

🐾 APPLY YOUR KNOWLEDGE

1. An area of study that has interested psychologists is *massed versus distributed practice*, i.e. whether learning is better if you practise something repeatedly all in one go (massed) or space your periods of practice (distributed). This topic has been studied in different settings; for example:

   Study 1: Participants were required to recall nonsense syllables on 12 occasions spread over either three days or 12 days (Jost, 1897). Recall was higher when spread over 12 days. This finding has been supported by subsequent research.

   Study 2: Post office workers had to learn to type postcodes either using massed or distributed practice (Baddeley and Longman, 1978). Distributed practice was again found to be superior.

   Present arguments for why each of these studies could be viewed as having high and low external validity.

2. Select **one or more** studies that you are familiar with and explain why you think the study might be:
   - High in internal validity
   - Low in internal validity
   - High in external validity
   - Low in external validity

CAN YOU?   No. 7.2

1. Give an example of a confounding variable in the context of a named study. (2 marks)
2. Briefly explain why it is important to control extraneous variables in a study. (2 marks)
3. Distinguish between extraneous variables and confounding variables. (3 marks)

Return to hypotheses and other things

A hypothesis is a statement of what the researcher believes to be true. Strictly speaking it is not a research *prediction*. It should not be stated in the future tense (i.e 'this will happen…'). At the end of a study the researcher decides whether the evidence collected supports the hypothesis or not.

A hypothesis is also not the same as the aims of a research study. Aims are an initial statement of what the researcher plans to investigate whereas the hypothesis is a formal and testable statement of the relationship between variables.

That's a recap of what you know so far, so you are ready for the next instalment on hypotheses…

▲ Babies who sleep more do better than babies who sleep less – a directional hypothesis, but how would you operationalise it?

KEY TERMS

Confederate An individual in a study who is not a real participant and has been instructed how to behave by the investigator.

Directional hypothesis States the direction of the predicted difference between two conditions or two groups of participants.

Non-directional hypothesis Predicts simply that there is a difference between two conditions or two groups of participants, without stating the direction of the difference.

Pilot study A small-scale trial run of a study to test any aspects of the design, with a view to making improvements.

DIRECTIONAL AND NON-DIRECTIONAL HYPOTHESES

Let's consider a different experiment to our TV on/off study – we might consider the effects of lack of sleep on school performance. That is our research aim, i.e. to see if lack of sleep affects school performance.

We might propose the following hypothesis: People who have plentiful sleep (an average of eight hours or more hours per night over a period of one month) have better marks in class tests than people with a lower sleep average. (Note that this hypothesis has been operationalised.)

The hypothesis above is a **directional hypothesis** – it states the expected *direction* of the results, i.e. you are stating that people who sleep well do *better* on class tests.

If you changed the hypothesis to 'People who have plentiful sleep (an average of eight hours or more hours per night over a period of one month) have *lower* marks in class tests than people with a lower sleep average', this is still a directional hypothesis – you are then stating that the results are expected to go in the opposite direction.

A **non-directional hypothesis** states that there is a difference between two conditions but does not state the direction of the difference: People who have plentiful sleep (an average of eight hours or more hours per night over a period of one month) have *different* marks on class tests than people with a lower sleep average. We may well have a hunch that lack of sleep affects performance but have no real evidence to suggest whether this would be a positive or a negative effect.

Here are two more examples:

Directional hypothesis	People who do homework without the TV on produce *better* results from those who do homework with the TV on.
Non-directional hypothesis	People who do homework with the TV on produce *different* results from those who do homework with no TV on.

Note that the IV and DV haven't been operationalised in the above examples.

Which should you use?

Why do psychologists sometimes use a directional hypothesis instead of a non-directional one (or vice versa)? Psychologists use a directional hypothesis when past research (a theory or a study) suggests that the findings will go in a particular direction. It makes sense then to frame the hypothesis in the direction indicated.

Psychologists use a non-directional hypothesis when there is no past research or past research is contradictory. Non-directional hypotheses may be more appropriate if the study is exploring a new area, where informed expectations about how people might behave have yet to be established through research.

A very shy guy goes into a pub and sees a beautiful woman sitting at the bar. After an hour of gathering up his courage, he finally goes over to her and asks, tentatively, 'Um, would you mind if I chatted with you for a while?'

She responds by yelling, at the top of her voice, 'NO! I won't sleep with you tonight!' Everyone in the bar is now staring at them. Naturally, the guy is hopelessly embarrassed and slinks back to his table.

After a few minutes, the woman walks over to him and apologises. She smiles and says, 'I'm sorry if I embarrassed you. You see, I'm a psychology student, and I'm studying how people respond to embarrassing situations.'

To which he responds, at the top of his voice, 'What do you mean £200?!'

Pilot studies and the aims of piloting

If you conducted the study on page 178 (or any other studies) yourself you are probably aware that there were flaws in your research design. Did you realise that there would be flaws beforehand? Or did some of the flaws become apparent during or after conducting the experiment?

Scientists deal with this problem by conducting a **pilot study** first. A pilot study is a small-scale trial run of a research design before doing the real thing. It is done in order to find out if certain aspects of the design do or don't work. For example, participants may not understand the instructions or they may guess what an experiment is about. They may also get bored because there are too many tasks or too many questions.

If a researcher tries out the design using a few typical participants they can see what needs to be adjusted without having invested a large amount of time and money in a full-scale study.

Note that the results of any such pilot study are irrelevant – the researcher is not interested in what results are produced – the researcher is simply seeing to what extent the procedures need fine tuning.

Confederates

Sometimes a researcher has to use another person to play a role in an experiment or other investigation. For example, you might want to find out if people respond differently to orders from someone wearing a suit compared with someone dressed in casual clothes.

In this experiment the IV would be the clothing worn by a person who has been briefed to behave in a certain way by the experimenter. The experimenter would arrange for this person to give orders either dressed in a suit or dressed casually. This person is called a **confederate**.

Milgram's study on obedience (see page 24) used a confederate to play the role of the experimenter and another to play the role of the learner. In Asch's study on conformity (see page 20) the confederates pretended to be other participants.

> **Insider tip…**
>
> *Exam questions about pilot studies rarely ask you to explain what a pilot study is – you are more likely to be asked how a researcher would conduct one or why a researcher might conduct a pilot study. Make sure you deal with 'how' or 'why' in such questions.*

CAN YOU?   No. 7.3

1. Briefly explain what is meant by a 'pilot study'. (2 marks)
2. Briefly explain why a researcher might use a pilot study. (2 marks)
3. Briefly explain how a pilot study might be conducted. (2 marks)
4. Distinguish between a directional and non-directional hypothesis. (2 marks)
5. Briefly explain why a researcher would choose to use a non-directional hypothesis rather than a directional hypothesis. (2 marks)

▲ The woman on the left (a confederate) talks 'blirtatiously' (loudly and effusively) to see what effect this has on the person who is studying.

🐾 APPLY YOUR KNOWLEDGE

1. Read the statements below and identify which are aims and which are hypotheses. (1 mark each)
   a. Younger people have better memories than older people.
   b. To see if blondes have more fun than brunettes.
   c. Do people who sleep with a teddy bear sleep longer than people who don't?
   d. Positive expectations lead to differences in performance.
   e. Men with beards are more attractive.
   f. Lack of sleep may affect schoolwork.

2. For each of the following, decide whether it is a directional or non-directional hypothesis. (1 mark each)
   a. Boys score differently on aggressiveness tests than girls.
   b. Students who have a computer at home do better in exams than those who don't.
   c. People remember the words that are early in a list better than the words that appear later.
   d. People given a list of emotionally charged words recall fewer words than participants given a list of emotionally neutral words.
   e. Hamsters are better pets than budgies.
   f. Words presented in a written form are recalled differently from those presented in a pictorial form.

3. Now write your own. Below are research aims for possible experiments. For each one identify and operationalise the IV and DV and then write **two** hypotheses: a directional one and a non-directional one. (1 mark each)
   a. Do girls watch more television than boys?
   b. Do teachers give more attractive students higher marks on essays than students who are less attractive?
   c. A researcher believes older people sleep more than younger people.
   d. Do people rate food as looking more attractive when they are hungry?
   e. A teacher wishes to find out whether one maths test is harder than another maths test.

4. Select **one** of the experiments from question 3.
   a. Explain *why* you would conduct a pilot study for this experiment. (2 marks)
   b. Describe *how* you would do it. (2 marks)

Experimental design

On this spread we are going to find out a little more about experiments. As you know by now an experiment has an independent variable (IV) and a dependent variable (DV). In order to find out whether the IV did affect the DV we always need a comparison condition – a condition where there is a different level of the IV.

For example, consider the sleep experiment. If you only got data on people who slept more than eight hours a night that wouldn't help you to know anything about their performance unless you have another condition to compare them with (people who slept less than eight hours). The two levels of the IV are therefore: (1) 'sleep eight hours or more' and (2) 'sleep less than eight hours'.

The same is true for the experiment looking at the effects of watching TV while doing your homework – the two levels of the IV are 'TV on' and 'TV off'.

The way that the two levels of the IV are delivered is called **experimental design**.

TYPES OF EXPERIMENTAL DESIGN

Type of experimental design	Evaluation: Limitations	Method of dealing with the limitations
Repeated measures design All participants receive all levels of the IV; for example: • Each participant does the task with the TV on, e.g. does a memory test. • Then, perhaps a week later, each participant does a similar test without the TV on. We compare the performance (DV) of the participant on the two tests.	1. The order of the conditions may affect performance (an **order effect**). For example, participants may do better on the second test because of a *practice effect* or because they are less anxious. Alternatively, in some situations participants may do worse on the second test because of being bored with doing the same test again *(boredom effect)*. 2. When participants do the second test they may guess the purpose of the experiment, which may affect their behaviour. For example, some participants may purposely do worse on the second test because they want it to appear as if they work less well in the afternoon.	Researchers may use two different tests to reduce a practice effect – though the two tests must be equivalent. This can be done by constructing a test of, say, 40 items and randomly allocating items to Test A and Test B. The main way that order effects are dealt with is using **counterbalancing** (see facing page). In order to avoid participants guessing the aims of a study, a cover story can be presented about the purpose of the test.
Independent groups design Participants are placed in separate (independent) groups. Each group does one level of the IV; for example: • Group A does the task with TV on (one level of the IV). • Group B does the task with no TV (the other level of the IV). We compare the performance (DV) of the two groups.	1. The researcher cannot control the effects of *participant variables* (i.e. the different abilities or characteristics of each participant). For example, participants in Group A might happen to have better memories than those in Group B. This would act as a confounding variable. 2. Independent groups design needs more participants than repeated measures design in order to end up with the same amount of data.	**Randomly allocate** participants to conditions which (theoretically) distribute participant variables evenly. Random allocation can be done by putting the participant names in a hat and drawing out the names so that every other person goes in Group A. See randomisation on page 193.
Matched pairs design A compromise is to use two groups of participants but match participants on key characteristics believed to affect performance on the DV (e.g. IQ or time spent watching TV). Then one member of the pair is allocated to Group A and the other to Group B. The procedure is then the same as for independent groups. It is important to realise that the characteristics for matching *must* be relevant to the study. In other words you wouldn't need to match participants on gender if you were testing memory – unless there was some evidence that gender was a potential confounding variable.	1. It is very time-consuming and difficult to match participants on key variables. The researcher probably has to start with a large group of participants to ensure they can obtain matched pairs on key variables. 2. It is not possible to control all participant variables because you can only match on variables known to be relevant, but it could be that others are important. For example, in a memory experiment you might match on memory abilities but later find that some of the participants had been involved in a teaching programme to boost memory skills and you should have matched on this.	Restrict the number of variables to match on to make it easier. Conduct a pilot study to consider key variables that might be important when matching.

Evaluation: Strengths

You can work out the strengths of each experimental design by looking at the limitations of the other designs.

For example, one limitation of repeated measures is that participants do better on one condition than the other condition because of a practice effect. Therefore one strength of independent groups and matched pairs designs is that these designs avoid such order effects, i.e. there would be no practice effect because each participant only does one condition.

Identify **two** strengths for each design listed here.

In a repeated measures design there are two (or more) levels of the IV. Each level is called a 'condition'. Instead of levels there may be an experimental condition and a control condition.

In an independent groups or matched pairs design each group does one condition – the experimental group does the experimental condition and the control group does the control condition.

KEY TERMS

Counterbalancing An experimental technique used to overcome order effects when using a repeated measures design. Counterbalancing ensures that each condition is tested first or second in equal amounts.

Experimental design A set of procedures used to control the influence of factors such as participant variables in an experiment.

Independent groups design Participants are allocated to two (or more) groups representing different levels of the IV. Allocation is usually done using random techniques.

Matched pairs design Pairs of participants are matched in terms of key variables such as age and IQ. One member of each pair is allocated to one of the conditions under test and the second person is allocated to the other condition.

Order effect In a repeated measures design, an extraneous variable arising from the order in which conditions are presented, e.g. a practice effect or fatigue effect.

Random allocation Allocating participants to experimental groups or conditions using random techniques.

Repeated measures design Each participant takes part in every condition under test, i.e. each level of the IV.

COUNTERBALANCING

Counterbalancing ensures that each condition in a repeated measures design is tested first or second in equal amounts. If participants do the same memory test first in the morning and then in the afternoon, we might expect them to do better on the second test because they have had some practice – or they might do worse because they are bored with the task. These are called order effects, which can be dealt with using counterbalancing.

There are two ways to counterbalance order effects. In each case, we have two conditions:

- Condition A – test done in the morning.
- Condition B – test done in the afternoon.

Way 1. AB or BA

Divide participants into two groups:
- Group 1: each participant does A then B.
- Group 2: each participant does B then A.

Note that this is still a repeated measures design even though there are two groups of participants, because comparison will be made for each participant on their performance on the two conditions (morning and afternoon).

Way 2. ABBA

This time, all participants take part in each condition twice.
- Trial 1: Condition A (morning)
- Trial 2: Condition B (afternoon)
- Trial 3: Condition B (afternoon)
- Trial 4: Condition A (morning)

Then we compare scores on trials 1 and 4 with trials 2 and 3. As before, this is still a repeated measures design because we are comparing the scores of the same person.

🐾 APPLY YOUR KNOWLEDGE

1. For each of the following experiments a–f, identify the experimental design that has been used. (1 mark each)
   When trying to decide, it might help you if you ask yourself:
   - Would the findings be analysed by comparing the scores from the same person or by comparing the scores of two (or more) groups of people?
   - If it is two or more groups of people then ask 'Are the people in the different groups related (i.e. matched) or not?'
   a. Boys and girls are compared on their IQ test scores.
   b. Hamsters are tested to see if one genetic strain is better at finding food in a maze than another.
   c. Reaction time is tested before and after a reaction time training activity to see if test scores improve after training.
   d. Students are put in pairs based on their GCSE grades and then one member of the pair is given a memory test in the morning and one in the afternoon.
   e. Three groups of participants are given different word lists to remember, in order to find out whether nouns, verbs or adjectives are easier to recall.
   f. Participants are asked to give ratings for attractive and unattractive photographs.

2. For each of the following studies identify the experimental design used and explain **one** limitation and **one** strength of using this experimental design in this study.
   a. Craik and Lockhart's study of elaborative rehearsal (page 47). (1 mark + 2 marks + 2 marks)
   b. Godden and Baddeley's study of content-dependent forgetting (page 54). (1 mark + 2 marks + 2 marks)
   c. Moscovici's study of minority influence (page 32). (1 mark + 2 marks + 2 marks)
   d. A study of drug treatment versus placebo (see page 115). (1 mark + 2 marks + 2 marks)

Insider tip…

Exam questions often ask you to identify the experimental design used in a particular study. When students see the phrase 'experimental design' in an exam question they often can't remember what 'experimental design' means. Here's one way to remember – in the middle of the word 'experimental' are the letters RIM, which stand for Repeated, Independent and Matched pairs.

CAN YOU? No. 7.4

1. Briefly explain what is meant by 'independent groups design'. (2 marks)
2. Name **one** other type of experimental design and explain how it might be used. (2 marks)
3. Explain **one** limitation of using a matched pairs design to study minority influence. (3 marks)

Laboratory and field experiments

An experiment permits us to study cause and effect. Experiments differ from non-experimental methods because they involve the manipulation of one variable (the independent variable – IV), while trying to keep all other variables constant. If the IV is the only thing that is changed then it must have caused any change in the dependent variable (DV).

There are different kinds of experiments. We will start by looking at two kinds: laboratory (lab) experiments and field experiments. All experiments have one thing in common: they all have an independent variable and a dependent variable.

*Note that it is possible to do research in a **laboratory** which is not experimental. For example, **controlled observations** may be conducted in a laboratory (we will look at these on page 198).*

*Note also that there are field studies as well as field experiments. Any study which is conducted in a natural environment is called a **field study** – it is only a field experiment if there is an IV that has been manipulated by an experimenter.*

▲ A psychology lab might look like the room above. The main characteristic of a lab is that it is an environment where variables can be easily controlled – the independent variable can be easily manipulated, the dependent variable can be easily measured and extraneous/confounding variables can be controlled.

Just because a research study is conducted in such an environment does not mean it is a laboratory experiment. It might be a natural or a quasi-experiment, something you will study on the next spread.

Don't pay homage to formal terms*

As we have already said, learning about research methods is a bit like learning a foreign language. You have to learn to use a whole new vocabulary and you have to learn the meaning of this vocabulary. The problem with the vocabulary is that people often focus too much on the words and fail to really grasp the underlying meaning. This is the case with the terms 'field' and 'lab' experiment. It isn't always easy to decide whether a study is one or the other. What matters more are the underlying issues of whether the participants were aware they were being studied, whether the task was contrived and so on. So don't get too hung up on the terms – focus on what was going on.

*An excellent phrase 'invented' by Hugh Coolican (2004) to explain this problem.

LABORATORY AND FIELD EXPERIMENTS

Laboratory experiment

A **laboratory experiment** is an experiment conducted in a *special environment* where variables can be *carefully controlled*. Participants are *aware* that they are taking part in an experiment, though they may not know the true aims of the study.

It is this awareness of being in a study that contributes to the contrived nature of such studies – participants may alter their behaviour because they know it is being recorded.

Laboratory experiments also often involve quite artificial materials such as consonant syllables (Peterson and Peterson's study of STM; see page 44) and this again makes the experience less like everyday life.

In addition, of course, the laboratory environment may seem artificial and uncomfortable – but remember it is by no means the environment alone which contributes to the contrived nature of lab experiments.

Field experiment

A **field experiment** is conducted in a more natural (or 'ordinary') environment, i.e. in 'the field' (as distinct from 'a field' – 'the field' is anywhere outside a laboratory). As with the laboratory experiment, the IV is still deliberately manipulated by the researcher and the researcher measures the DV.

A key feature of a field experiment is that participants are usually not aware that they are participating in an experiment. For this reason their behaviour may be more natural.

Field or lab experiment?

Sometimes it isn't very easy to work out whether a study is a laboratory or field experiment.

On page 58 we described the weapon focus study (Johnson and Scott, 1976). The study might seem, on the surface, to be a lab experiment: it was conducted under controlled conditions in a room unfamiliar to the participants. But the actual behaviour that was being measured (the participants' ability to identify the man running through the room) reflected natural behaviour. The participants were not aware that it was this behaviour that was being studied and therefore were behaving naturally. So this makes the study more like a field experiment.

KEY TERMS

Field experiment A controlled experiment conducted outside a laboratory. The IV is still manipulated by the experimenter, and therefore causal relationships can be demonstrated. Field experiments tend to have lower internal validity (more difficult to control extraneous and confounding variables) and higher external validity (greater mundane realism). Participants are usually unaware that they are participating in an experiment; thus their behaviour may be more natural and they are less likely to respond to cues from the experimenter.

Laboratory experiment An experiment carried out in a controlled setting. Lab experiments tend to have high internal validity because good control over all variables is possible. They tend to have low ecological validity because participants are aware they are being studied and also the tasks involved tend to be more artificial.

EVALUATION/DISCUSSION

Laboratory experiments

Strengths
- Laboratory experiments are high in internal validity because extraneous variables can be controlled. This means that we can be confident that any observed change in the DV is due to the IV.

Limitations
- Participants usually are aware that their behaviour is being studied. This leads participants to search for cues about the aims of the experiment and may affect the participants' behaviour, reducing 'realness' (ecological validity).
- The IV or DV may be operationalised in such a way that it doesn't represent everyday experiences, i.e. it is low in mundane realism. For example, using film clips to test eyewitness memory is not like the 'real' experience of an accident (see Loftus and Palmer on page 56). This leads to low ecological validity.
- Low ecological validity can also be explained in terms of the setting. Participants may feel uncomfortable in an unknown and artificial environment. This means they may not behave as they usually would.

The considerable strengths of lab experiments are limited by the fact participants are less likely to behave as they would in everyday life.

Field experiments

Strengths
- Participants are not likely to be aware that their behaviour is being studied. This means they don't respond to demand characteristics and therefore their behaviour may be more 'natural'. (Note this is not always true, e.g. see Godden and Baddeley's divers study on page 54).
- A field experiment takes place in a more natural setting (e.g. a classroom at school), so participants may be more relaxed.

Limitations
- Many of the problems outlined above for laboratory experiments may also arise in field experiments. For example, the IV in a field experiment may lack mundane realism. Therefore, field experiments are not *necessarily* more like everyday life than lab experiments.
- It is more difficult to control extraneous variables.
- There is a major ethical issue – if participants don't know they are being studied, it is difficult to debrief them. This raises ethical issues with manipulating and recording their behaviour.

The benefits of a 'more natural' research environment may therefore be offset by other issues to do with control and ethics.

Take care – do not assume lab experiments are low in ecological validity and field experiments are high. In some situations the reverse is true.

CAN YOU? No. 7.5

1. Briefly explain what is meant by a 'laboratory experiment'. (2 marks)
2. Briefly explain what is meant by a 'field experiment'. (2 marks)
3. Identify **two** differences between laboratory and field experiments. (2 marks)
4. Briefly explain **one** similarity between laboratory and field experiments. (2 marks)
5. Discuss laboratory and field experiments. In your answer include some examples of both. (6 marks)

🐾 APPLY YOUR KNOWLEDGE

Answer the questions for the experiments A–F described below.
1. Identify the IV and DV. (2 marks)
2. Was the task required of participants contrived? (1 mark)
3. Was the study conducted in a natural setting? (1 mark)
4. Was the setting high or low in mundane realism? (1 mark)
5. Did the participants know they were being studied? (1 mark)
6. Were the participants brought into a special situation, or did the experimenter go to them? (1 mark)
7. What relevant variables might not have been controlled? (1 mark)
8. Do you think this was a lab or field experiment? (1 mark)

Study A Bushman (1988) tested the effects of perceived authority on obedience. A female researcher, dressed either in a 'police-style' uniform, as a business executive or as a beggar, stopped people in the street and told them to give change to a male researcher for an expired parking meter. People obeyed most when she was in the 'police' uniform, whereas obedience rates were much lower in the other two conditions. When interviewed afterwards, people claimed they had obeyed the woman in uniform because she appeared to have authority.

Study B Participants were asked to wait in a room before an experiment began. There was a radio playing either good or bad news and a stranger was present. When they were asked to rate the stranger, the degree of liking was related to the kind of news they had been listening to, showing that people like others who are associated with positive experiences (Veitch and Griffitt, 1976).

Study C The participants were children aged from three to five years. Each child was taken on its own to an experimental room where there were lots of toys including, in one corner, a five-foot inflatable Bobo doll and a mallet. The experimenter invited the 'model' (another adult) to join them and then left the room for about 10 minutes. Half of the children watched the model playing aggressively with the Bobo doll while the others watched the model play non-aggressively with the doll. Later they were given an opportunity to play with toys including the Bobo doll and were observed through a one-way mirror. The children who saw the aggressive behaviour were more likely to behave aggressively (Bandura *et al.,* 1961; see page 128).

Study D One group of school pupils were given information about how their peers had performed on a maths task. They were either told that their peers had done well or done poorly on the test. The children were later given a maths test in class. Those who expected to do well on the maths test did better than those led to expect to do poorly (Schunk, 1983).

Study E Researchers were asked to study what factors led to increased worker productivity at the Hawthorne Electrical factory. The study found that increased lighting levels led to increased productivity – but then also found that decreased lighting led to increased productivity (Roethlisberger and Dickson, 1939). The researchers finally realised that the persistent increase in productivity was not related to lighting conditions at all (the IV) but because the workers were responding positively to the attention they were receiving and this was enhancing their performance.

Study F Participants were tested in their teaching room and given consonant syllables (e.g. SXT) and then asked to count backwards until told to stop. Then participants were asked to recall the consonant syllable. The counting interval was used to prevent the consonant syllables being rehearsed. When the counting interval was three seconds, participants could recall most of the consonant syllables; when it was 18 seconds they couldn't recall many consonant syllables (Peterson and Peterson, 1959; see page 44).

Natural and quasi-experiments

There are two further types of experiment – a **natural experiment** and a **quasi-experiment**. Both of these are not 'true' experiments because the independent variable (IV) is not deliberately manipulated. This means that it is not possible to claim that changes in the dependent variable (DV) are caused by the independent variable.

▲ What is natural?

Natural means 'derived from nature, not made or caused by humankind'.

In a field experiment the thing that is natural is the environment – meaning that it hasn't been engineered by the experimenter.

In a natural experiment the thing that is natural is the IV. In a natural experiment the environment may not be natural – for example, the DV may be tested in a lab.

KEY TERMS

Natural experiment A research method in which the experimenter has not manipulated the independent variable (IV) directly. The IV would vary whether or not the researcher was interested. The researcher records the effect of the IV on a dependent variable (DV) – this DV may be measured in a lab. Strictly speaking, an experiment involves the deliberate manipulation of an IV and random allocation to conditions by the experimenter – neither of which apply to a natural experiment and therefore causal conclusions can only tentatively be drawn.

Quasi-experiments Studies that are 'almost' experiments. The independent variable is actually not something that varies at all – it is a condition that exists. The researcher records the effect of this 'quasi-IV' on a dependent variable (DV). As with a natural experiment, the lack of manipulation of the IV and the lack of random allocation means that causal conclusions can only tentatively be drawn.

NATURAL AND QUASI-EXPERIMENTS

Natural experiment

A natural experiment is conducted when it is not possible, for ethical or practical reasons, to deliberately manipulate an IV. Therefore it is said that the IV varies 'naturally'. The DV may be tested in a laboratory.

Consider these examples:

- **Effects of institutionalisation** On page 86 we discussed the studies of Romanian orphans and the effect their early experiences had on their subsequent emotional and intellectual development. The IV in such a study may be adoption either before or after the age of six months. It would not be ethical to deliberately control this IV – deciding that some babies might be adopted early but others would have to wait in order for researchers to study the effects. In these studies the DV might be behaviour in the Strange Situation or performance on an IQ test. Both of these would probably be tested in a lab.
- **Effects of TV** Before 1995 people living on the small island of St. Helena in the middle of the Atlantic had no TV. The arrival of TV gave researchers a chance to see how exposure to Western programmes might influence behaviour – overall, Charlton *et al.* (2000) found no difference in either pro- or anti-social behaviour after the introduction of Western TV. In this study the IV was no TV and later exposure to TV.

  This IV was not controlled by the researchers – they took advantage of something which would be practically quite difficult to control. The DV was measures of pro- and anti-social behaviour using questionnaires, observations and psychological tests.

Quasi-experiment

In a quasi-experiment the IV is also naturally occurring and the DV may be measured in a lab. The key feature is that the IV has not been made to vary by anyone. It is simply a difference between people that exists.

Consider these examples:

- **Gender differences** Sheridan and King (1972) tested obedience by asking male participants to give genuine electric shocks of increasing strength to a puppy. They found that 54% of male participants delivered the maximum (non-fatal) shock, but the obedience rate for females was a staggering 100%! The IV in this study was gender – a difference that cannot be manipulated and thus not a 'true' IV.
- **Locus of control** On page 30 we looked at the consequences of having an internal or external locus of control. The IV is internal or external locus of control. This is a personal attribute of the individuals, not something that was caused to vary by the situation. In one study (Hutchins and Estey, 1978) the DV was performance in a simulated prisoner-of-war camp situation.

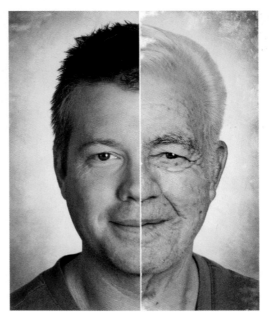

◄ Many studies in psychology compare the behaviour of older and younger people, for example on the accuracy of their eyewitness testimony. In such studies the IV is age. This is a 'condition' of the individual and therefore such studies are quasi-experiments.

It is not age that has caused the behaviour but characteristics that vary with age such as, for example, the likelihood that some participants may have dementia.

EVALUATION/DISCUSSION

There are several reasons why researchers cannot draw cause-and-effect conclusions from natural and quasi-experiments.

No manipulation of the IV

The lack of control over the IV means that we cannot say for certain that any change in the DV was caused by the IV.

For example, if there were uncontrolled confounding variables, then observed changes in the DV might not be due to the IV. Remember, though, that poor experimental design may make causal conclusions unjustified in a laboratory or field experiment – so causal conclusions are not guaranteed in those more controlled situations either.

This means that any conclusions about cause and effect can only be tentative.

Random allocation

In an experiment with an independent groups design participants are randomly allocated to conditions. This is not possible in natural or quasi-experiments.

This means that participant variables may differ between the two groups. For example, in the study on the effects of institutionalisation (see facing page) there may be other variables that changed systematically with the IV that were not controlled, such as friendliness of the baby. It might be that the infants adopted early were chosen because they were more outgoing than those adopted later. This confounding variable of friendliness might explain why that group of babies was emotionally better adjusted than the late adopted group.

This lack of random allocation in natural and quasi-experiments means there may be uncontrolled confounding variables.

Unique characteristics of participants

The sample studied in any natural or quasi-experiment may have unique characteristics.

For example, in the St. Helena study (on the facing page) the people were part of a particularly helpful and pro-social community, and this might explain why violence on TV didn't affect their behaviour whereas, in other studies, the advent of TV did have an effect.

The unique characteristics of the sample mean that the findings can't be generalised to other groups of people (i.e the studies may be described as having low population validity).

CAN YOU? No. 7.6

1. Briefly explain what is meant by a 'natural experiment'. (2 marks)
2. Briefly explain what is meant by a 'quasi-experiment'. (2 marks)
3. Explain the difference between a field experiment and a natural experiment. (3 marks)
4. Discuss the use of natural experiments in psychological research. Give examples in your answer. (6 marks)

Comparing different types of experiment

	Strengths	Limitations
Laboratory experiment To investigate causal relationships between an IV and DV under controlled conditions.	• Well controlled, so extraneous/confounding variables are minimised, thus higher internal validity. • Can be easily replicated, demonstrating external validity.	• Artificial, a contrived situation. Participants may not behave as they would in everyday life, leading to lower ecological validity. • Participants may know they are being studied which creates demand characteristics (see next page). • Materials may lack mundane realism.
Field experiment To investigate causal relationships between an IV and DV in less controlled, more natural surroundings.	• Less artificial, usually higher mundane realism and higher ecological validity. • Participants are usually not aware of being studied.	• Less control of extraneous/confounding variables, reduces internal validity. • More time-consuming and thus more expensive.
Natural experiment To investigate relationships between an IV and DV in situations where IV cannot be directly manipulated for ethical or practical reasons.	• Allows research where IV can't be manipulated for ethical or practical reasons. • Enables psychologists to study 'real' problems such as the effects of a disaster on health (increased mundane realism and ecological validity).	• Cannot demonstrate causal relationships because IV not directly manipulated. • Random allocation not possible, therefore there may be confounding variables that can't be controlled, a threat to internal validity. • Can only be used where conditions vary naturally.
Quasi-experiment To investigate relationships between an IV and DV in situations where IV is a characteristic of the person (e.g. age or gender or level of depression).	• Allows comparisons between types of people.	• Participants may be aware of being studied, creating demand characteristics and reducing internal validity. • The dependent variable may be a fairly artificial task, reducing mundane realism.

 APPLY YOUR KNOWLEDGE

Six studies are described below. For each study: (a) identify the IV and DV (2 marks); (b) identify whether it is a laboratory, field, natural or quasi-experiment (1 mark); (c) explain your decision (2 marks); and (d) explain why you think the study would have high or low validity (2 marks).

1. Two primary schools use different reading schemes. A psychological study compares the reading scores at the end of the year to see which scheme was more effective.
2. Children take part in a trial to compare the success of a new maths programme. The children are placed in one of two groups – a group receiving the new maths programme or a group receiving the traditional one – and taught in these groups for a term.
3. The value of using computers rather than books is investigated by requiring children to learn word lists, either using a computer or with a book.
4. People who score high on the authoritarian personality scale are compared with people low on the authoritarian personality scale in terms of how willing they are to obey orders in a Milgram-type study.
5. The effect of advertisements on gender stereotypes is studied by asking participants to look at ads with women doing feminine tasks or neutral tasks and then asking them about gender stereotypes.
6. A study investigates the anti-social effects of TV by monitoring whether people who watch a lot of TV (more than five hours a day) are more aggressive than those who don't.

More problems with experiments

There are a number of problems that arise in experiments that threaten the internal validity of an experiment. We have considered extraneous and confounding variables already. On this spread we consider more issues that may act as extraneous or confounding variables.

▶ Participants may want to offer a helping hand. If they know they are in an experiment they usually want to please the experimenter and be helpful, otherwise why are they there? This sometimes results in them being over-cooperative – and behaving artificially.

However, some participants react in the opposite way – the 'screw you' effect where a participant deliberately behaves in a way that spoils an experiment.

Participants or subjects?

In early psychological research the people in the studies were called 'subjects'. In the 1990s there was a move to use the term 'participant' instead of 'subject'.

One reason for the change of terminology is that the term 'participant' reflects the fact that such individuals are not passive members of a study but are actively involved. They search for cues about what to do and this may mean that they behave as researchers expect rather than as they would in everyday life. The use of the term 'participants' acknowledges this active involvement.

A further reason for the change is that the term 'subject' implies that those involved must be obedient and are powerless whereas, in fact, psychologists owe them a great deal for their willingness to take part – it is an equal partnership.

DEMAND CHARACTERISTICS

Participants want to be helpful and therefore they pay attention to cues in the experimental situation that may guide their behaviour. Consider this study by Martin Orne:

> Participants had to sit in a room on their own for four hours. One group of participants were asked at the beginning of the study to sign a form releasing the experimenter from responsibility if anything happened to them during the experiment. They were also given a panic button to push if they felt overly stressed. The other group were given no information to arouse their expectations. The first group showed extreme signs of distress during isolation. This can only be explained in terms of expectations created by the situation. (Orne and Scheibe, 1964)

Orne invented the term **demand characteristics** to describe the effect of expectations and defined them as:

> The totality of cues that convey the experimental hypothesis to the [participant] become determinants of the [participant's] behaviour. (Orne, 1962)

Everyday demand characteristics

Watching a football game at home you might sit relatively quietly, but on a football ground you would chant and jump up and down. These different situations create different expectations and 'demand' different behaviours.

Experimental demand characteristics

In an experiment, participants are often unsure about what to do. They actively look for clues as to how they should behave in that situation. These clues are demand characteristics – which collectively convey the experimental hypothesis to participants. For example:

- A participant is given two memory tests (repeated measures): one in the morning and one in the afternoon. Participants might try to guess why they are being given two tests and correctly work out that the study is looking at the effects of time of day on performance. This might lead the participant to try to perform the same on each test.
- Boys and girls are compared to see who is more friendly. A questionnaire is used to assess friendliness. It is quite apparent that the questions are about friendships. This leads participants to guess the purpose of the questionnaire. The girls want to help and give answers showing how friendly they are. The boys are a bit contrary and give answers that show how unfriendly they are.

In both cases the result is that participants do not behave as they would usually. They have altered their behaviour as a consequence of cues in the research situation. Thus demand characteristics may act as an extraneous (confounding) variable.

INVESTIGATOR EFFECTS

Investigator effects are any cues (other than the IV) from an investigator that encourage certain behaviours in the participant, and which might lead to a fulfilment of the investigator's expectations. Such cues act as extraneous or confounding variables.

Consider this study by Robert Rosenthal and Kermit Fode (1963):

> Students were asked to train rats to learn the route through a maze. The students were told that there were two groups of rats: one group consisted of 'fast learners' having been bred for this characteristic, while the other comprised 'slow learners'. In fact, there were no differences between the rats. Despite this, the findings of the study showed that the supposedly brighter rats actually did better. When the students were asked afterwards about their rats, those with 'fast learning' rats described them as smarter, more attractive and more likeable than the descriptions given by the other group of students. The only explanation can be that the students' expectations affected the rats' performance.

So even rats were affected by the investigator's expectations. How?

Investigators unconsciously encourage participants by, for example, spending more time with one group of participants or being more positive with them. For example, research has found that males are more pleasant and friendly with female participants than with other male participants (Rosenthal, 1966).

Alternatively (with human participants) the way in which an investigator asks a question may *lead* a participant to give the answer the investigator 'wants' (similar to leading questions; see page 56).

Indirect investigator effects

There are also indirect investigator effects, such as the 'investigator experimental design effect'. The investigator may operationalise the measurement of variables in such a way that the desired result is more likely, or may limit the duration of the study for the same reason.

The 'investigator loose procedure effect' refers to situations where an investigator may not clearly specify the standardised instructions and/or standardised procedures which leaves room for the results to be influenced by the experimenter.

▲ An example of demand characteristics.

Clever Hans was a stallion owned by Wilhelm Von Osten. Hans demonstrated an astonishing ability with arithmetic. Someone would ask a simple arithmetic question, for example 'What is 7 times 4?' and they would then start counting aloud. When they reached 28 the horse would start stamping its hooves. However, rigorous testing showed that he was not adding, he was responding to subtle unconscious cues from his owner – Wilhelm was communicating expectations which acted as demand characteristics. The reason the horse did as expected was because of the cues, not his ability. Fulfilling expectations is the outcome of demand characteristics.

DEALING WITH THESE PROBLEMS

Single blind design

In a single blind design the participant is not aware of the research aims and/or of which condition of the experiment they are receiving. This prevents the participant from seeking cues about the aims and reacting to them.

Double blind design

In a double blind design both the participant *and* the person conducting the experiment are 'blind' to the aims and/or hypotheses. Therefore the person conducting the investigation is less likely to produce cues about what he/she expects.

Experimental realism

If the researcher makes an experimental task sufficiently engaging the participant pays attention to the task and not the fact that they are being observed.

Other extraneous variables (EVs)

Participant variables

A participant variable is any characteristic of individual participants. Participant variables are not the same as participant effects. Demand characteristics are an effect of participants' behaviour, whereas a participant variable is a characteristic of participants.

Participant variables act as extraneous variables only if an independent groups design is used. When a repeated measures design is used, participant variables are controlled. In a matched pairs design participant variables are hopefully controlled.

Participant variables include age, intelligence, motivation, experience, gender and so on. Students often identify gender as an extraneous variable and it may be. For example Alice Eagly (1978) reported that women may be more conformist than men. This means that having more women than men in one condition of an experiment might mask the effects of the IV. However, it is important to realise that gender only acts as an EV in some circumstances. For example, we would not control gender in a memory experiment unless we had a reason to expect that it would matter. When considering participant variables as EVs we need only focus on those that are relevant to the task.

Situational variables

Situational variables are those features of a research *situation* that may influence participants' behaviour and thus act as EVs or confounding variables. One example of a situational variable is order effects, which were described on page 84. Improved participant performance may be due to practice (a confounding variable) rather than the IV.

Situational variables are only confounding if they vary systematically with the IV, for example if all members of one group are tested in the morning and all members of the second group are tested in the afternoon.

APPLY YOUR KNOWLEDGE

1. Orne's panic button study (see facing page) is an example of demand characteristics. Identify the demand characteristics in this study. (2 marks)

2. Asch's study of conformity (see page 20) has been criticised in terms of demand characteristics. Identify the demand characteristics in this study. (2 marks)

3. In the two studies listed below give an example of a possible: (a) demand characteristic; (b) investigator effect; (c) participant variable; and (d) situational variable. (1 mark each)

   For each one, if you can, suggest how the problem might be dealt with.

   Study 1 Participants' memory was tested in the morning and in the afternoon, to see if there was any difference in their ability to recall numbers.

   Study 2 Participants were given a list of adjectives describing Mr Smith. One group had positive adjectives first, followed by negative adjectives. The other group had the adjectives in reverse order. They were all then asked to describe Mr Smith.

KEY TERMS

Demand characteristics A cue that makes participants unconsciously aware of the aims of a study or helps participants work out what the researcher expects to find.

Investigator effect (sometimes referred to as investigator or experimenter bias). Anything that an investigator does that has an effect on a participant's performance in a study other than what was intended. This includes direct effects (as a consequence of the investigator interacting with the participant) and indirect effects (as a consequence of the investigator designing the study). Investigator effects may act as a confounding or extraneous variable.

Insider tip…

The only specialist terms used on this spread that are in the specification are the two highlighted in dark blue above – this means that exam questions can only use these terms. The other terms may be useful to use in any discussion of research methods or even when criticising research studies.

CAN YOU?   No. 7.7

1. Briefly explain what is meant by 'demand characteristics'. (2 marks)
2. Explain what is meant by 'investigator effects'. Use an example in your answer. (3 marks)
3. Briefly explain how a researcher might deal with the effects of demand characteristics. (2 marks)

Sampling

By now you should realise that the people who are studied in a research investigation are called participants. This is generally a small group of people, maybe only 20 or 30 people. How does a psychologist select this group of people? The process is called **sampling** and there are a variety of techniques that can be used to obtain the sample of people actually used in the study.

KEY TERMS

Bias A systematic distortion.

Generalisation Applying the findings of a particular study to the population.

Opportunity sample A sample of participants produced by selecting people who are most easily available at the time of the study.

Population The group of people that the researcher is interested in. The group of people from whom a sample is drawn. The group of people about whom generalisations can be made.

Random sample A sample of participants produced by using a random technique such that every member of the target population being tested has an equal chance of being selected.

Sampling The method used to select participants, such as random, opportunity and volunteer sampling, or to sample behaviours in an observation such as event or time sampling.

Stratified sample A sample of participants produced by identifying subgroups according to their frequency in the population. Participants are then selected randomly from the subgroups.

Systematic sample A sample obtained by selecting every nth person (where n is any number). This can be a random sample if the first person is selected using a random method; you then select every nth person after that.

Volunteer bias A form of sampling bias (distortion) because volunteer participants have special characteristics, such as usually being more highly motivated than randomly selected participants.

Volunteer sample A sample of participants that relies solely on volunteers to make up the sample. Also called a self-selected sample.

POPULATIONS AND SAMPLES

In any study the **population** is the group of individuals a researcher is interested in, for example 'babies in the Western world', 'people in the UK' or 'young people living in Bristol'. At the end of the study the researcher wants to be able to make a statement about this population of people.

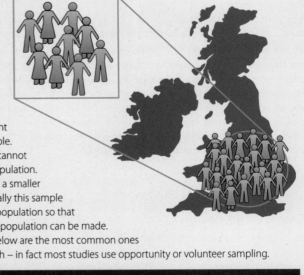

The researcher obviously cannot study all the people in the population. Instead the researcher selects a smaller group, called the sample. Ideally this sample will be representative of the population so that **generalisations** about the population can be made.

The sampling methods below are the most common ones used in psychological research – in fact most studies use opportunity or volunteer sampling.

Sampling method	Strengths	Limitations
Opportunity sample Recruit those people who are most convenient or most available, for example people walking by you in the street or students at your school.	The easiest method because you just use the first suitable participants you can find, which means it takes less time to locate your sample than if using one of the other techniques.	Inevitably biased because the sample is drawn from a small part of the population. For example, if you selected your sample from people walking around the centre of a town on a Monday morning then it would be unlikely to include professional people (because they are at work) or people from rural areas.
Random sample See 'random techniques' on facing page.	Unbiased; all members of the target population have an equal chance of selection.	Need to have a list of all members of the population and then contact all of those selected, which may take some time.
Stratified sample Subgroups (or strata) within a population are identified (e.g. boys and girls, or age groups: 10–12 years, 13–15, etc.). Participants are obtained from each of the strata in proportion to their occurrence in the population. Selection from the strata is done using a random technique.	Likely to be more representative than other methods because there is a proportional and randomly selected representation of subgroups.	Very time consuming to identify subgroups, then randomly select participants and contact them.
Systematic sample Use a predetermined system to select participants, such as selecting every nth person from a phonebook (where n = any number). The numerical interval is applied consistently.	Unbiased as participants are selected using an objective system.	Not truly unbiased/random unless you select a number using a random method and start with this person, and then select every nth person.
Volunteer sample Advertise in a newspaper or on a noticeboard or on the internet.	Gives access to a variety of participants (e.g. all the people who read a particular newspaper) which may make the sample more representative and less biased.	Sample is biased in other ways because participants are likely to be more highly motivated and/or with extra time on their hands. They might be more highly motivated to be helpful, or more broke and needing the money offered for participation. This results in a **volunteer bias**.

*A sampling method is about how participants are identified, NOT about who eventually takes part. Whatever the sampling method, it may be that some participants refuse to take part, which then leaves the researcher with a **biased** sample – a sample of only those who are willing participants.*

However, this doesn't apply in most field experiments – when participants aren't aware they are being studied, they can't refuse.

Random techniques

People tend to use the word 'random' to mean 'whatever comes into my head'. In science the word random has a very specific meaning; it means that each item in a population has an equal chance of being selected. There are various random techniques that are used to obtain a random sample (or also to achieve random allocation of participants to groups).

The lottery method

The easiest way to obtain a random selection is to draw numbers or names 'out of a hat'. This is sometimes called the lottery method. There are three important steps:

1. Obtain a list of all the people in the population. This may simply be the names of all the people in your school.
2. Put all the names in a lottery barrel or hat.
3. Select the number of names required.

If a researcher is using this method for random allocation of participants to groups then they might put the first 10 names drawn in group A and the second 10 names in group B.

Random number table

An alternative random technique is to use a printed table of random numbers (see example below of numbers from a much larger table).

1. This time every member of the population is given a number.
2. The starting position in the table is determined blindly by placing your finger anywhere.
3. If your population is less than 100 you only need two digit numbers so read the table two digits at a time. Using the table below you would select person 19, 58, 93 and so on. If your population consists of only 80 people then you would ignore number 93 and carry on.

19589 36938 38006 34802 44415 89017 02094 15980 74323 99294
97821 28797 35870 41210 25188 73254 02499 88208 47673 02552
11356 38059 57949 98279 24174 99607 73308 25646 68631 66235
20306 84653 18169 91062 98943

Random number generators

Calculators have functions that generate random numbers as do computers and apps on phones.

1. Number every member of the population.
2. Using, for example, Microsoft Excel type =RAND(100) to get a random number between 1 and 100.

Insider tip...

Mathematical skills
About 10% of your exam questions (at AS or A Level) will relate to mathematical concepts. There is a full list of these on page 210. The list includes the principles of sampling as applied to scientific data, for example explaining how a random or stratified sample could be obtained from a population.

Bias

Bias means 'distorted' in some way. You will come across lots of biases in psychological research: experimenter bias, interviewer bias, observer bias, social desirability bias and two that relate to sampling – sample bias and volunteer bias.

A sample bias describes the fact that, even though all sampling methods aim to produce a representative sample, they are inevitably biased or distorted. For example, an opportunity sample differs from the population because it only represents one particular group of people – the people who happen to be easily available to the researcher.

A volunteer bias describes the fact that people who volunteer to take part in research are likely to be different to other members of the population and this distorts or biases the data they produce.

▲ It may look like a fishbowl but it is actually a piece of scientific equipment used to select a random sample.

🐾 APPLY YOUR KNOWLEDGE

Identify the sampling method in each of the studies below and in each case identify **one** strength of using that sampling method for that study. Each question is worth 3 marks.

1. A researcher wishes to study memory in children aged between five and 11. He contacts the headmaster of his local primary school and arranges to test the children in the school.
2. A study on sleep habits identifies various subgroups in the population and then randomly selects members from each subgroup.
3. A university department conducts a study of mobile phone use in adolescents, using a questionnaire. The questionnaire is given to a group of students in a local comprehensive school. The sample is selected by placing all the students' names in a container and drawing out 50 names.
4. A class of psychology students conducts a study on memory. They put up a notice in the sixth-form common room asking for participants who have an hour to spare.
5. A researcher studied IQ in primary school children by selecting the first five names in each class register for every school he visited.

CAN YOU?　No. 7.8

1. Explain the difference between a population and a sample. (3 marks)
2. Identify **one** sampling method used in psychological research and explain how a sample would be obtained using this method. (3 marks)
3. Briefly explain how bias is a problem in opportunity sampling. (2 marks)
4. Briefly explain what is meant by 'generalisation'. (2 marks)
5. Give **one** limitation of using volunteer sampling. (2 marks)

Ethical issues

What is an *issue*? It is a conflict between two points of view. In psychology, an ethical issue is a conflict between:

1. what the researcher needs to do in order to conduct useful and meaningful research, and
2. the rights of participants.

Ethical issues are conflicts about what is acceptable. Everyone conducting psychological research, including psychology students, is expected to be aware of their responsibility to ensure participants are treated in an ethically appropriate manner. Whenever you conduct any research you must ensure that you deal properly with all ethical issues.

The BPS

Ethics are standards that concern any group of professional people – solicitors, doctors and teachers all have documents advising what is expected of them in terms of right and wrong in their jobs. These are sometimes referred to as codes of ethics.

Psychologists in the UK are advised by the British Psychological Society (BPS). In the US there is the American Psychological Association (APA), in Canada the Canadian Psychological Association (CPA), and so on.

The most recent *Code of Ethics and Conduct* (BPS, 2009) identifies four principles:

1. *Respect* for the dignity and worth of all persons. This includes standards of **privacy** and confidentiality and **informed consent**. Intentional deception (lack of informed consent) is only acceptable when it is necessary to protect the integrity of research and when the deception is disclosed to participants at the earliest opportunity. One way to judge acceptability is to consider whether participants are likely to object or show unease when debriefed. Participants should be aware of the right to withdraw from the research at any time.
2. *Competence* – psychologists should maintain high standards in their professional work.
3. *Responsibility* – psychologists have a responsibility to their clients, to the general public and to the science of psychology. This includes protecting participants from physical and psychological harm as well as debriefing at the conclusion of their participation.
4. *Integrity* – psychologists should be honest and accurate. This includes reporting the findings of any research accurately and acknowledging any potential limitations. It also includes bringing instances of misconduct by other psychologists to the attention of the BPS.

ETHICAL ISSUES

Informed consent

From the researcher's point of view informed consent means revealing the true aims of the study – or at least telling participants what is actually going to happen. However, revealing the details might cause participants to guess the aims of a study. For example, a psychologist might want to investigate whether people obey a male teacher more than a female teacher. If the participants are told the aim of this experiment before the study takes place, it might change the way they behave – they might try to be equally obedient to both. Researchers therefore may not always want to reveal the true aims or even the full details of what is going to happen.

From the participant's point of view they should be told what they will be required to do in the study so that they can make an informed decision about whether they wish to participate. This is a basic human right, established during the Nuremberg war trials: in the Second World War Nazi doctors conducted various experiments on prisoners without their consent and the war trials afterwards decided that consent should be a right for participants involved in any study.

Even if researchers have sought and obtained informed consent, that does not guarantee that participants really do understand what they have let themselves in for. Epstein and Lasagna (1969) found that only a third of participants volunteering for an experiment really understood what they had agreed to take part in.

Another problem is the requirement for the researcher to point out any likely benefits or risks of participation. Researchers are not always able to accurately predict the risks or benefits of taking part in a study.

Deception

From the researcher's point of view as we have just seen, it can be necessary to deceive participants about the true aims of a study, otherwise participants might alter their behaviour and the study could be meaningless. A distinction, however, should be made between withholding some of the details of the research aims (reasonably acceptable) and deliberately providing false information (less acceptable).

From the participant's point of view deception is unethical – the researcher should not deceive anyone without good cause. Perhaps more importantly, deception prevents participants being able to give informed consent. They may agree to participate without really knowing what they have let themselves in for and they might be quite distressed by the experience.

Deception can also lead people to see psychologists as untrustworthy. It might further mean that a participant may not want to take part in psychological research in the future.

Diana Baumrind (1985) argued that deception is morally wrong on the basis of three generally accepted ethical rules in Western society: the right of informed consent, the obligation of researchers to protect the welfare of the participant, and the responsibility of researchers to be trustworthy. However, others point out that sometimes deception is relatively harmless, for example a participant may have little reason to refuse to take part in a memory study (no distress, quick experiment) and therefore the deception seems less objectionable.

KEY TERMS

Confidentiality Concerns the communication of personal information from one person to another, and the trust that the information will be protected.

Deception A participant is not told the true aims of a study (e.g. what participation will involve) and thus cannot give truly informed consent.

Informed consent Participants must be given comprehensive information concerning the nature and purpose of the research and their role in it, in order that they can make an informed decision about whether to participate.

Privacy A person's right to control the flow of information about themselves.

Protection from harm During a research study, participants should not experience negative physical or psychological effects, such as physical injury, lowered self-esteem or embarrassment.

Right to withdraw Participants can stop participating in a study if they are uncomfortable in any way. This is especially important in cases where it was not possible to give fully informed consent. Participants should also have the right to refuse permission for the researcher to use any data they produced.

The right to withdraw

From the researcher's point of view if participants do leave during the study this will bias the results because the participants who have stayed are likely to be more obedient, or they might be more hardy – leading to a biased sample.

From the participant's point of view the **right to withdraw** from a study is important. If a participant begins to feel uncomfortable or distressed they should be able to withdraw. This is especially important if a participant has been deceived about the aims and/or procedures. However, even if a participant has been fully informed, the actual experience of taking part may turn out to be rather different, so they should be able to withdraw.

Sometimes the right to withdraw is compromised by payment of participants or some other reward (psychology students are often given university credits for taking part in research). In such cases participants may feel less able to withdraw.

Protection from physical and psychological harm

From the researcher's point of view studying some of the more important questions in psychology may involve a degree of distress to participants. It is also difficult to predict the outcome of certain procedures (such as in the Stanford Prison Experiment; see page 22); therefore it is difficult to guarantee **protection from harm**.

From the participant's point of view nothing should happen to them during a study that causes harm. There are many ways harm can be caused to participants, some physical (e.g. getting them to smoke, or drink coffee excessively) and some psychological (e.g. making them feel inadequate, or embarrassing them). It is considered acceptable if the risk of harm is no greater than a participant would be likely to experience in ordinary life, and if participants are in the same state after a study as they were before, unless they have given their informed consent to be treated otherwise.

Confidentiality

From the researcher's point of view it may be difficult to protect **confidentiality** because the researcher wishes to publish the findings. A researcher may guarantee anonymity (neither the researcher or anyone else is able to connect data obtained with any specific participant) but even then it may be obvious who has been involved in a study. For example, knowing that a study of children in hospital was conducted on the Isle of Wight could permit some people to be able to identify participants because the target group has been narrowed down.

From the participant's point of view the Data Protection Act makes confidentiality a legal right. It is only acceptable for personal data to be recorded if the data are not made available in a form that identifies the participants.

Privacy

From the researcher's point of view it may be difficult to avoid invasion of privacy when studying participants without their awareness, for example in a field experiment.

From the participant's point of view people do not expect to be observed by others in certain situations, for example when in the privacy of their own homes, while they might expect this when sitting on a park bench in public.

CAN YOU?   No. 7.9

1. One ethical issue is 'protection from harm'. Explain situations where apparent harm might be considered acceptable. (4 marks)
2. Identify **one** other ethical issue in psychological research and explain why it is an issue. (3 marks)
3. Discuss the role of the British Psychological Society's code of ethics. (8 marks)
4. Discuss ethical issues in the design and conduct of psychological studies. Refer to examples of studies in your answer. (12 marks AS, 16 marks A)

Confidentiality and privacy – what's the difference?

The words 'confidentiality' and 'privacy' are sometimes used interchangeably, but there is a distinction between them. Confidentiality concerns the communication of personal information from one person to another, and the trust that this information will then be protected. Privacy refers to a zone of inaccessibility of mind or body, and the trust that this will not be 'invaded'. In other words, we have a right of privacy. If this is invaded, confidentiality should be respected.

▲ Middlemist *et al.* conducted a field experiment in a men's urinal. There were three conditions: a confederate stood either immediately next to a participant, one urinal away, or there was no confederate. An observer recorded the onset of micturation times (how long participants took before they started to urinate as an indication of how comfortable the participant felt). Some psychologists regard this as an important study of personal space.

🐾 APPLY YOUR KNOWLEDGE

Ethical issues are *issues* because there are no easy answers. On the right are descriptions of various studies. When considering them it might be useful to discuss your thoughts in small groups and then present your views to the class. In each study:

1. Identify any ethical issues raised in the study. (2 marks)
2. Consider to what extent they are acceptable from the researcher's point of view. (2 marks)
3. Consider to what extent they are acceptable from the participants' point of view. (2 marks)
4. Decide whether you think the study was ethically acceptable, or not, giving your reasons. (2 marks)
5. Suggest what you think the researcher might have done to make the study more ethically acceptable. (3 marks)

Study A – In the Stanford Prison Experiment (see page 22) the researchers took great care to gain informed consent. However, the participants did not know the amount of psychological distress that would be caused by participating.

Study B – Craik and Lockhart (see page 47) conducted a study on memory. The participants were not informed of the true aims of the study (to compare deep with shallow processing) and were not told they would have to recall the words.

Study C – Middlemist *et al.* (1976) investigated personal space (see above).

Study D – Piliavin *et al.* (1969) investigated the behaviour of bystanders in an emergency situation to see how quickly they would offer help to someone (a confederate) who collapsed on a New York subway train. The confederate either acted as if he was drunk or as if he was disabled. Observers recorded how long it took for anyone to offer help. There was no opportunity to debrief participants.

Study E – Orne (1962) observed that people behave in quite unusual ways if they think they are taking part in a psychology experiment. For example, he asked participants to add up columns of numbers on a sheet of paper and then tear the paper up and repeat this again. Some were willing to continue the task for over six hours!

Dealing with ethical issues

Embedded in any discussion of ethical issues (on the previous spread) are ways of dealing with these issues. For example, the issue of informed consent is dealt with by asking participants to give their informed consent; the issue of protection from harm is dealt with by ensuring that people are in the same state after a study as they were before unless they have consented. The BPS code of practice identifies issues and at the same time suggests how these issues are dealt with. Therefore there are some overlaps between the previous spread and this one.

The most obvious way of dealing with ethical issues is through the use of codes of practice (guidelines) produced by a professional organisation. Psychologists, like other scientists, have other ways of dealing with ethical issues such as the use of ethics committees, the consideration of costs and benefits and punishment.

Insider tip...

Issues versus guidelines
Issues are not the same as guidelines even though informed consent is both an issue and a guideline. An issue is a conflict; a guideline is a means of resolving this conflict.

Note that debriefing is not an issue, it is a way of dealing with ethical issues such as deception, psychological harm and lack of informed consent.

STRATEGIES TO DEAL WITH ETHICAL ISSUES

Ethical guidelines (code of conduct)

The BPS regularly updates its **ethical guidelines (code of conduct)**. The current version is the 'Code of Ethics and Conduct' (BPS, 2009); see below. The intention of such guidelines is to tell psychologists which behaviours are not acceptable and to give guidance on how to deal with ethical dilemmas.

Cost-benefit analysis

In a **cost-benefit analysis** we judge the costs of doing the research against the benefits. The costs and benefits may be judged from a participant's point of view, where we might list distress and loss of time versus payment for participation and a feeling of having contributed to scientific research.

Alternatively we can judge costs and benefits in terms of society at large and then can consider the value in improving people's lives versus the possibility that individuals may be harmed in the process.

We can also judge costs/benefits in terms of the group to which an individual belongs – when research is done to investigate cultural differences, the research may not harm the individual but the findings may lead to biased treatment of the individual's cultural group (for good or bad).

▲ Psychologists who behave unethically are not sent to prison – it is not a criminal offence. However, they may be barred from psychological research or practice, which affects their livelihood.

Ethics committees

Most institutions where research takes place have an **ethics committee** which must approve any study before it begins. The committee looks at all possible ethical issues raised in any research proposal and at how the researcher suggests that the issues will be dealt with, weighing up the benefits of the research against the possible costs to the participants. Members of the committee often include lay people as well as experts in the field.

Punishment

If a psychologist does behave in an unethical manner, such as conducting unacceptable research, then the BPS reviews the research and may decide to bar the person from practising as a psychologist. It is not a legal matter (the psychologist won't be sent to prison).

EVALUATION/DISCUSSION

Ethical guidelines

Strengths
- The 'rules and sanctions' approach of BPS and APA ethical guidelines has strengths in terms of the clarity it offers.

Limitations
- The BPS/APA guidelines are inevitably rather general because of the virtual impossibility of covering every conceivable situation that a researcher may encounter.
- The approach tends to close off discussions about what is right and wrong because the answers are provided.
- Guidelines also absolve the individual researcher of any responsibility because the researcher can simply say, 'I followed the guidelines so my research is acceptable'. The Canadians take a slightly different approach – they present a series of hypothetical dilemmas for psychologists to discuss.

The strength of the Canadian approach is that it stimulates debate, encouraging psychologists to engage deeply with ethical issues rather than just following rules.

Cost-benefit analysis

Limitations
- The problem with a cost-benefit analysis is that it is difficult, if not impossible, to predict both costs and benefits prior to conducting a study. It is difficult to assess costs and benefits even after conducting a study. How are costs and benefits quantified? How much does personal distress cost?
- Diana Baumrind (1959) also argued that the cost-benefit approach could be said to legitimise unethical practices. For example, it suggests that deception and harm *are* acceptable in many situations *provided* the benefits are high enough.

This means that the cost-benefit approach solves nothing because you simply exchange one set of dilemmas (the ethical issues) for another.

The BPS *Code of ethics and conduct*

The BPS code of ethics identifies ethical issues (see previous spread) but also relates to conduct.

On informed consent

Failure to make full disclosure prior to obtaining informed consent requires additional safeguards to protect the welfare and dignity of the participants.

Research with children (under age 16), or with participants who have impairments that limit understanding and/or communication, to the extent that they are unable to give their consent, requires special safe-guarding procedures.

On deception

The central principle is the reaction of participants when deception is revealed; if this leads to discomfort, anger or objections from participants then the deception is inappropriate.

On protection from harm

If harm, unusual discomfort or other negative consequences for the individual's future life might occur, the investigator must obtain the disinterested approval of independent advisors, inform the participants, and obtain real, informed consent from each of them.

TRY THIS

One way to become more expert in answering questions in this area is to get lots of practice. You could, of course, comb through all the sample questions relating to ethical issues (and their resolution), or alternatively you could set up your own ethics committee and start reviewing a few research scenarios.

Start by dividing your class into groups. Each group should devise a study, the procedures of which raises one of the ethical issues on the previous spread, and which would make an ethics committee have to think about whether such a study would be acceptable. The group should also identify how they would deal with the ethical issue in question.

Then, each group should present their proposal to an ethics committee, role-played by members of your class. The ethics committee will consider whether the way in which the group has proposed dealing with the ethical issue is appropriate, and then suggest improvements that would make the study more ethically acceptable.

Try this until everyone has had the chance to have designed a study *and* been on the ethics committee. After this exercise, your 'dealing with ethical issues' skills will be more finely honed.

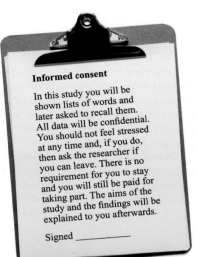

Informed consent

In this study you will be shown lists of words and later asked to recall them. All data will be confidential. You should not feel stressed at any time and, if you do, then ask the researcher if you can leave. There is no requirement for you to stay and you will still be paid for taking part. The aims of the study and the findings will be explained to you afterwards.

Signed _____

▲ Participants are asked to sign an informed consent form to indicate they have been informed and are freely consenting to take part.

DEALING WITH SPECIFIC ETHICAL ISSUES

Ethical issue	How to deal with it	Limitations
Informed consent	• Participants are asked to formally indicate their agreement to participate by, for example, signing a document which contains comprehensive information concerning the nature and purpose of the research and their role in it. • An alternative is to gain **presumptive consent**. • Researchers must also offer the right to withdraw.	• If a participant is given full information about a study this may invalidate the purpose of the study. • Even if researchers have obtained informed consent, that does not guarantee that participants really do understand what they have let themselves in for. • The problem with presumptive consent is what people expect that they will or will not mind can be different from actually experiencing it.
Deception	• The need for deception should be approved by an ethics committee, weighing up benefits (of the study) against costs (to participants). • Participants should be fully **debriefed** after the study. This involves informing them of the true nature of the study. Participants should be offered the opportunity to discuss any concerns they may have and to withhold their data from the study – a form of retrospective informed consent.	• Cost-benefit decisions are flawed because they involve subjective judgements, and the costs and/or benefits are not always apparent until after the study. • Debriefing can't turn the clock back – a participant may still feel embarrassed or have lowered self-esteem.
The right to withdraw	• Participants should be informed at the beginning of a study that they have the right to withdraw.	• Participants may feel they shouldn't withdraw because it will spoil the study. • In many studies participants are paid or rewarded in some way, and may not feel able to withdraw.
Protection from harm	• Avoid any risks greater than experienced in everyday life. • Stop the study if harm is suspected.	• Harm may not be apparent at the time of the study and only judged later with hindsight.
Confidentiality	• Researchers should not record the names of any participants. • They should use numbers or false names to represent individual participants.	• It is sometimes possible to work out who the participants were using information that has been provided, for example the geographical location of a school. In practice, therefore, confidentiality may not be fully possible.
Privacy	• Do not study anyone without their informed consent unless it is in a public place and public behaviour (e.g. it would exclude couples' intimate moments in a park).	• There is no universal agreement about what constitutes a public place.

KEY TERMS

Cost-benefit analysis A systematic approach to estimating the negatives and positives of any research.

Debriefing A post-research interview designed to inform participants of the true nature of the study and to restore them to the state they were in at the start of the study. It may also be used to gain useful feedback about the procedures in the study. Debriefing is not an ethical issue; it is a means of dealing with ethical issues.

Ethical guidelines (code of conduct) A set of principles designed to help professionals behave honestly and with integrity.

Ethics committee A group of people within a research institution that must approve a study before it begins.

Presumptive consent A method of dealing with lack of informed consent or deception, by asking a group of people who are similar to the participants whether they would agree to take part in a study. If this group of people consents to the procedures in the proposed study, it is *presumed* that the real participants would also have agreed.

🐾 APPLY YOUR KNOWLEDGE

Re-examine the five studies on the previous spread and consider how a researcher might deal with the ethical issues in each case. (3 marks each)

CAN YOU? No. 7.10

1. Describe **one** way that psychologists have dealt with ethical issues in psychological research. (3 marks)
2. Discuss how psychologists deal with ethical issues in psychological research. Refer to examples of research studies in your answer. (12 marks AS, 16 marks A)

Observational techniques

In an observational study a researcher watches or listens to participants engaging in whatever behaviour is being studied. The observations are recorded. On this spread we will look at the main types of observation and, on the next spread, we will look at issues related to the design of observational studies.

One important aspect of observations worthy of note is that they are often used in an experiment as a means of measuring the dependent variable. Therefore observations are less of a research method and more of a technique to use in conjunction with other research methods.

Observation with Bobo

In the study by Bandura *et al.* (see page 128) the behaviour of the children was observed at the end to determine how aggressive they were (the dependent variable). The toys were arranged in a fixed order for each child. The experimenter sat quietly in the corner working while the child played for 20 minutes. The child was observed through a one-way mirror by another researcher. A second observer was present for half of the participants and recorded his observations independently. This enabled **inter-observer reliability** to be calculated (see below).

The observers did not know which condition the child had participated in (except if the child had been in one of the sessions with the male model who was one of the observers). The observers recorded what the child was doing every five seconds (providing 240 observations). Responses were recorded in the following categories and produced an 'aggression score' for each child:

Imitative aggression responses:
- *Physical*: any specific acts imitated.
- *Verbal aggression*: any phrases imitated.
- *Non-aggressive verbal responses*: Such as saying 'He keeps coming back for more'.

Partially imitative responses:
- *Mallet aggression*: uses mallet on toys other than Bobo.
- *Sits on Bobo doll* but not aggressively.

Non-imitative aggressive responses:
- Punches Bobo doll.
- *Non-imitative physical and verbal aggression*: aggressive acts directed at toys other than Bobo, saying hostile things not said by the model.
- Aggressive gun play.

Inter-observer reliability

Observations should be consistent (i.e. reliable), which means that ideally two observers should produce the same record. The extent to which two (or more) observers agree is called inter-observer reliability. A general rule is that if there is more than 80% agreement on the observations, the data have high inter-observer reliability.

TYPES OF OBSERVATION

Naturalistic and controlled observation

In a **naturalistic observation**, behaviour is studied in a natural situation where *everything has been left as it is normally*. In other words the researcher does not interfere in any way with what is happening. Examples might include watching an infant playing in their normal (i.e. 'natural') environment. This might be a nursery school if that is an environment that the infant is used to. Observing an animal in a zoo could be considered a naturalistic observation because the environment is normal to them.

In a **controlled observation**, some variables in the environment are regulated by the researcher, reducing the 'naturalness' of the environment and, most importantly, the naturalness of the behaviour being studied. Participants are likely to know they are being studied and the study may be conducted in a laboratory.

A controlled observation allows the researcher to investigate the effects of certain things on behaviour, for example in Bandura's study of social learning theory (see left) various toys were present to see how the children would interact with these (note that this study was an experiment and observation was used to assess the dependent variable). Such 'things' are not the same as independent variables unless another group of participants had a different set of toys as a comparison.

Overt and covert observation

In both naturalistic and controlled observations the person being observed may be aware of the observations. This is called an **overt observation**. Since this is likely to have an effect on the naturalness of participants' behaviour, observers try to be as unobtrusive as possible. They may even use one-way mirrors so they are hidden from view – but the study would still be classed as overt if participants knew beforehand that they were being observed.

In a **covert observation** participants do not have any knowledge of being observed, at least not before or during the study. They may be informed afterwards.

Participant and non-participant observation

In most cases an observer is merely watching (or listening to) the behaviour of others and acts as a **non-participant**. The observer observes from a distance and does not interact with the people being observed.

The alternative is **participant observation**. In this case the observer is part of the group being observed. In both covert and overt observations the observer may be a participant, unbeknown to the people being observed.

KEY TERMS

Controlled observation A form of investigation in which behaviour is observed but under conditions where certain variables have been organised by the researcher.

Covert observations Observing people without their knowledge. Knowing that behaviour is being observed is likely to alter a participant's behaviour.

Inter-observer reliability The extent to which there is agreement between two or more observers involved in observations of a behaviour.

Naturalistic observation An observation carried out in an everyday setting, in which the investigator does not interfere in any way but merely observes the behaviour(s) in question.

Non-participant observation The observer is separate from the people being observed.

Observer bias Observers' expectations affect what they see or hear. This reduces the validity of the observations.

Overt observation Observational studies where participants are aware that their behaviour is being studied.

Participant observation Observations made by someone who is also participating in the activity being observed, which may affect their objectivity.

Insider tip...

Students often get confused between a naturalistic observation and a natural experiment – in any experiment there is an independent and dependent variable. Naturalistic observations do not have these variables but might be used in an experiment as a means of measuring the dependent variable.

Observational studies in general

Strengths

- Observational studies have high validity: they record what people actually do rather than what they *say* they do.
- Observations may capture spontaneous and unexpected behaviour.
- Observations are often used as a way to measure the DV in an experiment and therefore are a fundamental method of gathering data.

Limitations

- There is the serious issue of **observer bias**. It is difficult to be objective when making observations because what people observe is distorted by their expectations of what is likely or what they would hope to see. Using more than one observer may reduce the risk of observer bias affecting the validity of the observations.
- Only observable behaviour is recorded and not information about what people think or feel.

Therefore data from observations must be interpreted carefully.

Naturalistic and controlled observation

Strengths

- Naturalistic observation gives a realistic picture of spontaneous behaviour. Therefore, it is likely to be high in ecological validity (though this may be less so if participants know they are being observed).
- In a controlled observation an observer can focus on particular aspects of behaviour.

Limitations

- In a naturalistic observation there is little control of all the other things that are happening, which may mean that something unknown to the observer may account for the behaviour observed.
- In a controlled observation the control comes at the cost of the environment feeling unnatural and participants' behaviour also being less natural as a result.

Therefore there is a trade-off between ecological validity and control.

Overt and covert observation

Strengths

- In covert observations participants are unaware of being observed and thus their behaviour is more natural.

Limitations

- For overt observations participants are aware of being studied which may affect the naturalness of their behaviour – they may respond to demand characteristics.
- In covert observation, there are important ethical issues – it is acceptable to observe people in a public place as long as the behaviours being observed are not private ones, such as kissing your boyfriend.
- Covertly observed participants by definition cannot give consent, although it may be possible to seek retrospective consent.

Both methods have contrasting strengths and limitations.

Participant and non-participant observation

Strengths

- Participant observation may provide special insights into behaviour from the 'inside' that may not otherwise be gained.
- In non-participant observation observers are likely to be more objective because they are not part of the group being observed.

Limitations

- Participant observation is more likely to be overt and thus have issues of participant awareness.
- Non-participant observation is more likely to be covert and then there are ethical issues, as discussed above.

Researchers therefore need to weigh up these strengths and limitations when designing observational research.

APPLY YOUR KNOWLEDGE

In each of the studies described below, decide whether the study involved observations that were: (a) naturalistic or controlled (1 mark); (b) overt or covert (1 mark); (c) participant or non-participant (1 mark); or (d) ethically acceptable (explain your answer) (2 marks).

Study A Mary Ainsworth studied infant attachment patterns using the Strange Situation (see page 80). Infants and a caregiver were placed in a room with a pre-determined and fixed set of toys. They were observed through a one-way mirror so that the infants wouldn't be disturbed by the observer's presence. Caregivers gave informed consent.

Study B Mary Ainsworth (1967) also studied 26 mothers and their infants who lived in six villages in Uganda. She observed the mothers in their own homes interacting as they normally would with their infants.

Study C One study observed boys and girls aged three to five years during their free-play periods at nursery school. The researchers classified activities as male, female or neutral and recorded how playmates responded. The researchers found that children generally reinforced peers for sex-appropriate play and were quick to criticise sex-inappropriate play (Lamb and Roopnarine, 1979).

Study D Festinger *et al.* (1956) recorded the behaviour of a religious cult expecting visitors from outer space (see below left).

Study E Middlemist *et al.* (1976) observed men's behaviour in a toilet; see page 195.

Study F Moore (1922) spent weeks walking round New York, writing down everything he heard and uncovering some interesting exchanges between people he observed.

Study G Rosenhan (1973) conducted a classic study on insanity. Sane individuals pretended to hear voices and were admitted to mental hospitals. While in hospital they noted down the behaviour of the staff in the institution and the patients.

Visitors from outer space

In the 1950s the social psychologist Leon Festinger read a newspaper report about a religious cult that claimed to be receiving messages from outer space. These messages predicted that the end of the world would take place on a certain date in the form of a great flood. The cult members were going to be rescued by a flying saucer so they all gathered with their leader, Mrs Keech. Festinger was intrigued to know how the cult members would respond when they found their beliefs were unfounded, especially as many of them had made their beliefs very public.

In order to observe this first-hand, Festinger and some co-workers posed as converts to the cause and were present on the eve of destruction. When it was apparent that there would be no flood, the group leader Mrs Keech said that their prayers had saved the city. Some cult members didn't believe this and left the cult, whereas others took this as proof of the cult's power (Festinger et al., 1956).

CAN YOU? No. 7.11

1. Briefly explain what is meant by 'participant observation'. (2 marks)
2. Explain the difference between a naturalistic observation and a controlled observation. (4 marks)
3. Identify and briefly explain **one** ethical issue related to covert observations. (3 marks)
4. Give **one** limitation and **one** strength of using non-participant observation as a method of collecting data. (2 marks + 2 marks)

Observational design

You learned on the previous spread that observational studies can be naturalistic or controlled – and can be overt/covert and participant/non-participant. There is a fourth dimension, which is structured or unstructured.

The key thing to understand is that naturalistic observations can be structured. This might appear to be at odds with the definition that 'everything is free to vary' in a naturalistic observation – but this description applies to the environment that the participant is in; the way that the observations are *recorded* can be very structured in the ways described on this spread.

TRY THIS

Try this to understand how difficult observation actually is. Work with a partner and take it in turns to observe each other. One of you will be Person A and the other will be Person B.
- Person A should have a difficult task to do (e.g. answering one set of questions in this book).
- Person B should have a boring task to do (e.g. copying from a book).

Each person should spend five minutes on their task, while the other person observes them. The observer should note down everything their partner does.

KEY TERMS

Behavioural categories Dividing a target behaviour (such as stress or aggression) into a subset of specific and operationalised behaviours.

Event sampling An observational technique in which a count is kept of the number of times a certain behaviour (event) occurs.

Sampling The method used to select participants, such as random, opportunity and volunteer sampling, or to select behaviours in an observation such as event or time sampling.

Structured observation A researcher uses various systems to organise observations, such as behavioural categories and sampling procedures.

Time sampling An observational technique in which the observer records behaviours in a given time frame, e.g. noting what a target individual is doing every 15 seconds or 20 seconds or 1 minute. The observer may select one or more behavioural categories to tick at this time interval.

Insider tip…

Don't get confused about sampling procedures here and those discussed on page 192. It's really the same thing – using a method to select what to focus on. In the case of sampling on page 192 we are selecting participants. Here we are selecting which behaviours to record.

UNSTRUCTURED AND STRUCTURED OBSERVATIONS

You might think that making observations is easy, but if you tried the activity on the left you should now realise it is difficult for two main reasons:
- It is difficult to work out what to record and what not to record.
- It is difficult to record everything that is happening.

Unstructured observations

The researcher records all relevant behaviour but has no system, as in the activity on the left. The most obvious problem with this is that there may be too much to record. Another problem is that the behaviours recorded will often be those which are most visible or eye-catching to the observer but these may not necessarily be the most important or relevant behaviours.

Researchers do sometimes use this approach in situations, for example, where research has not been conducted before as a kind of pilot study to see what behaviours might be recorded using a structured system.

Structured observations

Observational techniques, like all research techniques, aim to be objective and rigorous. For this reason it is preferable to use **structured observations**, i.e. various 'systems' to organise observations. The two main ways to structure observations are using **behavioural categories** and **sampling** procedures.

Behavioural categories

One of the hardest aspects of the observational method is deciding how different behaviours should be categorised. This is because our perception of behaviour is often seamless; when we watch somebody perform a particular action we see a continuous stream of action rather than a series of separate behavioural components.

In order to conduct systematic observations, a researcher needs to break up this stream of behaviour into different behavioural categories. What is needed is operationalisation – breaking the behaviour being studied into a set of components. For example, when observing infant behaviour, we can have a list including things like smiling, crying and sleeping, etc., or, when observing facial expressions, including different combinations of mouth, cheeks, eyebrows, etc., such as those shown on the facing page.

Behavioural categories should:
- be *objective*: the observer should not have to make inferences about the behaviour, but should just record explicit actions.
- cover *all possible component behaviours* and avoid a 'waste basket' category.
- be *mutually exclusive*, meaning that you should not have to mark two categories at one time.

Sampling procedures

When conducting an unstructured observation the observer should record every instance of the behaviour in as much detail as possible. This is useful if the behaviours of interest do not occur very often. However, in many situations, continuous observation is not possible because there would be too much data to record; therefore there must be a systematic method of sampling observations:
- **Event sampling** Counting the number of times a certain behaviour (event) occurs in a target individual or individuals, for example counting how many times a person smiles in a 10-minute period.
- **Time sampling** Recording behaviours in a given time frame. For example, noting what a target individual is doing every 30 seconds or some other time interval. At that time the observer may tick one or more categories from a checklist.

TRY THIS

At the top of the page we suggested you tried to observe your partner while they performed a difficult or easy task. Redo your observations of your partner but this time use time and event sampling.

Some examples

Secure attachment in pets

Topál *et al.* (1998) used the Strange Situation technique (see page 80) to explore the attachments between dogs and their owners. For 10,000 years dogs have been bred for certain traits, among them their willingness to become attached to their owners. This makes it quite likely that dogs and owners will behave like infants and caregivers. The presence of a caregiver (the owner) should reduce anxiety and increase willingness to explore in the dog.

In this study owners and their dogs went through the episodes of the Strange Situation. The owners were not informed of the aims of the study beforehand. Their behaviour was videotaped so that the behaviours could be analysed afterwards.

There were eight behavioural categories (see below). Two observers sampled the behaviour every 10 seconds, rating each category on a scale of 1 to 5 where 5 meant they were very confident about this observation.

The findings of the study were that dogs, like people, were either securely or insecurely attached.

▼ The list of behavioural categories used to assess dogs and their owners. Such a list is called a behaviour checklist or a coding system (because each behaviour is given a code to make it easier to record).

EXPO	exploration when with owner
EXPS	exploration when with stranger
PLYO	playing when with owner
PLYS	playing when with stranger
PASO	passive behaviours when with owner
PASS	passive behaviours when with stranger
CONTO	physical contact with the owner
CONTS	physical contact with the stranger
SBYO	standing by the door when with owner
SBYS	standing by the door when with stranger

Facial expressions

Paul Ekman and colleague (1978) have developed the coding system below to record non-verbal behaviours. This can be used to investigate, for example, what expressions are shown on a person's face when they are lying.

▼ The Facial Action Coding System (FACS) for observing facial expressions (Ekman and Friesen, 1978).

Code	Description	Code	Description
1	Inner brow raiser	26	Jaw drop
2	Outer brow raiser	27	Mouth stretch
4	Brow lowerer	28	Lip suck
5	Upper lid raiser	41	Lip droop
6	Cheek raiser	42	Slit
7	Lid tightener	43	Eyes closed
9	Nose wrinkler	44	Squint
10	Upper lip raiser	45	Blink
11	Nasolabial deepener	46	Wink
12	Lip corner puller	51	Head turn left
13	Cheek puffer	52	Head turn right
14	Dimpler	53	Head up
15	Lip corner depressor	54	Head down
16	Lower lip depressor	55	Head tilt left
17	Chin raiser	56	Head tilt right
18	Lip puckerer	57	Head forward
20	Lip stretcher	58	Head back
22	Lip funneler	61	Eyes turn left
23	Lip tightener	62	Eyes turn right
24	Lip presser	63	Eyes up
25	Lips part	64	Eyes down

▲ Outer brow raiser.

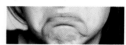

▲ Lip corner depressor.

You can see illustrations of all the other codes at www-2.cs.cmu.edu/afs/cs/project/face/www/facs.htm.

🐾 APPLY YOUR KNOWLEDGE

1. In each of the following observations state which sampling procedure would be most appropriate and explain how you would do it. (3 marks each)

   a. Recording instances of aggressive behaviour in children playing in a school playground.
   b. Vocalisations (words, sounds) made by young children.
   c. Compliance to controlled pedestrian crossings by pedestrians.
   d. Litter-dropping in a public park.
   e. Behaviour of dog owners when walking their dogs.

2. In the study of attachment behaviour in dogs (above):

   a. Identify the sampling procedure used. (1 mark)
   b. Explain why the behaviours were videotaped. (1 mark)
   c. Explain why two observers recorded behaviours. (1 mark)

3. A group of students decided to study student behaviour in the school library.

   a. Suggest **one or more** hypotheses that you might investigate. (2 marks)
   b. List **five** behavioural categories you might include in a behaviour checklist. (3 marks)
   c. Identify a suitable sampling procedure and explain how you would do it. (3 marks)
   d. How could you observe the students so that they were not aware that they were being observed? (2 marks)
   e. What ethical issues might be raised in this observational study? (2 marks)
   f. For each issue identified in your answer to (e), explain how you could deal with this issue and whether this would be acceptable. (3 marks)
   g. Explain in what way this study would be a naturalistic observation. (2 marks)
   h. Are the observations structured or unstructured? (1 mark)

CAN YOU? No. 7.12

1. Explain what is meant by 'time sampling'. Include an example in your answer. (3 marks)
2. Explain the difference between event sampling and time sampling. (3 marks)
3. Explain how behavioural categories are used in observational research. Use examples in your answer. (3 marks)

Self-report techniques

Psychologists aim to find out about behaviour. One way to do this is to conduct experiments. Another method is by observation – called a non-experimental method. Another non-experimental method or technique is to ask people questions about their experiences and/or beliefs. These are called self-report techniques because the person is reporting their own thoughts/feelings. This includes questionnaires and interviews. A **questionnaire** can be given in a written form or it can be delivered in real-time (face-to-face or on the telephone), in which case it is called an **interview**.

An example of using interviews

In Europe, a woman was near death from a rare type of cancer. There was one drug that the doctors thought might save her. It was a form of radium that a pharmacist in the same town had recently discovered. The drug was expensive to make but the pharmacist was charging 10 times what the drug cost him to make. He paid €400 for the radium and charged €4,000 for a small dose of it. The sick woman's husband, Heinz, went to everyone he knew to borrow the money, but he could only get together about €2,000. He told the pharmacist that his wife was dying and asked him to sell it cheaper or let him pay later. But the pharmacist said, 'No. I discovered the drug and I'm going to make money from it'. Heinz got desperate and broke into the man's store to steal the drug for his wife.

Lawrence Kohlberg (1978) used the scenario above to investigate moral views. He used a structured interview to elicit answers to the following:

- Should Heinz steal the drug? Why or why not?
- If the interviewee favours stealing, ask: 'If Heinz doesn't love his wife, should he steal the drug for her?' Why or why not?
- If the interviewee favours not stealing, ask: 'Does it make a difference whether or not he loves his wife?' Why or why not?
- Suppose the person dying is not his wife but a stranger. Should Heinz steal the drug for the stranger? Why or why not?

A study may consist solely of a questionnaire or interview but often these techniques are used as a means of measuring the dependent variable (DV). Consider these two examples:

The aims of a study may be to find out about smoking habits in young people. The researcher would design a questionnaire to collect data about what people do and why. In this case the whole study consists of a questionnaire. It is the research method.

On the other hand, the aims of a study might be to see if children who are exposed to an anti-smoking educational programme have different attitudes towards smoking than children not exposed to such a programme. The researcher would use a questionnaire to collect data about attitudes to smoking, but the analysis would involve a comparison between the two groups of children – an experimental study using a questionnaire as a research technique to measure the DV.

QUESTIONNAIRES AND INTERVIEWS

Questionnaires

A questionnaire is a set of written questions. It is designed to collect information about a topic or topics.

Questions permit a researcher to discover what people think and feel; a contrast to observations which rely on 'guessing' what people think and feel on the basis of how they behave. With a questionnaire you can ask people directly – whether they give you truthful answers is another matter.

Questionnaires can be an objective and scientific way of conducting research but this involves more than just thinking up some questions. Design is important, which is discussed on the next spread.

Questionnaires are always pre-determined, i.e. structured, whereas an interview can be structured or unstructured.

A structured interview

A **structured interview** has pre-determined questions; in other words it is essentially a questionnaire that is delivered face-to-face (or over the telephone) with no deviation from the original questions. It is conducted in real-time – the interviewer asks questions and the interviewee replies.

Unstructured interview

An **unstructured interview** has less structure! Basically this 'structure' refers to the pre-determined questions. In an unstructured interview new questions are developed during the course of the interview. The interviewer may begin with general aims and possibly a few pre-determined questions but subsequent questions develop on the basis of the answers that are given.

This is sometimes called a *clinical interview* because it is a bit like the kind of interview you might have with a doctor. He or she starts with some pre-determined questions but further questions are developed as a response to your answers.

KEY TERMS

Interview A research method or technique that involves a face-to-face, 'real-time' interaction with another individual and results in the collection of data.

Interviewer bias The effect of an interviewer's expectations, communicated unconsciously, on a respondent's behaviour.

Questionnaire Data are collected through the use of written questions.

Social desirability bias A distortion in the way people answer questions – they tend to answer questions in such a way that presents themselves in a better light.

Structured interview Any interview in which the questions are decided in advance.

Unstructured interview The interview starts out with some general aims and possibly some questions, and lets the interviewee's answers guide subsequent questions.

Self-report techniques

Strengths

- The key strength is that all self-report techniques allow access to what people think and feel, to their experiences and attitudes.

Limitations

- People may not supply truthful answers. It's not that people deliberately lie, but they may simply answer in a socially desirable way (called a **social desirability bias**). For example, if asked whether you are a leader or a follower, many people would prefer not to class themselves as a follower even if they are.
- People sometimes simply don't know what they think or feel, so they may make their answer up, and thus their answers lack validity.
- The sample of people used in any study using self-report may lack representativeness and thus the data collected cannot be generalised.

Despite these limitations, self-report techniques are an important way of gathering information about people's thoughts, attitudes and experiences.

Questionnaire

Strengths

- Once designed and tested, questionnaires can be distributed to large numbers of people relatively cheaply and quickly. This enables a researcher to collect data from a large sample of people.
- Respondents may be more willing to give personal information in a questionnaire than in an interview, where they may feel self-conscious and more cautious.

Limitations

- Questionnaires are only filled in by people who can read and write and have the time to fill them in. This means that the sample is biased.

Therefore, although questionnaires are a powerful way of gathering a large amount of information, issues of design, distribution and bias need to be thought through carefully.

Structured interview

Strengths

- The main strength of a structured interview (as well as a questionnaire) is that it can be easily repeated because the questions are standardised. This means answers from different people can be compared.
- This also means that they are easier to analyse than an unstructured interview because answers are more predictable.

Limitations

- Comparability may be a problem in a structured interview (but not a questionnaire) if the same interviewer behaves differently on different occasions or different interviewers behave differently (low reliability).
- A limitation of both structured and unstructured interviews is that the interviewer's expectations may influence the answers the interviewee gives (a form of investigator effect called **interviewer bias**).

The many benefits of structured interviews therefore depend on having skilled interviewers and avoiding interviewer bias as far as possible.

Unstructured interview

Strengths

- More detailed information can generally be obtained from each respondent than in a structured interview. This is because the interviewer tailors further questions to the specific responses.

Limitations

- Unstructured interviews require interviewers with more skill than a structured interview because the interviewer has to develop new questions on the spot. The requirement for well-trained interviewers makes unstructured interviews more expensive to produce compared with structured interviews.
- Such in-depth questions may be more likely to lack objectivity than predetermined ones because of their instantaneous nature, with no time for the interviewer to reflect on what to say.

Therefore, while unstructured interviews allow researchers to gain deeper insights into the respondent's feelings and thoughts, there are issues of objectivity and cost to consider.

 UPGRADE

'Can You?' questions 2 and 3 below share a common feature, i.e. they ask for the *difference* between two things. The general rule of these 'Explain **one** difference between X and Y' questions is for students to say something about X, say something about Y, and then draw another distinction between them.

So, for example, in a question that asks you to explain **one** difference between a questionnaire and an interview, you might say... '*A questionnaire is a set of written questions designed to collect information about a topic. An interview involves a face-to-face interaction with another individual*'. This tells us something about each, but as yet doesn't say anything about the difference between the two in order to gain the full 3 marks.

When contrasting a questionnaire and an interview (i.e. giving a difference between the two types of self-report technique), it is important to compare in terms of the same thing. For example, you could point out that... '*Questions are always predetermined (i.e. structured) in a questionnaire, whereas interviews can either be structured or unstructured, where new questions are developed during the course of the interview*'.

▲ Olly was sure that working with an attractive female interviewer wouldn't affect *his* behaviour.

🐾 APPLY YOUR KNOWLEDGE

1. A group of students wishes to study mobile phone use in people aged 14–18. Why might it be preferable to:
   a. Conduct an interview rather than a questionnaire? (2 marks)
   b. Conduct a questionnaire rather than an interview? (2 marks)
2. Imagine instead that the students wished to find out about drug taking. Answer the same questions a and b above. (2 marks each)
3. For each of the studies described in questions 1 and 2, suggest **two** ethical issues that should concern the students and suggest how they might deal with these. (2 marks + 2 marks)

CAN YOU? No. 7.13

1. Briefly explain what is meant by 'self-report techniques'. (2 marks)
2. Explain **one** difference between a questionnaire and an interview. (3 marks)
3. Explain **one** difference between a structured and an unstructured interview. (3 marks)
4. Give **one** limitation to using a questionnaire rather than a structured interview to collect data. (2 marks)

Self-report design

Questionnaires and interviews, like all methods and techniques used in psychological research, aim to be systematic and objective, i.e. a scientific tool. It is not simply a matter of asking participants a few questions – there are many design matters to consider. For example, there is the issue of leading questions, something you also have learned about in your study of eyewitness testimony (see page 56). The way a question is written may bias the response that is given, resulting in the collection of data that does not truly represent what a person actually thinks/feels.

"It's an internet survey asking if there are too many internet surveys."

KEY TERMS

Closed questions Questions that have a predetermined range of answers from which respondents select one. Tend to produce quantitative data – but, for example, Yes/No answers are qualitative. They then can be counted to produce quantitative data.

Open questions Questions that invite respondents to provide their own answers rather than select one of those provided. Tend to produce qualitative data.

Qualitative data Non-numerical data.

Quantitative data Data in numbers.

QUESTIONNAIRE CONSTRUCTION

Writing good questions

When writing questions there are three guiding principles:

1. **Clarity** Questions need to be written so that the reader (respondent) understands what is being asked. There should be no ambiguity. Something that is ambiguous has at least two possible meanings. For example 'Did you see the girl with the telescope?' could mean 'Did you see the girl when you were using the telescope?' or it could mean 'Did you see the girl who was using a telescope?'

   The use of double negatives reduces clarity. A double negative is when there are two negative words in one sentence, for example 'Are you against banning capital punishment?'

   A further issue is double-barrelled questions, for example asking 'Do you suffer from sickness and headaches?'

2. **Bias** Any bias in a question might lead the respondent to be more likely to give a particular answer (as in a leading question). The greatest problem is probably social desirability bias. Respondents prefer to give answers that make them look more attractive, nicer, more generous, etc. rather than being totally truthful.

3. **Analysis** Questions need to be written so that the answers are easy to analyse. If you ask 'What do you like most about your job?' or 'What makes you feel stressed at work?' you may get 50 different answers from 50 people. These are called **open questions**.

   Alternatively researchers can ask **closed questions** where the range of possible answers is fixed, such as listing five possible answers for respondents to choose from or asking a question with a yes/no/maybe answer. Such closed questions are easier to analyse but respondents may be forced to select answers that don't represent their real thoughts or behaviour.

Writing good questionnaires

A good questionnaire should contain good questions (above) but there are other things to consider as well:

- **Filler questions** It may help to include some irrelevant questions to distract the respondent from the main purpose of the survey. This may reduce demand characteristics (see page 190).
- **Sequence for the questions** It is best to start with easy ones, saving questions that might make someone feel anxious or defensive until the respondent has relaxed.
- **Sampling technique** i.e. how to select respondents. Questionnaire studies often use stratified sampling (see page 192).
- **Pilot study** The questions can be tested on a small group of people. This means the questions can later be refined in response to any difficulties encountered.

Examples of open questions

1 What factors contribute to making work stressful?
2 How do you feel when stressed?

Examples of closed questions

1 Which of the following makes you feel stressed? (You may tick as many answers as you like.)

☐ Noise at work   ☐ Lack of control
☐ Too much to do   ☐ Workmates
☐ No job satisfaction

2 How many hours a week do you work?

☐ 0 hours ☐ Between 1 and 10 hours
☐ Between 10 and 20 hours
☐ More than 20 hours

3 *Likert scale*

Work is stressful:
☐ Strongly agree ☐ Agree ☐ Not sure
☐ Disagree ☐ Strongly disagree

4 How much stress do you feel? (Circle the number that best describes how you feel.)

At work:
A lot of stress 5 4 3 2 1 No stress at all
At home:
A lot of stress 5 4 3 2 1 No stress at all
Travelling to work:
A lot of stress 5 4 3 2 1 No stress at all

5 Forced choice question

A The worst social sin is to be rude
B The worst social sin is to be a bore

Insider tip...

Don't make the mistake that many students make of thinking that open questions are only used in interviews and closed questions are only used in questionnaires – the consequence of thinking in this way is that, for example, when asked to give a limitation of a questionnaire, students give a limitation of a closed question which isn't correct unless you write 'One limitation of a questionnaire is that if closed questions are used.'

DESIGN OF INTERVIEWS

Many of the considerations on the facing page apply to interviews as well, for example seeking clarity in the questions asked and starting an interview with some general, easy questions to put the interviewer at ease.

Recording the interview

An interviewer may take notes throughout the interview to document answers but this is likely to interfere with their listening skills. It may also make the respondent feel a sense of evaluation because the interviewer may not write everything down and then the respondent feels that what they said was not valuable.

Alternatively interviews may be audio recorded or video recorded.

The effect of the interviewer

One of the strengths of conducting interviews rather than using a questionnaire is that the presence of an interviewer who is interested in the respondent's answers may increase the amount of information provided, even in an unstructured interview. This means that interviewers need to be aware of behaviours that demonstrate their 'interest'. This includes:

- **Non-verbal communication** Various behaviours such as sitting with arms crossed and frowning communicate disapproval and disinterest, whereas head nodding and leaning forward may encourage the respondent to speak.
- **Listening skills** An interviewer needs to know when and how to speak. For example they should not interrupt too often and when they do speak they should have a range of encouraging comments such as 'How interesting' to show they are listening.

Questioning skills in an unstructured interview

In an unstructured interview there are special skills to be learned about what kind of follow up questions should be asked. It is important to be aware of the questions already asked and avoid repeating them. It is also useful to avoid probing too much, for example after asking someone what an experience was like don't then say 'What was it really like?' It is also not helpful to ask 'Why?' too often. It is better to ask more focused questions – both for the interviewee and also, later, for the analysis of the answers.

EVALUATION/DISCUSSION

Open questions

Strengths

- Respondents can expand on their answers, which increases the amount and detail of information collected.
- Open questions can provide unexpected answers, thus allowing researchers to gain new insights into people's feelings and attitudes.

Limitations

- Most respondents may simply avoid giving lengthy complex answers; therefore, in practice, open questions may not actually provide detailed extra information.
- Open questions produce **qualitative data** (discussed on page 216), which are more difficult to summarise because there is likely to be a wide range of responses. This makes it harder to detect clear patterns and draw conclusions.

The benefits of open questions, in terms of detailed information gathered are therefore offset by difficulties detecting clear patterns.

Closed questions

Strengths

- Closed questions have a limited range of answers and produce **quantitative data**, which means the answers are easier to analyse using graphs and measures such as the mean.

Limitations

- Respondents may be forced to select answers that don't represent their real thoughts or behaviour. This means that the data collected lack validity.
- Participants may select 'don't know' or have a preference to answer yes (an acquiescence bias) and therefore the data collected are not informative.

The limitations of closed questions mean they are best used when straightforward, factual information is needed.

Psychological tests

A psychological test is a task or set of tasks that measures some aspect of human behaviour. For example:

- *IQ tests* measure intelligence.
- *Personality tests* assess personality type.
- *Mood scales* measure emotional state.
- *Attitude scales* report on people's feelings and opinions.
- *Aptitude scales* measures, for example, artistic or numerical ability.

Strictly speaking, psychological tests and attitude scales are not self-report techniques but they do commonly involve filling in a questionnaire, so many of the issues discussed on this and the previous spread are relevant.

Ceiling and floor effects

Test scores may not be accurate because of a ceiling effect. If all the questions on a test are easy then everyone will do well i.e. hit the ceiling. The reverse may sometimes be true, where all the questions are too hard and everyone does poorly, i.e. hits the floor (floor effect).

 APPLY YOUR KNOWLEDGE

1. A psychology student designed a questionnaire about attitudes to eating, including the questions below:

> (1) Do you diet? (circle your answer)
>   always   sometimes   never
> (2) Do you think dieting is a bad idea?
> (3) Explain your answer to question 2.

For each question above:
   a. State whether it is an open or closed question. (1 mark)
   b. State whether the question would produce quantitative or qualitative data. (1 mark)
   c. Give **one** limitation of the question. (2 marks)
   d. Suggest how you could improve the question in order to deal with your criticism. (2 marks)
   e. Write **one** further question that would produce quantitative data and **one** that would produce qualitative data. (1 mark + 1 mark)

2. You have been asked to construct questions for an interview about people's attitudes towards smoking.
   a. Write **one** closed question and **one** open question for this interview. (2 marks + 2 marks)
   b. When asking questions about smoking attitudes, what factors might be important in an interviewer's behaviour? (4 marks)
   c. An interviewer should avoid using leading questions. Give an example of a leading question that the interviewer might use for this interview. (2 marks)

CAN YOU?   No. 7.14

1. Identify and briefly explain **two** issues that are important in questionnaire construction. (2 marks + 2 marks)
2. Identify and briefly explain **two** issues that are important in the design of interviews. (2 marks + 2 marks)
3. Explain the difference between closed and open questions. Use examples in your answer. (4 marks)
4. Give **one** strength of using closed questions in an interview. (3 marks)

Correlations

The concept of a **correlation** should be familiar to you from GCSE maths. Strictly speaking, a correlation is a method used to analyse data, not a research method. A correlation is used to analyse the association between two variables, in this case called **co-variables**.

A study that uses a correlational analysis should be called 'a study using a correlational analysis'. However, that's a bit of a mouthful, so we generally just say 'a correlation' or a 'correlational study'.

A correlation is a systematic association between two **continuous variables**. Age and beauty co-vary. As people get older they become more beautiful. This is a **positive correlation** because the two variables *increase* together. You may disagree, and think that as people get older they become less attractive. You think age and beauty are systematically associated but it is a **negative correlation**. As one variable increases the other one decreases. Or you may simply feel that there is no relationship between age and beauty. This is called a **zero correlation**.

Correlational hypothesis

When conducting a study using a correlational analysis we need to produce a correlational hypothesis. This states the expected association between the co-variables (in an experiment we were considering the difference between two conditions of an independent variable).

In our example, age and beauty are the co-variables, so possible hypotheses might be:

- Age and beauty are positively correlated (positive correlation, directional hypothesis).
- As people get older they are rated as more beautiful (positive correlation, directional hypothesis).
- As people get older their beauty decreases (negative correlation, directional hypothesis).
- Age and beauty are correlated (positive or negative correlation, non-directional hypothesis).
- Age and beauty are not correlated (zero correlation, non-directional hypothesis). [This is actually a null hypothesis that states no relationship – not the same as no direction!]

Scattergrams

A correlation can be illustrated using a **scattergram**. For each individual we obtain two scores which are used to plot one dot for that individual – the co-variables determine the x and y position of the dot (x refers to the position on the x axis and y refers to the position on the y axis). The scatter of the dots indicates the degree of correlation between the co-variables.

Correlation coefficient

If you plot a scattergram, how do you know whether the pattern of dots represents a meaningful, systematic association? You can eyeball the graph and decide whether it looks like the dots form a line from top left to bottom right (strong negative correlation) or bottom left to top right (strong positive correlation). But this is a rather amateurish way of deciding whether there is a meaningful correlation.

Instead researchers use a statistical test to calculate the **correlation coefficient**, a measure of the extent of correlation that exists between the co-variables.

- A correlation coefficient is a number.
- A correlation coefficient has a maximum value of 1 (+1 is a perfect positive correlation and −1 is a perfect negative correlation).
- Some correlation coefficients are written with a minus sign (e.g. −.52), whereas others are written with a plus sign (e.g. +.52). The plus or minus sign shows whether it is a positive or negative correlation.
- The coefficient (number) tells us how closely the co-variables are related.

There is one final step and that is to find out if our correlation coefficient is **significant**. In order to do this we use tables of significance (such as the one on the left) which tell us how big the coefficient needs to be in order for the correlation to count as significant (meaningful).

▶ **Scattergrams.**
The top scattergram illustrates a positive correlation. The middle scattergram shows a negative correlation. The bottom scattergram is a zero correlation.

The correlation coefficients for all three graphs are: (1) +.76; (2) −.76; (3) −.006. The plus or minus sign shows whether it is a positive or negative correlation. The coefficient (number) tells us how closely the co-variables are related: −.76 is just as closely correlated as +.76.

Scattergrams showing the relationship between age and beauty

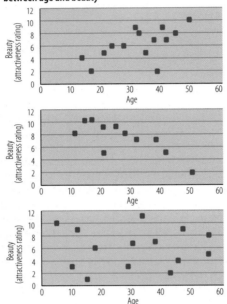

▶ **Table of significance.**
The table on the right gives an approximate idea of the values needed for a correlation to be considered significant. The more pairs of scores you have, the smaller the coefficient can be.

A coefficient of either −.45 or +.45 would be significant if there were 16 pairs of data, but not if there were 14 pairs.

The magnitude of the number informs us about significance, while the sign tells us which direction the correlation is in (positive or negative).

Significance table N =	
4	1.000
6	.829
8	.643
10	.564
12	.503
14	.464
16	.429
18	.401
20	.380
22	.361
26	.331
28	.317

These values are for Spearman's test of correlation.

Strengths

- Correlations are used to investigate trends in data. If a correlation is significant, then further investigation is justified (such as experiments). If correlation is not significant, then you can probably rule out a causal relationship.
- As with experiments, the procedures in a correlation can usually be easily repeated, which means that the findings can be confirmed.

Limitations

- In a correlation the variables are simply measured, no deliberate change is made. Therefore, no conclusion can be made about one co-variable *causing* the other. Consider, for example, a study that showed there was a positive correlation between students' attendance record at school and their academic achievement. A researcher could not conclude that the level of attendance *caused* the better achievement.
- This is additionally a limitation because people assume causal conclusions. This is a problem because such misinterpretation of correlations may mean that people design programmes for improvement based on false premises. For example, in the example above, a headteacher might mistakenly conclude that improving attendance would improve exam results.
- Furthermore the supposed causal connection may actually be due to **intervening variables**, unknown variables which can explain why the co-variables being studied are linked. In our example, it might be that students who do not attend are the ones who dislike school and their dislike of school also impacts on exam performance. Dislike of school may be the more important variable – and there may well be others.
- As with experiments, a correlation may lack internal/external validity. For example, the method used to measure academic achievement may lack validity or the sample used may lack generalisability.

The strength of correlational research therefore lies in investigating the extent of relationships between variables, which can be particularly useful in the early stages of research. However, it is imperative to avoid any causal inferences.

Linear and curvilinear

The correlations we have considered are all **linear** – in a perfect positive correlation (+1) all the values would lie in a straight *line* from the bottom left to the top right.

However, there is a different kind of correlation – a **curvilinear correlation**. The relationship is not linear, but curved. There is still a predictable relationship. For example, stress and performance do not have a linear relationship. Performance on many tasks is depressed when stress is too high or too low; it is best when stress is moderate (see the illustration on page 58).

KEY TERMS

Co-variable The two measured variables in a correlational analysis. The variables must be continuous.

Continuous variable A variable that can take on any value within a certain range. Liking football (on a scale of 1 to 10) is continuous whereas the football team a person supports isn't. The latter could be arranged in any order.

Correlation Determining the extent of an association between two variables; co-variables may not be linked at all (**zero correlation**), they may both increase together (**positive correlation**), or as one co-variable increases, the other decreases (**negative correlation**).

Correlation coefficient A number between −1 and +1 that tells us how closely the co-variables in a correlational analysis are associated.

Curvilinear correlation A non-linear relationship between co-variables.

Intervening variable A variable that comes between two other variables, which is used to explain the association between those two variables. For example, if a positive correlation is found between ice cream sales and violence this may be explained by an intervening variable – heat – which causes the increase in ice cream sales and the increase in violence.

Linear correlation A systematic relationship between co-variables that is defined by a straight line.

Scattergram A graphical representation of the association (i.e. the correlation) between two sets of scores.

Significance A statistical term indicating that the research findings are sufficiently strong for us to accept the research hypothesis under test.

🐾 APPLY YOUR KNOWLEDGE

Guiseppe Gelato always liked statistics at school and now that he has his own ice cream business he keeps various records. To his surprise he found an interesting correlation between his ice cream sales and aggressive crimes. He has started to worry that he may be irresponsible in selling ice cream because it appears to cause people to behave more aggressively. The table below shows his data.

All data rounded to 1000s	Jan	Feb	Mar	Apr	May	Jun	Jul	Aug	Sep	Oct	Nov	Dec
Ice cream sales	10	8	7	21	32	56	130	141	84	32	11	6
Aggressive crimes	21	32	29	35	44	55	111	129	99	36	22	25

a. Sketch a scattergram of Guiseppe's data. Make sure to label the axes and have a title for the scattergram. (3 marks)

b. What can you conclude from the data and the scattergram? (Conclusions are an interpretation of the findings.) (2 marks)

c. What intervening variable might better explain the relationship between ice cream and aggression? (1 mark)

d. Describe how you would design a study to show Guiseppe that ice cream does (or does not) cause aggressive behaviour. (You need to operationalise your variables, decide on a suitable research design and sampling method, etc.) (4 marks)

CAN YOU? No. 7.15

1. Briefly explain what is meant by a 'zero correlation'. (2 marks)
2. Explain the difference between experiments and correlations. (4 marks)
3. The data from a correlational study produces a scattergram with dots arranged in a line from bottom left to top right. Explain what kind of correlation this is. (1 mark)
4. A research study produced a negative correlation between two co-variables. Briefly explain what this means. (2 marks)

Other research methods

There remains one further research method/technique for us to study as part of the AS psychology specification – the method of **meta-analysis**. But there are many others that you will have encountered when reading about psychological research. Two of them – **case studies** and **content analysis** – are included in the full A Level specification. On this spread we look at these three methods/techniques as well as a few other types of study.

Sometimes a study is just a study

After reading this chapter you would be forgiven for thinking you had to classify every study you encountered as an experiment or an observation or a questionnaire and so on. This is not so – there are some occasions when a study doesn't fit into any of these categories. Milgram's baseline study is an example of this. It isn't an experiment (the shock levels were the dependent variable, measuring how obedient the person was). In essence it was an investigation of obedience. When evaluating investigations the same issues are still relevant – the sample of participants, the laboratory setting, the realism of the task and so on.

The multi-method approach

Another point to consider is that very few studies simply use one method. Many studies reported in this book use the *multi-method approach* – a combination of all sorts of different techniques and methods to investigate the target behaviour. For example, Schaffer and Emerson's study of infant attachment in 1964 (see page 72) was basically a non-experimental study, using naturalistic observation, interviews and rating scales, but it also included an experimental element.

KEY TERMS

Case study A research investigation that involves a detailed study of a single individual, institution or event. Case studies provide a rich record of human experience but are hard to generalise from.

Content analysis A kind of observational study in which behaviour is observed indirectly in written or verbal material such as interviews, conversations, books, diaries or TV programmes.

Effect size A measure of the strength of the relationship between two variables.

Meta-analysis A researcher looks at the findings from a number of different studies and produces a statistic to represent the overall effect.

Review A consideration of a number of studies that have investigated the same topic in order to reach a general conclusion about a particular hypothesis.

META-ANALYSIS

Systematic review

We have often mentioned **review** studies in this book where a systematic assessment of other studies has been conducted. For example, on page 44 we described a review by Cowan of studies of the capacity of STM and on page 135 deMaat *et al's* review of psychotherapy studies was mentioned.

A review of research involves identifying an aim and then searching for research studies that have addressed similar aims/hypotheses. This is done by looking through various databases which hold the details of research published in academic journals. A decision will be made about search criteria – deciding what kind of study will be included or excluded. For example, a review of attachment research might only include studies that have used the Strange Situation and/or only used infants under one year of age.

Meta-analysis

In some reviews a method of analysing the data is used, called a meta-analysis. This technique produces an **effect size** as the dependent variable in order to assess overall trends. We use effect sizes in our everyday lives, for example a weight-loss programme may boast that it leads to an average weight loss of 30 pounds. This is the size of the effect.

On page 61 we looked at a meta-analysis of 53 studies related to the cognitive interview (CI) (Köhnken *et al.,* 1999) which demonstrated the effectiveness of the CI compared with standard interviewing techniques. The effect size was 34%, which means that, of all the studies, the CI technique improved recall by 34%, when compared to using the standard interview technique.

A LEVEL ONLY ZONE

CASE STUDY

A case study involves the detailed study of a single individual, institution or event. It uses information from a range of sources, such as from the person concerned and also from their family and friends.

Many research techniques may be used – the people may be interviewed or they might be observed while engaged in daily life. Psychologists might use IQ tests or personality tests or some other kind of questionnaire to produce psychological data about the target person or group of people. They may use the experimental method to test what the target person/group can or can't do.

The findings are organised to represent the individual's thoughts, emotions, experiences and abilities. Case studies are generally longitudinal; in other words they follow the individual or group over an extended period of time.

On page 47 we described the case study of HM, a man who lost the ability to remember any new events due to damage done to his hippocampus. Over a period of 50 years his abilities were tested, and he was interviewed and observed in everyday life.

CONTENT ANALYSIS

A content analysis is what it says – the analysis of the content of something. For example a researcher might study the gender content of magazine advertisements and attempt to describe this content in some systematic way so that conclusions could be drawn.

Content analysis is a form of indirect observation, indirect because you are not observing people directly but observing them through the artefacts they produce. These artefacts can be TV programmes, books, songs, paintings, etc. The process involved is similar to any observational study; the researcher has to make design decisions about:

- Sampling method – what material to sample and how frequently (e.g. which TV channels to include, how many programmes, what length of time).
- The behavioural categories to be used. For example, in a content analysis of songs the behavioural categories might be: romantic, humorous, seasonal, adolescence and so on (i.e. ways to categorise the type of song).

EVALUATION OF META-ANALYSIS

Strengths

- Reviewing the results from a group of studies rather than from just one study can increase the validity of the conclusions drawn because they are based on a wider sample of participants.
- Often a group of studies on a similar topic produce rather contradictory results (e.g. some studies may find no effect, some studies a small effect, and others a larger effect). A meta-analysis allows us to reach an overall conclusion by having a statistic to represent the findings of different studies.

Limitations

- The research designs in the different studies sampled may also vary considerably, which means that the studies are not truly comparable. Putting them all together to calculate the effect size may not be appropriate, and thus the conclusions are not always valid.

Nevertheless, a meta-analysis can provide more powerful information about trends and research evidence than a single study can.

▼ ▶ Conducting a longitudinal study (Cara, right) eliminates participant variables (studying the same person over time). A cross-sectional study (below) can be conducted without waiting years for the individuals to get older. Cross-sectional studies may not just be related to age but could, for example, look at people from different professions.

Longitudinal and other methods

When a study is conducted over a long period of time it is said to be a longitudinal study (it's long!). The reason for such studies is to be able to observe long-term effects and to make comparisons between the same individual at different ages.

An alternative way to do this is to conduct a cross-sectional study. In this instance one group of participants of a young age is compared to another, older group of participants at the same point in time, e.g. in 2008.

In some investigations participants are required to take on a certain role and then their behaviour can be observed as if it were real life. For example, to pretend that they are a prison guard as in Zimbardo's study (see page 22). Role play is a form of controlled observation.

In cross-cultural studies psychologists compare behaviours in different cultures. This is a way of seeing whether cultural practices are related to behaviour. It is a kind of natural experiment where the independent variable is, for example, childrearing techniques in different cultures and the dependent variable is some behaviour, such as attachment.

EVALUATION OF A CASE STUDY

Strengths

- The method offers rich, in-depth data, so information that may be overlooked using other methods is likely to be identified.
- It is especially useful as a means of investigating instances of human behaviour and experience that are rare, for example investigating cases of people with brain damage, or how people respond to an event such as the London riots of 2011 (Reicher and Stott, 2011). It would not be ethical to generate such conditions experimentally.
- The complex interaction of many factors can be studied, in contrast with experiments where many variables are held constant.

Limitations

- It is difficult to generalise from individual cases as each one has unique characteristics.
- Case studies also often involve the recollection of past events as part of the case history and such evidence may be unreliable.
- Case studies are also only identified *after* a key event has occurred (such as damage to the brain) and we cannot be sure that the apparent changes observed were not present originally.

Therefore, while case studies can provide rich, detailed data and unique insights, they have limitations in terms of low reliability and generalisability.

EVALUATION OF CONTENT ANALYSIS

Strengths

- Content analysis is based on observations of what people *actually do* – real communications that are current and relevant, such as recent newspapers or children's books in print. This gives it high ecological validity.
- When sources can be retained or accessed by others (e.g. back copies of magazines or videos of people giving speeches), findings can be replicated.

Limitations

- Observer bias reduces the objectivity and validity of findings because different observers may interpret the meaning of the behavioural categories differently.

Therefore, content analysis has high ecological validity, but may lack reliability and internal validity.

🐾 APPLY YOUR KNOWLEDGE

1. Researchers reviewed studies on the effectiveness of antidepressants and found a difference depending on the severity of the depression. The effect size was 5% for mild depression, 12% for moderate depression and 16% for severe depression.
   a. Explain what an effect size of 5% means. (1 mark)
   b. What would you conclude from these findings? (2 marks)

2. A hospital is interested to find out why some patients with head injuries recover faster than others.
   a. Why would you recommend using a case study for this research? (2 marks)
   b. Suggest how you would conduct a case study in this situation. (3 marks)

3. A university department was given funding to investigate the stereotypes presented in children's books (age stereotypes, gender stereotypes, etc.). They were to compare books that children read today with those from 20 years ago to see if and how stereotypes had changed.
   a. Suggest three items that could be used as behavioural categories in this study. (3 marks)
   b. How might you ensure that two researchers were using the behavioural categories in the same way? (2 marks)

CAN YOU? No. 7.16

1. Briefly describe **one** example of a meta-analysis that you have studied. (2 marks)
2. Briefly explain **one** limitation of a meta-analysis. (2 marks)
3. Explain what is involved in a case study. (3 marks)

Mathematical skills

The specification for both AS and A Level psychology requires that, across all exams for each level, at least 25% of the marks will be from questions related specifically to research methods. Included in this 25% at least 10% of the marks must be related to mathematical skills.

What this means in practice is:

- AS Level – there are two exam papers of 72 marks each, with a total of 144 marks. Therefore at least 36 marks will be research methods questions (mainly on Paper 2 where there is a research methods section), of which at least 15 marks must relate to mathematical skills.
- A Level – there are three exam papers of 96 marks each, with a total of 288 marks. Therefore at least 72 marks will be research methods questions (mainly on Paper 2 where there is a research methods section), of which at least 30 marks must relate to mathematical skills.

◄ **Maths is number 1.**

The percentages given above indicate that research methods is NUMBER 1. It is considerably more important than any other of the psychological topics that you cover. For example, social influence questions are worth 17% of your final AS mark or 8% of your total A Level mark.

So, if you wish to do well in psychology, you need to embrace all areas of the specification (but particularly research methods!).

 APPLY YOUR KNOWLEDGE

Get comfortable with numbers

It may surprise you to know that lots of students are uncomfortable with even relatively simple mathematical skills such as representing a figure as a percentage or expressing a number as a fraction. Even symbols such as > or ≤ can strike fear into the heart of the average psychology student. When Mike used to teach A Level psychology students, he used to give them a statistical test called an 'independent *t* test' to work out, armed with nothing but a formula, a set of instructions and a calculator. After the initial panic had passed at the sight of the formula (see below), the sense of triumph when they reached the right answer after a few relatively simple steps was a joy to behold.

$$t = \frac{\overline{x}_1 - \overline{x}_2}{\sqrt{\frac{s_1^2 + s_2^2}{n}}}$$

We aren't going to ask you to work out an independent t test, but to simply generate lots of your own questions like the sample ones on this page. Practise working them out for yourself, and then work with others to answer each others questions. Share ideas for short-cuts and ways of remembering what the symbols mean, and soon you'll be more of a maths expert than you'll care to admit!

MATHEMATICAL REQUIREMENTS IN THE SPECIFICATION

Before you start to panic about maths skills read through this list of the skills that you will need for the 10% maths questions.

	Skills	Where this is covered (grey indicates the topic is not part of AS Level).
Arithmetic and numerical computation	Recognise and use expressions in decimal and standard form.	See facing page.
	Use fractions, percentages and ratios.	See facing page.
	Estimate results.	See facing page.
	Use an appropriate number of significant figures.	See facing page.
	Make order of magnitude calculations.	See facing page.
Handling data	Understand simple probability.	See page 218.
	Understand the principles of sampling as applied to scientific data.	See pages 192–193.
	Understand the mean, median and mode. Calculate arithmetic means.	See page 212.
	Understand measures of dispersion, including standard deviation and range.	See page 212.
	Use a scattergram to identify a correlation between two variables.	See page 206.
	Construct and interpret frequency tables and diagrams, bar charts and histograms.	See page 214.
	Know the characteristics of normal and skewed distributions.	See page 215.
	Understand the differences between qualitative and quantitative data.	See page 216.
	Understand the difference between primary and secondary data.	See page 217.
	Use a statistical test.	The sign test is covered on pages 218–219.
	Select an appropriate statistical test.	At A Level a number of statistical tests are covered and you will need to be able to decide when to use each test.
	Use statistical tables to determine significance.	See pages 214 and 219.
	Distinguish between levels of measurement.	See page 212.
Algebra	Understand and use the symbols: =, <, <<, >>, >, ∝, ~.	See facing page.
	Substitute numerical values into algebraic equations using appropriate units for physical quantities.	In our Year 2 book.
	Solve simple algebraic equations.	In our Year 2 book.
Graphs	Translate information between graphical, numerical and algebraic forms.	See pages 206 and 214.
	Plot two variables from experimental or other data.	See pages 206 and 214.

SOME BASIC MATHEMATICAL CONCEPTS

You are likely to have encountered at least some of the concepts outlined below in your maths course; therefore only brief explanations are provided.

Fractions

A **fraction** is a part of a whole number such as $\frac{1}{2}$ or $\frac{3}{4}$. We may want to present the results from a study as a fraction. For example, if there were 120 participants in a study and 40 of them were in condition A, what fraction of the participants is this?

To calculate a fraction we divide 40 by 120 $= \frac{40}{120}$.

To make a fraction more comprehensible we reduce a fraction by dividing the top number (the numerator) and the bottom number (the denominator) by the lowest number that divides evenly into both (the lowest common denominator).

In this case that number is 40, which results in a fraction of $\frac{1}{3}$.

Percentages

The term 'per cent' means 'out of 100' (cent means 100). Therefore 5% essentially means 5 out of 100 or $\frac{5}{100}$. We have converted the fraction to a **percentage**.

We can reduce this fraction to $\frac{1}{20}$.

Or we can write $\frac{5}{100}$ as a decimal = 0.05, because the first decimal place is out of 10 and the second is out of 100.

The decimal 0.5 would be 5 out of 10, not 5 out of 100.

To change a fraction to a percentage, divide the numerator by the denominator. For example, for the fraction $\frac{19}{36}$, we divide 19 by 36 (using a calculator) and get 0.52777778.

To make this into a percentage we multiply by 100 (move the decimal point two places to the right) and get 52.777778%.

Ratios

A **ratio** says how much there is of one thing compared to another thing.

Ratios are used in betting, so if you are a betting man or woman you will be at home. Odds are given as 4 to 1 (4:1), meaning that out of a total of five events you would be expected to lose four times and win once.

There are two ways to express a ratio. Either the way above, which is called a part-to-part ratio; or a part-to-whole ratio, which would be expressed as 4:5, meaning four losses out of five occurrences.

A part-to-whole ratio can easily be changed to a fraction: 4:5 is $\frac{4}{5}$.

Ratios can be reduced to a lowest form in the same way that fractions are, so 10:15 would more simply be 2:3 (both parts of the fraction have been divided by 5).

Estimate results

When doing any calculations it helps to estimate what the result is likely to be because then you can detect if you make a mistake.

Consider the fraction $\frac{19}{36}$. It is fairly close to $\frac{18}{36}$, which is the same as half (50%), therefore my answer should be slightly more than half.

The same thing could be done when dealing with big numbers. For example, to estimate the product of 185,363 times 46,208 I could round up 185,363 to 200,000 and round up 46,208 to 50,000.

Then I multiple 5×2 and add nine zeros = 10,000,000,000.

I know the actual answer will be smaller because I rounded both numbers up. The actual answer is 8,565,253,504.

Significant figures

In the example above there are a lot of digits, many of which are distracting! It would be a lot simpler if I told you that the answer was about eight billion (8,000,000,000). In this case I have given the answer to one **significant figure** and all the rest are zeros for less distraction.

Except that's not quite right. We can't just remove all the remaining figures without considering whether we have to round up. In our example, 8,500,000,000 would be half way between eight and nine billion and 8,565,253,504 should be rounded up to nine billion (1 significant figure). Two significant figures would be 8,600,000,000.

Let's consider the percentage on the left, 52.777778%, another awkward number. We might give that to two significant figures, which would be 53% (removing all but two figures and rounding up because the third figure is more than five). If we wanted to give this number to three significant figures it would be 52.8%. If the number was 52.034267% then three significant figures would be 52.0% – we have to indicate three figures.

Order of magnitude and standard form

When dealing with very large numbers it is sometimes clearer to just give two significant figures and then say how many zeros there are, thus focusing on the **order of magnitude**. The convention for doing this for 8,600,000,000 is 8.6×10^9 where 9 represents how many places we have moved the decimal point. To convert 0.0045 we write 4.5×10^{-3} (this is **standard form**).

Mathematical symbols

And finally, you deserve a reward if you have got this far! The symbols you need to be able to use are in the table below.

= and ~	< and <<	> and >>	≤	∝
Equal and approximately equal	*Less than and much less than*	*More than and much more than*	*Less than or equal to*	*Proportional to*

KEY TERMS

Fraction, percentage, ratio Methods of expressing parts of a whole.

Order of magnitude A means of expressing a number by focusing on the overall size (magnitude). This is done by expressing the number in terms of powers of 10.

Significant figure Refers to the number of important single digits used to represent a number. The digits are 'important' because, if removed, the number would be quite different in magnitude.

Standard form A means of expressing very large or very small numbers, a number between 1 and 10 multiplied by 10 (to the power of a number).

CAN YOU?   No. 7.17

1. Represent $\frac{3}{8}$ as a percentage. Give your answer to two significant figures. (2 marks)

2. A researcher wants to divide 4,526 by 42. Estimate what the result would be, explaining how you arrived at your answer. (2 marks)

3. Express 0.02 as a fraction. (1 mark)

4. Briefly explain what the following expression means: 'The number of girls < number of boys'. (1 mark)

Measures of central tendency and dispersion

The information collected in any study is called data or, more precisely, a 'data set' (a set of items). Data are not necessarily numbers; they could be words used to describe how someone feels. For the moment we are going to focus on numerical data, called **quantitative data**. Once a researcher has collected such data, the data needs to be analysed in order to identify trends or to see the 'bigger picture'. One of the ways to do this is *describing* the data, for example by giving an average score for a group of participants. For this reason such statistics are called descriptive statistics – they identify general patterns and trends.

▲ Finding the centre of your data – a measure of the centre or 'central tendency'.

Levels of measurement

Distinctions are made between different kinds of data.

- **Nominal** Data are in separate categories, such as grouping people according to their favourite football team (e.g. Liverpool, Inverness Caledonian Thistle, Oxford United, etc.).
- **Ordinal** Data are ordered in some way, for example asking people to put a list of football teams in order of liking. Liverpool might be first, followed by Inverness Caledonian Thistle, and so on. The 'difference' between each item is not the same, i.e. the individual may like the first item a lot more than the second, but there might only be a small difference between the items ranked second and third.
- **Interval** Data are measured using units of equal intervals, such as when counting correct answers or using any 'public' unit of measurement. Many psychological studies use 'plastic interval scales' where the intervals are arbitrarily determined and we can't therefore know for certain that there are equal intervals between the numbers. However, for the purposes of analysis, such data may be accepted as interval.
- **Ratio** There is a true zero point as in most measures of physical quantities.

MEASURES OF CENTRAL TENDENCY

Measures of central tendency inform us about central (or middle) values for a set of data. They are 'averages' – ways of calculating a typical value for a set of data. The average can be calculated in different ways, each one appropriate for a different situation.

Mean

The **mean** is calculated by adding up all the data items and dividing by the number of data items. It is properly called the arithmetic mean because it involves an arithmetic calculation. It can only be used with ratio and interval level data.

Median

The **median** is the middle value in an ordered list. All data items must be arranged in order and the central value is then the median. If there are an even number of data items there will be two central values. To calculate the median add the two data items and divide by two. The median can be used with ratio, interval and ordinal data.

Mode

The **mode** is the value that is the most common data item. With nominal data it is the category that has the highest frequency count. With interval and ordinal data it is the data item that occurs most frequently. To identify this the data items need to be arranged in order. The modal group is the group with the greatest frequency.

   If two categories or data items have the same frequency the data have two modes, i.e. are bi-modal.

MEASURES OF DISPERSION

A set of data can also be described in terms of how dispersed or spread out the data items are. These descriptions are known as **measures of dispersion**.

Range

The **range** is the arithmetic distance between the top and bottom values in a set of data. It is customary to add 1, so, for example, with the first data set below the range would be 15–3+1. The addition of 1 is because the bottom number of 3 could represent a value as low as 2.5 and the top number of 15 could represent a number as big as 15.5.

Consider the data sets below:

3, 5, 8, 8, 9, 10, 12, 12, 13, 15 mean = 9.5; range = 13 (15–3+1)
1, 5, 8, 8, 9, 10, 12, 12, 13, 17 mean = 9.5; range = 17 (17–1+1)

The two sets of numbers have the same mean but a different range, so the range is helpful as a further method of *describing* the data. If we just used the mean, the data would appear to be the same.

Standard deviation

There is a more precise method of expressing dispersion, called the **standard deviation**. This is a measure of the average distance between each data item above and below the mean, ignoring plus or minus values. It is usually worked out using a calculator. The standard deviations for the two sets of numbers above are 3.69 and 4.45 respectively (worked out using a calculator). You won't be asked to calculate a standard deviation in the exam.

▶ The mean number of legs that people have is 1.999. It would be better to use the mode to describe the average number of legs.

NOIR – an acronym to help remember the four levels of measurement of data: nominal, ordinal, interval and ratio.

EVALUATION OF MEASURES OF CENTRAL TENDENCY

The mean

Strengths
- The mean is the most sensitive measure of central tendency because it takes account of the exact distance between all the values of all the data.

Limitations
- This sensitivity means that it can be easily distorted by one (or a few) extreme values and thus end up being misrepresentative of the data as a whole.
- It cannot be used with nominal data.
- It does not make sense to use it when you have discrete values such as average number of legs.

Therefore, the mean is not always representative of the data as a whole and should always be considered alongside the standard deviation.

The median

Strengths
- The median is not affected by extreme scores.
- It is appropriate for ordinal (ranked) data.
- It can be easier to calculate than the mean.

Limitations
- The median is not as 'sensitive' as the mean because the exact values are not reflected in the final calculation.

The median therefore has strengths in that it can be used to describe a variety of data sets, including skewed data and non-normal distributions.

The mode

Stengths
- The mode is also unaffected by extreme values.
- It is much more useful for discrete data.
- It is the only method that can be used when the data are in categories, i.e. nominal data.

Limitations
- It is not a useful way of describing data when there are several modes.
- It also tells us nothing about the other values in a distribution.

As with all three measures of central tendency, the key is to use the mode only with data sets for which it is appropriate.

EVALUATION OF MEASURES OF DISPERSION

Range

Stengths
- The range is easy to calculate.

Limitations
- It is affected by extreme values.
- It fails to take account of the distribution of the numbers. For example, it doesn't indicate whether most numbers are closely grouped around the mean or spread out evenly.

The range is useful for ordinal data or with highly skewed data or when making a quick calculation.

Standard deviation

Strengths
- The standard deviation is a precise measure of dispersion because it takes all the exact values into account.
- It is not difficult to calculate if you have a calculator.

Limitations
- It may hide some of the characteristics of the data set (e.g. extreme values).

Therefore, the standard deviation is best used, together with the mean, to describe interval or ratio data which is normally distributed.

▶ In an American study 66% of students rated themselves as having a better sense of humour than the average person (Kruger and Dunning, 1999). This is called the better-than-average effect – other findings include 93% of a US sample rating their driving as better than average (Svenson, 1981) and 85% of students rating themselves as above average in their ability to get on with others (Alicke and Govorun, 2005).

🐾 APPLY YOUR KNOWLEDGE

1. For each of the following data sets, where appropriate calculate the mean, the median and/or the mode. (3 marks for each data set)
   a. 2, 3, 5, 6, 6, 8, 9, 12, 15, 21, 22
   b. 2, 3, 8, 10, 11, 13, 13, 14, 14, 29
   c. 2, 2, 4, 5, 5, 5, 7, 7, 8, 8, 8, 10
   d. cat, cat, dog, budgie, snake, gerbil
2. For each of the data sets (a–d) in question 1, state which of the three measures of central tendency would be most suitable to use and why. (2 marks for each data set)
3. Estimate the mean and standard deviation for the following data sets. (2 marks for each data set)
   a. 119, 131, 135, 142, 145, 147, 155, 156, 161, 163
   b. 0.15, 0.23, 0.28, 0.34, 0.34, 0.34, 0.36, 0.46
4. For each of the data sets (a–b) in question 3 explain what measure of central tendency might be preferable to use and explain why. (2 marks for each data set)
5. For each of the data sets (a–b) in question 3 explain what measure of dispersion might be preferable to use and explain why. (2 marks for each data set)
6. Look at the following two data sets. Which one do you think would have the smaller standard deviation? (1 mark)
   Data set A: 2 2 3 4 5 9 11 14 18 20 21 22 25
   Data set B: 2 5 8 9 9 10 11 12 14 15 16 20 25

KEY TERMS

Mean The arithmetic average of a data set. Takes the exact values of all the data into account.

Measure of central tendency A descriptive statistic that provides information about a 'typical' value for a data set.

Measure of dispersion A descriptive statistic that provides information about how spread out a set of data are.

Median The middle value of a data set when the items are placed in rank order.

Mode The most frequently occurring value or item in a data set.

Quantitative data Data measured in numbers.

Range The difference between the highest and lowest item in a data set. Usually 1 is added as a correction.

Standard deviation shows the amount of variation in a data set. It assesses the spread of data around the mean.

CAN YOU?   No. 7.18

1. Identify **one** measure of central tendency and explain how to calculate it for a set of data. (3 marks)
2. Briefly explain **one** strength and **one** limitation of using the mean to work out the central tendency of a data set. (2 marks + 2 marks)
3. Identify **one** measure of dispersion and explain how to calculate it for a set of data. (3 marks)
4. Explain why it is sometimes preferable to use the mode rather than the mean as a measure of central tendency. (3 marks)
5. Explain why it might be better to know the standard deviation of a data set rather than the range. (3 marks)

Display of quantitative data and data distributions

A picture is worth 1,000 words! Graphs and tables provide a means of 'eyeballing' your data and seeing the findings at a glance. Using graphs and tables are a way of describing data and therefore are also descriptive statistics, like measures of central tendency and dispersion. In fact we often display measures of central tendency and dispersion in a graph because it is easier to grasp the significance of the statistics in visual form.

Graph A

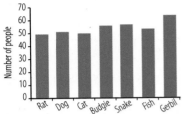

▲ A bar chart showing the students' favourite pets.

Graph B   **Graph C**

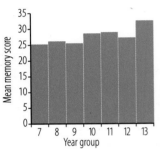   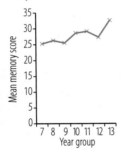

▲ A histogram showing the mean memory scores for each year group in a school (maximum score is 40).

▲ A line graph showing the same data as Graph B.

KEY TERMS

Bar chart A graph used to represent the frequency of data; the categories on the x-axis have no fixed order and there is no true zero.

Histogram Type of frequency distribution in which the number of scores in each category of continuous data are represented by vertical columns. There is a true zero and no spaces between the bars.

Negative skewed distribution Most of the scores are bunched towards the right. The mode is to the right of the mean because the mean is affected by the extreme scores tailing off to the left.

Normal distribution A symmetrical bell-shaped frequency distribution. This distribution occurs when certain variables are measured, such as IQ or the life of a light bulb. Such 'events' are distributed in such a way that most of the scores are clustered close to the mid-point; the mean, median and mode are at the mid-point.

Positive skewed distribution Most of the scores are bunched towards the left. The mode is to the left of the mean because the mean is affected by the extreme scores tailing off to the right.

Skewed distribution A distribution is skewed if one tail is longer than another, signifying that there are a number of extreme values to one side or the other of the mid-score.

DISPLAY OF QUANTITATIVE DATA

Graphs and tables should be simple so they can be read easily.
- They should clearly show the findings from a study.
- There should be a short but informative title.
- In a graph both axes should be clearly labelled. The x-axis goes across the page. In the case of a bar chart or histogram, it is usually the independent variable. The vertical, or y-axis, is usually frequency.
- Always use squared paper if you are hand-drawing graphs.

Tables

The measurements collected in a research study are referred to as 'raw data' – numbers that haven't been before any descriptive statistics have been carried out. These data can be set out in a table and/or summarised using measures of central tendency and dispersion. Such summary tables are more helpful for interpreting findings.

Bar chart

The height of each bar represents the frequency of each item. **Bar charts** are especially suitable for data that is not continuous, i.e. has no particular order such as Graph A on the left which is categorical or nominal data. In a bar chart a space is left between each bar to indicate the lack of continuity.

Histogram

A **histogram** is similar to a bar chart except that the area within the bars must be proportional to the frequencies represented (see Graph B). In practice this means that the vertical axis (frequency) must start at zero. In addition the horizontal axis must be continuous (therefore you can't draw a histogram with data in categories). Finally, there should be no gaps between the bars.

Line graph

A line graph, like a histogram, has continuous data on the x-axis and there is a dot to mark the middle top of where each bar would be and each dot is connected by a line (see Graph C).

Scattergram

A scattergram is a kind of graph used when doing a correlational analysis (see page 206).

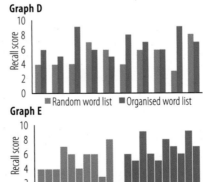

Graph D

■ Random word list   ■ Organised word list

Graph E

Random word list   Organised word list

Graph F

Random word list   Organised word list

◀ Participant number 1 in the random word group is placed next to participant number 1 in the organised word group. Students like to draw 'participant charts', but they are totally meaningless.

◀ The findings from each participant are shown in this graph. They are grouped together so that you can see all the scores from participants in the random word group and all the scores from the participants in the organised word group. This is slightly better than Graph D because we can just about tell that the random word list led to better recall – but a glance at the means (as in Graph F) shows this effortlessly.

◀ This graph shows the mean scores for each group. The findings are immediately obvious, which is the point of using a graph.

DATA DISTRIBUTIONS

When we plot frequency data the *y*-axis represents frequency and the *x*-axis is the item of interest as in a histogram (see facing page). When doing this for large data sets we can see an overall pattern of the data called a distribution.

Normal distribution

The **normal distribution** is a classic bell-shaped curve. It is the predicted distribution when considering an equally likely set of results. For example, if a light bulb has a mean lifetime of 100 hours we would expect some light bulbs to last a little less than this and some to last a little more. If we plot the lifetime of 1,000 light bulbs we would get a normal distribution.

Many human characteristics are normally distributed, such as shoe sizes or intelligence. A normal distribution has certain defining features:
- The mean, median and mode are all in the exact mid-point.
- The distribution is symmetrical around this mid-point.
- The dispersion of scores or measurements either side of the mid-point is consistent and can be expressed in standard deviations.

For any set of data that is normally distributed, 34.13% of the people will lie within one standard deviation below the mean and 34.13% will lie within one standard deviation above the mean. Therefore, a total of 68.26% will lie within one standard deviation above or below the mean. A total of 95.44% of people lie two standard deviations above or below the mean, which means that only 4.56% lie in the area beyond this; 2.28% are less than two standard deviations below the mean.

This concept underlies the idea of the statistical deviation model of abnormality (see page 98). People in the sections above or below two standard deviations are very unusual indeed.

Skewed distribution

In some populations scores are not distributed equally around the mean – this is **skewed distribution**. Consider a test of depression where 0–50 represents normal behaviour and 50+ represents clinical depression. If we plotted the distribution of scores for 100 people we would expect most scores to be towards the low end rather than the high end of this score range. This produces a **positive skewed distribution** as illustrated below right. The fact that there are a few extreme high scores has a strong effect on the mean, which is always higher than the median and mode in a positive skew.

The alternative is a **negative skewed distribution** (below left). This might happen if marks were plotted for an exam which was very easy so most people got a very high score.

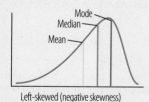

Left-skewed (negative skewness)

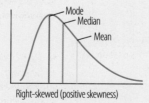

Right-skewed (positive skewness)

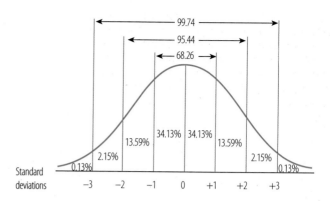

▲ The percentage of people in each part of the normal distribution curve is shown above.

Consider IQ. The mean score for IQ is 100 and one standard deviation is 15 points. If we tested a group of 1,000 people this is what we should find:
- Score between 85 and 115 (one standard deviation either side of the mean) = 683 people (68.26% of 1,000)
- Score between 70 and 130 = 954 people (95.44% of 1,000)
- Score less than 55 = 1 (0.13% of 1,000)

🐾 APPLY YOUR KNOWLEDGE

1. A psychologist conducted a study to look at whether watching certain films made children more helpful (one film was about being helpful, the other was neutral). Helpfulness was measured using a questionnaire. The mean score of children who watched the helpful film was 30.25 whereas the mean score for the neutral film was 24.62.
   a. Give each mean score to two significant figures. (2 marks)
   b. Sketch a bar chart showing these results. Label the bar chart carefully. (3 marks)
   c. The neutral film is described as a control condition. Explain why a control condition is used. (2 marks)
2. There are three graphs near the top of the facing page.
   a. For each graph state what conclusion you would draw. (1 mark each)
   b. What kind of data are displayed in each graph? (3 marks)
3. There are three further graphs at the bottom of the facing page.
   a. What can you conclude from Graph F? (1 mark)
   b. Write a title that would be suitable for this graph. (1 mark)
   c. What labels would be appropriate for the *y*-axis and the *x*-axis? (2 marks)
4. Explain why the mean is always lower than the mode in a negative skew. (2 marks)
5. What kind of skew would you get if a test had a ceiling effect? (1 mark)

▶ And to help you remember…

Left Foot
Negative Skew

Right Foot
Positive Skew

What not to do…
Imagine a study where one group of participants were given a list of 10 words to memorise where the words were in a random order (shown in the colour green). A second group were given the same words but organised into categories (shown in red).

Only one of the graphs on the left-hand page helps you see immediately what the findings are. Which is it?

CAN YOU? No. 7.19
1. Briefly explain **two** key differences between a bar chart and a histogram. (2 marks)
2. Briefly outline the characteristics of a normal distribution. (2 marks)
3. Explain the difference between a normal and a skewed distribution. (3 marks)

Types of data

We have already discussed **quantitative** and **qualitative data** (page 204). On this spread we are going to discuss these two types of data in more depth and also consider two other types of data: **primary** and **secondary data**.

The opposite of quantitative data is qualitative data. The former is numerical whereas the latter isn't. A different kind of distinction is made between primary and secondary data. The former is data collected by a researcher specifically for a current research project whereas the latter is data collected by someone else and/or for a different project than the current one.

▲ Painting in the style of *The Kiss* by Gustav Klimt.

Many studies produce a mix of quantitative and qualitative data. For example Stanley Milgram, in his obedience research (see page 24), found that 65% of participants were fully obedient (quantitative data) but he also reported the comments of observers (qualitative data), providing additional insights into the experience of participants:

'I observed a mature and initially poised businessman enter the laboratory smiling and confident. Within 20 minutes he was reduced to a twitching, stuttering wreck, who was rapidly approaching a point of nervous collapse. He constantly pulled on his earlobe, and twisted his hands. At one point he pushed his fist into his forehead and muttered "Oh God, let's stop it". And yet he continued to respond to every word of the experimenter, and obeyed to the end.'

QUANTITATIVE AND QUALITATIVE DATA

Quantitative data

Quantitative data is data that represents how much or how long, how many, etc. there are of something, i.e. behaviour is measured in numbers or quantities.

- The dependent variable in an experiment is quantitative.
- Closed questions in questionnaires collect quantitative data – numerical information about your age, how many hours you work in a week, how highly you rate different TV programmes.
- In an observational study a tally of behavioural categories is quantitative.

Qualitative data

Qualitative data can't be counted or quantified but it can be turned into quantitative data by placing the data in categories and then counting frequency. For instance, in the Milgram example below left we might count how many participants described themselves as stressed.

Sometimes people define qualitative data as being about what people think and feel, but quantitative questions can also concern what people think and feel.

Open questions in questionnaires may collect qualitative data – data that express the 'quality' of things. This includes descriptions, words, meanings, pictures and so on.

In an observational study researchers can describe what they see and this would be qualitative.

Quantitative data	Qualitative data
• Quantity	• Quality
• Deals with numbers	• Deals with descriptions
• Data which can be measured	• Data that is observed but not measured
• Psychologists develop measures of psychological variables	• Observing people through the messages they produce and the way they act
• Looking at averages and differences between groups	• Concerned with attitudes, beliefs, fears and emotions

The Kiss by Gustav Klimt	
• Painted between 1907 and 1908, when the artist was 45 years old	• Representative of a style of art called Art Nouveau
• Actual painting measures 180 × 180 cm	• Shows a couple locked in a kiss
• Bought for 25,000 crowns when it was first painted	• Shows how bright, beautiful and golden everything is when you first kiss someone
• It has 33% of its surface covered in gold leaf	• Painted in oil and gold leaf on canvas
• Listed as no. 12 on list of most popular paintings	• Probably his most famous work

A psychology class	
• 24 students	• Very enthusiastic about psychology
• 18 girls, 6 boys	• Mixture of boys and girls
• 72% gained Grade A on mock exam	• Hardworking students
• 10 plan to go on to study psychology at university	• School located in an innercity area
• Most psychology teachers are female	• Teacher's name is Mrs Jones

EVALUATION OF QUANTITATIVE AND QUALITATIVE DATA

Quantitative data

Strengths

- Quantitative data are easy to analyse, using descriptive statistics and statistical tests. This enables conclusions to be easily drawn.

Limitations

- Such data may oversimplify reality. For example, a questionnaire with closed questions may force people to tick answers that don't really represent their feelings. Therefore, the conclusions may be meaningless.

Overall, quantitative data allow researchers to produce reliable information that can be presented in a wide variety of ways (e.g. charts, graphs, statistics).

Qualitative data

Strengths

- Qualitative data provide rich and detailed information about people's experiences. This can provide unexpected insights into thoughts and behaviour because the answers are not restricted by previous expectations.

Limitations

- The complexity makes it more difficult to analyse such data and draw conclusions.

The power of qualitative data lies in helping researchers tease out the underlying meaning in what people do or say.

PRIMARY AND SECONDARY DATA

Both primary and secondary data may be quantitative and/or qualitative.

Primary data

Primary data is information observed or collected directly from first-hand experience. In the case of psychological research it is data collected by the researcher for the study currently being undertaken. The collection of primary data would involve designing the study, gaining ethical approval, piloting the study, recruiting and testing participants, and finally analysing the data collected and drawing conclusions.

The study might be an experiment, possibly with a questionnaire and/or an observational element to measure the dependent variable. Or the study could just involve a questionnaire or just an observation. The data collected would be specifically related to the aims and/or hypothesis of the study.

Secondary data

Secondary data is information that was collected for a purpose other than the current one. The researcher could use data collected by themselves but for a different study or collected by another researcher. The researcher might make use of government statistics, such as information about the treatment of mental health, or make use of data held by a hospital or other institution.

A correlation study often uses secondary data and review studies use secondary data, conducting a meta-analysis on such data.

🐾 APPLY YOUR KNOWLEDGE

1. On the facing page are descriptions of Klimt's painting *The Kiss* and of a hypothetical psychology class. Qualitative and quantitative descriptions are given of both. Try to do the same activity for the following:
   a. A television series. (6 marks)
   b. The town or city you live in. (6 marks)
   c. A major world event such as the London Olympics or the 9/11 bombing in New York. (6 marks)
2. Based on your answers to question 1, consider what kind of data is 'better':
   a. Outline the strengths and limitations of using quantitative data in the examples above. (3 marks + 3 marks)
   b. Outline the strengths and limitations of using qualitative data in the examples above. (3 marks + 3 marks)
3. In each of the following examples identify whether primary data or secondary data would be involved, or both. Explain your answers. (2 marks each)
   a. Zimbardo's study of social roles (page 22).
   b. Tarnow's study of aviation accidents (page 27).
   c. Study of HM (page 47).
   d. Schaffer and Emerson's study of infants (page 72).
   e. Minnesota parent–child study (pages 79 and 88).
   f. Jahoda's analysis of mental healthiness (page 100).

CAN YOU?　　　　　　　　　　　　　　　No. 7.20

1. Explain what is meant by 'quantitative data'. Give an example in your answer. (3 marks)
2. Give **one** strength of producing qualitative data in a questionnaire. (2 marks)
3. Distinguish between primary and secondary data. (3 marks)

EVALUATION OF PRIMARY AND SECONDARY DATA

Primary data

Strengths
- The great strength of generating primary data is the control the researcher has over the data. The data collection can be designed so it fits the aims and hypothesis of the study.

Limitations
- It is a very lengthy and therefore expensive process. Simply designing a study takes a lot of time and then time is spent recruiting participants, conducting the study and analysing the data.

Despite these limitations, collecting primary data is a key aim of most psychological research studies.

Secondary data

Strengths
- It is simpler and cheaper to just access someone else's data because significantly less time and equipment is needed.
- Such data may have been subjected to statistical testing and thus it is known whether it is significant.

Limitations
- The data may not exactly fit the needs of the study.

Despite being 'borrowed' data, secondary data plays an important role in much psychological research, including review studies, meta-analyses and correlational studies.

⬆ UPGRADE

Research methods exam questions often require expansion or application.

An exam question might say: Explain what is meant by 'quantitative data'. (3 marks)

The definition given in the 'Key Terms' would be enough for the first 2 marks, and to get the third mark, you might add an example of what counts as quantitative data e.g. the number of hours someone works in a typical week. This is expansion.

Or the question might refer to a study described in the stem, such as: Explain why quantitative data is a strength in this study. (3 marks)

In this case you would outline a limitation and then find an example in the stem of the question. This is an example of an application.

The key is to be prepared, be flexible, and be ready to give examples to get the full marks available.

KEY TERMS
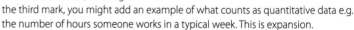

Primary data Information observed or collected directly from first-hand experience.

Qualitative data Information in words that cannot be counted or quantified. Qualitative data can be turned into quantitative data by placing them in categories and counting frequency.

Quantitative data Information that represents how much or how long, or how many, etc. there are of something, i.e. a behaviour is measured in numbers or quantities.

Secondary data Information used in a research study that was collected by someone else or for a purpose other than the current one. For example published data or data collected in the past.

Introduction to statistical testing

There are two kinds of statistics: descriptive statistics (such as averages and graphs) and inferential statistics. You may have heard the phrase **statistical test** – for example a newspaper might report that '*statistical tests show that women are better at reading maps than men*'. If we wanted to know if women are better at reading maps than men we could not possibly test all the women and men in the world, so we just test a small group of women and a small group of men. If we find that the sample of women are indeed better with maps than the sample of men, then we *infer* that the same is true for all women and men.

However, there are two key issues:

1. To make that inference we have to use statistical (inferential) tests that have been designed to work out the **probability (p)** of whether a particular set of data could simply have occurred by chance.
2. We may have found a difference between our two samples, but is this difference big enough? If you test any two groups of people it is extremely unlikely that, on average, they will perform identically. Therefore we need a test to establish whether the difference is big enough to be of **significance**.

Insider tip...

At this point of your course the only thing you need to know is how to do the sign test, a simple statistical test.

Don't be scared by the statistical bit. It really is a set of very simple steps.

In the second year of A Level psychology you will learn about other statistical tests and more about probability.

◀ One-tailed and two-tailed.

When looking up critical values a 'one-tailed test' is used for a directional hypothesis – when you look at a one-tailed cat you know which direction it is going. A two-tailed cat goes in both directions (non-directional hypothesis).

THE SIGN TEST

We are going to begin with a simple statistical test, the **sign test**. There are three things you will need to know:

1. When it is appropriate to use a sign test.
2. How to do the sign test.
3. How to report the conclusion that can be drawn.

When to use a sign test

- This is a test that is used when looking at paired or related data.
- The two related pieces of data could come from a repeated measures design, i.e. the same person is tested twice.
- The sign test can also be used with matched pairs design because the participants are paired and therefore count, for the purposes of statistics, as one person tested twice.

How to do the sign test

Let's imagine a study where we wanted to know whether people were happier after they had a holiday. To do this we ask people to rate their happiness on a scale of 1 to 10, where 1 is very unhappy and 10 is very happy. They do this before going on holiday and then do it again two weeks after they return (we wait two weeks for the initial euphoria of the holiday to wear off).

Step 1. State the hypothesis This is our hypothesis: people are happier after going on holiday than they were beforehand. This is a directional hypothesis and therefore requires a **one-tailed test**. If the hypothesis was non-directional then a **two-tailed test** is used – this will be clear later on.

Step 2. Record the data and work out the sign Record each pair of data and record a minus (−) for happier before and a plus (+) if happier after. This has been done in the table on the left.

Step 3. Find calculated value *S* is the symbol for the **test statistic** we are calculating. It is calculated by adding up the pluses and adding up the minuses and selecting the smaller value. In our case there are 10 pluses and 3 minuses and one zero. Therefore the less frequent sign is minus, so *S* = 3. This is called the **calculated value** because we calculated it!

▼ Table of results.

Participant	Happiness score before	Happiness score after	Difference (after–before)	Sign
1	6	7	1	+
2	3	4	1	+
3	4	6	2	+
4	8	6	−2	−
5	5	7	2	+
6	7	5	−2	−
7	5	7	2	+
8	5	8	3	+
9	4	7	3	+
10	8	5	−3	−
11	4	4	0	
12	8	9	1	+
13	6	7	1	+
14	5	6	1	+

Our study is a natural experiment – we are not paying for anyone to go on holiday. The independent variable is before and after a holiday; the dependent variable is happiness score. Just in case you wanted to know.

Calculated value The value of a test statistic calculated for a particular data set.

Critical value In an inferential test the value of the test statistic that must be reached to show significance.

One-tailed test Form of test used with a directional hypothesis.

Probability (p) A numerical measure of the likelihood or chance that certain events will occur.

Sign test A statistical (inferential) test to determine the significance of a sample of related items of data.

Significance A statistical term indicating that the research findings are sufficiently strong for us to accept the research hypothesis under test.

Table of critical values A table that contains the numbers used to judge significance. The calculated value of the test statistic is compared to the number in the table (called the critical value) to see if the calculated value is significant.

Test statistic A statistical test is used to calculate a numerical value. For each test this value has a specific name such as S for the sign test.

Two-tailed test Form of test used with a non-directional hypothesis.

Step 4. Find critical value of S

N = The total number of scores (ignoring any zero values).

In our case $N = 13$ (1 score omitted).

The hypothesis is directional; therefore a one-tailed test is used.

Now we use the **table of critical values** on the right and locate the column headed 0.05 for a one-tailed test and the row which begins with our N value.

For a one-tailed test, the **critical value** of $S = 3$.

Step 5. Is the result in the right direction?

If the hypothesis is directional we have to check that the result is in the expected direction.

In this case we expect people to be happier afterwards and should therefore have more pluses than minuses.

This was the case and therefore we can accept the hypothesis.

How to report the conclusion that can be drawn

If the calculated value is equal to or less than this critical value our result is significant.

In our case it is significant.

As the calculated value is significant we can conclude that people are happier after going on holiday than they were beforehand.

But wait – how certain are we that this is true? A statistical test only gives the *probability* that a particular set of data did not occur by chance. The level of significance we selected was 0.05. This means that there is a 0.05 or 5% probability that the result would have occurred even if holidays had no effects (0.05 is 5/100 or 5%).

Sometimes researchers wish to be more certain and use 0.01, for example, if testing the effect of a drug on treating a disease.

▼ Table of critical values of S.

Level of significance for a one-tailed test	0.05	0.01
Level of significance for a two-tailed test	**0.10**	**0.02**
N		
5	0	
6	0	0
7	0	0
8	1	0
9	1	1
10	1	1
11	2	1
12	2	2
13	3	2
14	3	2
15	3	3
16	4	3
17	4	4
18	5	4
19	5	4
20	5	5
25	7	7
30	10	9
35	12	11

Calculated value of S must be EQUAL TO or LESS THAN the critical value in this table for significance to be shown.

APPLY YOUR KNOWLEDGE

1. Edgar believes in extra sensory perception (ESP). One way to test this is using Zener cards (below). A pack contains 25 cards, five of each type. The sender looks at each card and 'sends' what he is seeing to a receiver (who can't see the card). At a chance level a person could guess five out of 25 correctly.

   He tested this for 20 friends and scored them as a 'plus' if they got more than five correct and a 'minus' if they got five or less right.

   He ended up with 15 pluses and five minuses. His hypothesis was directional. Is his result significant? Explain your answer.

2. Some political students believed that people rarely change their political stance. To test this they recorded political views at the beginning and end of the school year. Their data is shown below. Were they right – is it a non-directional hypothesis?

Participant	View at beginning of year	View at end of year
1	Conservative	Labour
2	Conservative	Lib-Dem
3	Labour	Labour
4	Labour	Labour
5	Labour	Lib-Dem
6	Lib-Dem	Lib-Dem
7	Conservative	Conservative
8	Labour	Labour
9	Labour	Lib-Dem
10	Lib-Dem	Conservative
11	Conservative	Conservative
12	Lib-Dem	Lib-Dem

CAN YOU? No. 7.21

1. Briefly explain what the letter N stands for in relation to statistical tests. (1 mark)
2. Explain the difference between the calculated value of S and the critical value of S. (3 marks)
3. Convert 5% to a decimal. (1 mark)
4. Explain when a sign test should be used. (3 marks)

The scientific process and peer review

Psychology, in common with all scientific subjects, develops its knowledge base through conducting research and sharing the findings of such research with other scientists. **Peer review** is an essential part of this process whereby scientific quality is judged prior to publication. It is in the interest of all scientists that their work is held up for scrutiny and any work that is flawed or downright fraudulent (as in the 'Cyril Burt affair' below) is detected and the results of such research are ignored.

Fraud in psychology

The Cyril Burt affair

In the early 1950s, the eminent British psychologist Sir Cyril Burt published results from studies of twins that was used to show that intelligence is inherited. Burt (1955) started with 21 pairs of twins raised apart, later increasing this to 42 pairs of twins. In a subsequent study Burt (1966) increased his sample to 53 pairs of identical twins raised apart, reporting an identical correlation to the earlier twin study of .771. The suspicious consistency of these correlation coefficients led Leon Kamin (1977) to accuse Burt of inventing data. When a *Sunday Times* reporter, Oliver Gillie (1976), tried and failed to find two of Burt's

▲ Sir Cyril Burt (1883–1971).

research assistants (who didn't actually exist), this appeared to confirm the underlying fraud and Burt was publicly discredited. These accusations have been challenged (e.g. Joynson, 1989) but the most recent view is that Burt was astonishingly dishonest in his research (Mackintosh, 1995).

The Burt affair is particularly worrying because his research was used to shape social policy.

Burt helped to establish the 11-plus examination used in the UK to identify which children should go to grammar school rather than secondary moderns. He argued that since IQ was largely inherited, it was appropriate to test and segregate children into schools suitable for their abilities.

Some more recent cases of fraud

In 2010 Professor Marc Hauser of Harvard University was found responsible for scientific misconduct related to a number of published scientific papers. His main area of research concerned cotton-top tamarin monkeys and their cognitive abilities. He appears to have drawn conclusions for which he has been unable to provide evidence.

In the light of such prominent cases of professional misconduct Leslie John and colleagues (2012) surveyed over 2,000 psychologists asking them to anonymously report their involvement in questionable research practices. They found that 70% said they cut corners in reporting data and 1% admitted to falsifying data. They concluded that questionable practices may constitute the prevailing research norm.

Aftermath

Such practices raise two key issues. First, there is the issue of lack of trust. In the future people are likely to be less trusting of scientific data.

Second is the problem that the data from such fraudulent studies remains published. Despite the fact the journals involved usually publish retractions (stating that the evidence is flawed and fraudulent), there are people who will continue to use the faulty data not knowing that it is discredited.

THE ROLE OF PEER REVIEW

The scientific process

The scientific method is described on page 181. It is important to understand that this is not the same as 'doing an experiment'. First of all it may involve observation or self-report, not just experiment. But more importantly, science is a *process* which enables humankind to get closer and closer to understanding how the world, and the people in it, function. Many elements of this process have evolved over the centuries to ensure that we uncover facts that can be relied on to build bridges, treat disease, raise psychologically healthy children and so on. One part of this process is peer review.

Peer review

Peer review (also called 'refereeing') is the assessment of scientific work by others who are experts in the same field (i.e. 'peers'). The intention of peer reviewing is to ensure that any research conducted and published is of high quality.

Usually there are a number of reviewers for each application/article/assessment. Their task is to report on the quality of the research and then their views are considered by a peer review panel.

The Parliamentary Office of Science and Technology (2002) suggests that peer review serves three main purposes:

1. **Allocation of research funding** Research is paid for by various government and charitable bodies. The overall budget for science research in the year 2015–16 was set at £5.8 billion (Gov.uk, 2014). The organisations spending this money obviously have a duty to spend it responsibly. Therefore, public bodies such as the Medical Research Council require reviews to enable them to decide which research is likely to be worthwhile.

2. **Publication of research in academic journals and books** Scientific or academic journals provide scientists with the opportunity to share the results of their research. The peer review process has only been used in such journals since the middle of the twentieth century as a means of preventing incorrect or faulty data entering the public domain. Prior to the idea of peer review, research was simply published and it was assumed that the burden of proof lay with opponents of any new ideas.

3. **Assessing the research rating of university departments** All university science departments are expected to conduct research and this is assessed in terms of quality (Research Excellence Framework, REF). Future funding for the department depends on receiving good ratings from the REF peer review.

Peer review and the Internet

The sheer volume and pace of information available on the Internet means that new solutions are needed in order to maintain the quality of information. Scientific information is available in numerous online blogs, online journals and, of course, *Wikipedia* (see facing page).

To a large extent such sources of information are policed by the 'wisdom of crowds' approach – readers decide whether it is valid or not, and post comments and/or edit entries accordingly. Several online journals (such as *ArXiv* and *Philica*) ask readers to rate articles. On *Philica*, papers are ranked on the basis of peer reviews and the peer reviews can be read by anyone. On the Internet, however, 'peer' is coming to mean 'everyone' – a more egalitarian system but possibly at a cost of quality.

EVALUATION OF PEER REVIEW

It is clear why peer review is essential – we need to have a means of establishing the validity of scientific research. While the benefit of peer review is beyond question, certain features of the process can be criticised. For example, Richard Smith, previous editor of the *British Medical Journal (BMJ)*, commented: 'Peer review is slow, expensive, profligate of academic time, highly subjective, prone to bias, easily abused, poor at detecting gross defects and almost useless at detecting fraud' (Smith, 1999). Let us pick up on a few of these criticisms.

Finding an expert

It isn't always possible to find an appropriate expert to review a research proposal or report.

This means that poor research may be passed because the reviewer didn't really understand it (Smith, 1999). In addition, reviewers may be biased towards prestigious researchers rather than less well-known names.

This emphasises the need to always take a rigorous and questioning approach both to the appointment of reviewers and to their work.

Anonymity

Reviewers may have their identity kept secret.

This aims to allow them to be honest and objective. However, it may have the opposite effect if reviewers use the veil of anonymity to settle old scores or bury rival research. Research is conducted in a social world where people compete for research grants and jobs, and make friends and enemies. Social relationships inevitably affect objectivity.

To combat these issues, some journals now favour open reviewing, where both author and reviewer know each other's identity.

Publication bias

Journals tend to prefer to publish positive results, possibly because editors want research that has important implications in order to increase the standing of their journal.

This results in a bias in published research that in turn leads to a misperception of the true facts. Furthermore, it appears that journals also avoid publishing straight replications of a study, a fundamental part of research validation. Ritchie *et al.* (2012) submitted a replication of a study on paranormal phenomena and found that it was not even considered for peer review.

This suggests that academic journals are as bad as newspapers for seeking eye-catching stories.

Preserving the status quo

Peer review results in a preference for research that goes with existing theory rather than dissenting or unconventional work.

Richard Horton (2000), a former editor of the medical journal *The Lancet*, made the following comment: 'The mistake, of course, is to have thought that peer review was any more than a crude means of discovering the acceptability – not the validity – of a new finding.'

Journals should be aware of the damaging effect of such bias.

Cannot deal with already published research

We noted on the facing page the problem that, once a research study has been published, the results remain in the public view even if they are later shown to be fraudulent or simply the result of poor research practices.

Therefore, peer review does not ensure that all data we are exposed to is valid. For example, Brooks (2010) points to peer-reviewed research that was subsequently debunked but nevertheless continued to be used in a debate in parliament.

This means that the general public need to be more critical in their acceptance of published information, even from reputable sources.

▲ Academic journals.

There are thousands of academic journals publishing over one million research papers each year. They differ from 'popular' magazines because they contain in-depth reports of research. The articles are written by academics and are peer reviewed. Several hundred such journals specifically relate to psychology, such as **The Psychologist, Archives of Sexual Behaviour***,* **Journal of Early Adolescence** *and* **British Journal of Psychology***.*

Academic textbooks are based on such articles – as you can see by looking in the references at the back of this book.

Wikipedia is peer-reviewed. This is achieved by having various levels of editor to check information that is posted. However, Wikipedia recognises that, while it may be simple to detect incorrect information, it is more difficult to recognise 'subtle viewpoint promotion' in a typical reference work. On the other hand, they point out that bias which would be unchallenged in a traditional reference work is more likely to be pointed out in Wikipedia. In addition, because Wikipedia is online, instant revision can take place when mistakes are spotted.

🐾 APPLY YOUR KNOWLEDGE

1. A psychologist wishes to publish his research in a mainstream psychology journal.
   a. Explain why it is desirable for this research study to be peer reviewed before publication. (4 marks)
   b. The research paper is rejected for publication. Suggest **two** reasons why it may have been rejected. (4 marks)
2. Consider a radio programme that you listen to or a magazine that you read:
   a. In what way are these likely to be peer reviewed? (2 marks)
   b. Do you think peer review is/would be beneficial to such media? Explain your answer. (3 marks)

CAN YOU?   No. 7.22

1. Explain why peer review is essential to the scientific process. (3 marks)
2. Briefly explain **two** criticisms of peer review. (2 marks + 2 marks)

Psychology and the economy

The mission statement for the British Psychological Society is to be 'responsible for the development, promotion and application of psychology for the public good'. This also relates to the economy of the country we live in. The 'economy' concerns the production, distribution and consumption of goods and services. On this spread we consider how psychology can contribute to the public good and a better economy.

MEET THE RESEARCHER

Daniel Kahneman (1934–) is a psychologist who was awarded the Nobel prize in 2002. What was unusual was that he got the prize for his contribution to economics. He grew up in Paris during the Nazi occupation of the city. After the war he moved to Israel and later to the US, initially conducting research on visual perception. From the 1970s he has collaborated with Amos Tversky looking at how people make decisions. This research led to a new area of research, behavioural economics, which has had a profound effect on the way people think about thinking.

Testing the availability heuristic

You can test the availability heuristic (see right) yourself by repeating a study by Tversky and Kahneman (1973). They read out male and female names to participants. Some of the names were famous names and some were not. Participants were then asked to estimate whether there were more male or female names in the list.

According to the availability heuristic, participants should say 'male' if there were a lot of famous male names in the list because then 'male' is more available, and the same would apply if there were a lot of famous female names in the list.

One group of participants heard 19 famous male names and 20 less famous female names. A second group of participants heard 19 famous female names and 20 less famous male names (to counterbalance any gender effect).

In the original study about 80% of participants' judgements were incorrect, having been influenced by the famous names being more available and thus tipping the balance.

If you do conduct this study you can use the sign test to analyse your findings. The table of data should look like the example below (obviously with your own data in it). The data are paired and thus suitable for the sign test.

Participant	Famous name category	Gender selected	Same?
1	male	female	−
2	male	female	−
3	male	male	+
4	male	female	−
5	male	male	+
6	male	male	+
7	female	female	+
8	female	female	+
9	female	male	−
10	female	female	+
11	female	male	−
12	female	female	+

ECONOMIC PSYCHOLOGY

The discipline of Economic Psychology is a blend of economics and psychology – seeking a better understanding of people's behaviour in their economic lives. The field is also referred to as 'behavioural economics' where researchers investigate the effects of social, cognitive and emotional factors on economic decisions. The field is primarily concerned with the rationality (or irrationality) of decisions relating to economics.

Irrational thinking

You have seen examples of irrational thinking in your studies of depression (page 108). But it isn't just depressed people who think irrationally – all of us do. Daniel Kahneman has led the field of research into everyday irrational thinking and uncovered, and explained, many fascinating aspects of this behaviour.

▲ Economic Psychology is a relatively new field in psychology. The field's journal began in 1981 – so it may not seem that new to you.

Availability heuristic

Take, for example, the availability heuristic ('heuristic' is a fancy word for 'rule'). People typically overestimate the likelihood of dying in a plane accident – the reason for such irrational thinking is because we often read about such accidents and therefore they are more *available* when making a probability judgement about the likelihood of being in such an accident. The *availability heuristic* is the rule that the likelihood of selecting something is related to its 'availability'.

The framing effect

Another example of irrational thinking is that people's decisions differ depending on whether a choice is presented as a gain or a loss. Tversky and Kahneman (1986) asked participants to choose between two treatments that were going to be used with 600 people suffering from a deadly disease. Two groups of participants were given the same facts about the success and failure rates of the treatment but the facts were 'framed' differently.

One group of participants were told that Treatment A would result in 400 deaths, whereas Treatment B would have a 33% chance that no one would die, and a 66% chance that all 600 would die.

A second group of participants were told that Treatment A would save 200 lives, whereas Treatment B had a 33% chance of saving everyone and a 66% of saving no one.

The first example is positive framing, and when participants were given this description 72% selected Treatment A.

When participants were given the same scenario but in a negative frame only 22% selected Treatment A.

Real-world influences

Understanding the systematic biases caused by such irrational thinking is important in improving our personal lives as well as the fabric of our society.

Economist Richard Layard (2014) says that Kahneman's work on understanding irrational thinking has transformed business. His ideas have been applied to almost any endeavour you can think of – decision-making in juries, treatment of mental health problems, financial advice, government programmes (see facing page) and so on.

APPLYING THE TOPICS IN THIS BOOK

There are many topics covered in this book that can be applied to improving the economy of our country and world. Here we consider a few of them but, to be honest, the list is endless.

Social change

In Chapter 1 we explored the topic of social change, discussing a number of examples where understanding of social influence has been used to improve behaviour. For example, on page 34 a campaign to reduce drink driving was discussed where attitudes and behaviour was changed by making people aware of social norms. Similar ideas have been used to reduce social stereotypes and smoking (page 18).

Such practices have the potential to bring about positive changes that will impact on the economy; however, this approach is limited to tasks where behaviour is moderated by social criteria.

Improving memory

In Chapter 2 you learned about the cognitive interview (page 60), a technique based on psychological research that has improved the amount of accurate information collected from eyewitnesses. In fact the whole topic of eyewitness memory research is focused on improving crime detection.

The implication for the economy is to be able to reduce expenses on wrongful arrests and to ensure that criminals are caught.

Attachment

Bowlby's theory and related research (page 78) on attachment opened the eyes of the world to the importance of emotional care in early child development. Unicef (see above right) indicate the continuing influence this has on developmental policies in ensuring the healthy development of children to becoming productive members of society and thus improving world economy. Before Bowlby's research people believed that physical care was all that was necessary.

Mental health

The McCrone report (McCrone *et al.*, 2008) estimated the direct costs of mental health in England at around £22.5 billion a year – that includes spending in health and social care and a variety of other agencies, but not the indirect costs of the impact on the criminal justice system and in lost employment. Of particular concern is the projected rise in dementia and a growing population of older people. Psychologists are increasingly turning their attention to research on dementia.

The McCrone report commented on the use of drugs versus psychotherapies, saying that 'the number of people receiving medication provides a much greater economic gain than psychological therapies, which may produce similar benefits compared to medication but are far more expensive'. Evidence-based research on effective drug therapies is important in reducing costs and helping people return to work.

Biopsychology

Neuroscience offers the possibility of revolutionising our understanding of the human brain. An American government report suggested that this may have practical economic benefits in the area of 'smart' machines, i.e. machines that will think like humans (NIH, 2013). This does not mean building human-like robots but just money-saving intelligent machines to deal with, for example, questions on the telephone or recognising faces at airports.

▲ The United Nations children's charity says: 'Science is changing the way we think about development policy and practice when it comes to young children… No one disputes that food and nutrition are vital for a baby's health and welfare…but what about stimulation? And a sense of security? How about love? Deprivation that stems from lack of care and nurture, exposure to domestic violence, abuse, and the effects of living through war can have just as detrimental an effect on brain development as a lack of food' (UNICEF, 2014).

 APPLY YOUR KNOWLEDGE

In 2008 Richard Thaler and Cass Sunstein published a book called *Nudge: Improving Decisions About Health, Wealth and Happiness* based on the research by Kahneman and others that human thinking is not rational. Thaler and Sunstein reasoned that a kind of 'soft paternalism' could be used to nudge people into making better decisions (better for them and better for society) without taking away their freedom of choice. For example, junk food might be placed on supermarket shelves above eye level or organ donation should be opt out rather than opt in.

Following this the UK government set up the *Behavioural Insights Team* with the aim of producing research which would help run the country better. The unit is also called the 'Nudge Unit'. Their research has included a project on the payment of car tax. Despite hefty penalties many people still don't pay. Based on psychological research, the Nudge Unit proposed that messages should be simpler; letters to non-payers should be personalised and more visual. This tripled the number of payments made.

In the case of organ donation the team conducted a randomised control trial comparing the effect of different messages on a government website. The message 'If you needed an organ transplant, would you have one? If so help others' was based on reciprocity and fairness and led to an increase in donors.

Using your knowledge of ethical issues, consider the costs and benefits of the work done by the Nudge Unit.

CAN YOU? | No. 7.23

1. Outline **one** example of how psychological research has been used to benefit the economy. (3 marks)
2. Discuss the implications of psychological research for the economy. (6 marks)

End-of-chapter review / CHAPTER SUMMARY

We have identified here the key points of the topics on the AQA (A) AS specification, i.e. the bare minimum that you need to know. You may want to fill in further details to elaborate and personalise this material.

EXPERIMENTS

THE EXPERIMENTAL METHOD

DESCRIPTION
- Aims are stated.
- There are two or more levels of the independent variable (IV), manipulated by the experimenter.
- The effect is measured on a dependent variable (DV) which is operationalised.
- Extraneous variables are controlled and procedures are standardised.
- The hypothesis states the relationship between the IV and DV.
- Causal conclusions can be drawn.

CONTROL OF VARIABLES

DESCRIPTION
- Confounding variables vary systematically with the IV, thus any change in the DV may be due to a confounding variable instead of the IV.
- Extraneous variables are nuisance variables and make it harder to detect change in the DV.
- Mundane realism is the extent to which features of a study mirror the real world.
- Generalisation – findings from a study may lack generalisability if the materials or environment lack mundane realism or if participants know they are being studied.
- Validity = legitimacy, genuineness.
- Internal validity – enhanced by control of confounding variables, high mundane realism.
- External validity – generalising to other situations (ecological validity), people (population validity) and historical periods (historical validity).

HYPOTHESES AND THINGS

DESCRIPTION
- Directional hypothesis states more, less, higher, lower, etc.
- Non-directional hypothesis does not state direction of difference.
- State direction if indicated by past research.
- Pilot study is a trial run with similar participants to test procedures and amend if necessary.
- Confederates are directed by a researcher to play certain roles in a study.

SAMPLING

DESCRIPTION
- Small group of people selected from a population.
- Opportunity sample – recruit those easily available.
- Random sample – use a random technique, e.g. lottery method or random number generator.
- Stratified sample – identify relevant subgroups, randomly select appropriate proportion from each subgroup.
- Systematic sample – select every *n*th person.
- Volunteer sample – people respond to an advertisement.

EVALUATION/DISCUSSION

Opportunity sample
- (+) Easy because participants are there.
- (−) Biased.

Random sample
- (+) Unbiased.
- (−) Takes time.

Stratified sample
- (+) Proportional, representative and unbiased.
- (−) Time consuming.

Systematic sample
- (+) Unbiased.
- (−) Not truly random.

Volunteer sample
- (+) Variety of participants.
- (−) Volunteer bias.

ETHICS

ETHICAL ISSUES

DESCRIPTION

From the researcher's point of view:
- Informed consent – may give away the aims.
- Deception – acceptable when information withheld, less acceptable if dishonest.
- The right to withdraw – biases the sample.
- Protection from psychological and physical harm – difficult to guarantee because unpredictable.
- Confidentiality – publication of findings may reveal identity even if anonymous.
- Privacy – hard to protect when participants studied without their awareness.

From the participant's point of view:
- Informed consent – basic human right based on knowing what is involved.
- Deception – prevents informed consent, may distrust psychologists in the future.
- The right to withdraw – compensates for situations involving deception.
- Protection from psychological and physical harm – risks should be no greater than everyday life.
- Confidentiality – a legal right (Data Protection Act).
- Privacy – even in a public place people may not wish to be observed.

DEALING WITH ETHICAL ISSUES

DESCRIPTION

Strategies include:
- Ethical guidelines – tell psychologists what is acceptable.
- Cost-benefit analysis – judged from the participant's perspective or perspective of society.
- Ethics committees – approve studies based on cost-benefit considerations.
- Punishment – may be barred from work as a psychologist.

Specific ethical issues:
- Informed consent – sign a form, presumptive consent, the right to withdraw.
- Deception – debriefing is required and the right to withhold data.
- The right to withdraw – part of informed consent.
- Protection from harm – researcher can stop the study.
- Confidentiality – maintain anonymity.
- Privacy – only acceptable in a public place.

EVALUATION/DISCUSSION

Ethical guidelines
- (+) Rules and sanctions approach offers clarity.
- (−) Can't cover everything.
- (−) Closes off discussion.
- (−) Absolves researcher of responsibility.

Cost-benefit approach
- (−) Can't predict costs/benefits beforehand.
- (−) Just creates new dilemmas (Baumrind).

- Informed consent – participants may not understand what is actually involved.
- Presumptive consent – hypothetical agreement is different from real agreement.
- Debriefing – can't turn the clock back; the harm is done.
- The right to withdraw – participants may feel they can't.
- Protection from harm – may only be apparent with hindsight.
- Confidentiality – people may work out identity.
- Privacy – lack of universal agreement about what counts as public.

EXPERIMENTS

EXPERIMENTAL DESIGN

DESCRIPTION

- Repeated measures – each participant is tested twice/experiences both levels of the IV.
- Independent groups – each participant is only tested on one level of the IV.
- Matched pairs – each participant is paired with another participant, each pair receives both levels of the IV.
- Counterbalancing – each condition is tested first or second in equal amounts, could be AB or BA, or ABBA.

EVALUATION/DISCUSSION

Repeated measures
- − Order effects (e.g. practice or boredom).
- − May guess aims of the study.
- + Can counterbalance.

Independent groups
- − Participant variables not controlled.
- − Need more participants.
- + Can use random allocation.

Matched pairs
- − Matching takes time.
- − May not account for all variables that matter.
- + Good compromise.

Strengths for each design can be worked out by looking at limitations of the other designs.

LABORATORY AND FIELD EXPERIMENTS

DESCRIPTION

- Laboratory experiment – study with an IV and DV, conducted in controlled environment.
- Field experiment – study with an IV and DV conducted in a more natural environment.
- In both kinds of experiment the IV may be contrived and thus reduce mundane realism.

EVALUATION/DISCUSSION

Laboratory experiment
- + High internal validity.
- − Usually aware of being studied.
- − Operationalisation of IV or DV may have low mundane realism.
- − Participants may feel uncomfortable in setting.

Field experiment
- + Usually not aware of being studied.
- + More natural setting, so more relaxed.
- − Operationalisation of IV or DV may have low mundane realism.
- − Difficult to control extraneous variables.
- − Difficult to debrief.

NATURAL AND QUASI-EXPERIMENTS

DESCRIPTION

- Natural experiment – the IV is natural insofar as it varies whether or not the researcher is there. The DV may be measured in a lab.
- Quasi-experiment – the IV is not a variable, it is a condition that exists such as age or having an external locus of control.

EVALUATION/DISCUSSION

Natural experiment
- + Used where IV can't be manipulated for ethical or practical reasons.
- + Can study 'real' problems.
- − Can't demonstrate causal relationships.
- − Random allocation not possible, so low internal validity.
- − Can only be used with existing conditions.
- − Participants may be aware of being studied.
- − Operationalisation of DV may have low mundane realism.

MORE PROBLEMS WITH EXPERIMENTS

DESCRIPTION

- Demand characteristics – cues in an experimental situation that convey hypothesis to participants, creating expectations about how to behave.
- Investigator effects – unconscious cues from investigator that affect participant's performance other than what was intended, including indirect effects, e.g. *investigator experimental design effect*.
- Single blind or double blind – minimise these problems.

OBSERVATIONS

OBSERVATIONAL TECHNIQUES

DESCRIPTION

- Naturalistic observation – everything is left as it is normally, in an everyday setting.
- Controlled observation – researcher regulates aspects of the environment.
- Overt observation – participants aware that they are being observed, whereas not aware during a covert observation (may be informed afterwards).
- Participant observation – observer is part of group being observed, whereas in non-participant observation observer watches from a psychological and probably physical distance.

EVALUATION/DISCUSSION

Observational studies in general
- + Show what people actually do.
- + Capture spontaneous behaviour.
- + Can be used to measure DV.
- − Observer bias (can be improved by having more than one observer and checking inter-observer reliability).
- − Don't provide insight into what people think.

Naturalistic observation
- + Realistic picture, high in ecological validity.
- − Little control, which makes conclusions difficult.

Controlled observation
- + Useful for focusing on particular behaviours.
- − Behaviour may be less natural.

Covert observation
- + Participants not aware of being studied and therefore more natural.
- − Ethical issues.

Overt observation
- − Affects naturalness of behaviour, demand characteristics.

Participant observation
- + May provide better insights.
- − Likely to be overt, so problems with naturalness.

Non-participant observation
- + More objective.
- − Likely to be covert, so ethical issues.

OBSERVATIONAL DESIGN

DESCRIPTION

- Unstructured observations – observer records everything.
- Structured observations – a system is used.
- Behavioural categories – target behaviour divided into individual behaviours that can be clearly identified, e.g. 'smile showing teeth' rather than 'be happy'.
- Sampling procedures – record events (event sampling) or record behavioural categories at time intervals (time sampling).

SELF-REPORT

SELF-REPORT TECHNIQUES

DESCRIPTION

- Questionnaire – data collected through written, fixed questions.
- Structured interview – questionnaire delivered face-to-face or over phone; in real-time.
- Unstructured questionnaire – may start with some predetermined questions and further questions developed in response to answers given.

EVALUATION/DISCUSSION

Self-report techniques
- (+) Access what people think and feel.
- (−) Answers may lack validity because of social desirability bias.
- (−) People also don't know what they actually think.
- (−) Sample may be unrepresentative.

Questionnaires
- (+) Collect data from large number of people.
- (+) People may be more willing to reveal confidential information than in an interview.
- (−) Can only be filled in by people who can write and have the time, biased sample.

Structured interview
- (+) Can be repeated exactly (as can a questionnaire), good for making comparisons between people.
- (+) Good for analysis.
- (−) May lack comparability between interviewers.
- (−) Interviewer bias.

Unstructured interviews
- (+) More detailed information.
- (−) More issues with interviewer skills and bias, more expensive because of training needed.
- (−) In-depth questions lack objectivity.
- (−) Interviewer bias.

SELF-REPORT DESIGN

DESCRIPTION

- Clarity of questions – avoid ambiguity, double negatives, double-barrelled questions.
- Bias – avoid leading questions and social desirability bias.
- Analysis – use closed or open questions.
- Other considerations – filler questions, leave anxiety-provoking questions until later, consider sampling technique, run a pilot study.
- Recording interviews – writing down answers may make interviewee feel evaluated.
- Effect of interviewer – non-verbal cues (e.g. crossing arms), listening skills (e.g. regulating comments).
- Questioning skills in unstructured interview – how and what questions to ask (e.g. not too probing or repetitive).

EVALUATION/DISCUSSION

Open questions
- (+) Respondents can expand answers, more detail provided.
- (+) Unexpected answers, new insights.
- (−) Respondents may not give full answers.
- (−) May be difficult to analyse.

Closed questions
- (+) Mainly quantitative data produced, easier to analyse and draw conclusions.
- (−) Forced choice means answer may not represent true thoughts.
- (−) Acquiescence bias leads to low validity.

CORRELATIONS

DESCRIPTION

- An analysis of association between continuous co-variables.
- Positive correlation – dots on scattergram from bottom left to top right, co-variables increase together.
- Negative correlation – top left to bottom right, as one co-variable increases the other decreases.
- Zero correlation – no significant association.
- Correlational hypothesis can be directional (positive or negative correlation) or null (zero correlation).
- Correlation coefficient is a number between +1 and −1 to show strength of correlation.

EVALUATION/DISCUSSION

- (+) Can investigate trends, which may justify further investigation or may rule out any causal link.
- (+) Procedures can be easily repeated, to confirm findings.
- (−) No causal relationship demonstrated.
- (−) People may act on erroneous causal conclusions, which may be dangerous.
- (−) Apparent correlations may be due to intervening variables.
- (−) Measurement of variables may lack validity or poor sampling may mean low generalisability.

OTHER RESEARCH METHODS

DESCRIPTION

- Meta-analysis – data analysed from a review of studies sharing the same aim/hypothesis, effect size (dependent variable) may be produced.
- (A03 plus) Case study – detailed study of a single individual, institution or event using many different research methods.
- (A03 plus) Content analysis – form of indirect observation of the artefacts people produce.

EVALUATION/DISCUSSION

Meta-analysis
- (+) Results from number of studies increases validity.
- (+) Balances out contradictory results and gives overall figure.
- (−) Studies may not be comparable.

Case study
- (+) In-depth data overlooked using other methods.
- (+) Good for studying rare events/behaviours.
- (+) Complex interactions can be studied.
- (−) Unique characteristics.
- (−) May involve recollection of past events.
- (−) There is generally no 'before' comparison.

Content analysis
- (+) Based on real events, high ecological validity.
- (+) Easily replicated if data is public.
- (−) May suffer from observer bias.

THE SCIENTIFIC PROCESS AND PEER REVIEW

DESCRIPTION

- Assessing the quality of research (peer review) is part of the process of science.
- Allocation of research funding – ensure it is spent on high-quality research.
- Research in academic journals and books – prevent incorrect data being published.
- Research rating of university departments – determined by REF peer review.
- Online journals (e.g. Philica) policed by 'wisdom of crowds'.

EVALUATION/DISCUSSION

- Finding an expert – for some topics there aren't suitable 'peers'.
- Anonymity – may help bury rival research.
- Publication bias – journals prefer to publish positive results.
- Status quo – preference against research that challenges accepted theories.
- Fraudulent research – remains in public domain.

PSYCHOLOGY AND THE ECONOMY

DESCRIPTION

- Economic psychology researches the effect of social, cognitive and emotional factors on economical decisions.
- Kahneman's research into irrational thinking has changed many aspects of professional life, e.g. juries, business.
- Examples of irrational thinking – availability heuristic, framing effect.
- Social change – e.g. use social norms to reduce drink driving.
- Improving memory – e.g. the cognitive interview reduces police costs.
- Attachment – understanding the importance of emotional care in infancy promotes a healthy adult population.
- Mental health – research on dementia and drug therapies saves money in an area of vast expenditure.
- Biopsychology – neuropsychology helps build smart, money-saving machines.

DISPLAY OF QUANTITATIVE DATA AND DATA DISTRIBUTIONS

DESCRIPTION
Display of quantitative data
- Tables and graphs must have a title and clear labels.
- Tables may contain measures of central tendency and dispersion.
- Bar chart – height of bar represents frequency, data on *x*-axis may not be continuous.
- Histogram – represents frequency of continuous data, true zero and bars next to each other.
- Line graph – frequency represented by a line rather than bars.
- Scattergram – shows correlation between co-variables.

Data distributions
- Normal distribution – symmetrical bell-shaped curve; mean, median and mode at mid-point; about 68% of people are one standard deviation above and below the mid-point, 95% within two standard deviations from mid-point.
- Positive skew – tail to right, occurs, e.g. when test too hard.
- Negative skew – tail to left, occurs, e.g. when test too easy.

TYPES OF DATA

DESCRIPTION
- Quantitative data – numerical, e.g. measuring a dependent variable, answers to closed questions.
- Qualitative data – can't be directly counted, non-numerical, e.g. answers to open questions.
- Primary data – collected by the researcher for current study, involves design of study to collect data.
- Secondary data – using data collected for a previous study, e.g. government statistics.

EVALUATION/DISCUSSION
Quantitative data
- (+) Easy to analyse, and draw conclusions.
- (−) May oversimplify reality.

Qualitative data
- (+) Detailed and possibly unexpected information.
- (−) More difficult to draw conclusions.

Primary data
- (+) Controlled by researcher and suits the needs of the study.
- (−) Time consuming to design and collect, so expensive.

Secondary data
- (+) Saves time and money.
- (+) May already have been subject to statistical testing.
- (−) May not fit exact needs of study.

INTRODUCTION TO STATISTICAL TESTING

DESCRIPTION
- When to use the test – the sign test is used with paired or related data.
- How to do the test – represent each pair of data with plus or minus, calculated value of *S* = least frequent sign.
- Look up critical value of *S* – need to know *N* and whether one-tailed test (directional hypothesis) or two-tailed test (non-directional hypothesis).
- Conclusion – if calculated value is less than or equal to critical value, the difference is significant.
- Probability level of 5% is commonly used.

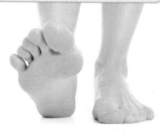

MATHEMATICAL SKILLS

DESCRIPTION
- Fractions – numerator and denominator, can be reduced to simplest form by dividing both by the lowest common denominator.
- Percentage is out of 100, can convert to a fraction by writing number/100 and reducing to simplest form.
- Can convert a fraction to a percentage by dividing denominator by numerator and move decimal place two places to right.
- Ratios can be part-to-part (e.g. 4:1) or part-to-whole (4:5), can reduce to simplest form or change to fraction.
- Estimate results – round your numbers up or down to produce a sum you can do in your head and then add the zeros.
- Significant figures – refers to the number of important digits used to represent a number.
- Order of magnitude – show number by giving one or two significant figures and powers of 10, e.g. 5.4×10^4 or 3.6×10^{-3} which are 540,000 and 0.0036.
- Mathematical symbols: $=, \therefore, <, \ll, \gg, >, \propto, \sim$.

MEASURES OF CENTRAL TENDENCY AND DISPERSION

MEASURES OF CENTRAL TENDENCY

DESCRIPTION
- Mean – add up all numbers and divide by *N*. Ratio and interval data only.
- Median – order all numbers and select mid-point. Ratio, interval and ordinal data.
- Mode – most common value or group. May be bi-modal. Can be used with all levels of measurement.

EVALUATION/DISCUSSION
Mean
- (+) Most sensitive because uses exact distance.
- (−) Distorted by extreme values.
- (−) Not appropriate for nominal data or discrete values.

Median
- (+) Not affected by extreme values.
- (+) Appropriate for ordinal data.
- (+) Can be easier to calculate than the mean.
- (−) Not as sensitive as mean.

Mode
- (+) Unaffected by extreme values.
- (+) More useful for discrete data.
- (+) Useful for nominal data.
- (−) Not good where many modal groups.
- (−) Tells nothing about other values/distribution.

MEASURES OF DISPERSION

DESCRIPTION
- Range – subtract lowest from highest and add a correction of 1.
- Standard deviation – average distance between each number and the mean.

EVALUATION/DISCUSSION
Range
- (+) Easy to calculate.
- (−) Affected by extreme numbers.
- (−) Doesn't reflect data distribution.

Standard deviation
- (+) Takes exact values into account.
- (+) Can be easily calculated with a calculator.
- (−) May be affected by extreme values.

The exam questions on research methods will be varied but are likely to involve some short answer questions (AO1), some application of knowledge questions (AO2), research methods questions (AO2) and possibly an extended writing question (AO1 + AO3). We have provided a selection of these kinds of questions.

AS AND A LEVEL QUESTIONS

0 1   Read the item below and then answer the questions that follow.

> A psychologist wanted to test the accuracy of eyewitness testimony when using different identification techniques. He wanted to compare the use of simultaneous line-ups with the use of sequential line-ups. Simultaneous line-ups involve a witness identifying a suspect when viewing everyone in the line-up at the same time. Sequential line-ups involve looking at one person at a time and deciding whether they are the offender or not. If not, the next person is viewed.
>
> The psychologist had 40 students volunteering to take part in his experiment. He divided them into two equal groups – one group viewed a simultaneous line-up, the other group viewed a sequential line-up. All participants were shown the same staged mugging on film. A week later participants returned to the laboratory to view the line-up.

(i)   Write a suitable hypothesis for this study.   **[3 marks]**

(ii)   Briefly outline how the psychologist could have conducted the same experiment using a repeated measures design.   **[4 marks]**

(iii) Identify **one** extraneous variable controlled by the psychologist and briefly explain why it was important to control it in this study.   **[3 marks]**

0 2   Read the item below and then answer the questions that follow.

> The results of the experiment are given in Table 1.
>
> Table 1: The number of correct and incorrect identifications for each type of line-up.
>
> | | Simultaneous line-up | Sequential line-up |
> | --- | --- | --- |
> | Correct identifications | 12 | 15 |
> | Incorrect identifications | 8 | 5 |

(i)   Calculate the percentage of participants who made a correct identification in the condition using simultaneous line-ups. Show your workings.   **[2 marks]**

(ii)   What do the data in Table 1 seem to suggest about the effect of different identification techniques on the accuracy of eyewitness testimony? In your answer, refer to whether this matches the hypothesis you wrote in Question 1 (i).   **[5 marks]**

0 3   Read the item below and then answer the questions that follow.

> The psychologist did some further analysis having recorded the amount of time that it took to make a correct identification for each type of line-up.
>
> The results of this analysis are given in Table 2.
>
> Table 2: The mean time for identification and the standard deviations for each type of line-up.
>
> | | Simultaneous line-up | Sequential line-up |
> | --- | --- | --- |
> | Mean time for identification | 12 mins 15 secs | 8 mins 32 secs |
> | Standard deviation | 3.5 | 1.8 |

(i) What conclusion could the psychologist draw about the effect of type of line-up on time taken to make a correct identification? Refer to both the mean scores and standard deviations as part of your answer.   **[4 marks]**

(ii) Sketch a graph to show the difference in average identification times between the two conditions.   **[4 marks]**

(iii) Identify and explain **one** potential problem with this study.   **[3 marks]**

0 4   Read the item below and answer the question that follows.

> The psychologist focused on the type of line-up and its effect on eyewitness accuracy.
>
> The accuracy of eyewitness testimony can also be affected by the anxiety experienced by a witness.

Design a self-report study to investigate the effect that anxiety has had on real-life eyewitnesses.

In your answer you should provide details of:

- where the sample is drawn from and how
- what type of self-report method is used and why
- the type of questions used including an example of one question that could be asked
- ethical issues to be considered.   **[10 marks]**

0 5   Read the item below and then answer the questions that follow.

> A researcher investigated the genetic basis of OCD by carrying out an adoption study. He advertised for adoptees who had been diagnosed with OCD and who had contact with both their biological parents and adoptive parents. Using his sample of 47 respondents, the researcher then contacted both sets of parents to ask whether any of them had been diagnosed with the disorder as well. The researcher found that 23% of the biological parents had been diagnosed with OCD compared to 4% of the adoptive parents.

(i) Identify the sampling method used to select the adoptees.   **[1 mark]**

(ii) State whether the researcher collected quantitative or qualitative data. Justify your answer.   **[2 marks]**

(iii) Outline **one** ethical issue that the researcher would have needed to consider when conducting this study.   **[3 marks]**

0 6   Read the item below and then answer the questions that follow.

> A psychologist wanted to compare the effectiveness of flooding and systematic desensitisation for treating phobias. She used a matched pairs design identifying sex, age and type of phobia as key variables. All participants were volunteers and agreed to be allocated to one of the two treatments at random. The psychologist decided to measure effectiveness through self-report. One month after treatment had finished, she asked her participants to rate how anxious they felt in the presence of their feared object or situation.

(i) Outline **one** reason for not using a repeated measures design in this investigation.   **[3 marks]**

(ii) Outline **one** reason for not using an independent groups design in this investigation.   **[3 marks]**

(iii) Identify **one** method of self-report that she could have used.   **[1 mark]**

(iv) Outline **one** strength and **one** limitation of using self-report in this study.   **[4 marks]**

(v) Give an example of a question she could ask after the treatment had finished. Indicate whether this is an open question or a closed question.   **[2 marks]**

We've provided answers by two students to some of the questions from pages 228–229 here, together with comments from an examiner about how well they've each done. **Green** comments show what the student has done well. Orange comments indicate areas for improvement.

01 Read the item below and then answer the questions that follow.

> A psychologist wanted to test the accuracy of eyewitness testimony when using different identification techniques. He wanted to compare the use of simultaneous line-ups with the use of sequential line-ups. Simultaneous line-ups involve a witness identifying a suspect when viewing everyone in the line-up at the same time. Sequential line-ups involve looking at one person at a time and deciding whether they are the offender or not. If not, the next person is viewed.
>
> The psychologist had 40 students volunteering to take part in his experiment. He divided them into two equal groups – one group viewed a simultaneous line-up, the other group viewed a sequential line-up. All participants were shown the same staged mugging on film. A week later participants returned to the laboratory to view the line-up.

(i) Write a suitable hypothesis for this study. *(3 marks)*

✓ Both the IV and DV are included.

Maisie's answer

There is a difference between the type of line-up and whether a correct identification is made or not.

! The answer doesn't make clear what difference is being looked at, as it states it is between levels of the IV rather than the number of correct identifications.

Examiner's comments

Limited answer and the IV (type of line-up) needs to be operationalised. *1/3 marks*

✓ Both the IV and DV are included and fully operationalised.

Ciaran's answer

There is a difference in the number of correct identifications made when suspects are placed in a simultaneous line-up or a sequential line-up.

Examiner's comments

A much better answer that clearly states the difference and operationalises the two variables. *3/3 marks*

(ii) Briefly outline how the psychologist could have conducted the same experiment using a repeated measures design. *(4 marks)*

✓ She understands the basic structure of a repeated measures design.

✓ Maisie understands the implications of switching to repeated measures.

Maisie's answer

This would mean that he would test participants twice — once using a simultaneous line-up and then using a sequential line-up. Obviously, he could not use the same suspect both times so he would use two different films, but they should both involve a mugging that happens in a similar way.

! Maisie could include more detail about the experiment, for example by explaining how long the psychologist would wait between the two conditions or how counterbalancing could be used.

Examiner's comments

The answer is accurate and is clearly repeated measures. However, it lacks a little depth and detail. Try to give answers detailed enough so someone could use it to replicate the experiment. *2/4 marks*

✓ Clear and comprehensive explanation of how the groups could be set up in a repeated measures design.

✓ Good detail.

✓ This is accurate and good detail, although the question does not specifically ask for it.

Ciaran's answer

The psychologist would select two films using different actors, and the films could involve two different types of crimes to make the findings more representative. If he had 40 students again then he could divide them into four groups of 10, and counterbalance the order of conditions as well as the film used. This means that the experiment would be set up in the following way.
Trial A: Watch Film 1 followed by sequential line-up, then watch Film 2 followed by simultaneous line-up.
Trial B: Watch Film 1 followed by simultaneous line-up, then watch Film 2 followed by sequential line-up.
Trial C: Watch Film 2 followed by sequential line-up, then watch Film 1 followed by simultaneous line-up.
Trial D: Watch Film 2 followed by simultaneous line-up, then watch Film 1 followed by sequential line-up.
Doing it this way should reduce order effects which are a problem with repeated measures design.

Examiner's comments

Ciaran gives a thorough account of how a repeated measures design could be used. He clearly understands the question and is capable of being flexible with his knowledge. Perhaps a little more than is needed for 4 marks but it would depend how long it took to write it. *4/4 marks*

(iii) Identify **one** extraneous variable controlled by the psychologist and briefly explain why it was important to control it in this study. *(3 marks)*

✓ Maisie highlights why it is important to control.

✓ Extraneous variable identified clearly.

✓ Good elaboration of the importance of controlling it.

Maisie's answer

The psychologist made all participants wait a week before doing the line-up. This is important because the time between witnessing the crime and identifying the suspect affects the chances of it being correct. For example, if some participants had been called back many weeks later there is more time for the information in their memories to have decayed or become distorted.

Examiner's comments

Maisie has identified an extraneous variable directly related to the study outlined and explained it. *3/3 marks*

! Ciaran seems to have misread the question as the task was clearly to find one that had been controlled rather than one that 'might' be controlled.

Ciaran's answer

The psychologist might have controlled noise because this could distract some participants. This would mean that this affected the dependent variable instead of the independent variable causing the change.

Examiner's comments

Ciaran needs to ensure he is answering the question asked specifically. *0/3 marks*

---

04 Read the item below and answer the question that follows.

> The psychologist focused on the type of line-up and its effect on eyewitness accuracy.
> The accuracy of eyewitness testimony can also be affected by the anxiety experienced by a witness.

Design a self-report study to investigate the effect that anxiety has had on real-life eyewitnesses.

In your answer you should provide details of:

- where the sample is drawn from and how
- what type of self-report method is used and why
- the type of questions used, including an example of one question that could be asked
- ethical issues to be considered. *(10 marks)*

✓ 'Appropriate question.

✓ Maisie makes it clear where she would get the sample, the method she would use and specifically how she would pick them.

✓ A good justification. The more you can explicitly make it relevant to the scenario the better. For example, Maisie could explain why she thinks they might get upset.

Maisie's answer

My investigation would use a volunteer sample of eyewitnesses which I would collect by putting an advert in a courtroom and choosing the first 10 that reply. One ethical consideration is gaining consent. The advert would explain the purpose of my study so they knew what they were consenting to, but I would also make it clear that they could withdraw at any point. My preferred method would be an unstructured interview because I think this appropriate when dealing with something sensitive such as crime and anxiety. I would be able to tailor the questions to suit the personality of my interviewee, and reassure them if they were getting upset or clarify a question if it did not make sense. I would also be using open questions because they would allow me to go into more depth about how each person felt, and to what degree they thought their testimonies were accurate rather than just asking if they were accurate or not. One question I could ask is 'When the crime was being committed, how did you feel?'. To be safe, I would tape record the interviews so that I could play them back to a colleague and together we would summarise the main findings which should improve reliability.

Examiner's comments

Maisie has given a thorough and well thought out answer with enough detail to be implemented successfully. All required elements are included. *10/10 marks*

! Method identified but not the reasons why.

! It is very unclear to whom Ciaran would be sending this to, initially.

Ciaran's answer

I would use a questionnaire and send this out to people. They would only have to return it if they had been a witness to a crime. The questionnaire would use pre-set questions with multiple choice answers such as 'Did the crime cause you anxiety? Yes/No'. This would make it easier to analyse people's answers. The ethical issue I would consider is confidentiality as the questionnaires could be anonymous.

✓ The type of question and an appropriate example given.

! One ethical consideration highlighted. The requirement is for 'ethical issues' so more than one is needed.

Examiner's comments

Ciaran has not given enough detail and it would be hard to implement this study with success. For example, there is no explanation as to whom to send the questionnaire to, initially. There is also no justification for the method. *4/10 marks*

Problem corner
Expert advice on students' big worries

These pages highlight some of the common problems that concern students while studying A Level Psychology as well as in exams. If repeated across topics these mistakes could have an impact on your final result.

The good news is that there are often simple solutions or rules to help you avoid making these mistakes, and *The Complete Companions* Team is here to guide you through them!

Assessment objectives (AOs): Picking the right one

Dear Complete Companions Team,

I don't understand why I did badly in the mocks when I really know the material.

Susie, A Level student

Examiner insight
One of the big mistakes students make every year is choosing the wrong approach to some of the questions. They display the 'wrong' AO and therefore lose out on most, or all, of the marks. Here is our advice.

Assessment objectives (AOs) relate to the skills you need to demonstrate to the examiner.

Look out for the command word in the question, as this should tell you what the examiner is looking for in your answer.

The AOs are split into three skills and these are as follows:

AO1: Demonstrating knowledge and understanding, often referred to as 'description'
This skill is about showing your understanding and knowledge. For AO1, you don't need to evaluate, you just need to describe.

    Key command words that indicate AO1: Identify, name, outline, describe, explain how.

AO2: Application of knowledge and understanding
This is about applying what you know. This could be to do with a piece of research, conversation, implications or research methods.

    Key command words that indicate AO2: This is harder to pin down to particular words as AO2 can be indicated in different ways. 'Suggest how' is a common start to a question that signifies AO2.

AO3: Evaluation, analysis and interpretation
Your answer must go beyond simply describing a study or theory. It could include strengths and weaknesses, criticisms (positive and/or negative), ethical issues, methodological issues, applications and so on.

    Key command words that indicate AO3: Discuss, evaluate, any question that refers to strengths or limitations or criticisms. As with AO1, explain can be used here too.

Responding effectively to the AOs
Recognising the different AOs in a question, and knowing how to respond to them is vital as doing this effectively will undoubtedly maximise your marks.

There are some relatively simple steps you can take to achieve this:
(i)   Recognise the key command words and respond appropriately (see above).
(ii) Know the right sort of material to provide for each AO (i.e. description, application or evaluation/discussion).
(iii) Know the right sort of balance for each AO in a question. For example, is it all AO1, equal amounts of AO1 and AO3, more AO3 than AO1?
(iv) Respond in the right way, e.g. by adding detail in AO1 (if required), linking AO2 material effectively to the scenario or conversation and by elaborating your AO3, or making it more discursive if a 'Discuss' question.

AO2 application questions:
Applying your knowledge and understanding

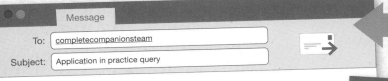

To: completecompanionsteam
Subject: Application in practice query

Dear Complete Companions Team

How can I get high marks on questions with a scenario or conversation?

Thank you
Magnus, A Level student

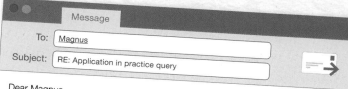

To: Magnus
Subject: RE: Application in practice query

Dear Magnus

You need to show the examiner that you can apply what you know to the scenario in the question and not simply give a generic answer. We have attached some notes to this email which should help you.

Best paws forward

The Complete Companions Team

Let's look at two types of AO2 application questions:

1. One type of application question is where the **whole** answer needs to be related to the stem and there are no marks for simply outlining the theory/study/concept. Here is an example:

> Nadia is passionate about a charity that supports children living in developing countries. However, most of her classmates want to raise money for an animal charity. The class is due to vote for the class charity at the end of the week.
>
> Using your knowledge of minority social influence, explain **two** ways in which Nadia could try to persuade her classmates to vote for her charity. [6 marks]

This question asks you to apply what you already know about minority influence (the role of flexibility, consistency and so on) to Nadia and what she could do. Let's have a look at three different answers:

Answer 1:
For a minority to be successful, they have to make sure that they are consistent. This means that they give the same message every time and everyone in the minority does the same thing. This was shown in Moscovici's green/blue slide study and it showed that if a group was more consistent, they were more likely to influence others.

For people to be persuaded, a minority must also be flexible in their views and not too dogmatic. If the minority seems too unwilling to listen to others then the majority will be less likely to follow them. There should also be a level of commitment where the minority shows that they are willing to sacrifice for the cause too — like the suffragettes. This is what Nadia should do.

> All the marks in this question are for AO2. This answer is mainly descriptive and explains how minorities in general are able to persuade people. The last sentence is not enough to gain marks for application as the answer does not engage with the stem throughout.

Answer 2:
Nadia could put together her arguments very carefully to try and convince her classmates to vote for her charity. For example, she could make a brochure with personal stories about some of the children in the countries she wants to help. This would make her classmates more interested in helping because they can put a face to the name and it stops the children being anonymous in the eyes of the people reading the brochure.

A second way she could persuade her classmates to vote for her charity is to have a debate. She could present her arguments for the children's charity while another classmate presents arguments for the animal charity. If she can make her arguments persuasive enough and presents them consistently then the views of the class will change from the majority position to her minority position.

Let's put those together and see what an answer based on psychological knowledge applied to the scenario would look like.

Although this answer engages with the stem throughout, it doesn't go beyond common sense. As this isn't based much on the knowledge of minority influence, it would gain very little credit.

Answer 3:

When Nadia is putting across her arguments about why the rest of the class should vote for her charity, she needs to be **consistent**, not changing her mind all the time. This will make the rest of the class consider her point of view more carefully, and why she believes the children's charity is the more worthy cause. The importance of consistency in this sort of situation was highlighted in a study by Wood et al. (1994), who found that when minorities were consistent in expressing their position they tended to be more influential.

As well as being consistent, Nadia needs to be **flexible** in the way she puts her argument across. Research by Mugny (1982) has shown that flexibility is more effective at changing the views of the majority opinion than being rigid and inflexible. Nadia is more likely to change her classmates' minds if she shows she is prepared to compromise, perhaps acknowledging that both charities are worthy causes and that perhaps they can support both. However, if she is too flexible, she risks being seen as inconsistent, which would make it less likely that the class will accept her arguments.

This answer combines an understanding of the psychology behind how a minority influences a majority (using terms such as 'consistent' and 'flexible') with the scenario that has been given. Where the research by Wood is mentioned, for it to be creditworthy there would need to be some link to Nadia. There is always more that *could* be said, but this answer would be good enough to get full marks.

2. A second type of AO2 application question asks you to outline a theory, approach or evaluation point and then simply refer to the scenario or stem as just **part** of the answer. You could come across it as a short question or a longer essay-style question. Here is an example of the short version:

> Alfie watched his older brother, Charlie, tidy up his toys and get praised for doing so by his parents. Alfie went to his room and started to tidy up his toys.
>
> What is meant by the term 'vicarious reinforcement'? Refer to Charlie and Alfie in your answer. [4 marks]

Only part of the marks will be for AO2, while the remainder will be given for an accurate description of vicarious reinforcement (AO1). You need to make sure you give a clear definition, and link it explicitly to Charlie and Alfie.

Make sure you explain how their behaviour fits the definition.

Vicarious reinforcement is learning by observing someone else being reinforced for a behaviour, for example, if we see someone get rewarded, we are likely to imitate. Alfie paid attention to Charlie (the model) getting praise, which was positive reinforcement for Charlie. Alfie then starts to tidy up his toys too in the hope he might get the same praise.

This answer gives a clear definition and shows good use of technical vocabulary (AO1). The third sentence links effectively to the Charlie and Alfie scenario (AO2). This combined helps to make this a full-mark answer (4 marks).

Applying knowledge of research methods: Practical skills

Dear Complete Companions Team,

How do I show the examiner that I can apply my knowledge of research methods? I struggle with linking what I've learned in class to a particular study.

Examiner insight

Something that seems apparent from answers in the research methods section is that students are not equipped to apply their knowledge as well as they should be. In the past, students were asked to conduct coursework to show their practical skills but this is no longer the case. Here is our advice.

One thing that could make a real difference here is if you go out and conduct your own research. You should attempt to design, carry out and analyse a number of small-scale studies to help you practise the application which is so important.

In your design you could include:

- Title
- Aim
- Hypothesis and justification for choosing a directional or non-directional one
- Method chosen (such as lab experiment, observation or interview)
- Strengths and limitations of choosing that method within the context of the study
- Research design chosen and justification for why
- Sampling method and an explanation of how it would be done
- Justification for the sampling method in this context
- The way the data will be recorded

- Any stimulus materials needed
- Standardised instructions
- Any potential problems that might be faced including ethical issues as well as how these would be dealt with
- Any unexpected problems faced
- Strengths of the research
- What you found and how it relates to your hypothesis
- What statistical test you would use and why (at AS there is only one test you would use)
- Overall conclusion

Although this seems a long list, it can be done in a very basic form and it could be repeated for a number of simple studies. However, the aim of this exercise is to make it specific to the study you are conducting rather than being a list of generic statements.

There are lots of suggestions for research projects in Chapter 7 but here are a few more:

1 An easy lab experiment could be one to do with memory. It could be as simple as asking people to learn a list of words while listening to music and when in silence. You can decide whether to do repeated measures (don't forget counterbalancing!) or independent groups. You could extend it to include other types of music or sounds.

2 You could use a questionnaire that has already been created, such as one related to the locus of control, Authoritarian Personality or attachment types. Alternatively, you could create a questionnaire about something simple like mobile phone use or the amount of revision students do. Try to include open and closed questions. You could even go on to correlate the amount of revision with the score in a mock exam or last test (if done with classmates).

3 Interviews can be difficult if you are shy but, as your study can be based on anything, choose something you are comfortable with. You could base it on the questionnaire that you do, and interview a couple of people in more depth.

4 In Year 2 there is an option you might be studying on relationships and an easy study to conduct is on the matching hypothesis. You could get photos of long-term couples (wedding photography websites are a good resource for this) and then ask people to rate how attractive they believe the individuals are. Again you could ask people to rate both partners or just one. You then compare to see whether there is a correlation between the mean rating given to each of the individuals. The matching hypothesis states that people get together with individuals of a similar level of attractiveness to themselves.

How to distinguish effectively in your answers

Examiner insight

One common error students make when asked to distinguish between things is that they simply explain what each one is without explicitly pointing out the difference.

The command word 'distinguish' is asking you what the difference is between two ideas or concepts.

The easy way to show that you are distinguishing is to use 'whereas', 'however' or 'on the other hand'. For example, 'Structured interviews have a set of predetermined questions that are asked in the same order for each participant, whereas unstructured interviews do not'.

You also need to ensure that what you are 'distinguishing' is comparable, otherwise it won't make much sense or get many marks. For example, 'Structured interviews have a set of predetermined questions that are asked in the same order for each participant, whereas unstructured interviews are more time consuming'. Whether or not questions are predetermined, on the one hand, and how much time an interview takes, on the other, are not comparable factors.

Let's look at an exam question and how to answer it:

> Distinguish between insecure-avoidant and insecure-resistant attachment. [3 marks]

The insecure-avoidant child avoids intimacy and shows little concern when separated from the primary caregiver. However, insecure-resistant children both seek and resist intimacy, and so are distressed when separated yet may resist being picked up.

Also, avoidant children tend to have low stranger anxiety whereas insecurely attached children have high stranger anxiety.

These are good examples of using language to show that a distinction is being made.

The same traits – emotional response, separation anxiety and stranger anxiety – are described and contrasted for both attachment types.

Common misconceptions: Bowlby's theories (see Chapter 3, pages 78 and 85)

Examiner insight

Many students find it difficult to distinguish between Bowlby's maternal deprivation hypothesis and his monotropic theory of attachment. Students either get confused and use aspects of both, or alternatively simply choose the wrong one, which obviously has a big impact on the marks they are able to get.

It is understandable to get confused between Bowlby's two theories because one is an extension of the other. Bowlby developed the maternal deprivation theory first and then, over a number of years, extended this to the monotropic theory of attachment. The handy lists below will help you reinforce your understanding of the features that are specific to each theory.

Maternal deprivation

- Focus is on the negative effects of deprivation
- Critical period for separation to have an effect: under the age of two and a half years (if no substitute available)
- Consequence: frequent prolonged separations may lead to emotional maladjustment later in life
- Affectionless psychopathy may be an outcome (44 thieves study)

Theory of attachment

- Focus is on the benefits of attachment
- Critical period for formation of attachment: between 3 and 6 months
- Consequence: internal working model of relationships later in life
- Social releasers elicit caregiving
- Monotropy, one primary attachment figure

Let's look at how this might be used effectively in an exam question that is taken from the 2017 AS paper 1. The answer below is focused and accurate and would gain the full 3 marks.

> Outline Bowlby's theory of maternal deprivation. [3 marks] (AQA, 2017)

Bowlby's theory of maternal deprivation suggests that if a child is deprived of maternal care for a prolonged length of time or experiences frequent prolonged separations, then this may lead to emotional maladjustment later in life, such as the individual becoming an affectionless psychopath. If this deprivation/separation happens in the critical period of the first two and a half years or so then it is more likely to have these negative effects.

The start is accurate and focused on the key aspect of the theory rather than formation of attachment.

The general consequence is mentioned first and then some specific and accurate effects are added.

Reference to the critical period is specifically about the negative impact.

Common misconceptions:
Reinforcement and operant conditioning

Message

Dear Complete Companions Team,
I have been trying to understand reinforcement and operant conditioning. I keep getting the different aspects muddled up though and can never remember how punishment and negative reinforcement are different.

Reinforcement 'encourages' or 'strengthens' a behaviour – and makes it happen more frequently. Punishment, on the other hand, 'discourages' or 'weakens' a behaviour, making it less likely to be shown.

Let's look at some examples.

Positive reinforcement

Frankie gets £5 (pleasant stimulus) for tidying his room (behaviour). This is likely to increase how often Frankie tidies his room.

Negative reinforcement

Grace tidies her room (behaviour) to stop her mother from nagging her to do it (unpleasant stimulus).

Punishment – aims to reduce frequency of, or stop, a behaviour

When he hits his brother with his toy lightsaber (behaviour), Charlie has it taken off him for the rest of the day (punishment). Charlie wants to keep his toy, so this decreases how likely he is to hit his brother.

Let's take a look at an exam question on this topic.

> Using an example, outline **one** type of reinforcement used in learning theories. [3 marks]

Type of reinforcement clearly identified.

Accurate description of what it is.

Answer 1:

Positive reinforcement is where something pleasant happens after a person performs a particular behaviour. Because they are being rewarded for their behaviour they are more likely to do it again. An example would be when a child is praised for being polite, they are then more likely to be polite again in the future.

Clear, accurate example to illustrate the outline.

Accurate effect stated, and explanation given.

Examiner's comments
Good, accurate answer with the right amount of detail. *3 marks*

Clearly Identified.

Incorrect explanation.

Answer 2:

Negative reinforcement is when something negative follows after a person has done something. As a result they are less likely to act in the same way in the future. An example would be if somebody was told off for doing something, they would probably not do it again.

The example is for punishment, not negative reinforcement.

Examiner's comments
The second answer shows the classic mistake of confusing negative reinforcement with punishment. The only part that is potentially relevant in this answer is the 'telling off', but this would need to be in the context of doing something more (the reinforcement part) to avoid being told off rather than less (punishment). *0 marks*

Tips for writing successful answers to extended writing questions

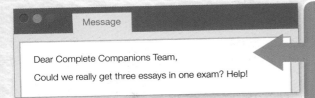

Message

Dear Complete Companions Team,

Could we really get three essays in one exam? Help!

Examiner insight

There are likely to be between two and four essays across the two AS papers, and between five and seven 16-mark essays across the three A Level papers. They could appear in any section, so don't panic if there are three in one paper. This just means the other papers will have more short questions - the total number of marks remains the same!

Writing essays is key to your exam success, so read on to discover the five tips for success and how to avoid making some of the common mistakes that are made each year in the exams.

1 Read the question fully. Then read it again. Then briefly plan how you will set out your answer before… reading it again. Writing an essay you have prepared earlier is unlikely to answer the question effectively. Your knowledge must be selected and shaped for the actual question.

2 Step back and plan. This will help you to write a clear, coherent answer. Take time to think before you start writing. Dissect the question. For example, let's look at the following 12-mark question:

> Outline research into the effect of situational variables on obedience and discuss what this tells us about why people obey.   [12 marks] (AQA, 2017)

> This is the topic – 'research' includes theories and studies so you can focus on either, or both.

> This shows that you have more than one thing to do.

> This is another command word but this time it is to do with AO3.

> This is a command word – it is asking for AO1.

> This is what you need to relate the AO3 to – do situational factors effectively tell us why people do, or do not, obey?

3 Get the right balance between assessment objectives. As a rule of thumb, for a 12-mark question there are usually 6 marks for AO1 and 6 for AO3. However, if there is a stem then AO2 is also needed, which means fewer marks for AO3, but marks for AO1 remain the same.

Make sure that you balance your answer appropriately. Students often spend too long describing a theory or studies, especially if they know them really well, but this can mean they leave little time for evaluation. Remember that the maximum number of marks for AO1 is 6 – be selective!

4 Use research studies in the right way. Some essay questions will ask you to discuss 'research', where you might refer to a theory and/or research studies in your answer. Some questions might ask you to discuss 'research studies', where you must both describe and evaluate research studies. Other questions will ask you to outline and evaluate a 'theory'. There would be no marks in such a question for describing studies, unless they are being used explicitly to evaluate the theory itself.

Here's an example:

> Describe and evaluate social learning theory.   [12 marks AS/16 marks A]

Although this might seem like a fairly straightforward question, it is clear from previous exams that students find it difficult to separate social learning theory (SLT) and the Bobo doll study. Detailed descriptions of the study alone are not creditworthy – you must link any evaluation of the study back to SLT itself. For example, something like this:

There might have been demand characteristics as it was such a controlled environment that they might have guessed what they were expected to do. Also, the task was unusual as to watch a model beat up a toy in that way would not be something they are likely to experience in day-to-day life. Therefore the study might not be useful in telling us how learning occurs in real life situations.

This is a good evaluation point for Bandura's study, but it is not related back to SLT and so would not be credited. Evaluation points like this could be used more effectively by saying things such as 'if theories are based on these studies then it might affect the validity of the theory itself'.

5 Elaborate effectively. Comments like 'It lacks ecological validity' or 'It was unethical' without further clarification will get few, if any, marks. Equally, a list of basic points like 'They had a limited sample as it only used males', 'It was done in a lab so there was lots of control' or 'There are other explanations that this did not consider' will not get beyond basic marks – no matter how many of them you write.

Practice developing every evaluation point to make it more effective. You can follow the approach we have used throughout this book or, if you would like to introduce other points of evaluation, you could elaborate these in various ways, including:

- State your point – is this positive or negative? For example, a study may be limited in some way (negative) or have led to important applications (positive).

- Is there evidence to back up the claim you are making? What is this evidence?

- What does this point mean for the thing being evaluated (e.g. does it strengthen or weaken a line of argument?) or does it have consequences or implications?

- If you are being asked to 'Discuss' you could introduce counterarguments or challenges to this particular critical point.

Use paragraphs. Examiners will follow your argument more easily if they aren't faced with a 'wall of words'.

Essay focus: The 'Discuss' instruction

Dear Complete Companions Team,

When a question asks me to 'discuss' something, is this different from 'outline and evaluate'?

Examiner insight

Students often lose marks on 'Discuss' questions as they answer as if the question is a simple 'Outline and evaluate'. This means that the AO3 is not effective enough. Use the guidance below to help develop a more discursive style for 'Discuss' questions.

Yes!

In a simple 'outline and evaluate' question you can just write all the AO1 then all the AO3, and AO3 points could all be strengths or all limitations of a theory.

A 'discuss' question requires you to go a little further and, well... *discuss* the topic. For example, you could offer counterarguments, or perhaps consider the implications of a particular critical point.

Let's look at an example of a 'Discuss' question:

Discuss the Authoritarian Personality explanation of obedience.   [8 marks]

The A01 part is to *describe* the Authoritarian Personality explanation of obedience.

As there are only 3 marks for A01 here, about 60–75 words would suffice (e.g. link between obedience and F-scale, right-wing authoritarianism, Elms and Milgram findings).

The 'discuss' instruction requires you to go deeper with your AO3, looking beyond just the strengths and/or limitations of the explanation.

As well as stating any strengths or limitations of the Authoritarian Personality explanation, you should also have some more 'discursive' AO3 content. This might include Milgram's counterargument that situational factors are more important than personality in obedience, or Middendorp and Meloen's claim that education is the main causal factor in both Authoritarian Personality *and* obedience.

Examiner insight

A common mistake that students make with this question is discussing the Authoritarian Personality without linking this explicitly to obedience. This would seriously limit the number of marks awarded because it isn't answering the question. So, ALWAYS read the question carefully and respond accordingly.

Good luck!

References

Abernethy, E.M. (1940) The effect of changed environmental conditions upon the results of college examinations. *Journal of Psychology, 10,* 293–301.

Abravanel, E. and DeYong, N. (1991) Does object modeling elicit imitative-like gestures from young infants? *Journal of Experimental Child Psychology, 52,* 22–40.

Adorno, T.W., Frenkel-Brunswik, E., Levinson, D.J. and Sanford, R.N. (1950) *The Authoritarian Personality.* New York: Harper and Row.

Aggleton, J.O. and Waskett, L. (1999) The ability of odours to serve as state-dependent cues for real-world memories: Can Viking smells aid the recall of Viking experiences? *British Journal of Psychology, 90(1),* 1–7.

Ainsworth, M.D.S. (1967) *Infancy in Uganda: Child Care and the Growth of Love.* Baltimore: Johns Hopkins University Press.

Ainsworth, M.D.S., Bell, S.M. and Stayton, D.J. (1971) Individual differences in Strange Situation behavior of one year olds. In H.R. Schaffer (ed.) *The Origins of Human Social Relations.* New York: Academic Press.

Ainsworth, M.D.S., Blehar, M.C., Waters, E. and Wall, S. (1978) *Patterns of Attachment: A Psychological Study of the Strange Situation.* Hillsdale, NJ: Lawrence Erlbaum.

Akers, R.L. (1998) *Social Learning and Social Structure: A General Theory of Crime and Deviance.* Boston: Northeastern University Press.

Al-Kubaisy, T., Marks, I.M., Logsdail, S., Marks, M., Lovell, K., Sungur, M. and Araya, R. (1992) Role of exposure homework in phobia reduction: A controlled study. *Behavior Therapy, 23,* 599–621.

Albucher, R.C., Abelson, J.L. and Nesse, R.M. (1998) Defense mechanism changes in successfully treated patients with obsessive compulsive disorder. *American Journal of Psychiatry, 155,* 558–9.

Alicke, M.D. and Govorun, O. (2005) The better-than-average effect. In M.D. Alicke, D.A. Dunning, J.I. Krueger. *The Self in Social Judgment: Studies in Self and Identity.* Hove: Psychology Press.

Allen, V.L. and Levine, J.M. (1969) Consensus and conformity. *Journal of Experimental Social Psychology, 5,* 389–99.

Alloy, L.B. and Abramson, L.Y. (1979) Judgment of contingency in depressed and non-depressed students: Sadder but wiser? *Journal of Experimental Psychology, 108,* 441–85.

Altemeyer, R. (1981) *Right-Wing Authoritarianism.* Winnipeg: University of Manitoba Press.

Anderson, J.R. (2000) *Learning and Memory: An Integrated Approach.* New York: John Wiley and Sons.

Anderson, R.C. and Pichert, J.W. (1978) Recall of previously unrecallable information following a shift in perspective. *Journal of Verbal Learning and Verbal Behavior, 17,* 1–12.

Andrewes, D. (2001) *Neuropsychology from Theory to Practice.* Hove: Psychology Press.

Andsager, J.L., Bemker, V., Choi, H.-L. and Torwel, V. (2006) Perceived similarity of exemplar traits and behaviour: Effects on message evaluation. *Communication Research, 33,* 3–18.

Annese, J., Schenker-Ahmed, N.M., Bartsch, H., Maechler, P., Sheh, C., Thomas, N., Kayano, J., Ghatan, A., Bresler, N., Frosch, M.P., Klaming, R. and Corkin, S. (2014) Postmortem examination of patient H.M.'s brain based on histological sectioning and digital 3D reconstruction. *Nature Communications, 5(1),* 3122, 1–9.

Arliss, J.M., Kaplan, E.N. and Galvin, S.L. (2005) The effect of the lunar cycle on frequency of births and birth complications. *American Journal of Obstetric Gynecology, 192(5),* 1462–4.

Asch, S.E. (1956) Studies of independence and conformity: I. A minority of one against a unanimous majority. *Psychological Monographs: General and Applied, 70(9),* 1–70.

Aschoff, J., Fatranska, M., Giedke, H., Doerr, P., Stamm, D. and Wiser, H. (1971) Human circadian rhythms in continuous darkness: Entrainment by social cues. *Science, 171,* 213–15.

Ashton, H. (1997) Benzodiazepine dependency. In A. Baum, S. Newman, J. Weinman, R. West and C. McManus (eds) *Cambridge Handbook of Psychology, Health and Medicine.* Cambridge: Cambridge University Press.

Atkinson, R.C. and Shiffrin, R.M. (1968) Human memory: A proposed system and its control processes. In K.W. Spence and J.T. Spence (eds) *The Psychology of Learning and Motivation, Vol. 2.* London: Academic Press.

Avtgis, T.A. (1998) Locus of control and persuasion, social influence, and conformity: A meta-analytic review. *Psychological Review, 83,* 899–903.

Babyak, M.A., Blumenthal, J.A., Herman, S., Khatri, P., Doraiswamy, P.M., Moore, K.A., Craighead, W.E., Baldewicz, T.T. and Krishnan, K.R. (2000) Exercise treatment for major depression: Maintenance of therapeutic benefit at 10 months. *Psychosomatic Medicine, 62,* 633–8.

Baddeley, A.D. (1966a) The influence of acoustic and semantic similarity on long term memory for word sequences. *Quarterly Journal of Experimental Psychology, 18,* 302–9.

Baddeley, A.D. (1966b) Short-term memory for word sequences as a function of acoustic, semantic and formal similarity. *Quarterly Journal of Experimental Psychology, 18,* 362–5.

Baddeley, A.D. (1986) *Working Memory.* Oxford: Clarendon Press.

Baddeley, A.D. (1997) *Human Memory: Theory and Practice.* Hove: Psychology Press.

Baddeley, A.D. (2000) The episodic buffer: A new component of working memory? *Trends in Cognitive Sciences, 4(11),* 417–23.

Baddeley, A.D. (2004) *Your Memory: A User's Guide* (new illustrated edn). Buffalo, NY: Firefly Books.

Baddeley, A.D. and Hitch, G.J. (1974) Working memory. In G.H. Bower (ed.) *The Psychology of Learning and Motivation, Vol. 8.* London: Academic Press.

Baddeley, A.D. and Hitch, G.J. (1977) Recency re-examined. In S. Dornic (ed.) *Attention and Performance.* New Jersey: Erlbaum.

Baddeley, A.D. and Longman, D.J.A. (1978) The influence of length and frequency on training sessions on the rate of learning type. *Ergonomics, 21,* 627–35.

Baddeley, A.D., Thomson, N. and Buchanan, M. (1975) Word length and the structure of short-term memory. *Journal of Verbal Learning and Verbal Behavior, 14,* 575–89.

Bahrick, H.P., Bahrick, P.O. and Wittinger, R.P. (1975) Fifty years of memory for names and faces: A cross-sectional approach. *Journal of Experimental Psychology: General, 104,* 54–75.

Bandura, A. (1986) *Social Foundations of Thought and Action: A Social Cognitive Theory.* Englewood Cliffs, NJ: Prentice-Hall.

Bandura, A. and Rosenthal, T.L. (1966) Vicarious classical conditioning as a functioning of arousal level. *Journal of Personality and Social Psychology, 3,* 54–62.

Bandura, A., Ross, D. and Ross, S.A. (1961) Transmission of aggression through imitation of aggressive models. *Journal of Abnormal and Social Psychology, 63,* 575–82.

Bandura, A. and Walters, R. (1963) *Social Learning and Personality Development.* New York: Holt, Rinehart and Winson Inc.

Banuazizi, A. and Movahedi, S. (1975) Interpersonal dynamics in a simulated prison: A methodological analysis. *American Psychologist, 30,* 152–60.

Barrett, H. (1997) How young children cope with separation: Toward a new conceptualisation. *British Journal of Medical Psychology, 70,* 339–58.

Bates, G.W., Thompson, J.C. and Flanagan, C. (1999) The effectiveness of individual versus group induction of depressed mood. *Journal of Psychology, 133(3),* 245–52.

Baumrind, D. (1959) Conceptual issues involved in evaluating improvement due to psychotherapy. *Psychiatry, 22,* 341–8.

Baumrind, D. (1964) Some thoughts on ethics of research: After reading Milgram's 'Behavioral study of obedience'. *American Psychologist, 19,* 421–3.

Baumrind, D. (1985) Research using intentional deception: Ethical issues revisited. *American Psychologist, 40(2),* 165–74.

Bavalier, D., Corina, D., Jezzard, P., Padmanabhan, S., Clark, V.P., Karni, A., Prinster, A., Braun, A., Lalwani, A., Rauscheeker, J.P., Turner, R. and Neville, H. (1997) Sentence reading: A functional MRI study at 4 Tesla. *Journal of Cognitive Neuroscience, 9,* 664–86.

Beardsley, T. (1997) The machinery of thought. *Scientific American, August,* 58–63.

Beck, A.T. (1967) *The Diagnosis and Management of Depression.* Philadelphia, PA: University of Pennsylvania Press.

Beck, A.T. (1976) *Cognitive Therapy and Emotional Disorders.* New York: International Universities Press.

Bègue, L., Beauvois, J.-L., Courbet, D., Oberlé, D., Lepage, J. and Duke, A.A. (2014) Personality predicts obedience in a Milgram paradigm. *Journal of Personality* (published online 24 June 2014).

Bekerian, D.A. and Bowers, J.M. (1983) Eye-witness testimony: Were we misled? *Journal of Experimental Psychology, Learning, Memory and Cognition, 9,* 139–45.

Belsky, J. and Rovine, M. (1987) Temperament and attachment security in the Strange Situation: A rapprochement. *Child Development, 58,* 787–95.

Bickman, L. (1974) Clothes make the person. *Psychology Today, 8(4),* 48–51.

Bifulco, A., Harris, T. and Brown, G.W. (1992) Mourning or early inadequate care? Re-examining the relationship of maternal loss in childhood with adult depression and anxiety. *Development and Psychopathology, 4,* 433–49.

Billett, E.A., Richter, M.A. and Kennedy, J.L. (1998) Genetics of obsessive compulsive disorder. In R.P. Swinson, M.M. Antony, S. Rachman and M.A. Richter (eds) *Obsessive Compulsive Disorder: Theory, Research and Treatment*. New York: Guilford.

Blass, T. (1999) The Milgram paradigm after 35 years: Some things we now know about obedience to authority. *Journal of Applied Social Psychology, 29*, 955–78.

Bond, R. (2005) Group size and conformity. *Group Processes and Intergroup Relations, 8(4)*, 331–54.

Bothwell, R.K., Brigham, J.C. and Pigott, M.A. (1987) An exploratory study of personality differences in eyewitness memory. *Journal of Social Behavior and Personality, 2*, 335–43.

Bowlby, J. (1944) Forty-four juvenile thieves: Their characters and their home life. *International Journal of Psychoanalysis, 25*, 1–57, 207–28.

Bowlby, J. (1951) *Maternal Care and Mental Health*. Geneva: World Health Organization.

Bowlby, J. (1953) *Child Care and the Growth of Love*. Harmondsworth: Penguin.

Bowlby, J. (1958) The nature of the child's tie to his mother. *International Journal of Psycho-Analysis, XXXIX*, 1–23.

Bowlby, J. (1969) *Attachment and Love, Volume 1: Attachment*. London: Hogarth.

Bowlby, J., Ainsworth, M., Boston, M. and Rosenbluth, D. (1956) The effects of mother–child separation: A follow-up study. *British Journal of Medical Psychology, 29*, 211.

Boyke, J., Driemeyer, J., Gaser, C., Buchel, C. and May, A. (2008) Training-induced brain structure changes in the elderly. *The Journal of Neuroscience, 28(28)*, 7031–5.

BPS (2009) Code of Ethics and Conduct. *See* www.bps.org.uk/system/files/documents/code_of_ethics_and_conduct.pdf (accessed January 2015).

Brandimote, M.A., Hitch, G.J. and Bishop, D.V.M. (1992) Influence of short-term memory codes on visual processing: Evidence from image transformation tasks. *Journal of Experimental Psychology: Learning, Memory and Cognition, 18*, 157–65.

Braun, K.A., Ellis, R. and Loftus, E.F. (2002) Make my memory: How advertising can change our memories of the past. *Psychology and Marketing, 19(1)*, 1–23.

Brazelton, T.B. (1979) Evidence of communication during neonatal behavioral assessment. In M. Bullowa (ed.) *Before Speech: The Beginning of Interpersonal Communication*. Cambridge: Cambridge University Press.

Bregman, E.O. (1934) An attempt to modify the emotional attitudes of infants by the conditioned response technique. *Journal of Genetic Psychology, 45*, 169–98.

Bretherton, I. and Muholland, K. (1999) Internal working models in attachment relationships: A construct revisited. In J. Cassidy and P. Shaver (eds) *Handbook of Attachment: Theory, Research and Clinical Applications*. New York: Guilford Press.

Broca, P. (1865) Sur le siège de la faculté du language articulé. *Bulletin of Social Anthropology, 6*, 337–93.

Brooks, M. (2010) We need to fix peer review now. New Scientist blog. *See* www.newscientist.com/blogs/thesword/2010/06/we-need-to-fix-peer-review-now.html (accessed February 2012).

Buhr, E.D., Yoo, S.-H. and Takahashi, J.S. (2010) Temperature as a universal resetting cue for mammalian circadian oscillators. *Science, 330(6002)*, 379–85.

Burger, J.M. (2009). Replicating Milgram: Would people still obey today? *American Psychologist, 64(1)*, 1–11.

Burgess, H.J., Crowley, S.J., Gazda, C.J., Fogg, L.F. and Eastman, C.I. (2003) Preflight adjustment to eastward travel: 3 days of advancing sleep with and without morning bright light. *Journal of Biological Rhythms, 18(4)*, 318–28.

Burnett, S., Bird, G., Moll, J., Frith, C. and Blakemore, S.J. (2009) Development during adolescence of the neural processing of social emotion. *Journal of Cognitive Neuroscience, 2*, 1736–50.

Burt, C.L. (1955). The evidence for the concept of intelligence. *British Journal of Psychology, 25*, 158–77.

Burt, C.L. (1966) The genetic determination of differences in intelligence: A study of monozygotic twins reared together or apart. *British Journal of Psychology, 57*, 137–53.

Bushman, B.J. (1988) The effects of apparel on compliance: A field experiment with a female authority figure. *Personality and Social Psychology Bulletin, 14(3)*, 459–67.

Buss, D.M. (1989) Sex differences in human mate preferences: Evolutionary hypotheses tested in 37 cultures. *Behavioral and Brain Sciences, 12*, 1–49.

Campbell, J.D. and Fairey, P.J. (1989) Informational and normative routes to conformity: The effect of fraction size as a function of norm extremity and attention to the stimulus. *Journal of Personality and Social Psychology, 57*, 457–68.

Carré, J., Muir, C., Belanger, J. and Putnam, S.K. (2006) Pre-competition hormonal and psychological levels of elite hockey players: relationship to the home advantage. *Physiology and Behavior, 89*, 392–8.

Ceraso, J. (1967) The interference theory of forgetting. *Scientific American, 217*, 117–24.

Chan, A. (1985) *Children of Mao*. London: Macmillan.

Charlton, T., Gunter, B. and Hannan, A. (eds) (2000) *Broadcast Television Effects in a Remote Community*. Hillsdale, NJ: Lawrence Erlbaum.

Chase, W.G. and Simon, H.A. (1973) The mind's eye in chess. In W.G. Chase (ed.) *Visual Information Processing*. New York: Academic Press.

Choy, Y. and Schneier, F.R. (2008) New and recent drugs for anxiety disorders. *Primary Psychiatry, 15(12)*, 50–6.

Choy, Y., Fyer, A.J. and Lipsitz, J.D. (2007) Treatment of specific phobia in adults. *Clinical Psychology Review, 27*, 266–86.

Christianson, S.-Å. (1992) Emotional stress and eyewitness memory: A critical review. *Psychological Bulletin, 112*, 284–309.

Christianson, S.-Å. and Hubinette, B. (1993) Hands up! A study of witnesses' emotional reactions and memories associated with bank robberies. *Applied Cognitive Psychology, 7*, 365–79.

Cohn, D., Cohn, G.L. and Wang, W. (2014) After decades of decline, a rise in stay-at-home mothers. *See* www.pewsocialtrends.org/2014/04/08/after-decades-of-decline-a-rise-in-stay-at-home-mothers (accessed August 2014).

Comer, R.J. (1998) *Abnormal Psychology* (2nd edn). New York: WH Freeman.

Comer, R.J. (2002) *Fundamentals of Abnormal Psychology* (3rd edn). New York: Worth.

Coolican, H. (2004) Personal communication.

Cooper, G., Hoffman, K., Powell, B. and Marvin, R. (2005) The circle of security intervention. In L. Berlin, Y. Ziv, L. Amaya-Jackson and M. Greenberg (eds) *Enhancing Early Attachments: Theory, Research, Intervention, and Policy*. New York: Guilford Press.

Corkin, S. (2002) What's new with the amnesic patient H.M.? *Nature Reviews Neuroscience, 3*, 153–60.

Cotter, D., Mackay, D., Landau, S. *et al.* (2001) Reduced glial cell density and neuronal size in the anterior cingulate cortex in major depressive disorder. *Archives of General Psychiatry, 58*, 545–53.

Cowan, N. (2001) The magical number 4 in short-term memory: A reconsideration of mental storage capacity. *Behavioral and Brain Sciences, 24(1)*, 87–114.

Craik, F.I.M. and Lockhart, R.S. (1972) Levels of processing: A framework for memory research. *Journal of Verbal Learning and Verbal Behavior, 11*, 671–84.

Craik, F.I.M. and Tulving, E. (1975) Depth of processing and the retention of words in episodic memory. *Journal of Experimental Psychology, 104*, 268–94.

Craske, M.G., Kircanski, K., Zelikowsky, M., Mystkowski, J., Chowdhury, N. and Baker, A. (2008) Optimizing inhibitory learning during exposure therapy. *Behaviour Research and Therapy, 46*, 5–27.

Crockett, M.J., Clark, L., Tabibnia, G., Lieberman, M.D. and Robbins, T.W. (2008) Serotonin modulates behavioral reactions to unfairness. *Science, 320*, 1739.

Csikszentmihalyi, M. and Hunter, J. (2003) Happiness in everyday life: the uses of experience sampling. *Journal of Happiness Studies, 4*, 185–99.

Cuijpers, P., Berking, M., Andersson, G., Quigley, L., Kleiboer, A. and Dobson, K.S. (2013) A meta-analysis of cognitive-behavioural therapy for adult depression, alone and in comparison with other treatments. *Canadian Journal of Psychiatry, 58*, 376–85.

Czeisler, C.A., Duffy, J.F., Shanahan, T.L., Brown, E.N., Mitchell, J.F., Rimmer, D.W., Ronda, J.M., Silva, E.J., Allan, J.S., Emens, J.S., Dijk, D.-J. and Kronauer, R.E. (1999) Stability, precision and near-24-hour period of the human circadian pacemaker. *Science, 284*, 2177–81.

Dambrun, M. and Valentine, E. (2010) Reopening the study of extreme social behaviors: Obedience to authority within an immersive video environment. *European Journal of Social Psychology, 40(5)*, 760–73.

de Maat, S., de Jonghe, F., Schoevers, R. and Dekker, J. (2009) The effectiveness of long-term psychoanalytic therapy: A systematic review of empirical studies. *Harvard Review of Psychiatry, 17*, 1–23.

de Maat, S., de Jonghe, F., Schoevers, R. and Dekker, J. (2009) The effectiveness of long-term psychoanalytic therapy: A systematic review of empirical studies. *Harvard Review of Psychiatry, 17*, 1–23.

DeJong, W, Schneider, S.K., Towvim, L.G., Murphy, M.J., Doerr, E.E., Simonsen, N.R. and Scribner, R.A. (2006) A multisite randomized trial of social norms marketing campaigns to reduce college student drinking. *Journal of Studies on Alcohol, 67*, 868–79.

Danaher, P.J., Bonfrer, A. and Dhar, S. (2008) The effect of competitive advertising interference on sales for packaged goods. *American Marketing Association, XLV*, 211–25.

Dando, C. and Milne, B. (2009) The cognitive interview. In R. Kocsis (ed.) *Applied Criminal Psychology: A Guide to Forensic Behavioral Sciences*. Charles C. Springfield, IL: Thomas Publishers.

de Maat, S., Dekker, J., Schoevers, R. and de Jonghe, F. (2006) Relative efficacy of psychotherapy and pharmacotherapy in the treatment of depression: A meta-analysis. *Psychotherapy Research, 16*, 562–72.

Deffenbacher, K.A. (1983) The influence of arousal on reliability of testimony. In S.M.A. Lloyd-Bostock and B.R. Clifford (eds) *Evaluating Witness Evidence*. Chichester: Wiley.

Deffenbacher, K.A., Bornstein, B.H., Penrod, S.D. and McGorty, E.K. (2004) A meta-analytic review of the effects of high stress on eyewitness memory. *Law and Human Behavior, 28*, 687–706.

Di Nardo, P.A., Guzy, L.T. and Bak, R.M. (1988) Anxiety response patterns and etiological factors in dog-fearful and non-fearful subjects. *Behaviour Research and Therapy, 26(3)*, 245–51.

Doi, T. (1973) *The Anatomy of Dependence*. New York: Kodansha International. (Amae no kozo, Japanese text, published in 1966).

Dollard, J. and Miller, N.E. (1950) *Personality and Psychotherapy*. New York: McGraw-Hill.

Dronkers, N.F., Plaisant, O., Iba-Zizen, M.T. and Cabanis, E.A. (2007) Paul Broca's Historic Cases: High Resolution MR Imaging of the Brains of Leborgne and Lelong. *Brain, 130(5)*, 1432–41.

Duffy, J.F., Rimmer, D.W. and Czeisler, C.A. (2001) Association of intrinsic circadian period with morningness-eveningness, usual wake time and circadian phase. *Behavioral Neuroscience, 115*, 895–9.

Durkin, K. and Jeffery, L. (2000). The salience of the uniform in young children's perception of police status. *Legal and Criminological Psychology, 5(1)*, 47–55.

Eagly, A.H. (1978) Sex differences in influenceability. *Psychological Bulletin, 85*, 86–116.

Elabd, C., Cousin, W., Upadhyayula, P., Chen, R.Y., Chooljian, M.S., Li, J., Kung, S., Jiang, K.P. and Conboy, I.M. (2014) *Nature Communications, 5*, 4082.

Ekman, P. and Friesen, W.V. (1978) *Manual for the Facial Action Coding System*. Palo Alto, CA: Consulting Psychology Press.

Elbert, T., Heim, S. and Rockstroh, B. (2001) Neural plasticity and development. In C.A. Nelson and M. Luciana (eds) *Handbook of Developmental Cognitive Neuroscience*. Cambridge, MA: MIT Press.

Elkin, I., Parloff, M.B., Hadley, S.W. *et al.* (1985) NIMH Treatment of Depression Collaborative Research Program. Background and research plan. *Archives of General Psychiatry, 42*, 305–16.

Ellis, A. (1957) *How to Live with a 'Neurotic'*. Hollywood, CA: Wilshire Books.

Ellis, A. (1962) *Reason and Emotion in Psychotherapy*. New York: Lyle Stuart.

Ellis, A. (1994) *Reason and Emotion in Psychotherapy, Revised and Updated*. Secaucus, NJ: Carol Publishing Group.

Ellis, A. (2001) *Overcoming Destructive Beliefs, Feelings, and Behaviours: New Directions for Rational Emotive Behaviour Therapy*. New York: Prometheus Books.

Elms, A. and Milgram, S. (1966) Personality characteristics associated with obedience and defiance toward authoritative commands. *Journal of Experimental Research in Personality, 2*, 282–9.

Engels, G.I., Garnefski, N. and Diekstra, R.F.W. (1993) Efficacy of rational emotive therapy: A quantitative analysis. *Journal of Consulting and Clinical Psychology, 61(6)*, 1083–90.

Epstein, L.C. and Lasagna, L. (1969) Obtaining informed consent: Form or substance. *Archives of Internal Medicine, 123*, 682–8.

Ericsson, K.A. (2006) The influence of experience and deliberate practice on the development of superior expert performance. *The Cambridge Handbook of Expertise and Expert Performance, 38*, 683–703.

Eslinger, P.J. and Damasio, A.R. (1985) Severe disturbance of higher cognition after bilateral frontal lobe ablation: Patient EVR. *Neurology, 35(12)*, 1731–41.

Evans, R.M. and Marain, C. (1996) Taking your medication: A question of timing. *American Medical Association*, 3–8.

Farah, M.J., Peronnet, F., Gonon, M.A. and Giard, M.H. (1988) Electrophysiological evidence for a shared representational medium for visual images and visual percepts. *Journal of Experimental Psychology: General, 117*, 248–57.

Fazey, J.A. and Hardy, L. (1988) *The Inverted-U Hypotheses: A Catastrophe for Sport Psychology*. British Association of Sport Sciences Monograph No. 1, National Coaching Foundation, Leeds.

Fedorenko, E., Duncan, J. and Kanwisher, N. (2012) Language-selective and domain-general regions lie side by side within Broca's area. *Current Biology, 22(21)*, 2059–62.

Feeney, J.A. (1999) Adult romantic attachment and couple relationships. In J. Cassidy and P.R. Shaver (eds) *Handbook of Attachment: Theory, Research and Clinical Applications*. New York: Guilford Press.

Fein, S., Goethals, G.R. and Kugler, M.B. (2007) Social influence on political judgments: The case of presidential debates. *Political Psychology, 28(2)*, 165–92.

Fennis, B.M. and Aarts, H. (2012) Revisiting the agentic shift: Weakening personal control increases susceptibility to social influence. *European Journal of Social Psychology, 42*, 824–31.

Festinger, L., Riecken, H.W. and Schachter, S. (1956) *When Prophecy Fails*. Minneapolis: University of Minnesota Press.

Fisher, R.P. and Geiselman, R.E. (1992) *Memory Enhancing Techniques for Investigative Interviewing: The Cognitive Interview*. Springfield IL: Charles C. Thomas.

Fisher, R.P., Geiselman, R.E. and Raymond, D.S. (1987) Critical analysis of police interviewing techniques. *Journal of Police Science and Administration, 15*, 177–85.

Fisher, S. and Greenberg, R. (1996) *Freud Scientifically Appraised*. New York: John Wiley.

Foster, R.A., Libkuman, T.M., Schooler, J.W. and Loftus, E.F. (1994) Realism and eyewitness person identification. *Applied Cognitive Psychology, 8*, 107–21.

Foster, R.G. and Roenneberg, T. (2008) Human responses to the geophysical daily, annual and lunar cycles. *Current Biology, 18(17)*, 784–94.

Fox, J. and Bailenson, J.N. (2009) Virtual self-modeling: The effects of vicarious reinforcement and identification on exercise behaviors. *Media Psychology, 12*, 1–25.

Fraley, C.R. (2002) Attachment stability from infancy to adulthood: Meta-Analysis and dynamic modeling of developmental mechanism. *Personality and Social Psychology Review, 6(2)*, 123–51.

Frank, R.A., Kromelow, S., Helford, M.C. and Harding, C. (1997, August) Primary caregiving father families: Do they differ in parental activities? Paper presented at the annual meeting of the American Psychological Association, Chicago, IL.

Freud, S. (1909) Analysis of phobia in a five-year-old boy. In J. Strachey (ed. and trans.) *The Complete Psychological Works: The Standard Edition* (vol. 10). New York: Norton, 1976.

Frodi, A.M., Lamb, M., Leavitt, L. and Donovan, W. (1978) Fathers' and mothers' responses to infant smiles and cries. *Infant Behavior and Development, 1*, 187–98.

Fromm, E. (1973). *The anatomy of human destructiveness*, New York: Fawcett Crest Books.

Frost, N. (1972) Encoding and retrieval in visual memory tasks. *Journal of Experimental Psychology, 95*, 317–26.

Gabbert, F., Memon, A. and Allan, K. (2003) Memory conformity: Can eyewitnesses influence each other's memories for an event? *Applied Cognitive Psychology, 17(5)*, 533–43.

Gamson, W.A., Fireman, B. and Rytina, S. (1982) *Encounters with Unjust Authority*. Homewood, IL: Dorsey Press.

Gardner, L.I. (1972) Deprivation dwarfism. *Scientific American, 227(1)*, 76–82.

Gava, I., Barbui, C., Aguglia, E., Carino, D., Churchill, R., De Vanna, M. and McGuire, H. (2007) Psychological treatments versus treatment as usual for obsessive compulsive disorder (OCD). *Cochrane Database of Systematic Reviews, 2*, Article no. CD005333.

Gazzaniga, M.S. (1998) The split brain revisited. *Scientific American, 279(1)*, 50–5.

Geiger, B. (1996) *Fathers as Primary Caregivers*. Westport, CT: Greenwood.

Geiselman, R.E., Fisher, R.P., Firstenberg, I. Hutton, L.A., Sullivan, S.J., Avetissain, I.V. and Prosk, A.L. (1984) Enhancement of eyewitness memory: An empirical evaluation of the cognitive interview. *Journal of Police Science and Administration, 12(1)*, 74–80.

Gillie, O. (1976) Crucial data faked by eminent psychologist. *Sunday Times*, 24 October 1976, London.

Godden, D.R. and Baddeley, A.D. (1975) Context-dependent memory in two natural environments. *British Journal of Psychology, 66*, 325–31.

Goodwin, D.W., Powell, B., Bremer, D., Hoine, H. and Stern, J. (1969) Alcohol and recall: State-dependent effects in man. *Science, 163*, 1358.

Gov.uk (2014) *See* www.gov.uk/government/publications/science-and-research-funding-2015-to-2016 (accessed January 2015).

Gray, J.A. (1988) *The Psychology of Fear and Stress*. 2nd edn. New York: Cambridge University Press.

Griffiths, M.D. (1994) The role of cognitive bias and skill in fruit machine gambling. *British Journal of Psychology, 85*, 351–69.

Grossmann, K.E. and Grossmann, K. (1991) Attachment quality as an organizer of emotional and behavioural responses in a longitudinal perspective. In C.M. Parkes, J. Stevenson-Hinde and P. Marris (eds) *Attachment across the Life Cycle*. London: Tavistock/Routledge.

Gründl, M. (2007) Beautycheck – Causes and Consequences of Human Facial Attractiveness. *See* www.uni-regensburg.de/Fakultaeten/phil_Fak_II/ Psychologie/Psy_II/beautycheck/english/index.htm (accessed January 2015).

Guiton, P. (1966) Early experience and sexual object choice in the brown leghorn. *Animal Behaviour, 14*, 534–8.

Hagerty, M. (1999) Testing Maslow's Hierarch of Needs: National quality of life across time. *Social Indicators Research, 46*, 249–71.

Halberg, F., Cornélissen, G., Wall, D. *et al.* (2002) Engineering and governmental challenge: 7-day/24-hour chronobiological blood pressure and heart rate screening. *Biomedical Instrumentation and Technology, 36(I and 2)*, 89–122 and 183–97.

Halford, P. and Milne, R. (2005) The identification performance of forensic eyewitnesses exposed to weapons and violence. Paper presented at the 15th European Conference of Psychology and Law, Vilnius (June).

Hammen, C.L. and Krantz, S. (1976) Effect of success and failure in depressive cognitions. *Journal of Abnormal Psychology, 85*, 577–86.

Haney, C., Banks, W.C. and Zimbardo, P.G. (1973) A study of prisoners and guards in a simulated prison. *Naval Research Review, 30*, 4–17.

Harasty, J., Double, K.L., Halliday, G.M., Kril, J.J. and McRitchie, D.A. (1997) Language-associated cortical regions are proportionally larger in the female brain. *Archives of Neurology, 54*, 171–6.

Harlow, H.F. (1959) Love in infant monkeys. *Scientific American, 200(6)*, 68–74.

Harrison, P.J. (2000) Postmortem studies in schizophrenia. *Dialogues in Clinical Neuroscience, 2(4)*, 349–357.

Harter, S., Stocker, C. and Robinson, N.S. (1996) The perceived directionality of the link between approval and self-worth: The liabilities of a looking glass self-orientation among young adolescents. *Journal of Research on Adolescence, 6*, 285–308.

Haslam, S.A. and Reicher, S.D. (2012) Contesting the 'nature' of conformity: What Milgram and Zimbardo's studies really show. *PLoS Biology, 10(11)*.

Hay, D.F. and Vespo, J.E. (1988) Social learning perspectives on the development of the mother–child relationship. In B. Birns and D.F. Hay (eds) *The Different Faces of Motherhood*. New York: Plenum.

Hazan, C. and Shaver, P.R. (1987) Romantic love conceptualised as an attachment process. *Journal of Personality and Social Psychology, 52*, 511–24.

Heermann, J.A., Jones, L.C. and Wikoff, R.L. (1994) Measurement of parent behavior during interactions with their infants. *Infant Behavior and Development, 17*, 311–21.

Heimann, M. (1989) Neonatal imitation, gaze aversion and mother–infant interaction. *Infant Behavior and Development, 12*, 495–505.

Hitch, G. and Baddeley, A.D. (1976) Verbal reasoning and working memory. *Quarterly Journal of Experimental Psychology, 28*, 603–21.

Hodges, J.R. and Patterson, K. (2007) Semantic dementia: A unique clinicopathological syndrome. *Lancet Neurology, 6*, 1004–14.

Hoffman, H.S. (1996) *Amorous Turkeys and Addicted Ducklings: A Search for the Causes of Social Attachment*. Boston, MA: Author's Cooperative.

Horton, R. (2000) Genetically modified food: Consternation, confusion and crack up. *Medical Journal of Australia, 172*, 148–9.

Hughes, D.G. (1977) Circadian rhythm of plasma cortisol in Antarctica. *British Antarctic Survey, Bulletin 46*, 77–84.

Humphrey, J.H. (1973) *Stress Education for College Students*. Hauppauge, NY: Nova.

Hutchins, C.W. Jr. and Estey, M.A. Jr. (1978) *The Relationship Between Locus of Control and Resistance in a Simulated Prisoner of War Compound*. San Diego, CA: Naval Health Research Center.

Huttenlocher, P.R. (2002) *Neural Plasticity: The Effects of Environment on the Development of the Cerebral Cortex*. Cambridge, MA: Harvard University Press.

Irish, M., Hornberger, M., Lah, S., Miller, L., Pengas, G., Nestor, P.J., Hodges, J.R. and Piguet, O. (2011) Profiles of recent autobiographical memory retrieval in semantic dementia, behavioural-variant frontotemporal dementia, and Alzheimer's disease. *Neuropsychologia, 49*, 2694–702.

Isabella, R.A., Belsky, J. and van Eye, A. (1989) The origins of infant–mother attachment: An examination of interactional synchrony during the infant's first year. *Developmental Psychology, 25*, 12–21.

Jacobs, J. (1887) Experiments in prehension. *Mind, 12*, 75–9.

Jaffe, J., Stern, D. and Perry, J. (1973) 'Conversational' coupling of gaze behavior in prelinguistic human behavior. *Journal of Psycholinguistic Research, 2*, 321–9.

Jahoda, M. (1958) *Current Concepts of Positive Mental Health*. New York: Basic Books.

Jenicke, M.A. (1992) New developments in treatment of obsessive compulsive disorder. In A. Tasman and M.B. Riba (eds) *Review of Psychiatry* (vol. 11). Washington, DC: American Psychiatric Press.

Jenness, A. (1932) The role of discussion in changing opinion regarding matter of fact. *Journal of Abnormal and Social Psychology, 27*, 279–96.

John, L.K., Loewenstein, G. and Prelec, D. (2012) Measuring the prevalence of questionable research practices with incentives for truth-telling. *Psychological Science, 23(5)*, 524–32.

Johnson, C. and Scott, B. (1976) Eyewitness testimony and suspect identification as a function of arousal, sex of witness, and scheduling of interrogation. Paper presented at the American Psychological Association Annual Meeting, Washington, D.C.

Jost, A. (1897) Die assoziationsfestigkeit in iher abhängigheit von der verteilung der wiederholungen. *Zeitschrift für Psychologie, 14*, 436–72.

Joynson, R.B. (1989) *The Burt Affair*. London: Routledge.

Kagan, J. (1984) *The Nature of the Child*. New York: Basic Books.

Kamin, L.J. (1977). *The Science and Politics of IQ*. Harmondsworth: Penguin.

Kane, M.J. and Engle, R.W. (2000) Working-memory capacity, proactive interference, and divided attention: Limits on long-term retrieval. *Journal of Experimental Psychology: Learning, Memory, and Cognition, 26*, 336–58.

Katz, J. (2008) Are you crazy enough to succeed? Obsessive and compulsive behaviors can make you – or break you. *Men's Health*. See www.msnbc.msn.com/id/25415322 (accessed March 2009).

Kebbell, M.R. and Wagstaff, G.F. (1996) Enhancing the practicality of the cognitive interview in forensic situations. *Psycoloquy* (online serial), *7(6)*. See www.cogsci.ecs.soton.ac.uk/cgi/psyc/newpsy?7.16 (accessed January 2015).

Kelman, H. (1958) Compliance, identification, and internalization: Three processes of attitude change. *Journal of Conflict Resolution, 1*, 51–60.

Kempermann, G., Kuhn, H.G. and Gage, F.H. (1998) Experience-induced neurogenesis in the senescent dentate gyrus. *Journal of Neuroscience, 18*, 3206–12.

Klein, D.F., Zitrin, C.M., Woerner, M.G. and Ross, D.C. (1983) Treatment of phobias: II. Behavior therapy and supportive psychotherapy: Are there any specific ingredients? *Archives of General Psychiatry, 40*, 139–45.

Klein, K.E. and Wegmann, H.M. (1974) The resynchronization of human circadian rhythms after transmeridian flights as a result of flight direction and mode of activity. In L.E. Scheving, F. Halberg and J.E. Pauly (eds) *Chronobiology*. Tokyo: Igaku Shoin.

Kleitman, N. (1969) Basic rest–activity cycle in relation to sleep and wakefulness. In A. Kales (ed.) *Sleep Physiology and Pathology*. Philadelphia, PA: Lippincott.

Koepke, J.E., Hamm, M., Legerstee, M. and Russell, M. (1983) Neonatal imitation: Two failures to replicate. *Infant Behavior and Development, 6*, 97–102.

Kohlberg, L. (1978) Revisions in the theory and practice of moral development. *Directions for Child Development, 2*, 83–8.

Köhnken, G., Milne, R., Memon, A. and Bull, R. (1999) The cognitive interview: A meta-analysis. *Psychology, Crime and Law, 5*, 1–35.

Koran, L.M., Hanna, G.L., Hollander, E., Nestadt, G. and Simpson, H.B. (2007) Practice guideline for the treatment of patients with obsessive compulsive disorder. *American Journal of Psychiatry, 164(7)*, 5–53.

Kruger, J. and Dunning, D. (1999) Unskilled and unaware of it: How difficulties in recognising one's own incompetence lead to inflated self-assessments. *Journal of Personality and Social Psychology, 77(6)*, 1121–34.

Kühn, S., Gleich, T., Lorenz, R.C., Lindenberger, U. and Gallinat, J. (2014) Playing Super Mario induces structural brain plasticity: Gray matter changes resulting from training with a commercial video game. *Molecular Psychiatry, 19*, 265–71.

Kushner, M.G., Kim, S.W., Donahue, C., Thuras, P., Adson, D., Kotlyar, M., McCabe, J., Peterson, J. and Foa, E.B. (2007) D-cycloserine augmented exposure therapy for obsessive compulsive disorder. *Biological Psychiatry, 62*, 835–8.

Kuyken, W. and Tsivrikos, D. (2009) Therapist competence, co-morbidity and cognitive-behavioral therapy for depression. *Psychotherapy and Psychosomatics, 78*, 42–8.

Lamb, M.E. (1997) Fathers and child development: An introductory overview and guide. In M.E. Lamb (ed.) *The Role of the Father in Child Development*, 3rd edn. New York: John Wiley and Sons, Inc.

Lamb, M.E. and Roopnarine, J.L. (1979) Peer influences on sex-role development in preschoolers. *Child Development, 50*, 1219–22.

Langlois, J.H. and Roggmann, L.A. (1990) Attractive faces are only average. *Psychological Science, 1*, 115–21.

LaRooy, D., Pipe, M.E. and Murray, J.E. (2005) Reminiscence and hypermnesia in children's eyewitness memory. *Journal of Experimental Child Psychology, 90(3)*, 235–54.

Lashley, K.S. (1930) Basic neural mechanisms in behavior. *Psychological Review, 37*, 1–24.

Laughlin, P.R. (1996) Group decision making and collective induction. In E.H. White and J. Davis (eds) *Understanding Group Behaviour, Vol. 1: Consensual Action by Small Groups*. Hillsdale, NJ: Erlbaum.

Layard, R. (2014) Interview in 'Dabiel Kahneman changed the way we think about thinking. But what do other thinkers think of him?' *The Observer*, 16 February.

Le Mare, L. and Audet, K. (2006) A longitudinal study of the physical growth and health of post-institutionalized Romanian adoptees. *Paediatrics and Child Health, 11*, 85–91.

Lee, A. and Harley, V.R. (2012) The male fight–flight response: A result of SRY regulation of catecholamines? *Bioessays. 34(6)*, 545–7.

Lifton, R.J. (1986) *The Nazi Doctors: Medical Killing and the Psychology of Genocide*. New York: Basic Books.

Linkenbach, J.W. and Perkins, H.W. (2003) Most of us are tobacco free: An eight-month social norms campaign reducing youth initiation of smoking in Montana. In H.W. Perkins (ed.) *Social Norms Approach to Preventing School and College Age Substance Abuse: A Handbook for Educators, Counselors, and Clinicians*. San Francisco, CA: Jossey-Bass.

Loftus, E.F. and Palmer, J.C. (1974) Reconstruction of automobile destruction: An example of the interaction between language and memory. *Journal of Verbal Learning and Verbal Behavior, 13*, 585–9.

Loftus, E.F., Loftus, G.R. and Messo, J. (1987) Some facts about 'weapon focus'. *Law and Human Behaviour, 11*, 55–62.

Logie, R.H. (1995) *Visuo-Spatial Working Memory.* Hove, UK: Lawrence Erlbaum Associates, Ltd.

Logie, R.H. (1999) State of the art: Working memory. *The Psychologist, 12*, 174–8.

Lorenz, K.Z. (1935) Der kumpan in der umwelt des vogels. *Journal of Ornithology, 83*, 137–213. Published in English (1937) The companion in the bird's world. *Auk, 54*, 245–73.

Lorenz, K.Z. (1952) *King Solomon's Ring: New Light on Animal Ways.* New York: Thomas Y. Crowell.

Luborsky, L., Rosenthal, R., Diguer, L., Andrusyna, T.P., Berman, J.S., Levitt, J.T., Seligman, D.A. and Krause, E.D. (2002) The Dodo Bird verdict is alive and well – mostly. *Clinical Psychology – Science and Practice, 9*, 2–12.

Luborsky, L., Singer, B. and Luborsky, L. (1975) Comparative studies of psychotherapies. *Archives of General Psychiatry, 32*, 995–1008.

Lucas, T., Alexander, S.A., Firestone, I.J. and Baltes, B.B. (2006) Self-efficacy and independence from social influence: Discovery of an efficacy-difficulty effect. *Social Influence, 1(1)*, 58–80.

Lutz, A., Greischar, L.L., Rawlings, N.B., Ricard, M. and Davidson, R.J. (2004) Long-term meditators self-induce high-amplitude gamma synchrony during mental practice. *Proceedings of the National Academy of Science, U S A. 101*(46): 16369–73.

Mackie, D.M. (1987) Systematic and nonsystematic processing of majority and minority persuasive communications. *Journal of Personality and Social Psychology, 53*, 41–52.

Mackintosh, J. (ed.) (1995) *Cyril Burt: Fraud or Framed?* Oxford: Oxford University Press.

Magnusson, A. (2000) An overview of epidemiological studies on seasonal affective disorder. *Acta Psychiatrica Scandinavica, 101(3)*, 176–84.

Maguire, E.A., Gadian, N.G., Johnsrude, I.S., Good, C.D., Ashburner, J., Frackowiak, R.S.J. and Frith, C.D. (2000) Navigation-related structural changes in the hippocampi of taxi drivers. *Proceedings of the National Academy of Science, 97(8)*, 4398–403.

Main, M. (1999) Attachment theory: Eighteen points with suggestions for future research. In J. Cassidy and P.R. Shaver (eds) *Handbook of Attachment: Theory, Research, and Clinical Applications.* New York: Guilford Press.

Main M. and Solomon J. (1986) Discovery of an insecure disoriented attachment pattern: Procedures, findings and implications for the classification of behavior. In Brazelton T., Youngman M., *Affective Development in Infancy.* Norwood, NJ: Ablex.

Main, M. and Solomon, J. (1990) Procedures for identifying infants as disorganized/disoriented during the Ainsworth Strange Situation. In M. Greenberg, D. Cicchetti and E. Cummings (eds) *Attachment in the Preschool Years: Theory, Research and Intervention.* Chicago, IL: University of Chicago Press.

Main, M. and Weston, D.R. (1981) The quality of the toddler's relationship to mother and father: Related to conflict behaviour and the readiness to establish new relationships. *Child Development, 52*, 932–40.

Maina, G., Albert, U. and Bogetto, F. (2001) Relapses after discontinuation of drugs associated with increased resistance to treatment in obsessive compulsive disorder. *International Clinical Pharmacology, 16(1)*, 33–8.

Maki, P.M. and Henderson, V.W. (2012) Hormone therapy, dementia, and cognition: The Women's Health Initiative 10 years on. *Climacteric, 15(3)*, 256–62.

Mandel, D.R. (1998) The obedience alibi: Milgram's account of the Holocaust reconsidered. *Analyse and Kritik: Zeitschrift fur Sozialwissenschaften, 20*, 74–94.

Maner, J.K. and Miller, S.L. (2014) Hormones and social monitoring: Menstrual cycle shifts in progesterone underlie women's sensitivity to social information. *Evolution and Social Behavior, 35(1)*, 9–16.

Marian, V., Neisser, U. and Rochat, P. (1996) Can 2-month-old infants distinguish live from videotaped interactions with their mother? *Emory Cognition Project Report #33.*

Markus, H.R. and Kitayama, S. (1991) Culture and the self: Implications for cognition, emotion and motivation. *Psychological Review, 98*, 224–53.

Marx, K. and Engels, F. (1848) The Communist Manifesto. London: The Communist League.

Maslow, A.H. (1943) A theory of human motivation. *Psychological Review, 50(4)*, 370–96.

Mauro, R. (1984). The constable's new clothes: Effects of uniforms on perceptions and problems of police officers. *Journal of Applied Social Psychology, 14(1)*, 42–56.

McCrone, P., Dhanasiri, S., Patel, A., Knapp, M. and Lawton-Smith, S. (2008) *Paying the Price: The Cost of Mental Health Care in England to 2026.* London: The King's Fund.

McGeoch, J.A. and McDonald, W.T. (1931) Meaningful relation and retroactive inhibition. *American Journal of Psychology, 43*, 579–88.

McGrath, T., Tsui, E., Humphries, S. and Yule, W. (1990) Successful treatment of a noise phobia in a nine-year-old girl with systematic desensitization *in vivo. Educational Psychology, 10*, 79–83.

Mello, E.M. and Fisher, R.P. (1996) Enhancing older adult eyewitness memory with the Cognitive Interview. *Applied Cognitive Psychology, 10*, 403–17.

Meltzoff, A. N. (2005) Imitation and other minds: The 'Like Me' hypothesis. In S. Hurley and N. Chater (eds) *Perspectives on Imitation: From Neuroscience to Social Science.* Cambridge, MA: MIT Press.

Meltzoff, A.N. and Moore, M.K. (1977) Imitation of facial and manual gestures by human neonates, *Science, 198*, 75–8.

Meltzoff, A.N. and Moore, M.K. (1983) Newborn infants imitate adult facial gestures. *Child Development, 54*, 702–9.

Menzies, L., Achard, S., Chamberlain, S.R., Fineberg, N., Chen, C.-H., del Campo, N., Sahakian, B.J., Robbins, T.W. and Bullmore, E. (2007) Neurocognitive endophenotypes of obsessive compulsive disorder. *Brain, 130(12)*, 3223–36.

Michaels, J.W., Blommel, J.M., Brocato, R.M., Linkous, R.A. and Rowe, J.S. (1982) Social facilitation and inhibition in a natural setting. *Replications in Social Psychology, 2*, 21–4.

Middendorp, C.P. and J.D. Meloen (1990) The authoritarianism of the working class revisited. *European Journal of Political Research, 18*, 257–67.

Middlemist, D.R., Knowles, E.S. and Matter, C.F. (1976) Personal space invasions in the lavatory: Suggestive evidence for arousal. *Journal of Personality and Social Psychology, 33*, 541–6.

Milgram, S. (1963) Behavioral study of obedience. Journal of Abnormal and Social Psychology, 67(4), 371–8.

Milgram, S. (1974) *Obedience to Authority: An Experimental View.* London: Tavistock Publications.

Milgram, S., Bickman, L. and Berkowitz, L. (1969) Note on the drawing power of crowds of different size. *Journal of Personality and Social Psychology, 13(2)*, 79–82.

Miller, G.A. (1956) The magic number seven, plus or minus two: Some limits on our capacity for processing information. *Psychological Review, 63*, 81–93.

Milne, R. and Bull, R. (2002) Back to basics: A componential analysis of the original cognitive interview mnemonics with three age groups. *Applied Cognitive Psychology, 16*, 1–11.

Moore, H.T. (1922) Further data concerning sex differences. *Journal of Abnormal and Social Psychology, 17*, 210–14.

Morfit, N.S. and Weekes, N.Y. (2001) Handedness and immune function. *Brain Cognition, 46(1–2)*, 209–13.

Mori, K. and Arai, M. (2010) No need to fake it: Reproduction of the Asch experiment without confederates. *International Journal of Psychology, 45(5)*, 390–7.

Morris, P.E., Gruneberg, M.M., Sykes, R.N. and Merrick, A. (1981) Football knowledge and the acquisition of new results. *British Journal of Psychology, 72*, 479–83.

Moscovici, S. (1980) Toward a theory of conversion behavior. In L. Berkowitz (ed.), *Advances in Experimental Social Psychology, 13*, 209–39. New York: Academic Press.

Moscovici, S., Lage, E. and Naffrenchoux, M. (1969) Influence of a consistent minority on the responses of a majority in a colour perception task. *Sociometry, 32*, 365–80.

Mowrer, O.H. (1947) On the dual nature of learning: A re-interpretation of 'conditioning' and 'problem-solving'. *Harvard Educational Review, 17*, 102–48.

Mugny, G. (1982) *The Power of Minorities.* London: Academic Press.

Müller, G.E. and Pilzecker, A. (1900) Experimentelle beiträge zur lehre vom gedächtnis. *Zeitschrift der Psychologie, 1*, 1–288.

Murray, L. and Trevarthen, C. (1985) Emotional regulation of interactions between two-month-olds and their mothers. In T.M. Field and N.A. Fox (eds), *Social Perception in Infants.* Norwood, NJ: Ablex Publishers.

Nairne, J.S. (2002) The myth of the encoding-retrieval match. *Memory, 10*, 389–95.

Nairne, J.S., Whiteman, H.L. and Kelley, M.R. (1999) Short-term forgetting of order under conditions of reduced interference. *Quarterly Journal of Experimental Psychology, 52A*, 241–51.

Nelson, T.O. and Rothbart, R. (1972) Acoustic savings for items forgotten from long-term memory. *Journal of Experimental Psychology, 93*, 357–60.

Nemeth, C. and Brilmayer, A.G. (1987) Negotiation vs. influence. *European Journal of Social Psychology, 17*, 45–56.

Nemeth, C.J. (2010) Minority influence theory. In P. Van Lange, A. Kruglanski and T. Higgins (eds), (2009) *Handbook of Theories of Social Psychology.* New York: Sage, 362–78.

Nestadt, G., Samuels, J., Riddle, M., Bienvenu III, O.J., Liang, K.-Y., LaBuda, M., Walkup, J., Grados, M. and Hoehn-Saric, R. (2000) A family study of obsessive compulsive disorder. *Archives of General Psychiatry, 57*, 358–63.

Nevis, E.C. (1983) Using an American perspective in understanding another culture: Towards a hierarchy of needs for the PRC. *Journal of Applied Behavioural Science, 19*, 249–64.

NIH (2013) Brain research through advancing innovative technologies (BRAIN) working group. *See* www.braininitiative.nih.gov/index.htm (accessed December 2014).

Nisbett, R.E. and Wilson, T.D. (1977) Telling more than we can know: Verbal reports on mental processes. *Psychological Review, 84*, 231–59.

Nolan, J.M., Schultz, P., Cialdini, R.B., Goldstein, N.J. and Griskevicius, V. (2008) Normative social influence is underdetected. *Personality and Social Psychology Bulletin, 34(7)*, 913.

Öhman, A., Eriksson, A. and Olofsson, C. (1975) One-trial learning and superior resistance to extinction of autonomic responses conditioned to potentially phobic stimuli. *Journal of Comparative and Physiological Psychology, 88*, 619–27.

Oltmanns, T.F., Neale, J.M. and Davison, G.C. (1999) *Case Studies in Abnormal Psychology*. New York: John Wiley and Sons.

Orne, M.T. (1962) On the social psychology of the psychological experiment: With particular reference to demand characteristics and their implications. *American Psychologist, 17*, 776–83.

Orne, M.T. and Holland, C.H. (1968) On the ecological validity of laboratory deceptions. International Journal of Psychiatry, *6*, 282–93.

Orne, M.T. and Scheibe, K.E. (1964) The contribution of nondeprivation factors in the production of sensory deprivation effects: The psychology of the 'panic button'. *Journal of Abnormal and Social Psychology, 68*, 3–12.

Öst, L.G. (1987) Age of onset in different phobias. *Journal of Abnormal Psychology, 96*, 223–9.

Ozaki, N., Goldman, D., Kaye, W.H., Plotnicov, K., Greenberg, B.D., Lappalainen, J., Rudnick, G. and Murphy, D.L. (2003) Serotonin transporter missense mutation associated with a complex neuropsychiatric phenotype, *Molecular Psychiatry, 8*, 933–6.

Parliamentary Office of Science and Technology (2002) Postnote: Peer Review September 2002, *182*. See www.parliament.uk/post/pn182. pdf (accessed December 2008).

Pauls, D.L. and Leckman, J.F. (1986) The inheritance of Gilles de la Tourette's syndrome and associated behaviours. Evidence for autosomal dominant transmission. *New England Journal of Medicine, 315(16)*, 993–7.

Pavlov, I. (1927) *Conditioned Reflexes: An Investigation of the Physiological Activity of the Cerebral Cortex*. Translated and edited by G.V. Anrep. London: Oxford University Press.

Penton-Voak, I.S., Perrett, D.I., Castles, D.L., Kobayashi, T., Burt, D.M., Murray, L.K. and Minamisawa, R. (1999) Menstrual cycle alters face preference. *Nature, 399(6738)*, 741–2.

Perkins, H.W. and Berkowitz, A.D. (1986) Perceiving the community norms of alcohol use among students: Some research implications for campus alcohol education programming. *International Journal of the Addictions, 21*, 961–76.

Perrin, S. and Spencer, C. (1980) *The Asch effect – A child of its time. Bulletin of the BPS, 33*, 405–6.

Perry, G. (2012) *Behind the Shock Machine: The untold story of the notorious Milgram psychology experiments*. Brunswick, Victoria: Scribe Publications.

Peterson, L.R. and Peterson, M.J. (1959) Short-term retention of individual verbal items. *Journal of Experimental Psychology, 58*, 193–8.

Piaget, J. (1962) *Play, Dreams, and Imitation in Children* (original work published in French in 1927). London: Routledge and Kegan Paul.

Pickel, K.L. (1998) Unusualness and threat as possible causes of 'weapon focus'. *Memory, 6*, 277–95.

Pigott, T.A., Pato, M.T., Bernstein, S.E., Grover, G.N., Hill, J.L., Tolliver, T.J. and Murphy, D.L. (1990) Controlled comparisons of clomipramine and fluoxetine in the treatment of obsessive compulsive disorder. *Archives of General Psychiatry, 47*, 926–32.

Piliavin, I.M., Rodin, J. and Piliavin, J.A. (1969) Good Samaritanism: An underground phenomenon. *Journal of Personality and Social Psychology, 13*, 1200–13.

Posada, G. and Jacobs, A. (2001) Child–mother attachment relationships and culture. *American Psychologist, 56(10)*, 821–2.

Prior, V. and Glaser, D. (2006) *Understanding Attachment and Attachment Disorders: Theory, Evidence and Practice*, Child and Adolescent Mental Health Series. London: Jessica Kingsley Publishers.

Quinton, D., Rutter, M. and Liddle, C. (1984) Institutional rearing, parental difficulties and marital support. *Psychological Medicine, 14*, 107–24.

Radke-Yarrow, M., Cummings, E.M., Kuczynski, L. and Chapman, M. (1985) Patterns of attachment in two- and three-year-olds in normal families and families with parental depression, *Child Development, 56(4)*, 884–93.

Rasmussen, S.A. and Eisen, J.L. (1992) The epidemiology and clinical features of obsessional compulsive disorder. *Psychiatric Clinics of North America, 15*, 743–58.

Raval, V., Goldberg, S., Atkinson, L., Benoit, D., Myhal, N., Poulton, L. and Zwiers, M. (2001) Maternal attachment, maternal responsiveness and infant attachment. *Infant Behaviour and Development, 24*, 281–304.

Rees, C. and Wallace, D. (2015) The myth of conformity: Adolescents and abstention from unhealthy drinking behaviors. *Social Science & Medicine, 125*, 151–162.

Refinetti, R. (2006) Variability of diurnality in laboratory rodents. *Journal of Comparative Physiology A, 192(7)*, 701–14.

Reicher, S. and Haslam, S.A. (2006) Rethinking the psychology of tyranny: The BBC prison study. *British Journal of Social Psychology, 45*, 1–40.

Reicher, S. and Stott, C. (2011) *Mad mobs and Englishmen? Myths and Realities of the 2011 Riots.* Kindle edition: Robinson

Reitman, J.S. (1974) Without surreptitious rehearsal, information in short-term memory decays. *Journal of Verbal Learning and Verbal Behaviour, 13*, 365–77.

Ritchie, S.J., Wiseman, R. and French, C.C. (2012) Failing the future: Three unsuccessful attempts to replicate Bem's 'retroactive facilitation of recall' effect. *PLoS ONE, 7(3)*, e33423. doi:10.1371/journal.pone.0033423.

Robertson, J. and Bowlby, J. (1952) Responses of young children to separation from their mothers. *Courier Centre International de Enfance, vol. 2*, 131–42.

Roethlisberger, F.J. and Dickson, W.J. (1939) *Management and the worker: An account of a research program conducted by the Western Electric Company, Chicago*. Cambridge, MA: Harvard University Press.

Rogers, C. (1951) *Client-centered Therapy: Its Current Practice, Implications and Theory*. London: Constable.

Rogers, C. (1959) A theory of therapy, personality and interpersonal relationships as developed in the client-centered framework. In S. Koch (ed.) *Psychology: A Study of a Science. Vol. 3: Formulations of the Person and the Social Context*. New York: McGraw Hill.

Rogers, L.J., Zucca, P. and Vallortigara, G. (2004) Advantages of having a lateralized brain. *Proceedings of the Royal Society B: Biological Sciences, 271(Suppl 6)*, S420–S422.

Rosenhan, D.L. (1973) On being sane in insane places. *Science, 179*, 250–8.

Rosenthal, R. (1966) *Experimenter Effects in Behaviour Research*. New York: Appleton.

Rosenthal, R. and Fode, K.L. (1963) The effect of experimenter bias on the performance of the albino rat. *Behavioural Science, 8(3)*, 183–9.

Rosenzweig, S. (1936) Some implicit common factors in diverse methods of psychotherapy. *American Journal of Orthopsychiatry, 6*, 412–15.

Rothbaum, F., Weisz, J., Pott, M., Miyake, K. and Morelli, G. (2000) Attachment and culture: Security in the United States and Japan. *American Psychologist, 55*, 1093–104.

Ruchkin, D.S., Grafman, J., Cameron, K. and Berndt, R.S. (2003) Working memory retention systems: A state of activated long-term memory. *Behavioral and Brain Sciences, 26(6)*, 709–28.

Russell, M.J., Switz, G.M. and Thompson, K. (1980) Olfactory influences on the human menstrual cycle. *Pharmacology, Biochemistry and Behavior, 13*, 737–8.

Rutter, M. (1981) *Maternal Deprivation Reassessed* (2nd edn). Harmondsworth, Middlesex: Penguin.

Rutter, M. (1995) Clinical implications of attachment concepts: Retrospect and prospect. *Journal of Child Psychology and Psychiatry, 36(4)*, 549–71.

Rutter, M. and Sonuga-Barke, E.J. (2010) X Conclusions: Overview of findings from the era study, inferences, and research implications. *Monographs of the Society for Research in Child Development, 75(1)*, 212–29.

Sagi, A., van IJzendoorn, M.H., Scharf, M., Koren-Karie, N., Joels, T. and Mayseless, O. (1994) Stability and discriminant validity of the Adult Attachment Interview: A psychometric study in young Israeli adults. *Developmental Psychology, 30*, 771–777.

Schacter, D.L., Kaszniak, A.W., Kihlstrom, J.F. and Valdiserri, M. (1991) The relation between source memory and aging. *Psychology and Aging, 6(4)*, 559–68.

Schaffer, H.R. and Emerson, P.E. (1964) The development of social attachments in infancy. *Monographs of the Society for Research in Child Development, 29(3 Serial No. 94)*, 1–77.

Schneider, E.B., Sur, S., Raymont, V., Duckworth, J., Kowalski, R.G., Efron, D.T., Hui, X., Selvarajah, S., Hambridge, H.L. and Stevens, R.D. (2014) Functional recovery after moderate/severe traumatic brain injury: A role for cognitive reserve? *Neurology, 82(18)*, 1636–42.

Schultz, P.W., Khazian, A. and Zaleski, A. (2008) Using normative social influence to promote conservation among hotel guests. *Social Influence, 3*, 4–23.

Schultz, P.W., Nolan, J.M., Cialdini, R.B., Goldstein, N.J. and Griskevicius, V. (2007) The constructive, destructive, and reconstructive power of social norms. *Psychological Science, 18(5)*, 429–34.

Schunk, D.H. (1983) Reward contingencies and the development of children's skills and self-efficacy. *Journal of Educational Psychology, 75*, 511–18.

Scoville, W.B. and Milner, B. (1957) Loss of recent memory after bilateral hippocampal lesions. *Journal of Neurology, Neurosurgery, and Psychiatry, 20*, 11–21.

Seligman, M.E.P. (1970) On the generality of the laws of learning. *Psychological Review, 77*, 406–18.

Shallice, T. and Warrington, E.K. (1970) Independent functioning of verbal memory stores: A neuropsychological study. *Quarterly Journal of Experimental Psychology, 22*, 261–73.

Sheridan, C.L. and King, K.G. (1972) Obedience to authority with an authentic victim. *Proceedings of the 80th Annual Convention of the American Psychological Association, 7*, 165–6.

Shutts, K., Banaji, M. and Spelke, E. (2010) Social categories guide young children's preferences for novel objects. *Developmental Science, 13(4)*, 599–610.

Siegel, L.J. and McCormick, C. (2006) *Criminology in Canada: Theories, Patterns, and Typologies* (3rd edn). Toronto: Thompson.

Simon, H.A. (1974) How big is a chunk? *Science, 183*, 482–8.

Simons, A.D., Gordon, J.S., Monroe, S.M., and Thase, M.E. (1995) Toward an integration of psychologic, social, and biologic factors in depression: Effects on outcome and course of cognitive therapy. *Journal of Consulting and Clinical Psychology, 63*, 369–77.

Simpson, J., Collins, W.A., Tran, S. and Haydon, K. (2007). Attachment and the experience and expression of emotion in romantic relationships: A developmental perspective. *Journal of Personality and Social Psychology, 92(2)*, 355–67.

Singer, L.M., Brodzinsky, D.M., Ramsay, D., Steir, M. and Waters, E. (1985) Mother–infant attachments in adoptive families. *Child Development, 56*, 1543–51.

Skene, D.J. and Arendt, J. (2007) Circadian rhythm sleep disorders in the blind and their treatment with melatonin. *Sleep Medicine, 8(6)*, 651–5.

Skinner, B.F. (1938) *The Behavior of Organisms: An Experimental Analysis*. New York: Appleton-Century.

Skodak, M. and Skeels, H. (1949) A final follow-up study of 100 adopted children. *Journal of Genetic Psychology, 75*, 85–125.

Slade, A., Grienenberger, J., Bernbach, E., Levy, D. and Locker, A. (2005) Maternal reflective functioning and attachment: Considering the transmission gap. *Attachment and Human Development, 7*, 283–92.

Sloane, R.B., Staples, F.R., Cristol, A.H., Yorkston, N.J. and Whipple, K. (1975) *Short-term Analytically Oriented Psychotherapy vs Behaviour Therapy*. Cambridge, MA: Harvard University Press.

Smith, P.B., Bond, M.H. and Kagitcibasi, C. (2006) *Understanding Social Psychology across Cultures Living and Working in a Changing World*. Oxford: Sage.

Smith, R. (1999) Opening up BMJ peer review. *British Medical Journal, 318*, 4–5.

Smith, S. and Vela, E. (2001) Environmental context-dependent memory: A review and meta-analysis. *Psychonomic Bulletin and Review, 8(2)*, 203–20.

Smith, S.M. (1979) Remembering in and out of context. *Journal of Experimental Psychology: Human Learning and Memory, 5*, 460–71.

Soomro, G.M., Altman, D.G., Rajagopal, S. and Oakley-Browne, M. (2008). Selective serotonin re-uptake inhibitors (SSRIs) versus placebo for obsessive compulsive disorder (OCD). *Cochrane Database of Systematic Reviews, 1*. See http://summaries.cochrane.org/CD001765/selective-serotonin-re-uptake-inhibitors-ssris-versus- placebo-for-obsessive-compulsive-disorder-ocd (accessed June 2012).

Spangler, G. (1990) Mother, child, and situational correlates of toddlers' social competence. *Infant Behavior and Development, 13*, 405–19.

Spector, P.E. (1983) Locus of control and social influence susceptibility: Are externals normative or informational conformers? *Journal of Psychology: Interdisciplinary and Applied, 115(2)*, 199–201.

Sperry, R.W. and Gazzaniga, M.S. (1967) Language following surgical disconnection of the hemispheres. In C. H. Milikan (ed.) *Brain Mechanisms Underlying Speech and Language*. New York: Grune and Stratton.

Spiers, H.J., Burgess, N. and Maguire, E.A. (2001) Hippocampal Amnesia: A Review. *Neurocase, 7*, 357–82.

Spitz, R.A. and Wolf, K.M. (1946) Anaclitic depression. *Psychoanalytic Study of the Child, 2*, 313–42.

Squire, L.R., Ojemann, J.G., Miezin, F.M., Petersen, S.E., Videen, T.O. and Raichle, M.E. (1992) Activation of the hippocampus in normal humans: A functional anatomical study of memory. *Proceedings of the National Academy of Science, 89*, 1837–41.

Sroufe, L.A., Egeland, B., Carlson, E. and Collins, W.A. (2005) *The Development of the Person: The Minnesota Study of Risk and Adaptation from Birth to Adulthood*. New York: Guilford.

Staub, E. (1989) The roots of evil: Personality, social conditions, culture and basic human needs. *Personality and Social Psychology Review, 3*, 179–92.

Sue, D., Sue, D. and Sue, S. (1994) *Understanding Abnormal Behaviour* (4th edn). Boston: Houghton Mifflin.

Sue, D.W. and Sue, D. (2008) *Counseling the Culturally Diverse: Theory and Practice* (5th edn). Hoboken, NJ: John Wiley and Sons, Inc.

Sukel, K. (2007) Basal ganglia contribute to learning, but also certain disorders. See www.dana.org/news/brainwork/detail.aspx?id=6028 (accessed March 2009).

Svenson, O. (February 1981). Are we all less risky and more skillful than our fellow drivers? *Acta Psychologica, 47(2)*, 143–8.

Szaflarski, J.P., Holland, S.K., Schmithorst, V.J. and Byars, A.W. (2006) An fMRI study of language lateralisation in children and adults. *Human Brain Mapping, 27(3)*, 202–12.

Szasz, T.S. (1974) *Ideology and Insanity*. Harmondsworth: Penguin.

Szechtman, H., Sulis, W. and Eilam, D. (1998) Quinpirole induces compulsive checking behavior in rats: A potential animal model of obsessive compulsive disorder (OCD). *Behavioural Neuroscience, 112(6)*, 1475–85.

Tajiri, N., Kaneko, Y., Shinozuka, K., Ishikawa, H., Yankee, E., McGrogan, M., Case, C. and Borlongan, C.V. (2013) Stem cell recruitment of newly formed host cells via a successful seduction? Filling the gap between neurogenic niche and injured brain site. *PLoS ONE, 8(9)*.

Takahashi, K. (1990) Are the key assumptions of the 'strange situation' procedure universal? A view from Japanese research. *Human Development, 33*, 23–30.

Tarnow, E. (2000) Towards the zero accident goal: assisting the first officer: Monitor and challenge captain errors. *Journal of Aviation/Aerospace Education and Research, 10(1)*, 1–11.

Taylor, S.E., Klein, L.C., Lewis, B.P., Gruenewald, T.L., Gurung, R.A. and Updegraff, J.A. (2000) *Psychological Review, 107(3)*, 411–29.

Thaler, R.H. and Sunstein, C.R. (2008) *Nudge: Improving Decisions About Health, Wealth and Happiness*. New Have, CT: Yale University Press.

Tonnessen, F.E., Lokken, A., Hoien, T. and Lundberg, I. (1993) Dyslexia, left-handedness, and immune disorders. *Archives of Neurology, 50*, 411–16.

Topál, J., Miklósi, A., Csányi, V. and Dóka, A. (1998) Attachment behaviour in dogs (Canis familiaris): A new application of Ainsworth's (1969) Strange Situation Test. *Journal of Comparative Psychology, 112(3)*, 219–29.

Touitou, Y., Reinberg, A. and Touitou, D. (2017) Disruption of adolescents' circadian clock: The vicious circle of media use, exposure to light at night, sleep loss and risk behaviors. *Life Sciences*, 173, 94–106.

Triplett, N. (1897) The dynamogenic factors in pacemaking and competition. *American Journal of Psychology, 9*, 507–33.

Trojano, L. and Grossi, D. (1995) Phonological and lexical coding in verbal short-term memory and learning. *Brain and Cognition, 21*, 336–54.

Tronick, E.Z., Morelli, G.A. and Ivey, P.K. (1992) The Efe forager infant and toddler's pattern of social relationships: Multiple and simultaneous. *Developmental Psychology, 28*, 568–77.

Trudeau, R. (1997) Monthly and daily patterns of deaths. *Statistics Canada Health Reports, 9(1)*.

Tucker, A.M., Dinges, D.F. and Van Dongen, H.P.A. (2007) Trait inter-individual differences in the sleep physiology of healthy young adults. *Journal of Sleep Research, 16(2)*, 170–80.

Tükel, R., Gürvit, H., Öztürk, N., Özata, B., Ertekin, B.A., Ertekin, E., Baran, B., Kalem, Ş.A., Büyükgök, D. and Direskeneli, G.S. (2013) COMT Val158Met polymorphism and executive functions in obsessive-compulsive disorder. *Journal of Neuropsychiatry and Clinical Neuroscience, 25(3)*, 214–21.

Tulving, E. and Pearlstone, Z. (1966) Availability versus accessibility of information in memory for words. *Journal of Verbal Learning and Verbal Behavior, 5(4)*, 381–91.

Tulving, E. and Psotka, J. (1971) Retroactive inhibition in free recall: Inaccessibility of information available in the memory store. *Journal of Experimental Psychology, 87*, 1–8.

Tulving, E. and Thomson, D. (1973) Encoding specificity and retrieval processes in episodic memory. *Psychological Review, 80(5)*, 352–73.

Turk, D.J., Heatherton, T.F., Kelley, W.M., Funnell, M.G., Gazzaniga, M.S. and Macrae, C.N. (2002) Mike or me? Self-recognition in a split-brain patient. *Nature Neuroscience, 5(9)*, 841–2.

Turner, E.H., Matthews, A.M., Linardatos, E., Tell, R.A. and Rosenthal, R. (2008) Selective publication of antidepressant trials and its influence on apparent efficacy. *New England Journal of Medicine, 358(3)*, 252–60.

Turner, M.J. (2014) Smarter thinking in sport. *The Psychologist, 27–8*, 596–9.

Turner, R.J. and Lloyd, D.A. (1995) Lifetime traumas and mental health: The significance of cumulative adversity. *Journal of Health and Social Behaviour, 36*, 360–76.

Tversky, A. and Kahneman, D. (1973) Availability: A heuristic for judging frequency and probability. *Cognitive Psychology, 5(1)*, 207–33.

Tversky, A. and Kahneman, D. (1986) Rational choice and the framing of decisions. *The Journal of Business, 59(4, 2: The Behavioural Foundations of Economic Thery)*, S251–S278.

Twenge, J., Zhang, L. and Im, C. (2004) It's beyond my control: A cross-temporal meta-analysis of increasing externality in locus of control, 1960–2002. *Personality and Social Psychology Review, 8*, 308–19.

Ulrich, M.S. (2003) Risk and protective factors – school and peer domains. In B.E. Kappel (ed.) *Youth Violence, a Literature Review: From Risk to Resiliency Utilizing a Developmental Perspective*. Toronto: CTI Canadian Training Institute.

Underwood, B.J. (1957) Interference and forgetting. *Psychological Review, 64*, 49–60.

UNICEF (2014) Neuroscience is redefining early childhood development. *See* http://blogs.unicef.org/2014/09/20/neuroscience-is-redefining-early-childhood-development (accessed September 2014).

Van Dyne, L. and Saavedra, R. (1996) A naturalistic minority influence experiment: Effects on divergent thinking, conflict, and originality in work-groups. *British Journal of Social Psychology, 35*, 151–68.

Van IJzendoorn, M.H. and Kroonenberg, P.M. (1988) Cross-cultural patterns of attachment: A meta-analysis of the Strange Situation. *Child Development, 59*, 147–56.

Van IJzendoorn, M.H. and Sagi, A. (2001) Cultural blindness or selective inattention? *American Psychologist, 56*, 824–5.

Van IJzendoorn, M.H., Schuengel, C. and Bakermans-Kranenburg, M.J. (1999) Disorganised attachment in early childhood: Meta-analysis of precursors, concomitants, and sequelae. *Development and Psychopathology, 11*, 225–49.

Vance, D.E. (1995) Belief in lunar effects on human behavior. *Psychological Reports, 76(1)*, 32–4.

Veitch, R. and Griffitt, W. (1976) Good news, bad news: Affective and interpersonal effects. *Journal of Applied Social Psychology, 6*, 69–75.

Vetter, C., Juda, M., Lang, D., Wojtysiak, A. and Roenneberg, T. (2011) Blue-enriched office light competes with natural light as a zeitgeber. *Scandinavian Journal of Work, Environment & Health, 37(5)*, 437–45.

Vogel, E.K., Woodman, G.F. and Luck, S.J. (2001) Storage of features, conjunctions, and objects in visual working memory. *Journal of Experimental Psychology: Human Perception and Performance, 27(1)*, 92–114.

Von Dawans, B., Fischbacher, U., Kirschbaum, C., Fehr, E. and Heinrichs, M. (2012) The social dimension of stress reactivity: Acute stress increases prosocial behavior in humans. *Psychological Science, 23*, 651–60.

Wall, P.D. (1977) The presence of ineffective synapses and circumstances which unmask them. *Philosophical Transactions of the Royal Society London, 278*, 361–72.

Watson, J.B. and Rayner, R. (1920) Conditioned emotional reactions. *Journal of Experimental Psychology, 3*, 1–14.

Wells, G.L. and Olson, E. (2003) Eyewitness identification. *Annual Review of Psychology, 54*, 277–95.

White, D.W. and Woollett, A. (1992) *Families: A Context for Development*. London: Falmer.

Wickens, D.D., Dalezman, R.E. and Eggemeier, F.T. (1976) Multiple encoding of word attributes in memory. *Memory and Cognition, 4(3)*, 307–10.

Wittenbrink, B. and Henley, J.R. (1996) Creating social reality: Informational social influence and the content of stereotypic beliefs. *Personality and Social Psychology Bulletin, 22*, 598–610.

Wolpe, J. (1958) *Psychotherapy by Reciprocal Inhibition*. Stanford, CA: Stanford University Press.

Wood, W., Lundgren, S., Ouellette, J., Buscerne, S. and Blackstone, T. (1994) Minority influence: A meta-analytic review of social influence processes. *Psychological Bulletin, 115*, 323–45.

Xie, J., Sreenivasan, S., Korniss, G., Zhang, W., Lim, C. and Szymanski, B. K. (2011) Social consensus through the influence of committed minorities. *Physical Review E, 84(1)*, 011130.

Yuille, J.C. and Cutshall, J.L. (1986) A case study of eyewitness testimony of a crime. *Journal of Applied Psychology, 71*, 291–301.

Zeanah, C.H., Smyke, A.T., Koga, S.F.M., Carlson, E. and The BEIP Core Group (2005) Attachment in institutionalized and non-institutionalized Romanian children. *Child Development, 76*, 1015–28.

Zebrowitz, L.A. (1997) *Reading Faces: Window to the Soul?* Boulder, CO: Westview Press.

Zeigarnik, B. (1927) Über das Behalten von erledigten und unerledigten Handlungen. *Psychologische Forschung, 9*, 1–85.

Zhang, X., Gainetdinov, R.R., Martin Beaulieu, J.-M., Sotnikova, T.D., Burch, L.H., Williams, R.B., Schwartz, D.A., Ranga, K., Krishnan, R. and Caron, M.G. (2005) Loss-of-function mutation in tryptophan hydroxylase-2 identified in unipolar major depression. *Neuron, 45*, 11–16.

Glossary/index

Calley, Ltt. William 26

capacity This is a measure of how much can be held in memory. It is represented in terms of bits of information, such as number of digits. 44, 45, 62

caregiver Any person who is providing care for a child, such as a parent, grandparent, sibling, other family member, childminder and so on. 73
–infant interactions 70–1, 90

case study A research investigation that involves a detailed study of a single individual, institution or event. Case studies provide a rich record of human experience but are hard to generalise from. 208, 209, 227

catastrophe theory 59

ceiling and floor effects 205

central executive Monitors and coordinates all other mental functions in working memory. 48, 49

central nervous system (CNS) Comprises the brain and spinal cord. It receives information from the senses and controls the body's responses. 148, 149, 170

Charlton, T. 188

chronotherapeutics 165

circadian rhythm A pattern of behaviour that occurs or recurs approximately every 24 hours, and which is set and reset by environmental light levels. 164–5, 171
in blind people 168

Circle of Security Project 81

classical conditioning Learning through association. A neutral stimulus is consistently paired with an unconditioned stimulus so that it eventually takes on the properties of this stimulus and is able to produce a conditioned response. 105, 140
and explanations of attachment 76, 77
Pavlov's research 126
and phobias 104, 105, 106, 107
strengths and limitations 127

Clever Hans 191

closed questions Questions that have a predetermined range of answers from which respondents select one. Produces quantitative data. 204, 205

co-variable The two measured variables in a correlational analysis. The variables must be continuous. 206, 207

Code of Ethics and Conduct (BPS) 194, 196

coding (also 'encoding') The way information is changed so that it can be stored in memory. Information enters the brain via the senses (e.g. eyes and ears). It is then stored in various forms, such as visual codes (like a picture), acoustic codes (sounds) or semantic codes (the meaning of the experience). 44, 45, 62

coding systems 201

cognitive Relates to mental processes such as perception, memory and reasoning. 130, 131

cognitive approach 130–1, 141
determinism 138
to explaining depression 108–9, 117
nature and nurture 138
overview 139
scientific methods 131, 139
to treating depression 110–11, 117

cognitive-behavioural therapy (CBT) A combination of cognitive therapy (a way of changing maladaptive thoughts and beliefs) and behavioural therapy (a way of changing behaviour in response to these thoughts and beliefs). 109, 110–11, 117
for OCD 109
sport and 111

cognitive interview A police technique for interviewing witnesses to a crime, which encourages them to recreate the original context of the crime in order to increase the accessibility of stored information. Because our memory is made up of a network of associations rather than of discrete events, memories are accessed using multiple retrieval strategies. 60–1, 63, 66

cognitive neuroscience An area of psychology dedicated to the underlying neural bases of cognitive functions. 130, 131, 141

collectivist cultures 21, 73, 82

commitment The degree to which members of a minority are dedicated to a particular cause or activity. The greater the perceived commitment, the greater the influence. 32, 33

Communist Manifesto 35

compliance occurs when an individual accepts influence because they hope to achieve a favourable reaction from those around them. An attitude or behaviour is adopted not because of its content, but because of the rewards or approval associated with its adoption. 18, 19

computer model Refers to the process of using computer analogies as a representation of human cognition. 130, 131

concordance rate A measure of genetic similarity. In a sample of, for example, 100 twin pairs, one twin of each pair has a phobic disorder. The number of times their other twin also shows the illness determines the concordance rate, so if 40 have phobic disorder, then the concordance rate is 40%. 112, 113

conditions of worth Conditions imposed on an individual's behaviour and development that are considered necessary to earn positive regard from significant others. 136, 137

confederate An individual in a study who is not a real participant and has been instructed how to behave by the investigator. 182, 183

confidentiality Concerns the communication of personal information from one person to another, and the trust that the information will be protected. 194, 195, 197
as distinct from privacy 195

conformity A form of social influence that results from exposure to the majority position and leads to compliance with that position. It is the tendency for people to adopt the behaviour, attitudes and values of other members of a reference group.
Asch's study 20–1, 30, 36
effect 56
resisting 30
to social roles 22–3, 36
types and explanations 18–19, 36
variables affecting 20–1, 36

confounding variable A variable under study that is not the IV but which varies systematically with the IV. Changes in the dependent variable may be due to the confounding variable rather than the IV, and therefore the outcome is meaningless. To 'confound' means to cause confusion. 75, 180

congruence If there is similarity between a person's ideal self and self-image, a state of congruence exists. A difference represents a state of incongruence. 136, 137

consistency Minority influence is effective provided there is stability in the expressed position over time and agreement among different members of the minority. 32, 33

content analysis A kind of observational study in which behaviour is observed indirectly in written or verbal material such as interviews, conversations, books, diaries or TV programmes. 208, 209, 227

context-dependent forgetting 54

continuity hypothesis The idea that emotionally secure infants go on to be emotionally secure, trusting and socially confident adults. 78, 79
and cultural bias 83

continuous variable A variable that can take on any value within a certain range. Liking football (on a scale of 1 to 10) is continuous whereas the football team a person supports isn't. The latter could be arranged in any order. 206, 207

control Refers to the extent to which any variable is held constant or regulated by a researcher. 180
of variables 180–1, 224

controlled observation A form of investigation in which behaviour is observed but under conditions where certain variables have been organised by the researcher. 198, 199

core body temperature 164

corpus callosum 158

correlation Determining the extent of an association between two variables; co-variables may not be linked at all (**zero correlation**), they may both increase together (**positive correlation**), or as one co-variable increases, the other decreases (**negative correlation**). 206–7, 226

correlation coefficient A number between −1 and +1 that tells us how closely the co-variables in a correlational analysis are associated. 206, 207

correlational hypothesis 206

cost–benefit analysis A systematic approach to estimating the negatives and positives of any research. 196, 197

counterbalancing An experimental technique used to overcome order effects when using a repeated measures design. Counterbalancing ensures that each condition is tested first or second in equal amounts. 184, 185

covert observations Observing people without their knowledge. Knowing that behaviour is being observed is likely to alter a participant's behaviour. 198, 199

critical period A biologically determined period of time, during which certain characteristics can develop. Outside of this time window such development will not be possible. 78, 79, 84

critical value In an inferential test the value of the test statistic that must be reached to show significance. 219

cross-cultural studies 83, 137, 209

cross-sectional studies 209

cues are things that serve as a reminder. They may meaningfully link to the material to be remembered or may not be meaningfully linked, such as environmental cues (a room) or cues related to your mental state (being sad or drunk). 54, 55

cultural relativism The view that behaviour cannot be judged properly unless it is viewed in the context of the culture in which it originates. 98, 99, 101, 116

Cultural Revolution, China 28

cultural variations The ways that different groups of people vary in terms of their social practices, and the effects these practices have on development and behaviour. 73, 82–3, 91